Applied Sport Management Skills

SECOND EDITION

Robert N. Lussier, PhD
Springfield College

David C. Kimball, PhD
Elms College

Human Kinetics

Library of Congress Cataloging-in-Publication Data

Lussier, Robert N.
 Applied sport management skills / Robert N. Lussier, PhD, Springfield College, David C. Kimball, PhD, Elms College. -- Second edition.
   pages cm
 Includes bibliographical references and index.
 1. Sports--Management. 2. Sports administration. I. Kimball, David Charles, 1959- II. Title.
 GV713.L87 2014
 796.06'9--dc23

                          2013014794

 ISBN-10: 1-4504-3415-0
 ISBN-13: 978-1-4504-3415-7

Acquisitions Editor: Myles Schrag; **Developmental Editor:** Kevin Matz; **Assistant Editors:** Amy Akin and Casey A. Gentis; **Copyeditor:** Joyce Sexton; **Indexer:** Susan Danzi Hernandez; **Permissions Manager:** Dalene Reeder; **Graphic Designer:** Nancy Rasmus; **Graphic Artist:** Kathleen Boudreau-Fuoss; **Cover Designer:** Keith Blomberg; **Photograph (cover):** AP Photo/John Minchillo; **Photo Production Manager:** Jason Allen; **Art Manager:** Kelly Hendren; **Associate Art Manager:** Alan L. Wilborn; **Printer:** Sheridan Books

Printed in the United States of America   10   9   8   7   6   5   4   3

The paper in this book is certified under a sustainable forestry program.

Human Kinetics
Website: www.HumanKinetics.com

United States: Human Kinetics
P.O. Box 5076
Champaign, IL 61825-5076
800-747-4457
e-mail: humank@hkusa.com

Canada: Human Kinetics
475 Devonshire Road Unit 100
Windsor, ON N8Y 2L5
800-465-7301 (in Canada only)
e-mail: info@hkcanada.com

Europe: Human Kinetics
107 Bradford Road
Stanningley
Leeds LS28 6AT, United Kingdom
+44 (0) 113 255 5665
e-mail: hk@hkeurope.com

Australia: Human Kinetics
57A Price Avenue
Lower Mitcham, South Australia 5062
08 8372 0999
e-mail: info@hkaustralia.com

New Zealand: Human Kinetics
P.O. Box 80
Torrens Park, South Australia 5062
0800 222 062
e-mail: info@hknewzealand.com

E5763

To my wife, Marie, and our six children:
Jesse, Justin, Danielle, Nicole, Brian, and Renee

– RNL

To my wife, Amy, and our two children:
Carly and Jacob

– DCK

CONTENTS

PART IV Leading

PART V Controlling

TO THE STUDENT

Unlike most college textbooks, this book takes a how-to approach to management, because research has shown that knowledge is more likely to be implemented when it is acquired from learning by doing rather than simply from learning by reading, listening, or thinking. Sport management and business management leaders and researchers are calling for studies that can be applied by sport managers on the job and are asking for management development of skills to actually put those principles into action. To that end, we have written a textbook that focuses on applying sport management principles and fostering practical skills.

Objectives of the Book

This book uses a three-pronged approach, with these objectives:

- To teach you the important principles, concepts, research, and theories of management
- To develop your ability to apply the management principles to sport organizations
- To develop your management skills in your personal and professional lives

The book offers some unique features to further each of these three objectives, as summarized in the following table.

- **Management principles**: Throughout this book, you will learn management principles and concepts used in sport organizations and will read about the difficulties and

Features of This Book's Three-Pronged Approach

Principles (learning about management)	• Text discussion of concepts and theories, based on business and sport research • Figures • Learning Outcomes • Key Terms • Chapter Summary • Review and Discussion Questions
Application (applying the concepts)	• Opening cases with applications throughout the chapter • Sport examples • Time-Outs—applications of concepts to your sport or work experience • Applying the Concept • Cases • Sports and Social Media Exercises • Game Plan for Starting a Sport Business • Internet exercises—on companion web study guide
Skill development (job and personal)	• Developing Your Skills • Pop-up questions related to practicing managers • Self-Assessments • Step-by-step behavior models for handling management functions • Skill-Builder Exercises

challenges managers face. Your knowledge of management concepts is vital to your success as a manager.

- **Application of management principles**: Understanding theory and concepts is essential before moving to the next level: applying the concepts. If you don't understand the concepts, how can you develop the critical thinking skills you need to apply them? As shown in the table, this book offers eight features to help you develop the critical thinking skills you will need to apply the concepts.

- **Development of management skills**: The third and highest-level objective is to develop the management skills that you can use in your personal and professional lives, as both a leader and a follower. You can develop your management skills, and this book offers five features to help you do so.

Web Study Guide

A web study guide has been created specifically to supplement the text. This study guide includes internet resources and exercises and matching activities for the Key Terms. Also, features in the textbook can be completed online at the web study guide and may be sent to the professor if he or she wishes. All of the Time-Outs, Review and Discussion Questions, Applying the Concepts, Self-Assessments, Sports and Social Media Exercises, Game Plan for Starting a Sport Business exercises, and Cases may be completed online. The major advantage to completing the Self-Assessments online is that the program will automatically compute and report the score for you. Additionally, the Applying the Concepts, Self-Assessments, and Key Terms are interactive exercises. Finally, the Time-Outs, Review and Discussion Questions, Sports and Social Media Exercises, Game Plan for Starting a Sport Business exercises, and Cases are PDFs that can be downloaded and filled out.

Practice and Flexibility

As with sport and just about everything in life, you cannot become skilled by simply reading about or trying something once. You need discipline, you have to practice, and you have to keep repeating it. The great football coach Vince Lombardi said that leaders are made by effort and hard work.[1] If you want to develop your management skills, you must not only learn the concepts in this book but also practice with the applications and Skill-Builder exercises. But most important, to be successful, you need to practice using your skills in your personal and professional lives. We hope the variety of sport industries covered in the textbook motivates you to find internships, part-time jobs, full-time jobs, and long and successful careers in sport.

This book has so many features that it is unlikely that all of them can be covered in the course during a semester. Your instructor will select the features that best meet the course objectives and the amount of time available, but you may want to cover some or all of the other features on your own or with the assistance of others outside class.

Sport management is a growing field, and this growth has created the need for a book that teaches people how to be sport managers. Most people using this book will not be professional athletes; they will be managers in sport industries. Thus, our purpose is to provide a fully integrated textbook with a companion web study guide (www.HumanKinetics.com/AppliedSportManagementSkills) that constructively applies the principles of business management to the sport industry. We provide a meticulous and comprehensive overview of management topics with an in-depth focus on how to manage sport organizations. We provide thorough coverage of the principles of management combined with robust sport applications and exercises to develop sport management skills that students can use in their personal and professional lives. Adopters of *Applied Sport Management Skills, First Edition* and reviewers clearly agree that the book is the best on the market for developing sport management skills.

Organization and the North American Society for Sport Management (NASSM)

The book is organized based on the traditional four management functions—planning, organizing, leading, and controlling—but it is well grounded in sport contexts. We also rely on the principles of the North American Society for Sport Management (NASSM). The book covers all of the topics of interest to NASSM members, which are listed in its mission statement (sport marketing, chapter 13; future directions in management, chapters 1-14; employment perspectives, chapter 1 and the appendix; management competencies, chapters 1-14; leadership, chapters 8-12; sport and the law, chapter 7; personnel management, chapter 7; fund-raising, chapter 13; facility management, chapter 14; organizational structures, chapters 5-7; finance, chapter 13; and conflict resolution, chapter 8).

Three-Pronged Approach

As indicated in the title of the book, *Applied Sport Management Skills,* the book presents the principles of management, sport applications of the principles, and skill development. Following is a list of features for each prong. Examples of these features as they appear in the text are also shown on pages x-xi.

Principles of Management

The text uses several features to present the principles of management:

- Research—The references at the end of the book are primarily from two subjects: from business, the Academy of Management's four journals; and from sport management, NASSM's *Journal of Sport Management.*

- Learning Outcomes—Each chapter begins with a list of Learning Outcomes stating what students will be able to do through studying the chapter. The outcomes are also highlighted throughout the chapter.

- Key Terms—Important terms are listed in the opening of the chapter and defined within the chapter (terms appear in boldface). Students can also complete an interactive Key Terms matching exercise at the book's companion web study guide.

Applying the Concept activities require students to determine the management concept being illustrated in an example.

Self-Assessments help students gain knowledge about themselves.

Key Terms are listed at the start of the chapter and appear in boldface in the text.

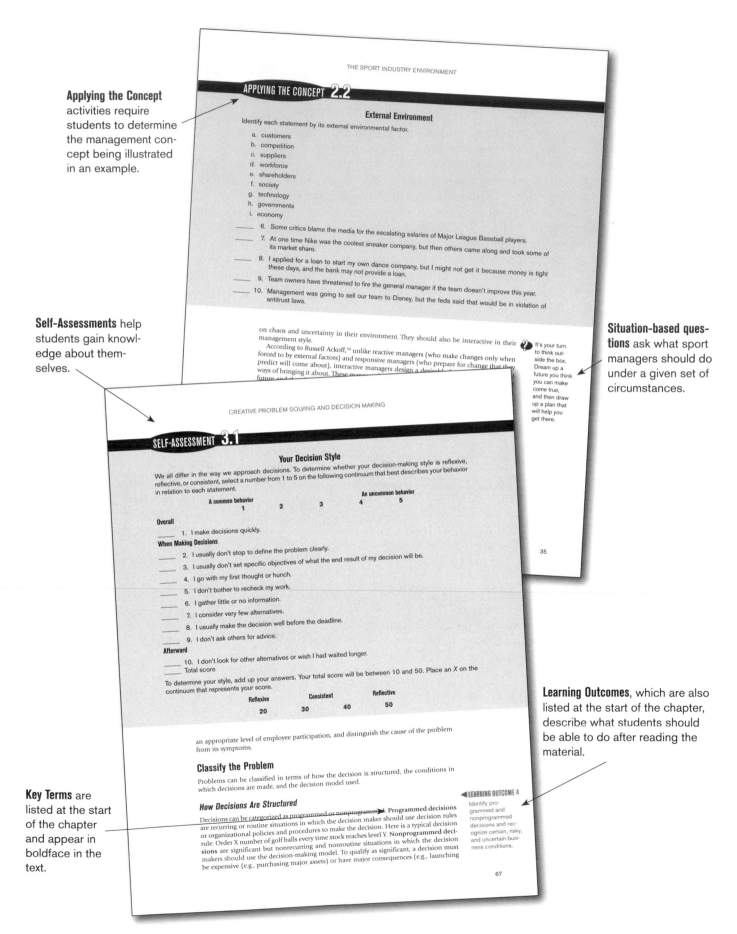

APPLYING THE CONCEPT 2.2

External Environment

Identify each statement by its external environmental factor.

a. customers
b. competition
c. suppliers
d. workforce
e. shareholders
f. society
g. technology
h. governments
i. economy

_____ 6. Some critics blame the media for the escalating salaries of Major League Baseball players.

_____ 7. At one time Nike was the coolest sneaker company, but then others came along and took some of its market share.

_____ 8. I applied for a loan to start my own dance company, but I might not get it because money is tight these days, and the bank may not provide a loan.

_____ 9. Team owners have threatened to fire the general manager if the team doesn't improve this year.

_____ 10. Management was going to sell our team to Disney, but the feds said that would be in violation of antitrust laws.

on chaos and uncertainty in their environment. They should also be interactive in their management style.

According to Russell Ackoff,[34] unlike reactive managers (who make changes only when forced to by external factors) and responsive managers (who prepare for change that they predict will come about), interactive managers design a desirable future and bring it about. These managers...

It's your turn to think outside the box. Dream up a future you think you can make come true, and then draw up a plan that will help you get there.

Situation-based questions ask what sport managers should do under a given set of circumstances.

SELF-ASSESSMENT 3.1

Your Decision Style

We all differ in the way we approach decisions. To determine whether your decision-making style is reflexive, reflective, or consistent, select a number from 1 to 5 on the following continuum that best describes your behavior in relation to each statement.

A common behavior			An uncommon behavior	
1	2	3	4	5

Overall

_____ 1. I make decisions quickly.

When Making Decisions

_____ 2. I usually don't stop to define the problem clearly.

_____ 3. I usually don't set specific objectives of what the end result of my decision will be.

_____ 4. I go with my first thought or hunch.

_____ 5. I don't bother to recheck my work.

_____ 6. I gather little or no information.

_____ 7. I consider very few alternatives.

_____ 8. I usually make the decision well before the deadline.

_____ 9. I don't ask others for advice.

Afterward

_____ 10. I don't look for other alternatives or wish I had waited longer.

_____ Total score

To determine your style, add up your answers. Your total score will be between 10 and 50. Place an X on the continuum that represents your score.

Reflexive	Consistent		Reflective
20	30	40	50

an appropriate level of employee participation, and distinguish the cause of the problem from its symptoms.

Classify the Problem

Problems can be classified in terms of how the decision is structured, the conditions in which decisions are made, and the decision model used.

How Decisions Are Structured

Decisions can be categorized as programmed or nonprogrammed. **Programmed decisions** are recurring or routine situations in which the decision maker should use decision rules or organizational policies and procedures to make the decision. Here is a typical decision rule: Order X number of golf balls every time stock reaches level Y. **Nonprogrammed decisions** are significant but nonrecurring and nonroutine situations in which the decision makers should use the decision-making model. To qualify as significant, a decision must be expensive (e.g., purchasing major assets) or have major consequences (e.g., launching

◀ **LEARNING OUTCOME 4**

Identify programmed and nonprogrammed decisions and recognize certain, risky, and uncertain business conditions.

Learning Outcomes, which are also listed at the start of the chapter, describe what students should be able to do after reading the material.

Learning Aids at the end of each chapter include a summary, review questions, case studies, skill-builder exercises, sports and social media exercises, and exercises for starting a sport business.

Developing Your Skills gives an overview of the skills that are emphasized in a chapter.

LEARNING AIDS

CHAPTER SUMMARY

1. Describe the Big Five personality traits.
   Five continuum traits exist: extrovert and introvert (the extroversion trait); cooperative and competitive (the agreeableness trait); dependable and not dependable (emotionalism); dependable and not dependable (conscientiousness); stable and unstable (emotionalism); and willingness and unwillingness to try new things (openness to experience).

2. Understand the perception process and the two factors on which it is based.
   Perception is the process of selecting, organizing, and interpreting information from the external environment. How we do this is based on internal individual factors that include our personality and our attitudes. The second factor in the perception process is the information itself.

3. Explain how personality, perception, and attitude are related and why they are important.
   Our personalities affect our perceptions and our attitudes. Perception affects attitudes, and vice versa. Changing self-esteem and adjusting attitudes actually change single personality traits such as optimism. Personality, perception, and attitude are important because combined, they directly affect behavior and performance.

4. State what job satisfaction is and why it is important.
   Job satisfaction is a person's attitude toward her job. Job satisfaction is important because it has direct relationships with absenteeism, turnover, and performance.

5. Define power and explain the difference between position and personal power.
   Power is the ability to influence others' behavior. Position power is derived from top management and delegated down the chain of command, whereas personal power is derived from the followers based on the individual's behavior.

6. Explain how reward power, legitimate power, and referent power differ.
   The difference is based on how the person with power influences others. Reward power is the user's ability to influence others with something of value to them. Legitimate [power] ... and is a type of position power. Referent ... power relationship with others.

... related.
... ehavior of others. Politics is the process of ... tical skills are a part of power.

... coalitions have in common.
... s are all political behaviors. Networking ... cial or business advantage. Reciprocity is ... iances and then use them to accomplish ... ple with similar objectives who together ... ectives.

... es.
... n resolve it. Accommodators resolve con- ... orcers use aggressive behavior to get their ... assertive give-and-take concessions. Col- ... est solution that is agreeable to all parties.

... statement that maintains your owner- ... statement, (3) agreeing on the conflict,

DEVELOPING YOUR SKILLS

The most important resource of any organization is its people—human resources (HR). You need to understand the HR laws and regulations—the rules of the game—to be a successful sport manager. HR managers need to recruit and select talented employees and players to win games. They also need good managers and coaches to train and develop the human resources. In addition, they need to evaluate the HR performance, retain top talent, and possibly engage in union negotiations. On a more personal level, in this chapter, you can develop your skills by using the models to interview candidates, train HR, and assess their performance. You may also consider HR management as a sport management career.

REVIEWING THEIR GAME PLAN

Finding Job Openings in Sport Management

The goal of many sport management students is to work in the sport industry. How do you make this career goal happen? Learn to work with HR departments. The HR department of an organization is involved in the entire hiring process. This includes helping write the criteria for the job opening, posting the advertisement in various publications and on websites, selecting the initial set of candidates, interviewing the candidates, and negotiating a salary and benefit package for the chosen candidate.

The first step in job searching is to research the field of interest. Conduct a broad search of current job openings to gain some insight into the various types of positions that HR departments are trying to fill. As of this writing, the following were six available positions advertised at www.teamworkonline.com.

1. Executive Director, Golden State Warriors Community Foundation - Golden State Warriors (Oakland, CA)
2. Vice President of Sales and Marketing - Sportsdigita (Minneapolis, MN)
3. Ms&E Corporate Ticket Account Executive - Sacramento Kings (Sacramento, CA)
4. Creative Services Coordinator - New Orleans Hornets (New Orleans, LA)
5. Premium Seating Manager - Sacramento Kings (Sacramento, CA)
6. Assistant, Human Resources - Memphis Grizzlies (Memphis, TN)

The sixth position listed was specifically in the field of human resources. The HR assistant for the Memphis Grizzlies of the NBA provides assistance in recruitment and staffing, personnel records, employee relations, benefits, and training. Starting as an assistant in HR can lead to a career as the vice president of HR for an organization. Would you like to work in HR?

For current information on job openings in sport management, please visit www.teamworkonline.com. (For more information on careers in sport management, see the appendix.)

Reviewing Their Game Plan features real-world sport organizations and managers.

Human Resources
Management Process and Department

LEARNING OUTCOME 1
Describe the four parts of HR management.

Every team and organization is only as good as its players and workers. Thus, the key driver of business success is HR management practices of hiring and developing great people. HR management is about helping the entire organization understand and manage its people, and you should be

TIME-OUT 1 Describe your experiences with the HR department in the organization you work for or play for.

Time-Outs are open-ended questions that relate the text concepts to students' experiences.

- Chapter Summary—Each chapter ends with a summary, which lists the Learning Outcomes with their answers.

- Review and Discussion Questions—Approximately 15 questions appear after the Chapter Summary. Students can also complete these questions online at the book's companion web study guide.

Applications to Sport

Each chapter includes eight types of applications that provide students an opportunity to apply the management principle to actual sports and sport organizations to develop critical thinking skills through the following features:

- Reviewing Their Game Plan—Each chapter begins with an opening case featuring real-world sport organizations and their managers. Throughout the chapter, examples illustrate how the organization uses the text concepts.

- Sport examples—As the concepts are presented, we provide many examples of how real-world sport organizations use the principles of management. We discuss a variety of organizations, including professional, college, and high school teams, and provide examples from sport businesses, such as Nike, and nonprofit organizations, such as the YMCA and Jewish Community Center. Review any chapter for examples.

- Time-Outs—Open-ended questions require students to explain how the text concepts apply to their own sport and work experiences. Students can draw from sport experience at any level as well as present, past, summer, full-time, or part-time employment. The questions help students bridge the gap between theory and their real world. The Time-Outs can be completed online at the book's companion web study guide.

- Applying the Concept—Each chapter contains a series of two to five Applying the Concept boxes that require the student to determine the management concept being illustrated in a specific sport example. The Applying the Concept boxes offer an interactive experience for the student at the book's companion web study guide.

- Cases—Following the Review and Discussion Questions, an actual manager and sport organization are described. The student learns how the manager or organization applies the concepts from the chapter. Each Case is followed by approximately 10 multiple-choice questions and some open-ended questions to aid students in applying the concepts to the sport organization. See any chapter for an example. The Case Questions can be answered online at the book's companion web study guide.

- Sports and Social Media Exercises—These Internet-based exercises are new to the second edition. Each chapter contains activities that expose students to the role of social media in managing a sport organization. Students are required to use popular social media sites such as Facebook, Twitter, and LinkedIn. Many chapters also require students to learn about social media from less well-known sport-related sites. These exercises can also be completed at the book's companion web study guide.

- Game Plan for Starting a Sport Business—Each chapter requires sport students to perform a managerial activity associated with owning their own sport business. Students are required to plan a sport business, develop an organizational structure, formulate ideas on how they will lead their employees, and control the quality and financial aspects of their sport business. These exercises can also be completed at the book's companion web study guide.

- Internet Exercises—Included in the web study guide are Internet Exercises. Several of the exercises require students to visit a sport organization and answer questions to gain a better understanding of sport management. For examples, visit www.Human Kinetics.com/AppliedSportManagementSkills.

Skill Development

The difference between learning about management and learning to be a sport manager is the acquisition of skills. Each chapter includes five features that provide students with the opportunity to apply management principles to develop sport management skills they can use in their personal and professional lives.

- Developing Your Skills—In the chapter opener, students are given an overview of the skills they can develop through the chapter.

- Situation-based questions—Usually related to the opening case, these questions build managerial competencies by asking what the sport manager should do in a given situation.

- Self-Assessment exercises—Each chapter includes at least one Self-Assessment. Students complete the Self-Assessments to gain personal knowledge. Many of the assessments are tied to exercises within the book, thus enhancing the impact of the activities. All information for completing and scoring the assessments is contained within the text, but the book's companion web study guide also offers students an interactive format for completing these exercises.

- Behavior models—Some of the tables and figures are behavior models that include step-by-step guidelines for handling situations. Models include how to set objectives and set priorities, how to prepare for and conduct a job interview and train employees, how to negotiate and handle a conflict, how to give motivational praise and delegate, and how to coach an employee to increase performance and to discipline when needed. Almost all of the behavior models are used in exercises to develop the skill.

- Skill-Builder Exercises—Each chapter contains at least two exercises to develop skills that can be used in students' personal and professional sport management lives. There are three primary types of exercises: individually-focused, group-focused, and role-playing exercises. For some examples of exercise topics, see the preceding list of behavior models, which are part of the exercises, and the end of any chapter for actual exercises.

Ancillary Support

To ensure fully integrated support for every faculty member, the following ancillaries are available to adopters of *Applied Sport Management Skills, Second Edition* at www.Human Kinetics.com/AppliedSportManagementSkills.

- Instructor guide—Each chapter includes a chapter outline, a lecture outline for class lecture enhancement, definitions of key terms, Learning Outcome answers, Time-Out sample answers, answers to Review and Discussion Questions, Applying the Concept answers, answers to Case Questions, and suggestions for using the Skill-Builders, Sports and Social Media Exercises, and Game Plan for Starting a Sport Business exercises, as well as tips for grading students' answers to these exercises.

- Test package—Each chapter includes two sets of questions. In the first set, there are approximately 25 true or false questions, 25 multiple-choice questions, and several essay questions that were all written specifically for the test package. They do not appear in the textbook activities. The second set of questions includes items taken verbatim from the text: Applying the Concept questions, Review and Discussion Questions, Learning Outcomes, and Time-Outs.

- Presentation package—More than 360 PowerPoint slides are provided that can be used to enhance class lectures. They include text, figures, and tables.

- Web study guide—Created specifically to supplement the text, this includes Internet resources and exercises and matching

eBook
available at
your campus bookstore
or HumanKinetics.com

activities for the Key Terms. Also, features in the textbook can be completed online at the web study guide and may be sent to the professor if he or she wishes. All of the Time-Outs, Review and Discussion Questions, Applying the Concepts, Self-Assessments, Sports and Social Media Exercises, Game Plan for Starting a Sport Business exercises, and Cases may be completed online. The major advantage to completing the Self-Assessments online is that the program will automatically compute and report the score for the student. These resources are especially helpful for teaching the course online. The Applying the Concepts, Self-Assessments, and Key Terms are interactive exercises. The Time-Outs, Review and Discussion Questions, Sports and Social Media Exercises, Game Plan for Starting a Sport Business exercises, and Cases are PDFs that can be downloaded and filled out.

Changes in This New Edition

- The text has been thoroughly updated. More than 80% of the references are new to this edition. The references continue to use a strong balance of sport research (NASSM's *Journal of Sport Management*) and business research (Academy of Management's four journals).
- New Sports and Social Media Exercises have been added to each chapter.
- New Game Plan for Starting a Sport Business exercises have been added to each chapter.
- The Developing Your Skills sections have all been revised to more clearly focus on the skills that can be developed through the chapter.
- The opening cases and end-of-chapter cases have been either updated or replaced with new cases.
- New, current sport examples of how the principles in the text are used in the real world of sports have been added to each chapter.

Contact Us With Feedback

We wrote this book for you. Let us know what you think of it. Specifically, how can it be improved? We will respond to your feedback. If we use your suggestion for improvement, your name and college or university will be listed in the acknowledgments section of the next edition.

Dr. David Kimball
Director of Sport Management
Elms College
291 Springfield Street
Chicopee, MA 01013
413-265-2572
kimballd@elms.edu

Introduction to Sport Management

The first chapter introduces you to the management functions and skills that you need to understand in order to be an effective sport manager. The North American Society for Sport Management (NASSM), a key organization guiding the growth of the field of sport management, is also described. In chapter 2, internal environment factors (management, mission, resources, the systems process, and structure) are analyzed in the context of how they are changing within sport organizations. At the same time, the rapidly changing features of the external environment (customers, competition, suppliers, the workforce, shareholders, society, technology, the economy, and governments) are analyzed in light of how they change sport organizations—with specific regard to organizations' goals of reaching their fans or customers. The chapter also includes many examples of the ethical situations that sport organizations and their players are facing (such as steroids in Major League Baseball).

Managing Sports

LEARNING OUTCOMES

After studying this chapter, you should be able to

1. describe career opportunities in sport management;

2. describe a sport manager's responsibilities;

3. define the five management skills;

4. define the four management functions;

5. explain the interpersonal, informational, and decisional roles of management;

6. diagram the hierarchy of management levels;

7. describe general, functional, and project managers; and

8. explain how skills and functions differ by management level.

KEY TERMS

sport management	people skills	organizing
sport manager	communication skills	leading
manager's resources	conceptual skills	controlling
performance	decision-making skills	management roles
management skills	management functions	levels of management
technical skills	planning	types of managers

Organizing Leading Controlling Planning Organizing Leading Controlling Planning Organizing Lea
ntrolling Planning Organizing Leading Controlling Planning Organizing Leading Controlling Planning Org
Leading Controlling Planning Organizing Leading Controlling Planning Organizing Leading Contro
lanning Organizing Leading Controlling Planning Organizing Leading Controlling Planning Organi
ading Controlling Planning Organizing Leading Controlling Planning Organizing Leading Controlling Pla
ganizing Leading

DEVELOPING YOUR SKILLS

The first step in developing your sport management skills is to understand what managers are responsible for, what it takes to be a successful leader, what sport managers do, and how managers differ. To develop your skills, observe effective leaders and copy their behavior, and complete the Skill-Builder exercises at the ends of the chapters. You can also apply the principles of management by taking on leadership roles in your classes, in your job, and on your team—practice does make perfect.

REVIEWING THEIR GAME PLAN

Sports Authority is headquartered in Englewood, Colorado. Sports Authority (SA) is the number-one U.S. sporting goods chain with more than 460 stores in 45 states. SA sells a full line of sport and fitness equipment, bikes, and athletic shoes and apparel, with a focus on premium brands. Sports Authority knows that its customers are passionate about sports.

Instead of resting on its nearly 100-year history, SA has continued to expand its retail model. For example, SA also rents skis and snowboards. Although these rental products are not offered at every store, their availability shows that SA tailors store offerings based on the geographical location. Successful retail operations depend on merchandising and marketing skills. The company successfully uses a marketing strategy of inserting weekly fliers into the local Sunday newspapers around the country.

Sports Authority's 2003 merger with Gart Sports changed the retail sporting goods marketplace. Gart Sports is the owner of the Sportmart and Oshman's chains. This merger led to SA's assuming the number-one position in the U.S. sporting goods industry. Sports Authority is owned by Leonard Green & Partners.

The company's website, sportsauthority.com, is operated by GSI Commerce, Inc. Although not all that well known to consumers, GSI provides Internet service for e-commerce and interactive marketing solutions to more than 200 well-known brands and retailers across 15 merchandise categories.

Sports Authority has locations in Japan through a partnership with AEON Co. In 1995, AEON (formerly JUSCO) acquired a stake in SA. AEON is a large Japanese retailer (for example, it also acquired Talbots retail fashion stores) that provided SA with access to the large Japanese market.

It is safe to say SA is applying good sport management skills. Remember to consider the positive management skills exhibited at SA while you read future chapters.

References: www.sportsauthority.com, www.hoovers.com, www.gsicommerce.com, and www.aeon.info.

The Sport Industry

Sports are a big part of the U.S. and world economies and have strong links to other economic sectors,[1] and the number of sport managers has increased over the years.[2] Even fantasy sports have grown to more than 20 million participants.[3] What does this mean in terms of jobs? For one thing, it means lots of them—coaches for children's swimming and soccer teams, accountants at retail chains, athletic directors at schools and universities, and managers at whitewater rafting companies. And jobs mean opportunities in management, because good managers are crucial if sport organizations are to retain and motivate the kinds of employees who will make their programs thrive.[4]

Think about jobs that made you love going to work and jobs that made you dread the end of the weekend. Did management figure in your answer? Very likely it did, because managers set the tone at work, create the culture of the organization, and literally have the power to make or break it. You are taking this course because you are interested in a career in sport management. This means you already have energy, ambition, a desire to make a difference, people skills, and some leadership skills. Now it's time to put your energy and ambition to work. Being involved in sport, you most likely realize the importance of working well with people as a team. Teachers, coaches, and exercise leaders work with groups, so it is critical to understand team dynamics.[5] Management skills can be developed,[6] and this book will help you hone the skills you have and develop new ones. The skills that you develop through this course will serve you well in both your personal life and your professional life. So let's get going.

What Is Sport Management?

Let's begin this section by talking about jobs in sport management, then read an interview with a sport manager, and end with a discussion of the sport manager's resources.

Sport management is relatively young as an academic discipline.[7] The number of sport management programs in North America and Canada grew from only 20 in 1980 to over 200 by 2011.[8] A major reason for the growth in academic programs is the understanding that the value of sport depends on the ways in which sport is managed.[9] In sport, as in other businesses, managers determine organizational performance both on and off the playing field.[10] Sport management programs train people for management positions in such areas as college athletics, professional teams, fitness centers, recreational centers, coaching, officiating, marketing, youth organizations, and sporting goods manufacturing and retailing. There are many different careers in the sport industry. The following are some examples:

Athletic directors (ADs) and their assistants hold excellent administrative jobs in college sport management. Every college needs an athletic director. Another collegiate position is sport information director. These professionals are responsible for managing and distributing information about their college teams. This textbook frequently refers to the position of an athletic director as an example of managing sports.

Stadiums and arenas need general managers, business managers, operations managers, box office managers, and event managers to run their organizations. These jobs are exciting if you like to help produce live sporting events.

Sport marketing agencies manage corporate-sponsored events. Sports like golfing and NASCAR rely heavily on sport sponsorships and need managers to make sure their products gain attention at sponsored events.

Sport marketing agencies and independent agents represent athletes, handling the business side of affairs for the athlete.

Sport broadcasting includes careers in daily sport news programs, all-sports radio, and live game broadcasts. All-sports radio stations have become very popular and are an excellent place to find an internship. The Internet has opened up positions managing websites and providing statistical data for sport teams.

Recreation management is a broad term for careers such as athletic directors at YMCAs and Jewish Community Centers, directors of public parks and recreation, workers in leisure fields such as in fitness centers, and directors of activities at resorts.

Sporting goods manufacturers such as AND1 and Wilson need employees in sales, operations, human resources, and finance. Sporting goods stores such as Sports Authority need purchasing agents and accountants and employees to staff the human resources (HR) department at their headquarters. Managers are also needed to operate each store.

The most obvious career path is working in professional leagues. Major League Baseball (MLB), the National Football League (NFL), the National Basketball Association (NBA), and the National Hockey League (NHL) are professional leagues in the United States that sport management students often dream about when planning their careers. An internship with these professional teams is a good way to get started. However, in almost all situations you will be required to start at the bottom of the organization and work your way up the ladder. Newer professional leagues such as MLS (Major League Soccer), MLL (Major League Lacrosse), and AFL and AFL2 (arena football) offer additional opportunities to work for professional teams.

◀ LEARNING OUTCOME 1
Describe career opportunities in sport management.

Management study in sport is composed of subdisciplinary aspects of management science and business administration and subprofessional aspects with application to theory and practice.

Thus, sport management is a multidisciplinary field that integrates the sport industry and management. Therefore, if you go to the back of the book and look at the references, you will find that most of the references are from the top-tier *Journal of Sport Management* and the Academy of Management's four journals. As you can see by the number of references throughout each chapter, this book is based on research.

Interview With a Sport Manager

Cheryl Condon, athletic director for Elms College (Chicopee, Massachusetts), started as an admissions counselor at Elms. She has always loved and lived sports, and she pursued her passion by coaching Elms' women's softball team. Her successes as coach and her management skills did not go unnoticed, and she was eventually promoted to athletic director.

Question: Although opportunities to play sports have never been greater for women, opportunities in management are still few and far between. How did you prepare for the job of athletic director (AD) of a small college?

Answer: With my background in coaching and being around sports for so many years, I have the experience to do my job professionally and properly. I've been around sports all my life.

Question: Before you were an AD, you were an admissions counselor. How did your career path evolve?

Answer: The previous AD left for a similar position at another college. I interviewed for the position and was fortunate enough to be selected by the search committee. I was very fortunate to be able to move from a career in recruiting student-athletes into an administrative sport position. I believe that the key reason I was able to get the position was the extra effort I put into coaching the women's softball team. Coaching was not one of my required job responsibilities, and the college realized my commitment to sports by my extra efforts to make the team a success.

Question: What responsibilities do you have as an AD?

Answer: Many, many responsibilities. Hiring coaches, scheduling gymnasiums and fields for teams to practice and play regular-season games, arranging for van and bus transportation to away games, printing tickets and game programs, acquiring advertisers for the game programs, fund-raising, and watching many games. When I watch the games, I appreciate all the work that my staff and the students have put into making the event a success.

Question: Now you are about to take on different responsibilities as director of intramural sports. Why make the change?

Answer: The number of teams at my college is increasing, and the new AD will be responsible for managing even more budgets, teams, coaches, and game logistics. However, my college has never had any intramural sports. I want to get the whole student body more involved in sports on a daily basis, and I think an intramural program is the way to bring this about.

Question: What do you think is the most important issue for sport managers?

Answer: Ethics. Sport managers need to live by a high moral code. They need to make sure the physical environment is safe for all athletes and fans. They need to conduct themselves in a professional managerial role whether they are on or off the athletic field.

Sport Manager's Responsibilities

Without resources, you don't have an organization, and the resource-based view says that the better the resources, the more successful the organization.[11] A **sport manager** is responsible for achieving the sport organization's objectives through efficient and effective use of resources. So that we start with a good perspective on what sport managers are all about, let's take a closer look at a couple of these terms. *Efficient* means getting the maximum out of your available resources. *Effective* means doing the right thing (following the proper strategy) to attain your objective; it also describes how well you achieve the objectives. The **manager's resources** include human, financial, physical, and informational resources.

◀ LEARNING OUTCOME 2
Describe a sport manager's responsibilities.

Human Resources

People are a manager's most valuable resource. If you don't take care of your people, your organization will not be successful. As a manager, you will endeavor to recruit and hire the best people available. These athletes and employees must then be trained to use the organization's other resources to maximize productivity. Whether you are managing a team of players or a team of employees, they will not be productive if they cannot work well together. Throughout this book we focus on how you can work with others to accomplish your organization's objectives. It is people who come up with the creative ideas and technologies to improve the use of the other three resources.[12]

Financial Resources

Most managers have budgets. Their budgets state how much it should cost to operate their department, store, or team for a set period of time. In other words, a budget tells you what financial resources you have available to achieve your objectives. As a manager, you will be responsible for seeing that your department does not waste resources. You may see flush financial times and lean ones. When times are flush, budgets expand, but you must still watch them carefully to make sure resources are not squandered. When times are lean, you may need to find new avenues to finance your team or department, and you may have to cut budgets.[13] Cheryl Condon disperses her budget very creatively to make sure that each sport at Elms has a chance to have a successful season.

Physical Resources

Getting the job done requires effective and efficient use of physical resources. For a retailer like Sports Authority, physical resources include store buildings (more than 100 of them), the merchandise it sells, the fixtures that display the merchandise, and the computers used to record sales and inventory. Sports Authority's physical resources also include supplies such as price tags, hangers, and charge slips.

Managers are responsible for keeping equipment in working condition and for making sure that materials and supplies are readily available. Current sales and future business can be lost if Sports Authority's physical resources are not available when needed or are not used and maintained properly.

Informational Resources

Managers need all kinds of information. Sports Authority's managers need to know how sales in Fairfax, Virginia, and in Nashua, New Hampshire, compare. These managers need to know which suppliers will get them golf balls fastest and most cheaply. They need to track health care insurance costs for all their employees. Computers store and retrieve information like this for all of Sports Authority's stores and for the home office in Englewood, Colorado. When managers at Sports Authority check their voice mail, give employees directions on setting up displays, and attend the district meeting with store walk-through, they are using informational resources.

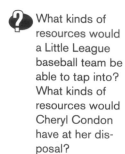 What kinds of resources would a Little League baseball team be able to tap into? What kinds of resources would Cheryl Condon have at her disposal?

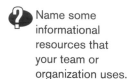 Name some informational resources that your team or organization uses.

Increasing the speed at which information is disseminated through organizations is crucial as a means of getting products to consumers faster (and ahead of the competition) and as a way to compete in the global economy. This means taking advantage of new technologies, and thus you as a manager must stay abreast of new information technologies.[14]

 TIME-OUT 1 Categorize the resources used by one of your present or past coaches or managers.

What Does It Take to Be a Successful Manager?

We don't have a short, simple answer for you. Over the years, numerous researchers have devoted their careers to answering this question. However, we can tell you that **performance** is a measure of how well managers achieve organizational objectives. Managers are responsible for meeting these objectives and are evaluated on how well they meet them. This means that managers must marshal their available resources effectively, efficiently, and creatively. Next we discuss qualities of good and poor managers, the five skills that all managers need, a list of topics of interest to North American Society for Sport Management (NASSM) members, and the findings of the Ghiselli study.

Traits of Good Managers and Poor Ones

In a Gallup survey conducted for the *Wall Street Journal*, 782 top executives in 282 large corporations were asked, "What are the most important traits for success as a supervisor?"[15] Before you read their answers, complete the Self-Assessment on page 10 to find out if you have what they think it takes.

The executives in the Gallup poll listed integrity, industriousness, and the ability to get along with people as the three most important traits of successful managers. A more recent study also reported integrity as the most important trait.[16] Other traits of successful managers included business knowledge, intelligence, leadership ability, education, sound judgment, ability to communicate, flexibility, and ability to plan and set objectives. According to these executives, managers who fail have a limited viewpoint, are unable to understand others, do not work well with others, are indecisive, lack initiative, do not assume responsibility, and lack integrity. They also lack the ability to change, are reluctant to think independently, cannot solve problems, and have too strong a desire to be popular (which prevents them from making tough decisions).

 **TIME-OUT 2** Think about a coach and a manager you know and explain what makes them good managers or poor ones. In what ways are they alike? In what ways do they differ? Give examples to support your conclusions.

Management Skills

People with strong management skills are in demand (hence this book's focus on skill building). Gaining experience in the workplace and completing programs and courses similar to this one will help you develop these skills.[17] As with all endeavors worth pursuing, the key to success is perseverance. If you persevere, you can develop and hone strong management skills. So don't leave your newly acquired skills at the classroom door—use them in your daily life.

More than 30 years ago, Robert Katz conducted a study that is still widely used today. Katz found that effective administrators have strong technical skills, strong people skills, and strong conceptual skills. Over the years other researchers have added administrative, communication, political, and problem-solving and decision-making skills. For our purposes, we paraphrase Katz and define **management skills** to include (1) technical skills, (2) people skills, (3) communication skills, (4) conceptual skills, and (5) decision-making skills (see figure 1.1). Technical skills are primarily concerned with things; people and communication skills are concerned with people; and conceptual and decision-making skills are primarily concerned with ideas.

Technical skills are the ability to use methods and techniques to perform a task. When managers work on budgets, they use spreadsheet software, so they need computer skills; they also need some knowledge of accounting (a great deal of accounting has to do with budgets and finances). Sports Authority's managers need computer skills just to open the store, and of course they also need these skills when they record transfers and sales.

Most people get promoted to their first management position primarily because of their technical skills. Because technical skills vary widely from job to job, developing these skills is not the primary focus of this book. However, in our discussion of controlling skills (chapters 13 and 14), we give you a brief overview of the financial and budgetary tools you will use as a manager.

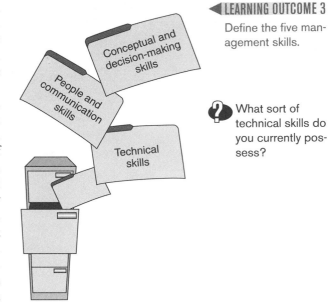

FIGURE 1.1 Management skills.

◀ **LEARNING OUTCOME 3**

Define the five management skills.

? What sort of technical skills do you currently possess?

People skills are the ability to work well with people. Today, people want a partnership relationship rather than the outdated superior–subordinate relationship.[18] Not only do employees want to participate in management; management encourages group decision making (see chapter 3). Your people skills are what will make athletes, parents, employees, and other coaches want to work with you and for you. **Communication skills** are the ability to get your ideas across clearly and effectively. Without communication skills, you cannot be an effective team member or manager. With the increased use of teams comes the need for good people skills to help groups stay on task and stay motivated. Another key area of people skills is political savvy—"street smarts" help you manage teams, develop a power base and political skills, manage conflict, and improve employee performance. The combination of people skills and communication skills is referred to as interpersonal skills. Our interpersonal relationships lead to gaining influence.[19] Students have been found to have weak interpersonal skills.[20] However, our interpersonal skills can be developed.[21] Throughout this book, in the Skill-Builders and other exercises, you will learn to work with diverse people, hone your people skills, improve your communication skills, and motivate and lead others. As director of the athletic department at Elms, Cheryl Condon has many stakeholders (see chapter 2) to satisfy—she wouldn't last a minute if she didn't have great people skills and great communication skills.

Conceptual skills are the ability to understand abstract ideas. Another term for conceptual skills is systems thinking, or the ability to understand an organization or department as a whole and the relationships among its parts. Sport managers regularly run projects and special events that require project management conceptual skills to pull it all together.[22] **Decision-making skills** are the ability to select alternatives to solve problems. The success of CEOs and coaches at all levels is based on the decisions they make, especially about the employees and players that they recruit and play; and when CEOs and coaches don't win, they sometimes get fired.[23] The success of any organization is based on its ability to solve problems and make decisions.[24] Decisions determine the success or failure of people and organizations,[25] so organizations are including employees in decision making,[26] and they are training their people to improve their decision-making skills.[27] An important part of Cheryl's job is to decide what facilities

 TIME-OUT 3 Think about a coach and a manager you know and list the management skills they use on the job. Be specific and try to identify each of the five skills discussed here.

SELF-ASSESSMENT 1.1

Management Traits

Objective: To practice assessing yourself objectively

Preparation: The following questions relate to key qualities that successful managers have. Rate yourself on each item by writing the number (1-4) that best describes your behavior for that item.

Not very descriptive of me			Very descriptive of me
4	3	2	1

_____ 1. I enjoy working with people. I prefer to work with others rather than work alone.

_____ 2. I can motivate others. I can get people to do things they may not want to do.

_____ 3. I am well liked. People enjoy working with me.

_____ 4. I am cooperative. I strive to help the team do well rather than to be the star.

_____ 5. I am a leader. I enjoy teaching, coaching, and instructing people.

_____ 6. I want to be successful. I do things to the best of my ability to be successful.

_____ 7. I am a self-starter. I get things done without having to be told to do them.

_____ 8. I am a problem solver. If things aren't going the way I want them to, I take corrective action to meet my objectives.

_____ 9. I am self-reliant. I don't need the help of others.

_____ 10. I am hardworking. I enjoy working and getting the job done.

_____ 11. I am trustworthy. If I say I will do something by a set time, I do it.

_____ 12. I am loyal. I do not do or say things to intentionally hurt my friends, relatives, or coworkers.

_____ 13. I can take criticism. If people tell me negative things about myself, I give them serious thought and change when appropriate.

_____ 14. I am honest. I do not lie, steal, or cheat.

_____ 15. I am fair. I treat people equally. I don't take advantage of others.

(Add up your total score.)

The lower your score, the better your chances of succeeding in management. If you are interested in being a manager someday, look closely at your scores on integrity (items 11-15), industriousness (items 6-10), and ability to get along with people (items 1-5) both in this course and in your personal life. As a start, review the traits listed in the text, and work to improve them. Which are your strongest and weakest traits? Think about how you can improve in the weaker areas or, preferably, write a plan.

to use, which marketing strategies will work, which coaches fit with Elms' objectives, and which student-athletes she should recruit.

North American Society for Sport Management (NASSM) Topics

The North American Society for Sport Management (NASSM) is the major professional association for sport management college and university academics. NASSM's website (www.nassm.com) lists sport management programs worldwide. The programs that have been reviewed by the Sport Management Program Review Council and have met the required approval standards are indicated. Some schools elect to go through the review and others don't.

APPLYING THE CONCEPT 1.1

Management Skills

Identify the skill used in each situation:

a. technical skills

b. people skills

c. communication skills

d. conceptual skills

e. decision-making skills

_____ 1. The ability to see the game as a whole and the interrelationship of the players

_____ 2. The ability to motivate athletes to do a good job

_____ 3. The ability to perform departmental jobs such as ticket taker

_____ 4. The ability to correct a problem

_____ 5. The ability to write effective memos and letters

NASSM is actively involved in supporting and assisting professionals working in the fields of sport, leisure, and recreation. The purpose of NASSM is to promote, stimulate, and encourage study, research, scholarly writing, and professional development in sport management—both theoretical and applied aspects. There are also regional affiliates. Sport management scholarly research is published in NASSM's *Journal of Sport Management* through Human Kinetics. Topics of interest to NASSM members include the following[28]:

- Sport marketing (we briefly discuss marketing in chapter 13)
- Future directions in management (current and future trends are discussed throughout the book)
- Employment perspectives (we have already listed jobs, and we discuss careers in sport management in the appendix)
- Management competencies (the focus of every chapter is on developing your management skills)
- Leadership (we discuss leading in five chapters, 8-12)
- Sport and the law (we discuss employment law in chapter 7)
- Personnel management (we discuss human resource management in chapter 7)
- Facility management (we discuss facility management in chapter 14)
- Organizational structures (we discuss organizing in chapters 5-7)
- Fund-raising (we briefly discuss fund-raising in chapter 13)
- Conflict resolution (you will learn how to resolve conflicts in chapter 8)

The focus of the book is on management, with a heavy dose of leadership. Reading the list of topics, you may realize that your school offers entire courses in some of these areas because NASSM influences sport management curriculum. You may be required to complete multiple courses to gain knowledge and skills in these areas.

Management Ability

In his classic 1971 study, Professor Edwin Ghiselli identified six traits as important for managers, although not all are necessary to succeed as a manager.[29] They are, in reverse order of importance, (6) initiative, (5) self-assurance, (4) decisiveness, (3) intelligence, (2) need for occupational achievement, and (1) supervisory ability. The number-one trait, supervisory ability, requires skills in planning, organizing, leading, and controlling. Ghiselli's four areas of supervisory ability are more commonly referred to today as the management functions; we discuss them in the next section and throughout the book.

What Do Sport Managers Do?

Sport managers do lots of things, as you can well imagine, but the things they do can be classified into the four functions of management and 10 management roles.

LEARNING OUTCOME 4 ▶

Define the four management functions.

Management Functions

Managers get the job done through others. They also plan, organize, lead, and control to achieve organizational objectives—these are the four **management functions.**

This book is organized around the four management functions. Each function serves as a title for a part of the book, and two to five chapters are devoted to developing skills in each function. Here, and in later chapters, we examine each function separately. However, keep in mind that the four functions together compose a system; they are interrelated and are often performed simultaneously.

What planning functions does your team or organization perform? Which managers are responsible for different aspects of planning?

Planning

Planning is typically the starting point in the management process. To succeed, organizations need to plan.[30] The people who work for organizations, from the CEO to the summer intern, need goals and objectives as well as plans by which they will achieve their goals and objectives. **Planning** is the process of setting objectives and determining in advance exactly how the objectives will be met. Managers schedule the work that employees perform and also develop budgets. At Sports Authority, managers schedule employees' work rotations so that high-volume times in stores are well covered, and these managers also select the merchandise that Sports Authority will sell. Performing the planning function well requires strong conceptual and decision-making skills.

Organizing

Successful managers also design and develop systems to implement plans. **Organizing** is the process of delegating and coordinating tasks and resources to achieve objectives. Managers allocate and arrange resources. An important part of allocating human resources is assigning people to various jobs and tasks. At Elms, Cheryl Condon plans for regular-season games, holiday tournaments, and postseason games. To do this, she has to organize the athletic department employees (including janitors, coaches, assistants, team doctors, equipment people, and ticket takers) so that they cover every game. An important part of organizing, sometimes listed as a separate function, is staffing, which is the process of selecting, training, and evaluating employees; Cheryl is responsible for staffing her teams. Effective organizing requires both conceptual and decision-making skills as well as people skills and communication skills.

Leading

Managers work with employees daily as they perform their tasks. **Leading** is the process of influencing employees to work toward achieving objectives. Managers not only must communicate their objectives to employees but also must motivate employees to achieve the objectives. An important part of Cheryl's job at Elms is to communicate objectives and then motivate and lead individuals and teams. Cheryl coaches her employees as they perform their jobs. Effective leaders have strong people skills and strong communication skills.

Controlling

The way we know if we are achieving our objective is to monitor our progress through controlling.[31] **Controlling** is the process of establishing and implementing mechanisms to ensure that objectives are achieved. An important part of controlling is measuring progress and taking corrective action when necessary. Cheryl controls throughout each sporting season. She and the coaches monitor the progress of each team and make adjustments in the team rosters. Effective controlling requires technical skills (you have to use appropriate measures) as well as conceptual and decision-making skills.

 TIME-OUT 4 Using the coach and manager you've analyzed in previous Time-Outs, give examples of how they perform each of the four management functions.

Nonmanagement Functions

All managers perform the four functions of management as they and their team get the work done. However, many managers also perform nonmanagement, or employee, functions. If Cheryl makes a photocopy of the athletic department budget she is working on, she is performing a nonmanagement function. Many managers are called working managers because they perform both management and employee functions. If you walk into a Sports Authority store during its busy hours, it is not uncommon to see managers waiting on customers and running the cash registers. They also may filling in for employees out sick, at lunch, or on break.

Management Functions as a System

Management functions do not work in a linear fashion. Managers do not plan, then organize, then lead, and then control. The functions are both separate and interrelated, calling for conceptual skills. Managers often perform these functions simultaneously. In addition, each function depends on the others. For example, if you start with a poor plan, your objective will not be met even though things are well organized, well led, and well controlled. Also, if you start

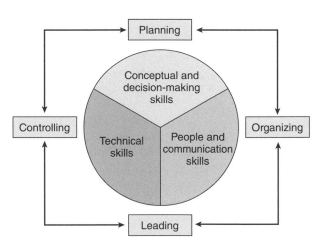

FIGURE 1.2 Management skills and functions.

with a great plan but are poorly organized or poorly led, you will probably not meet your objective. Plans without controls are rarely implemented effectively. Figure 1.2 illustrates this process. Remember, management functions are based on setting (planning) and achieving (organizing, leading, and controlling) objectives.

Management Roles

Henry Mintzberg identified 10 roles that managers undertake to accomplish their planning, organizing, leading, and controlling functions. A role is a set of expectations of how one will behave in a given situation. How well managers implement the management roles affects

APPLYING THE CONCEPT 1.2

Management Functions

Identify which function fits the situation described.

a. planning
b. organizing
c. leading
d. controlling
e. nonmanagement

_____ 6. Coach Sally shows Kelly how to kick a ball.

_____ 7. Coach Tom determines how many players were hurt during the first half of the game.

_____ 8. Ace forward Jason has missed practice several times. Coach Dave is discussing the situation with Jason to get him to understand that he cannot continue to miss practice.

_____ 9. Coach Sheryl is interviewing applicants for the position of physical therapist.

_____ 10. Coach Terry is fixing a broken weight training machine.

their performance.[32] Mintzberg categorized the 10 management roles as shown in figure 1.3.[33] **Management roles** are the roles managers undertake to accomplish the management functions, including interpersonal, informational, and decisional.

LEARNING OUTCOME 5 ▶

Explain the interpersonal, informational, and decisional roles of management.

Interpersonal Roles

Interpersonal roles include figurehead, leader, and liaison. When managers play interpersonal roles, they use their people skills and their communication skills. Managers are figureheads when they represent the organization or department in ceremonial and symbolic activities. Cheryl Condon played the figurehead role at the Elms when she granted an interview to one of the authors. Managers are leaders when they motivate, train, communicate with, and influence others. Throughout the day, Cheryl functions as a leader when she directs players to prepare for the upcoming game. Managers are liaisons when they interact

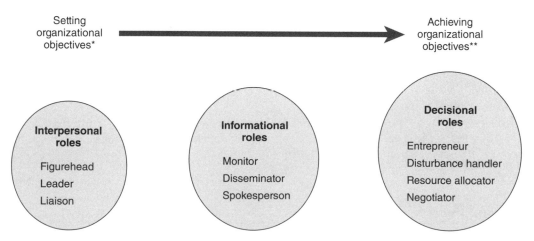

FIGURE 1.3 Ten roles managers play. *Note that the starting point is with setting objectives. **Managers play the necessary role while performing management functions to achieve objectives.

with people outside their unit to gain information and favors. Cheryl plays liaison when she solicits local businesses to place advertisements in game programs.

Informational Roles

Informational roles include monitor, disseminator, and spokesperson. When managers play informational roles, they use their people skills and communication skills. Managers are monitors when they read and talk to others to gather information. Cheryl continually monitors her situation by following the performance of other local colleges and other Division III teams in her league. Managers are disseminators when they send information to others. They are spokespersons when they provide information to people outside the organization. Cheryl is both disseminator and spokesperson when she gives interviews to the local newspaper.

Decisional Roles

Decisional roles include entrepreneur, disturbance handler, resource allocator, and negotiator. When managers play decisional roles, they use their conceptual and decision-making skills. Decision-making skills are important and are needed for success in the decisional roles.[34] Deciding who gets the organization's limited resources is an important role and one of its biggest challenges that affects success.[35] Managers are entrepreneurs when they innovate and when they improve products, systems, or services. Cheryl demonstrates an entrepreneurial spirit in her desire to start an intramural sport program. Managers are disturbance handlers when they take corrective action to diffuse disputes or crises. Cheryl is a disturbance handler when she negotiates a settlement between a coach and the coach's players. Managers are resource allocators when they schedule, request authorization, and perform budgeting and programming activities. Cheryl is a resource allocator when she authorizes departmental budgets and the purchases made against these budgets. Managers are negotiators when they represent their department or organization during nonroutine transactions to gain agreement and commitment. After Elms went coeducational in 1999, Cheryl played a major role as a negotiator when she helped the college add teams for male students.

 TIME-OUT 5 Using the coach and manager you've analyzed in previous Time-Outs, give examples of how they perform their management roles.

How Do Managers Differ?

At various levels of management, different management skills are needed, different management functions are performed, and different roles are played. Managers who work for large organizations typically have very different jobs than those who work for small organizations; this also holds true for managers who work for for-profit and nonprofit organizations.

Three Levels of Management

The three **levels of management** are top, middle, and first-line management (see figure 1.4).

◀ LEARNING OUTCOME 6
Diagram the hierarchy of management levels.

Top Managers

These executives have titles such as chairman of the board, chief executive officer (CEO), president, or vice president. Top managers manage the entire organization or major parts of it. They develop and fine-tune the organization's mission, objectives, strategies, and long-term plans. They report to other executives or the board of directors and supervise the activities of middle managers. The president of Elms College is a top manager. Most organizations have relatively few top management positions.

APPLYING THE CONCEPT 1.3

Management Roles

Identify the role played by management in each situation.

    a. interpersonal

    b. informational

    c. decisional

_____ 11. Baseball Commissioner Bud Selig discusses the players' contract with union representatives.

_____ 12. An Adidas HR manager shows a new hire how to fill out a form.

_____ 13. The Cincinnati Reds' Walt Jocketty reads *Street & Smith's* with his cup of coffee first thing in the morning.

_____ 14. Cheryl Condon develops new total quality management techniques.

_____ 15. The Oakland Raiders' sales and ticket managers discuss a complaint with a customer.

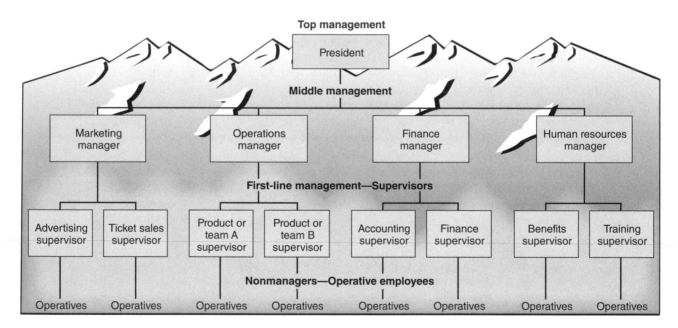

FIGURE 1.4   Management levels and functional areas.

Middle Managers

People holding these positions have titles such as general manager, athletic director, sales manager, branch manager, and department head. Middle managers implement top management's strategies by developing short-term operating plans. They generally report to executives and supervise the work of first-line managers. Cheryl Condon is a middle manager at Elms College.

First-Line Managers

Examples of the titles at this level include coach, assistant coach, academic advising coordinator, ticket manager, event manager, supervisor, and office manager. These managers implement middle managers' operational plans. They generally report to middle managers. Unlike managers at the other two levels of management, first-line managers do not supervise other managers; they supervise operative employees.

Operatives

The workers who compose the teams that managers lead do not hold management positions. Operatives, as we use the term here, are the people who report to first-line managers. Operatives work in the concessions, take tickets, make the products, wait on customers, and perform repairs.

 TIME-OUT 6 Think about a sport organization you are familiar with and identify the levels of management in the organization by level and title. Does this organization use all three levels? Why or why not?

Types of Managers

The three **types of managers** are general, functional, and project managers. Top-level and some middle managers are general managers because they supervise the activities of several departments. Middle and first-line managers are often functional managers who supervise the activities of related tasks. The four most common functional management areas are marketing, operations and production, finance and accounting, and human resources. Marketing managers are responsible for selling and advertising products and services. Production managers are responsible for making products such as basketballs, whereas operations managers are responsible for providing a service. However, both product and service organizations now use the broader term *operations*. Accounting managers are responsible for tracking sales and expenses (accounts receivable and payable) and for determining profitability, whereas financial managers are responsible for obtaining funding and for investing. The term *finance*, as commonly used, includes both accounting and financing activities. Human resources managers are responsible for forecasting future employee needs and recruiting, selecting, evaluating, and compensating employees. They also ensure that employees follow legal guidelines and regulations.

◀ **LEARNING OUTCOME 7**
Describe general, functional, and project managers.

 TIME-OUT 7 Which type of manager have you worked for? Write a job description for this person and categorize the tasks he or she performs by function.

Management Skills

All managers need technical skills, people and communication skills, and conceptual and decision-making skills. However, the need for these skills varies by level of management. Various studies have determined the skill needs at each level of management, and it is generally agreed that the need for people skills and communication skills is fairly constant across all three levels. Top-level managers have a greater need for conceptual and decision-making skills; first-line managers need better technical skills. This is logical—as managers move up the corporate ladder, they are less concerned with the daily details of conducting business and more concerned with the big picture, and big-picture thinking requires conceptualizing and strategizing. First-line managers focus on the detail—the day-to-day creation of the product or service. Middle managers typically need a balance of all three skills, but this varies from organization to organization.

◀ **LEARNING OUTCOME 8**
Explain how skills and functions differ by management level.

Management Functions

As noted earlier, every manager plans, organizes, leads, and controls. However, the time spent on each function varies by level of management. Studies of the amount of time managers spend on each function are inconclusive. However, it is generally agreed that first-line managers spend more time leading and controlling, middle-level managers spend equal time on all four functions, and top managers spend more time planning and organizing. Table 1.1 summarizes the differences by management levels.

Managing Large Businesses and Small Businesses

Table 1.2 lists the major differences between large and small businesses. These are general statements, and many large and small businesses share certain characteristics. Small business can be defined in numerous ways. The Small Business Administration (SBA) definition will suffice for our purposes: A small business is independently owned and operated, is not dominant in its field, and has fewer than 500 employees. Elms College is a small business.

Managing For-Profits and Not-For-Profits

Are managers' jobs the same in for-profit and not-for-profit organizations? Yes—whether you work for your local Little League team (nonprofit) or for the Brazilian World Cup champions (for-profit), you need the same management skills, perform the same management functions, and play the same roles.

That said, the two types of organizations do exhibit key differences. These are mainly seen in how they measure performance, how they staff their organizations, and how they get funds. The primary measure of performance in for-profit organizations is, well, profit. In addition, organizations that are in business to make money must pay their workers. Nonprofit organizations measure performance differently—for example, by whether they

TABLE 1.1   Skills and Functions Performed by Management Level

Management level	Primary management skills needed	Primary management functions performed
Top	Conceptual and decision-making skills	Planning and organizing
Middle	Balance of all skills	Balance of all four
First line	Technical and people skills	Leading and controlling

TABLE 1.2   Functions and Roles in Large and Small Businesses

Functions and roles	Large businesses	Small businesses
Planning	Commonly have formal written objectives and plans with a global business focus.	Commonly have informal objectives and plans that are not written with a global focus.
Organizing	Tend to have formal organization structures with clear policies and procedures, with three levels of management. Jobs tend to be specialized.	Tend to have informal structures without clear policies and procedures, with fewer than three levels of management. Jobs tend to be general.
Leading	Managers tend to be participative, giving employees a say in how they do their work and allowing them to make more decisions.	Entrepreneurs tend to be autocratic and want things done their way, often wanting to make decisions.
Controlling	Tend to have more sophisticated computerized control systems.	Tend to use less sophisticated control systems and to rely on direct observation.
Important management roles	Resource allocator.	Entrepreneur and spokesperson.

can pay for the team's swimming pool rental fees, whether team membership is increasing, and whether they are reaching their stakeholders (such as inner-city kids). Typically, many of the staff of nonprofits are unpaid volunteers. Nonprofits also commonly conduct fund-raisers and get money from the government, whereas for-profits don't. When funds are cut back, many school and college athletic programs depend on fund-raising.[36] Many athletic associations, such as the National Collegiate Athletic Association (NCAA) and the YMCA, are organized as nonprofits. However, you can also be a sport manager in a government organization, such as the University of California at Los Angeles (UCLA), or in the recreation department of your hometown.

In the past, it was common to classify both nongovernment and government organizations together in one group called not-for-profits. However, the trend is to distinguish not-for-profits into nongovernment organizations (NGOs) and government organizations. Three primary areas of difference among for-profit, NGOs, and government organizations relate to ownership and profits, revenues, and staffing. See table 1.3 for a list of differences among them.

TABLE 1.3 Differences Among For-Profit, Not-For-Profit, and Government Organizations

Function	For-Profit	Not-For-Profit (NGO)	Government
Ownership and profits	The primary universal measure of performance is bottom-line profit. Owners are entitled to take profits out of the firm.	Organizations are mission driven; as in all businesses, profits are the objective. However, any excess revenue remains in the organization. There are no individual owners.	Organizations are mission driven; profits are not the goal. Ownership is an entity of a function of government.
Revenues	Money comes into the business primarily through sales.	Money often is raised through donations, grants, memberships, and investments, as well as sales or fees.	Money is raised through taxes, fees, and sales.
Staffing	Employees are primarily all paid employees.	Many NGOs rely on both volunteer workers and paid employees to accomplish their mission.	Employees are primarily all paid employees; however, some entities rely on volunteers.

Source: Dr. Kathryn Carlson Heler, Professor Springfield College, 2010. Used with permission.

APPLYING THE CONCEPT 1.4

Differences Between Management Levels

Identify the level of management in each situation.

  a. top

  b. middle

  c. first line

_____ 16. Coaches the professional players

_____ 17. Owns the team

_____ 18. Spends time motivating and developing skills

_____ 19. Is the athletic director reporting to the president

_____ 20. Has a more balanced need for the management skills and functions

Objectives of the Book

This book takes a "how-to" approach to sport management, as research has shown that knowledge is more likely to be implemented when it is acquired from learning by doing, rather than from learning by reading, listening, or thinking.[37] This book uses a three-pronged approach, with these objectives:

- To teach you the important concepts of sport management
- To develop your ability to apply the sport management concepts through critical thinking
- To develop your sport management skills in your personal and professional lives

The book offers some unique features to further each of these three objectives, as summarized in table 1.4.

TABLE 1.4 Features of This Book's Three-Pronged Approach

Features that present sport management concepts	• Chapter text • Key Terms • Learning Outcomes • Chapter Summaries • Review and Discussion Questions
Features that help you apply what you learn	• Reviewing Their Game Plan cases • Sport organizational examples • Time-Outs • Applying the Concepts • Cases
Features that foster skill development	• Self-Assessments • Step-by-step models for handling sport management functions • Sports and Social Media Exercises • Game Plan for Starting a Sport Business • Skill-Builder exercises

Practice

When it comes to sport, we don't have to tell you about the need for practice. The great football coach Vince Lombardi said that leaders are made by effort and hard work. If you want to develop your sport management skills, you must not only learn the concepts in this book but also practice with the applications and Skill-Builder exercises.[38] But most important, to be successful, you need to practice using your sport management skills in your personal and professional lives just as you do in sports.

@ TAKE IT TO THE NET

Please visit www.HumanKinetics.com/AppliedSportManagementSkills and go to this book's companion web study guide, where you will find the following:

A list of websites associated with the concepts in this chapter

Exercises that you will need Internet access to complete

Online versions of chapter exercises and end-of-chapter learning aids

An exercise that helps you define the Key Terms

LEARNING AIDS

CHAPTER SUMMARY

1. Describe career opportunities in sport management.

    Sport management is a multidisciplinary field that integrates sport and management. Sport management programs train interested people for management positions in such areas as college athletics, professional teams, fitness centers, recreation centers, coaching, officiating, marketing, youth organizations, and sporting goods manufacturing and retailing.

2. Describe a sport manager's responsibilities.

    Sport managers are responsible for achieving organizational objectives through efficient and effective use of resources. Sport managers use their organization's human, financial, physical, and informational resources to achieve the objectives.

3. Define the five management skills.

    The five management skills are technical skills, people and communication skills, and conceptual and decision-making skills. Technical skills are the ability to use methods and techniques to perform a task. People skills are the ability to work well with people. Communication skills are the ability to get your ideas across clearly and effectively. Conceptual skills are the ability to understand abstract ideas, and decision-making skills are the ability to select alternatives to solve problems.

4. Define the four management functions.

    The four management functions are planning, organizing, leading, and controlling. Planning is the process of setting objectives and determining in advance exactly how the objectives will be met. Organizing is the process of delegating and coordinating tasks and resources to achieve objectives. Leading is about influencing employees to work toward achieving objectives. Controlling is the process of establishing and implementing mechanisms to ensure that the organization achieves its objectives.

5. Explain the interpersonal, informational, and decisional roles of management.

    Managers play the interpersonal role when they act as figureheads, leaders, and liaisons. Managers play the informational role when they act as monitors, disseminators, and spokespersons. Managers play the decisional role when they act as entrepreneurs, disturbance handlers, resource allocators, and negotiators.

6. Diagram the hierarchy of management levels.

    The three levels are top, middle, and first-line management.

7. Describe general, functional, and project managers.

    General managers supervise the activities of several departments or units. Functional managers supervise related activities such as marketing, operations, finance, and human resources management. Project managers coordinate employees and other resources across several functional departments to accomplish a specific task.

8. Explain how skills and functions differ by management level.
    Top managers have a greater need for conceptual and decision-making skills. Middle managers need a balance of all skills. First-line managers need better technical skills.

REVIEW AND DISCUSSION QUESTIONS

1. What is sport management? Name some possible career opportunities available to sport management majors.

2. What are the five management skills? Do all sport managers need these skills?

3. What are the four functions of management? Do all sport managers perform all four functions?

4. What are the three management roles? Do all sport managers perform all three roles?

5. What are the three types of managers? How do they differ?

6. Is it more important for a sport manager to be efficient or effective? Can you be both?

7. Should a sport management course focus on teaching students about sports or about management? Explain your answer.

8. Can college students develop their management skills through a college course? Why or why not?

9. Do you believe that sport management theory is or should be as precise as physics or chemistry? Explain your answer.

10. What are three career paths in sport management that you find interesting?

11. Why is it important to take this management course?

12. Are you interested in being a manager?

13. Some people say that hard skills (technical, finance, quantitative analysis) are more important for managers than soft skills (people and communication skills), and some say the opposite is true. What is your view?

14. Is your college professor a manager? Why or why not?

CASE

Special Teams to Special Leader at Under Armour

Under Armour is one pretty dry company! Under Armour's mission is to provide technically advanced products engineered with superior fabric construction, exclusive moisture management, and proven innovation. Under Armour produces highly technical gear marketed to provide climate control for athletes.

Founded in 1996 by former University of Maryland football player Kevin Plank, Under Armour is the originator of performance apparel—gear engineered to keep athletes cool, dry, and light throughout the course of a game, practice, or workout. Amazingly, Under Armour pretty much created the entire high-end performance apparel market on its own.

While Plank was a special teams captain of the University of Maryland football team, he grew tired of his sweaty T-shirt. He wanted to create the ultimate T-shirt, one that wouldn't absorb moisture. Nearly 10 years later, Plank developed his unique synthetic fiber concept to create one of the most unusual lines of sporting goods products since the founding of Nike.

Where did Under Armour find the nerve to compete against a giant like Nike? Kevin Plank.

It seemed as if overnight, Under Armour was available in all the major sporting goods stores, such as Modell's, Dick's Sporting Goods, and Sports Authority. In addition, professional leagues and their players became avid users of the unique clothes.

Plank oversees all operations and strategic planning, including sales and marketing, production management, forecasting, and general management functions. Today, Under Armour has more than 800 employees. The company has successfully added athletic cleats to diversify its product line. Under Armour even added an a new athletic sneaker to compete directly against Nike and Adidas.

Under Amour signed a five-year, $17.5 million contract with the University of Maryland in 2008 to outfit every varsity team. The company created a marketing stir with its uniforms for the Maryland Terrapins football team. The uniforms are designed to look like the state flag. Some felt that the decision to make a uniform with such an unusual design was a response to the creative Nike uniforms worn by the Oregon Ducks.

Lisa Delpy Neirotti, director of George Washington University's sports management MBA program, thought it was a brilliant move. "It's like anything in business . . . being a little bit different . . . gets attention and people talk about it."[39]

For current information on Under Armour, use the Internet to conduct a name search for Under Armour and visit its website at www.underarmour.com.

Case Questions

1. As CEO, Kevin Plank needs technical skills more than he needs conceptual skills.
   a. true
   b. false

2. Kevin Plank is a general manager.
   a. true
   b. false

3. Which resources play the most important role in Under Armour's success?
   a. human
   b. physical
   c. financial
   d. informational

4. Which management skills did Kevin Plank call into play for the various situations discussed in the case?
   a. technical skills
   b. people and communication skills
   c. conceptual and decision-making skills

5. Which management functions are Under Armour's managers performing in the preceding situations?
   a. planning
   b. organizing
   c. leading
   d. controlling
   e. all of the above

6. Which management role did Kevin Plank primarily play in Under Armour's journey to success?

    a. interpersonal—leader

    b. informational—monitor

    c. decisional—negotiator

7. As CEO, Kevin Plank spends most of his time

    a. planning and organizing

    b. leading and controlling

    c. balancing the above

8. Which area of sport management is Under Armour's primary focus?

    a. sport broadcasting

    b. stadium and arena management

    c. recreation management

    d. sporting goods manufacturing

9. Use the Internet to list new Under Armour products.

10. Is Kevin Plank the type of manager who would be successful in other sport organizations? Explain.

SKILL-BUILDER EXERCISES

Skill-Builder 1.1: Getting to Know You

Objectives

- To get acquainted with your classmates and instructor
- To get a feel for what this course is all about

Activities

1. Break into groups of five or six, preferably with people you don't know. State your name and tell two or three significant things about yourself. After everyone has finished, ask other students questions about themselves (5-8 minutes).

2. a. Can anyone in your group call the others by name? If so, they should do so. If not, have every member repeat his or her name. Take turns calling each other by name. Do this until everyone knows each other's first name (1-2 minutes).

    b. Brainstorm ways you can improve your ability to remember names (4-8 minutes).

3. Elect a spokesperson or recorder for your group. Look over the following categories and develop several statements or questions you would like to ask the instructor; then hand in your list (5-10 minutes).

    a. Expectations: What do you hope to learn from this course?

    b. Doubts or concerns: Is there anything about the course that you don't understand? Express any doubts or concerns that you may have or ask questions for clarification.

    c. Getting to know your instructor: Make a list of questions about your instructor's background, experience, or expectations.

4. The instructor responds to class questions (10-20 minutes).

Apply It (2-4 minutes)

What did I learn from this exercise? How will I use this knowledge?

_____

_____

_____

Skill-Builder 1.2: Comparing Managers

Objective

To better understand the differences between good and poor managers

Activities

Recall the best supervisor or boss you ever worked for and the worst one you ever worked for. Compare these two people by writing brief notes in the following chart about each person's management skills and ability to perform the four management functions.

	Best boss	Worst boss
Technical		
People and communication		
Conceptual and decision making		
Planning		
Organizing		
Leading		
Controlling		

Management Skills and Functions

After you consider your experiences with a good boss and a poor one, what do you believe are the key differences between good and poor managers?

_____

_____

_____

Apply It (2-4 minutes)

What did I learn from this exercise? How will I use this knowledge?

_____

_____

_____

SPORTS AND SOCIAL MEDIA EXERCISES

Did you ever wonder why you elected to take a course in sport management? Have you selected sport management as your major in college? Everyone who selects a major should conduct research on the field of study chosen. This exercise starts with some general areas of social media research and gets more specific as the textbook progresses.

1. Search "sport management" on www.youtube.com. What subjects related to sport management did you find?

   _____

   _____

   _____

2. Students like to use Facebook for their own personal social media purposes. Review your Facebook site and see if you have a friend who is connected to a field within sport. Networking is important in getting a job and career progressions, so work at developing your sport connections online and in person.

   _____

   _____

   _____

GAME PLAN FOR STARTING A SPORT BUSINESS

Most students think about entering sport management with the idea of working with their favorite professional team as their goal. But did you ever consider starting your own sport business? Being an entrepreneur means you are willing to take risks and create your own business, manage your business, and market your products or services to your customers. The hardest part is often just reviewing your options and finding the product or service you would like to sell to create happy customers. Much as a team needs a game plan, you need one to start your own sport business.

Every great business starts with research on potential ideas for starting one's own business. Use every resource you can find (professors, parents, career services, entrepreneurship magazines, sport magazines, the Internet, nassm.org, this textbook, the sports section of your local newspaper, and so on) to locate three possible sport businesses you would like to research this semester. Remember, this is your project, and you should find a sport business that fits your own goals. Your professor may need to agree that your idea is legal, is ethical, fits well with the course, and has enough supporting research to ensure you can complete the exercises. But, in the end, the business should reflect your own personality, goals, and motivation. Try to find three business concepts you would like to consider. In future chapters, you will be asked to select only one of these options to write your game plan. Good luck!

1. Sport business idea 1: What research led you to select this business concept?

   _____

   _____

2. Sport business idea 2: What research led you to select this business concept?

   _____

   _____

3. Sport business idea 3: What research led you to select this business concept?

   _____

   _____

The Sport Industry Environment

Globalization, Ethics, and Social Responsibility

Controlling Planning Organizing Leading Controlling Planning Organizing Leading Controlling Planning
zing Leading Controlling Planning Organizing Leading Controlling Planning Organizing Leading C
g Planning Organizing Leading Controlling Organizing Planning Organizing Leading Planning O
g Leading Controlling Planning Organizing Leading Controlling Planning Organizing Leading Controlling
ng Organizing Leading Controlling Planning Organizing Leading Controlling Planning Organizing Leading
lling Planning Organizing Leading Controlling Planning Organizing Leading Controlling Planning O

LEARNING OUTCOMES

After studying this chapter, you should be able to

1. describe the five components of the internal environment;

2. explain the two primary principles of total quality management;

3. explain how factors in the external environment affect the internal business environment;

4. state the differences between domestic, international, and multinational businesses;

5. list the lowest- and highest-risk ways to take a business global;

6. explain the stakeholders' approach to ethics; and

7. discuss the four levels of social responsibility in business.

KEY TERMS

internal environment	customer value	joint venture
mission	total quality management (TQM)	direct investment
stakeholders	external environment	ethics
systems process	international business	stakeholders' approach to ethics
structure	multinational corporation (MNC)	social responsibility
quality	global sourcing	

DEVELOPING YOUR SKILLS

Top-level managers routinely analyze their company's environment and management practices and those of their competitors. Analyze the company you work for in terms of its internal environment (What is its mission? What resources does it use to make and deliver its products or services?) and external environment (How does it get and treat customers? Who are its competitors?). Are the employees ethical, and is the firm socially responsible?

REVIEWING THEIR GAME PLAN

German-born Dirk Nowitzki was considered a "soft" player when his NBA Dallas Mavericks lost in the NBA Finals in 2006. Turns out he was really a superstar when he led the Mavericks to the NBA Championship in 2011. In the process, his work ethic also helped to bring NBA basketball to Germany.

As in most European countries, German sport is dominated by the citizenry's love of football (called soccer in the United States). But Dirk is a true German hero for having gone to America over 13 years ago, living up to the German tradition of hard work, and becoming an athletic champion.

The interesting aspect is that Yao Ming from China was expected to lead the NBA into global prominence. Ming was paid handsomely to be Adidas–Reebok's spokesman in China. Although the 7 footer had a good career, he couldn't quite shake his proneness to injury and struggled to stay healthy in the middle of his career. Still, China is a country with over a billion people, and they do like American basketball. It was easy to select Yao as the man to bring basketball to the Far East.

Dirk, a 7 footer himself, had a different journey. Not quite as tall as Yao or wide as Shaquille O'Neal, Dirk has the look of a tall, slender forward instead of a monster center. He always had a smooth jump shot for a tall man. He ran up and down the court like a more agile smaller player. He scored a lot of points, but it always seemed as though there was someone else scoring more points—Michael Jordan, Allen Iverson, Dwyane Wade, or LeBron James.

German national basketball team coach Dirk Bauermann says that Nowitzki's success in winning an NBA championship "crowns a long journey." He says "there is no one who has earned the championship more than Dirk."[1]

German soccer coach Joachim Löw also offered his congratulations on "an outstanding achievement for which I have great respect."[2]

In 2011, Dirk rose to new heights and led his Mavericks to the championship. He heard that people in his hometown of Würzburg, Germany, followed his every move. Dirk's father said "It is something really special for Dirk because he is finally recognized in America too as a real sporting great."[3]

Will Dirk's newfound fame help to spread NBA basketball in Germany? Will other European players be recruited in hopes of finding the next Dirk?

LEARNING OUTCOME 1 ▶

Describe the five components of the internal environment.

Internal Environment

Profit and not-for-profit organizations are created to produce goods and services that create value for customers. The term *product* is commonly used to mean both goods and services, because many products have an element of both. The organization's **internal environment** includes the factors within its boundaries that affect its performance. They are called internal factors because the organization has control over them, as opposed to external factors, which are outside its control. An important responsibility of managers is to match the internal environment to the external environment.[4] The five internal environment factors that you will learn about in this section are management, mission, resources, the systems process, and structure (see figure 2.1).

Management

Managers are responsible for their organization's performance. They plan, organize, lead, and control. The leadership style they use and the decisions they make affect the performance of the entire organization.[5] Effective managers develop their organization's internal environment with a culture of success and constantly scan the external environment for business opportunities.[6] Clearly, the Dallas Mavericks would not be the hot team it is today if team owner Mark Cuban didn't continually scrutinize both environments.

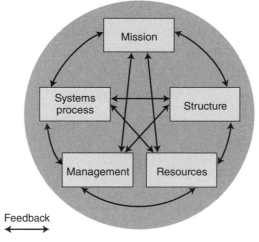

Feedback

FIGURE 2.1 The internal environment.

 Which environmental factors are important to a general manager of the Dallas Mavericks?

Mission

The organization's **mission** is its purpose or reason for being. The mission provides identity by answering the question, Who are we as an organization?[7] Developing the mission is the responsibility of top management. Shorter mission statements are easier to understand and carry out. For an example, see the YMCA's mission statement. What is your college's or university's mission?

Missions should be relevant to all stakeholders.[8] **Stakeholders** are people whose interests are affected by organizational behavior. There are internal (within the organization) and external (outside the organization) stakeholders. Managers must make trade-offs when stakeholder interests conflict.[9] For example, professional athletes want more pay, and fans want lower cost to attend a game. Wages and prices (tickets, food and drinks, parking) affect image and attendance.

A mission can also be defined as the outcome that the organization strives to attain. The other internal environmental factors—management, resources, systems process, and structure—are the means the organization uses to achieve its ends (see figure 2.2). Managers develop the mission statement and set objectives, but they are also one of the means to the ends. As a sport manager, you may not write the mission statement, but you will definitely be responsible for helping to achieve it.

TIME-OUT 1 State the mission of a sport organization. Does it differ in any way from the missions of other types of organizations?

Mission

YMCA stands for Young Men's Christian Association. It is a world-wide Christian, ecumenical, voluntary movement for women and men with special emphasis on, and the genuine involvement of, young people, that seeks to share the Christian ideal of building a human community of justice with love, peace, and reconciliation for the fullness of life for all creation.

YMCAs work for social justice for all people, irrespective of religion, race, gender or cultural background.

The World Alliance was established in 1855 with its first World Conference in Paris. The conference drew up the Paris Basis, the YMCA's mission statement, which made the World Alliance of YMCAs a pioneer of ecumenism.

Courtesy of World Alliance of YMCAs.

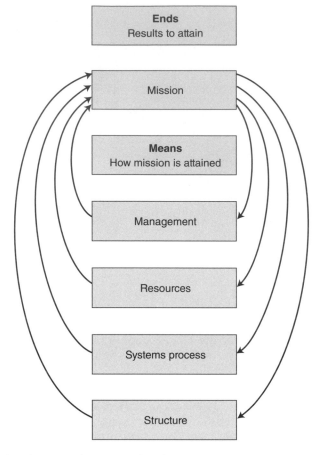

FIGURE 2.2 Internal environmental means and ends.

Resources

Organizations need resources to accomplish their mission. Performance-based differences among firms can be seen in how they acquire and use their resources.[10] For example, the team that gets and develops the best players wins more games. As stated in chapter 1, organizational resources include human, financial, physical, and informational resources. Human resources—the organization's workforce—are responsible for achieving the organization's mission and objectives. The YMCA's physical resources include fitness centers, swimming pools, gymnasiums, and inexpensive temporary housing. The Y's financial resources are used to purchase and maintain its physical resources and to pay employees. Informational resources include a YMCA directory and local YMCA websites. As a manager, you will use these four resources to achieve your organization's mission.

Systems Process

The **systems process** is the method used to transform inputs into outputs. The final outputs are organizations' products. To be successful, firms strive to accelerate the systems process to increase performance through teamwork.[11]

As shown in figure 2.3, the systems process has four components:

1. **Inputs:** Inputs provide the organization with operating necessities. They are the organization's resources (human, financial, physical, and informational). At the YMCA, the primary input is the labor of thousands of employees who provide services to Y members.

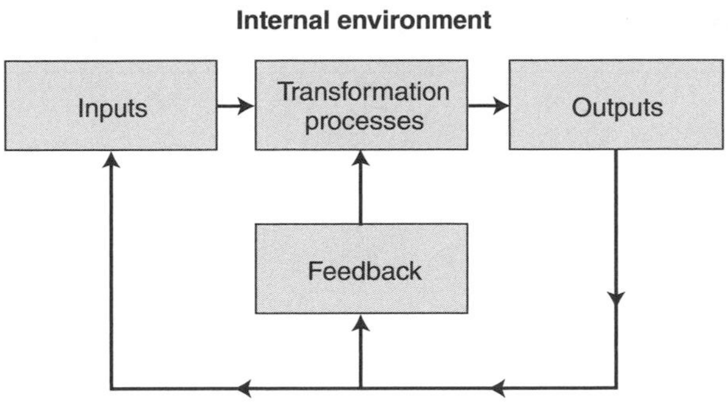

Internal environment

FIGURE 2.3   The systems process.

2. **Transformation processes:** Inputs must be transformed into outputs. At the YMCA, employees work (input) to provide services (transformation) such as fitness instruction, after-school sport programs, and database management to members.

> **TIME-OUT 2**
> Describe the systems process for an organization you have worked for or a team you have played on.

3. **Outputs:** Outputs are the different levels of satisfaction experienced by each member. At the Y, the desired output is that members experience improvements in spirit, mind, and body.

4. **Feedback:** Feedback ensures that the inputs and transformation process produce the desired results (outputs), and it can lead to innovation.[12] Y members are asked to complete satisfaction surveys on the services they receive.

Structure

An organization's **structure** is the way in which it groups its resources to accomplish its mission. The structure may be organized as departments—finance, marketing, production, and personnel. Each department affects the organization as a whole, and each department affects every other department. Organizations strive mightily to structure their resources effectively so that they can achieve their main objective—to transform inputs into outstanding outputs.[13] As a manager you will be responsible for some part of the organization's structure—perhaps a department or a team within the department. You will learn more about organizational structure in chapters 5 through 7.

Quality in Sport

Quality is a crucial issue for every organization, as quality resources can lead to breakthrough innovation.[14] Quality is an internal factor because organizations can control the quality of their products. Proponents of total quality management (TQM) believe that customers (fans in the case of many sport organizations) assess the **quality** of the organization's outputs by comparing what they require (or want) from the product or service with their actual use of, or experience with, the product or service.[15] Accordingly, **customer value** is the benefits that customers obtain if they buy a product or service. From the viewpoint of TQM, customers aren't buying only the product or service itself. They are also buying the benefit (value) they expect to derive from it.[16] Value therefore motivates us to buy or not to buy products or services. When fans buy tickets to a New York Yankees versus Anaheim Angels game, they expect to watch a high-quality game because star players such as Alex Rodriguez and Derek Jeter will be playing for their teams. Sport organizations pay close attention to quality and value because these are what attract—and retain—fans and customers.

◀**LEARNING OUTCOME 2**
Explain the two primary principles of total quality management.

Internal Environment

Match each statement with the internal environmental factor it pertains to.

a. management
b. mission
c. resources
d. systems process
e. structure

_____ 1. We take these chemicals and make them into a liquid, which then goes into these molds. When it's hard, we've got golf balls.

_____ 2. We deliver pizza and buffalo wings to the basketball tournament.

_____ 3. The people here make this team what it is.

_____ 4. As we grew, we added a new department for human resources services.

_____ 5. Management does not trust us. All the major decisions around here are made by top-level managers.

Total quality management is a management philosophy that stresses quality within the organization. **Total quality management (TQM)** is the process through which everyone in the organization focuses on the customer in order to continually improve product value. TQM uses a systems perspective because it views quality as the responsibility of everyone in the organization—not simply that of a single, self-contained department (the quality control department). The two primary principles of TQM are (1) to deliver customer value and (2) to continually improve the system and its processes. (We discuss quality and TQM in more detail in chapters 6 and 13.)

LEARNING OUTCOME 3 ▶

Explain how factors in the external environment affect the internal business environment.

External Environment

The organization's **external environment** includes factors outside its boundaries that affect its performance. Although managers can control the organization's internal environment, their influence over what happens outside the organization is limited, so they need to monitor the environment to continuously improve.[17] The external environment includes nine factors.

Customers

Customers purchase products and tickets, and without them, organizations cannot exist. Here's an example of a company outside the sport industry that capitalized on professional sport, specifically the star athlete, to get customers. When changing tastes dented Campbell's canned-soup sales, Campbell's changed its tune. For the past 10 years, the company has aired a very successful ad campaign using star athletes—and their mothers. The most recent lineup of athletes (and their moms) includes Maurice Jones-Drew (Jacksonville Jaguars) and Devin Hester (Chicago Bears). Former NFL legends Jerome Bettis (Pittsburg Steelers) and Tony Dungy (Indianapolis Colts) participated in a program encouraging dads to get off the couch and be more active on the field.[18]

Competition

Organizations must vie with their competitors for customers and fans. To beat the competition, competitor analysis is needed.[19] In professional sport, a competitive imbalance between teams can affect their leagues and spectator interest.[20] Free agency, introduced in the 1970s, changed the competitive balance of professional teams.[21] Teams with more financial resources, such as the New York Yankees, benefited.

 TIME-OUT 3 Give an example of how one sport firm's competitors have affected the firm's performance.

Suppliers

The resources of organizations often come from outside the firm. Organizations buy resources from suppliers. Many sport teams' merchandise sales are important sources of revenue. Most teams have suppliers make the merchandise, and poor-quality and out-of-stock items can result in lost sales revenue. Starting in 2012, Nike was scheduled to be the official on-field apparel company for the NFL. Reebok previously had the NFL on-field apparel contract. The NFL felt that using Nike would allow the league to select from the larger breadth of global apparel products offered by Nike.[22] Effective managers recognize that suppliers are a key factor in their success and develop close working relationships with them.[23]

Workforce

An organization's employees have a direct impact on its performance. How can teams win without star athletes? The better the employee or player, the higher the pay, and free agency has increased salaries.[24] The Texas Rangers agreed to pay shortstop Alex Rodriguez approximately U.S.$22 million a year for 10 years.[25] Management recruits its workforce from the available labor pool, which of course is outside its boundaries and is therefore an external factor. The capability of an organization's employees is determined partially by the quality of the available labor pool (how many Dirk Nowitzkis are there?).

 How are the skills needed by Maverick employees similar to those needed by YMCA employees, and how are they different?

Unions are a key source of employees for many organizations. Unions are also considered an external factor because they become a third party when they negotiate with organizations for wages and benefit packages. Dallas Maverick players are members of the National Basketball Players Association, whereas YMCA employees don't belong to a major union. Unions have the power to strike, and strikes mean lost revenues, lost wages, and lost goodwill. Fortunately, MLB has negotiated labor contracts, and the 2000s so far have been a time of relative peace between owners, players, and their unions. However, the 2012 NBA basketball season was in serious jeopardy after the owners locked out the players. The two sides remained firmly divided over what percentage of revenue the players should receive, whether teams should have a hard cap (a specific dollar amount) on payrolls, and how owners should share their money.[26]

Shareholders

Shareholders are the owners of corporations because they have purchased a share (stock) in the corporation. Although shareholders do vote for the corporation's board of directors, they must hold vast quantities of stock to influence the choice of directors.

The Disney Corporation owns ESPN. Consequently, the shareholders of Disney receive reports on the rising and falling fortunes of ESPN, ESPN2, ESPNEWS, ESPN Classic, *ESPN Magazine*, and the ESPN Zone, which is a chain of sport-themed restaurants that use the ESPN name. Although Disney shareholders certainly don't run the various ESPN media broadcasts on a daily basis, they will most assuredly take an interest if the stations are not profitable.

Society

We exert pressure on organizations. Individuals and groups lobby businesses for change, and they often get it. People who live near factories don't want them to pollute the environment and have forced tougher pollution requirements. Society expects business to be socially responsible and ethical and in that context has become increasingly concerned with player salaries. The Texas Rangers' paying Alex Rodriguez (A-Rod) U.S.$22 million a year led to questions. Will fans continue to pay higher and higher ticket prices to foot the bill for player salaries that have shot into the stratosphere? Will American families be priced out of the all-American pastime? Are athletes proper role models for our children?

Technology

The rate of technological change will continue to increase. Few organizations operate today as they did even a decade ago. Products not envisioned a few years ago are now fixtures in our lives. The computer has changed the way sport organizations conduct and transact business, and computers are a major part of every firm's systems process. Sports by their very nature are interactive, and fans (by their very nature) want to be part of the action. The web feeds this desire with message boards and fantasy leagues.[27] Professional athletes use Twitter to communicate directly with their fans. Although using Twitter allows fans to learn more about their favorite payers, it also creates an environment in which the athlete can say and do things that are not

TIME-OUT 4

Give an example of how technology has affected several different sport organizations.

professional. Nevertheless, athletes such as Chad "Ochocinco" can have a million fans following their every movement.[28]

Economy

Organizations have no control over economic growth, inflation, interest rates, or international exchange rates, yet these factors have a direct impact on performance. Sports are an important part of the economy of many countries,[29] and economic development has provided larger sections of the public with access to sport facilities.[30] In general, as measured by gross domestic product (GDP), U.S. businesses do better when the economy is growing than during times of decreased GDP, or recession. When business activity is slow, fewer fans attend games at the stadium. When interest rates are high, it costs more to borrow money; and with inflation, prices of tickets and other products go up.

Governments

U.S. federal, state, and local governments all set laws and regulations that businesses must obey. For example, the U.S. government previously allowed MLB teams to require players to sign renewal clauses (the reserve system) prohibiting them from negotiating contracts with other teams; however, the government later removed the exemption, and today many MLB players are free agents.[31] The governmental environment is sometimes referred to as the political and legal environment, and the United States has national-level governmental sport policy.[32]

Chaos in the External Environment and Interactive Management

Managers need to be aware of environmental influences.[33] In many industries, the external environment changes at an incredibly fast pace and is often chaotic. Chaos theory (as used in business) refers to the need for managers to adapt quickly to a constantly changing environment. A firm's mission or overall priorities and goals may need to change for the firm to align itself with its external environment. Today's managers must be able to thrive

APPLYING THE CONCEPT 2.2

External Environment

Identify each statement by its external environmental factor.

a. customers

b. competition

c. suppliers

d. workforce

e. shareholders

f. society

g. technology

h. governments

i. economy

_____ 6. Some critics blame the media for the escalating salaries of Major League Baseball players.

_____ 7. At one time Nike was the coolest sneaker company, but then others came along and took some of its market share.

_____ 8. I applied for a loan to start my own dance company, but I might not get it because money is tight these days, and the bank may not provide a loan.

_____ 9. Team owners have threatened to fire the general manager if the team doesn't improve this year.

_____ 10. Management was going to sell our team to Disney, but the feds said that would be in violation of antitrust laws.

on chaos and uncertainty in their environment. They should also be interactive in their management style.

According to Russell Ackoff,[34] unlike reactive managers (who make changes only when forced to by external factors) and responsive managers (who prepare for change that they predict will come about), interactive managers design a desirable future and then invent ways of bringing it about. These managers believe they can create a significant part of their future and thereby control how it will affect their organization. They try to prevent (not merely prepare for) threats and to create (not merely exploit) opportunities. Interactive managers thus make things happen for their own benefit and for that of their stakeholders.

 It's your turn to think outside the box. Dream up a future you think you can make come true, and then draw up a plan that will help you get there.

Conducting Sport Business in a Global Environment

In this section, we discuss how to classify businesses in the global economy, the importance of understanding cultural differences, ways to take a business global, and some of the risk in sport management.

As businesses grow, the complexity of their internal and external environments increases, especially when a business competes globally.[35] (For a review of the organizational environment including globalization, see figure 2.4.) So you're thinking, "Well, this sure doesn't affect the YMCA!" Think again. The YMCA movement stretches far beyond the United States. YMCAs are at work in more than 120 countries around the world, serving more than 45 million people. About 230 U.S. YMCAs maintain relationships with Ys in other countries. This means finding out about (not a small task in itself) and then complying with the rules and regulations of countries with vastly different economies, workforces, and

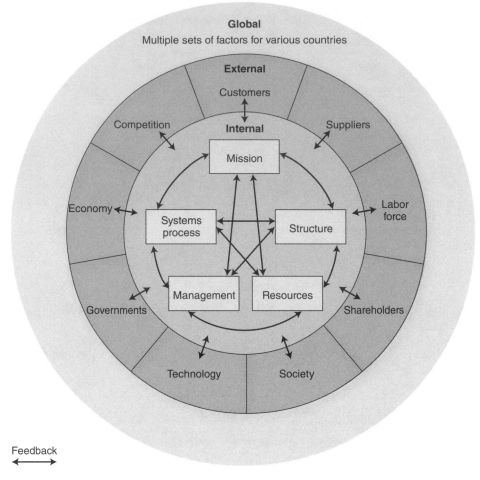

FIGURE 2.4 The business environment.

cultures—an immense undertaking even for a business that's been around as long as the Y. The globalization of sport allows sport management programs to have an international focus through teaching, research, service, and directly working in other countries.[36] College curriculums are fostering a global perspective, because business wants to hire students with international knowledge and experience.[37]

Internationalization is not new to sport, because the Olympic Games were held centuries ago in Greece,[38] and the Games are now run by the International Olympic Committee (IOC).[39] The NHL has had U.S. and Canadian teams, and tennis and golf tournaments have been global for many years. Although many of the same sports are played around the world, how they are regulated and managed varies greatly.[40] Organizations that help coordinate global sport include the International Sport Management Alliance, which in turn includes the North American Society for Sport Management (NASSM) (discussed in chapter 1), the European Association for Sport Management, the Sport Management Association of Australia and New Zealand, the Fédération Internationale de Football Association (FIFA), and the IOC, to name a few.[41]

LEARNING OUTCOME 4 ▶

State the differences between domestic, international, and multinational businesses.

Classifying Business in a Global Environment

There are three classifications of businesses in a global environment. A domestic firm conducts business in only one country, although it may have to compete against global firms at home. The local gym competes for members with the global YMCA. An **international business** is primarily based in one country but transacts business in other countries. The common international business model is importing and exporting from the home country. Ferrari sport cars are made in Italy and imported for sale by car dealers in other countries. A **multinational corporation (MNC)** has significant operations in more than one country.

Understanding International Cultural Differences and GLOBE

To be successful in the global village, it is important to understand and be able to work with people from different cultures.[42] Local and regional cultural patterns greatly affect the popularity of certain sports. Organizational leaders must be aware of cultural issues to avoid expensive errors like the time Nike used a design on the soles of its shoes that meant Allah in Arabic, which caused an embarrassing and expensive recall.

GLOBE stands for Global Leadership and Organizational Behavior Effectiveness, which is an ongoing cross-cultural investigation of leadership and national culture. The GLOBE research team used data from 825 organizations, with 18,000 managers, in 62 countries to identify nine dimensions in which national cultures are diverse. (See table 2.1 for a list

TABLE 2.1   GLOBE Dimensions

Dimension	Low	Moderate	High
Assertiveness People are tough, confrontational, and competitive.	Switzerland New Zealand	Ireland Philippines	Spain United States
Future orientation People plan, delaying spending today to invest in the future.	Russia Argentina	Slovenia India	Netherlands Canada
Gender differences People have great gender role differences.	Sweden Denmark	Brazil Italy	Egypt China
Uncertainty avoidance People are uncomfortable with ambiguity or the unknown.	Bolivia Hungary	Mexico United States	Austria Germany
Power distance People accept power inequality differences.	South Africa Netherlands	England France	Spain Thailand
Societal collectivism Teamwork is encouraged (vs. individualism).	Greece Germany	Hong Kong United States	Japan Singapore
In-group collectivism People take pride in membership (family, team, organization).	Denmark New Zealand	Israel Japan	China Morocco
Performance orientation People strive for improvement and excellence.	Russia Venezuela	England Sweden	Taiwan United States
Humane orientation People are fair, caring, and kind to others.	Singapore Spain	United States Hong Kong	Indonesia Iceland

Adapted from M. Javidan and R.J. House, 2001, "Cultural acumen for the global manager: Lessons from Project GLOBE," *Organizational Dynamics, Spring:* 289-305.

of the dimensions with examples of country ratings.) The GLOBE dimensions illustrate that managers need to lead in a manner that is based on the culture.

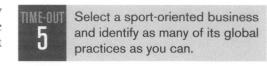

TIME-OUT 5

Select a sport-oriented business and identify as many of its global practices as you can.

LEARNING OUTCOME 5 ▶

List the lowest- and highest-risk ways to take a business global.

Taking a Sport Business Global

Since the 1990s, the question is no longer whether our businesses should go global. Rather, the question is how we go global and how fast.[43] Some would argue that the globalization of the sport industry should be termed the "Americanization of sports." Why? Because as industries go global, they typically follow the dominant market player, and for the time being in sport, that is America. Indeed, U.S. corporate sports currently appear to have a dominant position. In 2007, the NFL played a regular-season game in London between the Miami Dolphins and New York Giants.[44] In 2011, the NFL expanded to offering two regular-season games in England. Likewise, the NHL draws a large percentage of its players from Europe.

Sport businesses go global in six ways—by global sourcing, importing and exporting, licensing, contracting, engaging in joint ventures, and making direct investment. In figure 2.5, these six approaches are mapped by cost and risk and by whether they tend to be the strategy of international businesses or that of MNCs.

Global Sourcing

Global sourcing is the use of worldwide resources for inputs and transformation. It is also called outsourcing. The difference between domestic managers and global managers lies in where they look for the best deal on inputs and where they think inputs can be most advantageously transformed into outputs. Some U.S. colleges and most professional teams don't just search for talent in the United States; they have scouts all over the world looking for the best athletes. Some U.S. college grads who can't make it to the pros in the United States go to Europe to play. Both international corporations and MNCs use global sourcing. The Dallas Mavericks used global sources to determine that it was worthwhile to select Dirk Nowitzki in the first round of the 2008 NBA draft.

Importing and Exporting

With importing, domestic firms buy products from foreign firms and sell them at home. U.S. retailers must thus import Adidas (based in Germany) sneakers in order to sell them. With exporting, domestic firms sell their products to foreign buyers. Companies like Spalding export their products to almost every country in the world, and professional sport teams sell their team products globally as well. China is now the world's number-one exporter.[45]

Licensing

Under a licensing agreement, one company allows another to use its intellectual assets, such as brand name, trademarks, technology, pat-

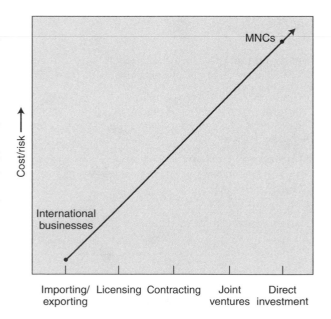

FIGURE 2.5 Taking your business global. Note: Global sourcing can be used alone (at low cost and risk), but is commonly used with the other approaches.

ents, or copyrights. For a fee, Disney allows companies around the world to make all kinds of products using the ESPN brand, and so do professional sport teams.

Contracting

With global contract manufacturing, a company hires a foreign firm to manufacture the goods but the company retains the marketing process. Nike uses this approach because it doesn't own any manufacturing facilities. Contract manufacturers make products for Nike, and Nike sells them in retail stores globally. On the other hand, Nike is criticized for allowing sweatshops to manufacture its products while making large profits. Virtually every professional sport team contracts its merchandise.

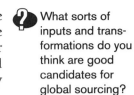 What sorts of inputs and transformations do you think are good candidates for global sourcing?

Joint Venture

A **joint venture** is created when firms share ownership (partnership) of a new enterprise. Dentsu of Japan announced the launch of Football Media Services (soccer). The service is a joint venture with Infront Sports & Media. Infront was to handle the distribution of Asian broadcast rights to all FIFA events between 2007 and 2014. The companies expected to be stronger together than when they had competed against each other in the past.[46]

Direct Investment

Direct investment occurs when a company builds or purchases operating facilities (subsidiaries) in another country. This is a common strategy for large MNCs.[47] Contracting and direct investment are also called offshoring. In 1991, to globalize American football, the NFL developed the NFL Europe subsidiary. However, on June 29, 2007, the NFL owners decided that it was not worthwhile to invest more money in NFL Europa (the last name the league was known by) just to gain the few advantages of keeping the league afloat.[48] A major factor in the failed venture was culture, because Europeans prefer soccer, which resulted in low ticket and merchandise sales. Again, you need to understand global culture.

Risks in Global Sport Management

Even as the number of globally watched sporting events grew by leaps and bounds in the 1990s, the threat of injury to athletes at international competitions was not a major concern during that time. However, the September 11, 2001, terrorist attacks in the United States sharply and forever changed this thinking. Preventing and dealing with violence and fan control around and in the facility are an important part of sport management.[49] It is impossible to ensure a risk-free environment at sporting venues. Incidents will happen and emergencies will arise. What matters is how managers prepare for, respond to, and recover from emergencies at a sporting venue.

Four issues have been highlighted as areas in which sport management students could conduct further research regarding the impact of global sport management. First, large global corporations are using developing countries' workforce to manufacture sportswear and sport equipment. Second, we are seeing an increase in the number of athletes whose country of birth and origin are no longer a limitation to where the athlete plays and competes. A third area is the role of extremely large global organizations such as FIFA, the IOC, and the NBA in organizing sports worldwide. And fourth, students of sport management should understand how globalization will affect their careers.[50]

Ethics in Sport Management

Ethics refers to the standards of right and wrong that influence behavior. Today, ethics is a major concern in businesses themselves and among the public[51]; thus ethical understanding is an important competency.[52] In this section, we discuss ethics in sports, explain why ethical behavior pays, discuss why good people do unethical things, provide some simple guidelines for ethical behavior, and discuss how you can manage employee ethics.

An organization's ethics are the collective behavior of its employees. If each employee acts ethically, the actions of the organization will be ethical too. The starting place for ethics, therefore, is you. Are you an ethical person? It's an important question, and one that you should devote some thought to. To help answer this question, complete the ethics Self-Assessment next.

Unfortunately, there is no shortage of unethical behavior in sports. Some unethical behavior can be attributed to the players themselves and a lack of judgment. For instance, a charge against Floyd Landis of doping during the Tour de France stripped Landis of his victory. Lance Armstrong had his seven titles taken away and admitted to doping. Are athletes singled out because of their fame? Whether this is so or not, the player's reputation can be ruined and the accusation may not even be true. Barry Bonds and Roger Clemens (baseball) were accused of doping but not proved guilty. Some people believe they will not get into the Hall of Fame because of the scandal.

The list of athletes who have had trouble with the law is lengthy. Athletes need to realize that young people look up to them as role models. Because of a number of scandals, ethics have received much attention in business and sport journals,[53] and colleges are being held responsible for developing ethical leaders.[54] Many academics believe that teaching ethics can help improve ethical behavior decisions,[55] although this view is controversial.

Another ethical issue is ticket scalping.[56] The tremendous success of ticket resellers such as StubHub has made scalping tickets seem like a normal aspect of buying tickets. The New England Patriots are one team strongly against the practice of reselling tickets. The Pats contend that reselling tickets at greater than U.S.$2 above face value plus various service fees is illegal. However, scalping tickets is now legal in most states.

Yes, Ethical Behavior Does Pay

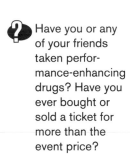

Have you or any of your friends taken performance-enhancing drugs? Have you ever bought or sold a ticket for more than the event price?

Recent years have seen an increased awareness of ethics, or the lack of it, in the sport industry. Not many days go by without the media reporting on some scandal involving unethical behavior. Laws and regulations exist to govern business behavior, but ethics go beyond legal requirements. Although unethical behavior may result in short-term gains, in the long run people often get caught and pay the price. Unethical behavior is often very costly to business.[57] Ethics scandals hurt the company's performance, access to important resources, and reputation.[58] Thus, recruiters are seeking ethical job candidates, and graduates are applying to organizations that have ethical products, ethical practices, and reputations for being ethical.[59] So yes, ethical behavior does pay.[60]

Why Good People Use Unethical Behavior

Unfortunately, it is not always easy to distinguish between ethical and unethical behavior. A gift in one country is a bribe in another, and in some countries bribes are standard business practice. So when in doubt, ask. On the other side, people sometimes act in their own interest and do whatever it takes to get what they want.[61] Four important factors contribute to a person's electing to use ethical or unethical behavior: personality, moral development, the situation, and justification.

Personality

In chapter 8, you will learn more about personality and attitudes. For now, you probably already realize that because of their personalities, some people have a higher level of ethics than others, because integrity is considered a personality trait. Unfortunately, a culture of lying and dishonesty has infected American business and society as these behaviors have become more acceptable. Pragmatism is on the increase, which asserts that there are no absolute principles or standards, no objective truth, and no objective reality. Truth simply

Ethics of Whistle-Blowing

Objective

To practice thinking ethically

Preparation

Respond to the same set of statements twice. In your first responses, focus on your own behavior and the frequency with which you use it. In the first column, place the number (1-5) that represents how often you did, do, or would do the behavior if you had the chance. These numbers will allow you to determine your level of ethics. Be honest—students will not share their ethics scores.

In your second responses, focus on current or past coworkers. Place an *O* on the line after the number if you observed someone doing this behavior. Also place a *W* on the line if you blew the whistle on this behavior within the organization or externally.

Column 1: **Frequently**   **Never**

                  1   **2**   **3**   **4**   **5**

Column 2: **O (observed)**   **W (reported)**

College

_____ 1. _____ Cheating on homework assignments

_____ 2. _____ Trying to pass off someone else's work as your own work

_____ 3. _____ Cheating on exams

Team (or replace with work terms)

_____ 4. _____ Coming to practice late

_____ 5. _____ Leaving practice early

_____ 6. _____ Taking longer breaks than allowed

_____ 7. _____ Calling in sick to skip practice when not sick

_____ 8. _____ Socializing or goofing off during practice rather than working diligently

_____ 9. _____ Socializing or goofing off during games

_____ 10. _____ Using the team phone to make personal calls

_____ 11. _____ Using the team copier for a personal purpose

_____ 12. _____ Mailing personal things through the team mail

_____ 13. _____ Taking home team supplies and keeping them

_____ 14. _____ Taking home team equipment without permission for personal use and returning it

_____ 15. _____ Giving team merchandise to friends or allowing them to take merchandise without saying anything

_____ 16. _____ Falsifying reimbursement paperwork for meals and travel or other expenses

_____ 17. _____ Drinking alcohol the night or day before games

_____ 18. _____ Taking spouse or friends out to eat and charging the expense to the team

_____ 19. _____ Taking a spouse or friend on business trips and charging the expense to the team

_____ 20. _____ Taking illegal drugs to enhance performance (or being high at work)

To determine your ethics score, add up your numbers. Your total will be between 20 and 100.

Place your score here _____ and circle it on the following continuum.

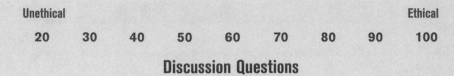

| Unethical | | | | | | | | Ethical |
| 20 | 30 | 40 | 50 | 60 | 70 | 80 | 90 | 100 |

Discussion Questions

1. For the college items 1 through 3, who is harmed and who benefits from these unethical behaviors?

   _____

2. For team items 4 through 20, select the three unethical behaviors (circle their numbers) you consider the most serious. Who is harmed and who benefits by these unethical behaviors?

   _____

3. If you observed unethical behavior but didn't report it, why did you not do so? If you did blow the whistle, why did you do so? What was the result?

   _____

   _____

   _____

4. As a manager it is your responsibility to hold your team to high standards of behavior. If you know employees are behaving unethically, will you take action to enforce compliance with your organization's code of ethics?

   _____

   _____

   _____

   _____

 As you could be asked in court, do you tell the truth, the whole truth, and nothing but the truth?

becomes saying whatever it takes to get what you want or make you feel good.[62] Some people lie deliberately, with the attitude that lying is no big deal; some people don't even realize that they are liars. In a national U.S. poll, 48% of workers admitted to cutting corners on quality control, covering up incidents, abusing or lying about sick days, lying to or deceiving customers, cheating on expense accounts, and paying or receiving kickbacks. But personality alone is not a good predictor of unethical behavior.[63]

Moral Development

A second factor affecting ethical behavior is moral development, which refers to distinguishing right from wrong and choosing to do the right thing. Moral development affects people's ethical decisions.[64] Lack of moral development is considered one of the many reasons for unethical behavior.[65] There are three levels of personal moral development.

At the first level (preconventional), a person chooses right and wrong behavior based on self-interest and the likely consequences of the behavior (reward or punishment). Those whose ethical reasoning has advanced to the second level (conventional) seek to maintain expected standards and live up to the expectations of others. Perceived peer behavior has the largest effect on behavior decisions. This involves following the crowd, giving in to peer pressure, and complying with group norms. Those at the third level (postconventional) make an effort to do the right thing regardless of what others think or do.

Although most of us have the potential to reach the third level of moral development, only about 20% of people reach this level. Most people behave at the conventional level, whereas some do not advance beyond the first level. But sport management scholars call for moral sensitivity[66] and state that we have a moral obligation to do the right thing.[67] So we need to raise moral standards. What level of moral development do you consider yourself to have reached? What can you do to further your moral development?

The Situation

A third factor affecting ethical behavior is situational forces. Unsupervised people in highly competitive situations who are under high pressure regarding bottom-line results are more likely to engage in unethical behavior.[68] Some people cook the books for one period, figuring they will make it up the next period, only to dig themselves into a hole they can't get out of. People also consider the chances of getting caught and the penalty.[69] Unethical behavior occurs more often when there is no formal ethics policy or code of ethics and when unethical behavior is not punished; unethical behavior is especially prevalent when it is rewarded. Some people simply make up their own rules. They cheat, lie, waffle, or claim naïveté, not only because it is to their advantage but also because they create their own rationale for what is acceptable.[70] People are also less likely to report unethical behavior (blow the whistle) when they perceive the violation as not being serious or when they are friends of the offender.

Justification

Most people understand right and wrong behavior and have a conscience. So why do good people do bad things? When people behave unethically, it usually is not because they have a character flaw or were born bad. Few people see themselves as unethical, so they justify their behavior by determining whether the action was rationally or reasonably acceptable.[71] We all want to view ourselves in a positive manner. Therefore, when we behave unethically, we often justify the behavior so that we don't have a guilty conscience or feel remorse. People at the preconventional and conventional levels of moral development more commonly use the following thinking processes to justify their unethical behavior.

- **Moral justification** is the process of reinterpreting immoral behavior in terms of a higher purpose. The terrorists who struck the United States on September 11, 2001, killed innocent people—as do terrorists elsewhere—yet they believe that their killing is for the good and that they will go to heaven for their actions. People who behave unethically (lie about a competitor to hurt its reputation, fix prices, steal confidential information, take performance-enhancing drugs) say that they do so for the good of the organization or its employees.

- **Conventional rationalization** is using the excuse that "everyone does it."[72] "We all take bribes and kickbacks; it's the way we do business." "They don't pay me enough, so I deserve it." "We all take merchandise home (steal)." Have you said any of these things?

- **Displacement of responsibility** is the process of blaming one's unethical behavior on others. "I was only following orders; my boss told me to inflate the figures." Would you perform unethical behavior if asked to do so?

- **Advantageous comparison** is the process of comparing oneself to others who are worse. "I only call in sick when I'm not a few times a year; Tom and Ellen do it all the time." "We pollute less than our competitors do." Do you use this one?

- **Disregard for or distortion of consequences** is the process of minimizing the harm caused by the unethical behavior. "No one will be hurt if I take the drugs, and I will not get caught. And if I do, I'll just get a slap on the wrist anyway." Was this the case at Enron? Have you ever been caught and punished?

- **Attribution of blame** is the process of claiming that the unethical behavior was caused by someone else's behavior. "It's my coworker's fault that I repeatedly hit him. He called me a [blank]—so I had to hit him." Do you take responsibility for your actions?

- **Euphemistic labeling** is the process of using words to make the behavior sound acceptable. *Terrorist group* sounds bad, but *freedom fighter* sounds justifiable. *Misleading* or *covering up* sounds better than *lying*. How is your vocabulary?

Being pragmatic by changing the rules or bending the truth to whatever works for you or makes you feel good often leads to unethical behavior. Unethical behavior that you justify might give you some type of short-term gain. But in the long run, you sabotage your own consciousness, undermine your own pride, and open yourself up to the risk of harm. Such harm can include the loss of trust, reputation, and friends; receiving disciplinary action or being fired; facing lawsuits; and going to jail.[73]

As a sport manager, you may hear employees justify their unethical behavior using these methods. How will you handle these employees? Throughout this book you will learn how to manage people, and in chapter 13 you will learn how to coach and discipline employees.

Simple Guidelines to Ethical Behavior

Every day in your personal and professional life you face decisions in which you can make ethical or unethical choices. You make your choices based on your past experiences with parents, teachers, friends, coaches, managers, and teammates or coworkers. Your life history shapes your conscience, which helps you choose right and wrong in a given situation. The following are some guidelines that can help you make the right decisions.

Golden and Platinum Rules

The golden rule is to treat others as you would have them treat you. Treating people the way you want to be treated can lead to ethical behavior. But in today's diverse global world, not everyone wants to be treated the way you do. So the new platinum rule was developed, which says to treat other people as they want to be treated. These are simple rules to remember, but they are often broken. Do you follow these rules? Imagine what a great world this would be if everyone followed these rules.

Four-Way Test

Rotary International developed the four-way test to frame our thinking and business actions in an ethical manner. When you are faced with an ethical dilemma, ask yourself the following about your choice: (1) Is it the truth? (2) Is it fair to all concerned? (3) Will it build goodwill and better friendship? (4) Will it be beneficial to all concerned? If you can answer yes to these questions, you are probably making an ethical choice.

For example, a former coach of the women's basketball team at Howard University was found to be in violation of rules governing recruitment inducements. The coach knowingly improperly paid for an airline ticket for a prospective student-athlete to visit the university. The coach then approached the players on her team, requesting that they provide false information about the visit.[74] The National Collegiate Athletic Association (NCAA) ruled that the coach did not pass this test. The coach was trying to hide the truth, and her own team would no longer be able to trust her. The penalty to the university for this infraction was to limit the coach's athletic responsibilities, and the coach was fired. Would you ask others to lie for you? Would you lie for others?

LEARNING OUTCOME 6 ▶

Explain the stake-
holders' approach
to ethics.

Stakeholders' Approach to Ethics

Under the **stakeholders' approach to ethics,** when making decisions you try to create a win–win situation for all relevant stakeholders so that everyone benefits from the decision. (Of course, this is not always possible—we'll deal with that in a moment.) The higher up in management you go, the more stakeholders you have to deal with. So in muddy situations, ask yourself two simple questions: Am I proud to tell my stakeholders of my decision? Am I justifying my answer? If you are proud and not justifying, then your decision is probably ethical. If you are not proud or you keep rationalizing your decision, it may not be ethical. If you are still unsure whether a decision you are considering is ethical, talk to your boss, higher-level managers, ethics committee members, or other people whose ethics you trust. A reluctance to ask others for advice may be a signal that your choice is unethical.

Sometimes decisions must be made that do not benefit all stakeholders—layoffs, for example. Yet even layoffs can—and should—be done ethically. Companies can, for example, offer severance pay and outplacement services to help the employees get jobs with other organizations.

What stakeholders did the Red Sox disappoint when they lost their big stars like Manny Ramirez, Johnny Damon, and Pedro Martinez? What stakeholders did they satisfy when they successfully rebuilt their team?

Going Beyond the Stakeholders' Approach to Ethics

We hope you can be among the few who go beyond the ethical guidelines. Some managers, called servant leaders, go beyond creating a win–win situation and make self-sacrifices for others' benefit. Most likely your parents, a coach or two, and others have made sacrifices to help you get to where you are today. How often do you look out for number one without concern for, or at the expense of, others? How often do you do things with your friends that they want to do but you don't enjoy doing? How often do you go out of your way to help others without expecting anything in return? If students were volunteering in great numbers, some schools and college would not have added community service requirements for graduation. If you were required to perform community service, did you do so regretfully or cheerfully?

Managing Ethics

Managers develop their organization's guidelines for ethical behavior, set the example, and enforce the rules they want to play by. But ultimately, individuals are responsible for their own behavior and must pay the consequences, including being fired and going to jail.

Codes of Ethics

Codes of ethics (also called codes of conduct) state the importance of conducting business in an ethical manner and provide guidelines for ethical behavior. Most large businesses and sport organizations have written codes of ethics. Knowing and following the code can help keep you honest and out of trouble. On page 46 is the code of ethics for the National Association of Sports Officials (NASO).

Support and Example of Top Management

It is the responsibility of management from the top down to develop codes of ethics, to ensure that employees are taught what is and is not considered ethical behavior, and to enforce the company's code of ethics. However, managers' primary responsibility is to lead by example. Managers, especially top managers, set the standard because employees tend to imitate managers' behavior.[75] During the 2002 scandal involving the IOC, some of the top IOC members were corrupt and others followed their lead, and still others in the IOC allowed this unethical behavior to continue by ignoring it. Eventually measures were taken to stop the unethical behavior.[76]

Coaches and physical education teachers hold a special responsibility when it comes to "talking the talk" of ethical behavior in sports. Paul "Bear" Bryant, former football coach at the University of Alabama, once stated, "We have the opportunity to teach intangible lessons to our players that will be priceless to them in future years. We are in a position to teach these young people intrinsic values that cannot be learned at home, school, or any place outside of the athletic field."[77]

Enforcing Ethical Behavior

If employees are not punished for unethical behavior, they will continue to pursue questionable business practices. To help keep people honest, many organizations create ethics

NASO's Code of Conduct for Sport Officials

1. Officials shall bear a great responsibility for engendering public confidence in sports.

2. Officials shall be free of obligation to any interest other than the impartial and fair judging of sports competitions.

3. Officials shall hold and maintain the basic tenets of officiating, which include history, integrity, neutrality, respect, sensitivity, professionalism, discretion, and tactfulness.

4. Officials shall master both rules of the game and mechanics necessary to enforce the rules and shall exercise authority in an impartial, firm, and controlled manner.

5. Officials shall uphold the honor and dignity of the profession in all interactions with student-athletes, coaches, school administrators, colleagues, and the public.

6. Officials shall display and execute superior communication skills, both verbal and nonverbal.

7. Officials shall recognize that anything that may lead to a conflict of interest, either real or apparent, must be avoided. Gifts, favors, special treatment, privileges, employment, or a personal relationship with a school or team that can compromise the perceived impartiality of officiating must be avoided.

8. Officials shall prepare themselves both physically and mentally, shall dress neatly and appropriately, and shall comport themselves in a manner consistent with the high standards of the profession.

9. Officials shall not be party to actions designed to unfairly limit or restrain access to officiating, officiating assignments, or association membership. This includes selection for positions of leadership based on economic factors, race, creed, color, age, sex, physical handicap, country, or national origin.

10. Officials shall be punctual and professional in the fulfillment of all contractual obligations.

11. Officials shall work with each other and their governing bodies in a constructive and cooperative manner.

12. Officials shall resist every temptation and outside pressure to use their position as an official to benefit themselves.

13. Officials shall never participate in any form of illegal gambling on sports contests, may never gamble on any sporting even in which they have either direct or indirect involvement, and may never gamble on events involving high school athletics.

14. Officials shall not make false or misleading statements regarding their qualifications, rating, credentials, experience, training, or competence.

15. Officials shall accept responsibility for all actions taken.

Reprinted, by permission, from NASO.

committees. Such committees act as judge and jury to determine whether unethical behavior has occurred and what the punishment should be for violating company policy. A recent trend is the establishment of ethics offices, in which a director or vice president reports directly to the CEO, establishes ethics policies, listens to employees' complaints, conducts training, and investigates abuses such as sexual harassment. For example, one of the corrective actions that can be taken when a university is in violation of an NCAA rule is to add an assistant director position in the compliance office to increase the understanding of NCAA rules on campus.

 TIME-OUT 6 Examine a recent scandal in the sport industry, preferably a local one, and identify which decisions led to unethical behavior and why.

As a means of enforcing ethical behavior, employees should be encouraged to blow the whistle on questionable behavior. Whistle-blowing occurs when employees expose what they believe to be unethical behavior by fellow employees. Historically, this has been a

APPLYING THE CONCEPT 2.3

Stakeholders

Identify each statement by its stakeholder.

a. employees
b. customers
c. society
d. competitors
e. suppliers
f. government

_____ 11. We're going to fight this—we do not want a baseball stadium downtown!

_____ 12. I bought an ice-level seat for the hockey game. The glass shattered in my face when a player was checked into the boards, causing me injury.

_____ 13. The town board is very political, so you have to play games if you want to get a liquor license for home games.

_____ 14. I'm sorry to hear your retail sales are down at your sporting goods stores, because that means we'll have to cut back production on team T-shirts.

_____ 15. I bid on the job, but another printer got the contract to print the programs for home games.

dicey action to take. Whistle-blowers have ended up being harassed on the job and even losing their jobs. However, companies are coming around to the idea that listening to whistle-blowers is in their best interest; it is also illegal to retaliate against whistle-blowers.

How do you feel about reporting unethical behavior to your managers? What if they are the ones engaging in the behavior—would you go outside the organization to report them? It's not an easy decision, because we have a deeply embedded cultural reluctance to "tattle." It would behoove you to give this some thought, however, because you will most likely face this dilemma at work. As pointed out in the Self-Assessment, you probably already have.

Social Responsibility

Corporate social responsibility (CSR) has become important within the sport industry.[78] Sports are a significant social institution to a community. Consequently, sports affect economic and social issues in our society.[79] It is important for sport organizations to act in an ethical manner. Ethics and social responsibility are often discussed together because they are so closely related and are both important.[80] Ethical behavior is often socially responsible, and social responsibility is usually ethical. **Social responsibility** is the conscious effort to operate in a manner that creates a win–win situation for all stakeholders. In this section, we discuss the need to be a good corporate citizen, why it pays to be socially responsible, the four levels of social responsibility, and sustainability.

Being a Good Corporate Citizen

Socially responsible companies step up to society's plate and determine ways they can marshal resources and make a difference. Corporate citizenship involves a commitment to improve community well-being through discretionary business practices and contributions

Do you shop at Walmart? If you don't think Walmart is ethical and socially responsible, should you shop there anyway?

of corporate resources. Organizations invest employee time and money in pro bono work, philanthropy, support for community education and health, and protection of the environment.[81] For customers and fans, such companies endeavor to provide safe products and services with customer value and a safe environment at athletic events. There are many ways that responsible companies can work to improve the quality of life for people in a society.

Boston Red Sox top-level managers and star players work closely with the Dana-Farber Cancer Institute to help children, and Indianapolis Colts football players work with kids. The Red Sox often have current and former Dana-Farber patients throw out the first pitch at their home ballgames. Dana-Farber and the Red Sox also sell a license plate with the Red Sox logo to raise funds for patient care and cancer research. Socially responsible companies go to great lengths to provide employees with safe working conditions with adequate pay and benefits. Some organizations of all sizes focus on the triple bottom line—making a profit for shareholders, benefiting society, and helping the environment.[82]

 What charities does your favorite team support?

Does It Pay to Be Socially Responsible?

Although research is inconsistent on support for a clear link between social responsibility and the bottom line, many companies would answer with a resounding yes! The value of the goodwill engendered by being a good corporate citizen is difficult to quantify in financial statements, but company stakeholders benefit, and that is a win–win situation for the company. Virtually all large international corporations engage in socially responsible ways because they benefit by increased sales and market share; strengthened brand positioning; enhanced corporate image and clout; increased ability to attract, motivate, and retain employees; decreased operating costs; and increased appeal to investors and financial analysts.[83]

Levels of Corporate Social Responsibility

Figure 2.6 illustrates the four levels of social responsibility in the continuum from the lowest level to the highest one; next we discuss these levels and define the social audit.

Social Obstruction

At this level, managers deliberately perform, or request employees to perform, unethical or illegal business practices. For example, Bruce Pearl, head basketball coach at the University of Tennessee, was fired in March of 2011 for recruiting violations. Pearl admitted lying to NCAA investigators when they were looking into possible recruiting violations committed by the Tennessee coaching staff.[84]

LEARNING OUTCOME 7 ▶ ### Social Obligation

Discuss the four levels of social responsibility in business.

At this level managers meet only the minimum legal requirements. Compliance is an approach in which firms rely on easy solutions and resist voluntarily initiating socially responsible programs. The 18th-century economists Adam Smith and Milton Friedman theorized that when a business makes a profit, it is being socially responsible because it is providing jobs for employees and goods and services for customers. Thus, a corporation has no responsibility to society beyond that of obeying the law and maximizing profits for shareholders. Although this level is ethical, most firms today operate at a higher level.

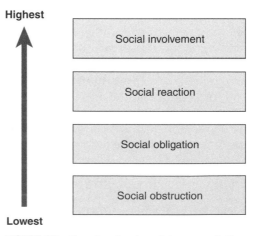

FIGURE 2.6 Four levels of social responsibility.

Social Reaction

Here, managers respond to appropriate societal requests. The most common type of social reaction takes place when civic groups ask companies for donations for the arts, college scholarships, or antidrug programs; sponsorship of sport teams; or the use of company facilities for meetings or sport teams. For example, each year SportsStuff and other retailers give merchandise to the Holy Cross Athletic Association to raffle off to raise money for its sport teams.

TIME-OUT 7 Select a sport organization and identify its level of social responsibility for a current issue.

Social Involvement

At this level, managers voluntarily initiate socially responsible acts. As discussed earlier, most major international corporations have social-involvement programs. The NFL has been active with the United Way for the past 35 years to strengthen local communities. Owners, players, coaches, and staff are currently helping with childhood obesity and creating healthier lifestyles.[85] It would be very difficult to find any professional sport team that is not involved in some worthwhile cause. For example, England's Liverpool Football Club (the world's most famous soccer team, which was acquired by the Boston Red Sox), worked closely with UNICEF in China to help teach children the real facts about HIV/AIDS.

Social Audit

Although not a level of social responsibility, a social audit measures corporate social responsibility. Businesses often set social objectives and then measure whether they have

APPLYING THE CONCEPT 2.4

Social Responsibility

Identify each statement by its level of social responsibility.

- a. social obstruction
- b. social obligation
- c. social reaction
- d. social involvement

_____ 16. We agree—a Boys & Girls Club downtown would help develop new sport programs in our city. We'll give you U.S.$1,000 to get the ball rolling.

_____ 17. I'm disappointed with the reading levels of players coming from our local high school. Betty, I want you to contact the principal and see if you can work together to develop a program to improve reading skills.

_____ 18. Bill, the auditor will be here next week, so we'd better make sure that the hockey equipment we took from inventory does not show up as missing.

_____ 19. We reviewed factory workers' hourly labor rates in Vietnam because of the bad press we were receiving. Now we pay higher than the minimum wage in Vietnam, which is more expensive for our company.

_____ 20. As of June 1 the new regulations go into effect. We will have to cut the amount of waste we dump into the river by half. Get the lowest bidder to pick up the other half and dispose of it.

met their objectives. Many corporations include a social audit in their annual reports. Although certain organizations maintain their social responsibilities at a given, consistent level, others score at different levels for different issues. In place of or in addition to the social audit, many organizations present information about their social responsibility activities on their websites. Where to find the social information varies. Some companies provide links from their home page and others include the information in their "About Us" link.

Sustainability

Sustainability is meeting the needs of today without sacrificing future generations' ability to meet their needs.[86] Thus, focusing on sustainability is being socially responsible. Society expects sustainability, or for managers to use resources wisely and responsibly; protect the environment; minimize the amount of air, water, energy, minerals, and other materials found in the final goods we consume; recycle and reuse these goods to the extent possible rather than drawing on nature to replenish them; respect nature's calm, tranquility, and beauty; and eliminate toxins that harm people in the workplace and communities.[87] Business, society, and governments are working to sustain our environment through sustainable development.[88] However, getting businesses and governments to cooperate is very difficult.

Professional sport organizations are becoming more active in developing sustainable management business practices. For example, NASCAR is focused on cutting costs by recycling, conserving, and generating its own energy. NASCAR has also implemented green initiatives such as collecting used fuel, planting trees to offset carbon emissions, and even using sheep to cut the infield grass.[89] Professional sport teams such as the St. Louis Cardinals and the Seattle Mariners recycle and conserve energy. The Portland Trail Blazers, the Miami Heat, and the Orlando Magic play in energy-efficient arenas certified by the United States Green Building Council. NASCAR suppliers, such as Coca-Cola, have significantly increased their efforts to recycle waste at sporting events.[90]

@ TAKE IT TO THE NET

Please visit www.HumanKinetics.com/AppliedSportManagementSkills and go to this book's companion web study guide, where you will find the following:

A list of websites associated with the concepts in this chapter

Exercises that you will need Internet access to complete

Online versions of chapter exercises and end-of-chapter learning aids

An exercise that helps you define the Key Terms

LEARNING AIDS

CHAPTER SUMMARY

1. Describe the five components of the internal environment.

Management refers to the people responsible for an organization's performance. Mission is the organization's purpose or reason for being. The organization uses human, physical, financial, and informational resources to accomplish its mission. The systems process is the organization's method of transforming inputs into outputs. Structure refers to the way in which the organization groups its resources to accomplish its mission.

2. Explain the two primary principles of total quality management.

The two primary principles of total quality management are to (1) focus on delivering customer value and (2) continually improve the system and its processes. To be successful, businesses must continually offer value to attract and retain customers. Without customers you don't have a business.

3. Explain how factors in the external environment affect the internal business environment.

Customers should determine what products the business offers, for without customer value there are no customers or business. Competitors' business practices, such as features and prices, often have to be duplicated to maintain customer value. Poor-quality inputs from suppliers result in poor-quality outputs without customer value. Without a qualified workforce, products and services will have little or no customer value. Shareholders, through an elected board of directors, hire top managers and provide directives for the organization. Society pressures the business to perform or not perform certain activities, such as pollution control. The business must develop new technologies, or at least keep up with them, to provide customer value. Economic activity affects the organization's ability to provide customer value. For example, inflated prices lead to lower customer value. Governments set the rules and regulations that business must adhere to.

4. State the differences between domestic, international, and multinational businesses.

Domestic firms do business in only one country. International firms are primarily based in one country but transact business with other countries. Multinational corporations have significant operations in more than one country.

5. List the lowest- and highest-risk ways to take a business global.

Importing-exporting is the lowest-risk strategy, and direct investment is the highest-risk strategy. Global sourcing can be part of either method.

6. Explain the stakeholders' approach to ethics.

In this approach to ethics, organizations create a win–win situation for the relevant parties affected by the decision. If as a manager you are proud to tell relevant stakeholders of your decision, it is probably ethical. If you are not proud or keep rationalizing your decision, it may not be ethical.

7. Discuss the four levels of social responsibility in business.

Social responsibility can be divided into four levels, which range from low to high. At the low end, social obstruction, managers behave unethically and illegally. At the next level, social obligation, managers meet only the minimum legal requirements. With social reaction, managers respond to societal requests. At the highest level, social involvement, managers voluntarily initiate socially responsible acts.

REVIEW AND DISCUSSION QUESTIONS

1. Do most sport organizations focus on creating customer value? Use specific examples to defend your position.

2. Do you think that all sport organizations should use TQM? Why or why not?

3. Describe the relationship between management and an organization's mission, resources, systems process, and structure. Which of these internal factors are ends and which are means?

4. What technological breakthrough in sports has had the greatest impact on the quality of your life, and why?

5. Should government regulation of sport and business be increased, be decreased, or remain the same? Defend your position.

6. Categorize a few sport companies you are familiar with as international or multinational.

7. For the companies you listed in question 6, identify their methods of going global.

8. Do you believe that ethical behavior pays off in the long run? Why or why not?

9. What guides your behavior now? Will you use one of the ethical guides from the text? If yes, which one and why?

10. Can ethics be taught and learned? Defend your position.

11. How do companies benefit from being socially responsible? Give some examples.

12. If you were a CEO, what level of social responsibility would you aspire to? How might you go about attaining it?

13. Has Alex Rodriguez demonstrated that he is worth U.S.$30 million a year? Does his ethical behavior on and off the field have anything to do with this?

14. Research what socially responsible activities Alex Rodriguez is involved with off the playing field.

15. If you can't control the external environment, why be concerned about it anyway?

16. Should people in the United States make an effort to buy products made in America? If yes, how should "made in America" be defined?

CASE

Ethics and the 2012 London Olympics

The scandals associated with the 2002 Salt Lake City Olympics (the bribery involved in the site location process and the judging practices used to award the figure skating medals, among others) forced the IOC to reevaluate its practices. The IOC faced two problems that had been difficult to manage. First, there was the long-standing problem of illegal doping by athletes. Second, the committee looking to bring the Olympics to Beijing in 2008 had to address long-standing human rights violations attributed to China's leaders. Issues of further concern included a lack of media freedom and free speech and the mistreatment and torture of human rights activists. The 2008 Olympic torch relay was slightly delayed by protestors in major cities such as London and San Francisco. Protesters were concerned about human rights issues in China. Still, the IOC hoped that media attention would be on sports and not human rights problems.[91]

The IOC president, Belgium's Jacques Rogge, said that the reforms implemented in the wake of the 1999 Salt Lake City bribes-for-votes scandal strengthened the IOC by widening its committee base (which originally included only national VIPs) to include heads of major international sport federations and athletes.

One of the challenges ahead was the fight against doping: Rogge commented, "You can win many battles but the war is more difficult. You find ways to discover drugs but there are new drugs coming." He hailed the collaboration between the World Anti-Doping Agency and governments, which "have means we don't have like customs and police investigations." However, he also noted, "The end of this fight is very far from now. The war is very difficult. But with the new World Anti-Doping Agency, there is a very good collaboration now between the world of sport and governments. For the last few years, governments have become very interested in this fight."[92]

The 2008 Beijing Olympics turned out to be a big success. The opening ceremonies were spectacular; the U.S. men's basketball team "redeemed" themselves by winning a gold medal; Chinese and U.S. women gymnasts both won hard-earned gold medals; and U.S. swimmer Michael Phelps broke many Olympic records by winning eight gold medals.

With regard to the management of the Games, only one unfortunate incident resulted in a death; a family member of the U.S. volleyball team. A sole individual, working alone, attacked the tourist for reasons still unknown.

In summary, concerns with environmental issues, freedom of speech, and the high use of banned drugs did not materialize.

The 2012 Summer Olympic Games were held in London, England. Rogge has tried to help the Olympic movement be more transparent and open about their activities. However, the memories of the 2002 Salt Lake Games still linger. He has also watched the bidding race for the 2018 FIFA World Cup, which has led to the suspension of two members over allegations of wrongdoing among committee members.[93] Potentially much worse, there were riots in the streets of London in August of 2011. The riots were started by demonstrators who felt that police used too much force when they killed a local Englishman. Two important soccer games were postponed. Although the riots were a blemish on the London Games, it seemed that the streets of London were back to being an orderly tourist attraction.[94]

For details on the planning, implementation, and results of the London 2012 Olympic Games, visit the official website at www.london2012.com/.

Case Questions

1. The Olympics provide a quality product with customer value.
   a. true
   b. false

2. The Olympics have shareholders.
   a. true
   b. false

3. Technology has had a major effect on the Olympics.
   a. true
   b. false

4. Officials connected with the Olympics have been accused of unethical practices.
   a. true
   b. false

5. Beijing 2008 Olympics managers made themselves ready to strongly enforce ethical behavior.
   a. true
   b. false

6. Which of the following external factors is the primary pressure facing the Olympics?
   a. customers and competition
   b. society and governments
   c. suppliers and labor
   d. economy and competition
   e. stakeholders and technology

7. What level of social responsibility does the IOC practice?
   a. social obstruction
   b. social obligation
   c. social reaction
   d. social involvement

8. Are the Olympics a domestic, an international, or a multinational sport organization?

9. What management procedures could the IOC implement before the 2016 Games to prevent any scandals?

10. Using the www.rio2016.com website, learn all you can about what type of activities volunteers can perform at the Rio Olympics.

11. Have the changes in monitoring procedures stopped the doping problems of Olympic athletes? Can you provide any examples of athletes who were removed from the Games because of doping?

SKILL-BUILDER EXERCISES

Skill-Builder 2.1: Analyzing Organizational Environment and Management Practices

Objective

To develop your ability to analyze an organization's business and management practices

Preparation

Select a sport organization, preferably one for which you have worked or played, and answer the following questions. You may need to contact people in the organization to answer some of the questions.

Internal Environment

1. Identify the organization's top managers and briefly discuss their leadership style.

   _____
   _____
   _____

2. State the organization's mission.

   _____
   _____
   _____

3. Identify some of its major resources.

   _____

4. Explain its systems process. Discuss how it maintains quality and customer value.

   _____
   _____
   _____

5. Identify the organization's structure by listing its major departments.

   _____

External Environment

As you answer the following questions, state how each external factor affects the organization.

1. Identify the organization's target customers.

   _____

2. Identify its major competitors.

_____

3. Identify its major suppliers.

_____

4. From what labor pool does the organization recruit most of its workforce?

_____

5. Is the organization publicly held? If yes, on which stock exchanges is it listed? If no, who owns it?

_____

6. Describe the ways in which the organization affects society (at the local, state, and national levels) and also the ways in which society affects it.

_____

_____

_____

7. Describe some technologies that the organization and its industry niche have used in the past, use now, and may use in the future. Is the organization a technology leader?

_____

_____

_____

8. Identify which governments affect the organization, and list some major laws and regulations that it must abide by.

_____

_____

_____

9. Explain how the economy affects the organization.

_____

_____

_____

Globalization

1. Is the organization a domestic, an international, or a multinational company? If it is international or multinational, list and briefly describe (a) some of its global activities (e.g., import and export) and (b) some of its business practices (e.g., management style, strategy).

_____

_____

_____

Ethics

1. Does the organization have a formal code of ethics? If yes, describe the code and how it is used and disseminated to employees. If no, how does it manage ethical issues?

_____

_____

_____

2. Does management lead by example? How are ethical behaviors encouraged? How are the rules enforced?

_____

_____

_____

Social Responsibility

1. On which level of social responsibility does the organization operate? Identify some of the things it does to be a good corporate citizen.

_____

_____

_____

In-Class Application

Complete the preceding skill-building preparation before class.
   Choose one (10-30 minutes):

Break into groups of three to five members and present your answers to the preceding questions.

Select one student's example and as a group present it to the entire class.

Conduct informal, whole-class discussion of student findings.

Wrap-Up

Take a few minutes to write your answers to the following questions:
What did I learn from this experience? How will I use this knowledge?

_____

_____

As a class, discuss student responses.

Skill-Builder 2.2: Cultural Diversity Awareness

Procedure 1 (4-6 minutes)

You and your classmates will share your international experience and nationalities. Start with people who have lived in another country, then move to those who have visited another country, and follow with discussion of nationality (e.g., I am half French and Irish but have never been to either country). The instructor or a recorder will write the countries on the board until several countries and nationalities are listed or the time is up.

Procedure 2 (10-30 minutes)

You and your classmates will share your knowledge of cultural differences between the country in which the course is being taught and those listed on the board. This is a good opportunity for international students and those who have visited other countries to share their experiences. For example, in Spain, most people have a 2-hour lunch break and go home for a big meal and may take a nap. In Japan, people expect to receive and give gifts. You may also discuss cultural differences within the country.

Wrap-Up

Take a few minutes to write your answers to the following questions:
What did I learn from this experience? How will I use this knowledge?

_____

_____

SPORTS AND SOCIAL MEDIA EXERCISES

1. Search "Richard Lapchick" on www.youtube.com. What sport management subjects does Richard Lapchick study? List three of his achievements.

   _____

   _____

   _____

2. Use the blog http://sportsmanagementdegree.org/2010/top-50-sports-business-blogs to find information about ethics and global issues related to sport management.

   _____

   _____

   _____

GAME PLAN FOR STARTING A SPORT BUSINESS

Analyze your three business ideas. Which idea do you think has the most global opportunity? Ethical opportunity?

1. Sport business idea 1:

   _____

   _____

2. Sport business idea 2:

   _____

   _____

3. Sport business idea 3:

   _____

   _____

PART II

Planning

Planning is the first of the four management functions that organize this book. The first area of planning discussed is creative problem solving and decision making (chapter 3). Using the process of defining the problem or opportunity, setting objectives and criteria, generating alternatives, selecting the most feasible alternative, implementing the decision, and then controlling the results is a time-tested method of improving decision making. Chapter 4 covers the long-term strategic planning process; FIFA and Nike are highlighted to emphasize the need to analyze an ever-changing external environment for business opportunities. The competitive advantage a sport organization has today might be eliminated in the near future due to poor strategic planning at the corporate level, business level, or functional level of an organization.

Creative Problem Solving and Decision Making

LEARNING OUTCOMES

After studying this chapter, you should be able to

1. describe how meeting objectives, solving problems, and making decisions are connected;

2. explain how management functions, decision making, and problem solving relate;

3. list the six steps in decision making;

4. identify programmed and nonprogrammed decisions and recognize certain, risky, and uncertain business conditions;

5. know when to use the different decision models and when to make decisions as a group or as an individual;

6. state the difference between an objective and "must" and "want" criteria;

7. explain how creativity and innovation differ;

8. describe the three stages in the creative process; and

9. explain how quantitative and cost–benefit analyses facilitate selecting alternatives.

KEY TERMS

problem	programmed decisions	creative process
problem solving	nonprogrammed decisions	devil's advocate
decision making	decision-making conditions	brainstorming
reflexive decision style	criteria	synectics
reflective decision style	creativity	nominal grouping
consistent decision style	innovation	consensus mapping

DEVELOPING YOUR SKILLS

The decisions you make will affect your sport management career. Problem solving and decision making are crucial skills of effective managers. By following the six steps in the decision-making model presented in this chapter, you can improve your ability to solve problems and make decisions.

REVIEWING THEIR GAME PLAN

Evaluating Adidas' Decision to Acquire Reebok—Seven Years Later

For the past 80 years, legendary soccer players trotted around playing fields all over the world, from Seoul to Manchester to Sao Paulo to Kabul, sporting the three-stripe Adidas logo on their footwear. Yet, caught in the downdraft that swept through the athletic footwear industry in the 1990s, Adidas—the original sport brand—somehow lost its firm footing on the bottom line. By 1993 Adidas was losing roughly U.S.$100 million per year. Company management realized that "the original authentic sport brand" was looking a wee bit tired and, well, dowdy. Dowdy doesn't make it in the sport brand market, so Adidas set about putting the buzz back into its products, status and personality back into its advertising (witness its blanket coverage in the World Cup), and good business practices back into its distribution systems. It also moved boldly into new industries. Adidas merged with Salomon, purchased TaylorMade, and strode confidently into the ski, golf, and bike markets. Maybe too boldly—by 1999, with U.S. sales off 7.5%, the company struggled under its heavy debt burden.

Enter CEO Herbert Hainer, whose mandate was to grow Adidas' sales to a healthier market share. Hainer defended the company's 1997 purchase of Salomon, saying, Yes, I would say we paid too much for Salomon, but it fit with our strategy. There isn't another sporting goods company with as wide an assortment of premium brands. Optimism aside, Adidas has some difficult obstacles to overcome if it is to move within striking distance of Nike, whose market share is holding steady in the U.S. athletic footwear market.

In 2005, Adidas decided that Salomon no longer fit into its mix of products, and Adidas sold the Salomon division. Soon after, Adidas made an even bigger acquisition—Reebok. Adidas would benefit from Reebok's associations with the NBA and NFL. Plus, Adidas could use Reebok spokesperson Yao Ming to reach the huge market in China. Yao did represent Reebok in China until his 2011 retirement from the NBA.

As happens with many large acquisitions, it has taken some time for Adidas to fully integrate Reebok into its corporate culture. In 2011, CEO Hainer reported on the continued success of the Adidas–Reebok combination. Many new technologically advanced running shoes (such as adiZero Adios) have helped propel Adidas to higher profits in the running market. Reebok has seen increased profit in North America with Zig technology footwear.[1]

The Adidas–Reebok merger still appeared to be a success in 2011. However, some experts feel that consumers view Reebok only as a women's fitness shoe company. In reality, Reebok focuses on different market segments such as the men's fitness market and classic footwear for both genders, while also strengthening its women's fitness markets.[2]

Nike continues to dominate the footwear and sportswear market. Adidas and Reebok together still do not equal the size of Nike. Adidas is marketed as a lightweight form-fitting running shoe. Reebok is targeted as footwear with comfort. Some experts continue to worry that Reebok could actually lower the athletic image of Adidas.[3]

Another potential problem was Reebok's claim that toning shoes improved overall body tone. Toning shoes were designed with a rocking chair type of sole with the goal of helping women customers tone their overall body. Apparently, the research Reebok conducted was not enough to support the claim with the Federal Trade Commission (FTC). Adidas settled with the FTC with the goal of improving the toning product in the future.[4]

For current information on Adidas, visit www.adidas.com.

An Overview of Problem Solving and Decision Making

Problem solving and decision making are important skills.[5] In fact, decision making is one of the five important management skills (chapter 1), and conceptual skills aid in decision making.[6] Top management decisions have a direct effect on the success of the organization.[7] Sport managers need to make decisions about large-scale mega-events, such as the Olympics. Important decisions require comprehensive knowledge about the economic impact on the host community and whether it is realistic to expect that objectives can be met.[8]

We all make decisions in our personal and professional lives. As coaches and managers we teach and encourage our players and employees to make good decisions because the success of the individual, team, and organization is based on the decisions we make. Clearly, team performance is based on the selection decisions of the coaches and athletes and the decisions they make on and off the field.[9] The good news is that—as with all management skills—you can develop your problem-solving and decision-making abilities. The sport industry does make some poor decisions. The New England Patriots have been known to be very well managed during the Bill Belichick era. However, there has been a high level of volatility of the team's decision making in the defensive secondary since 2007. The Patriots spent a lot of money acquiring defensive secondary players with a low ratio of success. They had some success with players such as draft pick Patrick Chung, but they made poor decisions in acquiring expensive players such as Shawn Springs and Leigh Bodden.[10]

We just explained the importance of problem solving and decision making. Now let's continue this section and discuss the relationships among objectives, problem solving, and decision making; the relationships among the management functions, decision making, and problem solving; and the six steps of the decision-making model that will help you make better decisions. You will also learn about your own decision-making style and understand the need to use the ethical guidelines from the previous chapter when making decisions.

 Adidas' CEO, Herbert Hainer, is famous for trusting his gut. Do you think that most CEOs follow their gut, or do they go for facts and figures? Why? Does time (the ivory tower, feet on the desk, let's ruminate about this context) produce better decisions, or does pressure (on the front lines under fire) bring the clarity that makes for wiser decisions? Is decision making something that you can learn?

Objectives, Problem Solving, and Decision Making

◀ **LEARNING OUTCOME 1**
Describe how meeting objectives, solving problems, and making decisions are connected.

You and your boss will sometimes set objectives together, and your boss will sometimes assign objectives for you and your team to achieve. When you don't meet your objectives, you have a problem. When you have problems, you must make decisions. The better you can develop plans that prevent problems before they occur, the fewer problems you will encounter and the more you will be able to take advantage of opportunities.

A **problem** exists when objectives are not being met. In other words, you have a problem when a difference exists between what is happening and what you and your team want to happen. **Problem solving** is the process of taking corrective action to meet objectives. **Decision making** is the process of selecting a course of action that will solve a problem.

Your first decision concerns whether to take corrective action. Some problems cannot be solved, and others do not deserve the time and effort it would take to solve

| TIME-OUT 1 | Give an example of an objective from your manager or coach that was not met. Identify the problem created and the decision that prevented the objective from being met. |

them. Therefore, you will sometimes accept the problem or change the objective. However, it's your job to achieve organizational objectives, so to be successful, you must figure out how.

Management Functions, Decision Making, and Problem Solving

◀ **LEARNING OUTCOME 2**
Explain how management functions, decision making, and problem solving relate.

In chapter 1 you learned that all managers perform the same four functions—they plan, organize, lead, and control. To perform each of these functions, managers must make decisions. Keep in mind that every action is preceded by a decision. As planners, managers decide on the objectives they want to pursue and when, where, and how the objectives will be met. As organizers, managers decide what to delegate and how to coordinate the department's resources, including whom to hire and how to train and evaluate them (staffing). As leaders, managers must decide how best to influence employees to meet objectives. As controllers, managers assess whether—and how well—objectives are being met and how to take corrective action.

Also, recall that management has the systems effect because the decisions made in each functional area also affect other areas.

Adidas saw opportunity in new markets. Its objective? Provide a broader selection of sporting goods than its competitors. Its decision? Enter the skiing, golf, and cycling markets. However, Adidas' decision to diversify has not been without problems. Adidas thus faces important decisions—how best to share skills, abilities, and resources.

Decision-Making Model

To navigate important decisions, managers are often taught to follow the steps of the classical decision-making model.[11] The model consists of six steps (see figure 3.1). Each step is presented in detail in separate sections after this overview section. In the real world you will not always proceed in the conveniently sequenced manner implied in figure 3.1. At any step in the process you may find yourself returning to a prior step to make changes. Let's say you have gotten to implementation, but it isn't going well. Perhaps this time you simply need to tweak the implementation plan, but other times you will need to backtrack and select a new alternative or even change your original objective. A problematic implementation may reveal that you haven't defined the problem precisely enough, and you may have to return to square one.

The Dallas Cowboys believe they have a shorter decision-making process within their football team. The club owner, Jerry Jones, does not hire a general manager. This means the Cowboys can eliminate the step in a normal decision-making process in which a general manager has to get permission to sign or drop a player. Fewer people in the decision-making process should mean that decisions are made faster. However, not having an experienced general manager can prove costly if the owner does not have the experience to draft or trade for the correct players the club needs in order to improve.[12]

LEARNING OUTCOME 3 ▶

List the six steps in decision making.

Following the steps laid out in figure 3.1 will not guarantee that you make good decisions. However, using these steps increases your chances of success. Think of it like this: Using the model will not result in a goal every time, but it will increase the number of goals you achieve during the season. Consciously use these six steps for important decisions in your daily life, and you will improve your ability to make effective decisions.

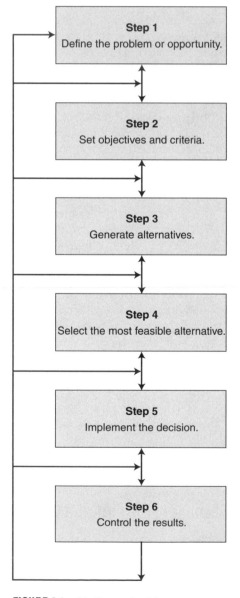

FIGURE 3.1 Making a decision.

APPLYING THE CONCEPT 3.1

Making Decisions

Identify which step in the decision process each statement represents.

a. step 1   c. step 3   e. step 5

b. step 2   d. step 4   f. step 6

_____ 1. We brainstorm to solve problems.

_____ 2. Betty, is the machine that makes baseball caps still jumping out of sequence, or has it stopped?

_____ 3. I don't understand what the new owners are trying to accomplish.

_____ 4. What symptoms have you observed that indicate the team has a problem?

_____ 5. Break-even analysis should help us in this situation.

Decision-Making Styles

Before you learn about the three styles, find out whether your decision-making style is more reflexive, reflective, or consistent by completing the following Self-Assessment.

Reflexive Decision Style

Decision makers who use the **reflexive decision style** "shoot from the hip"—that is, they make snap decisions without taking the time to get all the information they need and without considering many alternatives. On the positive side, reflexive decision makers are decisive—they do not procrastinate and sometimes score on short-lived opportunities. On the negative side, making quick decisions often results in poor decisions. Hasty decisions, without adequate information, are a dangerous form of "business roulette." If you use a reflexive style for important decisions, you may want to slow down and spend more time gathering information and analyzing more alternatives. Resist your natural tendency to jump in too quickly.

Reflective Decision Style

Decision makers who use the **reflective decision style** are slow to decide, gathering considerable information and analyzing numerous alternatives. On the positive side, they certainly don't make hasty decisions. On the negative side, they waste valuable time and other resources and often miss out on short-lived opportunities. Too much information can lead to paralysis, and being too slow to make decisions with employees can result in their viewing you as wishy-washy and indecisive. If you use a reflective style, think about what Andrew Jackson said: Take time to deliberate—absolutely—but when the time for action comes, stop thinking and get moving.

Consistent Decision Style

Decision makers who use the **consistent decision style** don't rush and don't waste time. They know when they need more information and when it's time to stop analyzing and get moving. In this fast-paced global environment, speed is important. Many managers believe it is better to move fast, using adequate information, and make a few mistakes than to move too slowly and miss opportunities. Consistent decision makers also boast the best decision-making record. Not surprisingly, they typically follow the steps outlined in figure 3.1, so maybe you should too.

Jerry Seeman, former referee and senior director of officiating for the NFL, personified consistent decision making. According to Seeman, being on the field is like being in a fishbowl: Everyone is waiting for your decision. Above all, you have to keep your cool. One of the biggest errors that officials fall into is making calls too quickly—because when things happen in a split second, it can be tempting to throw a penalty flag before you know what happened. That's why officials need to work in cruise control and consult with each other to get information from different angles. Using the consistent style to make calls may upset some who want a split-second decision, without consultation or watching the tape, but bad calls will make everyone angry and result in poor performance reviews.

Decisions in major sporting events are often made under time pressure. As the day of the event nears, event organizers have to make quick decisions.[13] Each decision is more important than the next as the event is closer to actually taking place.

NFL quarterbacks have to make many quick decisions, since they handle the ball on every offensive play. New York Giants quarterback Eli Manning has a history of making inconsistent decisions. Eli did lead his team to victory in the 2008 and 2012 Super Bowls. However, he also led the NFL in interceptions in 2010. His coach, Mike Sullivan, worked on Manning's leadership, accuracy, and decision-making processes. Eli spent extra time in the off-season working on improving the mental and physical aspects of his game. Sullivan attributed Manning's 2011 success to "making great decisions, being smart with the football, and being accurate."[14]

Tony Romo is another NFL quarterback whose decision-making skills are questioned. Romo has frequently made poor decisions during the crucial last quarter of important games. The response of the Dallas Cowboys' management is that Romo is involved in many dramatic plays—some work out, and some end up poorly. As with Manning, it seems as if more off-season training needs to be about improving decision-making processes.[15]

Ethics and Social Responsibility in Decision Making

There has been a call for the application of ethics in decision making.[16] People make the decision, in most cases, to use ethical or unethical behavior and to be, or not to be, socially responsible.[17] Recall from the last chapter that one of the touchiest ethical issues in sport involves the use of illegal drugs, including steroids, to enhance performance as well as just to get high. A major trap with drugs is that some athletes are looking to get an advantage over competitors, so they take drugs. Others find out and rationalize that they have to take the drug too in order to compete. Others take drugs under peer pressure. The final result is that no one has the advantage, but they are all on drugs and don't stop while competing unless they have to, usually because of suspension from the sport, injury, health problems, or death. Can the vicious cycle ever end?

As an old ad stated, no kid says, "I'm going to grow up to be a drug addict." But those who take drugs all justify it by saying, "I can handle it, there is nothing wrong with it, and nothing will happen to me." You can probably think of at least one person who took drugs and did suffer consequences, and that person's team, school, friends, and family suffered consequences as well. Many good coaches have helped prevent drug use and helped people quit, but some coaches have ignored drug use, encouraged it, or even given players drugs.

The decisions we make can affect the rest of our lives, and those of others, and we need to consciously follow our ethical guidelines (chapter 2) during each step of the decision-making process. Now let's learn how to perform each step of the model so that we can use it in our personal and professional lives to make important decisions.

Step 1: Define the Problem or Opportunity

In the first step in your decision process, you define the problem you want to solve or the opportunity you want to capitalize on. As suggested by William Shakespeare, we should actively search for opportunities. This step requires that you classify the problem, select

SELF-ASSESSMENT 3.1

Your Decision Style

We all differ in the way we approach decisions. To determine whether your decision-making style is reflexive, reflective, or consistent, select a number from 1 to 5 on the following continuum that best describes your behavior in relation to each statement.

A common behavior			An uncommon behavior	
1	2	3	4	5

Overall

_____ 1. I make decisions quickly.

When Making Decisions

_____ 2. I usually don't stop to define the problem clearly.

_____ 3. I usually don't set specific objectives of what the end result of my decision will be.

_____ 4. I go with my first thought or hunch.

_____ 5. I don't bother to recheck my work.

_____ 6. I gather little or no information.

_____ 7. I consider very few alternatives.

_____ 8. I usually make the decision well before the deadline.

_____ 9. I don't ask others for advice.

Afterward

_____ 10. I don't look for other alternatives or wish I had waited longer.

_____ Total score

To determine your style, add up your answers. Your total score will be between 10 and 50. Place an X on the continuum that represents your score.

Reflexive	Consistent		Reflective	
20	30	40	50	

an appropriate level of employee participation, and distinguish the cause of the problem from its symptoms.

Classify the Problem

Problems can be classified in terms of how the decision is structured, the conditions in which decisions are made, and the decision model used.

How Decisions Are Structured

Decisions can be categorized as programmed or nonprogrammed. **Programmed decisions** are recurring or routine situations in which the decision maker should use decision rules or organizational policies and procedures to make the decision. Here is a typical decision rule: Order X number of golf balls every time stock reaches level Y. **Nonprogrammed decisions** are significant but nonrecurring and nonroutine situations in which the decision makers should use the decision-making model. To qualify as significant, a decision must be expensive (e.g., purchasing major assets) or have major consequences (e.g., launching

◀ LEARNING OUTCOME 4

Identify programmed and nonprogrammed decisions and recognize certain, risky, and uncertain business conditions.

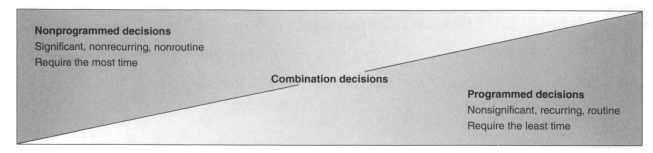

Nonprogrammed decisions
Significant, nonrecurring, nonroutine
Require the most time

Combination decisions

Programmed decisions
Nonsignificant, recurring, routine
Require the least time

FIGURE 3.2   The continuum of decision structure.

 Name a recent programmed decision and a nonprogrammed decision made by your firm or team.

a new product or laying off employees). Adidas made a nonprogrammed decision when it purchased Salomon, TaylorMade, and Reebok.

Nonprogrammed decisions should take longer to make than programmed decisions. Note also that decisions fall along a continuum from totally programmable to totally nonprogrammable, with numerous combinations of the two types in between (see figure 3.2).

You must be able to differentiate between the two types of decisions, because they alert you to the time and effort you should be spending. Upper-level managers typically make more nonprogrammed decisions than do lower-level managers, who tend to make programmed decisions.

Decision-Making Conditions

Decisions are made in an environment of certainty, risk, or uncertainty; these elements are called **decision-making conditions.** When managers make decisions in a certain environment, they know the outcome of each alternative in advance. When managers make decisions in a risky environment, they don't know each outcome in advance but can assign probabilities of occurrence to each one. In an uncertain environment, lack of information or knowledge makes the outcomes unpredictable so that probabilities cannot be assigned easily.

In the rapidly changing global environment, managers are dealing with more uncertainly than in the past.[18] Adidas' purchase of Salomon was made in risky conditions; Adidas entered the skiing market, with which it had little management experience. This moved the company into building and selling skiing equipment, which was quite different from selling footwear and apparel. Decisions made in risky conditions are the purview of upper-level management. When decisions are made in uncertain conditions, it is difficult to determine which resources will solve the problem or create or capitalize on an opportunity. Although risk and uncertainty can never be eliminated, they can be reduced. The key is for event decision makers working in an increasingly fast-paced environment to plan for the event (come game time) by having risk assessments and contingency plans.[19] In the real world, conditions can't always be neatly categorized as certain, risky, or uncertain. As shown in figure 3.3, the conditions are on a continuum.

LEARNING OUTCOME 5 ▶

Know when to use the different decision models and when to make decisions as a group or as an individual.

Decision Models

The two primary decision models are the classical rational model and the bounded rationality model. The rational model uses "optimizing"—that is, it endeavors to select the best possible alternative. The bounded rationality model, a subset of the rational model, uses "satisficing"—it selects the first alternative that meets certain specified minimal criteria. Figure 3.1 presents the rational model. With satisficing, only parts, or none, of the model would be used.

TIME-OUT 3 Analyze a recent decision of your organization, and decide which decision model your managers used. Identify the environmental conditions and the type of decision (programmed or nonprogrammed).

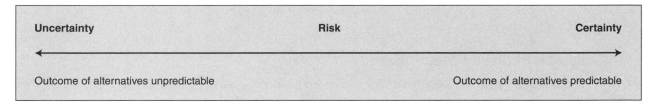

FIGURE 3.3   The continuum of the decision-making environment.

The more unstructured the decision and the higher the risk and uncertainty, the greater the need to conduct the research required in the rational model. Planning a sporting event ends with a more rational model as the event gets closer to happening.[20]

Thus, you want to optimize when you make nonprogrammed decisions in uncertain or high-risk conditions (follow the rational six-step model), and you should satisfice when you make programmed decisions in low-risk or highly certain conditions (use the bounded rationality model without following all six steps of the model).

Select an Appropriate Level of Employee Participation

When a problem arises, managers must choose the best people to solve it. Usually, only key people who are directly involved with the problem should participate in the solution process. Because current trends favor increased employee participation, the question is not whether managers should encourage employees to problem solve and make decisions but rather when and how employees should participate in the process. Decision making is often delegated by sport managers.[21] To begin, let's examine individual and group decision making. Note, however, that even though the trend is toward group decision making, some people don't want to participate.

APPLYING THE CONCEPT 3.2

Classify the Problem

Classify the following problems according to the type of decision and the environmental conditions in which the decision is being made.

   a. programmed, certain

   b. programmed, uncertain

   c. programmed, risky

   d. nonprogrammed, certain

   e. nonprogrammed, uncertain

   f. nonprogrammed, risky

_____   6. When I graduate from college, I will buy an existing fitness center rather than work for someone else.

_____   7. Sondra, a small business owner of a health center, has experienced a turnaround in her business; it's now profitable. She wants to be able to keep her excess cash accessible in case she needs it to cover shortfalls. How should she invest it?

_____   8. Every 6 months, a purchasing agent selects new materials for the soccer balls his company makes.

_____   9. In the early 1970s, investors decided to start the World Football League.

_____ 10. A manager in a department with high turnover hires a new employee.

The key to successful group decisions is to avoid the pitfalls and capitalize on the strengths of the group process.

Upsides of Group Decision Making

When group members participate in the decision process, six advantages often accrue:

1. **Better-quality decisions:** The saying "two heads are better than one" can be an important strength of group decision making. Groups often do a better job of solving complex problems than would the best individual in the group going solo. Thus, groups do well with nonprogrammed decisions in risky or uncertain conditions.

2. **More information, more alternatives, and heightened creativity and innovation:** Groups typically bring more information to the table than do individuals. Group members bring different points of view to bear on the problem and are thus able to generate more alternatives. Creative, innovative ideas (and products) emerge from the synergy of members' building on each other's ideas.[22]

3. **Better understanding of the problem and the decision:** When people participate in the decision-making process, they gain a fuller understanding of the alternatives and why the final selection was made. This makes implementation easier.

4. **Greater commitment to the decision:** People involved in a decision are more committed to making the implementation succeed.[23]

5. **Improved morale and motivation:** Teams help meet social needs. "Ownership" of the process, the decision, and the results improves morale and motivates people. Why? Because participation in the process is rewarding and personally satisfying. Encouraging group participation says, "We value your input."

6. **Good training:** Participation in decision making trains people to work in groups by developing group-process skills. Group participation helps employees better understand problems faced by the organization, and this results in greater productivity.

Downsides of Group Decision Making

Careful leadership is required to avoid the following pitfalls of group decision making:

1. **Wasted time and slower decision making:** It takes longer for groups to reach consensus, and employees who are solving problems and making decisions are not on the job producing. Because group involvement costs the organization time and money, for programmed decisions in certain or low-risk business conditions, individual decision making is generally more cost-effective.

2. **Satisficing:** Groups are more likely to satisfice than individuals, especially when groups are not run effectively. Members may take the attitude, "Let's be done with this." Part of the reason groups satisfice is that members in poorly run groups don't feel responsible for the outcome. Individuals stand alone—and stand out—when they and they alone must make the decision. In groups, no one person gets the blame—or the credit—for the decision.

3. **Domination by subgroup or individual and goal displacement:** Group dynamics can be destructive if not managed properly. Cliques can develop, and destructive conflict can be the result. Also, cliques (or an individual member) can dominate the process and nullify the decision. Goal displacement occurs when an individual or clique tries to get its decision accepted, or dominates for personal reasons, rather than trying to find the best solution.

4. **Conformity and groupthink:** Members may feel pressured to go along with the group's decision without raising reasonable criticisms because they fear rejection or they don't want to cause conflict. Groupthink occurs when members withhold differing views in order to appear to be in agreement. This nullifies one of the strong points of effective groups—their diversity. Conformity is especially problematic in highly cohesive groups because members can put getting along ahead of finding the best solution. Conformity is

less problematic in groups that value diversity because members seek and embrace differing viewpoints.

Group decision making generally works well with nonprogrammed decisions made in conditions of risk or uncertainty. Individual decision making works well with programmed decisions in low-risk or certain conditions. See figure 3.4 for an illustration.

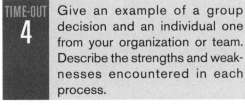

TIME-OUT 4

Give an example of a group decision and an individual one from your organization or team. Describe the strengths and weaknesses encountered in each process.

Distinguish Symptoms From the Cause of the Problem

To distinguish symptoms from causes, first observe the situation, and then describe recent occurrences in simple terms (do this purposefully—simplicity will clarify your thinking). This will help you determine the cause of the problem. For example, Sam, your star first baseman, has been sick or late more times in the last month than in the past 2 years. So what is the problem? If your answer is absenteeism or tardiness, you are confusing symptoms with the cause. Symptoms only indicate that there is a problem; they don't tell you what is causing the problem. Why is Sam late and missing? If the causes of problems are not

1. Categorize the decision.

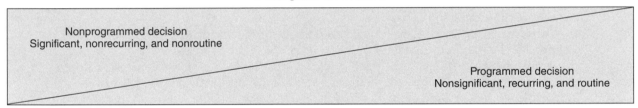

2. Check the conditions in the environment.

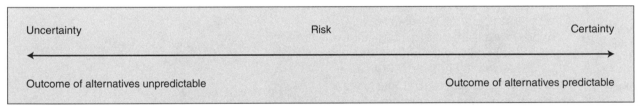

3. Choose the decision model.

4. Choose the level of participation.

FIGURE 3.4 Four continuums in classifying the decision.

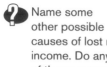 Name some other possible causes of lost net income. Do any of these causes fit the situation at Adidas-Reebok?

found out and addressed directly, problem symptoms often reappear.

At Reebok the problem symptom was lower net income. The causes (notice that there are several), as defined by Adidas, were use of smaller low-end retailers, overcapacity to produce products from Indonesian factories, and the inability to reach the higher-end target markets. The price that Adidas paid for Reebok and the timing of that purchase were not optimal. Remember that defining the problem is the key to successful solutions and strategies. When making nonprogrammed decisions in high-risk or uncertain conditions, take your time and clearly distinguish symptoms from causes.

TIME-OUT 5 Define a problem your organization or team is facing or an opportunity it would like to capitalize on. Clearly distinguish the problem symptoms from the problem causes.

LEARNING OUTCOME 6 ▶

State the difference between an objective and "must" and "want" criteria.

Step 2: Set Objectives and Criteria

Once you have defined the problem, you need to set an objective that states the end result in solving the problem or capitalizing on the opportunity.[24] An objective answers the question, "Why am I doing this?"[25] so that the objective states what the individual, group, or organization intends to accomplish. In the next chapter, you will learn how to set effective objectives. One goal of Adidas is to reduce purchasing costs. This will help the company reduce overall production costs.

When writing an objective, you should also specify the criteria for achieving the objective. **Criteria** are the standards that must be met to accomplish the objective. It is a good idea to distinguish between "must" and "want" criteria. "Must" criteria have to be met to achieve the objective, whereas "want" criteria are desirable but not absolutely necessary. Thus, every acceptable alternative (and there may be several that are acceptable in the initial stages of the decision process) has to meet the "must" criteria; thereafter, you must decide which alternative meets the most "want" criteria. With satisficing, you select the first acceptable alternative; with optimizing, you endeavor to select the best possible option, one that meets as many "want" criteria as possible.

 Go to a recent Adidas annual report and find a company objective that addresses an opportunity in the marketplace. Can you write an objective for Adidas to achieve with regard to successfully merging Adidas and Reebok?

Suppose your team manager has quit and you must hire a new one. Your objective is to hire a manager by June 30. Your "must" criteria include, among other things, 5 years' experience as a team manager. Your "want" criterion is that the new manager be from a minority group. That is, you want to hire a minority employee but will not hire someone with less than 5 years' experience. In addition, if a significantly more qualified nonminority person applies for the job, that person will be offered the job. In this situation you would optimize the decision following the six steps of the model, rather than satisfice. We discuss criteria again later in this chapter.

TIME-OUT 6 List the qualifications for a job at an organization that you are familiar with and distinguish between "must" and "want" criteria.

Step 3: Generate Alternatives

After you and your team have defined the problem and set objectives and criteria, it is time to generate alternatives. Often there is more than one way to solve a problem, so don't shortchange yourself—explore your alternatives.[26] Also, base your alternatives on evidence, not just opinion.[27]

With a programmed decision, step 3 can be skipped because the alternative has already been selected. However, with nonprogrammed decisions, the time and effort invested in generating alternatives pay off handsomely. In this section, we examine innovation and creativity, the use of information and technology to generate alternatives, and group methods for generating creative alternatives.

Use Innovation and Creativity

Creativity is a way of thinking that generates new solutions to problems and new ways to approach opportunities. Creativity leads to better performance.[28] Unfortunately, employees may have good ideas on the job, but if they are not implemented, they are not innovations. An **innovation** alters what is established by introducing something new. Today, organizations are pressured to innovate to meet customer requirements.[29]

Creative people think outside the box. Let's be fair to Adidas. The company took a risk in purchasing Salomon and TaylorMade at premium prices. It entered the equipment business even though its experience was in footwear and apparel. However, its managers were creative and tried an innovative approach.

◀ LEARNING OUTCOME 7
Explain how creativity and innovation differ.

Creative Process

Intelligence and creativity are not highly correlated—that is, creative thinking hails from a broad continuum of people.[30] It is also possible to enhance your own creative juices. The three stages in the **creative process** are (1) preparation, (2) incubation and illumination, and (3) evaluation. Following these stages, which we discuss next, can get your creative juices flowing.

◀ LEARNING OUTCOME 8
Describe the three stages in the creative process.

1. **Prepare:** Get others' opinions, feelings, and ideas, but also get the facts. Look for new angles. Dream big (you can always scale back). At this stage, don't limit your thinking—take the attitude that everything goes. Also, don't judge your own ideas or those of others—nothing throws cold water on creative brainstorming like criticism. (Criticism comes later.)

2. **Incubate (and incubate again) and illuminate (and incubate again):** Take a break and let ideas incubate[31]; sleep on your idea. Not to worry—you are working on the problem, just subconsciously. Allowing your idea to incubate gives you insight you might not gain otherwise. Your subconscious workings are powerful—trust them!

3. **Evaluate . . . and then *re*evaluate:** Now you and your team can criticize. But rethink what you mean by "criticize"—make it creative, and never let it get personal. In one useful approach, playing **devil's advocate,** some group members defend the idea that is on the table while others try to come up with reasons why it won't work.

Use Information and Technology

Technology leads to innovation.[32] Unlike previous managers, you have a new world of tools to use for problems and opportunities. You will also have a new problem, however—too much information and too many tools.

When you are generating alternatives, the following question will come up frequently: How much information do we need and where should we get it? There is no simple answer. The more important the decision, the more information you need (generally). However, too much information can paralyze the decision process. That is, the decision becomes too complex, and you don't get to the optimal alternative. Therefore, it behooves you to think about what constitutes useful information.

Useful information has four characteristics: (1) timeliness, (2) quality, (3) completeness, and (4) relevance (see figure 3.5). Timely information is information that you get in time to make your decision. High-quality information is accurate, whereas false information misleads and results in bad decisions. Sometimes group members withhold information or give false or incomplete

TIME-OUT 7 Think about some problem whose solution you were particularly proud of (or some other solution that really impressed you as outstanding). Break down the solution process into parts—do the three stages discussed here apply to this solution?

information. Why? To push the group toward the decision they want. Complete information is of course complete—no holes, no gaps. Relevant information pertains to the group's objectives. Having a clear objective and good criteria helps you chuck irrelevant information.

Get Groups to Use Creativity and Innovation

As noted earlier, the pitfalls of group dynamics include satisficing, domination issues, and groupthink. As a manager, you can help your group avoid these difficulties. A variety of methods are available to help you make the group effective and the experience valuable. Figure 3.6 lists five widely used methods.

Brainstorming

In **brainstorming,** group members generate as many alternatives as they can in a short time. Here is how it works. The group is presented with a problem and asked to develop as many solutions as possible. A short time period (10-20 minutes) is specified. Members are encouraged to make wild, off-the-wall suggestions. They can build on suggestions made by others. They are not to react in any way—favorably or unfavorably—to any contribution.

When selecting members for a brainstorming group, include diverse people—your goal, after all, is to get diverse ideas. Five to 12 people make a good-sized group for brainstorming. Everyone is given an equal voice—status differences should be ignored. Janitors have

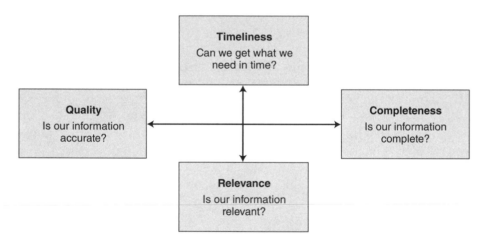

FIGURE 3.5 Characteristics of useful information.

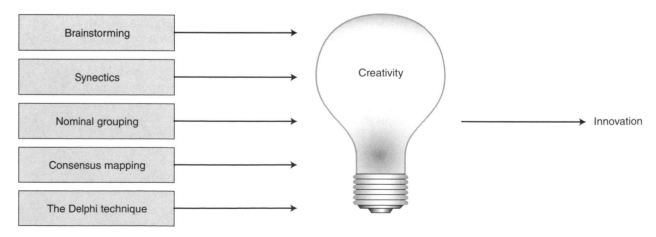

FIGURE 3.6 Methods that foster creativity and innovation in groups.

just as much to contribute to this process as CEOs. Alternatives are evaluated only after idea generation ends. Brainstorming is popular because it works.

Synectics

In **synectics,** novel alternatives are generated through role-playing and fantasizing. Synectics focuses on generating novel ideas rather than a large number of ideas.[33] The exact nature of the problem is purposefully not stated initially so that group members avoid preconceptions.

Nolan Bushnell wanted to develop a new concept in family dining, so he had a group discussion on leisure activities having to do with eating out. The idea that came out of this synectic process was a restaurant–electronic game complex where families could entertain themselves while eating pizza and hamburgers. The complex is called Chuck E. Cheese ShowBiz Pizza Time.

Nominal Grouping

In **nominal grouping,** a structured voting method is used to generate and evaluate alternatives. This process involves six steps:

1. List ideas: Each participant generates ideas in writing.
2. Record the ideas: Each member suggests an idea. This continues in a round-robin manner until all ideas are posted. The leader then presents the ideas to the group.
3. Clarify the ideas: Alternatives are clarified through a guided discussion, and additional ideas are listed.
4. Rank the ideas: Each member rank-orders the top three ideas; low-ranked alternatives are eliminated.
5. Discuss the rankings: Rankings are discussed for clarification, not persuasion. During this step, participants explain their choices and their reasons for making them.
6. Vote: A secret vote is taken to select the alternative.

Used properly, nominal grouping minimizes domination, goal displacement, conformity, and groupthink.

Consensus Mapping

Consensus mapping develops group agreement on a problem solution. If a consensus cannot be reached, the group does not make a decision. Consensus mapping, often just called consensus, differs from nominal grouping because competitive battles in which votes are taken and a solution is forced on members of the group are not allowed. The Japanese call this approach *ringi.* Consensus mapping can be used after brainstorming. The principal difference is that in consensus mapping the group categorizes or clusters ideas rather than choosing a single solution. A major benefit of consensus mapping is that the group "owns" the solution, so members are more committed to implementing it.

 TIME-OUT 8 Give examples of problems in your organization or team for which brainstorming, nominal grouping, or consensus mapping would be appropriate.

Delphi Technique

In the Delphi technique, a series of confidential questionnaires are used to refine a solution. Responses from the first questionnaire are analyzed and resubmitted to participants in a second questionnaire. This process may continue for five or more rounds before a consensus emerges. Delphi group members typically are recruited from the "best of the

APPLYING THE CONCEPT 3.3

Using Groups to Generate Alternatives

For each situation, identify the most appropriate technique.

- a. brainstorming
- b. synectics
- c. nominal grouping
- d. consensus mapping
- e. Delphi technique

_____ 11. A consultant leads a group of company employees and young soccer players to come up with ideas for new cleats.

_____ 12. Our team is suffering from morale problems.

_____ 13. We need new matching desks for the 10 of us in this office.

_____ 14. We need to reduce waste in the production department to cut cost and increase productivity.

_____ 15. Top managers are projecting future trends in the retail sporting goods industry as part of their long-range planning.

best" and are widely acknowledged as experts in their field, and—this is important—they are outsiders, not from the organization that is hiring them. Because of the nature of the process, they may never need to come together.

Upper-level managers commonly use synectics and the Delphi technique in their non-programmed decision making. Brainstorming, nominal grouping, and consensus mapping are frequently used at the department level with work groups. Whichever of these methods suits your decision situation, be sure to guard against responses that snuff out creativity. Ahead is a list of examples of "killer" statements. If a team member makes a killer statement, make sure everyone realizes that such negative attitudes are counterproductive.

Use Decision Trees

So you've got some alternatives—now what do you do? You might make a decision tree, which is a diagram of alternatives. The tree gives you a visual tool to work with, which makes it easier for some people to analyze the alternatives.

Great Ways To Kill Creativity

It can't be done.

We've never done it.

Has anyone else tried it?

It will not work in our department (or company or industry).

It costs too much.

It isn't in the budget.

Let's form a committee.

To construct a decision tree, write down every alternative you can think of that could solve the problem you are grappling with. For each alternative, list potential outcomes. Next, list the choices (decisions) to be made with each alternative. Continue doing this, breaking each alternative into subalternatives, until you are satisfied you have explored each alternative in enough detail. At Adidas, alternatives generated in the decision process included (among many others) doing nothing, developing a new advertising campaign, introducing new footwear products, creating new unrelated products, and creating new related products.

Why do you think doing nothing was considered an alternative? Play devil's advocate with this alternative, and defend doing it and rejecting it.

Step 4: Select the Most Feasible Alternative

At this point you may be wondering why steps 3 and 4 of the decision process (generating alternatives and selecting one) are separate steps. There is a good reason for this: Generating and evaluating alternatives at the same time often leads to satisficing.

Notice that step 4 says "the most feasible"; the most feasible alternative may not always be the best alternative, because we have limited resources. For example, NCAA Division III teams have limited budgets and pay for coaches, so these teams generally can't attract and hire coaches with the same experience as those hired by Division I and pro teams. So they hire the most feasible coaches, which are often internal employees, including team graduates who know the college athletic program.[34]

As you and your group evaluate alternatives, "think forward" and try to predict possible outcomes by synthesizing information. Be sure to make evidence-based decisions.[35] Use the objectives and criteria you developed in step 2 of the decision process to critique each alternative. Then compare how each alternative measures up against your other alternatives. To assist you in this process, become familiar with (if not adept at) two types of techniques: quantitative and cost–benefit analyses. To get you started, we present a brief overview here.

◀ **LEARNING OUTCOME 9**

Explain how quantitative and cost–benefit analyses facilitate selecting alternatives.

Quantitative Analyses

Quantitative techniques use mathematical analysis to assess alternative solutions. Microsoft Excel spreadsheets and other software make this process easier. The field of sport management is increasingly using quantitative methods. Recall the movie *Moneyball*, about the Oakland Athletics baseball team and its general manager Billy Beane. Its focus is the team's modernized, quantitative analytical, sabermetric approach to assembling a competitive baseball team, despite Oakland's disadvantaged revenue situation.[36]

Break-Even Analysis

This kind of analysis involves forecasting the volume of sales and the cost of production. The break-even point occurs at the level where no profit or loss results. As managers at Adidas evaluated each alternative, they no doubt computed how many pairs of Tim Duncan basketball sneakers would have to be sold to break even. To do this, these managers factored in costs as diverse as the cost of Duncan's promotional contract, the cost of shipping the shoes from China, and the research that went into their design.

What other factors might have been critical in Adidas' break-even analysis?

Capital Budgeting

These techniques are used to analyze alternative investments in major long-term assets. Building a new stadium is a major capital budgeting decision for any NFL or MLB team. The payback approach calculates the number of years it will take to recover the initial cash investment. The goal here is to find the quickest payback. Another technique computes the average rate of return. It is useful when yearly returns of various alternatives differ. A more sophisticated technique, discounted cash flow, takes into account the time value of money. It assumes that a unit of currency today is worth more than the same unit in the future. To assess alternatives, organizations like Adidas often direct staff statisticians and financial analysts to perform discounted cash flow analyses. Adidas also uses capital budgeting techniques to decide what machines it should purchase for its factories.

Go to www.adidasgroup.com to look at the company's financial statements. Do the notes to the statements tell what type of analyses the accountants use?

Queuing Theory

This technique addresses waiting time. Using too many employees to wait on customers or fans is an inefficient use of resources and is costly. Too few employees providing service can also be costly if poor service drives customers away. Queuing theory helps organizations balance these two costs. Event managers use queuing theory to determine the optimum number of ticket takers to reduce customers' waiting time when entering an event or game. Retail stores use queuing theory to determine the optimum number of checkout clerks, and production departments use it to schedule equipment maintenance.

Probability Theory

Analysts use probability theory to help managers make decisions in risky environmental conditions. A probability for the chance of success or failure is assigned to each alternative. Expected value, which is the payoff or profit from each combination of alternatives and outcomes, is then calculated. Usually done on a payoff matrix or decision tree, the assigned probability of the outcome is multiplied by the assigned benefit or cost. Probability theory is used to determine whether and how much to expand facilities, to select the most profitable use of finances, or to determine the amount of inventory to stock. On a simple level, some coaches and fans assign a probability (50%) of winning. As an exercise in critical thinking, use probability theory to choose a hypothetical job.

TIME-OUT 9 Choose two or three decisions of various importance facing your team, and decide whether break-even analysis, capital budgeting, queuing theory, or probability theory is an appropriate technique to use in your decision process.

APPLYING THE CONCEPT 3.4

Selecting a Quantitative Technique

Choose the appropriate technique to use in each situation:

a. break-even analysis

b. capital budgeting

c. queuing theory

d. probability theory

_____ 16. Claudia needs to repair the swimming pool's filtering system or replace it with a new one.

_____ 17. Ben is investing money for the team.

_____ 18. Employees at a sporting goods store sometimes hang around with nothing to do, and at other times they work for hours without stopping.

_____ 19. A bicycle shop owner wants to know how many times a bike must be rented out to make it worth purchasing.

_____ 20. Fans had to wait so long in the ticket line that they missed most of the first quarter of the game.

Quantitative techniques	Cost-benefit analysis
Objective	Subjective
Maximum use of math	Minimum use of math

FIGURE 3.7 Comparison of analysis techniques.

Cost–Benefit Analysis

Quantitative methods objectively compare alternatives by using various mathematical techniques. (But no technique is ever completely objective; each method has to start with underlying assumptions that are, by their very nature, subjective.) Even with use of mathematical techniques, managers tend to use at least some subjective intuition when judging alternatives. As effective as these math techniques are, circumstances don't always allow their use. Sometimes it is impossible to assign a probability to a benefit received for a cost. How much is a human life worth? Cost–benefit analysis can combine subjective methods and mathematical techniques to compare alternative courses of action. Also called pros and cons analysis, cost–benefit analysis looks at the advantages (benefits) and the disadvantages (costs) of each alternative. However, you need to be careful in judging the alternatives, and be sure to make evidence-based decisions.[37] Figure 3.7 compares quantitative techniques and cost–benefit analysis.

Agawam High School baseball coach Peter Clark (and most other good coaches) sits athletes down and goes over the pros and cons of their play, their focus, their attitude, and their behavior on or off the field. Likewise, each of us has, at one time or another, thought about the pros and cons of a situation facing us without writing them down—and this works (often very well) for small, nonconsequential decisions. However, for important, nonprogrammed decisions, laying them out on paper and formalizing your analysis will improve the quality of your decision. Try this technique on a current dilemma and see how this method focuses your thinking and clarifies your courses of action.

Cost–benefit analysis is more subjective than quantitative analysis. Therefore, groups that use cost–benefit analysis must consciously endeavor to sidestep group dynamics that can ambush subjective analysis. Playing devil's advocate, for example, can help groups avoid satisficing, dominance issues, and groupthink. Groups should also carefully consider how alternatives should be presented, because the order of discussion can affect decisions (people typically remember best what they hear first and last). Also, alternatives poorly or negatively presented tend not to be selected.

Whichever method you use to analyze alternatives, keep your end goal in mind—that of selecting the optimal alternative that meets the criteria you and your team have established. If none of the alternatives meet the criteria, you have two options: (1) Return to step 2 and change the criteria, or (2) return to step 3 and generate more alternatives. It appears that Adidas has changed its criteria for selecting an athlete to endorse its footwear. The Kobe shoe line was quite successful, and it had a youthful, three-time world champion star as its sponsor. However, L.A. Lakers player Kobe Bryant's contract with Adidas—worth an estimated U.S.$40 million over 5 years—came to an end. By not re-signing Bryant, Adidas made it clear that its new criteria involved finding star players who could work as a team to represent the company. The current endorsers include the San Antonio Spurs' Tim Duncan, Chicago Bulls' Derrick Rose, and the Orlando Magic's star Dwight Howard. Adidas is currently heavily marketing Rose's adiZero Rose 2 footwear line since he was the 2011 NBA MVP.

 TIME-OUT 10 Describe a recent decision in your organization in which cost–benefit analysis would have been particularly appropriate, and lay out a few of its pros and cons.

 How accurate do you think general managers can be in deciding which player will become the next marketing superstar?

Every year Adidas needs to generate new endorser alternatives based on new criteria. In 2007, the possible alternatives were to sign top draft picks Greg Oden or Kevin Durant. Durant had a game similar to that of former Chicago Bulls superstar Michael Jordan, whereas Oden was a rare center with size and skill. It turned out that Oden was injury prone and struggled to play many games. Durant went on to be one of the NBA's top scorers even in his rookie year.

Step 5: Implement the Decision

Selecting an alternative is useless without an effective plan, implementation, and follow-up. The final two steps in the decision-making process are about implementing and controlling. Before you can implement a decision, you need a plan. Once you have chosen an alternative, it is time to develop a plan of action that includes a schedule for the implementation. We examine the details of planning in the next chapter.

How you implement your plan is crucial to its success or failure. Part of the reason decisions fail is that the decisions were never implemented. The most promising alternative will fall flat on its paper face if its implementation is not carefully thought out and then carefully carried out. Communicating the plan to all employees is also critical. (We discuss effective communication in chapter 10.) Delegating (discussed in chapter 5) is also key to smooth implementation. You may need multiple implementation plans. Adidas, for example, developed a plan to sell TaylorMade golf clubs, a plan to advertise them, and a plan to distribute the clubs at the retail level.

Judging from Adidas' results with its Taylor-Made clubs, do you think the implementation went smoothly?

Step 6: Control the Results

Control methods should be developed during planning. Establish checkpoints to determine whether the chosen alternative is solving the problem. If not, consider corrective action. More important, if the implementation continues to go poorly, don't remain with your decision—that is, change your tack. For example, if a team is losing, it often tries different plays and players in various positions to score and win. When managers will not admit that they made a bad decision and take evasive action (to avoid the inevitable collision with failure), they are escalating their commitment. When you make a poor decision, humble yourself. Admit the mistake and strive to rectify it. Review your decision process.

As an example of corrective action, after the 2002 Salt Lake City Winter Olympic Games scandal, the International Olympic Committee separated planning and controlling of the Olympic Games site selection. In hopes of making all stakeholders more accountable, the IOC decided to give the control function to an external board while giving the internal managers the management functions.[38]

Another example of a situation that needs corrective action involves NCAA Division III teams. These teams have limited budgets, so they tend to hire inexperienced coaches who don't always do a good job.[39] These coaches need to be trained or replaced, and the good ones tend to move to better jobs, so the hiring decision process starts again. We discuss the process for making good human resource management decisions in chapter 7.

It will be several years before Adidas' managers can determine whether their decision to diversify into new markets was a wise one. Although moving into Salomon's ski business didn't go as well as planned, the fit with Adidas' traditional lines of footwear appears to justify the company's entrance into growing markets such as golfing.

As we bring this chapter to a close, you should understand your decision-making style and how to use the decision-making model when making important nonprogrammed decisions—define the problem, set objectives and criteria, generate alternatives, select the most feasible alternative, implement the decision, and control the results.

@ TAKE IT TO THE NET

Please visit www.HumanKinetics.com/AppliedSportManagementSkills and go to this book's companion web study guide, where you will find the following:

A list of websites associated with the concepts in this chapter

Exercises that you will need Internet access to complete

Online versions of chapter exercises and end-of-chapter learning aids

An exercise that helps you define the Key Terms

LEARNING AIDS

CHAPTER SUMMARY

1. Describe how meeting objectives, solving problems, and making decisions are connected.

   Managers are responsible for setting and achieving organizational objectives. When managers do not meet objectives, problems result. When problems exist, decisions must be made about what, if any, action must be taken.

2. Explain how management functions, decision making, and problem solving relate.

   When managers plan, organize, lead, and control, they make decisions. When managers are not proficient in these functions, they are part of the problem, not part of the solution.

3. List the six steps in decision making.

   (1) Define the problem or opportunity, (2) set objectives and criteria, (3) generate alternatives, (4) select the most feasible alternative, (5) implement the decision, and (6) control the results.

4. Identify programmed and nonprogrammed decisions and recognize certain, risky, and uncertain business conditions.

   Programmed and nonprogrammed decisions differ in how often they recur, whether they are routine, and their level of significance. Nonprogrammed decisions are nonrecurring, nonroutine, highly significant decisions. Programmed decisions are recurring, routine, and less significant decisions.

   Decisions are made in environmental conditions that are certain (you know the outcome of each alternative), risky (you can assign probabilities of success or failure to the outcomes), or highly uncertain (you cannot assign probabilities of success or failure to the outcomes).

5. Know when to use the different decision models and when to make decisions as a group or as an individual.

   Use the rational model with group decision making when a nonprogrammed decision must be made in high-risk or uncertain conditions. Use the bounded rationality model when you work solo on programmed decisions made in low-risk and certain conditions. Note, however, that this is a general guide; there are always exceptions to the rule.

6. State the difference between an objective and "must" and "want" criteria.

   An objective is the end result you want from your decision. "Must" criteria are the requirements that an alternative has to meet to be selected. "Want" criteria are desirable but are not absolutely necessary.

7. Explain how creativity and innovation differ.

   Creativity is a way of thinking that generates new ideas. Innovation is the implementation of new ideas.

8. Describe the three stages in the creative process.

   The three stages are (1) preparation, (2) incubation (take a break from the problem and let your subconscious work on it) and illumination (recognize when the light bulb goes on), and (3) evaluation (critique your idea to make sure it is a good one).

9. Explain how quantitative and cost–benefit analyses facilitate selecting alternatives.

   Quantitative analysis uses math to select objectively the alternative with the highest value. Cost–benefit analysis combines subjective analysis with some math, although alternatives don't necessarily have to be quantified to be compared (as in the pros and cons approach).

REVIEW AND DISCUSSION QUESTIONS

1. Why are problem solving and decision making important in sports?

2. Why is it necessary to determine the decision structure and the conditions surrounding the decision?

3. Why do organizations use groups to solve problems and make decisions?

4. Which pitfall of group problem solving and decision making is most common?

5. Is a decrease in ticket sales or profits a symptom or a cause of a problem?

6. Would setting a specific maximum price to spend on a cycle exercise machine be an objective or a criterion?

7. Are creativity and innovation really important to a soccer team?

8. We have all made decisions using information that was not timely, high quality, complete, or relevant—we are human, after all. Reflect on a decision your team made with poor information. What was the result?

9. What is the major difference between nominal grouping and consensus mapping?

10. Why are generating alternatives and selecting alternatives separate steps in the decision process?

11. Have you ever used any of the techniques discussed in the text to analyze an alternative? If so, which one? If not, how might you have improved on a recent decision using one of these techniques?

12. Should managers be ethical in their decision making? If so, how should ethics be used in decision making?

13. Have you, or do you know anyone who has, experienced escalation of commitment to a bad decision? If yes, explain.

CASE

Draft-Day Decision Making

How would you make the decision on what player to pick if you had the number 1 NFL draft pick? The 2011 NFL draft posed quite a dilemma for Ron Rivera, the new coach for Carolina.

Option 1:

Was quarterback Cam Newton from Auburn worth the top draft spot? Recent number 1 quarterback picks had been big busts. Ryan Leaf and JaMarcus Russell received huge contracts and were even bigger busts. Cam Newton doesn't fit the exact quarterback model. He looks like a bodybuilder and thus seems to have some mobility—but he is a big moving target. He also has a slightly different passing motion. Even with those limitations, Cam was very successful in leading Auburn University to the NCAA National Championship in 2010-2011.

Option 2:

A range of other quarterbacks with their own weaknesses looked very interesting. Blaine Gabbert, Andy Dalton, and Christian Ponder all offered a more classic style of playing quarterback while staying in the pocket. But none of these quarterbacks seemed to have a great combination of quarterback experience, mobility, and a rifle passing arm.

Option 3:

General managers had previously decided that running backs could be picked up lower in the draft due to their need for a strong offensive line to create holes for them to run between. Plus, the likelihood of running backs' getting hurt and having a shortened career is quite high. Mark Ingram from Alabama was rated the highest running back in all of the mock drafts held before the actual draft day.

Option 4:

Wide receivers had been a position that general managers considered more important in the last few years. Quarterbacks cannot be successful unless they have some good targets to throw to. Receivers normally need to be tall and rangy to make it easier for the QB to find them. However, some teams have successfully used smaller players. A.J. Green from Georgia and Julio Jones from Alabama were the top-rated wide receivers.

Option 5:

Football teams often select nonglamour athletes in the first couple of rounds. Offensive and defensive linemen, linebackers, and safeties are often selected according to what the team's biggest need is. Auburn defensive tackle Nick Fairley and Clemson defensive end Da'Quan Bowers were the top two lineman prospects.

Option 6:

Then again, Tom Brady was picked by the New England Patriots in the sixth round of the draft—the 199th pick! So, maybe the top five teams should trade away their pick and receive two or three lower-number picks and look for their own Brady.

So, what did the Carolina Panthers decide? How did the decision turn out? For current information on the Carolina Panthers and to find out whether their draft-day strategy appears to be working, go to www.panthers.com/index.html.

Case Questions

1. Ron Rivera's draft pick decision was a programmed decision.
    a. true
    b. false

2. The rational model is appropriate for this decision.
    a. true
    b. false

3. Ron Rivera needed to set objectives and criteria.
   a. true
   b. false

4. Creativity and innovation are not crucial in the draft pick.
   a. true
   b. false

5. The environmental conditions facing the Carolina Panthers were
   a. certain
   b. risky
   c. uncertain

6. The information given in the case discussion lacks the _____ that the Panthers needed to make a decision.
   a. timeliness
   b. completeness
   c. quality
   d. relevance

7. _____ would have been appropriate for generating alternatives for the Panthers.
   a. brainstorming
   b. synectics
   c. nominal grouping
   d. consensus mapping
   e. the Delphi technique
   f. none of these

8. Which method would have been most appropriate for Ron Rivera's decision process?
   a. a quantitative technique
   b. cost–benefit analysis

9. Do you believe that Rivera would have been creative if he had selected Cam Newton?
   a. yes
   b. no

10. Classify Ron Rivera's desire to improve his football team.
    a. objective
    b. criterion

11. List the pros and cons for each alternative from Ron's perspective, which may be different from yours. State the pros and cons of trading the first pick versus using it.

12. Which alternative would you select if you were in the general manager's shoes?

SKILL-BUILDER EXERCISES

Skill-Builder 3.1: Using the Six-Step Decision Process

Objective

To develop your problem-solving and decision-making abilities

Preparation

Select a problem or opportunity that you would like to address. (Remember, a problem exists when your objectives are not being met. In other words, are what is happening and what you want to happen different?) Choose any aspect of your life—work, college, sports, a relationship, a purchase you wish to make, or where to go on a big date, to name a few possibilities. Use the following outline to help you work through the decision process.

Step 1: Define the Problem or Opportunity

Decision structure: Is the decision programmed or nonprogrammed?

_____

Decision conditions: Are they uncertain, risky, or certain?

_____

Decision model: Which model is appropriate—rational or bounded rationality?

_____

Level of participation: Should you make this decision solo or use a group?

_____

Symptoms versus cause: List the symptoms and causes. Now state the problem simply.

_____

_____

_____

Step 2: Set Objectives and Criteria

What do you want to accomplish with this decision?

My objective:

_____

"Must" criteria:

_____

"Want" criteria:

_____

Step 3: Generate Alternatives

What information do you need? (Remember, information must be timely, high quality, complete, and relevant to be useful.)

_____

_____

Will technology help you or hinder you?

_____

_____

If you are using a group, will you brainstorm, use nominal grouping, or do consensus mapping?

_____

Generate at least three alternatives, and list them here.

_____

_____

_____

Step 4: Select the Most Feasible Alternative

Is quantitative or cost–benefit analysis appropriate?

_____

List the pros and cons of each alternative.

_____

_____

_____

On a separate piece of paper, make a decision tree.

Step 5: Implement the Decision

Write a plan for implementing the decision (you may wish to skim chapter 4). State the control methods you will use to assess the results.

_____

_____

_____

_____

_____

_____

_____

Step 6: Control the Results

Make notes about what (if any) progress you are making in solving your problem. Indicate whether corrective action seems advisable, and if necessary, return to prior steps in the decision process. Think about how you can avoid escalation of commitment.

_____

_____

_____

_____

In-Class Application

Complete the preceding skill-building preparation before class.
Choose one:

- Break into groups of three to five members. Go through the six decision steps. At each step, group members give feedback by pointing out errors, suggesting how to improve the written statements, generating additional alternatives, listing pros and cons not thought of, and stating alternatives they would select.
- Conduct informal, whole-class discussion of student experiences.

Wrap-Up

Take a few minutes to write your answers to the following questions:

What did I learn from this experience? How will I use this knowledge?

_____

_____

_____

_____

As a class, discuss student responses.

Skill-Builder 3.2: Decision-Making Styles

Objective

To better understand decision-making styles

Preparation

You should have completed the decision-making styles Self-Assessment exercise in the chapter.

In-Class Application

Complete the preceding skill-building preparation before class.

- Break into groups of four to six members. One at a time, state if you were more reflexive or reactive. Review the 10 questions and determine which one or two had the greatest similarity in response and the greatest diversity. Discuss strategies that reflexive and also reactive decision makers can use to be more consistent.
- Options. Each group shares its answers to the questions.

Wrap-Up

Take a few minutes to write your answers to the following questions:

What did I learn from this experience? How will I use this knowledge?

_____

_____

_____

_____

As a class, discuss student responses.

SPORTS AND SOCIAL MEDIA EXERCISES

1. Use the following link to better understand the 12 key findings on the use of social media.
   www.jeffbullas.com/2010/04/05/12-key-findings-on-social-media%E2%80%99s-impact-on-business-and-decision-making-by-ceos-and-managers
   What are the 12 key findings?

   _____

2. If you were the marketing director for the Kansas City Chiefs in the NFL, which of the findings would you use to increase the use of social media in your organization?

_____

_____

_____

GAME PLAN FOR STARTING A SPORT BUSINESS

It is time to use the six steps to making a decision that you learned in this chapter. Follow the steps to decide which of your three sport business ideas from chapter 1 you are going to operate this semester.

1. Define the problem or opportunity:

_____

2. Set objectives and criteria:

_____

3. Generate alternatives:

_____

4. Select the most feasible alternative:

_____

5. Implement the decision:

_____

6. Control the results:

_____

Strategic and
Operational Planning

LEARNING OUTCOMES

After studying this chapter, you should be able to

1. explain how strategic and operational plans differ;
2. describe the differences between corporate-, business-, and functional-level strategies;
3. explain why organizations analyze industries and competitive situations;
4. explain why organizations analyze the company situation;
5. discuss how goals and objectives are similar but not the same;
6. describe how to write objectives;
7. describe the four corporate-level grand strategies;
8. describe the three growth strategies;
9. discuss the three business-level adaptive strategies; and
10. list the four functional-level operational strategies.

KEY TERMS

strategic planning	SWOT analysis	corporate growth strategies
operational planning	competitive advantage	merger
strategic process	goals	acquisition
strategy	objectives	business portfolio analysis
three levels of strategies	management by objectives (MBO)	adaptive strategies
situation analysis	grand strategies	operational strategies

Organizing   Leading   Controlling   Planning   Organizing   Leading   Controlling   Planning   Organizing   Lea
ntrolling   Planning   Organizing   Leading   Controlling   Planning   Organizing   Leading   Controlling   Planning   Org
Leading   Controlling   Planning   Organizing   Leading   Controlling   Planning   Organizing   Leading   Contr
lanning   Organizing   Leading   Controlling   Planning   Organizing   Leading   Controlling   Planning   Organ
ding   Controlling   Planning   Organizing   Leading   Controlling   Planning   Organizing   Leading   Controlling   Pla
nizing   Leading

DEVELOPING YOUR SKILLS

Effective managers develop sound strategic plans and set achievable objectives. Does the organization you work for or play for have a plan? What are the objectives it intends to achieve this year? In 2 years? In 5 years? In this chapter, by following the steps in the strategic process, you can improve your strategic planning skills. At the more personal level, follow the steps of the writing objectives model to develop effective objectives for your personal, sport, and professional lives.

REVIEWING THEIR GAME PLAN

Building the House of FIFA

Whole regions, peoples, and nations across the globe share neither mores, culture, language, nor religion, but they do share a passion—football. Not to be confused with American-style football, football (soccer to Americans) is not only the world's number-one game but is also a "major player" on the international scene and in commerce and politics. With more than 200 million active players, the game also constitutes a substantial chunk of the global leisure industry. Whole nations (from Yemen to Germany to Brazil to South Korea and Japan) dream about winning the World Cup, and their citizens pay money (and lots of it!) to travel to see matches, to see them at home, to wear shoes like those of their favorite players (whose status makes that of movie stars pale in comparison), and to buy numerous football products.

FIFA (Fédération Internationale de Football Association) is one reason for the world's love affair with football. Founded in Paris in 1904, it has survived the turmoil of two world wars and today includes 204 member organizations, making it the biggest and most popular sport federation in the world.

In 1998, at the 51st FIFA Ordinary Congress in Paris, Joseph Blatter (Switzerland) succeeded João Havelange (Brazil) as the eighth FIFA president. This victory elevated Blatter, who had served FIFA in various positions for 23 years, to the highest rung on the international football scene. Blatter is a versatile and experienced proponent of international sport diplomacy (this is crucial with a global sport like soccer) and is totally committed to serving football, FIFA, and the world's youth.

With the new president came a fresh strategic approach to issues facing world football. Blatter lost no time in presenting his vision of FIFA's future priorities and has worked tirelessly to win widespread approval in FIFA's Congress and Executive Committee. His vision is wide ranging and ambitious and includes the following:

• IFA's Goal Program, which seeks to educate and support national associations by providing aid for special projects to further develop football in the given country.

• FIFA's Quality Concept initiative, whose goal is to improve the actual football (soccer ball).

• Development of coaching, refereeing, and administration courses to help national football associations. Special emphasis is placed on the need for football associations to have proper communication and good media relations—otherwise known as marketing and event planning.

• An aggressive stance against player doping. An ethical code against doping was developed. The last three World Cups have been dope free and a real success story after years of players with doping problems.

In pursuing these goals, Blatter speaks frequently of the need for a renewed sense of solidarity in the world of football. His House of FIFA, a "virtual house," features values crucial to FIFA's future (and future strength) as a global institution: Its foundation is the trust generated by the closely knit FIFA family; its walls are its efficiently managed organization based on the principles of democracy, solidarity, and quality whose goal is to support and protect the game; and its roof is its universality, which binds everything together. FIFA's slogan—For the Good of the Game—speaks to these ideas and guides its activities.

However, President Blatter was barely reelected as president of FIFA in June of 2011. Preceding the elections, there were allegations of payoffs before the vote to host the 2018 and the 2022 World Cup games. The payoffs were to influence the sites selected for the

2018 and 2022 games. Ultimately, the decision was to hold the 2018 World Cup games in Russia and the 2022 World Cup games in Qatar.[1]

Blatter has also been accused of making poorly worded remarks about some of the biggest issues that FIFA faces. He has offended female players by saying they should dress in a more feminine way, as they do in volleyball, if they want to increase the popularity of the sport. He also offended LGBT (lesbian, gay, bisexual, and transgender) people by saying they should refrain from sexual activities during the 2022 World Cup games in Qatar, where homosexuality is illegal.[2]

For current information on FIFA, visit www.fifa.com.

An Overview of Strategic and Operational Planning

◀ LEARNING OUTCOME 1
Explain how strategic and operational plans differ.

Strategic leadership and planning are major determinants of organizational performance. There is a relationship between formal plans and team performance. Planning is one of the most important tasks managers do, and it is crucial today. Planning has three major benefits: speedier decision making, better management of resources, and clearer identification of the action steps needed to reach important goals. The North American Society for Sport Management expects sport management students to learn how to plan.[3]

> **TIME-OUT 1**
> State one objective from a strategic plan and one from an operational plan for a sport organization you are familiar with (preferably one you work for or play for). Know that you will be asked to analyze this same organization in other Time-Outs in this chapter.

Top-level management and the board of directors have the primary responsibility for strategic planning.[4] Sport governance is the responsibility for the overall direction of sport organizations. National organizations, such as the United States Olympic Committee (USOC), state high school athletics associations, and professional sport teams need to provide direction to their organizations. Strategic development is a key component of corporate governance. One key issue is that CEOs need to work closely with their board of directors to make sure that important strategic goals are reached.[5]

However, poor planning of the use of organizational resources can lead to failure. For every 10 products introduced, eight fail. What is the reason for this high rate of failure? Poor planning. If you fail to plan, you plan to fail. A prime example is the now-defunct XFL, which was the World Wrestling Federation's attempt to develop a new professional football league. The XFL failed to assess the control that the NFL has over player talent. Although the XFL was able to secure some television coverage, the quality of the players and ultimately of the game itself was not high enough to make watching worthwhile. Better planning might have led to creating an alternative football league, such as the Arena Football League (AFL), instead of competing directly against the NFL. The AFL is played indoors, on a much shorter field than regular football, and uses nets on the goalposts to help keep the ball in play.

The 2010 Ryder Cup golf competition was held at the Celtic Manor golf course in Newport, Wales. It was planned by Sun Mountain Sports as a key moment to dress captain Corey Pavin and his American team during wet weather. Unfortunately, the company's RainFlex gear did not hold up well in the rainy weather and did not keep the players dry.[6] Sun Mountain Sports owner, Rick Reimers, used Facebook to explain the poor implementation of what had appeared to be a good plan:

> Sun Mountain Sports is very sorry for the way our rain suits performed at the Ryder Cup. We will apologize to Corey and Lisa Pavin and the U.S. team at our earliest opportunity, and hope they will accept our heartfelt apology for the stress this must have caused. We are evaluating what happened. Our RainFlex,

introduced in 2006, has been extensively and successfully used by over 150 tour players, the 2009 Presidents Cup team, the 2007 and 2009 Walker Cup teams and thousands of PGA professionals. We believed, as Corey must have, that our RainFlex, built with quiet, stretchable, breathable fabric would be an advantage to the U.S. team. That it was not is a great disappointment. It was just not enough for the torrential rains at Celtic Manor.[7]

Although planning alone won't secure the success of new ventures, planning increases the probability of survival. Good planning is based on conceptual and decision-making skills. Before we examine the planning process and the various levels of strategic planning, complete the Self-Assessment to determine how well you plan.

SELF-ASSESSMENT 4.1

Effective Planning

Indicate how well each statement describes your behavior by placing a number from 1 to 5 on the line before the statement.

Describes me				Does not describe me
5	4	3	2	1

_____ 1. I have a specific end result to accomplish whenever I start a project of any kind.

_____ 2. When setting objectives, I state only the end result to be accomplished; I don't specify how the result will be accomplished.

_____ 3. I have specific and measurable objectives; for example, I know the specific grade I want to earn in this course.

_____ 4. I set objectives that are difficult but achievable.

_____ 5. I set deadlines when I have something I need to accomplish, and I meet the deadlines.

_____ 6. I have a long-term goal (what I will be doing in 3-5 years) and short-term objectives to get me there.

_____ 7. I have written objectives stating what I want to accomplish.

_____ 8. I know my strengths and weaknesses, am aware of threats, and seek opportunities.

_____ 9. I analyze a problem and alternative actions, rather than immediately jumping right in with a solution.

_____ 10. I spend most of my day doing what I plan to do, rather than dealing with emergencies and trying to get organized.

_____ 11. I use a calendar, appointment book, or some form of to-do list.

_____ 12. I ask others for advice.

_____ 13. I follow appropriate policies, procedures, and rules.

_____ 14. I develop contingency plans in case my plans do not work out as I expect.

_____ 15. I implement my plans and determine whether I have met my objectives.

Add up the numbers you assigned to the statements to see where you fall on the following continuum.

Effective planner					Ineffective planner
75	65	45	35	25	15

Don't be too disappointed if your score isn't as high as you would like. All of these items are characteristics of effective planning. Review the items that did not characterize you. After studying this chapter and doing the exercises, you can improve your planning skills.

Strategic Process

In **strategic planning**, management develops a mission and long-term objectives and determines in advance how they will be accomplished. Long-term generally means longer than 1 year. In **operational planning**, management sets short-term objectives and determines in advance how they will be accomplished. Short-term objectives are those that can be met in 1 year or less. Much of team management is evolving from a focus on winning as a means of realizing short-term profits to a focus on strategic management of the team brand as a means of realizing long-term appreciation in franchise value.

Strategic planning and operational planning differ primarily by time frame and by the management level involved. Strategic plans are typically developed for 5 years and are reviewed and revised every year so that a 5-year plan is always in place. Top-level managers develop strategic plans. Operational plans are developed for time frames of 1 year or less; middle managers or first-line managers develop operational plans.

The strategic process is about developing both the long-range and short-range plans that will enable the organization to accomplish its long-range objectives. If we use the means and ends analysis (chapter 2), top managers determine the ends, and middle- and lower-level managers find the means to accomplish the ends. Hosting major sport events requires long-term strategic plans that are well coordinated with short-term plans. The investments must fit into the city's long-term plan to make the event economically successful.[8] The Olympic Games require extensive long- and short-term planning by the IOC and the cooperation of the host country and city.[9]

In the **strategic process**, managers (1) develop the mission, (2) analyze the environment, (3) set objectives, (4) develop strategies, and (5) implement and control the strategies. Developing strategies takes place at three levels. As you can see from figure 4.1, the process is not a linear one. Managers continually return to previous steps and make changes—planning is an ongoing process. Also note that management performs the four management functions—planning, organizing, leading, and controlling—in the strategic process.

Levels of Strategies

◄ LEARNING OUTCOME 2

Describe the differences between corporate-, business-, and functional-level strategies.

An organization's **strategy** is its plan for pursuing its mission and achieving its objectives. The **three levels of strategies** are corporate, business, and functional. We examine these three levels in more detail later in this chapter. Here we simply define them to give you an overview.

Corporate-level strategy is the organization's plan for managing multiple lines of businesses. Many large companies are actually several businesses. Adidas, for example, sells footwear, golf equipment, and cycling products—the company treats each product line as a separate line of business.

Adidas has been implementing its corporate-level strategy by entering new markets via key acquisitions. In 2011, as part of its

> **TIME-OUT 2**
>
> List the lines of business your organization is involved in.

Strategic Business Plan Route 2015, Adidas acquired Five Ten, a leading performance brand in outdoor action sports. "We are very excited to join forces with Five Ten. Five Ten is a leading brand in the technical outdoor market and within the outdoor action sport community. Climbers, mountain bikers and other outdoor athletes around the world highly value their products," said Rolf Reinschmidt, Senior Vice President adidas Outdoor.[10]

Business-level strategy is the organization's plan for managing one line of business. Each of Adidas' businesses has its own strategy for competing in its market. In golf, "TaylorMade-adidas Golf's aim is to be the leading performance golf company in the world in terms of sales and profitability. It combines three of golf's best-known and respected brands: TaylorMade, adidas Golf and Ashworth." TaylorMade is the market

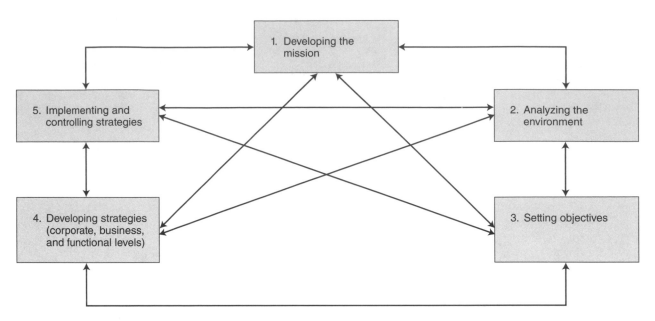

FIGURE 4.1   The strategic process.

leader in the metalwoods category, adidas Golf develops high-performance footwear and apparel, and Ashworth is an authentic golf-inspired lifestyle brand complementing adidas Golf's position.[11]

Functional-level strategy is the organization's plan for managing one area of the business. Functional areas include marketing, finance and accounting, operations and production, human resources, and others depending on the specific line of business. Managers in each of Adidas' business lines are involved with these functional areas. For example, TaylorMade-adidas Golf has combined product marketing, brand communication, and retail marketing into one fully integrated global marketing team. It has used Twitter and Facebook to make sure TaylorMade-adidas Golf reaches the social media generation.[12] Figure 4.2 shows the relationships among corporate-, business-, and functional-level strategies.

Development of the Mission

Name three ways FIFA is fulfilling its mission and three areas in which it could improve.

Developing the organization's mission is the first step in the strategic process. The mission provides the foundation on which the plan, via the four remaining steps, will be constructed. The organization's mission, as noted in chapter 2, defines who the organization is and why it exists. The mission describes management's vision (which may be a separate statement) for the company—where the company is headed and why. FIFA's mission is stated as "Develop the game, touch the world, build a better future." "We see it as our mission to contribute towards building a better future for the world by using the power and popularity of football. This mission gives meaning and direction to each and every activity that FIFA is involved in—football being an integrated part of our society."[13]

The field of sport management is monitored by the North American Society for Sport Management (NASSM). NASSM's mission is to actively be involved in supporting and assisting professionals working in the fields of sport, leisure, and recreation. The purpose of NASSM is to promote, stimulate, and encourage study, research, scholarly writing, and professional development in the area of sport management—both theoretical and applied aspects.[14] NASSM membership has increased significantly over the years, which is a sign that it is achieving its mission of helping members interested in sport management. NASSM has a strategic plan, which its members continue to discuss and update.

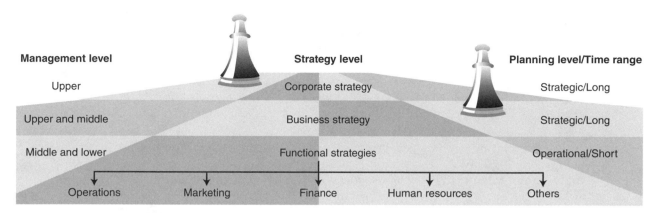

FIGURE 4.2 Strategic planning.

Analysis of the Environment

To create value, a strategy must fit with the capabilities of the firm and its external environment. The organization's internal and external environmental factors (chapter 2) are analyzed as step 2 in the strategic process, which determines the fit. Another term for analyzing the environment is situation analysis. A **situation analysis** draws out those features in a company's environment that most directly frame its strategic window of options and opportunities. The situation analysis has three parts: analysis of the company's industry and its competition, analysis of the company's particular situation, and analysis of the company's competitive advantage (or lack thereof). Companies with multiple lines of business conduct environmental analyses for each line of business.

Industry Analysis and Five Competitive Forces

Industries vary widely in their business makeup, competitive situation, and growth potential. Different sport management strategies are needed in different areas.[15] To determine whether an industry is worth entering requires answers to such questions as "How large is the market? What is the growth rate? How many competitors are there?" Thus, competitive analysis is important to strategic planning.[16] Callaway Golf Company, for example, faces strong competition from Acushnet (Titleist brand), Adams Golf (Tight Lies Fairway Woods), TaylorMade, and Orlimar (TriMetal Fairway Woods).

Michael Porter uses the idea of five competitive forces to analyze the competitive environment.[17]

1. Rivalry among competing firms: Porter calls this "the scrambling and jockeying for position." Businesses compete for customers by price, quality, and speed (responding to new styles and models and getting these products quickly to retailers). Nike, Adidas-Reebok, Puma, and Fila are rivals in the athletic footwear industry. All four of these companies need to anticipate the moves of their competitors. They also need to be aware of newer competitors such as Under Armour and Li Ning.

2. Potential development of substitute products and services: This occurs when companies from other industries try to move into the market. For example, Reebok and Skechers emerged as the leaders in the toning shoe market. The rocker bottom–shaped athletic footwear is marketed as footwear that tones the body when worn during walking. Although there are arguments that this type of footwear does not do what is claimed, it still has grown into a billion dollar market. Adidas settled with the Federal Trade Commission (FTC) on claims about the success of toning shoes, but will reenter the market with new technology and research to support the benefits of wearing these shoes.[18]

◀ **LEARNING OUTCOME 3**
Explain why organizations analyze industries and competitive situations.

95

In the early 2000s, Crocs slip-on shoes became popular in water sports and as a fashion item. Crocs normally come in bright colors and are easily recognizable. Crocs formed an alliance with the NFL to sell its shoes in professional team colors.

Clothing manufacturers such as Tommy Hilfiger have attempted to enter the sneaker market using their fashion brand to their advantage. Also, "brown shoe" companies, such as Dr. Martens, persuaded many younger buyers to buy hiking-style sneakers instead of the traditional sport sneakers. The brown shoe companies were quite successful in stealing sales in the mid- to late 1990s.

3. Potential entry of new competitors: How difficult and costly is it for new businesses to enter the industry? Does a company need to defend itself against new competition? Under Armour, founded in 1996, has successfully entered the high-performance apparel industry. Li Ning is a famous Chinese gymnastics Olympian who started his own footwear and sportswear company. In China, Li Ning is second in sales only to Nike. In 2011, Ning formed an alliance with the digital commerce company Acquity Group of Chicago to enter the U.S. market. Li Ning plans to using Shaquille O'Neal to represent its products.[19]

4. Bargaining power of suppliers: The success of companies selling a product is often based on its suppliers, so this is an important relationship.[20] How dependent is the business on its suppliers? If the business has only one major supplier and no available alternatives, the supplier has great bargaining power. Conversely, a business can have bargaining power over the supplier. For example, Nike doesn't manufacture its own sneakers; it uses private contractors in Vietnam to produce the sneakers. Workers are paid very low wages, which indirectly gives Nike a great deal of power over these often helpless factory workers. In effect, because Nike can easily switch factories, it controls the suppliers. Nike faced a tremendous amount of pressure to improve working conditions in Asia where its shoes are manufactured. Nike did not address the poor working conditions as quickly as expected from such a powerful company. However, Nike has spent the last 20 years improving the working conditions. Nike or inspection specialists that it hires regularly check factory conditions such as air quality and the age of employees, and the company works with suppliers to limit overtime. Nike learned that corporate social responsibility (CSR) practices can help maintain and even improve profitability.[21]

5. Bargaining power of consumers: Satisfied customers are the key to long-term success. How much does the business depend on the consumer? Consumers of footwear have power because they can shift to other manufacturers on a mere whim or because of a new style, better price, higher quality, greater convenience, and a host of other reasons. However, consumers lose power when they are loyal to a business like Nike and want to buy only Nike footwear. Because there are many consumers who want Nike products, Nike is in a strong position as long as it continues to offer appealing products. But companies such as Reebok create new products, such as its new Zig technology used in designing footwear, to persuade consumers to switch to their products. Reebok can also put its footwear on sale to help entice consumers to switch.

Companies use analyses of the industry and their competitors primarily at the corporate level when they are deciding which lines of business they should consider entering (or exiting) and how to allocate resources

 TIME-OUT 3 Using figure 4.3 as a guide, do a simple five-forces competitive analysis for your organization.

among their product lines. (We will return to this topic later in the chapter.) Nike bought Bauer, a hockey equipment manufacturer, because the company decided that this was an attractive industry. See figure 4.3 for a competitive analysis of Nike's decision.

LEARNING OUTCOME 4 ▶

Explain why organizations analyze the company situation.

Analysis of the Company Situation

Managers use analyses of the company situation when they develop business strategies and when they determine which issues need to be addressed in the next three steps of the strategic process. A complete company situation analysis has five steps, as shown in figure 4.4.

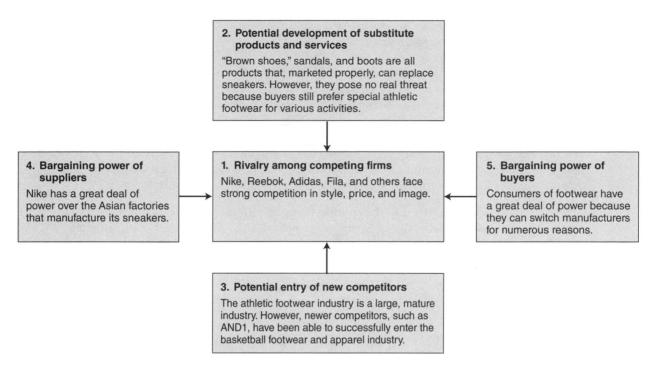

FIGURE 4.3   Nike's five-forces competitive analysis.

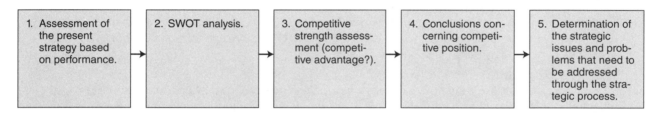

FIGURE 4.4   Steps in the analysis of the company situation.

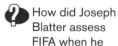

- **Step 1: Assess present strategy.** This assessment can be a simple comparison or a complex analysis of performance (wins, championships, attendance, market share, sales, net profit, return on assets, and so on) over the past 5 years.

- **Step 2: Analyze SWOTs.** A highly recommended strategic tool, **SWOT** (**S**trengths, **W**eaknesses, **O**pportunities, **T**hreats) **analysis** is used to assess strengths and weaknesses in an organization's internal environment and opportunities in its external environment. (See chapter 2 for a discussion of internal and external environments.) "Nike's Company Situation Analysis" includes a SWOT analysis.

- **Step 3: Assess competitive strength.** For a strategy to be effective, it must be based on a clear understanding of competitors. The emergence of motor sports (NASCAR) and professional wrestling (WWE), for example, as major competitors in the 1990s caught professional sport leagues such as the NBA and NFL by surprise and made an already competitive marketplace even tougher. The NBA's and NFL's strategies and research missed this demand. In such situations, management has got to wonder, "What else are we missing?" Some industry experts believe that showing MLB World Series games online at night has limited the ability of younger fans to follow the games. Even one or two weekend day games would allow children to watch and enjoy a championship series and become loyal fans of the game.

Looking at critical success factors can help improve a company's assessment of its competition. Critical success factors (CSFs) are key, pivotal activities that the business must perform

How did Joseph Blatter assess FIFA when he became the president of the association?

List three strengths and three weaknesses of your organization.

well if it is to win its race. It is imperative that management compare its CSFs for each product line to those of each of its major competitors. This takes a great deal of business acumen and objectivity. Organizations typically use one of two approaches. The first (and simpler) approach rates each CSF from 1 (weak) to 10 (strong) and tallies the ratings to rank competitors. The second approach uses the same rating system but weights the CSFs by importance, with the weighted total equal to 1.00. The weight is multiplied by the rating to get a score for each firm on each factor. Scores are totaled to determine the final rankings. "Nike's Company Situation Analysis" shows weighted CSF rankings for Nike, Under Amour, and Adidas-Reebok.

What issues did Joseph Blatter and FIFA decide to improve on?

- **Step 4: Make conclusions.** The questions here are simple to ask but not always so easy to answer. How is the business doing compared with its competition? Is our market share improving or slipping?

- **Step 5: Decide what issues to address.** Using information developed in steps 1 to 4, management now asks, "What needs to be done to improve our competitive position?"

Nike's Company Situation Analysis

1. Present Strategy Assessment

   Nike's present strategy is working well. Nike is profitable and continues to be the leading company in the sport footwear and apparel industry. So far, the company has been able to hold off strong competitors such as the recently merged Adidas–Reebok combination. Diversification into the golf industry has been successful, which is attributable to Nike's foresight in signing Tiger Woods as its spokesperson fairly early in his brilliant career.

2. SWOT Analysis

   Strengths: Nike's strength is its reputation for high-quality and innovative footwear. Nike is also known for its innovative marketing. Nike ads are part of the pop culture—an impressive achievement. Famous campaigns feature Bo Jackson, Michael Jordan, and Tiger Woods. The Nike "Swoosh" is highly recognizable worldwide. Nike's recent comeback has been greatly helped by increased sales of Nike apparel. Nike+ works with Apple products to help runners calculate their distance and speed. NikeiD allows customers to design their own footwear.

   Weaknesses: Tiger Woods' personal troubles off the golf course and his lack of winning on the golf course threatens to slow down Nike's gain in market share in the golf industry. Improved research and development by Adidas-Reebok threatens the perception that Nike is the technology leader in the footwear industry. Another area of some concern is that global sales, for example in Europe and Asia, have increased at a much faster pace than domestic sales in the United States.

   Opportunities: Nike has an opportunity to capitalize on its own Nike+ technology. This is a sensor placed in Nike footwear that interacts with Apple's iPod to record the distance a runner has completed and the calories that have been burned. Another opportunity will be to capitalize on an endorsement deal with LeBron James after his NBA Playoffs and Championship Series appearances. NikeiD is a unique website that allows consumers to design their own footwear. It is a fun and creative site that could be further marketed.

   Threats: The lingering recession in the United States in 2012 was troubling for Nike since its products are often higher priced than those of competitors. Competitors such as Under Armour and Adidas-Reebok have been able to secure contracts with colleges, the NBA, the NFL, and the NHL for their apparel businesses.

3. Competitive Strength Assessment

   As illustrated in table 4.1, each factor is rated on a weighted scale (rating 1 [low] to 10 [high] for each firm—rating × weight). Quality is determined to be the most important criterion, with a weight of 0.50, followed by marketing and price at a weight of 0.25 each. In terms of quality, Nike, Under

Armour, and Adidas all have a perfect score of 10: 10 multiplied by the weight of 0.50 equals a score of 5.0. Thus, all three companies have superior-quality products. Overall, Nike is the strongest company at 9.50, followed by Adidas at 9.25; Under Armour is a 9.00. Scores are determined by executives at the companies, students in a class, or (in this case) authors. Scoring is based on completing a SWOT and should foster debate. The authors lowered the score for Nike's marketing since it really hasn't been unique since Michael Jordan retired and Tiger Woods failed to win any major golf tournaments.

TABLE 4.1 Nike's Company Situation Analysis

Critical success factors	Weight	Nike	Under Armour	Adidas-Reebok
Quality	0.50	10 = 5.0	10 = 5.0	10 = 5.0
Marketing	0.25	9 = 2.25	8 = 2.0	8 = 2.0
Price	0.25	9 = 2.25	8 = 2.0	9 = 2.25
	1.00	9.50	9.00	9.25

4. Conclusions About Competitive Advantage

Nike's advantage lies in name recognition and quality image in many different markets. The Nike name and Swoosh logo continue to be worldwide status symbols.

Nike is the leading (and hence strongest) competitor and will remain so through continual improvement of the technology used in its footwear, equipment, and apparel lines. Continued growth in these divisions will be supported by new and creative marketing campaigns. However, Nike needs to monitor the success of the recent merger of Adidas and Reebok, which created a competitor nearly as large as Nike. At the same time, Nike needs to shift market share in the high-performance athletic apparel market away from Under Armour. Nike is a latecomer to this market, so gaining an edge here might take longer than Nike expects.

5. Determination of Strategic Issues

Nike needs to focus on (1) improving U.S. footwear sales, (2) continuing to increase international sales, (3) building U.S. sales in its high-performance athletic apparel, and (4) improving the sustainability of the environment as a source of innovation and growth for the company.

Competitive Advantage

Strategic planning helps organizations create a competitive advantage.[22] **Competitive advantage** specifies how the organization offers unique customer value. It answers the questions, "What makes us different from our competition?" and "Why

TIME-OUT
5
Describe your organization's competitive advantage. If you don't think it has one, state how it resembles its competitors in its products or services.

should a person buy our product or service rather than the competition's?" A sustainable competitive advantage (1) distinguishes the organization from its competitors, (2) provides positive economic benefits, and (3) cannot be readily duplicated. The key to producing sustainable competitive advantage is effective management of people. Many organizations focus on quality as a means to beat the competition.

If you ever consider starting your own business, be sure to answer these questions: "What will make my business different from the competition? Why should a person buy my product or service rather than the competition's?" If you don't have answers to these crucial questions, go back to the drawing board! Why? Because your business is very likely to join the ranks of failed businesses, those that don't have a competitive advantage and don't have a strategic plan for developing one. The Self-Assessment later in the chapter will help you determine whether you have what it takes to be a successful entrepreneur, and in the exercise you will develop a strategic plan for a new business.

Finding core competencies and benchmarking go hand in hand with developing competitive advantage. A core competency is what a firm does well—in other words, its strengths. Management that focuses on core competencies can create new products and services that take advantage of the company's strengths. Through benchmarking, you compare your firm with its competitors, as was done in the situational analysis.

Setting of Objectives

Setting objectives is the third step in the strategic process. Individuals, teams, and organizations need goals to be successful.[23] For strategies to succeed, management must commit to a carefully thought-out set of objectives. The idea is to set objectives that are compatible with the mission and that address strategic issues identified in the situation analysis. Objectives are then prioritized so that the organization can focus on the more important ones.[24] (In chapter 5 you will learn how to prioritize.)

Keep in mind that objectives are end results that you wish to attain—they do not tell others how to accomplish the objectives. Therefore, setting objectives is just the beginning of your task, because you need to develop plans to achieve your objectives. That is also why you need to know the difference between goals and objectives, how to write objectives, criteria for effective objectives, and the concept of management by objectives (MBO), all of which we examine in the following discussion.

Determining Goals and Objectives

LEARNING OUTCOME 5 ▶
Discuss how goals and objectives are similar but not the same.

Some people use the terms goals and objectives synonymously—this is not a good idea. Precise language makes for precision thinking, which of course enhances your ability to accomplish your organization's mission. **Goals** state general targets to be accomplished. **Objectives** state what is to be accomplished in specific and measurable terms by a certain target date. Goals are your target; objectives guide your development of operational plans and help you know if you are achieving the target. Goals thus translate into objectives. Likely goals and objectives for Nike's apparel and footwear divisions give a few likely goals for Nike as a whole.

Writing Objectives

LEARNING OUTCOME 6 ▶
Describe how to write objectives.

Successful people set goals that they then strive to attain, and they write explicit objectives to help them get there. The writing of the objectives is itself a clarifying and focusing endeavor and is one reason why motivational gurus and career counselors swear by written objectives. Remember New Year's resolutions? Well, think about making some "career resolutions." The *Wall Street Journal* notes that if you don't have career objectives, your resolution should be to get some.[25] The Skill-Builder at the end of this chapter will help get you started. To keep your focus on your end goals, post your objectives on your desk or wall.

 TIME-OUT 6 State one of your organization's goals, and list the objectives it is using to attain the goal.

So, you're chewing your pencil and can't quite get going? Here's a simple way (which we adapted from Max E. Douglas' model) to get your creative juices flowing.

1. Start with the word *to:*

   To—

2. Attach an action verb—typical ones are *increase, improve, enter, revive* (you get the picture):

   —obtain—

3. Now think of a single, specific result that you want to achieve and that can be measured:

—a batting average of 300—

4. Choose a target date.

—during the 2015 season.

This is too simple, you say? What do you think managers do when they write objectives? Table 4.2 shows one of Nike's objectives diagrammed. We'll show you some other examples when we discuss criteria.

TIME-OUT
7

Using the guidelines given here, write one objective that your organization should pursue.

Using Criteria to Write Objectives

You've seen one of Nike's objectives diagrammed. Now let's look a little more critically at what makes an objective useful. An objective must lead to a single result that is specific and measurable and must include a target date. These criteria are discussed next.

TABLE 4.2   Writing Objectives

To write an objective	Nike's objective
1. Start with *to*.	To
2. Add an action verb.	increase
3. Insert a single, specific, and measurable result.	the sales of eco-friendly footwear by 5%
4. Choose a target date.	by November 2015.

Writing Objectives

Goals

To increase sales of international markets

To increase sales in the U.S. apparel business

To view sustainability (of the environment) as a source of innovation and growth for the company, not just as a responsibility

To use sport as a tool for youth inclusion

Objectives

We continue to be very pleased with the underlying strength of our international businesses. Our objective is to increase sales of our international businesses by 7% to 9% in each quarter of the next fiscal year (2015).

As we expected, the U.S. apparel business improved last quarter, recording the first year-on-year increase in 2 years. Over the next year, we expect double-digit growth (10-13%) in U.S. apparel as our team sales continue to grow and we make further progress by developing our high-performance apparel business. Our objective is to increase sales by 10% to 13% in apparel in 2015.

By 2015, all Nike footwear will meet the company's new environmental design standard and reduce materials used by 10%. We believe that all youth should be able to play sports. One of our objectives in this area is to donate U.S.$1 million to help build new playgrounds in five different parks in Oregon State by 2015.

1. **Single result**: Write each objective so that it describes only one result. This prevents you from writing vague, meaningless, complicated objectives. Aim for clarity, simplicity, and explicitness. Vague or convoluted objectives can be misunderstood, and you want everyone involved to understand the objective. Later, you will have the luxury of stating that the objective was met or not met. If your objective involves multiple possible results, you're going to sound wishy-washy and apologetic when you are reduced to saying that the objective was partially met, somewhat but not quite met, or almost met. Because there is nothing like an example to drive home a point, let's look at the objectives written by OB Iffy and OB Sharp, two young floating managers who work for various organizations.

> **OB Iffy**: To increase sales by 25% and to achieve a 5.4% market share.
>
> (Sales of what? Market share of what? And by when? What if Iffy meets one goal but not the other—is this objective met or not met?)
>
> **OB Sharp**: To increase tennis racket sales by 25% by December 2015.
>
> To achieve a 5.4% market share of tennis rackets by 2015.

2. **Specific result**: State the exact level of performance expected. Years ago, research showed that people with specific goals perform better than those with general goals.

> **OB Iffy**: To maximize profits in 2015.
>
> (How much is "maximize"? Is this gross profit or net profit?)
>
> To recycle 40% by year end 2015.
>
> (40% of what—glass, paper, ideas?)
>
> **OB Sharp**: To earn a net profit of U.S.$15 million in 2015.
>
> To recycle 40% of all paper waste by year end 2015.

3. **Measurable result**: If you can't measure your progress, you're going to have trouble determining whether your objective has been met.

> **OB Iffy**: Perfect service for every customer.
>
> (Perfect by whose standards? How do you measure perfect service?)
>
> **OB Sharp**: To attain 90% "excellent" in customer satisfaction ratings for 2015.

4. **Target date**: Set a date for accomplishing the objective. Deadlines make all of us focus earlier and try harder.

> **OB Iffy**: To achieve attendance of 4 million fans.
>
> (For every game? For all time?)
>
> **OB Sharp**: To achieve attendance of 4 million fans for the 2015 MLB season.
>
> **OB Iffy but Getting Better**: To double international business to U.S.$5 billion annually within 5 years.
>
> (Will anyone remember the date 5 years from now?)
>
> **OB Sharp**: To double international business to U.S.$5 billion annually by year end 2015.
>
> **OB Sharp**: To keep rejected products to less than 1%. (Note: Some objectives are ongoing and therefore do not require a target date.)

In addition to the "must" criteria (a single result that is specific and measurable and has a target date), three "want" criteria will help you achieve objectives: a realistic objective that is set by the team and that has team commitment.

5. **Realistic objective**: A number of studies show that people perform better when they work toward realistic objectives. That is, the objective should be difficult, but it must also be achievable. People do less well when the objective is too difficult (we often don't try or we give up when we believe something is impossible), when the objective is too easy (we just meet the objective and hold back performance), and when the objective is an open-ended, do-your-best instruction (most people don't do their best but say they did). When

we read an objective, it is often difficult to determine whether it is realistic. What is realistic to one person may be unrealistic to another. Thus, this criterion is subjective and therefore is a "want" criterion for objectives.

6. **Team-set objective**: Work groups that set their own objectives generally outperform groups that are assigned objectives (chapter 3), but we must use the appropriate level of participation for the group's capabilities. Because it is not always appropriate for groups to set objectives, this is also a "want" criterion.

7. **Team commitment to the objective**: A team that commits to an objective will work harder to achieve it. Participation in the decision-making and problem-solving process that usually precedes the setting of an objective is often key in attaining team commitment (see chapter 3). Team commitment is also a "want" criterion because commitment will vary from individual to individual, and sometimes you will have to set objectives that your group or team will not like.

For a review of these key criteria, see figure 4.5. Teams and sport organizations can train all of their employees and managers to write SMART (Specific, Measurable, Achievable, Results-Based, and Time-Specific) objectives.

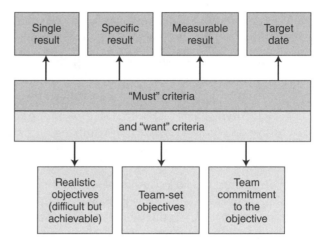

FIGURE 4.5 Key criteria for achieving objectives.

Using Management by Objectives

Management by objectives (MBO) is the process by which managers and their teams jointly set objectives, periodically evaluate performance, and reward according to the results. Other names for MBO include work planning and review, goals management, goals and controls, and management by results. There are three steps in the MBO process.

- **Step 1: Set individual objectives and plans**. With each subordinate, the manager jointly sets objectives. These objectives are the heart of the MBO program and should meet the criteria discussed earlier.

- **Step 2: Give feedback and evaluate performance**. Communication is a key factor in the success or failure of MBO. Thus, the manager and employee must meet frequently to review progress. The frequency of evaluations depends on the individual and the job performed. However, most managers probably do not conduct enough review sessions.

- **Step 3: Reward according to performance**. Employees' performance should be measured against their objectives. Employees who meet their objectives should be rewarded through recognition, praise, pay raises, and promotions.

Former head football coach Lou Holtz (currently a motivational speaker, author of five books, and ESPN commentator) is known for turning around Arkansas and Minnesota teams and leading the University of Notre Dame's previously struggling Fighting Irish to a national championship. Holtz is a strong believer in setting objectives, stating that all good performance starts with clear goals. He used MBO to motivate players. Holtz had players set objectives and then he approved them, reviewed them during the season and gave feedback, and rewarded (primarily with playing time) players who were accomplishing the objectives.[26] Do you have clear, well-written objectives? Skill-Builder 4.1 on page 120 will help you write objectives using the model.

Corporate-Level Strategy

After the mission is developed, the environmental analysis is completed, and objectives are set, the organization's strategy (step 4 in the planning process) is developed at the corporate, business, and functional levels. In this section, you will learn about corporate-level strategy: grand strategies, corporate growth strategies, and portfolio analysis.

Grand Strategies

LEARNING OUTCOME 7 ▶

Describe the four corporate-level grand strategies.

Strategies are commonly put into typologies,[27] as we present here. An organization's **grand strategies** are its corporate strategies for growth, stability, turnaround and retrenchment, or a combination thereof. Each grand strategy reflects a different objective.

- **Growth:** Companies with a growth strategy aggressively attempt to increase their size through increased sales. We will return to growth strategies in a moment. The sport industry is growing, and many organizations have growth strategies.

- **Stability:** Companies with a stability strategy endeavor to hold and maintain their present size or to grow slowly. Many companies are satisfied with the status quo. Some college and pro teams, such as the Red Sox, virtually sell out every game. With no real growth in ticket sales, they seek to keep fans coming.

- **Turnaround and retrenchment:** A turnaround strategy is an attempt to reverse a declining business as quickly as possible. A retrenchment strategy is the divestiture or liquidation of assets. We list them together because most turnarounds involve retrenchment. Turnaround strategies attempt to improve cash flow by increasing revenues, decreasing costs, and selling assets. Converse, the longtime maker of athletic footwear, tried numerous turnaround strategies to save that company. Following years of declining sales, the company filed for Chapter 11 bankruptcy protection in 2001. Footwear Acquisition purchased the company, intending to continue operations. But CVEO Corporation (which now owned Converse) went on to sell the company in the United States and Canada to Nike. Nike is looking to take ownership of the Converse brand in other regions. Nike has since returned Converse to profitability and is in the process of opening Converse stores in major U.S. cities. Converse had sales of a billion dollars in 2010.[28]

TIME-OUT 8 State your organization's grand strategy.

- **Combination:** A corporation may simultaneously pursue growth, stability, and turnaround and retrenchment across its different lines of business. We discuss this idea in more detail in the business portfolio analysis section.

Corporate Growth Strategies

LEARNING OUTCOME 8 ▶

Describe the three growth strategies.

TIME-OUT 9 Identify the growth strategies that your organization uses. Are they working?

Companies that want to grow have three major options. **Corporate growth strategies** include concentration, backward and forward integration, and related and unrelated diversification. Figure 4.6 summarizes an organization's choices when its grand strategy is growth.

- **Concentrate:** An organization with a concentration strategy grows its existing lines of business aggressively. Sports Authority, for example (see chapter 1), continues to open new stores.

- **Integrate:** An organization with an integration strategy enters *forward* or *backward* lines of business. In forward integration, the line of business is closer to the final customer. In backward integration, the line of business is farther away from the final customer. Some manufacturers, including Reebok, open factory stores and fitness centers to forward-

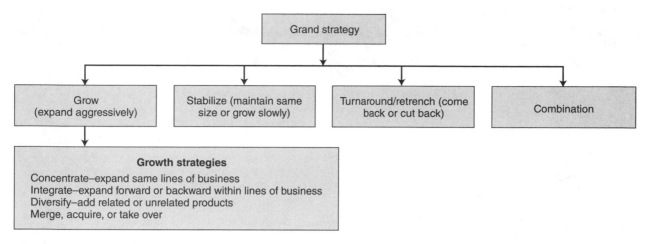

FIGURE 4.6 Corporate grand and growth strategies.

integrate; that is, they bypass traditional retail stores and sell their products directly to the customer.

- **Diversify:** An organization with a diversification strategy goes into *related* or *unrelated* lines of products. Nike pursued related diversification when it decided to add beach-style sport clothing (Hurley) as a business line. Figure 4.6 summarizes the grand strategies used at the corporate level.

- **Growth strategies include mergers and acquisitions:** Organizations also try to grow through mergers, acquisitions, and takeovers. Competing companies sometimes use mergers and acquisitions to compete more effectively with larger companies; to realize economies of size; to consolidate expenses; and to achieve access to markets, products, technology, resources, and management talent. In a **merger**, two companies form one new company. The Canadian Amateur Hockey Association and Hockey Canada merged to form the Canadian Hockey Association. In an **acquisition**, one business buys all or part of another business. Companies also use acquisitions to enter new lines of businesses—it is less risky to buy an established, successful business than it is to start a new one. Pepsi acquired Quaker Oats to get its sport drink, Gatorade, whereas Coca-Cola started its own POWERADE brand.

When a target company's management rejects an offer to be bought out by another company, the purchasing company can make a bid to the target company's shareholders to acquire it through a takeover—these are typically not friendly actions (hence the term *hostile takeover*).

Business Portfolio Analysis

You are no doubt familiar with the idea of individual investment portfolios. Businesses use the term *portfolio analysis* somewhat differently than would an individual investor. In **business portfolio analysis,** corporations determine which lines of business they will be in and how they will allocate resources among the different lines. As noted at the beginning of the chapter, a business line—also called a strategic business unit (SBU)—is a distinct business with its own customers that is managed reasonably independently of the corporation's other businesses. What constitutes an SBU varies from company to company—SBUs are variously divisions, subsidiaries, or single product lines. Adidas has divisions for footwear, cycling equipment, and golf equipment. Corporations use the environmental analysis they perform on each business line (step 2 in the strategic planning process) to analyze their portfolios. Another method, the BCG matrix, places each line of business in one matrix.

Corporate Growth Strategies

Identify the growth strategy used by each company.

a. concentration

b. forward integration

c. backward integration

d. related diversification

e. unrelated diversification

_____ 1. Spalding buys a rubber company to make the rubber it uses in its sneakers.

_____ 2. General Motors buys the Sea World theme park.

_____ 3. Dick's opens a new retail store in Worcester, Massachusetts.

_____ 4. Adidas opens its own retail stores.

_____ 5. Nike buys Bauer Hockey Equipment.

BCG Growth-Share Matrix

One popular method for analyzing corporate business portfolios is the Boston Consulting Group's (BCG) growth-share matrix. A BCG matrix for Nike is shown in figure 4.7. The four cells of the matrix are as follows:

Cash cows generate a lot of revenue. They may exhibit low growth, but they have high market share (e.g., Air Jordan sneakers). Cash cows typically use stability strategies (why put a sure thing at risk?). Air Jordan products (such as Men's Air Jordan Retro 3 Basketball Shoes) are selling briskly even after Jordan has been retired for more than 10 years.

Stars are emerging businesses with a rapidly growing market share. Corporations typically plow profits back into the star's products, in the hope that a star will eventually gain enough market share to become a cash cow. Stars often use growth strategies. The Nike+ GPS iPhone application technology used to monitor a runner's distance, pace, and calories burned has been a pleasant star because Nike expects the market for Nike+ to grow rapidly.

In 2011, Nike also took the significant step of opening its largest Asian distribution center in China. This will improve delivery to the important apparel market in China. China is Nike's second largest market after the United States, and growing.[29]

Question marks are new lines of business with a low market share in an expanding market that the corporation believes can be grown into stars. To make question marks into stars, corporations must make significant cash outlays; this requires using profits from their other lines of business. This commitment of resources is, of course, not without risk because question marks can

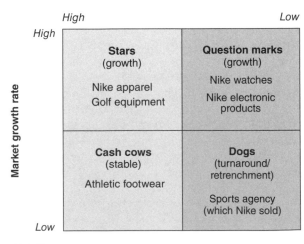

FIGURE 4.7 Nike's BCG matrix.

become dogs. Question marks use growth strategies to get to profitability fast. For example, Nike has been able to enter the collegiate baseball market with only two models of bats. However, the University of Alabama and other large institutions believe that Nike bats have left their team short on home run power. Universities that use Nike bats point to the fact that Nike has only one type of bat—the class A "aluminum alloy" bat. They feel that this type of bat does not wear out as fast as bats made of composite and other materials. A softening of the bat material actually helps bat performance by softening the walls and creating a trampoline effect.[30]

Dogs give low returns in a low-growth market, and to add insult to injury, they have low market share—nothing is going right with a dog. Therefore, corporations often divest or liquidate their dogs at some point when they determine that the dog is a hopeless case; for example, the World Wrestling Federation folded the XFL in 2001. Dogs require turnaround and retrenchment strategies.

The business portfolio analysis helps corporate-level managers figure out how to allocate cash and other resources among the organization's business lines (as well as which corporate strategies to use). Managers use profits from cash cows to fund question marks and sometimes stars. Any cash from dogs is also given to question marks and stars, as well as any resources from their sale.

Entrepreneurial Strategy Matrix

The BCG matrix works well with large companies with multiple lines of business. Sonfield and Lussier developed the entrepreneurial strategy matrix (ESM) for small businesses.[31] Before you read about the matrix, complete Self-Assessment 4.2.

The ESM identifies different combinations of innovation and risk for new ventures and then suggests ways to optimize performance. The matrix answers such questions as "What venture situation am I in?" and "What are the best strategic alternatives for a given venture?"

As we noted in an earlier chapter, innovation is the creation of something new and different. The newer and more different a product or service is, the higher its level of innovation. Risk is the probability of a major financial loss. Entrepreneurs need to determine the chances that their venture will fail and ascertain how serious the financial losses would be. Figure 4.8 shows how the ESM uses a four-cell matrix to assess innovation and risk.

The ESM suggests appropriate strategies for each cell (also shown in figure 4.8). Entrepreneurs use the first part of the matrix to identify which cell their firms are in. Then, based on their cell, they follow the suggested strategies.

Business-Level Strategy

Each line of business must develop its own mission, analyze its own environment, set its own objectives, and develop its own strategy. Corporate- and business-level strategies for organizations with a single business are the same. For organizations with multiple lines of business, linking corporate strategy with the business unit level is key to their success. Here we discuss adaptive strategies, competitive strategies, and the product life cycle.

Adaptive Strategies

◀ LEARNING OUTCOME 9

Discuss the three business-level adaptive strategies.

Miles and Snow developed adaptive strategies typologies back in 1978, and this has become one of the most widely tested, validated, and enduring strategy frameworks.[32] Because it can be confusing to use similar names for corporate- and business-level strategies, business-level strategies are commonly called adaptive strategies. These correspond to the grand strategies, but their emphasis is on adapting to changes in the external environment and entering new markets. Table 4.3 gives a

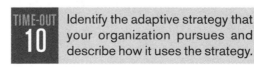
TIME-OUT 10 Identify the adaptive strategy that your organization pursues and describe how it uses the strategy.

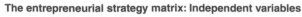

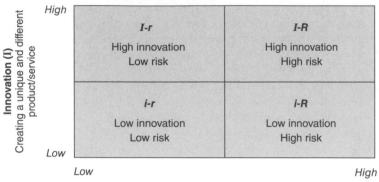

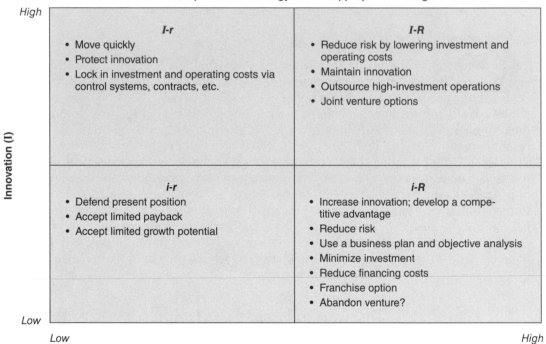

FIGURE 4.8 The entrepreneurial strategy matrix.

Reprinted from *Business Horizon*, Vol. 40, May-June, M.C. Sonfield and R.N. Lussier, "The entrepreneurial strategy matrix model for new and ongoing ventures," pgs. 73–77, Copyright 1997, with permission from Elsevier.

TABLE 4.3   Choosing an Adaptive Strategy

Rate of environmental change	Potential growth rate	Adaptive strategy	Corresponding grand strategy
Fast	High	Prospect	Grow
Moderate	Moderate	Analyze	Combination
Slow	Low	Defend	Stabilize

Do You Have Entrepreneurial Traits?

Objective

To assess your entrepreneurial qualities

Preparation

Would you like to be your own boss? Ever thought about operating your own business? This Self-Assessment will help you decide whether you've got what it takes to be a successful entrepreneur.

Entrepreneurial Qualities

Check the number on the scale that best describes you.

1. I have a strong desire to be independent

   I have a weak desire to be independent.

   | 6 | 5 | 4 | 3 | 2 | 1 |

2. I enjoy taking reasonable risks.

   I avoid risk.

   | 6 | 5 | 4 | 3 | 2 | 1 |

3. I usually don't make the same mistake twice.

   I often make the same mistakes.

   | 6 | 5 | 4 | 3 | 2 | 1 |

4. I need someone to motivate me to work.

   I am a self-starter.

   | 6 | 5 | 4 | 3 | 2 | 1 |

5. I seek out competition.

   I avoid competition.

   | 6 | 5 | 4 | 3 | 2 | 1 |

6. I prefer taking it easy and having lots of personal time.

   I enjoy working long, hard hours.

   | 6 | 5 | 4 | 3 | 2 | 1 |

7. I am confident of my abilities.

   I lack self-confidence.

   | 6 | 5 | 4 | 3 | 2 | 1 |

8. I need to be the best or the most successful.

   I'm satisfied with being average.

   | 6 | 5 | 4 | 3 | 2 | 1 |

9. I have a high energy level.

   I have a low energy level.

   | 6 | 5 | 4 | 3 | 2 | 1 |

10. I stand up for
 my rights.

I let others take
 advantage of me.

| 6 | 5 | 4 | 3 | 2 | 1 |

Scoring

Add your assessment numbers. Your total score will be between 10 and 60. Place your score on the following continuum.

Entrepreneurial Qualities:

Strong					Weak
60	50	40	30	20	10

Generally, the higher your score in this Self-Assessment, the better your chances of becoming a successful entrepreneur. Keep in mind, however, that simple paper-and-pencil assessments aren't always good predictors. If you scored low on this scale but you really want to start a business, you can still succeed. You may not have all the qualities that typically mark entrepreneurs, but you can develop them.

brief overview of the criteria used to select the three **adaptive strategies**—prospecting, defending, and analyzing. Also, be aware that the three strategies are on a continuum with the analyzer in between as shown in the table.[33] Each adaptive strategy reflects a different objective.

Prospect

The prospecting strategy calls for aggressively offering new products or entering new markets. Modell's continues to open new stores to enter new markets to compete with Dick's. The prospector strategy corresponds to the growth grand strategy and is appropriate for fast-changing environments with high growth potential.

Defend

When business segments use a defensive strategy, they stay with their current product line and markets and focus on maintaining or increasing market share. Defending resembles the stabilizing grand strategy and is appropriate in a slow-changing environment with low growth potential. Pepsi Gatorade is defending its position as the leading sport drink against the rival Coca-Cola POWERADE brand.

Analyze

The analyzing strategy is in the middle of the continuum between prospecting and defending. Business segments that analyze move into new markets cautiously and deliberately, or they seek new opportunities to offer a core product group. Analyzers tend to let the prospectors come out with the new products, and if it is a success they will come out with the same product. Analyzing resembles the combination grand strategy and is appropriate in moderately changing environments with moderate growth potential. Analyzers tend to outperform prospectors and defenders.[34] Coca-Cola and Pepsi were both well aware of Gatorade and analyzed its sales for years. With the growth of sport drinks, they both entered this market.

Although the adaptive strategies model has no turnaround and retrenchment, business units use this strategy when they cut back or stop sales of dogs by selling the line of business. If the firm does not replace its dogs with new products, it faces going out of business.

Competitive Strategies

Michael Porter identified three effective business-level competitive strategies: product differentiation, cost leadership, and focus.[35]

Product Differentiation

Companies that differentiate stress the advantages of their products over those of their competitors. Nike, Spalding, Reebok, Adidas, and others use their logos in prominent places on their products to differentiate them—indeed, the logos themselves become a selling feature. Differentiating strategies somewhat resemble prospecting strategies.[36] According to Coca-Cola, the three keys to selling consumer products are "differentiation, differentiation, differentiation," which the company accomplishes with great style through its scripted name logo and contour bottle.

Cost Leadership

Companies that use cost leadership strategies stress lower prices to attract customers. To keep prices down, such companies must have tight cost control and an efficient systems process. Cost leadership is commonly used by defenders.[37] Minor League Baseball (MiLB) offers inexpensive tickets to quality baseball games in order to compete with MLB. Some pro teams offer mini ticket packages to entice fans to buy tickets for a few games at a time. These teams hope to keep ticket prices at a slightly lower rate so that the fans turn into season ticket holders at a later date. Walmart became the world's largest company by using the cost leadership strategy, with its "smiling face" and "Always low pricing, Always" slogan. Walmart sells more sport and recreation goods than any other company in the world.

Although the adaptive strategy analyzer is an in-between strategy that is successful, Porter does not recommend mixing differentiation and cost leadership strategies (select one or the other), because this tends to lead to becoming stuck in the middle with lower performance.[38]

Focus

Companies that use a focus strategy target a specific regional market, product line, or buyer group. Within the target segment, or market niche, the firm may use a differentiation or

---

APPLYING THE CONCEPT 4.2

Adaptive Strategies

Identify the appropriate adaptive strategy for each situation.

    a. prospector
    b. defender
    c. analyzer

_____ 6. Industry leader Gatorade uses a primary strategy in the U.S. sport drink market.

_____ 7. Reebok comes out with a new zipper sneaker to compete with Nike's zipper sneaker.

_____ 8. Sports Authority opens restaurants in the state of Washington.

_____ 9. Wilson pioneers a baseball glove that can be folded up and put in your pocket.

_____ 10. Champion develops a strategy when other companies copy its sweatshirts.

cost leadership strategy. It would be very difficult to compete head on with *Sports Illustrated* or *Street & Smith's,* but lots of smaller magazines that focus on just one sport are making good profits, as are websites. The Women's National Basketball Association (WNBA) supports various women's issues and causes in order to gain loyalty from women. The focus strategy resembles the analyzing strategy.

Product Life Cycle

The product life cycle is the series of stages—introduction, growth, maturity, and decline—that a product goes through over its lifetime. The speed at which products go through their life cycle varies. Many products, like an MLB baseball or an NFL football, stay around for many years; however, the products and styles of the merchandise change. Fad products, like golfing products marketed to improve one's score, may last only a few months. Figure 4.9 gives appropriate portfolio analyses, grand strategies, and adaptive strategies for each life cycle stage for various Nike products.

Pricing strategies are important in order to grow and maintain market share. They also change over the product's life cycle. Prices typically are higher at the product's introduction because there is little, if any, competition. Product cost also declines with increased volume of sales because economies of scale allow lower prices, and prices drop as new competing products are offered to consumers.

Introduction

When a new product (a question mark in the business portfolio) is introduced, a prospector company endeavors to clearly differentiate the product but also uses a focus strategy. That is, the company will focus on getting customers to embrace the product. Resources will be used to promote (advertise) the product and to get production up and running. For example, the XFL embarked on a huge marketing blitz before the opening game of its new league. The XFL used saturation advertising in its TV spots and drummed up the interest of sport magazines, which then created a buzz through their analyses of the new league and its teams.

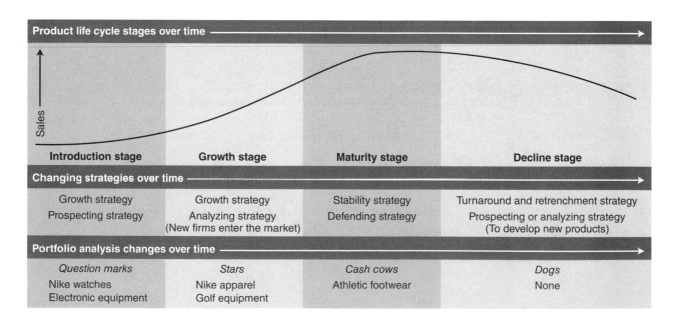

FIGURE 4.9　Nike's strategies for products at different life cycle stages.

Growth

During the growth stage, sales expand rapidly. When analyzer companies see that a prospector company is doing well, they may endeavor to bring out their own version of the product. Analyzer companies may use differentiation, focus, or cost leadership to gain market share during their product's growth stage. They focus on quality and systems process improvements to achieve economies of scale. They may lower prices, even though this reduces profit per unit, to gain market share. Minor League Baseball is growing in popularity, with attendance increasing at a rate of 5% per year—three times that of MLB—and there has been growth in the number of teams, both MLB-affiliated and independent league teams.

Maturity

When a product is mature, sales may grow slowly, level off, and even begin to decline. In a saturated market, the company's strategy changes to one of stability (a defensive strategy). Cost becomes an issue, and cost-cutting efforts are emphasized. The NBA has been a mature product for quite some time. Although the league has a loyal fan base, its TV ratings decreased—that is, until Michael Jordan returned for the 2001 season. Once Jordan retired for good, the NBA viewership decreased again. In his absence, the league has slowly increased viewership. Mature products are usually cash cows.

Decline

As the product nears the end of its life cycle, sales decrease. The company's strategy changes from that of stabilizer-defender to turnaround and retrenchment and possibly back to prospector and analyzer as the company begins to look for a replacement product. For example, if the NHL doesn't

TIME-OUT 11 Identify the life cycle stage for one of your organization's products. Is the strategy you identified in the Time-Out on page 107 appropriate for this stage of the product's life cycle? Explain.

Determine at what stage in the product life cycle FIFA and soccer itself are located.

solve its problems soon (maybe by securing better cable contracts and more marketable stars, with less fighting and more scoring), it may start on a decline from which it cannot recover. The XFL skipped the growth period entirely as it went from infant product to decline (one might say sudden death!). Fans did not take to the XFL combination of football and wrestling, and television viewership plunged. The XFL performed like a fad and moved into its decline in only the second week of the season. A product can be in decline and remain profitable for many years. In the business's portfolio, aging products are considered dogs and may be divested. The company becomes a prospector or analyzer again and begins to develop new (infant) products.

Grand strategies and adaptive strategies complement one another. Companies select their strategies based on their mission, the external environment, and their objectives.

Functional-Level Strategies

◀ **LEARNING OUTCOME 10**

List the four functional-level operational strategies.

Thus far we have examined long-range strategic planning. We now turn our attention to short-term operational strategies. **Operational strategies** are used by every functional-level department—marketing, operations, human resources, finance, among others—to achieve corporate- and business-level objectives. The primary task of functional-level departments is to develop and implement strategies that achieve the corporate- and business-level missions and objectives. These are the operational strategies that functional departments use as they do their work. They include the daily decisions and actions that make or break the team and organization. Research has shown that business failure almost always stems from decision-maker actions, including not taking any action, and not from bad luck or situational limitations.

Product Life Cycle

Select the life cycle stage of each product.

a. introduction

b. growth

c. maturity

d. decline

_____ 11. Baseball gloves

_____ 12. Racquetball rackets

_____ 13. Baseball caps

_____ 14. Skiing helmets

_____ 15. Recumbent exercise bicycles

In this section, we briefly describe the functional departments—marketing, operations, human resources, finance, and others—and how they are used based on the firm's strategy. You may have already taken (or probably will take) one or more entire courses devoted to each functional department.

Marketing Functions

The marketing department's primary responsibility is defining the target market, finding out what the customer wants, and figuring out how to add customer value. This department therefore is responsible for the four Ps—product, promotion, place, and price. The marketing department decides which products to provide, how they will be packaged, how they will be advertised, where they will be sold, how they will get there, and how much they will be sold for.

The sport mass media (such as *Sports Illustrated*, ESPN) has been very influential in promoting sport, and so have TV commercials, athlete endorsements, and venue signage. Brand identity is an important topic in sport that has four categories, or dimensions, of brand assets: brand awareness, brand loyalty, perceived quality, and brand associations. Companies budget large amounts of money to develop brands that stir excitement and cement customer loyalty. NASCAR hired a public relations agency to reconstruct its brand identity; the PR agency did this by using Dale Earnhardt, Jr., to promote the sport. To gain brand identity, many organizations develop trademark images like the Puma animal and slogans like "Wheaties, the Breakfast of Champions."

If the company is a prospector, marketing will plan for and implement new products and find new markets to enter. If the company is defending its products, marketing will focus on keeping these products in the consumer's "eye and heart." If the company is an analyzer, marketing will endeavor to find a balance between prospecting and defending. If the company identifies a product as a dog, marketing will be involved in the turnaround and retrenchment process and will look for smart and graceful ways to drop the product or exit the market.

Operations Functions

The operations (or production) department is responsible for systems processes that convert inputs into outputs. This department focuses on quality and efficiency as it produces the products that marketing determines will provide customer value. We return to the operations function in chapter 13.

If the company is prospecting for products, operations helps to plan and produce the new products. Aggressive growth may require new operations facilities. If the company is defending its products, operations endeavors to improve quality and efficiency and cut costs. If the company is an analyzer, operations ensures that a new product is successfully manufactured. Analyzers take a midrange approach between prospecting and defending. If turnaround and retrenchment are necessary, operations will find ways to reduce systems processes.

Human Resources Functions

Human resources (HR) departments work with all functional departments to recruit, select, train, evaluate, and compensate employees. HR commonly develops policies, procedures and rules for the entire organization.[39] We examine human resources more fully in chapter 7.

If the company is a prospector, human resources plans for, and then expands, the number of employees. In a stabilizer company, human resources works on improving the quality and efficiency of the workforce through training and empowerment programs. If the company is in the analyzer mode, human resources combines expansion and training activities. And, of course, in turnaround and retrenchment situations, human resources plans for and then implements layoffs.

Finance Functions

Finance departments perform at least two major functions. (1) They finance business activities by raising money through the sale of stock (equity) or bonds and loans (debt); they decide on the debt-to-equity ratio; and they pay off debt and pay out dividends (if any). (2) They record transactions, develop budgets, and report financial results (the income statement and balance sheet). A third function that finance departments perform in many organizations is optimizing the company's use of its cash reserves—that is, investing the company's cash as a means of making money. In the nonprofit sector, fund-raising is an important source of revenues. We discuss finance in chapter 13.

TIME-OUT 12 Describe the operational strategy of a functional area in your organization.

If the company is a prospector, finance raises money to cover the functional-area budgets, and dividends will be low, if any are paid. If the company is defending its market share, finance pays off debt and also generally pays a dividend. If the company is an analyzer, finance raises money and pays off debt. If the company finds itself in a turnaround situation, finance may endeavor to raise money and sell assets to pay for the comeback. In a retrenchment, finance sells assets but does not typically pay dividends or pays very low ones.

Other Functional Areas

Depending on the type of business, any number of other functional departments need strategies to achieve their objectives. One area that varies in importance depending on the nature of the company's business is research and development. Businesses that sell products usually allocate greater resources (budgets) for research and development than do service businesses. As another example, a team may have a ticket, food, or merchandise department.

Implementing and Controlling the Strategies

The first four steps in the strategic process involve planning. The fifth and final step involves implementing and controlling the strategies to ensure that the organization's

TIME-OUT 13 Describe some of the controls used in your organization.

APPLYING THE CONCEPT 4.4

Functional Strategies

Identify the function described in each statement.

  a. marketing
  b. operations
  c. finance
  d. human resources
  e. other

_____ 16. Cleans up and repairs the arena

_____ 17. Sends out the bills

_____ 18. Transforms inputs into outputs

_____ 19. Decides where the product will be sold

_____ 20. Manages labor relations

mission and objectives, at all three levels, are achieved. Top and middle managers are more involved with planning strategies, whereas the lower-level functional managers and employees implement the strategies on a day-to-day basis. Successful implementation of strategies requires effective and efficient support systems throughout the organization.

Executives in the United States have been credited with doing a great job of developing strategies but criticized for doing a poor job of implementing the strategies. One estimate is that only 10% of formulated strategies are successfully implemented. Game plans and plays are useless without good execution during the game, and so are business strategies. The implementation of strategic plans is often a stumbling block because organizations have difficulty translating business strategies into cohesive competitive strategies (results). The need for greater integration of corporate-, business-, and functional-level strategies has long been recognized. Another thorny issue is achieving greater cooperation across functional departments. It has been suggested that functional-level strategies should be developed for each stage of a product's life cycle; then these strategies can be used to integrate the functional areas.

Those in the trenches would say that if implementation isn't going well, strategic planners probably didn't do their job. Things that look good on paper are ultimately merely words and are not necessarily doable or practical. Another reason strategic plans fail is that they often end up buried in bottom drawers and no action is taken to implement the strategy. In chapters 5 through 12, you will learn how to implement strategy.

As strategies are implemented, they must also be controlled. Controlling establishes mechanisms to ensure that objectives are achieved in a timely and cost-efficient manner. Controlling also measures the department's progress toward achieving the objective and takes corrective action when needed. Budget issues are an important part of controlling, as is being flexible about the budget when necessary to meet new challenges in the environment. You will develop your controlling skills in chapters 13 and 14.

As we bring this chapter to a close, you should understand the strategic planning process; be able to complete an analysis of the environment; know how to set objectives using a model; understand corporate-, business-, and functional-level strategies; and understand the need to coordinate the three levels for successful implementation and control of the strategies.

@ TAKE IT TO THE NET

Please visit www.HumanKinetics.com/AppliedSportManagementSkills and go to the book's companion web study guide, where you will find the following:

A complete list of websites associated with the concepts in this chapter

Exercises that you will need Internet access to complete

Online versions of chapter exercises and end-of-chapter learning aids

An exercise that helps you define the Key Terms

LEARNING AIDS

CHAPTER SUMMARY

1. Explain how strategic and operational plans differ.

   They differ by time frame and management level involved. In strategic planning, a mission and long-range objectives and plans are developed. Operational plans state short-range objectives and plans. Upper-level managers develop strategic plans, and lower-level managers develop operational plans.

2. Describe the differences between corporate-, business-, and functional-level strategies.

   They primarily differ in focus, which narrows as strategy moves down the organization, and in the management level involved in developing the strategy. Corporate-level strategy focuses on managing multiple lines of business. Business-level strategy focuses on managing one line of business. Functional-level strategy focuses on managing an area of a business line. Upper-level managers develop corporate- and business-level strategy, and lower-level managers develop functional-level strategy.

3. Explain why organizations analyze industries and competitive situations.

   The industry and competitive situation analysis is used to determine the attractiveness of an industry. It is primarily used at the corporate level to decide which lines of business to enter and exit and how to allocate resources among the organization's lines of business.

4. Explain why organizations analyze the company situation.

   The company situation analysis is used at the business level to determine issues and problems that need to be addressed through the strategic process.

5. Discuss how goals and objectives are similar but not the same.

   Goals and objectives are similar because they both state what is to be accomplished. However, goals can be translated into objectives. They also differ in detail. Goals state general targets, whereas objectives state what is to be accomplished in specific and measurable terms with a target date.

6. Describe how to write objectives.

   (1) Start with the word *to;* (2) add an action verb; (3) insert a single, specific, and measurable result to achieve; and (4) set a target date.

7. Describe the four corporate-level grand strategies.

   Firms with a growth strategy aggressively pursue expansion. Firms with a stabilizing strategy maintain the same size or grow slowly. Firms with a turnaround strategy attempt a comeback; those that are retrenching decrease their size to cut costs so that they can survive. Firms with a combination strategy use all four strategies across different lines of business.

8. Describe the three growth strategies.

   Firms that concentrate endeavor to grow existing lines of business aggressively. Firms that integrate grow their lines forward or backward. Firms that diversify grow by adding related or unrelated products.

9. Discuss the three business-level adaptive strategies.

   A prospector company aggressively offers new products or services or aggressively enters new markets. Prospecting is a growth strategy used in fast-changing environments with high growth potential. A defender company stays with its product line and markets. Defending is a stable strategy used in slow-changing environments with low growth potential. An analyzer company moves into new markets cautiously or offers a core product group and seeks new opportunities. Analyzing is a combination strategy used in moderately changing environments with moderate growth potential.

10. List the four functional-level operational strategies.

    Companies develop operational strategies in four major functional areas: marketing, operations, human resources, and finance. Other functional-level strategies are developed as needed, depending on the organization's business and environment.

REVIEW AND DISCUSSION QUESTIONS

1. Explain why strategic planning and operational planning are important.

2. How do plans and strategies differ?

3. Should all sport organizations have corporate-, business-, and functional-level strategies? Why or why not?

4. Should a mission statement for an athletic department be customer focused? Why or why not?

5. Why would a situation analysis be part of the strategic process of redesigning a sport organization?

6. Why is competitive advantage important to sport organizations?

7. Are both goals and objectives necessary for managing a health club? Why or why not?

8. Develop a SWOT for the North American Society for Sport Management (NASSM).

9. As a manager or a coach, would you use MBO? Why or why not?

10. Which growth strategy would you say is the most successful? Defend your answer.

11. What is the difference between a merger and an acquisition?

12. Develop a BCG matrix for Adidas.

13. Why would a sport organization use a focus strategy rather than try to appeal to all customers?

14. Give examples of "other" functional departments.

15. Is it ethical to copy other teams' or companies' ideas through benchmarking?

CASE

Strategic Planning at AEG Worldwide

Companies of all sizes need to develop a corporate strategy. You can imagine how complex such strategies get when the organization is a media and sport conglomerate like AEG. AEG is a subsidiary of the privately managed Anschutz Company. You probably haven't heard of either AEG or the Anschutz Company, so you might be surprised to learn that they own such famous sporting arenas as the Los Angeles Staples Center and Toyota Sports Center; they serve as sport and entertainment booking agent for the Forum; and they own the Los Angeles Lakers (NBA), the Los Angeles Kings (NHL), the now defunct Los Angeles Riptide (Major League Lacrosse), and three Major League Soccer franchises. These are only a few of the 100 businesses owned by the Anschutz Company. All told, AEG owns 33 sport teams and 11 venues all around the world.

AEG's strategic plan focused on a growth strategy of developing a sport and entertainment empire. Its goal was a seamless distribution of sport and entertainment to as many markets across the United States as possible. An obvious focus was a concentrated strategy around Los Angeles. In comparison, AEG diversified to smaller arenas such as the XL Center in Hartford, Connecticut. The Connecticut Development Authority selected a local property owner, Northland Investment Corporation, and AEG to operate the aging civic center. AEG was to supply sport and entertainment content for 6 years starting in 2007.

AEG has also fulfilled the strategic goal of being a global player in the sport and entertainment industry. It developed incredible venues in both London and Berlin. The O2 in London was billed as a leisure and hospitality experience of a kind never before known in the United Kingdom. The centerpiece of the O2 is Europe's finest indoor music and sport venue—used for the 2012 Olympic events held in London. The complex is located near the Thames River and includes retail shops, restaurants, and music clubs.

To find current information about AEG Worldwide, visit www.aegworldwide.com. Be sure to check the Employment link to review current job openings. For more information specifically about O2 World, visit www.theo2.co.uk.

Case Questions

Select the best alternative for the following questions. Be able to explain your answers.

1. AEG does not have a competitive advantage over its competitors.

    a. true

    b. false

2. AEG's move into the sport and entertainment industry shows its turnaround strategy.

    a. true

    b. false

3. The information in this case refers primarily to

    a. strategic planning

    b. operational planning

4. Of the five competitive forces that AEG faces, the strongest is

    a. competitive rivalry

    b. threat of substitute products

    c. potential new entrants

    d. power of suppliers

    e. power of buyers

5. AEG's global grand strategy is

    a. growth

    b. stability

    c. turnaround and retrenchment

    d. combination

6. AEG's corporate growth strategy is
   a. concentration
   b. forward integration
   c. backward integration
   d. related diversification
   e. unrelated diversification

7. AEG's business-level adaptive strategy is
   a. prospecting
   b. defending
   c. analyzing

8. AEG's primary competitive strategy is
   a. differentiation
   b. cost leadership
   c. focus

9. Los Angeles Lakers games have been sold out for many years. Because of this, the Lakers have experienced little attendance growth at their games. At what stage of the product life cycle is this team currently placed?
   a. introduction
   b. growth
   c. maturity
   d. decline

10. Conduct an industry and competitive situation analysis for AEG using the five-forces competitive analysis. Use figure 4.3 on page 97 as an example.

11. Conduct a SWOT analysis for AEG.

12. Write some possible goals and objectives for AEG.

SKILL-BUILDER EXERCISES

Skill-Builder 4.1: Writing Objectives

Objective

To develop your ability to write effective objectives

Preparation

You will analyze and rewrite several ineffective objectives and then write nine new objectives.

Part 1

Analyze the following objectives. First, note the missing components and the criteria that haven't been met. Then rewrite the objective so that it meets all "must" criteria. Make sure that your rewrites contain the four parts noted in the text (infinitive, action verb, result, and target date).

1. To improve our company image by year end 2015

   Criteria missing: _____

   Improved objective: _____

   _____

2. To increase the number of fans by 10%

Criteria missing: _____

Improved objective: _____

_____

3. To increase profits during 2015

Criteria missing: _____

Improved objective: _____

_____

4. To sell 5% more hot dogs and 2% more soda at the baseball game on June 13, 2015

Criteria missing: _____

Improved objective: _____

_____

Part 2

Write three educational, personal, and career objectives that you want to accomplish. Your objectives can be as short-term as something you want to accomplish next week or as long-term as 20 years from now. Be sure your objectives meet the criteria given in the text for effective objectives.

Educational Objectives

1. _____

_____

_____

2. _____

_____

_____

3. _____

_____

_____

Personal Objectives

1. _____

_____

_____

2. _____

_____

_____

3. _____

_____

_____

Career Objectives

1. _____

_____

_____

2. _____
   _____
   _____
   _____

3. _____
   _____
   _____
   _____

In-Class Application

Complete the preceding skill-building preparation before class.

Choose one (10-30 minutes):

Break into groups of three to five members, and critique each other's objectives.

Hold an informal, whole-class discussion about writing objectives.

Wrap-Up

Take a few minutes to write your answers to the following questions:

What did I learn from this experience? How will I use this knowledge?

_____

_____

_____

As a class, discuss student responses.

Skill-Builder 4.2: Developing a Strategic Plan

Objective

To practice strategic planning

Preparation

As an individual or in a group of four to six, select a business that you would like to start someday, or dream up a single-line sport business that you think might have possibilities (because this is a mere exercise, let your imagination run to the out of the ordinary, even the wild) and give it a name (preferably a strange one—it's time to have some fun) and a location. An important part of any business plan is, of course, determining startup costs, but because financial analysis is beyond the scope of this course, we've got some good news for you: Money is not an issue because you just won the lottery and you've got U.S.$50 million burning a hole in your corporate pocket! All you have to do is develop a strategy. This exercise is not all about fun—using a (possibly) preposterous idea simply lets you focus on the process itself.

So let's get started.

What is your company's name? _____

Are you going to provide a product or service? _____

Describe your product or service. _____

Step 1: Develop a Mission

Write a mission for your business.

Step 2: Analyze the Environment

Do a five-forces competitive analysis on your industry's environment (model it after figure 4.3 on p. 97).

Five-Forces Competitive Analysis

1. Rivalry among competitors: _____

     _____

     _____

2. Threat of substitute products and services: _____

     _____

     _____

3. Potential new entrants: _____

     _____

     _____

4. Power of suppliers: _____

     _____

     _____

5. Power of buyers: _____

     _____

     _____

Now, do a company situation analysis.

Company Situation

1. SWOT analysis

Strengths	Opportunities
_____	_____
_____	_____
_____	_____
Weaknesses	Threats
_____	_____
_____	_____
_____	_____

   Competitive advantage (if any).

   Optional: Do a competitive strength assessment.

   Also, consider doing an ESM analysis, using figure 4.8 on p. 108 as a guide.

   _____

   _____

   _____

2. Describe your company's competitive position.

   _____

   _____

   _____

3. Determine issues and problems that you need to address through the strategic process.

   _____

   _____

   _____

Step 3: Set Objectives (List Three)

_____

_____

_____

Step 4: Develop Strategies

You're in a single line of business, so you don't need a grand strategy or a portfolio analysis. Think about your product's life cycle, and develop competitive strategies and adaptive ones for your product's infancy, growth period, maturity, and decline.

Strategy for the Infant Product

_____

_____

Strategy for the Growth Period

_____

_____

Strategy for the Mature Product

_____

_____

_____

Strategy for the Aging Product

_____

_____

Step 5: Implement and Control Strategies

How are you going to make these strategies happen?

_____

_____

In-Class Application

Complete the preceding skill-building preparation.
Choose one:

- As a group, present your strategic plan to the class. Plan and rehearse your presentation beforehand, and use whatever visual aids you think will enhance the presentation (three class periods).
- Conduct an informal, whole-class discussion of the pitfalls and strengths of strategic planning (10-30 minutes).

Wrap-Up

Take a few minutes to write your answers to the following questions:

What did I learn from this experience? How will I use this knowledge?

_____

_____

_____

_____

As a class, discuss student responses.

SPORTS AND SOCIAL MEDIA EXERCISES

1. Use Twitter or Facebook to see how many people follow the Green Bay Packers.

   _____

2. Use www.packers.com/team/staff/mark-murphy/1e6572d2-1c0e-496c-8743-9a15333aed42__ to search for any information on the Green Bay Packers' strategic plan.

   _____
   _____
   _____

GAME PLAN FOR STARTING A SPORT BUSINESS

A prospector company aggressively offers new products or services or aggressively enters new markets. Prospecting is a growth strategy used in fast-changing environments with high growth potential. Develop three potential prospector strategies for the business you have started in the prior chapters.

1. Prospector strategy 1 _____
2. Prospector strategy 2 _____
3. Prospector strategy 3 _____

PART III

Organizing

The organizing function is the second of the classic four functions of management. The process of organizing and delegating work (chapter 5) is essential to any sport organization. The organizing function is often more difficult to master than the other functions because it involves trying to make changes to the organizational structure and culture (chapter 6) that already exist in an organization. The human resources management process described in chapter 7 should be followed to ensure that a sport organization recruits, hires, trains, evaluates, and retains high achievers. The history of labor relations in Major League Baseball is also presented as an example of the blending of sport, legal issues, and collective bargaining.

Organizing
and Delegating Work

LEARNING OUTCOMES

After studying this chapter, you should be able to

1. explain how flat organizations and tall organizations differ;

2. describe liaisons, integrators, and boundary roles;

3. differentiate between formal and informal authority;

4. explain the four levels of authority;

5. describe the relationship between line and staff authority;

6. describe organization charts;

7. explain how internal departmentalization and external departmentalization differ;

8. state the similarities and differences between matrix and divisional departmentalization;

9. explain how job simplification and job expansion differ;

10. describe the job characteristics model and what it is used for;

11. set priorities; and

12. delegate.

KEY TERMS

span of management	line authority	departmentalization
responsibility	staff authority	job design
authority	centralized authority	job enrichment
delegation	decentralized authority	job characteristics model
levels of authority	organization chart	delegation model

DEVELOPING YOUR SKILLS

It is important to understand how sport firms are organized—the basic principles of organization, authority, organization charts, and types of departmentalization used to achieve the sport firm's mission and objectives. On a more personal level, in this chapter you will learn to organize yourself and set priorities by answering three questions, which can be part of a to-do list. By following the steps in the delegation model, you can improve on this skill as well.

REVIEWING THEIR GAME PLAN

Michael Fioretti is a master of the four functions of management: A day doesn't go by that Fioretti doesn't plan, organize, lead, and control. Fioretti has been co-owner of Sports World in Windsor, Connecticut, for the past 10 years.

Fioretti learned many years ago that to keep the programs alive and well he would need a strategic plan. His state-of-the-art sports dome was renovated after the roof collapsed during a winter snowfall. Fioretti and his partners had a vision, and they laid careful plans for bringing their vision to fruition. First they built the dome in a location that was in the scenic countryside of Connecticut. It was also located between two major cities: Hartford, Connecticut, and Springfield, Massachusetts. The dome was originally built as a soccer facility to help local teams practice during the winter. Fioretti has succeeded so well in developing a broad and loyal customer base that the dome is now used by area lacrosse and baseball, as well as many other sports, as a year-round training facility. The University of Connecticut uses the dome since it is close to the facility.

As co-owner, Fioretti organizes something every day. The staff need organizing to ensure that the dome, the membership desk, and the sport leagues are well serviced. He even has a new preschool with a teacher to recruit staff and children.

Fioretti's leadership skills were forged through many years of great customer service. Every team knows Michael because he is always around greeting, encouraging, mentoring, and coaching. His three daughters and two sons can also be seen working at the dome, helping to organize sport leagues. Local college students are hired as interns to gain experience managing and organizing a sport facility.

Control issues are just as important to Fioretti as they are to managers in other organizations. So he carefully oversees the budgets that need to be prepared for the different operational areas of the dome. He and his staff determine rental rates for the different indoor fields at various times of the day. Fioretti knows that knowledgeable, courteous, and enthusiastic staff are key to the center's success, so he pays special attention to developing his staff and hiring new employees. He finds that being the director of an indoor training facility is a busy and fulfilling career.[1]

For more information about Sports World, visit www.sportsworld.cc.

The Organizing Function

Organizing is the second function of management, and we defined it earlier (see chapter 1) as the process of delegating and coordinating tasks and resources to achieve objectives. Managers organize four resources—human, physical, financial, and informational. On a companywide basis, organizing is about grouping activities and resources. Effective managers know that organizing their team's resources and putting the right person in each position is instrumental in achieving objectives.

The organization's mission and strategy influence its structure, because the organization must be structured to meet the mission and strategy.[2] The organizational structure must be best suited to achieving objectives.[3] But how does management know the best organizational structure? Managers answer at least six key questions. The questions are listed in

TABLE 5.1   Organizing Questions

Questions for managers	Chapter topic (page number)
Whom should departments and individuals report to?	Chain of command (131); span of management and control (132)
How many individuals should report to each manager?	Span of management and control (132)
How should we subdivide the work?	Division of labor (133); departmentalization (139)
How do we get everyone to work together as a system?	Coordination (133)
At what level should decisions be made?	Centralized and decentralized authority (137)
How do we organize to meet our mission and strategy?	Departmentalization (139)

table 5.1, and the answers are discussed in more detail throughout the chapter under the topics indicated. In this section, we discuss eight organizational principles, listed under "Principles of Organization," that are commonly followed in organizations and help to answer two of the organizing questions.

Principles of Organization

Unity of command and direction

Chain of command

Span of management and control (flat and tall organizations)

Division of labor (specialization)

Coordination

Clarification of responsibilities and scope of authority

Delegation

Flexibility

Unity of Command and Direction

Unity of command means that each employee reports to only one boss. Having more than one boss can be confusing and frustrating when they want something different done now. Unity of direction means that all activities are directed toward the same objectives—winning the game. When a team doesn't pull together, it often loses the game.

Chain of Command

Chain of command, also known as the scalar principle, is the clear line of authority from the organization's top to its bottom. Everyone in a company needs to understand the chain of command—that is, whom they report to and who, if anyone, reports to them. The chain of command also identifies the formal path for communications. It forms the hierarchy described in organization

 TIME-OUT 1 Follow the chain of command from your present position (or a past one) to the top of your organization. Identify anyone who reported to you and to whom you reported; list that person's title, that person's boss's title, and so on, all the way to the top manager.

 Draw boxes to show the chain of command at Sports World as described in this paragraph.

charts, which we examine later in this chapter. Michael Fioretti is part of the chain of command that includes his investment partners and people below him (operational staff and teachers).

Team captains are the part of the chain of command that links coaches and players. Team captains in the NHL often have as much influence over their teammates as do the coaches.[4] Choosing the captain of a team, therefore, is not a decision to be taken lightly.

Span of Management and Control

The **span of management** (also called the span of control) has to do with how many employees report directly to a manager. The fewer employees supervised, the smaller or narrower is the manager's span of control. There is no optimal number of employees to manage. This span should be limited to a number that can be effectively supervised and depends on the nature of the work and the size of the business.[5] Typically, however, lower-level managers have a wider span of control than do higher-level managers. (Of course, *directly* is an operative word here—second-level managers are responsible for first levels in their department but also for all the staff under those first-level managers, even though they do not supervise them directly.)

Examining how an organization sets up its spans of management tells you a great deal about whether it is a flat or a tall organization. Flat organizations have very few levels of management, and these levels have wide spans of control. Tall organizations have many levels of management with narrow spans of control. Figure 5.1 illustrates these two different approaches. Notice that the flat organization has only two levels of management and the tall one has four. In recent years, organizations have been flattening their hierarchies by cutting as many levels of management as they can to speed up decisions and processes while cutting costs.

TIME-OUT 2 Think about a current boss or coach and describe his or her span of control. Describe your own span of control if you are a manager or coach. How many levels of management exist in your organization, and would you characterize it as flat or tall?

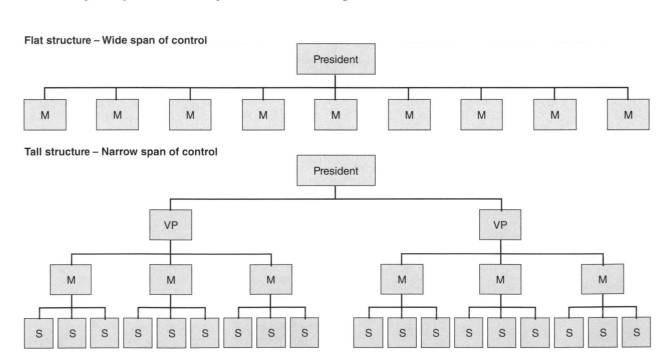

Flat structure – Wide span of control

Tall structure – Narrow span of control

FIGURE 5.1 The span of control in flat and tall organizations. Key: vice president (VP); manager (M); supervisor (S).

Norman Blake, from insurance giant USF&G, was hired to reorganize the U.S. Olympic Committee (USOC). Blake believed that the USOC was too hierarchical and too bureaucratic and that this facilitated its dispersal of money to Olympic sports without enough accountability. His solution was to flatten the USOC, move away from its management-by-committee style, and start paying for performance.[6] Interestingly, Blake lasted only 9 months in the position of CEO of the USOC. His reason for leaving so quickly was a lack of support for his strategic plan from the governing bodies of the different sports. In retrospect, Blake believed he might have fired staff too quickly and was too fast to implement his pay-for-performance (winning medals) strategy.[7]

By 2010, the USOC was still unorganized with regard to issues such as launching its own Olympic network. Chicago's bid to host the 2016 Games ended in an embarrassing fashion, and NBC Sports & Olympics Chairman Dick Ebersol and national governing body leaders wanted to change the USOC's leadership.

Patrick Sandusky, who ran the communications for the failed attempt by Chicago to host the 2016 Olympics, was hired by the USOC to help reorganize the USOC. Sandusky worked closely with new USOC Chairman Larry Probst and CEO Scott Blackmun. He advised both leaders to become more engaged with the media; he also encouraged them to create a more transparent organization and to build stronger relationships with the IOC and other national organizing committees. Sandusky also reorganized the communications department to focus on sponsor programs, community affairs, athlete services, and Olympic media operations.[8]

Division of Labor

◀ **LEARNING OUTCOME 2**
Describe liaisons, integrators, and boundary roles.

Division of labor occurs when jobs are organized by specialty—for example, accountants work in the accounting department, sales reps work in the marketing department, and football players are on the offensive or defensive squad. The MLB American League has specialized batting and pitching with its designated hitter. Managers usually perform less specialized functions as they move up the management ladder. Paul Lawrence and Jay Lorsch coined the terms *differentiation* and *integration*.[9] Differentiation is about organizing work groups into departments, and integration is about coordinating departmental activities.

Coordination

Coordination is about departments and individuals in an organization working together to accomplish strategic and operational objectives for its environment. Coordination is the process of integrating tasks and resources to meet objectives. Coordinating across jobs and departments requires systems-based analysis and conceptual skills. Michael Fioretti needs to coordinate use of the physical site (i.e., the indoor fields, concessions, parking lot, and preschool area) as well as the staff and cleaning schedules. This coordination must be undertaken with the goal of meeting the needs of the teams and players.

 What sorts of coordinating activities do you think would be involved in starting new group exercise classes at the dome?

Every aspect of the organizing function involves coordination, and coordination also requires cooperation. Examples of coordinating activities include the following:

- Direct contact among people from the same department or from different departments
- Liaisons who work in one department and coordinate information and activities with other departments
- Committees formed to organize just about everything—for example, constructing a new fitness facility
- Integrators, such as product or project managers, who don't work for a specific department but coordinate multiple-department activities
- Boundary roles in which staff (from sales, customer service, purchasing, and public relations, for example) work with people in the external environment

Sporting events typically require a great deal of coordination, and since September 11, 2001, security of sport has become more of a concern.[10] But not many event planners come up against the daunting challenges that the Salt Lake City 2002 Olympic Games faced after September 11. On a visit to Salt Lake City before the Games, homeland security director Tom Ridge said that during the Olympics, the city would be "one of the safest places on the globe." Roughly 15,000 people—including 10,000 national guards, state and local police, and federal officers—handled security operations during the Games. Ridge said, "This is the best planned, best coordinated, and best organized plan the world has ever seen."[11] Not a single security issue occurred during the entire 2-week experience.

The Vancouver Organizing Committee for the 2010 Olympics and Paralympics Winter Games did a great job planning the largest event in Vancouver history. In the months preceding the Games, much thought was put into school closures, transportation, and even ways to greet visitors. Everything went smoothly, and Vancouver had an atmosphere of one big party.[12]

Clarification of Responsibilities and Scope of Authority

Effective organizations know that to function well, management must ensure that each person's responsibilities in the organization are clearly defined, that employees are given the authority they need to meet these responsibilities (i.e., that their scope of authority should match their responsibilities), and that employees are held accountable for meeting their responsibilities. **Responsibility** is one's obligation to achieve objectives by performing required activities. Managers are responsible for the results of their organizations, divisions, or departments, and you have to trust others with responsibility.[13]

Authority is the right to make decisions, issue orders, and use resources. As a manager you will be given responsibility for achieving departmental objectives. You must also be given a certain level of authority if you are to get the job done. Authority is delegated. CEOs are responsible for the results of their entire organization, and they delegate authority down the chain of command to lower-level managers who are responsible for meeting operational objectives. Accountability is the evaluation of how well individuals meet their responsibilities.

Managers are accountable for everything that happens in their departments. As a manager, you will routinely delegate responsibility and authority for performing tasks, but your accountability stays with you.

Delegation

Delegation has to do with assigning responsibility and authority for accomplishing objectives. Responsibility and authority are delegated down the chain of command. To improve accountability, the IOC delegated the control function of decision making to a board and the management function to internal agents.[14] Delegation is an important skill for managers,[15] and we examine it on pages 149-152 in some detail.

Flexibility

Flexibility has to do with understanding that there are often exceptions to the rule. Going by the book is not always the way to get the best results.[16] Many managers focus on company rules rather than on creating customer satisfaction.[17] Let's say your sporting goods store has a rule that customers can receive a cash refund for returned merchandise only if they have the sales receipt. This is a good rule—it certainly protects your store from people who steal merchandise and return it for cash. But say that a well-known customer comes into the store and requests that you give him a cash refund for a baseball bat even though he doesn't have a sales slip. Should you follow the rules and lose a good customer or make an exception and make this good customer happy?

 TIME-OUT 3 Is your organization flexible? Explain why or why not.

APPLYING THE CONCEPT 5.1

The Organizing Function

Note which aspect of the organizing function is operative in each situation.

a. unity of command and direction

b. chain of command

c. span of management

d. division of labor

e. coordination

f. clarification of responsibility and authority

g. delegation

h. flexibility

_____ 1. Karl told me to pick up the team mail. When I got to the post office, I didn't have a key, so the postal worker wouldn't give me the mail.

_____ 2. The players on the football team are on either the offensive squad or the defensive squad.

_____ 3. My job can be frustrating. Sometimes my department manager tells me to do one thing, but my project manager tells me to do something else at the same time.

_____ 4. Middle manager: I want Sam, who works for Sally, to deliver this package, but I can't ask him to do it directly. I have to ask Sally to ask him.

_____ 5. There has been an accident in the game, and the ambulance is on the way. Jim, call Dr. Rodriguez and have her get to emergency room C in 10 minutes. Pat, get the paperwork ready. Karen, prepare room C.

Authority

Authority comes in many different forms and in many different styles. Understanding formal and informal authority, scope of authority, levels of authority, line and staff authority, and centralized and decentralized authority—the topics of this section—will help you become a more effective manager.

Formal and Informal Authority

◀ LEARNING OUTCOME 3

Differentiate between formal and informal authority.

Formal authority specifies relationships among employees. It is the sanctioned way of getting the job done. When your boss tells you what to do, that's formal authority. The organization chart outlines the lines of formal authority in the company. But most organization charts don't come close to describing organizational life, and it's not easy to understand how things really work through the informal organization.[18]

Informal authority comes from a constellation of collaborations, relationships, and networks.[19] If you note that someone is competent, is dependable, and continually comes up with strategies that get the job done, you (and others) are very likely to turn to that person for leadership—this is informal authority. It can be as powerful as formal authority—indeed, many times it is more powerful. Although it is not sanctioned (formally specified), it is very real. Informal authority can be used to overcome the burdens and limitations that formal authority imposes on employees. Informal authority often gets the job done and gets it done quicker.

Scope of Authority

People's formal scope of authority narrows the lower their job is in the organization chart. A CEO has more authority than a vice president, who has more authority than a manager, and so on. The Ohio State athletic director has more authority than the coaches, who have more authority than their assistant coaches and graduate assistants. Responsibility and authority flow down the organization, whereas accountability flows up the organization, as figure 5.2 illustrates.

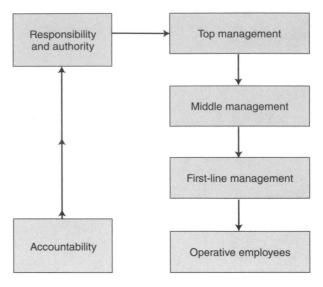

FIGURE 5.2   Scope of authority.

Levels of Authority

LEARNING OUTCOME 4 ▶

Explain the four levels of authority.

Every manager needs to know the scope of his formal authority. For example, what authority would the athletic director (AD) at Springfield High School (SHS) have to alter a medical record that she believes is in error? The **levels of authority** are informing authority, recommending authority, reporting authority, and full authority. Levels of authority vary from task to task. Let's examine the SHS AD's authority to hire a new basketball coach, illustrated under each level.

- **Informing authority.** At this level, team members can inform their leader of possible alternatives. The group leader then analyzes the alternatives and makes the decision. People in secretarial and clerical positions often have only informing authority because the job calls for gathering data for others. At the informing level of authority, the SHS AD would simply give the applications for the coaching job to the principal. Michael Fioretti has an administrative assistant who gathers and organizes data (writes schedules, updates brochures, and provides customer service to members).

- **Recommending authority.** At this level, team members generate alternative actions, analyze them, and recommend action. However, the members may not implement the recommendation without the OK of the group leader, who may require a different alternative if he doesn't agree with the recommendation. Committees are often given recommending authority. At the recommending level of authority, the SHS AD would give the top applications for the coaching job to the principal with a recommendation as to which candidate to hire.

- **Reporting authority.** At this level, each person in the group has the authority to select a course of action and carry it out. However, these group members routinely report their courses of action to their leader. At the reporting level of authority, the SHS AD would hire the coach and simply report doing so, maybe by introducing the coach to the principal.

- **Full authority.** At this level of authority, your boss may be coming to you for advice—you now have deep expertise in some area, and she trusts your judgment implicitly. You devise plans and carry them out with only a nod from your boss. At the full level of authority, the SHS AD would

TIME-OUT 4   Think about a task you do routinely for your company or team and describe your level of authority for this task in detail.

❓ Does Michael Fioretti have full authority over the entire dome?

simply hire the coach without telling the principal. Michael Fioretti has full authority to make decisions in the dome. However, full authority does not give full leeway—the implication is that you will act with sound judgment and within the confines laid out by your group members as to the direction they have decided to go.

Line and Staff Authority

Line authority is the responsibility to make decisions and issue orders down the chain of command. Operations and marketing are usually line departments, but some organizations also organize financial activities as line departments. Line managers are primarily responsible for achieving the organization's objectives, and their staff or team follows the directives that the line manager develops to achieve those objectives. SHS coaches are line managers because they are responsible for leading their team to victory.

◀ **LEARNING OUTCOME 5**
Describe the relationship between line and staff authority.

Staff authority is the responsibility to advise and assist other personnel. Human resources (HR), public relations, and management information systems are almost always staff departments. The line departments are internal customers of the staff departments. Therefore, the two types of departments have a collaborative partnership. When the SHS AD hires a new coach, the AD gets help from the HR department, which places the coaching job in newspapers and online and collects the applications. But HR doesn't select the new coach; the AD line manager does.

 TIME-OUT 5 Identify several line and staff positions in your company or team. State whether they are general or specialist staff positions.

The staff's primary role is to advise and assist, but situations occur in which they can give orders to line personnel. Functional authority is the right of staff personnel to issue orders to line personnel in established areas of responsibility. The SHS school financial manager can't tell the AD which coach to hire but has authority to require the AD to stay within the budget and fill out the proper paperwork when hiring the new coach. The AD can tell the coaches how to coach, but the financial manager can't.

Staff managers may have dual staff and line authority. For example, public relations (staff) managers advise and assist all departments in their organization. However, they also have line authority within their own department and issue orders (a line function) to their group. The SHS financial manager can tell the bookkeepers what to do.

There are also two types of staff. General staff work for only one manager. Often called "assistant to," they help the manager in any way needed. The SHS principal has an assistant principal who primarily takes care of discipline, but the AD has no assistant (though many colleges do have assistant ADs). Specialist staff help anyone in the organization who needs it. Human resources, finance, accounting, public relations, and maintenance offer specialized advice and assistance. The financial manager is a specialist who oversees the entire school system's budget, helping all those with budgets and giving monthly reports of spending and budget balance.

Centralized and Decentralized Authority

 TIME-OUT 6 What type of authority is most prevalent in your firm or team? Are there reasons that make this choice appropriate in this environment? Or is it not as effective as it could be? Explain.

The major difference between centralized and decentralized authority is who makes the important decisions. With **centralized authority,** important decisions are made by top managers. With **decentralized authority,** important decisions are made by middle- and first-level managers. The major advantages of centralization include control (uniform procedures are easier to control, and fewer risks are taken) and reduced duplication of work (fewer employees perform the same tasks). The major advantages of decentralization are efficiency and flexibility (decisions are made quickly by people who have first-hand knowledge of the situation) and development (managers are challenged and motivated to solve their own problems). Which type of authority works best? There is no simple answer. Authority is a continuum, and most organizations function as a blend of centralized and decentralized authority. Flat organizations tend to have decentralized authority.

With the exception of very small companies, which tend to be centralized, most organizations lie somewhere between the two extremes. The key to success seems to be finding the right balance between the two, the one that serves the business's environment contingencies and its business model best. For example, production and sales are often decentralized, whereas finance and labor relations are centralized to provide uniformity and control. The trend for top managers is toward decentralizing authority.[20]

Organizational Design

It's time we address how entire firms are organized. Organizational design is the arrangement of positions into work units or departments and the relationships among them. Here we discuss organization charts and departmentalization.

LEARNING OUTCOME 6 ▶

Describe organization charts.

Organization Chart

The formal authority structures that define working relationships between the organization's members and their jobs are illustrated in organization charts. An **organization chart** lays out the organization's management hierarchy and departments and their working relationships. As shown in figure 5.3, the boxes represent positions in the organization, and the lines indicate the reporting relationships and lines of communication. Note that organization charts do not show the day-to-day activities performed or the structure of the informal organization.[21] Figure 5.3, a hypothetical organization chart for a university, illustrates the following four major aspects of organizations.

- **The level of management hierarchy.** The board of regents and president are the top two levels of management; the vice presidents are middle-level management; and department managers, such as athletic facilities managers, are first-level management.

- **Chain of command.** As you follow the lines, you will see that the president reports to the board of regents. The vice presidents report to the president, and the department

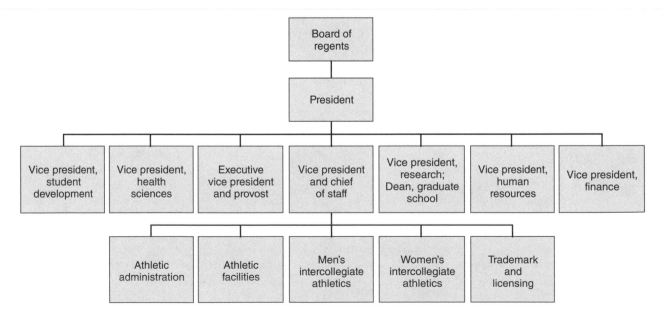

FIGURE 5.3   Organization chart for a university, highlighting athletic administration.

managers report to the vice presidents. A study focusing on New Zealand Football (soccer) found that the more the board of regents was involved in strategy, the more likely the board would be able to perform its strategic function. The study also found that it was important for the board and the CEO to share leadership.[22]

• **The division and type of work.** The chart divides the university by "product" by indicating different academic areas such as health sciences and graduate programs. Additionally, the university has divisions devoted to the administration such as university relations and university services. The university is also organized by functional area (finance and HR).

• **Departmentalization.** Organization charts show how the business of the firm is divided into permanent work units. The university's athletic departments are under the control of two people, the vice president for administration (not shown) and the chief of staff. The departments are athletic administration, athletic facilities, men's intercollegiate athletics, women's intercollegiate athletics, and trademark and licensing.

To develop a mind-set of better focus on the customer, some organizations use an upside-down chart with the customer at the top of the chart and management at the bottom. This reminds all the people in the organization that their job is to provide customer value, and it informs managers that their role is to support their teams in providing that value, not the other way around.

Departmentalization

Departmentalization is the grouping of related activities into work units. Departments may have an internal focus or an external one. Departmentalization around internal operations or functions and the resources needed to accomplish the unit's work is called functional departmentalization. External or output departmentalization is based on activities that

APPLYING THE CONCEPT 5.2

Authority

Identify the type of authority implied in each situation.

- a. formal
- b. informal
- c. level
- d. line
- e. staff
- f. centralized
- g. decentralized

_____ 6. I like my job, but it's frustrating when I recommend potential employees to the production and marketing managers and they don't hire them.

_____ 7. It's great working for a team that encourages everyone to share information.

_____ 8. Coaches here run their teams the way they want to.

_____ 9. I'm not sure if I'm supposed to get a list of company cars for Wendy or recommend one to her.

_____ 10. That is a great idea, Jean. I'll talk to Pete, and if he likes it, I'm sure he'll want us to present your idea to his boss.

focus on factors outside the organization; this is also called product or service, customer, and geographic or territory departmentalization.

Functional Departmentalization

Functional departmentalization organizes departments around essential input activities, such as production, sales, and finance. Virtually all sport companies use some form of functional departmentalization and have specialized functions such as finance departments and sales and marketing departments. An example is Spalding Sporting Goods, headquartered in Chicopee, Massachusetts. The first chart in figure 5.4 shows functional departmentalization.

Product or Service Departmentalization

This approach organizes departments around goods produced or services provided. Companies with multiple products commonly use product departmentalization. Retail stores like Sports Authority have product departments. The second chart in figure 5.4 exemplifies product departmentalization.

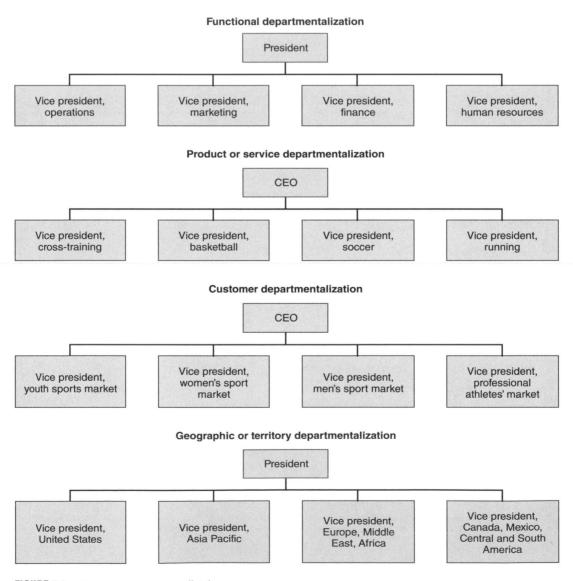

FIGURE 5.4 Types of departmentalization.

Customer Departmentalization

Customer departmentalization organizes departments around the needs of different types of customers. The product or service may be the same or slightly different, but the needs of the customer warrant different marketing approaches (in the type of packaging, sales staff, and so on). If Nike used customer departmentalization, it would divide its divisions into professional and amateur athletes—for example, its golf division would be organized to sell golf equipment to professional golfers and amateur golfers. Organizations that offer a wide variety of products often use customer departments, as do some nonprofit organizations. The third chart in figure 5.4 shows customer departmentalization.

Geographic or Territory Departmentalization

This type of departmentalization organizes departments by each area in which the enterprise does business. For example, Nike divides its financial reporting into four geographic regions. The EMEA division consists of Europe, the Middle East, and Africa. The Americas division includes Canada, Mexico, and Central and South America. The other two divisions are Asia Pacific and the United States.[23] Each region reports numbers for sales and expenses. The final chart in figure 5.4 organizes by geographic area.

Multiple Departmentalization

Many organizations, particularly large, complex ones, use several departmental structures to create a hybrid organization. Any mixture of structures can be used. Some organizations use functional departments with manufacturing facilities but organize sales by territory with separate sales managers and salespeople in different areas.

Matrix Departmentalization

Matrix departmentalization combines functional and product departmentalization. That is, staff are assigned to a functional department but work on one or more products or projects. The advantage of the matrix approach is its flexibility—the enterprise can temporarily and quickly reorganize for high-priority projects. The disadvantage is that every person has two managers—a functional boss and a project boss—which can make coordination difficult and can cause conflicts to arise because of the different objectives of multiple managers. Figure 5.5 shows a matrix structure.

◀ **LEARNING OUTCOME 8**

State the similarities and differences between matrix and divisional departmentalization.

Divisional Departmentalization

Divisional departmentalization is used for large companies that have semiautonomous strategic business units—companies within a company. For example, Adidas owns Reebok. You couldn't buy stock in Gatorade because it is a division of Pepsi, as are Frito-Lay snacks and Tropicana juices. The companies are sometimes called subsidiaries, and many companies have subsidiaries in other countries.

Athletic Director and Divisions and Conferences

TIME-OUT 7 Draw a simple organization chart for your company or team. Identify the type of departmentalization and staff positions used.

An important decision facing high school and college ADs (and pros as well) is which division and conference to compete in.[24] Let's focus on colleges that tend to be able to select the division level and then the conference. The conferences themselves, such as the Big Ten, ACC, Pac-12, Big East, SEC, and Big 12, do face an organizational issue when teams ask to enter the conference, or when some leave for another conference. Another option is to be independent and try to play any team you want to; Notre Dame is an example.

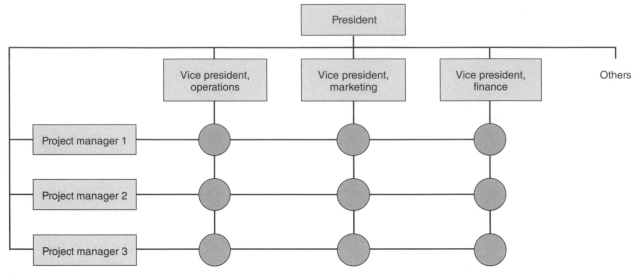

FIGURE 5.5 Matrix departmentalization.

Job Design

The work performed by organizations is grouped into functional departments, which are further grouped into jobs. **Job design** is the process of combining the tasks that each employee is responsible for completing. Job design is crucial because it affects job satisfaction and productivity. Empowering employees by involving them in the design of their own jobs increases productivity.

As you will learn in this section, jobs can be simple (and contain few tasks) or they can be expanded (and contain many tasks). A job characteristics model is used to design jobs.

LEARNING OUTCOME 9 ▶

Explain how job simplification and job expansion differ.

Job Simplification

Job simplification makes jobs more specialized and efficient. It is based on the organizing principle of division of labor. The idea behind job simplification is to work smarter, not harder. Job simplification is the process of eliminating, combining, or changing the work sequence to increase performance. Thus, job designers would break a job into steps to see if they can accomplish the following:

- Eliminate: Does the task have to be done at all? If not, don't do it.
- Combine: Combining tasks often saves time. Make one trip to the mail room at the end of the day instead of several throughout the day, if this makes sense.
- Change sequence: Changing the order of tasks can save time.

A major caveat is in order here. Jobs that are too simple bore people, and bored workers are neither productive nor empowered. However, used appropriately, job simplification can motivate people. Often, people don't hate the job, just some aspect of it. Rather than ignoring or simply putting up with aspects of their job that they don't like, sometimes employees can change their jobs.

Job Expansion

Job expansion makes jobs less specialized in order to empower workers and to make them more productive. Jobs can be expanded through job rotation, job enlargement, and job enrichment.

Departmentalization

Identify the organizing approach used in the following five charts.

a. function   c. customer   e. matrix

b. products and services   d. territory   f. division

_____ 11. All-Sports Consulting Company

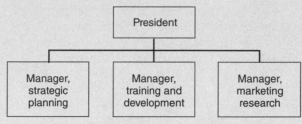

_____ 12. Fitness Publishing Company

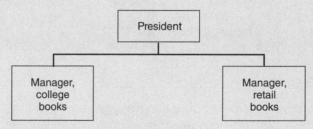

_____ 13. Worldwide Sporting Goods–USA

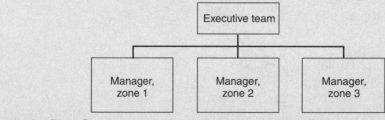

_____ 14. Best Company International

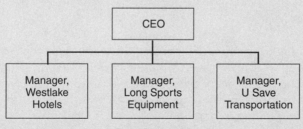

_____ 15. Production department of Golf Clubs Company

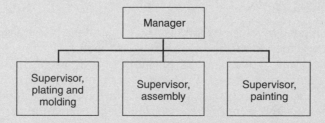

Job Rotation

In this approach, people perform different jobs for a set period of time. For example, employees making a sneaker on a New Balance assembly line could rotate so that they get to work on different parts. Many organizations develop conceptual skills in management trainees by rotating them through various departments.

TIME-OUT 8

Describe how you would simplify a job at your firm or company. Specify whether you are eliminating, combining, or changing the sequence of tasks.

Cross-training is related to job rotation. With cross-training, staff members learn to perform different jobs so they can fill in when someone is on vacation or sick. This also increases skills, which makes people more valuable to the organization.

Job Enlargement

This approach to job design adds more tasks in order to provide variety. For example, the New Balance sneaker workers could perform four tasks instead of just two. However, only adding more simple tasks to an already simple job is not a great motivator.

TIME-OUT 9

Describe how you would expand a job at your company or team. Specify whether you are using job rotation, job enlargement, or job enrichment.

Job Enrichment

Job enrichment builds motivators into a job to make it more interesting and challenging. Job enrichment, a hot topic in flat organizations, works when employees want their jobs enriched; but managers should consider that some employees are happy with their jobs the way they are. A simple way to enrich jobs is for the manager to delegate more variety and responsibility to employees.

Work Teams

The traditional approach to job design has been to focus on individual jobs. Today, the trend is shifting to designing jobs for work teams; or, rather, teams are redesigning members' jobs. Teamwork is as vital for successful companies as it is for successful NFL teams. Moving to work teams is a form of job enrichment. The two common types are integrated teams and self-managed teams.

Integrated Work Teams

These teams are assigned a number of tasks, and the team itself then assigns specific tasks to members and is responsible for rotating jobs. For example, Springfield College's AD has work teams coordinate facility management tasks. The teams decide who does what and how. The AD attends various meetings to see how the work is progressing and checks on quality of the finished process.

Self-Managed Work Teams

These teams are assigned an objective, and the team plans, organizes, leads, and controls the work in order to achieve that objective. Usually, self-managed teams operate without a designated manager; everyone on the team functions as both manager and worker. Teams commonly select their own members and evaluate each other's performance. The Springfield College facility management group mentioned previously can become a self-managed team by deciding what activities need to be coordinated and determining the most efficient sequence of activities. The team, not the AD, is responsible for checking its progress.

Work teams have been quite successful. Team-based systems are emerging as a key source of sustained competitive advantage. However, members need to be carefully trained to work together effectively as a team. In chapter 9 we examine in greater detail ways to help teams succeed.

TIME-OUT 10 Describe how your firm uses—or could use—work teams. Indicate whether the teams are integrated or self-managed.

Job Characteristics Model

◄ **LEARNING OUTCOME 10**

Describe the job characteristics model and what it is used for.

Developed by Richard Hackman and Greg Oldham, the job characteristics model provides a conceptual framework for designing enriched jobs.[25] Although it was developed in the late 1970s, the job characteristics model is commonly used and is still being researched. Individuals or a team can use the model to enrich jobs. The **job characteristics model** addresses core job dimensions, critical psychological states, and employees' growth need (their need to grow on the job) to improve the quality of working life for employees and productivity for the organization.

Core Job Dimensions

Five core dimensions determine a job's personal outcomes (quality of working life for employees) and work outcomes (productivity for the organization). By enhancing each dimension, you can increase both outcomes.

1. Skill variety is the number of diverse tasks required in the job and the number of skills used to perform the job.

APPLYING THE CONCEPT **5.4**

Job Design

Identify the job design implied in each situation.

a. job simplification

b. job rotation

c. job enlargement

d. job enrichment

e. work teams

f. job characteristics model

_____ 16. Jack, I think you need a challenge, so I want you to develop some new offensive plays.

_____ 17. Sales reps who have business lunches with clients that cost less than U.S.$20 no longer need to provide sales receipts.

_____ 18. We'd like to change your fitness center job so you can develop new skills, complete entire jobs by yourself so that the job is more meaningful, do the job the way you want to, and know how you are doing.

_____ 19. To make your athletic assistant job less repetitive, we're adding three new responsibilities to your job description.

_____ 20. I'd like you to learn how to run the stopwatch so that you can fill in for Ted while he's at lunch.

2. Task identity is the degree to which employees perform a whole identifiable task. Does the worker put together an entire golf club or just insert the grip on the end of the shaft?

3. Task significance is the perception of the task's importance to others—to the organization, the department, coworkers, or customers.

4. Autonomy is the degree to which employees have discretion to decide how to plan, organize, and control the task.

5. Feedback is the extent to which employees find out how well they perform their tasks.

Critical Psychological States

As the three critical psychological states—developed through the five core job dimensions—improve, so do the job's personal and work outcomes.

- Experienced meaningfulness of the work derives from (1) skill variety, (2) task identity, and (3) task significance. The greater these core dimensions, the greater the experienced meaningfulness of work.

- Experienced responsibility for outcomes of the work derives from (4) autonomy. The greater the autonomy, the greater the experienced responsibility for outcomes of the work.

- Knowledge of the actual results of the work activities derives from (5) feedback. The greater the feedback, the greater the knowledge of results of the work.

Performance and Work Outcomes   Employees with these psychological states benefit the organization because of their

- high motivation,
- high performance,
- high satisfaction with the work, and
- low absenteeism and turnover.

Employee Growth-Need Strength

A person's growth-need strength determines his interest in improving the five core dimensions. Figure 5.6 shows how this process works. Note that if a person is not interested in enriching his job, the job characteristics model will fail. We examine needs and motivation in more detail in chapter 11.

Organizing Yourself and Delegating Work

Successful managers set priorities and delegate work. Recall that planning entails setting objectives and that organizing is the process of delegating and coordinating resources to achieve those objectives. Thus, prioritizing is important, because some objectives and tasks are more important than others, and delegating is important because this is how you get the work done.

Now that you understand how organizations and jobs are designed, it's time to learn how to organize yourself by setting priorities and delegating work. Complete the Self-Assessment ahead to determine the priorities that are important to you personally.

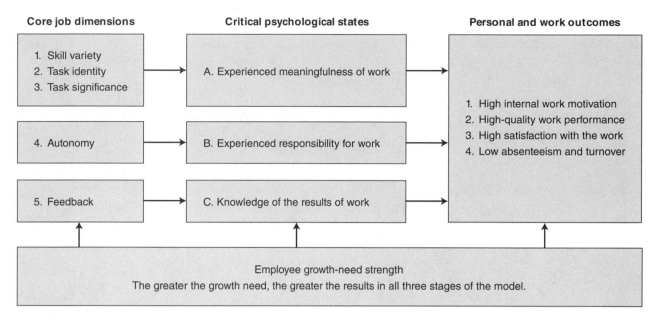

FIGURE 5.6 The job characteristics model.

Setting Priorities

◀ LEARNING OUTCOME 11

Set priorities.

As we have already noted, setting priorities is an important aspect of organizing anything—a department, a job, yourself.[26] At any given time, you must perform several tasks. Prioritizing makes this easier, and a to-do list is a good place to begin. List the tasks you need to do and then rate each one by importance. Then focus on accomplishing only one task at a time by its priority.

To begin, as a manager, ask yourself three questions:

1. Do I need to be personally involved? Often, you are the only one who can do the task, and you must be involved. But if your answer here is no, you don't need to answer the remaining questions for this particular task.

2. Is the task my responsibility or will it affect the performance or finances of my department? You must oversee the performance of your department and keep the finances in line with the budget.

3. Is quick action needed (for a deadline)? Should you work on this activity right now, or can it wait? Time is a relative term. The key is to start the task soon enough to meet the deadline. This may sound obvious, but people often miss deadlines simply because they start too late, so it bears repeating.

Assigning Priorities

With your answers to the three prioritizing questions in mind, you can now assign each task a priority.

- Delegate priority (D): Delegate the task if your answer to question 1 is no (N). The task will go on your coworker's to-do list with a priority.
- High priority (H): Assign a high priority for the task if you answered yes to all three questions (YYY).
- Medium priority (M): Assign a medium priority if you answered yes to question 1 but no to question 2 or question 3 (YNY or YYN).
- Low priority (L): Assign a low priority if you answered yes to question 1 but no to both questions 2 and 3 (YNN).

Your Personal Priorities

For the following 16 items, rate how important each one is to you on a scale of 0 (not important) to 100 (very important).

Not important					Somewhat important					Very important
0	10	20	30	40	50	60	70	80	90	100

_____ 1. An enjoyable, satisfying job

_____ 2. A high-paying job

_____ 3. A good marriage

_____ 4. Meeting new people, attending social events

_____ 5. Involvement in community activities

_____ 6. Relationship with spirituality or religion

_____ 7. Exercising, playing sports

_____ 8. Intellectual development

_____ 9. A career with challenging opportunities

_____ 10. Nice cars, clothes, home

_____ 11. Spending time with family

_____ 12. Having several close friends

_____ 13. Volunteer work for nonprofit organizations like the Cancer Society

_____ 14. Meditation, quiet time to think, pray

_____ 15. A healthy, balanced diet

_____ 16. Educational reading, TV, self-improvement programs

Transfer your rankings for each item to the appropriate column, and then add the two numbers in each column.

Professional	Financial	Family	Social
1. _____	2. _____	3. _____	4. _____
9. _____	10. _____	11. _____	12. _____
Totals _____	_____	_____	_____

Community	Spiritual	Physical	Intellectual
5. _____	6. _____	7. _____	8. _____
13. _____	14. _____	15. _____	16. _____
Totals _____	_____	_____	_____

The higher your total in any area, the more highly you value that area. The closer the numbers are in all eight areas, the more well-rounded you are.

Think about the time and effort you put into your top three priorities. Is your effort sufficient for you to achieve the level of success you desire in each area? If not, what can you do to change your level of effort? Is there any area that you believe you should value more? If yes, what can you do to give more priority to that area?

Consider how you value physical activity. Do you value exercise, playing sports, and eating properly as much as you thought you would? Do you think your valuing of physical activity can be transferred to community, spiritual, and intellectual pursuits? Is it realistic to expect that the values we learn in sport will transfer to other activities? Is sport, as Plato thought, a most valuable tool in instilling the right attitudes and values in young people? Or are we expecting too much from our passion for sports?

Prioritizing Your To-Do List

Figure 5.7 on page 150 is a quick way to prioritize your to-do lists—make copies of it and use it on your job as follows:

1. List the tasks to be performed.

2. Answer the three prioritizing questions. Note the deadline and the time needed to complete the task. You may also want to note a deadline for starting the task as well as its completion date.

3. Assign a priority (D, H, M, or L) to the task. The top left of the figure helps you do this at a glance. If you wrote D, note when the task should be delegated by.

4. Determine which task you should work on now. You may have more than one high-priority task, so select the most important one. When you have completed your high-priority tasks, start on the medium-priority ones, and finally work on your low-priority tasks.

TIME-OUT **11** Make a copy of figure 5.7, and use it to list three to five tasks you must complete in the near future and prioritize them.

You're not finished at this point—in fact, you've only just begun. You will need to continually update your list and add new tasks as they arise. As time passes, priorities change—medium- and low-priority items will become high-priority items.

As we note in chapter 14, if you deal with a wide variety of changing tasks and you need to carve out time for long-range planning, we strongly suggest that you use the time management system. Your prioritized to-do list dovetails neatly with that system. If your job is more routine and you basically plan for the short term, the to-do list will probably suffice to keep you both organized and focused. Skill-Builder 5.1 on page 157 uses the to-do list to help you develop your prioritizing skills.

Delegating

◀ LEARNING OUTCOME 12

Delegate.

When you delegate, you both assign the person responsibility for accomplishing a task and give her the authority to do what is needed. When delegating, you are coaching people to do the task.[27] An important part of coaching is delegating because, in most cases, you can't be a player. Directing people to do work that is part of their job description is *not* delegating. Delegating is about giving employees tasks that are not part of their regular job. The delegated task may eventually become a part of their job, or it may be a one-time task.

Why Should You Delegate?

Delegating gives you time to perform your high-priority tasks. Effective change requires direction, coaching, support, and then delegation. When more tasks are accomplished, productivity rises. Delegating work that people don't ordinarily do stretches them and improves their self-esteem, trains them for future opportunities, and eases the stress and burden on you. Wise delegation of work enriches jobs and improves personal and work outcomes. To help stop corruption, the IOC delegated separate tasks to different committees and internal agents to act as a method of checking on each other.[28]

What Stops Managers From Delegating?

Managers get used to doing things themselves—that's a habit and is easy to fix. More important, managers fear two things: (1) that the employee will fail to accomplish the task (thereby making things worse, not better), and (2) that the person will show them up. As we've noted, managers can delegate responsibility and authority, but they cannot

Prioritized To-Do List

Assigning a priority		Priority determination questions				
D Delegate priority	**N** No to question 1	1. Do I need to be personally involved?	2. Is it my responsibility or will it affect performance or finances of my department?	3. Is quick action needed?	Deadline/Time needed	Priority
H High priority	**YYY** Yes to all three questions					
M Medium priority	**YNY** or **YYN** Yes to question 1 and no to 2 or 3					
L Low priority	**YNN** Yes to question 1 and no to questions 2 and 3					
Task						

FIGURE 5.7   Prioritized to-do list.

From R. Lussier and D. Kimball, 2014, *Applied Sport Management Skills, Second Edition* (Champaign, IL: Human Kinetics).

delegate accountability. Another reason managers do things themselves is that they believe they can perform the task more efficiently than others and don't trust them to do it their way.[29] Perhaps they don't realize that delegating work is an important part of their job. Some managers don't know what to delegate, or don't know how to delegate (we'll teach you soon). If you want to be an effective manager, make delegating part of your job. But first learn when and what to delegate, and to whom.[30]

How Can Managers Know That They Delegate Too Little?

Several flags indicate that managers are delegating too little: (1) They take work home; (2) they perform employee tasks; (3) they are continually behind in their work; (4) they continually feel pressured and stressed; (5) they are always rushing to meet deadlines; (6) they rarely meet deadlines; and (7) their employees always seek approval before acting.

Getting to Delegating

An important part of delegating is knowing which tasks to delegate. Effective delegators know which work to delegate, when to delegate it, and the right person to delegate it to.

TIME-OUT 12 Think about a situation at work where you believe the manager isn't delegating enough. Identify the obstacle preventing the manager from delegating and list the flags that told you he or she isn't delegating enough.

What and When to Delegate

These two questions will make you feel very grateful that you have a prioritized to-do list, because their answers are natural fallouts of your list. To make sure you are approaching delegating correctly, here are the types of things you should consider delegating:

- Paperwork: Employees really can write reports, memos, and letters.
- Routine tasks: Employees really can check inventory, schedule, and order.
- Technical matters: Your top employees really can deal with technical questions and problems. (If they can't, it's time to train them!)
- Tasks with developmental potential: Employees like learning new things. Give them the opportunity to show the stuff they're made of.
- Problem solving: Train your people to solve their own problems. If they ask you what to do, ask them what they think they should do. More than likely they will have the answer and catch on that they don't need to run to you to make all the decisions. Your team will be more effective, and you will be less stressed.

What You Shouldn't Delegate

This is pretty clear-cut—do not delegate the following:

- Personnel matters: performance appraisals, counseling, disciplining, firing, and resolving conflicts
- Confidential activities (unless you have permission to do so)
- Crises—crises are why you are a manager, and you don't have time to delegate them anyway
- Activities assigned to you personally by your boss

Find the Right Person

This is where you earn your pay. You've got to know your people. If you choose wisely—that is, if the person has the skills, the growth-need strength, and the time to get the job done right by the deadline—you will have a happy employee and a happy result. If you choose unwisely, the person may fail (e.g., because of inexperience) through no fault of his own, and the job will still need doing. So, consider an employee's skills and the requirements of the job very carefully. Make sure the person has the temperament to work under pressure if a deadline is looming. When you hire employees, consider whether they can handle delegation.

Now It's Time to Delegate

The following four steps help ensure that the job you need done gets done and done right. Note how these steps mesh with the job characteristics model, core job dimensions, and critical psychological states. The **delegation model** steps are to (1) explain the need for delegating and the reasons for selecting the employee; (2) set objectives that define responsibility, the level of authority, and the deadline; (3) develop a plan; and (4) establish control checkpoints and hold employees accountable.

1. Explain why you are delegating this job and your reasons for selecting the person. We all like to know why—indeed, one can make a strong case that we *need* to know why. Remember the "experienced meaningfulness of work"? Here is where you give work meaning. And telling people why they've been chosen is a very natural and genuine way to make them feel valued. Be positive; make the person aware of how customers, your department, and she herself can benefit. Employees should be motivated, or at least willing, to do the task.

2. Set an objective that defines the person's responsibility, the scope of her authority, and the deadline. State the objective, the end result, and the deadline (see chapter 4). Define the employee's responsibility and level of authority.

3. Plan the task. Perhaps the employee can plan the task herself; perhaps she will need your help. This will depend on her experience and whether you are using this task to stretch her a bit. You (or she) may find it helpful to use a planning sheet (see figure 14.5 on p. 462).

4. Establish control checkpoints and hold employees accountable. Obviously for short, simple tasks, you don't need to set control checks. But you should check progress on tasks that have multiple steps or that will take some time to complete. Consider the person's abilities and experience. The lower her abilities or experience, the more frequently you should check on her work. The higher her abilities and experience, the less frequently you will need to check. The role-playing scenarios in Skill-Builder 5.2 on page 158 will give you some practice in delegating.

For complex tasks and projects, more formalized control and accountability benefit everyone concerned. For one thing, this creates a healthy flow of information. Discussing and agreeing on the form of progress checks (phone call, visit, memo, or detailed report) and their time frame (daily, weekly, or after specific steps are completed) before work begins will prevent future misunderstandings. It is also helpful to formalize control checkpoints in writing (possibly on the planning sheet itself), distributing copies of it so that everyone involved has a record. In addition, all involved should record pertinent control checkpoints on their calendars. If someone doesn't report as scheduled, find out why. Evaluate performance at each checkpoint and also on completion of the task to provide immediate feedback (sound familiar?—this is the "knowledge of the results of work" that we discussed earlier). Praising progress and successful completion of the task is always a good motivator. We will return to the subject of praise in chapter 11.

TIME-OUT **13** Think about a manager or coach for whom you have worked or played and analyze how well he or she delegates. Which steps did your manager or coach do well, and which steps could he or she do better?

Figure 5.8 summarizes the delegation process.

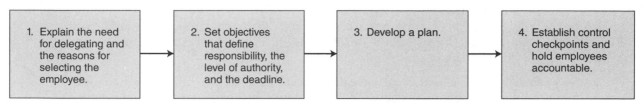

FIGURE 5.8 How to delegate.

@ TAKE IT TO THE NET

Please visit www.HumanKinetics.com/AppliedSportManagementSkills and go to the book's companion web study guide, where you will find the following:

A list of websites associated with the concepts in this chapter

Exercises that you will need Internet access to complete

Online versions of chapter exercises and end-of-chapter learning aids

An exercise that helps you define the Key Terms

LEARNING AIDS

CHAPTER SUMMARY

1. Explain how flat organizations and tall organizations differ.

   Flat organizations have fewer layers of management with wide spans of control. Tall organizations have many layers of management with narrow spans of control.

2. Describe liaisons, integrators, and boundary roles.

   Liaisons, integrators, and people in boundary roles are all coordinators. Liaisons and integrators coordinate internally, whereas people in boundary roles coordinate efforts with customers, suppliers, and other people in the external environment. Liaisons work in one department and coordinate with other departments, whereas integrators coordinate department activities without working for a specific department.

3. Differentiate between formal and informal authority.

   Formal authority specifies relationships among employees. It is the sanctioned way of getting the job done. Informal authority comes from the strength of relationships that evolve as people interact—it works through trust and respect. With centralized authority, top managers make important decisions; with decentralized authority, middle-level and first-line managers make important decisions.

4. Explain the four levels of authority.

   (1) Informing authority—the person simply presents an alternative. (2) Recommending authority—the person presents alternatives and suggests one. (3) Reporting authority—the person can take action in his own area of expertise and regularly informs the boss. (4) Full authority—the person takes action in his area of expertise and usually does not have to inform the boss.

5. Describe the relationship between line and staff authority.

   Staff advise and assist line personnel, who are responsible for making decisions and directing others down the chain of command.

6. Describe organization charts.

Organization charts show the organization's management hierarchy and departments and their working relationships. Organization charts also show the chain of command and type of work.

7. Explain how internal departmentalization and external departmentalization differ.

Internal departmentalization focuses on functions performed inside the organization. External departmentalization focuses on the product, the customer, or the territory in which the organization does business.

8. State the similarities and differences between matrix and divisional departmentalization.

Both are ways to set up departments. Matrix departments combine functional and product structures to focus on projects. Divisional departments are based on semiautonomous strategic business units and focus on portfolio management.

9. Explain how job simplification and job expansion differ.

Job simplification makes jobs more specialized by eliminating tasks, combining tasks, or changing the sequence of work. Job expansion makes jobs less specialized by rotating employees, enlarging the job, or enriching the job to make it more interesting and challenging.

10. Describe the job characteristics model and what it is used for.

This model is a conceptual framework for designing enriched jobs. It uses core job dimensions, critical psychological states, and employee growth-need strength to improve the quality of working life for employees and productivity for the organization.

11. Set priorities.

Setting priorities involves asking three questions: (1) Do I need to be personally involved? (2) Is the task my responsibility or will it affect the performance or finances of my department? (3) Is quick action needed? Delegate when you don't need to be personally involved. Assign a high priority when your answers to all three questions are yes (YYY). Assign a medium priority when your answer to question 1 is yes but no to questions 2 or 3 (YNY or YYN). Assign a low priority when your answer to question 1 is yes and your answers to questions 2 and 3 are no (YNN).

12. Delegate.

To delegate effectively, (1) explain why you are delegating the task and the reasons you chose this person to do the work; (2) clearly define responsibility, the person's scope of authority, and the deadline; (3) plan the task; and (4) establish control checkpoints and hold employees accountable.

REVIEW AND DISCUSSION QUESTIONS

1. What is the difference between unity of command and unity of direction?

2. What is the relationship between the chain of command and the span of management (span of control)?

3. What do the terms *differentiation* and *integration* mean?

4. What is the difference between responsibility and authority?

5. Can a coach delegate accountability to a player?

6. How does the scope of authority change through an organization, and what is the flow of responsibility, authority, and accountability?

7. What is the difference between a general staff person and a specialist staff person?

8. What does an organization chart show? What doesn't it show?

9. What is the difference between product and customer departmentalization?

10. What is job design and why is it necessary?

11. What is the difference between an integrated and a self-managed work team?

12. What is the importance of employee growth-need strength to the job characteristics model?

13. Why is it important to update priorities on a to-do list?

14. What is the first and most important question you ask to determine what and what not to delegate?

15. Explain why each of the four steps of delegating is necessary.

16. Why has there been a trend toward more team, network, virtual, and learning organizations? Is this a fad, or will it last?

17. Matrix structures violate the unity of command principle. Should companies not use the matrix structure?

18. Is centralized or decentralized authority better?

CASE

Building Championship Teams in Boston

Boston is known for beans and the Red Sox. In the last decade, Boston has also been known as a city of well-organized championship teams. What is the organizing secret that led to all four professional teams' winning a championship?

The Red Sox won the World Series in 2004 and 2007. The last time they had won a World Series was in 1918. Under the artful guidance of Terry Francona, known as a "player's manager," the team flourished with a "cowboy up" team philosophy.

Not to be outdone, the New England Patriots won three NFL Super Bowls in the decade of the 2000s. The Patriots won under the stern leadership of Bill Belichick. He is a no-nonsense type of coach who will release players who do not exhibit team spirit. He is also not afraid to release or trade valuable veterans before their contract expires even if it appears they have some good playing years left. It should be noted that Belichick drafted Tom Brady, his Hall-of-Famer-to-be quarterback, with the 199th pick of the football draft—a wise choice and decision by Belichick.

Meanwhile, the Boston Celtics rekindled the magic of early decades by winning the NBA Championship in 2008. Led by General Manager Danny Ainge and Coach Doc Rivers, the team turned a decade of losing into a season of glory by reorganizing around three aging veterans. Kevin Garnett was acquired from the Minnesota Timberwolves and Ray Allen was acquired from Seattle, and they blended extremely well with longtime Celtic Paul Pierce. Coach Rivers took over and created a team atmosphere where a young guard (Rajon Rondo) was able to develop to help assist the experienced veterans. The new "Big Three" reminded fans of the original "Big Three" of Larry Bird, Kevin McHale, and Robert Parrish and their championship seasons.

Lastly, the city of Boston was able to enjoy the reorganization of the NHL Boston Bruins. The Big Bad Bruins were led by Coach Claude Julien, who had been expected to be fired for another lackluster playoff loss. However, the Bruins got the hot hand and worked hard in the corners to win the NHL Stanley Cup in 2011. Julien's style of play (with players working together as a scrappy, hard-nosed team) took a little time for people to learn. But with the hot goaltending of Tim Thomas and some balanced scoring, the result was a championship in a hard-fought series against the Vancouver Canucks.

All four sport teams won with the simple philosophy that William Davidson successfully used to create championship teams in Detroit—letting managers do the job they were hired to do.

Davidson used the following three steps in working with people.

1. Find good people.

2. Give them latitude to probe for greatness over mediocrity.

3. Stay out of their way unless change seems necessary.[31]

For more information, visit redsox.com, bruins.nhl.com, celtics.com, and patriots.com. For more information about William Davidson, see http://www.nba.com/pistons/features/davidson_partone.html.

Case Questions

Select the best alternative for the following questions. Be able to explain your answers.

1. The partnership of Coach Bill Belichick and Tom Brady shows a great unity of direction.

   a. true

   b. false

2. What level of authority does General Manager Danny Ainge have with the Boston Celtics?

   a. informing

   b. recommending

   c. reporting

   d. full

3. What type of authority does the coach of the Boston Celtics have?

   a. line

   b. staff

4. If the Red Sox organization kept nearly all decision making at the top of the organizational structure, this authority would be

   a. centralized

   b. decentralized

5. Transferring managers from one team to another would be an example of

   a. simplification

   b. rotation

   c. enlargement

   d. enrichment

6. You would expect former Red Sox Manager Terry Francona, as a "player's manager," to be reluctant to delegate.

   a. true

   b. false

7. The Boston professional sport teams won seven championships in the decade of the 2000s. This is proof that a well-organized sport organization will always win the championship.

   a. true

   b. false

8. Bill Belichick lacks the skills to properly coordinate his team.
   a. true
   b. false

9. The Boston Bruins are well suited to be organized using a matrix approach.
   a. true
   b. false

10. The Boston Celtics and the Boston Red Sox should be organized by products.
    a. true
    b. false

11. Use the Internet to find out whether the Boston teams have won any new championships.

12. If professional teams are owned by wealthy businesspeople, would you expect most of the organizations to be centralized or decentralized?

SKILL-BUILDER EXERCISES

Skill-Builder 5.1: Setting Priorities

Objective

To develop your skill at setting priorities

Preparation

Congratulations! You just made first-line management in golf ball production at A Birdie in the Hand. A prioritized to-do list with 10 tasks is provided on page 160. Assign priorities to each task using the following steps.

1. List each task. (The 10 tasks for this Skill-Builder have been written in for you.)

2. Answer the three questions (see the box at the top right and use Y and N for yes and no). Because you aren't the actual manager of this department, do not fill in the deadline/time needed column.

3. In the priority column, assign a priority (D, delegate; H, high; M, medium; and L, low) to each task based on your answers to the three questions mentioned in step 2.

4. Determine which task you should complete now. You may have more than one high priority, so select the most important one.

In-Class Application

Complete the preceding skill-building preparation before class.

Choose one (10-30 minutes):

Break into groups of three to five members, and work to reach a group consensus on the 10 priorities. As a group, present your prioritized list to the class.

Hold an informal, whole-class discussion of student findings.

Wrap-Up

Take a few minutes to write your answers to the following questions:

What did I learn from this experience? How will I use this knowledge?

_____

_____

_____

_____

As a class, discuss student responses.

Skill-Builder 5.2: Delegating

Objective

To develop your ability to delegate

Preparation

Review the chapter material on delegating, and then familiarize yourself with the following scenarios.

Scenario 1

Camp counselor Grace: You are the head camp counselor at your college's training camp for left-handed, right-footed male and female cheerleaders. You've got your hands full with these all-star wannabes, and you can't do everything. Think of some tasks you can delegate to Mandy that will help these kids develop a cool, new style that works with their inherent lack of grace.

Camp counselor Mandy: You're new this year, and you've been stuck with the few good dancers in camp (who don't need any help)—but you really want to show that you can make something out of the wrong shoes (so to speak).

Scenario 2

Sally: You manage Golfers Go for It, a retail store that sells to the local golf set and is trying to move into the tennis market. Your favorite task is scheduling your sales clerks. You go to great lengths to accommodate everyone's requirements so you're "one happy crew," but it's taking more and more of your time. Your bosses have suggested that you delegate this task (you can't imagine why) to your assistant manager, Hector. Hector has never done any scheduling, but he appears willing and ready to take on the one task you really pride yourself on. Also, you've been reading this very useful book on sport management and are thinking that maybe its chapter 5, "Organizing and Delegating Work," has some pointers about delegating that you could use—especially the discussion on managers' fear of being shown up. Now you're thinking it's very possible you've been hiding behind the "I'm too busy" excuse to avoid developing some new sales initiatives that might really make the new tennis section a go. With these issues in mind, use the planning sheet on page 150 to plan how you will delegate staff scheduling to Hector.

Hector: You see this as an opportunity to streamline the system, but you also don't want to rock the boat.

Scenario 3

Seema: You and your two roommates, who are all-star athletes, are looking for two more roommates. Your name is on the rental lease, and you've handled this pesky task in the past, but you're really swamped this quarter with the Little League softball team you've been coaching in your free time. None of you can cook, but you all like to eat and are getting tired of takeout. Maybe the new roommates could teach you some things about cooking, or maybe they'll take over the cooking if you wash the dishes. Your rental house, the Castle, is the coolest and cheapest one near campus, so you expect a lot of calls. Plan how you will delegate this task to your roommates. Sara, the basketball star, is pretty shy, but Kate, the soccer forward, tends to procrastinate. You need two new renters in 2 weeks, or the three of you will have to make up the difference in the rent.

Sara: You know you've got to get over this shy business sometime, or you'll never make a good coach.

Kate: You see yourself as a successful international event planner but don't know how to get in gear.

In-Class Application

Choose one (10-30 minutes):
Break into groups of three or four. Take turns being the delegator and the "delegatee" with each scenario. Those of you not doing the role-play will observe the delegating process and provide an independent critique that might improve results.

Three sets of students volunteer to role-play the three scenarios for the entire class, with informal discussion following.

Wrap-Up

Take a few minutes and write your answers to the following questions:

What did I learn from this experience? How will I use this knowledge?

_____

_____

_____

_____

As a class, discuss student responses.

SPORTS AND SOCIAL MEDIA EXERCISES

1. The end-of-chapter case is about building championship teams in Boston. For this exercise, you want to research your favorite team and see if it has any social media links on its website.

   _____

   _____

2. Use Facebook to see if your favorite team has a presence. List three upcoming events for the public to meet team players.

   _____

   _____

3. Will you be able to attend any of these three events online?

   _____

   _____

GAME PLAN FOR STARTING A SPORT BUSINESS

Delegating is an art and a skill. Some managers are able to delegate many tasks to their employees. However, many managers feel their employees will never do the job as well as they could do it themselves. Describe what you would do to create a positive atmosphere of delegating in the sport company you started in prior chapters.

1. Key delegating issue 1 _____

2. Key delegating issue 2 _____

3. Key delegating issue 3 _____

Assigning a priority		Priority determination questions

D Delegate priority	**N** No to question 1
H High priority	**YYY** Yes to all three questions
M Medium priority	**YNY** or **YYN** Yes to question 1 and no to 2 or 3
L Low priority	**YNN** Yes to question 1 and no to questions 2 and 3

Task	1. Do I need to be personally involved?	2. Is it my responsibility or will it affect performance or finances of my department?	3. Is quick action needed?	Deadline/Time needed	Priority
1. Tom, the sales manager, told you that three customers stopped doing business with the company because your products have decreased in quality.					
2. Your secretary, Michele, told you there is a salesperson waiting to see you. He does not have an appointment. You don't do any purchasing.					
3. Molly, a vice president, wants to see you to discuss a new product to be introduced in 1 month.					
4. Tom, the sales manager, sent you a memo stating that the sales forecast was incorrect. Sales are expected to increase by 20% starting next month. There is no inventory to meet the unexpected sales forecast.					
5. Dan, the personnel director, sent you a memo informing you that one of your employees has resigned. Your turnover rate is one of the highest in the company.					
6. Michele told you that a Bob Furry called while you were out. He asked you to return his call, but wouldn't state why he was calling. You don't know who he is or what he wants.					
7. Phil, one of your best workers, wants an appointment to tell you about a situation that happened in the shop.					
8. Tom called and asked you to meet with him and a prospective customer for your product. The customer wants to meet you.					
9. John, your boss, called and said that he wants to see you about the decrease in the quality of your product.					
10. In the mail you got a note from Randolf, the president of your company, and an article from *Sports Business Journal.* The note says "FYI" (for your information).					

Sport Culture, Innovation, and Diversity

LEARNING OUTCOMES

After studying this chapter, you should be able to

1. identify the driving forces behind change;
2. list the four variables of change;
3. differentiate between fact, belief, and values;
4. describe the three components of organizational culture;
5. state the core values of TQM;
6. describe a learning organization;
7. explain how diversity can affect innovation and quality;
8. state how force-field analysis and survey feedback differ; and
9. explain the difference between team building and process consultation.

KEY TERMS

variables of change

management information
  systems (MISs)

stages in the change process

organizational culture

components of culture

core values of TQM

learning organization

organizational development (OD)

OD interventions

force-field analysis

survey feedback

team building

process consultation

161

DEVELOPING YOUR SKILLS

Change is a fact of life. Your ability (or inability) to change with the ever-shifting demands of the business environment may make (or break) your career. And if you are to succeed in management, one task you must learn to do—and do well—is to implement change. In this chapter, you will learn to identify and overcome resistance to change, which can mean the difference between a successful transition and a failed one. You will also need to work within the sport organization's culture; you will need to be able to work with a diversity of people; and you may be involved in an organizational development change intervention, such as team building.

REVIEWING THEIR GAME PLAN

Diversity Issues in Sport Management

The topic of diversity is certainly one of the most popular in the *Journal of Sport Management*. The titles of the articles should give you an appreciation for the wide spectrum of issues about diversity in sport management.

- "Lifting the Veils and Illuminating the Shadows: Furthering the Explorations of Race and Ethnicity in Sport Management" by Ketra Armstrong of California State University at Long Beach. A key component of this article is the changing view of diversity as a melting pot where people blend together to more of a kaleidoscope where people hold on to their unique differences.[1]

- "Gender and Sexually Suggestive Images in Sports Blogs" by Galen Clavio (Indiana University) and Andrea Eagleman (Indiana University and Purdue University). The authors discovered that males received significantly more photographic coverage in sport blogs than did females, and that female portrayals were far more likely to be suggestive.[2]

- "Race Relations Theories: Implications for Sport Management." One trend is the lack of African Americans in leadership positions even though they compose a large percentage of the athletes playing the actual sports.[3]

- "Understanding the Diversity-Related Change Process: A Field Study" by G. Cunningham. The results of this study indicate that for diversity issues to be successful, managers need to consider how they affect the entire organization.[4]

- "Perceptions of Gender in Athletic Administration: Utilizing Role Congruity to Examine (Potential) Prejudice Against Women" by Laura Burton (University of Connecticut), Heidi Grappendorf (North Carolina State University), and Angela Henderson (University of Northern Colorado). This article reviews the lack of women in senior-level athletic administration positions.[5]

Learning more about these articles from the *Journal of Sport Management* will help you to learn more about diversity in sport management.

Managing Change

New York Yankees former player and coach Yogi Berra once said, "The future ain't what it used to be."[6] Today, an organization's long-term success stands directly on the shoulders of its ability to manage change. Things are changing fast, and managers can't get stuck in the way they currently do business. Change leadership is an important skill. An important career question to ask yourself is, "Am I willing to constantly make changes?" If you answer no, don't expect to advance far in your career.

In this section, we discuss forces for change, variables of change, stages in the change process, resistance to change and how to overcome it, and a model for identifying and overcoming resistance.

Forces for Change

◀ LEARNING OUTCOME 1
Identify the driving forces behind change.

There are five different types of forces for change that we examine here: environmental, economic, social, demographic, and technological. We also provide examples of each type to illustrate how real-world sport organizations and managers respond to changes.

Environmental Forces

Today's business environment presents many challenges, often daunting ones, and as such it is a driving force behind change. As we noted in chapter 2, organizations interact continually with their external and internal environments. Factors in both environments require all manner of change, and effective organizations endeavor to "change the change" to their advantage. That is, they try to anticipate and predict change, to shape it if they can, and to prepare for it if they cannot shape it. This is a proactive (rather than reactive) approach. Dr. David Hoch, director of athletics at Loch Raven High School in Baltimore County, Maryland, suggests that athletic directors should deal proactively with problems that will be created by change without waiting until the change occurs.[7] An athletic director (AD) may face new budget restrictions, a new principal or superintendent, greater expectations from parents, or new technologies, such as blogs.

Economic Forces

Economic forces have changed so drastically that even players with average skills make millions of dollars per year. Baseball has become a sport where big-market teams like the New York Yankees and Boston Red Sox can generate more revenues than small-market teams like the Kansas City Royals and thus can afford to spend more money to acquire star players. And more star players mean more fan and media interest, which means even more money. Even though this economic change favors teams like the Yankees, they still need to properly evaluate the talent of available players. Because of the huge amount of money involved, management has very little margin for error when choosing players.

Social Forces

Sociology of sport is an academic discipline that has evolved significantly in the past 40 years.[8] Social forces also play an increasingly important role in managing a team. Most fans outside of the New York area consider the Yankees a bully of a team that is not willing to share revenues with small-market teams. The Yankees are viewed as a team that gets to buy whatever players it wants. The result is that most non-Yankee fans dislike the team, which makes it hard for any Yankee player or manager to be accepted outside of New York.

 Do you believe your college is a melting pot where people blend together? Or is it more like a kaleidoscope where people hold on to their unique differences?

At times, MLB has fallen behind NFL football as America's favorite sport. Baseball fans became leery of the game after the eight work stoppages between 1972 and 1994, which were caused by anger and mistrust between players and owners. Meanwhile, fans love the physical contact and fast action in football. The Super Bowl has become one of the single biggest sporting events in the world.

Demographic Forces

Statistical analysis of Tony Dungy's and Lovie Smith's teams (the Indianapolis Colts and Chicago Bears) coached against each other in the 2007 Super Bowl provides an interesting comparison between two large cities. In 2007, 37% of Chicago's residents who were 5 years or older, spoke a language other than English at home, compared with only 10% of Indianapolis' residents of the same age. The national U.S. average was 19%.[9] This difference is likely to increase over time as minorities increase. This will require the Chicago team to consider presenting its media and marketing materials in other languages. Teams must take into consideration the diverse populations in their marketplaces.

Technological Forces

Technology is very different today than it was only a few years ago.[10] The NFL has television contracts with ABC/ESPN, NBC, CBS, FOX, DirecTV, and the NFL Network. Each of the stations is allowed to broadcast games at various times during the weekend. For example, since 2006, ESPN has shown the Monday Night Football (MNF) game, which for 35 years was aired on ABC.

Although this was a major change in televising of the MNF game, the bigger threat is the creation of the NFL Network. The NFL Network is a new attempt by the NFL to control the viewership of its games. So far, the network is considered a premium cable channel, and acceptance has been slow. But if the network is successful, its growth could lead to the decline of the traditional media stations that cover the NFL.

The NFL Network gained some excellent exposure and goodwill near the end of the 2007 NFL season. The undefeated New England Patriots and the playoff-bound New York Giants were scheduled to meet in the last game of the season. The game was scheduled to be shown only on the NFL Network. Most fans would not be able to watch the game and were scrambling to find locations that had the NFL Network. But a few days before the game was to be played, Commissioner Roger Goodell announced that it would be simulcast on the major U.S. television networks NBC and CBS. The game was a huge ratings winner, and the NFL Network gained more positive exposure than if it had advertised in the Super Bowl itself.[11]

The NFL streamed the 2012 Super Bowl from Indianapolis to cellular phones. Although the game attracted around 111 million viewers, streaming the videos online allows fans to watch from different angles, replay popular commercials, and view parts of the game when they are away from the television.[12]

Management Functions and Change

Leaders manage change every workday.[13] Plans that they develop require changes. Organizing and delegating tasks often require employees to make changes. The hiring, orienting, and training of employees, and their performance evaluations,

TIME-OUT 1 Think about a change that the organization you work for or play for has faced recently, and identify the force driving the change.

may indicate that aspects of these employees' jobs, or their approaches to their jobs, must change. Dr. David Hoch at Loch Raven High School asked, "Have you ever thought about the changes that athletic directors encounter every year and the impact that they usually have? New athletes? New parents? New coaches? They all spell change and the possibility of having to adjust and react differently."[14]

LEARNING OUTCOME 2 ▶
List the four variables of change.

Variables of Change

The four **variables of change**—strategy, structure, technology, and people—refer to what organizations must adapt to, adjust, shift, or re-create to stay current, to keep or grow market share, or to remain viable as an organization as they are bombarded with changes they must address in the marketplace (see table 6.1). Because of the systems effect, effective managers consider what repercussions a shift in one variable will have on the remaining variables and plan accordingly.

TABLE 6.1 The Four Variables of Change

Strategy	Structure	Technology	People
Corporate (growth, stability, and turn-around and retrenchment)	Principles (unity of command and direction, chain of command, span of management, division of labor, coordination, balanced responsibility and authority, delegation, and flexibility)	Machines	Skills
Business level (prospecting, defending, and analyzing)	Authority (formal and informal, line and staff, and centralized and decentralized; levels of authority)	Systems process	Performance
Functional (marketing, operations, finance, and human resources)	Organizational design (departmentalization)	Information process	Attitudes
	Job design (job simplification, rotation, enlargement, enrichment, and work teams)	Automation	Behavior

Strategy

Organizations routinely adjust strategies in order to adapt to changes in their external and internal environments. For example, CYBEX International had a corporate goal to expand its market share in the fitness industry. To do this, the company needed to broaden its line of fitness equipment, so it merged with Trotter Inc., an undisputed leader in cardiovascular research and products. The different experiences and the deep expertise both companies brought to the table have turned out to be a good marriage. CYBEX is a publicly traded company, and you can visit its website at www.cybexintl.com.[15]

Structure

Structure typically follows strategy. In other words, a change in strategy changes structure. Over time, organizational structures evolve to adapt to emerging needs. We examined organizational structure in chapter 5; figure 5.3 on page 138 briefly summarizes key elements in organizational structure.

Technology

High-tech innovations—computers, faxes, e-mail, and the Internet—have increased the rate of change. Technology increases productivity and thus helps organizations gain competitive advantage. To gain this advantage, Olympic athletes, for example, look to their equipment suppliers (Nike, Spalding, Wilson, and many others) to provide cutting-edge shoes, bats, skis, and bicycles and to their trainers and therapists to provide cutting-edge training techniques and rehabilitation methods to facilitate recovery from injuries (for example, injuries that once sidelined players for a season now set them back mere days). Sport organizations routinely use the Internet for all manner of reasons—to provide websites so fans can follow the NFL (www.nfl.com), NBA (www.nba.com), and MLB (www.mlb.com); to get ideas on how to improve viewership or grow a fledgling swim team; and to find information on the latest coaching techniques. Once-obscure sports like curling, fencing, and Ultimate Frisbee can use the Internet to find new fans.[16]

Technology frequently drives change in strategy and structure. Here are a few examples of the innumerable ways technology affects changes:

- **Machines:** New machinery and equipment are introduced continually. In 2011, CYBEX International introduced the new CYBEX Bravo Functional Training System.[17]

- **Systems process:** How organizations transform inputs into outputs has been at the forefront of technological innovation. Companies use the latest in computer automation to build products free of defects. Wilson Sporting Goods in Humboldt, Tennessee, redesigned its production plant to better use a new conveyor system. With this redesign, Wilson reduced the time for sleeving a dozen balls (four packs of three balls) from 18 seconds to 5 seconds.[18]

- **Information process:** With the advent of the computer, organizations have radically changed the way they do business. **Management information systems (MISs)** are formal systems for collecting, processing, and disseminating information that aids managers in decision making. MISs centralize and integrate the organization's key information, such as finance, production, inventory, and sales. Departments plugged into MISs can better coordinate their efforts, and this translates into a more focused organization and higher productivity. For example, information communications technology helps physical education teachers record students' physical activities and graph their progress. E-mail and databases also help physical education departments with administrative duties.[19] MISs have been used to help MLB players extend their careers. Detroit Tigers starting pitcher Kenny Rogers threw 90 mile per hour (145 kilometer per hour) pitches at age 42; this was largely attributable to years of computer analysis and film study to learn how to transfer energy to his throwing arm from his legs in the most efficient way.[20] Just think about how much easier computers have made it to record and maintain all the statistics of each team and each player in all the sports at all levels.

  Moneyball, a book written by Michael Lewis in 2003 and made into a highly successful movie in 2011 starring Brad Pitt, was the author's quest to figure out why the low-budget 2002 Oakland A's were so successful. One key ingredient was the use of a large amount of statistical data to analyze the impact of a player. Billy Beane was the general manager of the A's. Beane believed, for instance, that winning could be more affordable if you found hitters with high on-base percentages and pitchers who got lots of ground outs. Beane used computer-generated analysis to determine what players were undervalued. It turned out the undervalued players were more likely to be players who had a high on-base percentage but not necessarily a high batting average. Beane followed the advice of sabermetricians, led by Bill James; their computer-generated data indicated that the statistics often used to measure ballplayers were not the correct set of data on which to base judgment of their future abilities.[21]

  ESPN used technology to develop a new quarterback rating from their Stats and Information group. The NFL passer rating system was over 40 years old. The new rating system included many more variables than the old system. The new system is sophisticated enough that successful plays in closely contested games are more valuable. For instance, a completed pass of 5 yards on third and 5 yields a first down. Less valuable is a completion of 8 yards on a third and 10. This does not lead to a first down, and a punt is necessary.[22]

- **Automation:** Computers and other machines have enabled organizations to replace people with robots. Automation has increased the speed of making athletic equipment and its quality and helped keep prices down. Automation takes away some jobs and adds others. It also changes the types of work people do. Pressing needs for better training, retraining, and higher levels of skill will continue to be seen for the foreseeable future.

People

People have always been, and always will be, a key variable of change.[23] Think of the ways changes affect you in your job, team, and school and how you effect changes in your job, team, and school. The day-to-day tasks that we do to perform our jobs have changed dramatically because of technology and the ensuing structural changes. As tasks change, our skills and performance have changed, and they will continue to change. Organizations often attempt to change our attitudes and behavior to improve the bottom line, grow market niche, and enhance productivity.

Changes in organizational culture are also considered a people variable, because people develop and implement changes in strategy and structure. We create, manage, and use technology; therefore, we are the organization's most important resource. This makes us both the organization's wild card and its ace in the hole when it comes to implementing change. Changes in the other three variables cannot work without the commitment, energy, and problem-solving abilities of people. So it is crucial to get input from those who will be affected by a change and to secure their commitment to its success. For example, an AD should inform and educate everyone involved with an upcoming change, such as a new budgeting form, to help reduce fears and reservations.

> **TIME-OUT 2**
>
> Describe a recent change in your organization or team and identify the variables of change affecting it or affected by it.

Stages in the Change Process

People in the midst of a change go through four distinct **stages in the change process**—denial, resistance, exploration, and commitment.

1. **Denial:** When people first hear rumors that change is coming, they go into denial—"It won't happen here!" Prudent managers manage change proactively; they don't wait until change rudely knocks on their door. They start addressing the change and its ramifications early on to both lessen the impact of the change and smooth the transition.

2. **Resistance:** Once people get over their initial shock and realize that change is inevitable, they resist it. It is important to understand that we all—in one way or another, and at one level or another—fear change. Change always takes us out of our comfort zone. Outside of our comfort zone, we may grow—but we also may fail.

APPLYING THE CONCEPT 6.1

Variables of Change

Identify the change variable involved in each situation.

a. strategy
b. structure
c. technology
d. people

_____ 1. We installed a new computer system to speed up the time it takes to bill ticket customers.

_____ 2. With the increasing number of pro basketball leagues, we're going to have to devote more time and effort to keeping our existing customers.

_____ 3. Jamie, I'd like you to consider getting a college degree if you're serious about a career in management with this team.

_____ 4. We're changing suppliers to get higher-quality components for our tennis rackets.

_____ 5. We are laying off some assistant coaches to increase the number of players reporting to one coach.

3. **Exploration:** When implementation is launched, people explore the change, often through training, and they begin to better understand how it will affect them. It is helpful to solicit input from affected individuals. Inviting and encouraging them to be part of the change process are key to successful implementation.

4. **Commitment:** Through exploration, people commit (or don't commit) to making the change a success. One's level of commitment can also change. Be alert for naysayers, and carefully and patiently address statements like "It's always been done this way." Tony Dungy, former coach of the Colts, is a genuinely nice guy, and his players responded by being committed to doing whatever it took to win.

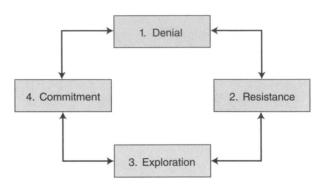

Figure 6.1 illustrates the change process. We present the stages as occurring in a circular fashion because change is rarely linear. People go back and forth—they waver in their resistance and commitment, as the arrows show.

FIGURE 6.1 Stages in the change process.

Resistance to Change and How to Overcome It

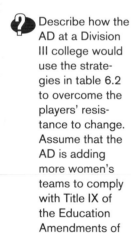

Describe how the AD at a Division III college would use the strategies in table 6.2 to overcome the players' resistance to change. Assume that the AD is adding more women's teams to comply with Title IX of the Education Amendments of 1972.

When change programs fail, it is usually because the people involved resist—even sabotage—the change.[24] Although U.S. law changed to give females equal rights to participate in sport (Title IX of the Education Amendments of 1972), people resisted, and some are still resisting.[25] As a manager, your job is to enact changes.[26] To do so, you need to understand why people resist and then find ways to counter resistance. See table 6.2 for an overview.

So, why do we resist change?

• **We fear uncertainty.** Fear of the unknown is a universal human trait, and people resist change in order to cope with their anxiety and fear of the unknown.[27] Learning anxieties underlie many people's resistance to change—the prospect of learning something new can conjure up old memories of failure and remind people that failure (however unlikely it might be) is possible.

• **We don't like to be inconvenienced.** We often don't want to disrupt our routines or the way things are because they are comfortable. At a minimum, change means having to learn new ways, and it may mean extensive training.

• **We always move to protect our self-interest.** This is also a universal human trait. When people hear about change, they ask, "How will it affect me?"[28] Of course people will

TABLE 6.2   Overcoming Resistance to Change

Why people resist change	How to overcome resistance
Uncertainty creates fear.	Create a trust climate.
Inconvenience is off-putting.	Develop a change plan.
Their self-interest is threatened.	State why change is needed and how it affects people.
They fear loss.	Create a win–win situation.
They don't want to lose control of their job.	Involve people and provide support.
	Follow through.

resist change if it threatens their self-interest. And we are usually more concerned about our own best interest than that of the organization.

- **We fear loss.** Change often brings loss of jobs, or it may require pay cuts[29]—witness older players who can no longer demand high salaries as they did when they were rising stars. A change in work assignments or schedules may mean losing valued social relationships. Aging athletes are often happy to prolong their career for a year or two just to spend more time with their teammates.

- **We like to be in control, or at least feel as if we're in control.** Actual or perceived losses in power, status, security, and especially control often come with change programs. Aging athletes often want to prolong their careers to keep control of their status as pro athletes.

TIME-OUT 3 Describe an instance in which you resisted change. Specify which of the five reasons were behind your resistance. Now, be your own manager and prescribe some proactive ways you could have overcome your initial reluctance.

Now you know why people resist change. The good news is that there are ways to alleviate their fears and overcome their resistance. Here are some key ones:

- **Create a trust climate.** You do this by carefully developing good relations with your team or work group. And don't forget to maintain those relations. You may have to ask your group to trust you to lead them through a change for which initial resistance is especially strong. Make sure your colleagues understand that you have their best interests in mind. Constantly look for better ways to do things. Encourage people to suggest changes and implement their ideas. They are valued members of your team—show it! It was evident that Tony Dungy's players trusted him to make the right moves during games.

- **Develop a change plan.** Successful implementation of change is no accident. Behind every successful implementation stands a good plan. Develop one and then use it. Identify possible resistance to change and plan ways to overcome it. View change from your team's position. Set clear objectives so that everyone knows exactly what to do during and after the change. And make sure your plan addresses the next four issues.

- **State why the change is necessary and how it will affect your group.** Communication is the key. People need to know all the whys and all the hows. "Why are we doing this? How will it affect us?" Give them the good news and the bad news. Be open, honest, and ethical in bringing about change. You've taken great care to build trust—don't squander it. Giving everyone the facts as early as you can not only prevents their fears but also helps them feel in control.[30] (Now they can make plans.) If the grapevine starts spreading incorrect information, correct the information quickly and firmly.

- **Create a win–win situation.** Obviously, you can't always do this, but often you can meet employee needs and achieve the objectives you've been given. Think about how you can answer the question everyone is thinking but nobody is asking: "What's in it for me?" People who see how they will benefit from a change will be more open to it. So, how do you create this win–win scenario? Read on. . . .

- **Involve people.** It's a fact—a group's commitment to change is critical to its success. Here's another fact—people who help develop change are more committed to the success of the change than are those who don't. It's about ownership and it's about control. Why do we like to own houses, cars, ice skates, golf clubs (rather than renting them, for example)? Because we can control their quality and their availability. The same goes for change at work, on the playing field—anywhere, in fact. If we feel we "own" the change, we feel in control, and we'll work like crazy to make it succeed.

- **Provide support.** Training is very important to successful change; therefore, it behooves you and your organization to provide as much training as you can before, during, and often after a change is made. Thorough training reduces anxieties, alleviates frustration, and helps people realize they will "have a life" after the change.

- **Follow through.** Many managers don't understand the need for tenacity and follow through. If a Little League or MLB coach sees a player drop his lead elbow as he swings the bat, do you think that simply telling the player once to change his technique is enough? Coaching in the office or on the field is all about persistent follow through to maintain and improve performance.

Model for Identifying and Overcoming Resistance

Before initiating change of any sort, savvy managers anticipate how their team will react.[31] Looking at three key components of the resistance itself—intensity, source, and focus—will help you understand why certain members of your group may be reluctant to change.[32]

Intensity

We all view change differently. Some of us even thrive on it, and others are upset by it. Most of us resist change at first but gradually accept it (with medium intensity), yet some of us resist it forever (with strong intensity). And we view different changes differently. Some of us think nothing of taking up bungee jumping, but we wouldn't want to give a formal presentation to our work group. As a manager of change, you need to prepare for the intensity of your group's response. Will their response be a strong one or a weak one, or will it be somewhere in between? Let's discuss the other two variables.[33]

LEARNING OUTCOME 3 ▶

Differentiate between fact, belief, and values.

Source

Resistance to change arises from three sources:

- **Facts:** All of us at one time or another have used facts to prove our point. Facts used correctly can help overcome our fear of the unknown.

- **Beliefs:** Facts can be proven; beliefs cannot. Beliefs are subjective opinions that can be shaped by others—they are our perceptions. How we perceive a situation colors whether we believe that a change will be beneficial or detrimental. People sometimes resist change by refusing to believe facts, even though they are proven. It is often hard to prove how a change will affect people, so the issue becomes a matter of their beliefs versus yours.

- **Values:** Values are what we believe are worth pursuing or doing.[34] What we value is extremely important to us. Values pertain to right and wrong behavior (ethics), and values help us decide what is important. Sometimes the facts collide with our values—in such situations, values often win.

Focus

When we resist change, we do so from three viewpoints—that is, we choose a focus:

- **Ourselves:** All of us ask, What's in it for me?[35] What will I gain or lose? When we perceive (correctly or incorrectly) that a proposed change will affect us negatively, we will resist the change.

- **Others:** After considering what's in it for us, or when the change does not affect us, we consider how the change will affect our friends, peers, and colleagues. If we believe the change will affect important others negatively, we may also be reluctant to embrace the change.

- **Work environment:** The work environment includes the physical setting, the work itself, and the climate. We like to be in control of our situation, and we resist changes that take away our feelings of control. Has a coach ever told you to change to another position that you didn't want to play? Has a manager asked you to do a task you didn't want to do?

Sources of resistance (fact → belief → value)

Focus of resistance (work → other → self)

1. **Facts about self**	4. **Beliefs about self**	7. **Values pertaining to self**
• I have never done the task before. • I failed the last time I tried.	• I'm too busy to learn it. • I'll do it, but don't blame me if it's wrong.	• I like the way I do my job now. Why change? • I like working in a group.
2. **Facts about others**	5. **Beliefs about others**	8. **Values pertaining to others**
• She has the best performance record in the department. • Other employees told me it's hard to do.	• He just pretends to be busy to avoid extra work. • She's better at it than I am; let her do it.	• Let someone else do it; I do not want to work with her. • I like working with him. Don't cut him from our department.
3. **Facts about the work environment**	6. **Beliefs about the work environment**	9. **Values pertaining to the work environment**
• We are paid only $8 an hour. • It's over 100 degrees.	• This is a lousy job. • The pay here is too low.	• I don't care if we meet the goal or not. • The new task will make me work inside. I'd rather be outside.

Intensity (high, medium, or low for each box)

FIGURE 6.2 Resistance matrix.

Based on Hultman 1979.

The resistance matrix in figure 6.2 gives examples for each component. Use the matrix to identify the intensity, source, and focus of your team. This will help you decide which strategies will lead people to buy into making the change work. Note that intensity is outside the matrix because it can be strong, moderate, or weak for the other nine components. In Skill-Builder 6.1 on page 189, you will use the resistance matrix to identify the source and focus of resistance to various changes.

 **TIME-OUT 4** Think about the situation you identified in the preceding Time-Out (p. 169), and then use the resistance matrix in figure 6.2 to determine your level of intensity, the focus of your resistance, and its source.

Organizational Culture

Organizational culture is the set of values, beliefs, and standards for acceptable behavior that its members share. Understanding an organization's culture helps you understand how it functions and how you should do things to fit in. Fit with the culture is one of the top criteria recruiters look for when hiring students. It's the shared understanding about the identity of an organization. Think of culture as the organization's personality. Sport team culture adds a special dimension to the idea of organizational culture, because teams form a special bond that is often very strong. With this bond come special ways of behaving or goofing off, a special determination to win, ways of dealing with winning and losing—in short, all the bonding mechanisms are in full display. Add to this mix the fans who closely identify with or idolize a particular team's culture, image, or personality, and you have many strong forces at play. NCAA Division I and III teams tend to have

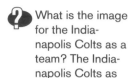

What is the image for the Indianapolis Colts as a team? The Indianapolis Colts as an organization?

distinctive cultures.[36] Think of "good guy" teams like the Seattle Mariners and "bad guy" teams like the Oakland Raiders.

Successful teams are often associated with having a strong team culture. "Sport team culture originated from the establishment and development of sports teams. The sport team culture with which all members voluntarily comply is the total of common faith, morality, spirit, ceremony, intelligence factor, and entertainment life. The function of the sport team culture is found in instructing people, construction of team standards, recovery, spiritual adjustment, and meeting psychological and social demand."[37]

Behavior

LEARNING OUTCOME 4 ▶

Describe the three components of organizational culture.

The three **components of culture** are behavior, values and beliefs, and assumptions.[38] Behavior is observable action—what we do and say. Artifacts are the results of our behavior and include written and spoken language, dress, and material objects. Behavior also includes rites, celebrations, ceremonies, heroes, jargon, myths, and stories. When you examine an organization's culture, you find that rites, corporate myths, jargon, and all the rest play an important part in defining that culture. Managers, particularly founders, have a strong influence on their organization's culture. The late Tom Yawkey of the Boston Red Sox, the late George Halas of the Chicago Bears, and the late Al Davis of the Oakland Raiders were legends in their own time and are legends still to fellow players, colleagues, and fans alike who relish the tales and anecdotes surrounding these enduring personalities.

Values and Beliefs

Values represent the way we think we ought to behave and identify what we think it takes to be successful. Beliefs can be expressed as if–then statements. (If I do X, then Y will happen.) Values and beliefs are the operating principles that guide decision making and behavior in an organization; they influence ethical or unethical behavior.[39] We observe values and beliefs only indirectly, through the behaviors and decisions they drive. Values and beliefs are often described in an organization's mission statement, but take care here—sometimes an organization's talk (its stated values and beliefs) doesn't match its walk (values and beliefs put into action).

Boston Red Sox Tom Yawkey and his family walked their talk. They believed in giving to charity, and they made sure their team gave both money and personal time to the Dana-Farber Cancer Institute. Before the 2002 baseball season, the Yawkey family sold the Red Sox to John Henry. This new management is carrying forward the Red Sox tradition by helping the Jimmy Fund. Even though Al Davis values his team's maverick image and goes to great lengths to maintain it, "bad boys" Oakland Raiders also donate substantial time to worthwhile causes in the Oakland area.

Assumptions

Assumptions are deeply ingrained values and beliefs whose truth we never question. Because our assumptions are the very foundation of our belief system, they are patently obvious to us—and we assume to everyone else—so we rarely discuss them. They are the automatic pilots that guide our behavior. Naturally, when our assumptions are challenged, we feel threatened. Question a teammate on why she does things certain ways: If she responds with a statement like "That's the way it has always been done," you have probably run into an assumption. Assumptions are often the most stable and enduring part of culture and the most difficult to change. For instance, although the Boston Red Sox team was known for supporting charities, the new owners challenged basic assumptions on how the team treated its fans and the media. Consequently, new owners have embraced both the media and the fans with new events that encourage players to get closer to both groups.[40] However, things don't always go this smoothly—some of the Red Sox pitchers (who were not scheduled to pitch) were drinking alcohol and eating fried chicken during games in the dugout in the 2011 season.[41]

Strong Cultures and Weak Cultures

Organizational cultures range from strong to weak. In organizations with strong cultures, people unconsciously share assumptions and consciously know the organization's values and beliefs. That is, they agree with the organization's assumptions, values, and beliefs and behave as expected. In organizations with weak cultures, many employees don't behave as expected—they don't share underlying assumptions. They question and challenge the beliefs. When people don't agree with the generally accepted values and beliefs, they may rebel and fight the culture. This can be destructive or constructive. Culture is both an entrenched phenomenon and a fluid one. Hence cultures resist change, but they also continually adapt to the times.

There is good news and bad news about strong cultures. Strong cultures make communication and cooperation easier and better. Unity is common, and consensus is easier to reach. The downside is potential stagnation and a lack of diverse opinion (no one thinks about alternative ways of doing things). The continually changing business environment requires that assumptions, values, and beliefs be questioned occasionally and changed when they no longer adequately address the needs of the marketplace.

TIME-OUT 5

Give examples of behaviors that show your organization's culture working. What values, beliefs, and assumptions underlie these behaviors? Does the organization have a strong culture or a weak one?

Successful organizations realize that managing culture is not a program with a starting and ending date. It is an ongoing endeavor called organizational development (OD). You will learn about OD later in this chapter.

A change in culture is a people change. To be effective, changes in culture have to occur in all three components (people's behavior, values and beliefs, and assumptions). A culture of success allows for change, and businesses that fail to move with the times lose their competitive advantage.

Culture is an important consideration when companies merge or acquire a business. A mismatch in cultures often leads to failed mergers and acquisitions. When larger businesses

APPLYING THE CONCEPT 6.2

Strong Cultures and Weak Cultures

Identify each statement as characteristic of an organization with (a) a strong culture or (b) a weak culture.

_____ 6. Walking around this athletic department during my job interview, I realized I'd have to wear a jacket and tie every day.

_____ 7. I'm a little tired of hearing about how our team founders conducted business. We all know the stories, so why do people keep telling them?

_____ 8. I've never met with so many people who all act so differently. I guess I can just be me rather than trying really hard to fit in.

_____ 9. It's hard to say what is really important in our department. Management says quality is important, but the supervisors force us to work too fast and they know we send out defective athletic equipment all the time just to meet orders.

_____ 10. I started to tell this ethnic joke and the other employees all gave me a dirty look.

acquire smaller companies, they often try to bring the smaller company's culture into alignment with their own culture, usually without much success. When developing or changing culture, remember that what you as a manager say doesn't count as much as what you measure, reward, and control—these three actions are powerhouses in influencing behavior. For example, managers who say that ethics are important but fiddle in a suspicious way with their financial statements have a hard time establishing a trust climate.

Innovation, Quality, and the Learning Organization

In chapter 3 we noted that creativity is a way of thinking that generates new ideas and that innovation is the implementation of a new idea. Two important types of innovations are product innovation (new things) and process innovation (new ways of doing things). You need to actively seek opportunities and to take action to create new products and processes. You have to be able to adapt your current practices and thinking and go for innovation. In fact, organizations are developing innovative climates.

Wilson Sporting Goods' mission statement is this: "In constant pursuit of innovative technologies and cutting edge design, to develop breakthrough products that enhance the performance of all athletes, from the enthusiastic novice to the seasoned professional." Wilson has innovated in golf balls with its "longest spin technology" (the world's first solid wood golf ball), "solid ball distance" (off-the-tee advance), and "wound ball spin" (shot-stopping spin around the green).[42]

NASCAR has often been viewed as an innovator in car design, body design, tire development, and radio communications between team members. For example, safety has been a major concern for NASCAR, accelerated by the death of Dale Earnhardt on the last lap of the 2001 Daytona 500. A new product innovation, shock-absorbing "soft walls," is being used to protect drivers. The walls will provide a cushion to any driver who happens to crash into them. Soft walls were first used in the 2002 Indianapolis 500 and were successful in reducing the impact on two drivers who hit the walls at speeds of almost 200 miles per hour (322 kilometers per hour). Watkins Glen is considering installing soft walls in certain dangerous sections after having had numerous accidents during the 2011 races.[43]

Process innovation occurs when coaches bring in new concepts regarding how games are played or how players should train for games. For example, computers are used extensively during preparation for football games, eliminating much of the time-consuming gathering of video and organizing of notes. Brian Billick, former head coach of the Baltimore Ravens, is known as a real innovator in this area. His coaches can call up any play on the computer that either their own team or a competitor has run in previous games. They can retrieve all plays called for a certain down and yardage combination (e.g., third down and 8 yards to gain) and what defense the other team played (e.g., a dime defense).

Coaches and players can use their iPads to play back video of plays as soon as they finish a game or while they are on an airplane flying home from a road game. The gambling industry has had success with apps for the iPhone to help speed up the betting process.[44]

 What product innovations have occurred in baseball in the past 10 years? What product innovations have occurred in football in the past 10 years?

Teams now hire video and computer personnel to document every play. However, teams that are overly aggressive in videotaping might be using illegal tactics. Bill Belichick, head coach of the New England Patriots, was caught on the sidelines videotaping the Jets' defensive signals in the first half of the opening game of the season. The NFL fined Belichick a record amount of U.S.$500,000, and the Patriots were fined U.S.$250,000 and lost one of their first-round draft picks. This incident is often referred to as Spygate.[45]

Organizations are always on the lookout for innovations that will help them hold their own against the competition and stay ahead of it. Successful companies know that innovation can be a powerful competitive advantage. The multimillion-dollar pursuit is to develop a culture that stimulates creativity and innovation.

Innovation

To be more innovative, firms are using the flat organization. As noted in chapter 5, flat organizations limit their bureaucracies (tall organizations have superfluous layers of management, which slows them down and makes them less able to move quickly on

TIME-OUT 6 Describe an innovation from an organization you have worked for or played for. Was it a product innovation or a process innovation?

opportunities); divide labor along generalist lines (not by specialties); and routinely use cross-functional teams to get the work done, to solve problems, and to identify opportunities. Flexibility is the name of their game. Systems are informal and authority is decentralized. Jobs are designed to be richer in content and in responsibility, and work teams are based on sociotechnical systems.

Large companies commonly create the small units so essential to innovation within the framework of their divisions. Innovative organizations commonly create separate systems for innovative groups, such as new venture units. They also recruit creative people and train their workforce to think creatively (yes, this can be done!). Their reward system encourages people to think about new ways to do things. Many organizations reward individuals and groups that come up with innovative ideas; cash, prizes (such as trips), praise, and (always) recognition encourage people to explore the less traveled path.

Quality

High-performing organizations believe that innovation and quality go hand in hand. In fact, the characteristics that make a corporate culture innovative are essentially the same characteristics found in organizations that pursue total quality management (TQM). Outdoor sport and mail-order catalog firm L.L. Bean established a total quality and human resources (TQHR) department that led the company's efforts to improve quality, efficiency, and customer service. The TQHR department has saved the company millions of dollars annually from process improvements.

◀ **LEARNING OUTCOME 5**
State the core values of TQM.

The **core values of TQM** involve a companywide focus on (1) delivering customer value and (2) continuously improving the system and its processes. TQM cultures emphasize trust, open communication, a willingness to confront and solve problems, openness to change, internal cooperation against external competition, and adaptability to the environment. In TQM organizations, people are the most important resource. Therefore, TQM organizations go to

 Do the Patriot teams led by Bill Belichick in the past several years fulfill the two core values of TQM?

APPLYING THE CONCEPT 6.3

Getting to Innovation

Check each statement that describes an innovative corporate culture.

_____ 11. We have a very tall organization in our local soccer league.

_____ 12. I tried for months to develop a stronger skate blade for hockey, but it didn't work. However, my boss thanked me profusely for trying.

_____ 13. It drives me nuts when I'm given a task and my boss tells me exactly how to do the job, down to crossing the T's and dotting the I's. Why can't I meet the objective my way for a change?

_____ 14. This athletic footwear company has a policy, procedure, and rule for everything under the sun.

_____ 15. We strive mightily to make sure that our coaches' jobs are broad in scope and that coaches have a lot of autonomy to get the job done their way.

great lengths to make sure their workforce gets the best training available, and they stress teamwork. Employees use cutting-edge technology and innovations to improve customer value. TQM cultures are strong cultures in which values support and reinforce the organization's strategic purpose—that of aligning people, processes, and resources to create value for customers through continuous improvement.

The late W. Edwards Deming developed 14 points that are pivotal in creating a TQM culture. Deming's points improve people's job satisfaction as well as product quality, productivity, effectiveness, and competitiveness.

The Learning Organization

LEARNING OUTCOME 6 ▶

Describe a learning organization.

Today's managers are knowledge workers, which is a change in the realm of management. Knowledge is a dominant source of competitive advantage, because knowledge leads to creativity and innovation action.

TIME-OUT 7 Identify whether TQM values are operative in your organization or team. Give specific examples to support your conclusions.

Success often comes from recognizing new opportunities through knowledge of a market, industry, or customers. The learning organization is based on knowledge. In a learning organization, all involved understand that the world is changing rapidly and that they must not only be aware of these changes but also adapt to the changes and, more important, be forces for change. The **learning organization** has a capacity to learn, adapt, and change as its environment changes to continuously increase customer value.

Organizations need to focus on building "corporate learning," which is a much broader idea than simply developing individual skills and knowledge. The learning organization appears to be an effective model for a fast-changing work environment. Learning organizations thus focus on developing good human resources (HR) policies that will ensure that they can recruit, retain, and develop the best and the brightest. Learning organizations see that knowledge flows horizontally—this increases corporate learning as everyone in the organization participates in the transfer, sharing, and leveraging of individual knowledge and expertise. Trust is a crucial part of the learning culture because only by trusting one another can workers fully exploit their own knowledge and expertise. Creating a learning organization demands strong leadership, team-based structures, a commitment to empower people, open information, strategies built through full employee participation, and a strong, adaptive culture.

LEARNING OUTCOME 7 ▶

Explain how diversity can affect innovation and quality.

Diversity

When we talk about diversity, we mean characteristics of individuals that shape their identities and their experiences in the workplace. Diversity refers to the degree of differences among members of a team or an organization. People are diverse in many ways. As workers, we are commonly classified by our race or ethnicity, religion, gender, age, and "other." A few of the "other" categories are military status, sexual preference, lifestyles, socioeconomic class, and work styles.

Effective organizational cultures value innovation, quality, and diversity. Quality and diversity have a special relationship. To improve the quality of their products and services, organizations must first understand and address the needs of their workforce, and this includes valuing diversity. Innovative organizations have long recognized the realities of the new workforce and how they affect efficiency and effectiveness. Thus, sport managers are promoting diversity for the benefits and value it brings to the organization.[46] In this section, we discuss the importance of diversity, valuing diversity, and gender diversity.

Importance of Diversity

Diversity is one of the most important issues for academics and sport mangers today.[47] Diversity programs have replaced most equal employment opportunity (EEO) and affirmative action programs. EEO stressed treating all employees equally, whereas affirmative action was created to correct the past exclusion of women and minorities from the workforce. Affirmative action programs established some percentages and quotas. Although quotas are no longer used, many organizations actively recruit a diverse workforce, because they now realize that such a workforce responds better to problems. In other words, diversity is a good strategy in gaining competitive advantage. People with diverse backgrounds bring diverse experiences and viewpoints to bear on problems, and more creative solutions are often the result. Diversity helps the individual, the group, and the organization.[48]

If you think that diversity doesn't really matter, or that it will not affect you, think again. The United States population continues to grow, with around 311.6 million people,[49] and it is rapidly diversifying.[50] However, the Caucasian population is not growing, as there is one birth for every death.[51] The population growth is coming from minorities, and more than half the growth is from Hispanics, as they are now the largest minority group.[52] Today, in 10 states, white children are a minority, and in 23 states, minorities now make up more than 40% of the child population.[53] One in 12 children (8%) born in America is an offspring of illegal immigrants; these children are U.S. citizens.[54] By around 2040, less than one-half of the total U.S. population will be Caucasian.[55] The diversification of America is clearly affecting us as individuals, as well as business and government. This trend isn't going to change, and you will witness the shifting percentages as you continue to age. Even if it wanted to, do you believe any pro team could function without minority employees and players?

If you think that prejudice and discrimination are no longer real problems, think again. Augusta National had a long history of refusing to allow female members.[56] Discrimination lawsuits now rank among the leading types of crises faced by business leaders. Discrimination is one of the more pressing issues in organizations today, including those in sport and leisure. Perhaps nowhere are discrimination and oppression more evident than in NCAA Division IA intercollegiate athletics.[57] Although Title IX opened the doors for equality of the sexes in the United States, female athletes often don't truly have equal support,[58] and women face constraints in sport organizations.[59] Also, there are negative attitudes toward lesbians and gay men, confirming sexual prejudice.[60]

Women and minorities are underrepresented in coaching and upper-level management positions of sport organizations.[61] Some people think that African Americans make good players but not good coaches, or that they don't want to coach. This stereotype is a myth.[62] However, maybe a new leadership style will be part of the future of NFL teams. The 2007 Super Bowl was a matchup between two coaches, the Indianapolis Colts' Tony Dungy and the Chicago Bears' Lovie Smith, who tended to use a servant management style. This means they first learned to lead themselves and then learned to lead their teams. Their persona was a much friendlier, kinder, supportive type of manager. Dungy and Smith didn't curse or sarcastically chew out players, which makes them stand out in the NFL's scream-and-holler culture. Both believe they can get their teams to complete more fiercely and score more touchdowns by giving directions calmly and treating players with respect.[63] Their method of leadership was not just a management style but a lifestyle philosophy. Their message is that life is as important as winning.

Tony Dungy was also known to gather the respect of his players. One former player, Marcus Jones, said that people just didn't want to let Tony down by losing a game. "He gives us enough space to where we can be our own people. At the same time, he's a no-nonsense guy." Marcus played for Dungy while on the Tampa Bay Buccaneers. Interestingly, Dungy was fired by the Buccaneers even though his team regularly made it to the playoffs.

Dungy's defensive coordinator, Monte Kiffin, commented, "You don't feel pressure coaching for him. You can just be yourself instead of wondering, 'What if I do something wrong and upset the coach?'"[64]

The Super Bowl matchup had the extra excitement of two African American men coaching against each other after having coached together. They became close friends when Dungy hired Smith as an assistant coach for the Tampa Bay Buccaneers. Lovie Smith said, "I think a lot about John Thompson (NCAA Basketball), Bill Russell (NBA)–black coaches who were able to win it for the first time. Again, and I speak for Tony Dungy when I say this, we are just happy as much as anything to lead our two teams with an opportunity to win it all."[65]

Valuing Diversity

Organizations have a moral obligation to accept all employees, irrespective of their individual differences.[66] When organizations value diversity, they focus on training everyone in their workforce—from all the different races and ethnicities, religions, ages, and abilities, as well as both men and women—to function together effectively so that all employees are treated fairly and justly. The interest in diversity arises from the notion that a diverse workforce can bring real, tangible benefits to the organization.[67] The goal is a climate of dignity and trust, and in such a climate everyone wins. The organization wins because its workforce has a synergy that is fertile ground for creativity and innovation, and this can only help the organization in its ultimate goal of continuously improving customer value. The workforce wins because work becomes a place people can enjoy and value for its fairness and team spirit and on which they can build a good life.

To attain this ideal climate, organizations need to find ways to manage diversity, because with diversity come numerous belief systems, mores, and culturally acceptable and unacceptable ways of behaving that sometimes conflict. Recall table 2.1 in chapter 2, which details some cultural differences.

Think about something as simple as pointing your finger. This is OK in some cultures—it is just a way to identify what you're referring to. But it is considered rude in other cultures and even obscene in some. Or take personal space—this varies around the world, and when personal space is violated, people get very uncomfortable. But we don't go around asking our colleagues whether we're in their personal space. Take winning in a team sport—different cultures handle winning and losing very differently. This is where diversity management and training come in. Don't look at diversity training and management as a pesky task to be merely tolerated—it is an opportunity to understand our world better and an opportunity for personal, professional, and organizational growth.

As shown in figure 6.3, a solid diversity management program requires four building blocks. The first and most important building block is the support and commitment of top management. People throughout the organization look to management to set the example. If top management is committed and actively supports diversity programs, others will follow their lead—hence the term diversity leadership. Diversity leaders and their teams develop the diversity policies and practices that the entire organization commits to. The final building block is, of course, diversity training. Skill-Builder 6.2 on diversity training will help examine your values and belief system about working in a diverse workforce.

Gender Diversity

Do you agree that there is a lack of women in senior-level athletic administration positions?

Before we discuss gender issues, complete the Self-Assessment to determine your attitude toward women in the workplace. Female readers should complete this assessment also; you may be surprised at what you learn!

Although women's sports are growing, it's hard to make social change to true equality between the sexes. Do women get equal treatment at work today? According to the U.S.

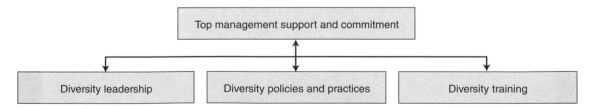

FIGURE 6.3 Managing diversity.

178

Census Bureau, despite the Equal Pay Act, which was passed more than 30 years ago and requires equal pay for the same job, women's earnings were 77.4% of men's in 2010, compared to 77.0% in 2009.[68] Some sport organizations have promoted women to high-level positions (e.g., the International Olympic Committee, the Canadian Interuniversity Sport organization, and the NCAA). Springfield College, which is known as the birthplace of basketball and where around one-third of the student body play on 27 intercollegiate athletic teams and more than 70% of the student body play intramural sports, had its first female AD in 2000. However, the glass ceiling is still a fact of life as women struggle to access middle and upper managerial jobs in commercial, voluntary, and nonprofit sport organizations.[69] According to the National Golf Foundation, golf is dominated by men.[70] Part of the reason is that men have the power in all types of sports and so far have been able to keep it.[71] Women have largely been limited to coaching other women, whereas men commonly coach both men and women. Men coach women's NCAA basketball and the WNBA, but women do not tend to coach men's NCAA basketball or the NBA. In youth sport in many areas, mothers are generally not role models, because it is much more common for the fathers to coach their daughters. Females are also much more willing to watch males play sports than males are to watch females.

Title IX was actively debated in 2007, which was the 35th anniversary of the landmark U.S. decision. The third prong stipulates that a school is in compliance if it "is fully and

SELF-ASSESSMENT 6.1

Women at Work

For each statement, select the response that best describes your belief. (Be honest!)

Strongly agree	Agree	Not sure	Disagree	Strongly disagree
5	4	3	2	1

_____ 1. Women lack the education necessary to get ahead.

_____ 2. Women's entering the workforce has caused rising unemployment among men.

_____ 3. Women are not mentally strong enough to succeed in high-pressure management jobs.

_____ 4. Women are too emotional to be effective managers.

_____ 5. Women managers have difficulty in situations calling for quick and precise decisions.

_____ 6. Women work to earn extra money rather than to support a family.

_____ 7. Women are out of work more often than men.

_____ 8. Women quit work or take long maternity leaves when they have children.

_____ 9. Women have a lower commitment to work than men.

_____ 10. Women lack the motivation to get ahead.

_____ Total

To determine whether you have a positive or negative attitude, total your score and place it on the following continuum.

Positive attitude				Negative attitude	
10	20	30	40	50	

Each statement represents a commonly held attitude about women in the workplace. However, research has shown all of these statements to be false. Such statements stereotype women unfairly and create glass ceilings.

effectively accommodating the interests and abilities of the underrepresented sex." The clarification allows institutions to use web-based surveys to demonstrate insufficient interest. Former world number-one female tennis player and current women's rights advocate Billie Jean King called the clarification ludicrous, suggesting that most females will not take the time to complete the surveys.[72]

A Title IX decision that carried a significant amount of damages was awarded during the 35th anniversary of the landmark decision. Lindy Vivas, a former Fresno State University volleyball coach, was awarded U.S.$5.85 million for having been illegally fired from her coaching position. A jury ruled that the school discriminated against her for speaking up on behalf of female athletes. The more Lindy Vivas asked for equal opportunity (adequate equipment and practice facilities) for her team, the more her male counterparts worked against her.[73]

Sexual Harassment

Women are also more commonly sexually harassed than men at work, and same-sex harassment also takes place at work. Sexual harassment is any unwelcome behavior of a sexual nature. Actions such as touching private body areas (defined for kids as the bathing suit area) or requiring sex for getting, keeping, or advancing on the job are considered sexual harassment the first time. With other sexual behavior, however, things are not always so clear, as illustrated in Applying the Concept ahead. When you are in doubt, tell the person not to repeat the behavior again or you will report the offense as sexual harassment; if the behavior is repeated, report it internally; and if no satisfactory action is taken, consider legal action with the Equal Employment Opportunity Commission (EEOC). For more information on sexual harassment, visit the EEOC website at www.eeoc.gov.

Mentoring

A word about mentoring is pertinent here. Mentors are highly skilled people who prepare promising employees for advancement; they function at every level of the organization. Mentoring enhances management skills, encourages diversity, and improves productivity. Mentoring programs also help women and minorities break the glass ceiling.

Skilled mentors can help you develop expertise, poise, confidence, and business savvy. Ask about mentoring opportunities at work. If your organization doesn't have a mentoring program, seek out a person whose professional attributes you admire and would like to emulate and ask him or her to mentor you.

APPLYING THE CONCEPT 6.4

Sexual Harassment

Check each behavior that would be considered sexual harassment in the workplace.

_____ 16. Jose tells Claire she is sexy and he'd like to take her out on a date.

_____ 17. Sue tells Josh he'll have to go to a motel with her if he wants that promotion.

_____ 18. Joel and Kathy hang pictures of nude men and women in their office cubicles in view of people walking by.

_____ 19. For the third time after being politely told not to, Jamal tells Anita a sexually explicit joke.

_____ 20. Ray puts his hand on his secretary Lisa's shoulder as he talks to her.

Organizational Development

Organizational development (OD) is the ongoing planned change process that organizations use to improve performance. HR departments (discussed in chapter 7) are usually responsible for OD. Change agents are people selected by HR management to be responsible for the OD program. Change agents may be members of the organization or hired consultants.

Lewin's Change Model

In the early 1950s, Kurt Lewin developed a model that is still used today to change people's behavior and attitudes. Lewin's change model consists of three steps (see table 6.3).

1. Unfreezing: This involves reducing the strength of the forces that maintain the status quo. Organizations often accomplish unfreezing by introducing information that shows discrepancies between desired performance and actual performance.

2. Moving: In this step, behavior begins to shift to the desired behavior. That is, people begin to learn the new desired behavior, and they also begin to embrace the values and attitudes that go with it. Shifts in strategy, structure, technology, and people or culture may be needed to attain the desired change.

3. Refreezing: The desired change becomes the new status quo. Reinforcement and support for the new behavior are often required for refreezing.

TABLE 6.3　Two Change Models

Lewin's change model	Comprehensive change model
Step 1: Unfreezing	Step 1: Recognize the need for change.
Step 2: Moving	Step 2: Identify possible resistance to the change and plan how to overcome it.
Step 3: Refreezing	Step 3: Plan the change interventions.
	Step 4: Implement the change interventions.
	Step 5: Control the change.

Comprehensive Change Model

Today's rapidly evolving business environment has necessitated expansion of Lewin's original model. The expanded model (also presented in table 6.3) involves the following actions:

1. Recognize the need for change. Clearly state the change needed—set objectives. Consider the systems effect—that is, how will the proposed change affect other areas of the organization?

2. Identify possible resistance to the change and plan how to overcome it. Use the resistance matrix in figure 6.2 on page 171, and then follow the guidelines in table 6.3.

3. Plan the change interventions. A careful diagnosis of the problem (step 2) often indicates the appropriate interventions. (Interventions are discussed next.)

4. Implement the interventions. Change agents oversee the interventions (from start to finish) to bring about the desired change.

5. Control the change. Follow up to ensure that the change is being implemented and maintained. Make sure the objective is met. If not, take corrective action.

Change Interventions

OD interventions are specific actions taken to implement specific changes. What follows is a brief survey of common interventions (see figure 6.4).

Training and Development

Most interventions include some form of training and development.[74] Training is the process of developing skills, behaviors, and attitudes that will enhance performance. MLB players, for example, spend the month of March in Florida and Arizona in spring training. During this time, teams work on developing hitting, pitching, and fielding skills. (We examine training and development in more detail in chapter 7.)

Force-Field Analysis

Particularly useful for small-group (4-18 members) problem solving, **force-field analysis** involves assessing current performance and then identifying the forces hindering change and those driving it. The result is a diagram that gives an overview of the situation (see figure 6.5 for an example). The process begins with an appraisal of current performance—this assessment appears in the middle of the

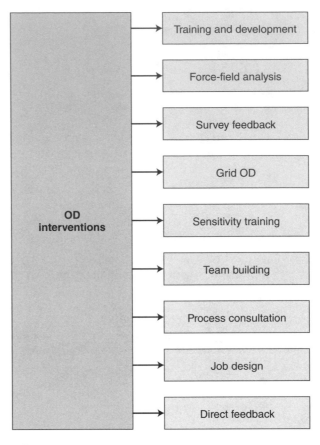

FIGURE 6.4 Organizational development interventions.

diagram. Forces that are holding back performance (hindering it) are listed at the left side of the diagram. The forces driving change are listed at the right side. Diagramming the situation clarifies thinking and helps change agents develop strategies. The basic thrust is to find ways to strengthen the driving forces and simultaneously diminish the hindering forces. The diagram often points the way to a promising strategy. As an example, we created a force-field diagram (see figure 6.5) for a hypothetical footwear company that has been losing market share. Our analysis indicates that the footwear company should focus on production and sales forecasting.

LEARNING OUTCOME 8 ▶

State how force-field analysis and survey feedback differ.

Survey Feedback

One of the oldest and most popular OD techniques, **survey feedback** uses a questionnaire to gather data that are used as the basis for change. Survey feedback is commonly used in step 1 of the change model. Different change agents use slightly different approaches; however, a typical survey feedback includes six steps:

1. Management and the change agent do preliminary planning to develop an appropriate survey questionnaire.

2. The questionnaire is administered to all members of the organization or unit.

3. The survey data are analyzed to uncover problem areas for improvement.

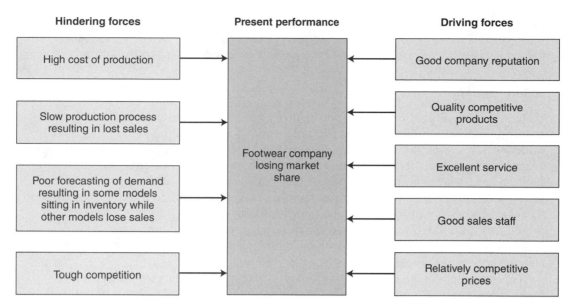

FIGURE 6.5 Force-field diagram for a footwear company.

4. The change agent presents the results to management.

5. Managers evaluate the feedback and discuss the results with their teams.

6. Corrective intervention action plans are developed and implemented.

Grid OD

Robert Blake and Jane Mouton have developed a packaged approach to OD. Grid OD is a six-phase program, with a standardized format, procedures, and fixed goals, designed to improve management and organizational effectiveness. The six phases are as follows:

Phase 1: Training. Teams of five to nine managers, ideally from different functional areas, are formed. During a weeklong seminar, team members assess their own leadership style by determining their position on the grid. (You will learn about the grid in chapter 12.) They work at becoming "9,9 managers" (also explained in chapter 12) who show high concern for production and people by developing skills in team building, communication, and problem solving.

Phase 2: Team development. Managers return to the job and use their new skills as 9,9 managers.

Phase 3: Intergroup development. Work groups improve their ability to cooperate and coordinate their efforts. This is fostered by joint problem-solving activities.

Phase 4: Organizational goal setting. Management develops a model for the overall organization that it will strive to achieve.

Phase 5: Goal attainment. The changes needed to become the model organization are determined and implemented.

Phase 6: Stabilization. The first five phases are evaluated to determine whether implementation is working, to stabilize positive changes, and to identify areas that need improving or altering.

Sensitivity Training

Sensitivity training includes a training group (a T-group) of 10 to 15 people. The training sessions have no agenda. People learn about how their behavior affects others and how others' behavior affects their own. Understanding each other's styles and qualities helps people get along better. The popularity of T-groups peaked in the 1970s as organizations questioned the on-the-job value gained through the training. Although T-groups are still used, they have largely been replaced by team building and process consultation.

LEARNING OUTCOME 9 ▶

Explain the difference between team building and process consultation.

Team Building

Team building is probably the most widely used OD technique, besides training; it includes training, and its popularity will continue to grow as more companies use teams. **Team building** helps work groups increase structural and team dynamics and thus performance. Team building is a powerful tool and a crucial one as well, because team effectiveness and ineffectiveness, both within teams and between teams, affect the results of the entire organization. Team building can be used as a comprehensive program, in which top executives first go through the program and then go through it with their middle managers, who then go through it with their groups, and so on throughout the organization. However, team building is more widely used by new or existing groups to pinpoint ways to improve effectiveness.[75]

Team-building activities are quite diverse—indeed, they use many techniques developed in coaching sports. Teams may play in a golf tournament, play a single game of baseball or rugby, or participate in an "autocross" competition in which teams are timed as they drive cars through obstacle-course drills until a winning team is determined. The activities are tied to classroom instruction on the principles of effective team building.

Team-building goals The goals of team-building programs also vary considerably, depending on the group's needs and the change agent's skills.[76] Typical goals include the following:

- To clarify the objectives of the team and the responsibilities of each team member
- To identify problems preventing the team from accomplishing its objectives
- To develop team problem-solving, decision-making, objective-setting, and planning skills
- To develop open, honest working relationships based on trust and an understanding of group members

Discuss a part of the team-building program that Tony Dungy used successfully.

The team-building program Team-building agendas and the length of time vary with team needs and the change agent's skills.[77] Typical programs go through six stages:

1. Climate building and goals: The program begins with change agents' establishing a climate of trust, support, and openness. Change agents discuss the program's purpose and goals based on data gathered before the program. Team members learn more about each other and share what they would like to accomplish through team building.

2. Structure and team dynamics evaluation: Team building endeavors to improve both how the work is done (structure) and how team members work together as they do the work (team dynamics). The team evaluates its strengths and weaknesses in both areas.

3. Problem identification: Change agents use interviews or feedback surveys to help the team identify its strengths and its weaknesses (areas it would like to improve). The team next lists several areas where it can improve and then prioritizes these areas in terms of how improving each area will help the team improve performance.

4. Problem solving: The team takes the top priority and develops a solution. It then moves down the priorities in order of importance. Force-field analysis may be used here for problem solving.

5. Training: Team building often includes some form of training that addresses the problems facing the group.

6. Closure: The program ends with a summary of what has been accomplished. Team members commit to specific improvements in performance. Follow-up responsibilities are assigned, and a meeting is scheduled to evaluate results.

Process Consultation

Process consultation is often used in the second stage of team building, but it is also commonly used as a separate, more narrowly focused intervention. **Process consultation** improves team dynamics. Whereas team building frequently focuses on how to get the job done, process consultation focuses on how people interact as they get the job done. Team dynamics (or processes) are about how the team communicates, allocates work, resolves conflict, and handles leadership and how leadership solves problems and makes decisions. Change agents observe team members as they work to give them feedback on the operative team processes. Under the change agent's guidance, the team discusses its processes and how to improve them. Training to improve group processes may also be conducted at this point. The ultimate objective is to train the group so that process consultation becomes an ongoing team activity. (We examine team dynamics in more detail in chapter 9.)

Job design, discussed in chapter 5, is also an OD intervention. Job enrichment, which is part of job design, is commonly used.

Direct Feedback

Situations can occur, particularly with rapidly changing technologies, that require a solution outside the company's core expertise. In these situations, outside consultants are often brought in to act as change agents and to recommend action directly. For example, some pro teams have hired IBM to set up their computer systems.

 TIME-OUT 8 Give an example of an OD intervention used recently in your firm or team. Was it effective? Why or why not?

APPLYING THE CONCEPT 6.5

OD Interventions

Identify the appropriate OD interventions for each situation.

a. training and development
b. force-field analysis
c. survey feedback
d. grid OD
e. sensitivity training
f. team building
g. process consultation
h. job design
i. direct feedback

_____ 21. We're not winning, our fans are leaving in droves, our costs are skyrocketing, the voters are unhappy about funding expensive stadiums that are often empty at games, and the players are about to go on strike.

_____ 22. Everyone can see that team morale is at an all-time low—but why?

_____ 23. We need a new scouting system; our present one isn't delivering the goods.

_____ 24. We've got a cutting-edge fitness machine and no one to run it.

_____ 25. We've got a lot of prima donna star athletes who are more interested in publicity than in winning.

@ TAKE IT TO THE NET

Please visit www.HumanKinetics.com/AppliedSportManagementSkills and go to this book's companion web study guide, where you will find the following:

A list of websites associated with the concepts in this chapter

Exercises that you will need Internet access to complete

Online versions of chapter exercises and end-of-chapter learning aids

An exercise that helps you define the Key Terms

LEARNING AIDS

CHAPTER SUMMARY

1. Identify the driving forces behind change.

   The forces for change come from the external and internal environment. Changes in economic, social, demographic, and technological forces require organizations to adapt to their environments.

2. List the four variables of change.

   Change occurs in strategies, structures, technologies, and people.

3. Differentiate between fact, belief, and values.

   Facts are provable statements that identify reality. Beliefs cannot be proven because they are subjective, not objective. Values address what is important to people.

4. Describe the three components of organizational culture.

   The three components are (1) behavior (the actions we take), (2) values (the way we think we ought to behave) and beliefs (if–then statements), and (3) assumptions (values and beliefs that are so deeply ingrained we never question their truth). The values, beliefs, and assumptions of an organization guide its decision making and behavior.

5. State the core values of TQM.

   The core values of TQM involve a companywide focus on (1) delivering customer value and (2) continuously improving the system and its processes.

6. Describe a learning organization.

   Learning organizations consciously create a culture in which people have the capacity to learn, adapt, and change with the environments to continuously increase customer value.

7. Explain how diversity can affect innovation and quality.

   A diverse workforce can be more innovative and also more effective at achieving quality.

8. State how force-field analysis and survey feedback differ.

   Force-field analysis is used by small groups to diagnose and solve specific problems. Survey feedback uses questionnaires with large groups to identify problems; the group does not work together to solve the problem. Force-field analysis is used to solve problems identified through survey feedback.

9. Explain the difference between team building and process consultation.

   Team building is broader in scope than process consultation. Team building improves both how the work is done and how team members work together as they do the work (team dynamics). Process consultation improves team dynamics.

REVIEW AND DISCUSSION QUESTIONS

1. How do the management functions relate to change?

2. How does the systems effect relate to the four variables of change?

3. List the four stages in the change process.

4. Which of the five reasons for resisting change do you believe is most common?

5. Which of the six ways to overcome resistance to change do you believe is the most important?

6. Select two sport organizations and discuss the differences between their cultures.

7. Discuss how the two types of innovations could be used by a manufacturer of golf balls.

8. Discuss how you would use team building to improve the effectiveness of a team you are playing on or have played for.

9. Do you agree with the core values of TQM? If not, how would you change them?

10. Do you believe that online surveys are an effective method for analyzing the effectiveness of Title IX in the United States?

11. Do you consider yourself to be a creative, innovative person? Why or why not?

12. How has diversity affected you personally?

13. Should men break the glass ceiling and promote more women to top positions? Why or why not?

14. Should the government get involved in breaking the glass ceiling? Why or why not? If yes, what should the government do? State pros and cons of government involvement.

15. Do you believe that it is acceptable for people who work together to date each other?

16. Do you have a mentor? Will you get one? Why or why not?

17. As a manager, which, if any, OD interventions will you use?

CASE

Big-Time ADs

Until the late 1970s, the job of a college AD was easy. In the old days, colleges often gave the AD job to the football coach when he retired.[78] Playing golf with alumni was a big part of the job then. The times, how they change!

To say that ADs have many more job responsibilities today is a bit of an understatement. ADs in the United States supervise coaching staff and teams, oversee million-dollar budgets and requisitions, work with coaches to schedule events and travel itineraries, help plan facilities, issue contracts for home contests, watchdog player eligibility, maintain records of players and insurance coverage for all athletes, manage crowd behavior at events (are you tired yet?), fund-raise, attend booster club meetings, supervise the sport information director, maintain marketing publications, attend professional meetings, develop staff, and conduct weekly meetings to monitor progress!

The AD job is just one of many positions in large U.S. collegiate organizations—college sports are big business today. The AD may have an associate director, a sport information director, academic advisors, ticket managers, and event managers. For instance, at Ohio State University, Gene Smith is in his seventh year as AD.[79] He oversees a department of more than 300 employees, 377 acres (1.52 square kilometers) of land, 16.9 million square feet (1.57 square kilometers) of buildings, 926 varsity athletes, and 36 varsity sports. His major constraint (besides human ability) is the National Collegiate Athletic Association rulebook. Ohio State must comply with these rules or face sanctions. Smith has a nine-person NCAA rules-compliance staff.

AD jobs are also more complicated because external factors are changing so rapidly. ADs must keep up with legal issues such as Title IX in the United States, which requires equal access to education (including athletics) for women. Recruiting athletes is increasingly competitive because more colleges actively pursue athletes as they endeavor to build winning teams. And unfortunately, athletes (like the wider population) face a wide variety of social problems such as AIDS, drug addiction, and sexual harassment.

Fund-raising is a constant endeavor—athletic operations are extremely expensive. The athletic department at Ohio State is expected to operate like a business and at least break even. As AD, Gene Smith uses the sales and marketing strategies of professional sport: seat licenses, luxury boxes, corporate sponsorships, new arenas, and high ticket prices. In fiscal year 2006, Ohio State's athletic department earned a profit of U.S.$2.9 million on revenues of U.S.$104.7 million. The football team alone brought in U.S.$60.7 million with a net profit of U.S.$28.4 million.[80]

However, the Ohio State football team was not to play in the postseason in 2012, and the program was to lose nine scholarships between 2012 and 2015 as a result of a scandal that cost football coach Jim Tressel his job. The NCAA found Ohio State guilty of failure to monitor the program after it said eight players had received cash from the owner of a tattoo parlor. AD Smith was surprised that the punishment was so severe.[81]

Would you like to be an AD? An assistant AD? A coach? A sport information director? Visit www.jobsatosu.com for information on jobs in Ohio State's athletic department.

Case Questions

Select the best alternative for the following questions. Be able to explain your answers.

1. The forces for change in an AD's job came from which environment?
   a. external
   b. internal
   c. both

2. The change variable in AD jobs has primarily been what type of change?
   a. strategy
   b. structure
   c. technology
   d. people

3. ADs in the United States are not obliged to provide equality for women's sports.
   a. true
   b. false

4. Part of the reason for change in an AD's job responsibilities was to make the athletic department more cost-effective.
   a. true
   b. false

5. The primary way to overcome resistance to change as an AD is by
   a. developing a trust climate
   b. planning
   c. stating why change is needed and how it will affect employees

d. creating a win–win situation

e. involving employees

f. providing support

g. all of the above

6. An AD's job should be organized around the principles of TQM.

a. true

b. false

7. Ohio State has learned to use professional marketing techniques such as corporate sponsorships to keep up with increasing costs in running an athletic department.

a. true

b. false

8. ADs perform which of the following job responsibilities?

a. helping plan facilities

b. watchdogging player eligibility

c. scheduling events

d. organizing travel itineraries

e. all of the above

9. Managing diversity is an important part of an AD's job.

a. true

b. false

10. ADs are in a position to mentor many employees.

a. true

b. false

11. In what sorts of situations do you think ADs use team-building skills?

SKILL-BUILDER EXERCISES

Skill-Builder 6.1: Identifying Resistance to Change

Objective

To develop your ability to identify resistance to change

Preparation

Following are 10 statements made by people who were asked to make a change. Identify the source and focus of their resistance using the matrix given in figure 6.2 on page 171. (Because it is difficult to identify intensity of resistance on paper, skip the intensity factor in this Skill-Builder. However, when you deal with people on the job, don't skip this step, because it is often very important.) Select the number (1-9) of the resistance matrix box that best describes the responses.

_____ 1. "But we've never done the butterfly stroke that way before—can't we just do it the way we've been doing it?"

_____ 2. Star tennis player Jill is asked by her coach to try Louise as her doubles partner. Jill's response: "Come on, coach, Louise is a lousy player. Betty is much better; please don't break us up."

_____ 3. Team manager Winny tells Mike to stop letting everyone on the team take advantage of him by sticking him with extra work. Mike's response: "But I want the team to like me—if I don't help people, they might not like me."

_____ 4. "I can't learn to use the new computer—I'm just a jock, and I'm not smart enough."

_____ 5. Star defensive back Chris is asked to help develop a rookie player: "Do I have to? I broke in our last rookie, Wayne. He and I are getting along really well."

_____ 6. Rookie Tina has an idea for a new soccer play. Coach Chuck quickly dismisses it—"Learning this new play would be a waste of time; our current plays are fine."

_____ 7. Diane organizes ticket sales. Her manager, Sue, directs her to take on a new responsibility—arranging the softball team's travel itinerary. Diane's response: "The job I'm doing now is more important."

_____ 8. "I don't want to play with that team. It has the lowest performance record in the league."

_____ 9. "Keep me in the kitchen part of the sports bar. I can't work the bar because drinking is against my religion."

_____ 10. "But I don't see why I have to stop showing pictures of racing car accidents to help sell tickets to our racing events. I don't think it's unethical. Our competitors do it."

In-Class Application

Complete the preceding skill-building preparation before class.
Choose one (10-30 minutes):

- Break into groups of three to five members and present your findings on the preceding questions. Try to reach a group consensus on the most probable resistance for each statement.
- Conduct informal, whole-class discussion of student findings.

Wrap-Up

Take a few minutes to write your answers to the following questions:
What did I learn from this experience? How will I use this knowledge?

_____

_____

_____

_____

As a class, discuss student responses.

Skill-Builder 6.2: Diversity Training

Objective

To increase your appreciation for the value of diversity and your understanding for what it feels like to be different

Preparation

Fill in the blanks. (You can elect not to share your responses in your group.)

Race and Ethnicity

1. My race: _____. My ethnicity: _____.

2. My name is _____. It is significant because it means _____ or I was named after _____.

3. One positive thing about being a _____ is _____.

4. One difficult or challenging thing about being a _____ is _____.

Religion

5. My religion: _____.

6. One positive thing about being a _____ is _____.

7. One difficult or challenging thing about being a _____ is _____.

Gender

8. My gender: _____.

9. One positive thing about being a _____ is _____.

10. One difficult or challenging thing about being a _____ is _____.

11. Men and women are primarily different in _____ because _____.

Age

12. My age: _____.

13. One positive thing about being my age is _____.

14. One difficult or challenging thing about being my age is _____.

Ability

15. I am of (high, medium, low) ability in college and on the job. I (do, don't) have a disability.

16. One positive thing about being of _____ ability is _____.

17. One difficult or challenging thing about being of _____ ability is _____.

Other

18. One major way in which I'm different from other people is _____
_____

19. One positive thing about being different in this way is _____
_____

20. One difficult or challenging thing about being different in this way is _____
_____

Prejudice, Stereotypes, Discrimination

21. Describe ways in which you have been prejudged, stereotyped, or discriminated against.

_____

_____

_____

_____

In-Class Application

Complete the preceding skill-building preparation before class.
Do each activity (10-30 minutes for each):

- Break into groups of three to five members. Strive to make your group as diverse as possible. If necessary, your instructor will reassign students to improve group diversity. Present your findings on the previous questions. Select a spokesperson to present one or two of your group's best examples for item 21 to the class.
- In your group, role-play the stereotyping situation assigned to you by your instructor. Discuss how it feels to be on the receiving end of stereotyping.
- Conduct informal, whole-class discussion of student findings.

Wrap-Up

Take a few minutes to write your answers to the following questions:
What did I learn from this experience? How will I use this knowledge?

_____

_____

_____

_____

As a class, discuss student responses.

SPORTS AND SOCIAL MEDIA EXERCISES

1. Does your local professional sport team have a diversity policy on its website?

_____

_____

2. If you were the marketing director for your local professional sport team, what forms of electronic media would you use to promote the diversity goals of your team?

_____

_____

_____

GAME PLAN FOR STARTING A SPORT BUSINESS

Building an organization with a diverse workforce doesn't just happen. Can you think of three strategies to help increase diversity in your new sport organization?

1. Diversity strategy 1 _____

2. Diversity strategy 2 _____

3. Diversity strategy 3 _____

Human Resources Management

LEARNING OUTCOMES

After studying this chapter, you should be able to

1. describe the four parts of HR management;

2. differentiate between a job description and a job specification and explain why they are needed;

3. state the two parts of attracting employees;

4. explain how hypothetical questions and probing questions differ;

5. state the purposes of orientation and training and development;

6. describe job instructional training;

7. define the two types of performance appraisals;

8. explain the concept "You get what you reward";

9. state the two major components of compensation;

10. describe how job analyses and job evaluations are used; and

11. give a brief history of labor relations in Major League Baseball.

KEY TERMS

human resources management

bona fide occupational
   qualification (BFOQ)

strategic human resources
   planning

job description

job specifications

recruiting

selection

assessment centers

orientation

training

development

vestibule training

performance appraisal

compensation

job evaluation

comparable worth

labor relations

salary caps

reserve clause

free agent

collective bargaining

strike

lockout

DEVELOPING YOUR SKILLS

The most important resource of any organization is its people—human resources (HR). You need to understand the HR laws and regulations—the rules of the game—to be a successful sport manager. HR managers need to recruit and select talented employees and players to win games. They also need good managers and coaches to train and develop the human resources. In addition, they need to evaluate the HR performance, retain top talent, and possibly engage in union negotiations. On a more personal level, in this chapter, you can develop your skills by using the models to interview candidates, train HR, and assess their performance. You may also consider HR management as a sport management career.

REVIEWING THEIR GAME PLAN

Finding Job Openings in Sport Management

The goal of many sport management students is to work in the sport industry. How do you make this career goal happen? Learn to work with HR departments. The HR department of an organization is involved in the entire hiring process. This includes helping write the criteria for the job opening, posting the advertisement in various publications and on websites, selecting the initial set of candidates, interviewing the candidates, and negotiating a salary and benefit package for the chosen candidate.

The first step in job searching is to research the field of interest. Conduct a broad search of current job openings to gain some insight into the various types of positions that HR departments are trying to fill. As of this writing, the following were six available positions advertised at www.teamworkonline.com.

1. Executive Director, Golden State Warriors Community Foundation - Golden State Warriors (Oakland, CA)

2. Vice President of Sales and Marketing - Sportsdigita (Minneapolis, MN)

3. Ms&E Corporate Ticket Account Executive - Sacramento Kings (Sacramento, CA)

4. Creative Services Coordinator - New Orleans Hornets (New Orleans, LA)

5. Premium Seating Manager - Sacramento Kings (Sacramento, CA)

6. Assistant, Human Resources - Memphis Grizzlies (Memphis, TN)

The sixth position listed was specifically in the field of human resources. The HR assistant for the Memphis Grizzlies of the NBA provides assistance in recruitment and staffing, personnel records, employee relations, benefits, and training. Starting as an assistant in HR can lead to a career as the vice president of HR for an organization. Would you like to work in HR?

For current information on job openings in sport management, please visit www.teamworkonline.com. (For more information on careers in sport management, see the appendix.)

LEARNING OUTCOME 1 ▶
Describe the four parts of HR management.

Human Resources Management Process and Department

Every team and organization is only as good as its players and workers. Thus, the key driver of business success is HR management practices of hiring and developing great people. HR management is about helping the entire organization understand and manage its people, and you should be

 TIME-OUT 1 | Describe your experiences with the HR department in the organization you work for or play for.

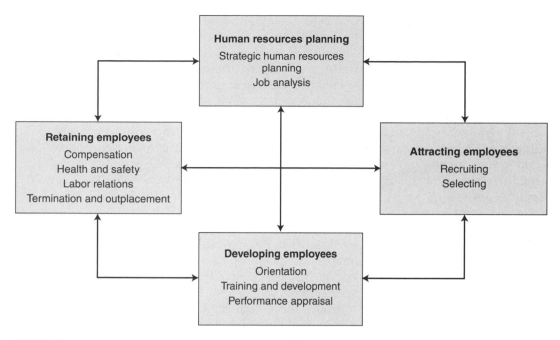

FIGURE 7.1 Managing human resources.

committed to treating your people well.[1] **Human resources management** (also known as staffing) consists of planning, attracting, developing, and retaining employees. HR practices affect firm performance. Figure 7.1 gives an overview of this four-part process; the arrows indicate how the parts mesh to create a systems effect. For example, how an organization compensates its employees affects the caliber of people it will attract; labor relations affect planning; job analysis affects training; and turnover affects attracting and developing employees. Thus, systems thinking is important to sport management.

One of the four major functional departments in organizations, the HR department is a staff department that advises and assists all other departments. Larger companies (usually about 100 or more employees) tend to have a separate HR department that plans HR practices for the entire organization. HR managers are responsible for developing HR practices and systems,[2] which you will learn about throughout this chapter.

Legal Environment

All organizations have to conduct business in accordance with the law. It is the job of the HR department to ensure that everyone in the organization complies with the law. The laws tell organizations what they must and must not do. Recall the importance of Title IX, which requires equality for females in sport in the United States.[3] Also, Title VII of the Civil Rights Act of 1964 *prohibits employment discrimination based on race, color, religion, sex and national origin.*[4] Just as all athletes should be treated fairly and justly, irrespective of differences, so should all employees.[5] The legal environment affects HR practices in significant ways, so understanding HR law is important to sport management. As a manager, you will most likely be involved in hiring employees; and if you break the law you and your organization can get into legal problems and end up in court, and you can even be sent to jail. This section teaches you the basics of HR equal employment opportunity law and what you can and can't ask candidates during employment recruiting.

Equal Employment Opportunity

Equal employment opportunity (EEO), a 1972 amendment to the U.S. Civil Rights Act of 1964, prohibits discrimination in the workplace on the basis of sex, religion, race or color, or national origin and applies to virtually all private and public organizations in the United States that employ 15 or more employees. Who is considered a minority by the EEO? Just about anyone who is not a white male, not of European heritage, or not adequately educated. Thus, in the United States, Hispanics, Asians, African Americans, American Indians, and Alaskan natives are minorities. Women are not a minority, but they also get protection. The EEO also protects disadvantaged young people, disabled workers (Americans With Disabilities Act), and people older than 40 years (Age Discrimination in Employment Act).[6]

Although the law protects women from discrimination in employment, they are not considered a legal minority in the United States because they make up half of the population and in some situations constitute a majority. Also, although overweight people are not a minority in the United States (127 million American adults are overweight, and nearly 70 million are obese), overweight people in the United States suffer discrimination in selection and hiring, promotions, earning potential, and compensation.[7]

The Equal Employment Opportunity Commission (EEOC), which is responsible for enforcing EEO mandates, has field offices across the United States and operates a toll-free line (1-800-USA-EEOC) around the clock to provide information on employee rights. It also has a website (www.eeoc.gov). If you are not sure whether your HR policies are legal, contact the EEOC.

The U.S. General Counsel is responsible for conducting EEOC enforcement litigation under Title VII, the Equal Pay Act, the Age Discrimination in Employment Act, and the Americans With Disabilities Act. Violation of antidiscrimination laws can lead to investigation by the EEOC or to class action or individual lawsuits. Courts find discrimination when selection criteria are vague, elusive, unstructured, undefined, or poorly conceived. As a manager, you should be familiar with your organization's EEO compliance. Although laws are in place and progress has been made, discrimination in HR practices still exists in the United States.

Preemployment Inquiries

No one in your organization—not recruiters, interviewers, other HR staff, or line managers—can legally ask discriminatory questions, either on the application or during interviews. Here are two rules to guide you:

1. Be sure that every question you ask is job related. When developing questions, make sure you have a purpose for using the information. Ask only for information that you plan to use in the selection process.

2. Ask all candidates the same general questions. Asking women and minorities different questions can lead to legal problems.

> **TIME-OUT 2** Have you or anyone you know ever been asked for discriminatory information when you were screened for a job? If yes, explain the situation.

The list under "Preemployment Inquiries" summarizes U.S. laws concerning what you can ask for during the selection process (lawful information you can use to disqualify candidates) and what you cannot ask for (prohibited information you cannot use to disqualify candidates). Complete the Applying the Concept box on page 198 for a better understanding of what questions are and are not legal to ask.

Actually, an organization can discriminate legally for a **bona fide occupational qualification (BFOQ)** for the job. A BFOQ allows organizations to base their hiring decisions on otherwise discriminatory attributes that are reasonably necessary to the normal operation of a particular organization. For instance, being a practicing Jew is not a BFOQ for a fitness instructor at a Jewish Community Center; however, being a practicing Jew is a BFOQ for a rabbi and teacher of Jewish religion classes. If challenged, the organization must provide evidence that the BFOQ is needed to do the job.

What BFOQ would an HR assistant for the Memphis Grizzlies have to be concerned with if she were trying to fill a senior equipment mechanic position?

Preemployment Inquiries

Topic	Can ask	Cannot ask
Name	Current legal name and whether the candidate has ever worked under a different name	Maiden name or whether the person has changed his or her name
Address	Current residence and length of residence there	Whether the candidate owns or rents his or her home
Age	Whether the candidate's age is within a certain range (if required for a particular job; for example, an employee must be 21 to serve alcoholic beverages); if hired, can ask for proof of age	How old are you? What is your date of birth? Can you provide a birth certificate? How much longer do you plan to work before retiring?
Sex	Candidate to indicate sex on an application if sex is a BFOQ	Candidate's sexual preference
Marital and family status	Whether candidate can adhere to the work schedule; whether the candidate has any activities, responsibilities, or commitments that may affect attendance	Specific questions about marital status or any question regarding children or other family issues
National origin, citizenship, or race	Whether the candidate is legally eligible to work in the United States, and whether the candidate can provide proof of status if hired	Specific questions about national origin, citizenship, or race of candidate or parents and relatives
Language	What languages the candidate speaks, writes, or both; can ask candidate to identify specific language or languages if these are BFOQs	What language the candidate speaks when off the job or how the candidate learned the language
Criminal record	Whether the candidate has been convicted of a felony; if the answer is yes, can ask other information about the conviction if the conviction is job related	Whether the candidate has ever been arrested (an arrest does not prove guilt); for information regarding a conviction that is not job related
Height and weight	Whether the candidate meets BFOQ height or weight requirements and whether the candidate can provide proof if hired	Candidate's height or weight if these are not BFOQs
Religion	Whether candidate is of a specific religion if religious preference is a BFOQ; whether the candidate must be absent for religious reasons or holidays	Candidate's religious preference, affiliation, or denomination if not a BFOQ
Credit rating or garnishments	For information if a particular credit rating is a BFOQ	Unless it is a BFOQ
Education and work experience	For information that is job related	For information that is not job related
References	For names of people who are willing to provide references or who suggested the candidate apply for the job	For a reference from a religious leader
Military record	For information about candidate's military service that is job related	Dates and conditions of discharge from the military; National Guard or reserve unit of candidate
Organizations	About membership in job-related organizations, such as unions or professional or trade associations	About membership in any non-job-related organization that would indicate candidate's race, religion, or the like
Disabilities	Whether candidate has any disabilities that would prevent him or her from performing the job being applied for	General questions about disabilities (focus on abilities, not disabilities)

Legal or Illegal Questions

Use "Preemployment Inquiries" to identify the following 10 preemployment questions as

a. legal (can ask)

b. illegal (cannot ask)

_____ 1. What languages do you speak?

_____ 2. Are you married or single?

_____ 3. How many dependents do you have?

_____ 4. Are you a member of the racecar drivers' union?

_____ 5. How old are you?

_____ 6. Have you been arrested for stealing on the job?

_____ 7. Do you own your own car?

_____ 8. Do you have any form of disability?

_____ 9. What type of discharge did you get from the military?

_____ 10. Can you prove you are legally eligible to work?

Human Resources Planning

HR develops the HR plans for the entire organization. HR practices guide employees as they carry out the mission, strategy, and objectives of the firm. **Strategic human resources planning** is the process of staffing the organization to meet its objectives. The job of the HR department is to provide people with the right skills at the right time to meet their goals.[8] If a company's strategy is growth, then employees will need to be hired. If its strategy is retrenchment, then there will be a layoff. One study found that few sport organizations have adopted a formal HR strategy, and HR practices vary widely across organizations.[9] Hiring strategies in professional sport are important elements affecting competitive balance among teams and revenue sharing.

General managers (GMs) of professional sport teams need to be involved in strategic HR management. The director of player development for professional teams typically spends time finding replacements for injured players, working on problems with the coaching staff, and preparing for contract negotiations. The GMs help to decide when a team releases an aging player, when a player is no longer worth a long-term contract, and which free agents are worth large amounts of cap money. If GMs don't answer these questions correctly, they will likely be fired.

LEARNING OUTCOME 2 ▶

Differentiate between a job description and a job specification and explain why they are needed.

Job Analysis

Strategic HR planning determines the number of people and skills needed, but it does not specify how each job is to be performed. An important part of HR planning is reviewing information about the job itself. Job design (chapter 5) is the process of developing and combining the tasks and activities that compose a particular job. *Job analysis* is the process of determining what the position entails and the qualifications needed to staff the position. Thus, job analysis is the basis for the job description and the job specifications.

The **job description** identifies the tasks and responsibilities of a position. In other words, it identifies what employees do all day to earn their pay. See the sample job description ahead for the athletic director of Division III Elms College.[10]

The next step is to determine **job specifications.** Job specifications identify the qualifications needed to staff a position. The job specifications thus identify the types of people needed. It answers the question, What competencies are important for performing the job?[11]

TIME-OUT 3

Perform a job analysis on your current job or one you recently held. Use your analysis to write a simple job description and job specifications. Were you given a realistic job preview when you were hired? Explain.

The process of planning and job analysis is an important first HR activity because it is your basis for the other three HR processes: attracting, developing, and retaining employees. If you don't understand the job, how can you select employees to perform it? How can you train them to do the job? How can you evaluate their performance? How do you know how much to pay them?

An essential part of job analysis is developing a *realistic job preview (RJP)*. The RJP provides the candidate with an accurate, objective understanding of the job. Research indicates that employees who believe they were given accurate descriptions are more satisfied and express a lower desire to change jobs than do those who believe they were not given an accurate job description. The RJP can lead to job satisfaction, which tends to improve performance.[12]

Attracting Employees

◀ LEARNING OUTCOME 3
State the two parts of attracting employees.

After hiring needs have been determined and jobs analyzed, the HR department typically recruits promising applicants, and line managers select people to fill positions. Thus, it is a good idea for you to understand the recruiting and selecting process even if you don't choose HR as your career. During your career you will be interviewed, and as a manager you will most likely conduct job interviews. This section discusses recruiting methods and the selection process and then teaches you how to prepare for and conduct a job interview. Although our focus is on hiring, many nonprofits (NGOs) also have to attract volunteers, who need to be recruited and selected, especially for mega-events like the Olympic Games.[13]

Recruiting

Recruiting is the process of attracting qualified candidates to apply for job openings. For an organization to fill an opening, possible candidates must be made aware that the organization is seeking employees. They must then be persuaded to apply for the jobs. For instance, recruiting and retaining sport management professors have been challenging in recent years. Professors with sport management doctorates are in short supply and in high demand as numerous colleges add new sport management programs to their offerings. Administrators have to use all types of recruitment methods to attract qualified new doctorate and experienced sport professors. The website higheredjobs.com is increasingly used by colleges and universities to recruit for sport-related positions.[14] Recruiting is conducted both internally and externally; figure 7.2 lists more possible recruiting sources.

General managers have to recruit players by selling unique factors to attract star athletes. GMs try to attract players by highlighting the nice weather, the large and enthusiastic fan base, the option to live in a large urban city, and so on. When LeBron James of the Cleveland Cavaliers became a free agent in 2010, he became part of one of the most public recruitment processes in sport. James ultimately decided to play with the Miami Heat. James left his hometown, Cleveland, to be part of Miami's plan to start him, Dwyane Wade, and Chris Bosh, who was another free-agent acquisition.[15]

NCAA football teams also need to recruit high school players to play at their universities. An ESPN study found that Florida, Texas, USC, Alabama, Florida State, Notre Dame, Georgia, LSU, Miami, Ohio State, and Oklahoma had had the best recruiting programs since 2007. Of course, recruiting great high school players to play in college is effective only if

Sample Job Description

Division III College

Position Description

Job Title: Athletic Director

Exempt (Y/N): Yes
Department: Athletics
Approved:
Incumbent:

Salary Level:
Supervisor: Vice President of Student Services
Date:
Status: Full-time, 12-month

General Responsibilities

The director is responsible for administering and developing the athletic programs and policies while supporting student athletes and coaches. He or she is responsible for all areas of compliance as applied to a Division III program.

Specific Responsibilities

- Administer all athletic programs.
- Develop athletic programs that reflect the vision outlined by the college.
- Make recommendations for the quality of all athletic programs.
- Ensure consistency between athletic programs, college policies, and strategic plan.
- Monitor compliance as it applies to the student athlete concept, the principles governing intercollegiate athletics, gender equity, NCAA Division III and conference regulations, and legislation.
- Develop marketing concepts in collaboration with the college marketing department.
- Develop and implement promotions and public relations programs in collaboration with the college marketing department.
- Plan and participate in fund-raising efforts.
- Work with the dean of academics and the dean of students to integrate and administer a high-quality athletics program.
- Supervise all summer sports camps for children.
- Manage and oversee department budgets.
- Lead and supervise direct reports.
- Develop and implement student athlete recruiting strategies that are in agreement with the approach and philosophy of the admissions office.
- Monitor recruiting efforts by coaches, making adjustments as needed.
- Monitor coaching styles to reflect the college philosophy surrounding student athletes, making adjustments as needed.
- Work collaboratively with the human resources office to ensure that college personnel policies and issues are handled with consistency.

These duties and responsibilities are required of this position. However, the list is not all-inclusive. Other responsibilities and duties may be assigned to meet mission or strategic plan requirements of the college, and cooperation of all personnel is expected.

Supervisory Responsibilities

- Administrative assistant
- Contest management
- Director, sport information
- Athletic trainers
- Full-time and part-time coaches

Qualifications and Requirements

Education, Experience, Skills

The ideal candidate for this position will have demonstrated skills and experience in strategic leadership, written and oral communications, creative approaches, problem solving, operations, and administration management. Qualifications include a master's degree in athletic administration, sports management, physical education, or a related field; 5 years of related experience in a college athletic department; and conference, coaching, and NCAA experience.

Standards of Performance

- Flexibility and adaptability: Is able and willing to support the strategic plan, mission, and vision of the college.
- Judgment and decision making: Demonstrates a proactive role in judgment and decision processes.
- Communication: Maintains effective internal and external communications.
- Planning and organizing: Demonstrates skills in managing all aspects of the athletic department.
- Procedural expertise: Adheres to the procedures and processes as established by the college.
- Management of projects: Demonstrates leadership skills in meeting desired outcomes and in oversight of projects.
- Goals and objectives: Develops and implements strategies that support the goals and objectives established by the athletic department and the college.
- Use of resources: Demonstrates a prudent use of all resources.
- Safety, security, environmental awareness: Consistently exhibits behavior and department oversight that promote the safety and security of people and facilities while ensuring responsible behavior for our environment, both on and off campus.
- Promotes the college's mission, purpose, and goals and understands the role of this position in achieving those goals.

Physical Demands and Work Environment

The physical demands described here are representative of those that must be met by an employee to successfully perform the essential functions of this job. Reasonable accommodations may be made to enable individuals with disabilities to perform the essential functions. The incumbent is exposed to a typical, climate-controlled office environment and various weather-related conditions (extreme temperature ranges, rain), typical office equipment (computer, printer, fax machine, telephones), usual sport equipment, and associated items. This position requires sitting, standing, bending, reaching, vision (near, distance), walking, lifting, climbing stairs, and manual dexterity to perform essential job functions.

Reprinted, by permission, from Elms College.

they learn to win games together. The top 10 recruiting universities have won their share of NCAA National Championships.[16]

Internal Recruiting

Internal recruiting involves filling job openings with current employees or personal referrals. Promotion from within and employee referrals are two common types of internal recruiting. Others include previous employees and previous applicants who can still be contacted. NCAA Division III teams have been criticized for doing too much internal recruiting of their own graduates and have been encouraged to expand their job searches.[17]

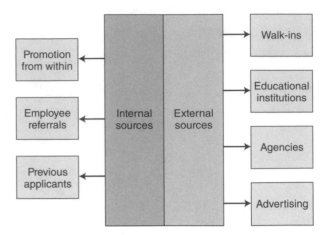

FIGURE 7.2 Recruiting sources.

TIME-OUT 4 Identify the recruiting sources used to hire you both for your current job and for previous jobs.

- **Promotions from within:** Many organizations post job openings on bulletin boards, in company newsletters, and on their websites. Current employees can then apply or bid for the open positions.

- **Employee referrals:** When job openings are posted internally, employees may be encouraged to refer friends and relatives for the positions. Typically, employees refer only good candidates. However, the government has stated that this referral method is not acceptable when current employees are predominantly white or male because it tends to perpetuate the present composition of the workforce, which results in discrimination.

External Recruiting

The following are external recruiting sources:

- **Walk-ins:** Sometimes good candidates come to the organization "cold" (i.e., without an appointment) and ask for a job. However, professionals tend to send resumes and cover letters requesting an interview.

- **Educational institutions:** Organizations recruit at high schools, vocational and technical schools, and colleges. Many schools offer career planning and placement services to aid students and potential employers. Take advantage of your career center. Educational institutions are good places to recruit people without prior experience.

- **Agencies:** There are three major types of agencies: (1) Temporary agencies, like Kelly Services, provide part- or full-time help for limited periods. They are useful for replacing employees who will be out for a short period of time or for supplementing the regular workforce during busy periods. (2) Public agencies are nationwide government state employment services in the United States. They generally provide job candidates to employers at no, or very low, direct cost. (3) Private employment agencies charge a fee for their services. Agencies are good for recruiting people with experience. *Executive recruiters* are a type of private agency often referred to as "headhunters." They specialize in recruiting managers or those with high-level technical skills, like engineers and computer experts, and tend to charge the employer a large fee.

- **Advertising:** It is important to use the appropriate media source to reach qualified candidates. A simple "Help Wanted" sign in the window may be appropriate for some positions, but newspaper ads will reach a larger audience. Professional and trade magazines are more suitable for specific skill categories.

Technology is changing how organizations recruit and select employees. Employers now routinely advertise on the Internet. Numerous websites match applicants and job opportunities. For instance, websites such as www.teamworkonline.com have become a very popular source of advertising open positions and finding new candidates. You may want to visit the website to find sport-related job openings; it has links to jobs and internships with the NBA, WNBA, NFL, NHL, and MLB. See the appendix for a list of sport management–related websites. Also, virtually every major organization's website has a link to career opportunities, with a list of job openings, most of which can be applied for online.

Selection Process

Selection is the process of choosing the most qualified applicant recruited for a job. Selection is a crucial activity because bad hiring decisions haunt an organization for years.

Organizations don't follow a universal, set sequence in their selection process. Nor do they use the same selection process for different jobs. That said, the selection process is typically composed of the application form, screening interviews, testing, background and reference checks, interviewing, and hiring. The selection process can be thought of as a series of hurdles that the applicant must overcome to be offered the job.

Application Form

The first hurdle is typically the job application form. The data that applicants provide on this form are compared with the job specifications. If they match, the applicant may progress to the next hurdle. Organizations use different application forms for different jobs. For professional jobs, resumes often replace the application form.

APPLYING THE CONCEPT 7.2

Recruiting Sources

Select the recruiting source that would be most appropriate for the five job openings described.

a. promotion from within

b. employee referrals

c. walk-ins

d. educational institutions

e. advertising

f. agencies

g. executive recruiters

_____ 11. You need a 1-month replacement for Jason, who was hurt on the job manufacturing hockey skates.

_____ 12. Bonnie, a first-line supervisor in the fitness center, is retiring in 2 months.

_____ 13. You need an engineer to design new fitness equipment with very specific requirements. There are very few people with the qualifications you want.

_____ 14. Your sales manager likes to hire young people without experience in order to train them to sell insurance to athletes.

_____ 15. The maintenance department for your athletic center needs someone to perform routine cleaning services.

Organizations also often use computers to scan application forms and resumes. Before sending a resume, find out whether the company you are applying to does this. If so, the HR department can give you specific instructions to make sure your information is scanned accurately.

Screening Interview

Specialists in HR departments often conduct interviews to screen candidates—those who they think are promising will continue in the selection process. This saves line managers precious time. Organizations also now use computers to conduct screening interviews.

Testing

Tests can be used by organizations when the tests meet EEO guidelines for validity (people who score high on the test do well on the job, and those who score low don't) and reliability (people taking the same test on different days get approximately the same score each time). Illegal tests can result in lawsuits. Testing achievement, aptitude, personality, and interest have all been deemed appropriate, as have physical exams. Many organizations are also testing for the use of illegal drugs, and candidates who fail are dropped from the search.

Both internal and external candidates for management positions are tested through assessment centers. **Assessment centers** are places where job applicants undergo a series of tests, interviews, and simulated experiences to determine their potential.

Background and Reference Checks

Carefully checking references to verify the information on a candidate's application form and resume helps organizations avoid poor hiring decisions. Unfortunately, many applications contain false statements about applicants' education and experience.

Interviewing

The interview is the most heavily weighted selection criterion and is usually the final hurdle in the selection process. Interviews give candidates a chance to learn about the job and size up the organization firsthand. (Is this a place where I want to work?) Interviews give managers a chance to size up candidates in ways that applications, tests, and references just don't. (Is he a people person? Is she a leader? Would he be more productive as a team player or as an independent contributor?) Because job interviewing is so important, in the next section we take you through the do's and don'ts of preparing for and conducting job interviews.

Hiring

After reviewing the information gathered, managers compare the candidates without bias and decide who is best suited for the job. Managers consider many criteria—qualifications, salary requirements, availability, issues of diversity in the department or organization. The chosen candidate is then contacted and offered the job. If he doesn't accept the offer—or accepts but leaves after a short period of time—the next best candidate is offered the job.

 **TIME-OUT 5** Create a simple table of the selection methods discussed in this section, and identify which ones were used for a job you were offered or for a position you were offered on a team you played for. If a test was used, specify the type of test.

SELF-ASSESSMENT 7.1

Career Development

The focus of this chapter is on hiring others. But let's take a few minutes to determine how ready you are to progress in your career.

Answer the questions on a scale from 1 to 5. Place the number (1-5) on the line before the question.

Does not describe me				Describes me
1	2	3	4	5

_____ 1. I know my strengths, and I can list several.

_____ 2. I can list several skills that I have to offer an employer.

_____ 3. I have career objectives.

_____ 4. I know the type of full-time job that I want next.

_____ 5. I have, or plan to get, part-time, summer, or internship experience related to my career objectives.

_____ 6. I have analyzed help-wanted ads or job descriptions and determined the most important skills I need to get the type of full-time job I want.

_____ 7. I know the proper terms to use on my resume to help me get the job I want (full-time, part-time, summer, internship).

_____ 8. I understand how my strengths and skills developed in school and on the job are transferable or how they can be used in jobs I apply for.

_____ 9. I can give examples (on a resume and during an interview) of how my strengths and skills can be used in the job I am applying for.

_____ 10. I can give examples (on a resume and during an interview) of suggestions or direct contributions I have made that increased performance, reduced time or cost, increased sales, or changed a process.

_____ 11. If I have limited job experience, I focus more on the skills I developed than on giving job titles, stating how the skills relate to the job I am applying for.

_____ 12. If I have limited job experience, I give details of how my college education, and the skills developed in college, relate to the job I am applying for.

_____ 13. I have a written job objective (preferably on a resume) that clearly states the type of job I want and the skills I will use on the job.

_____ 14. I have, or plan to have, a resume for every job I apply for (full-time, part-time, summer, or internship).

_____ 15. I plan to customize each resume, changing the skills and ways in which they are transferable, to each job I apply for, rather than use one generic resume for all jobs.

Add up your scores, place the number here _____, and put it on the following continuum.

Career ready						In need of career development
75	65	55	45	35	25	15

Interviewing

Interviewing is a skill you will use over and over, both as an interviewer and as an interviewee. Study this section carefully, and complete Skill-Builder 7.1 on page 226. Figure 7.3 lists the types of interviews and the types of questions used in them.

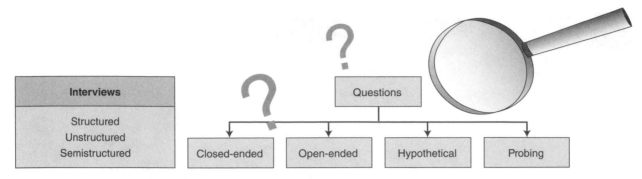

Interviews		Questions			
Structured					
Unstructured	Closed-ended	Open-ended	Hypothetical	Probing
Semistructured					

FIGURE 7.3 Types of interviews and questions.

Choosing the Type of Interview

The three types of interviews are based on structure. (1) In *structured interviews*, interviewers use a list of prepared questions to ask all candidates. (2) In *unstructured interviews*, interviewers do not use preplanned questions or a preplanned sequence of topics. (3) In *semistructured interviews*, interviewers ask questions from a prepared list but also ask unplanned questions; that is, interviewers depart from their prepared questions when they believe it is appropriate. HR people generally prefer semistructured interviews because they help

> **TIME-OUT 6** What types of job interviews have you participated in?

prevent discrimination (the prepared questions are asked of all candidates) and also give interviewers flexibility in pursuing lines of questioning and conversation that give them accurate assessments of candidates' motivation and attitudes. At the same time, the standard set of questions makes it easier to compare candidates. The amount of structure you should use in interviews depends on your experience and on the situation. The less experienced you are, the more structure will help you conduct effective interviews.

Formulating Questions

LEARNING OUTCOME 4 ▶
Explain how hypothetical questions and probing questions differ.

The questions you ask give you control over the interview; they allow you to dig out the information you need to make your decision. Make sure your questions all have a purpose and are job related. Ask all candidates for the same information.

Interviewers use four types of questions. (1) *Closed-ended questions* require a limited response, often a yes or no answer, and are appropriate for dealing with fixed aspects of the job. "Do you have a class I license and can you produce it if hired?" (2) *Open-ended questions* allow an unlimited response and are appropriate for determining abilities and motivation. "Why do you want to be a general manager for our company?" "What do you see as a major strength you can bring to our team?" (3) *Hypothetical questions* require candidates to describe what they would do and say in a given situation; these questions help you assess capabilities. "What would you do if a free-agent baseball player wanted his own private locker room?" (4) *Probing questions* require candidates to clarify some aspect of their background or some aspect brought up by the interviewer and help you understand an issue or point. Probing questions are not planned. "What do you mean by 'it was tough'?" "What was the dollar increase your team achieved in ticket sales?"

Preparing for the Interview

Going through the formalized procedure shown in figure 7.4 will help you improve your interviewing skills.

> **TIME-OUT 7** List the types of questions you have been asked when you interviewed for jobs, and give an example of each one.

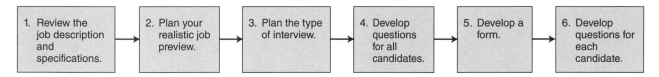

FIGURE 7.4 Preparing to interview.

1. **Review the job description and specifications.** You cannot conduct an effective interview if you do not thoroughly understand the job for which you are assessing applicants. If the job description and job specifications are outdated, or don't exist, conduct a job analysis.

2. **Plan your realistic job preview.** One of your jobs as interviewer is to help applicants understand what the job is and what they will be expected to do. They should know the job's "good news" and its "bad news." Use the job description to plan this preview. It often helps to give candidates a tour of the work area.

3. **Plan the type of interview.** What level of structure will you use? The interview should take place in a private, quiet place, without interruptions. It may be appropriate to begin in an office and then tour the facilities while asking questions. Plan when the tour will take place and what questions you will ask. Take your form with you if you intend to ask several questions.

4. **Develop questions for all candidates.** Use the job description and specifications to develop questions that relate to each job task and responsibility. Use a mixture of closed-ended, open-ended, and hypothetical questions. Don't be concerned about the order of questions; just write them down at this point. Now check that your questions are job related and nondiscriminatory. Ask them of all candidates.

5. **Develop a form.** Once you have a list of questions, determine the sequence. Start with the easy questions. One approach starts with closed-ended questions, moves to open-ended ones, and then moves to hypothetical ones, using probing questions as needed. Another approach structures the interview around the job description and specifications; the interviewer explains each and then asks questions relating to each responsibility.

Write your questions in sequence, leaving space for checking off closed-ended responses, for making notes on the responses to open-ended and hypothetical questions, and for writing follow-up questions. Add information gained from probing questions where appropriate. Recording the candidate's responses on this form will help guide you through the interview and help keep you on topic. Use a clean copy of the form for each candidate, and make a few extra copies to use when filling the same job in the future or to help you develop forms for other jobs.

6. **Develop questions for each candidate.** Review each candidate's application or resume. You will most likely want to verify or clarify some of the information given during the interview. "I noticed that you did not list any employment during 2012; were you unemployed during that time?" "On the application you stated you had computer training; what types of computer software are you trained to operate?" Be sure that these individual questions are not discriminatory—for example, don't ask only women whether they can lift a specific amount of weight; ask every candidate this question.

You can note individual questions on the standard form, writing them in where they may be appropriate to ask, or you can add a list at the end of the form.

Conducting the Interview

Following the steps in figure 7.5 will help make you an effective interviewer.

1. **Open the interview.** Endeavor to develop rapport with applicants. Put them at ease by talking about some topic not related to the job. Maintain eye contact in a way that is comfortable for you and for them.

FIGURE 7.5 Interviewing.

2. **Give your realistic job preview.** Be sure applicants understand the job requirements. Answer any questions they have about the job and the organization. If the job is not what they expected or want to do, allow applicants to disqualify themselves and close the interview at that point.

3. **Ask your questions.** Steps 2 and 3 can be combined if you like. To get the most out of a job interview, take notes on applicants' responses to your questions. Tell each applicant that you have prepared a list of questions and that you plan to take notes.

During the interview, applicants should do most of the talking. Give them a chance to think and respond. In addition to making sure the person fits the job requirements, you also need to determine whether the candidate fits the company and its culture. If someone doesn't give you all the information you need, ask an unplanned probing question. However, if it's obvious that the person doesn't want to answer the question, don't force it. Go on to the next question or close the interview. End with a closing question such as, "I'm finished with my questions. Is there anything else you want to tell me about or ask me?"

4. **Introduce top candidates to coworkers.** Introduce top candidates to people with whom they will be working to get a sense of their interpersonal skills and overall attitude. Introductions can also give you a sense about whether the person is a team player.

5. **Close the interview.** Be honest without making a decision during the interview. Don't lead candidates on. Thank them for their time, and tell them about the next step in the interview process, if any. Tell candidates when you will contact them—be specific, and keep your word. You might say, for example, "Thank you for coming in for this interview. I'll be interviewing over the next two days and will call [or e-mail] you with my decision by Friday of this week." (Be sure that you make that call; simple courtesy demands that you give applicants closure.) After the interview, jot down general impressions not covered by specific questions.

TIME-OUT 8

Use figure 7.5 to analyze an interview in which you were the job seeker. Did your interviewer use all the steps we have examined? If not, why might the interviewer have skipped some steps?

Avoiding Problems When Selecting

Sport managers often struggle with hiring decisions.[18] After all interviews are completed, compare each candidate's qualifications with the job specifications to determine who will be best for the job and will fit with the organizational members and culture. Gather coworkers' impressions of each candidate. Here are some tips for the selection process:

• Don't rush. Take your time—this is an important decision. Don't be pressured into hiring just any candidate. Find the best person available.

• Don't stereotype. Don't prejudge with assumptions, for example that overweight people are lazy. Don't leap to conclusions. Be objective and subjective; use analysis to match the best candidate to the job, but also trust your gut.

• Don't look for employees who are copies of you. Remember the tangible benefits of diversity (chapter 6). A department of your clones will not be an effective team. You want people with strengths that can offset your weaknesses.

- Don't look for "halos" and "horns." Don't judge a candidate on the basis of one or two favorable or unfavorable characteristics. Look at the total person and at the entire pool of candidates.

- Don't jump prematurely. Don't make your selection based solely on the person's application or resume, and don't decide right after interviewing a candidate who impressed you. Don't compare candidates after each interview. The order in which you interview applicants can be strongly influential. Be open-minded during all interviews, and make a choice only after you have finished all interviews. Compare all candidates on each job specification.

Developing Employees

After an organization has attracted employees, it must develop its employees by orienting and training them and also by appraising their performance: This is the third HR process. The topic of this section is orienting and training; in the next section, we discuss appraising performance.

Orientation

Orientation introduces new employees to the organization, its culture, and their jobs. Orientation is about learning the ropes. Effective orientation reduces the time needed to get new hires up to speed, reduces their new-job jitters, and gives them an accurate idea of what is expected of them. Good orientation and training programs reduce turnover and improve attitudes and performance. Allowing coworkers to help with orientation is a good idea because they can pass along unwritten rules of behavior and cultural norms in the organization.

Although orientation programs vary in formality and content, five elements are shared by effective programs:

1. Explaining what the organization does (products and services) and the department functions that the new person will be part of. Many organizations show videos to explain what the organization is all about.

2. Explaining what the new employee's job task and responsibilities are.

3. Going over the standing plans (policies, procedures, and rules) that need to be followed to get the job done.

4. Then giving the new employee a tour of the facilities.

5. Introducing the new employee to coworkers.

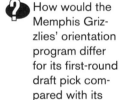

◀**LEARNING OUTCOME 5**
State the purposes of orientation and training and development.

How would the Memphis Grizzlies' orientation program differ for its first-round draft pick compared with its new ticket sales manager?

Professional leagues such as the NBA conduct orientation programs with rookie players to highlight complexities of being a professional player. The orientation includes discussions on the use of illegal drugs and fiscal responsibility.

TIME-OUT 9 Describe an orientation you participated in recently. Which elements of effective programs did it include? Which ones did it exclude?

Training and Development

Orientation and training often take place simultaneously. **Training** is about acquiring the skills necessary to perform a job. **Development** is ongoing education that improves skills for present and future jobs. The NBA has the NBA Developmental League to help young players improve their skills before entering the NBA.[19] Less technical than training, development endeavors to strengthen people skills, communication skills, conceptual abilities, and decision-making skills in managerial and professional employees. Today, ongoing training is required to help employees keep up with the latest trends, and training has been recognized as added value to both organizations and employees.

Getting back to sports, some people complain that U.S. colleges and universities are training foreign athletes to compete against Americans in the Olympics.[20] If you want to talk about cross-training, how about the fact that many of the workouts the NFL quarterbacks learn are straight from baseball, and that ex-MLB pitcher Tom House is teaching quarterbacks how to throw fastballs?[21]

Off the Job and on the Job

As the name implies, off-the-job training is conducted away from the worksite, often in a classroom setting. A common method is **vestibule training,** which develops skills in a simulated setting. Vestibule training is used to teach job skills when teaching at the worksite is impractical. In preparation for the regular season, MLB baseball players attend spring training in Florida and Arizona every spring to practice before playing on their home fields.

On-the-job training is done at the worksite with the same resources the employee uses to perform the job. Managers, or employees selected by the managers, usually conduct the training; and because of its proven track record, job instructional training is a popular method used in training worldwide. Spring training helps develop teams that are well coached and players who make fewer errors and have fewer injuries.

LEARNING OUTCOME 6 ▶

Describe job instructional training.

Job Instructional Training

Job instructional training (JIT) is composed of four steps (see figure 7.6). Remember that what *we* know well seems very simple to us, but new hires and athletes don't yet share this perspective.

1. Preparation of the trainee: Put trainees at ease as you create interest in the job and encourage questions. Explain the quantity and quality requirements and their importance.

2. Presentation of the task by the trainer: Perform the task yourself at a slow pace, explaining each step several times. Once trainees seem to have the steps memorized, have them explain each step as you perform the job at a slow pace. Write out complex tasks with multiple steps, and give trainees a copy.

3. Performance of the task by the trainee: Have trainees perform the task at a slow pace, explaining each step. Correct any errors and help them perform any difficult steps. Continue until they can perform the task proficiently.

4. Follow-up: Watch trainees perform the task and correct any errors or faulty work procedures before they become a habit. Be patient and encouraging. Tell trainees whom to go to for help with questions or problems. Gradually leave them alone. Begin by checking quality and quantity frequently, and then decrease the amount of checking based on the trainee's skill level.

Training Cycle

Figure 7.7 shows the steps in the training cycle. Following these steps ensures that training is systematic and thus effective.

TIME-OUT
10
Identify which JIT steps your trainer used to teach you your current job. Was the training on or off the job?

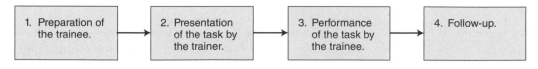

| 1. Preparation of the trainee. | → | 2. Presentation of the task by the trainer. | → | 3. Performance of the task by the trainee. | → | 4. Follow-up. |

FIGURE 7.6 Steps in job instructional training.

1. Conduct a needs assessment. Before you begin training, you must determine your staff's training needs. Based on your knowledge as a coach, what skills and plays do they need to work on?

2. Set objectives. Any training program should have well-defined, performance-based objectives. As with all plans, begin by determining the end result you want to achieve. Your objectives should meet the criteria discussed in chapter 4.

3. Prepare for training. Before conducting a training session, have written plans and all the necessary materials and equipment ready. If you have ever had an instructor come to class or a coach come to practice unprepared, you know why preparation before training is necessary for success.

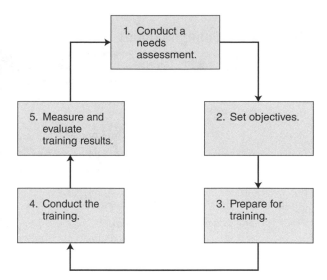

FIGURE 7.7 The training cycle.

Selecting the training method is an important part of your preparation. You have already learned about JIT. Table 7.1 lists various training methods. Whatever method you develop, break the task into steps. Write each step and go through the steps yourself to make sure they work.

4. Conduct the training. Have your written plan with you, as well as any other materials you will need.

5. Measure and evaluate training results. Linking training outcomes and results will make you more effective as a trainer. During training and at the end of the program, measure and evaluate the results to determine whether you achieved your objectives. If you met your goals, training is over. If you didn't meet your goals, either continue the training until your objectives are met or take employees off the job if they cannot meet the standards.[22] Revise and improve your written plans for future use.

Training Methods

Table 7.1 lists the various training methods available, many of which can be used as part of JIT. The third column lists the primary skill developed. However, some of the technical methods can be combined. Technical skill also includes acquiring knowledge that can be tested.

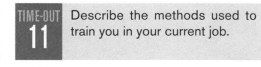

When selecting a training method, keep in mind the sequence of least effective to more effective training. People learn the least from what they read only, a little more from what they hear, and more from what they see. People learn better when combining what they see and hear, and they learn more when they talk with others. People learn much more from what they use and do in real life, and they learn even more when they teach someone else. We learn more by doing. Unfortunately, there is a big gap between knowing and doing. Filling this gap is the foundation of this book's focus on learning concepts, applying them, and developing skills that can be used in your personal and professional lives.

TABLE 7.1 Training Methods

Method	Definition	Skill developed
Written material	Trainees read manuals and books.	Technical
Lecture	Trainees listen to spoken instructions and class lectures.	Technical
Video	Trainees learn from television and class videos.	Technical
Question and answer	After using the other methods, the trainer asks the trainees questions about what they read, heard, and watched.	Technical
Discussion	A topic is presented and discussed.	Technical
Programmed learning	A computer or book is used to present material, followed by a question or problem. Trainees select a response and then are given feedback on their answers. Depending on the material presented, programmed learning may possibly develop people skills and conceptual skills.	Technical
Demonstration	Trainers show trainees how to perform the task. This is step 2 in JIT. Demonstrations can also be used to develop people skills and decision-making skills.	Technical
Job rotation	Employees learn to perform multiple jobs.	Technical and conceptual
Projects	Trainees learn via special assignments, such as developing a new product or a new team. Projects that require working with people and other departments also develop people skills and conceptual skills.	Technical
Role-playing	Trainees act out a possible job situation, such as handling a customer complaint, to develop skill at handling similar situations on the job.	People and communication
Behavior modeling	(1) Trainees observe how to perform the task correctly. This may be done via a live demonstration or a videotape. (2) Trainees role-play a situation using the observed skills. (3) Trainees receive feedback on how well they performed. (4) Trainees develop plans for using the new skills on the job.	People and communication
Cases	Trainees are presented with a situation and asked to diagnose and solve the problems involved. They are usually asked to answer questions. (Cases are included at the end of each chapter of this book.)	Conceptual and decision making
In-basket exercise	Trainees are given actual or simulated letters, memos, reports, and telephone messages typically found in the in-basket of a person holding the job they're being trained for. Trainees are asked what, if any, action they would take for each item and are told to assign priorities to the material.	Conceptual and decision making
Management games	Trainees manage a simulated company. They make decisions in small teams and get the results back, usually on a quarterly basis, over a period of several game "years." Teams are in an "industry" with several competitors.	Conceptual and decision making
Interactive video	Trainees sit at a computer and respond as directed.	Any of the skills

APPLYING THE CONCEPT 7.3

Training Methods

Select the most appropriate training method for the following situations.

a. written material
b. lecture
c. video
d. question-and-answer session
e. discussion

f. programmed learning
g. demonstration
h. job rotation
i. projects

j. role-playing
k. behavior modeling
l. management games
m. in-basket exercise
n. cases

_____ 16. Your large department has a high turnover rate. Staff must know the rules and regulations in order to sell high-quality bicycles.

_____ 17. In the athletic center you manage, you occasionally need to teach new employees how to handle problems they face daily.

_____ 18. Your boss has requested a special report.

_____ 19. You need your staff to be able to cover for each other as lifeguards at the center's swimming pool.

_____ 20. Your staff must know how to handle customer complaints about weather conditions at the ski resort you manage.

Performance Appraisals

◄ LEARNING OUTCOME 7
Define the two types of performance appraisals.

After people are hired and trained, organizations need to know how the new employees are working out. Is their performance outstanding or merely adequate? For hiring errors, dismissal may be needed.[23] The HR department is responsible for helping develop performance appraisals for long-term employee development, which is the topic for this section. Many workers and managers dread performance appraisals.[24] A major reason is that they are not conducted effectively. But if you follow our guidelines here, you can do a good job.

Performance appraisal is the ongoing process of evaluating employee performance. Performance appraisals (PAs) are a critical part of understanding and managing people. PAs come in two types—developmental and evaluative. _Developmental PAs_ are used to improve performance. _Evaluative PAs_ are used to decide pay raises, transfers and promotions, and demotions and terminations. Evaluative PAs focus on the past, whereas developmental PAs focus on the future. However, developmental plans are always based on evaluative PAs. The primary purpose of both types is to help employees continuously improve their performance. Most firms place the biggest emphasis on evaluation, which is a mistake because it doesn't develop employees.

When developmental and evaluative PAs are conducted together—which they commonly are—the developmental PA is often less effective, especially when an employee disagrees with the evaluation. Most managers are not good at both judging and coaching. Therefore, separate meetings make the two uses clear and make the process more productive for both employee and manager.

Performance Appraisal Process

Figure 7.8 shows the connection between the organization's mission and objectives and the performance appraisal process. The feedback loop indicates the need to control human

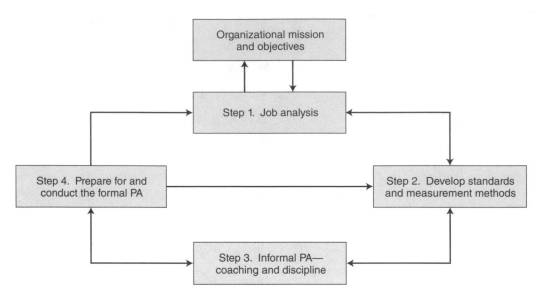

FIGURE 7.8 The performance appraisal process.

resources performance. Employees' performance should be measured against the achievement of the organization's mission and objectives (chapter 4).

1. **Analyze the job.** This includes working up the job description and job specifications. The responsibilities laid out in the job description should be ranked in order of importance.

2. **Develop standards and measurement methods.** After determining what it takes to do the job, you can develop standards and methods for measuring performance. (In the next section we describe several common measurement methods; we discuss how to set standards in chapter 13.)

3. **Carry out informal PAs through coaching and discipline.** Effective PA systems encompass more than just the once-a-year formal interview; appraising performance is an ongoing process. We all benefit from regular informal feedback on our performance. Coaching involves giving praise for a job well done to maintain performance and taking corrective action when standards are not met. Someone performing below standard may need daily or weekly coaching or discipline to meet standards. In chapter 13, we examine coaching and discipline in more detail.

4. **Prepare for and conduct the formal PA.** Follow the steps in figure 7.9, presented later in this section.

Performance Standards

Your employees need to know what the organization's standards are and what your standards are. Job performance must be defined precisely. Discrimination is prevalent within sport organizations.[25] Thus, although intuition is used in appraising performance, you need to use objective standards to help avoid discrimination. If you give an employee an average rating rather than a good one, you must be able to clearly explain why. Otherwise, you may face allegations of discrimination. The employee also needs to understand what she can do during the next appraisal period to earn a higher rating. If your standards are clear and you are coaching effectively, there should be no surprises during the formal PA. In chapter 13, you will learn how to set standards in the areas of quantity, quality, time, cost, and behavior.

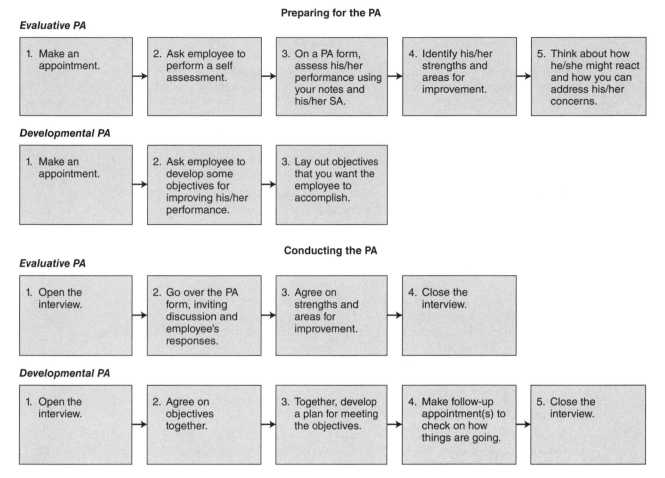

Preparing for the PA

Evaluative PA

1. Make an appointment.
2. Ask employee to perform a self assessment.
3. On a PA form, assess his/her performance using your notes and his/her SA.
4. Identify his/her strengths and areas for improvement.
5. Think about how he/she might react and how you can address his/her concerns.

Developmental PA

1. Make an appointment.
2. Ask employee to develop some objectives for improving his/her performance.
3. Lay out objectives that you want the employee to accomplish.

Conducting the PA

Evaluative PA

1. Open the interview.
2. Go over the PA form, inviting discussion and employee's responses.
3. Agree on strengths and areas for improvement.
4. Close the interview.

Developmental PA

1. Open the interview.
2. Agree on objectives together.
3. Together, develop a plan for meeting the objectives.
4. Make follow-up appointment(s) to check on how things are going.
5. Close the interview.

FIGURE 7.9 Steps in solid performance appraisals.

You Get What You Reward

◀ LEARNING OUTCOME 8
Explain the concept "You get what you reward."

All of us will do what we are rewarded for doing. We seek information concerning what activities are rewarded and then endeavor to do (or at least pretend to do) those things, often to the exclusion of activities not rewarded. The extent to which this occurs depends on the attractiveness of the rewards. For example, if a professor gives a class a reading list of several sources but tells students (or the students realize without being told) that they will not discuss those sources in class or be tested on them, how many students will acquire and read this list? How about if your professor tells that you A, B, and C from this chapter will be on the test, but X, Y, and Z will not? Would you spend equal time studying both groups? So clearly tell employees what you expect, and reward (or punish) accordingly.

Measurement Methods

People giving formal PAs often use a standard form (typically rating scales) developed by the HR department to measure employee performance. Table 7.2 lists commonly used PA measurement methods. Which PA method is best? This depends on your objectives, on the type of people in your group, on the work being evaluated, and on your organization's culture. Combinations usually work better than any one method. For developmental PAs, critical incidents and management by objectives (MBO) work well because they are tailored to the individual. For evaluative PAs, ranking methods work well because they help you select the best.

TABLE 7.2 Performance Appraisal Measurement Methods

Critical incidents file: Managers note an employee's positive and negative performance behavior throughout the performance period. This form of documentation is particularly necessary in today's litigious environment.	**Ranking:** Managers rank employee performance from best to worst. That is, managers compare employees to each other, rather than comparing each person to a standard measurement. An offshoot of ranking is the forced distribution method, which resembles grading on a curve. A predetermined percentage of employees are placed in performance categories: for example, excellent—5%; above average—15%; average—60%; below average—15%; and poor—5%.
Rating scale: Managers simply check off the employee's level of performance. Typical areas evaluated include quantity of work, dependability, judgment, attitude, cooperation, and initiative.	**Management by objectives (MBO):** Managers and the employee jointly set objectives for the employee, periodically evaluate the person's performance, and reward according to the results (see chapter 4 for details).
Behaviorally anchored rating scale (BARS): This method combines rating and critical incidents. It is more objective and accurate than the two methods separately. Rather than using ratings like *excellent, good, average, and poor*, managers choose from several statements the one that best describes the employee's performance for the given task. A good BARS makes standards clear.	**Narrative:** Managers write a statement about the employee's performance. The system varies. Managers may be allowed to write whatever they want, or they may be required to answer specific questions about performance. Narratives are often combined with another method.

The problem with most PA forms is that they include measures of non-performance-related stuff, like initiative, creativity, willingness to take responsibility, and promotability, which nobody really knows how to measure. As a result, employees try to please the boss rather than focus on results. Under these conditions, having a good relationship with your boss—not results—gets you ahead in the firm. Such measures are also very subjective. Successful PAs depend on your people skills as a manager and on your fair and objective analysis.

Performance Appraisal Interview

Always plan before you conduct PA interviews. Everybody comes out ahead when you are well prepared. Figure 7.9 gives you the steps you should follow in your all-important preparation and in the interview itself. When you conduct interviews, encourage employees to talk. You want them to feel free to talk and to share concerns; employees' feeling of freedom (or lack thereof) builds the trust (or distrust) that makes them more open (or closed) to viewing the evaluation objectively. Note that figure 7.9 presents the preparation and conduct of the evaluative and developmental PAs separately. We do this to show you how they differ and also how they resemble each other. Note the collaborative tone in the steps. Remember, you and the employee are on the same side—maximizing their potential is in the best interest of both of you.

As an employee, you should relish a development conversation, because it is your opportunity to improve your performance and thus get ahead in the organization. So be sure to leave your PA with a clear understanding of how to improve your performance for the next session.

Retaining Employees

We have discussed the HR processes of planning, attracting, and developing employees, so now we present the fourth and last process—retaining employees. Organizations must

APPLYING THE CONCEPT 7.4

Selecting Performance Appraisal Methods

Use table 7.2 to select the most appropriate PA method for the given situation.

a. critical incidents

b. rating scales

c. BARS

d. ranking

e. MBO

f. narrative

_____ 21. The roller-skating rink you started 6 years ago now has 10 employees. You're overworked, so you want to develop one PA form that you can use with every employee.

_____ 22. You've been promoted to middle management at Golf Balls Deluxe. You've been asked to select your replacement.

_____ 23. Winnie, who markets the new line of basketballs, isn't performing up to standard. You decide to talk to her about ways she can improve her performance.

_____ 24. You want to create a system for helping employees realize their potential.

_____ 25. Your roller-skating rink has grown to 50 employees. Some of them are concerned that the form you're using doesn't work well for the various jobs, so you've hired a professional to develop a PA system that is more objective and job specific. You have specifically asked him to develop more focused PA forms.

have HR systems in place to retain good people. High turnover rates can reduce productivity and profitability.[26] Replacing a good employee is expensive; costs vary depending on the job. Thus, organizations go to great lengths to keep the employees they have because it's the biggest way to save money.[27] If you became a manager of a Walmart sporting goods department, you'd face an 85% turnover rate of your staff. If you had 100 employees, 85 would have to be attracted and developed every year, so the organizing management function of interviewing and training would take up most of your time. In the nonprofit sector, retaining volunteers is also critical to many organizations, including the Olympic Games.

There are numerous strategies for retaining employees. People who believe they are being justly rewarded tend to stay with an organization. A good work environment keeps people. So do challenging work and good feedback.[28] And so does an informed and highly skilled HR department. Therefore, in this section we examine three areas that affect employee retention: compensation, health and safety, and labor relations. Because no company has 100% employee retention, we also discuss termination and outplacement.

Compensation

◀ LEARNING OUTCOME 10
State the two major components of compensation.

Compensation is the total cost of pay and benefits to employees. Compensation is pivotal in both attracting and retaining employees. Compensation schemes are also related to performance. For example, NCAA Division III has less funding and thus can have more challenges in attracting and retaining coaches than does Division I. An important strategic decision is the organization's pay level. Pay level refers to whether the organization aims at being a high-, medium-, or low-paying organization. Low-paying firms may save money by low-balling wages, but such savings can be lost to the high cost of turnover. However, Division III colleges can offer coaches and sport managers an opportunity to work in a smaller educational system, often in a rural atmosphere. Overall, sport managers need to be ethical and not discriminate when compensating employees.

Pay Systems

There are three general compensation methods, and organizations use all three. (1) Wages are paid on an hourly basis. (If you work 40 hours, you get paid your hourly wage times 40 hours.) (2) Salary is figured weekly, monthly, or annually but does not take into account the number of hours worked. (If you work 30 hours or 75 hours, your weekly salary stays the same.) (3) Incentives are paid for performance, which can motivate employees to higher levels of performance. Incentives include piece rate (pay based on production), commissions (pay based on sales), merit raises (the more productive workers get paid more), and bonuses. Two common bonuses include a specific reward for reaching an objective and profit sharing, in which employees get a part of the profits. Pay for performance is also commonly used. Professional athletes sometimes receive enormous salaries regardless of performance—MLB player Alex Rodriguez was the highest paid at U.S.$32 million for the 2012 season.[29] MLS soccer star David Beckham made $46 million in compensation (pay and sponsorships) in 2012.[30] However, many athletes are paid a base amount and then get incentive pay if they perform well—that is, if they reach a certain number of hits, touchdowns, quarterback sacks, or games played. General managers believe that incentive pay motivates players to excel—to give it their all.

LEARNING OUTCOME 10 ▶

Describe how job analyses and job evaluations are used.

Determining Pay

How much to pay each employee is a difficult decision that all organizations face. Some organizations use an external approach—they find out what other organizations pay for the same or similar jobs and set their pay based on that. Other organizations use an internal approach that involves job evaluation. **Job evaluation** determines the worth of each job relative to other jobs in the organization. Organizations commonly group jobs into pay grades. The higher the worth or grade of the job, the higher the pay. The two approaches are frequently used together. Comparable worth is yet another approach that has been around for a while but remains controversial. In **comparable worth,** jobs that are distinctly different but that require similar levels of ability, responsibility, skills, and working conditions are valued equally and paid equally. This means that many jobs traditionally held by women would rise in pay, even though we have previously valued them less than certain jobs traditionally held by men. In 2012, Congress considered a comparable-worth bill, but as in the past, it did not become a law.

Benefits

Benefits are the part of a compensation package that is not direct wages. They are also not merit based. Legally required benefits in the United States include workers' compensation to cover job-related injuries, unemployment compensation for when people are laid off or terminated, and Social Security for retirement. Employers match the amount the U.S. government takes out of each person's pay for Social Security. Benefits that are technically optional but that are offered in almost all large U.S. companies are health insurance; paid sick days, holidays, and vacations; and pension plans. Optional benefits (health insurance and pension plans) are commonly split between employee and employer or are paid completely by the employee. Other benefits less commonly offered include dental and life insurance, membership to fitness centers, membership in credit unions, and tuition reimbursement. Benefits such as elder care and child care are also on the increase as organizations focus on work–life issues.

The benefits portion of compensation packages has been increasing over the years,

TIME-OUT 12 Describe the compensation package offered by your employer.

primarily attributable to the high cost of health insurance. The benefits portion varies with the level of job from one-third to two-thirds of compensation, but it has been estimated that the average U.S. worker receives slightly more than 40% of her compensation from benefits.

Health and Safety

The U.S. Occupational Safety and Health Act (OSHA) of 1970 requires U.S. employers to pursue workplace safety. Employers must meet OSHA safety standards, maintain records of injuries and deaths attributable to workplace accidents, and submit to on-site inspections. HR departments commonly are responsible for ensuring the health and safety of employees. They work closely with other departments and often conduct new-hire training and ongoing training in this area as well as maintaining health and safety records. A growing area of concern is workplace uncivil behavior and violence. To learn more about the U.S. Department of Labor's OSHA, visit www.osha.gov.

 Do you think an HR assistant for the Memphis Grizzlies has to be concerned with OSHA?

As a manager, you must know the safety rules, make sure that your employees know them, and enforce them to prevent accidents. OSHA investigated the death of Minnesota Vikings offensive lineman Korey Stringer, who died of heatstroke during practice. OSHA determined that the Vikings managers were not to blame. They had given their athletes proper training on heat stress and provided ample water and a first aid truck.[31] Stringer's death led some teams to add some more safety measures, such as providing plenty of ice, water, and shade for all players.[32]

Labor Relations

◀ **LEARNING OUTCOME 11**
Give a brief history of labor relations in Major League Baseball.

Labor relations are the interactions between management and unionized employees. Labor relations are also called *union–management relations* and *industrial relations*. There are many more U.S. organizations without unions than there are with unions. Therefore, not all organizations include labor relations as part of their HR systems. Unions are organizations that represent employees in collective bargaining with employers. They are also a source of recruitment. In the United States, the National Labor Relations Act (also known as the Wagner Act, after its sponsor) established the National Labor Relations Board (NLRB) in 1935; this board conducts unionization elections, hears unfair labor practice complaints, and issues injunctions against offending employers.[33] (To learn more about the NLRB, visit www.nlrb.gov.)

There are typically five stages in forming a union, as figure 7.10 shows.

Union Organizing in Baseball

American baseball has outlasted panicky owners, spoiled players, scandal, and embarrassment for more than 100 years. America's national pastime thus provides a rich example of labor relations. Conflicts between baseball players and owners date back to the 1880s. Fans have endured five strikes since 1966, and the owners have locked players out three times. The following brief history provides a background for labor issues in pro sports.

Salary caps are the maximum amount of money a team can spend on players. Today, capologists are hired to help teams stay under the salary cap limit. The Denver Broncos hired longtime NFL player agent Mike Sullivan to run their salary cap as director of football administration. Denver hired Sullivan to direct the club's negotiating and structuring of all player contracts.[34]

However, back in the 1880s, MLB owners established the first salary cap in pro sport— their U.S.$2,000 salary cap was not peanuts, although it seems paltry today, even taking into account inflation. MLB's first challenge to its hold on the sport came in 1913, when Federal Base Ball (FBB) tried to start a new league. Eventually, FBB's major investors joined up with MLB.

Player–owner spats continued unabated, however. Have you heard of the Black Sox scandal? Eight White Sox players threw the 1919 World Series, supposedly because of owner

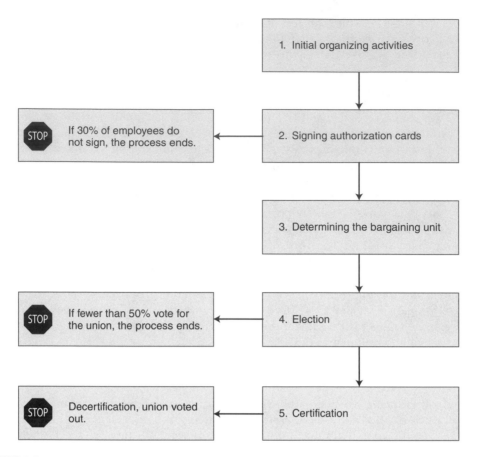

FIGURE 7.10 The union-organizing process.

Comiskey's stinginess.[35] Players who dared to criticize management's infamous reserve clause (which basically married players to their clubs for life with no chance of divorce) were called "persons of avowed Communist tendencies" by 1949 Brooklyn Dodgers executive Branch Rickey. The **reserve clause** allowed teams to automatically re-sign their players at the end of the season. By the 1950s, star players were creating their own associations to discuss such issues as minimum salaries and retirement pensions. However, these associations were not real unions, so the owners didn't take them seriously.

By the 1960s, baseball players began to believe that a players' union was the only way to negotiate better benefits. LA Dodgers star pitchers Sandy Koufax and Don Drysdale held out before the 1966 season. When they did sign, both players received substantial salary increases. Koufax settled for 1 year at U.S.$125,000, and Drysdale accepted U.S.$110,000.[36]

The late 1960s and early 1970s saw the players' union try to break management's infamous reserve clause. In 1969, St. Louis Cardinals star player Curt Flood asked for a substantial salary increase but instead found himself promptly traded to the Philadelphia Phillies. He sued to stay in St. Louis. This case went all the way to the U.S. Supreme Court, which ruled against Flood, citing the Federal Base Ball decision of 1915. The Flood case showed that the Supreme Court was unwilling to change the reserve system.[37]

A successful challenge to the reserve clause didn't occur until the 1970s. The first case came when Charles Finley, owner of the Oakland Athletics, withheld part of Catfish Hunter's U.S.$100,000 salary. Hunter's contract stipulated that half of his salary go toward purchasing an annuity in an insurance fund. Finley didn't pay because of a tax question, so he had not fulfilled the contract; and this allowed Hunter to become a **free agent,** a player who is free to negotiate a contract with any team. Catfish Hunter went on to sign a huge contract with the New York Yankees, and it was the beginning of the end for the reserve system.

Rather than sit out the 1975 season, Andy Messersmith of the Los Angeles Dodgers played under the standard contract that was renewed by the Dodgers, but he never signed it. Courts later ruled that when Messersmith chose to play at the Dodgers' option, but without signing the new contract, he became a free agent. Today, subsequent to several versions of free agency, free agents can sign with any team that will sign them, and the original team receives a draft pick.

Owners and players still tangle periodically. The 1976 baseball season started without a contract, so owners locked players out of spring training that year. Owners were subsequently found guilty in court of three instances of collusion. *Collusion* meant that the owners were guilty of working together to organize how they would bid or not bid for free-agent ballplayers. The 1994-1995 baseball season ended in a strike, and the World Series was cancelled. Even the 2002 season was played under the shadow of labor tensions and threats of a strike. Fortunately, the two sides were able to negotiate a last-minute settlement, and the 2002 season was completed as scheduled. Since 2002, there has been an ongoing investigation of the use of steroids in baseball. However, in terms of labor relations in baseball between owners and players, it has been a period of peaceful coexistence.

Collective Bargaining

Collective bargaining is the process whereby unions and management negotiate a contract that covers employment conditions at the organization. Contracts typically stipulate compensation, hours, working conditions, and health benefits. Contracts can include other issues—job security, for example, which is a hot issue for unions today. The NFL and the NFL Players Association met regularly before the 2011-2012 off-season as their previous contract was due to expire. However, the two sides could not agree, and a lockout situation occurred. The two sides finally reached an agreement late in the summer of 2011. When they agreed, there was a tender moment between the New England Patriots owner, Robert Kraft (whose wife had passed away days earlier), and player Jeff Saturday from the Indianapolis Colts. The two sides agreed on player health and safety issues; for example, players can remain in a medical plan for life, and $50 million was set aside for medical research and health care programs.[38] Retired players would receive $900 million to $1 billion over the next decade, with $620 million ticketed for pre-1993 retirees. Players can become unrestricted free agents after four accrued seasons.[39]

Another collective bargaining example is the 2011-2012 NBA season, which was shortened to a 66-game season. The NBA and the player's union had a difficult time negotiating a new labor contract. The league wanted to reduce player costs since it claimed that many teams were no longer profitable. The players wanted the rich teams to be able to spend money to help keep free-agency bidding competitive. The complicated final agreement allows the league to save $3 billion over 10 years while the players will still have a competitive free-agent market. Many experts felt that the NBA "won" the labor dispute since the players were struggling with the concept of not having a season.[40]

The NBA season eventually started on Christmas Day with great fanfare. The fans quickly returned to watching and attending NBA basketball games. The television ratings for the NBA Finals were the same as they had been the previous year—with one fewer game.[41]

To avoid a **strike** (employees refuse to go to work) or a **lockout** (management refuses to let employees in to work) and to handle grievances by either side, involved parties sometimes agree to use neutral third parties, called *mediators*, from the U.S. Federal Mediation and Conciliation Service. Mediators are neutral parties who help management and labor settle disagreements. In cases in which the two parties are unwilling to compromise but still want to avoid a strike or lockout, they may choose to call in an arbitrator. *Arbitrators* differ from mediators in that arbitrators' decisions are binding (must be followed). Arbitrators more typically work to settle grievances; mediators deal with impasses in collective bargaining.

The NHL arbitration process pits the team management (which downplays a player's worth) against a player's agent (who plays up the player's value). An independent arbitrator selects a 1- or 2-year award no more than 48 hours later. A team then has 48 hours to accept the award or walk away from it. Does player performance increase, decrease, or remain the same after a free agent changes teams?

Termination and Outplacement

Employees leave organizations in two ways: (1) voluntarily (for other jobs or for other reasons like retirement or health issues) and (2) involuntarily (because they are fired or are laid off). These employees usually need to be replaced. Employees who leave voluntarily are often interviewed to find out why they are leaving. The exit interview, usually conducted by the HR department, helps identify problem areas that may be causing turnover. Involuntary termination occurs in one of two ways—firing (when employees break important rules or are otherwise found wanting) and layoffs (which occur because of downturns in the economy or problems in the organization and through mergers and acquisitions). There is an ongoing research debate about an optimal level of turnover that is good for the organization.[42]

In 2007, the Carlsbad-based golf equipment company TaylorMade-adidas Golf cut its workforce by 41. The cuts were the result of determining how well the company's workforce met its needs.[43] When companies undergo layoffs, they sometimes offer outplacement services to help employees find new jobs. Why would companies bother? The reasons are simple—for goodwill (they may want to hire those people back someday) and to avoid wrongful-termination lawsuits.

As we bring this chapter to a close, you should understand the HR process of planning (job analysis and the HR legal requirements), attracting employees (recruiting and selecting), developing employees (orientation, training and development, and performance appraisal), and retaining employees (compensation, health and safety, labor relations, termination, and outplacement).

@ TAKE IT TO THE NET

Please visit www.HumanKinetics.com/AppliedSportManagementSkills and go to this book's companion web study guide, where you will find the following:

- A list of websites associated with the concepts in this chapter
- Exercises that you will need Internet access to complete
- Online versions of chapter exercises and end-of-chapter learning aids
- An exercise that helps you define the Key Terms

LEARNING AIDS

CHAPTER SUMMARY

1. Describe the four parts of HR management.

    The four parts are (1) human resources planning, (2) attracting employees, (3) developing employees, and (4) retaining employees.

2. Differentiate between a job description and a job specification and explain why they are needed.

    Job descriptions identify what a worker does on the job, whereas job specifications list the qualifications needed to do the job. Job analysis is an important basis for attracting, developing, and retaining employees.

3. State the two parts of attracting employees.

   The two parts are recruiting and selecting. Recruiting is about persuading qualified candidates to apply for job openings. Selecting is about choosing the most qualified applicant recruited for a job.

4. Explain how hypothetical questions and probing questions differ.

   Hypothetical questions are planned; they require candidates to describe what they would do and say in a given situation. Probing questions are not planned and are used to clarify responses.

5. State the purposes of orientation and training and development.

   Orientation introduces new employees to the organization, its culture, and their jobs. Training and development help employees acquire new skills that they will use to perform present and future jobs.

6. Describe job instructional training.

   Job instructional training includes (1) preparation of the trainee, (2) presentation of the task, (3) performance of the task by the trainee, and (4) follow-up.

7. Define the two types of performance appraisals.

   Developmental PAs are used to improve performance. Evaluative PAs are used to determine pay raises, transfers and promotions, and demotions and terminations.

8. Explain the concept "You get what you reward."

   People seek information concerning what activities are rewarded and then endeavor to do those things, often to the exclusion of activities not rewarded.

9. State the two major components of compensation.
   The two components are pay and benefits.

10. Describe how job analyses and job evaluations are used.

    Job analyses determine what the job should entail and the qualifications needed to staff the position. Job evaluations determine how to pay employees for their work.

11. Give a brief history of labor relations in Major League Baseball.

    MLB labor relations have been difficult for more than 100 years. Both managers and players have tangled over such issues as salary caps, reserve clauses, free agency, and benefits. The result has been a series of strikes and lockouts. The two sides tiptoed past another strike in 2002. Since 2002, aside from the ongoing investigation of steroid use in baseball, labor relations between owners and players have been peaceful.

REVIEW AND DISCUSSION QUESTIONS

1. How do you feel about bona fide occupational qualifications?

2. What are the components of a job analysis?

3. What do you think about promoting from within for pro baseball teams? Why would this work or not work?

4. Should the interview be the primary criterion in selecting a coach? Why or why not?

5. What website helps people find jobs in sport?

6. Suppose the firm you work for has an HR department. What does this mean for you as a manager? What services will this department typically provide? What will you still need to do?

7. How does setting objectives affect measuring and evaluating training results for a general manager? For a coach? For an athlete?

8. How does compensation help attract and retain employees? Why do some organizations elect to be low-paying organizations whereas others elect to be high-paying ones?

9. Why don't most employees realize how expensive benefits are and how much they contribute to compensation cost?

10. Do players expect more than they are worth? Or do management and owners take too large a share of the profits for themselves? What do their stances imply for the future of pro sports?

11. What is the difference between mediators and arbitrators?

12. Define the reserve clause and free agency.

13. Curt Flood's name is often associated with free agency. But what other players followed Flood to help create the process of free agency?

14. What is the difference between a strike and a lockout?

15. How do you feel about the saying that it's not what you know but who you know that counts in getting a job? Is using connections to get a job a form of positive discrimination? To reduce discrimination, should using connections to get a job be illegal?

16. What is your view of performance appraisals? How can they be improved?

17. What pay system do you prefer? What compensation do you expect after graduation? State the pay and the benefits you expect. Add up the pay and benefits to get your compensation. If you can't estimate the cost of benefits, use 30% of your pay (multiply your pay times 0.30 [which is the cost of benefits] and add the result to your pay).

CASE

Coach Jekyll and Coach Hyde

Bobby Knight is not an easy coach to fathom. One of the youngest coaches ever to achieve 700 wins in NCAA basketball, Knight argues that his style may not be pretty but his teams win. He is right about that. Knight achieved his 880th career win on January 1, 2007. He is currently second on the list of most career victories in NCAA Division I men's college basketball.[44]

Knight's coaching style is certainly not pretty—in fact, it is vocal, confrontational, and loaded with controversy.[45] Mention Bobby Knight, and chair throwing comes to mind (Indiana vs. Purdue, 1984-1985 season)—so does winning (Indiana was NCAA champion in 1976, 1981, and 1987).

Fans like winners, and Knight, a true basketball genius, built a large and loyal following in the state of Indiana. Knight was very successful at externally recruiting players. But there can be costs to winning, and sometimes they are too high. Knight's costs came home to roost in March 2000, when his high-visibility style got him into hot water. Knight's coaching style is to be highly energized and to control his team as much as possible. However, a former player, Neil Reed, asserted that in 1997 Knight choked him on the court. Allegations by other former Indiana players began to surface. Knight held on to his coaching position for a while but was fired in September 2000 for what university president Myles Brand considered a pattern of unacceptable behavior.

Of course, much of Knight's personnel information at Indiana is private. But it behooves us to wonder. Where was HR as his behavior began to deteriorate? Are some people above HR? Are some positions above the behavior parameters set for others? If so, is the organization still liable for unacceptable behavior from people in such positions? Did HR let Knight and the university down? Did Knight receive fair treatment? Was a program of progressive discipline or counseling undertaken before he was fired? Does he have a case against Indiana if he didn't receive counseling? Do his former players have a case against Indiana for allowing them to be endangered? Did the fact that Knight brought fame and fortune to the Indiana campus enter into Indiana's winking at his behavior? Should it have?

In 2001, Texas Tech reached outside the university in its search for candidates to coach the men's basketball team. Tech selected Knight, and he led the team to an NCAA tournament appearance. In November 2006, it appeared that Knight might have slipped into his old pattern. He gave a quick head slap to a player who was coming off the court after receiving an ill-advised foul. Although the incident caused a great deal of media attention, it quickly died out because most observers believed that the incident was a harmless attempt at making a point. Some have speculated that Knight receives attention for actions that would not be noticed if done by another coach. Overall, Knight led by being a fairly positive example at Texas Tech. He retired from coaching at Texas Tech in February 2008. Knight was able to hand off the coaching responsibilities to his son and assistant coach, Pat Knight. Coach Bobby Knight said he might have wished he had done a few things differently in his career, but he was proud of his teams, players, and accomplishments.

After nearly three seasons, Pat Knight was fired subsequent to losing a series of close games in the last few minutes. He gave the following speech at one of his last postgame interviews. "We've lost seven games in the last minute," he said, according to the Associated Press. "This program is competitive. But that's not for me. I mean, honestly, I'm going to be coaching here, I'm going to be coaching somewhere else. I've proven I can coach. I run a clean program, I don't cheat, my players graduate and we have discipline. So if you don't want me here there's going to be someone else that wants me."[46]

Pat Knight left Texas Tech for Lamar University. In 2012, at Lamar, Knight led the team to the NCAA men's basketball tournament for the first time since 2000. However, he also threw a temper tantrum at the end of the game toward his players for the poor quality of play and the lack of effort by his senior players. You can watch this 9-minute rant at www.nesn.com/2012/02/lavar-university-basketball-head-coach-pat-knight-goes-on-rant-reminiscent-of-his-fathers-tirades-vi.html.

For a multimedia presentation on Bobby Knight, see http://sportsillustrated.cnn.com/multimedia_central/news/2000/03/15/knight_mmc.

Case Questions

1. Which area of training would benefit Bobby Knight?
   a. technical training
   b. people skills and conceptual training

2. At Indiana, Knight's primary recruiting source for players was
   a. internal
   b. external

3. There were good employee relations between Bobby Knight and Indiana University.
   a. true
   b. false

4. Coach Pat Knight received a reserve clause after he was terminated.
   a. true
   b. false

5. Coach Knight's management style was to let his players run the team.
   a. true
   b. false

6. Knight left Indiana University for which reason?

   a. retirement

   b. another job

   c. breaking the rules

   d. layoffs

7. Internal recruiting occurred when Knight accepted the position at Texas Tech.

   a. true

   b. false

8. Texas Tech's replacement for Knight was his assistant coach, Pat Knight; this is an example of what recruiting method?

   a. walk-in

   b. educational institution

   c. agency

   d. promotion from within

9. Apparently, Texas Tech was comfortable with Bobby Knight's record at Indiana. Based on Knight's prior coaching behavior, this is an example of possibly not using _____ effectively.

   a. application form

   b. screening interview

   c. testing

   d. background check

10. Bobby Knight eventually met with Texas Tech's president to discuss the possibility of taking the coaching position. This is an example of which stage of the selection process?

    a. application form

    b. interview

    c. testing

    d. background check

11. Use the Lamar University website at the end of the case to learn about Knight's behavior during the past collegiate basketball season.

12. Why do you think there is such a high turnover rate among college coaches?

13. Do you believe that Indiana University gave Bobby Knight enough chances before they fired him?

SKILL-BUILDER EXERCISES

Skill-Builder 7.1: Selecting a Tennis Coach

Objective

To perform a job analysis and to develop your interviewing skills

Preparation

You're in your first year as a high school athletic director, and you have an opening for a tennis coach. Compensation, which is competitive with other schools in the area, is set in the budget and will be paid in one lump sum at the end of the season. You don't have a recruiting budget, so you do some internal recruiting and contact some athletic directors in your area to spread the word about the opening.

Your efforts yield three candidates. Here are their qualifications:

- Candidate A has taught history at your school for 10 years. He also coached tennis for 2 years, but it has been 5 years since he coached the team. You don't know why he stopped coaching or how good a job he did. He never played competitive tennis. However, someone told you he plays regularly and is pretty good. You guess he's about 35 years old.

- Candidate B supervises the graveyard shift for a local business. She has never coached before, but she was a star player in high school and college. She still plays in local tournaments, and you see her name in the paper now and then. You guess she is about 25 years old.

- Candidate C has been a basketball coach and physical education teacher at a nearby high school for the past 5 years. She has a master's degree in physical education. You figure it will take her 20 minutes to get to your school. She has never coached tennis but did play high school tennis. She currently plays tennis about once a week. You guess she is about 45 years old.

Preparing for the Interviews

Follow the steps given in figure 7.4 on page 207. For step 1, there are no job descriptions and specifications. Because there are only three candidates, you've decided to interview them all.

In-Class Application

Complete the preceding skill-building preparation before class, and bring your interview questions to class.

Choose one (1-2 hours):

- Break into groups of three and present the questions you developed. As a group, critique the various lists and then use the best questions to develop a PA form that you think best serves this situation. Now meet with another group and take turns using your master list to interview the three "candidates" from the other group. Allot no more than 15 minutes per interview (even though this is unrealistic in a real-world setting). (Follow the steps outlined in figure 7.5.) Observing members give feedback after each interview.

- Conduct informal, whole-class discussion of students' interview questions.

Wrap-Up

Take a few minutes to write your answers to the following questions:

What did I learn from this experience? How will I use this knowledge?

_____

_____

_____

_____

As a class, discuss student responses.

Skill-Builder 7.2: Resume

Objective

To develop a resume for getting a full-time, part-time, or summer job or an internship

Preparation

For help developing your resume, visit your college career center or the Proven Resumes website (www.provenresumes.com). Before finalizing your resume, improve it by using the following resume assessment. Bring three hard copies of your resume to class.

Resume assessment: Answer with yes, somewhat, or no.

1. Within 10 seconds, can a recruiter understand the job you are applying for and the qualifications (skills, experience, and education) you have to get the position?

2. Does the resume have an objective that clearly states the position you are applying for (such as sales rep)?

3. Does the resume list skills and experience that support your ability do the job? (For example, if you don't have sales experience, list sales skills developed on other jobs. List courses and explain how they developed your sales skills. List communication skills and product knowledge, explain that you enjoy meeting new people, and mention that you easily converse with people you don't know.)

4. If education is the major qualification for the job, does the resume include the skills developed or courses taken in school that will qualify you for the position applied for?

5. Does the resume clearly list accomplishments and valuable contributions made during education or experience?

In-Class Application

Complete the skill-building preparation and bring your resume to class.

Break into groups of three and give each other copies of your resume. Separately, each member assesses the resumes using the preceding five questions, providing a rating for each question (yes, somewhat, or no). Write rating and suggestions on each resume; correct any errors and offer ideas for improvement. After all members have made their written assessments, talk about recommended changes to improve each resume. Provide feedback to one group member at a time.

Wrap-Up

Take a few minutes to write your answers to the following questions:

What did I learn from this experience? How will I use this knowledge?

_____

_____

_____

_____

As a class, discuss student responses.

SPORTS AND SOCIAL MEDIA EXERCISES

Sign up for LinkedIn. LinkedIn is a free networking site. It is easy to sign up and learn how to connect to other professionals in your field on www.linkedin.com. Your task is to search for three sport management positions posted in the JOBS link.

_____

_____

_____

GAME PLAN FOR STARTING A SPORT BUSINESS

Hiring people to work for your organization is a real-life commitment on your part to build your organization. Look on LinkedIn to find three qualified people to help you manage your sport organization.

_____

_____

PART IV

Leading

Leading is the third function that is required for sport managers to be successful. Behavioral issues including power, politics, conflict, and stress are covered with regard to developing skills to handle these issues and ensure career success (chapter 8). The stages that groups go through to become a great team are presented to aid you in building your own great teams (chapter 9). Ways to develop communication skills for individual-level interactions and for broadcasting in radio, television, and the Internet are described in chapter 10. Traditional theories and models of motivation (chapter 11) and leadership (chapter 12) are presented, using sport managers and teams as examples. Great motivational leadership examples in sport, such as Phil Jackson of the Los Angeles Lakers, are discussed to help you learn how to motivate and lead others on and off the field.

Behavior in Organizations

Power, Politics, Conflict, and Stress

LEARNING OUTCOMES

After studying this chapter, you should be able to

1. describe the Big Five personality traits;

2. understand the perception process and the two factors on which it is based;

3. explain how personality, perception, and attitude are related and why they are important;

4. state what job satisfaction is and why it is important;

5. define power and explain the difference between position and personal power;

6. explain how reward power, legitimate power, and referent power differ;

7. understand how power and politics are related;

8. explain what networking, reciprocity, and coalitions have in common;

9. describe the five conflict management styles;

10. use collaboration to resolve conflict; and

11. explain the stress tug-of-war analogy.

KEY TERMS

organizational behavior (OB)	power	functional conflict
win–win situation	politics	initiators
personality	networking	BCF statements
perception	reciprocity	mediator
attribution	coalition	arbitrator
attitudes	conflict	stress
Pygmalion effect	dysfunctional conflict	stressors

DEVELOPING YOUR SKILLS

Effective leaders share at least one thing in common—they all have amazing people skills. People skills include understanding personality traits, perceptions, and attitudes and how they affect performance. In this chapter, you can develop your people skills through gaining and using power and organizational politics ethically. Models will also provide you with step-by-step guides so you can resolve conflicts and negotiate successfully to improve your performance. You can also develop your skill at recognizing the causes of stress and methods for reducing stress—fighting and winning the stress tug-of-war.

REVIEWING THEIR GAME PLAN

Applying Legitimate Power at the USADA

The goal of the USADA (United States Anti-Doping Agency) is to preserve the integrity of Olympic sport, preserve the integrity of competition, and ensure the health of athletes. Floyd Landis, the apparent winner of the 2006 Tour de France, fought with the USADA in court to keep his tour title. Some have called the race Tour de Chaos.[1]

The USADA tries to help athletes in four ways: The first is to conduct research on substances that are prohibited. The second is to educate athletes about the dangers of using banned substances and about policies concerning banned substances. The third is to develop quality and consistency in testing in and out of competition. The fourth is to maintain an adjudication system that relies on arbitrations before the American Arbitration Association (AAA)/Court of Arbitration for Sport under modified AAA commercial rules, which have been agreed to by the relevant stakeholders.

The USADA board consists of nine members, five of whom came from outside the Olympic family and four of whom (two each) were elected by the Athlete Advisory Council and the National Governing Body Council. The agency was created because the U.S. Olympic Committee's integrity had been questioned internationally for a number of reasons. So the USADA had some difficult organizational problems to solve. The group's work, helping athletes to behave ethically and to take care of their bodies, was bound to cause some conflict and stress.

The USADA lawyers treated the Landis case as they normally would, using the scientific facts generated from their lab testing. USADA attorney Richard Young said that the Landis case was just like dozens of other athlete doping cases in which tests indicated the use of a banned substance.

Landis was not the only rider in the 2006 Tour to be found guilty of doping. But he was the first to loudly appeal the finding. Landis used his case as a forum to expose the fraudulent way the USADA does business. Landis did everything in his own power to keep pressing that he had not used a banned substance. He steadfastly maintained his innocence among his circle of bicycling friends, in the global media, and in his arbitration appearances.

In September 2007, an arbitration panel upheld charges that Landis had used performance-enhancing drugs. Landis was stripped of his title by the International Cycling Union (ICU) and banned from competitive cycling for 2 years.[2] The 2007 Tour de France (which Landis agreed not to participate in because his case was still pending) itself was disgraced again as the leader Michael Rasmussen was eliminated from the event. His Rabobank team accused the rider of having lied about his whereabouts before the Tour to evade doping controls.

On June 30, 2008, Landis lost his final chance to regain his title when a three-person panel at the Court of Arbitration for Sport upheld the previous panel's decision.[3]

In a related case, Alberto Contador was stripped of his 2010 Tour de France title and was banned for 2 years after the Court of Arbitration for Sport suspended the three-time Tour champion. The court rejected his claim that his positive test for clenbuterol was caused by eating contaminated meat on a 2010 Tour rest day.[4]

Tour de France champion Lance Armstrong gave up fighting allegations that he used illegal substances during his reign as the champion of the tour and was stripped of his seven titles by the ICU.[5]

However, the use of performance-enhancing drugs in sport appears to still be a problem. MLB thought it had put the problem in the past after the Barry Bonds, Roger Clemens, and Mark McGwire era. Testing procedures were improved, and punishments to major and minor league players who tested positive were implemented. However, Manny Ramirez accepted a 50-game suspension in early 2009. Ryan Braun, 2011 National League player tested positive for a banned substance. The positive result came about from elevated levels of synthetic testosterone in Braun's system.[6] Braun denied taking a banned substance and was found not guilty since his sample had not been handled properly. The collection samples were not shipped for testing as soon as possible.[7] It should be noted that the new guidelines set up by MLB appear to have been effective in catching marginal players trying to improve their performance by using performance-enhancing drugs.[8]

Understanding the role that the USADA plays in Olympic sport is crucial for those who intend to pursue a career in sport administration. For more information about the USADA, visit www.usada.org.

Organizational Behavior

Have you ever wondered why you do certain things and why teammates and coworkers behave the way they do? This is what organizational behaviorists look at. Our behavior consists of what we say and do—in a word, our actions. **Organizational behavior (OB)** is the study of actions that affect performance in the workplace. Organizational behaviorists endeavor to explain and predict actions in the workplace and show how such actions affect performance. Considerable research has highlighted the importance of leader behaviors for team performance. Effective leaders attempt to create win–win situations. **Win–win situations** occur when organizations and their employees get what they want.

The better you understand OB, the more effectively you will work with others in teams both as a manager and as a worker. OB skills are based on people and communication management skills (chapter 1). OB skills are sometimes referred to as soft skills, and employers seek employees with these skills. In this chapter, you can develop your OB skills.

Three components—our personality, perception, and attitudes—drive our behavior. They are the foundations on which our behavior is built, and they are observable through our every action. Understanding how personality, perception, and attitude drive behavior gives you insight into how people will behave in certain situations. These are the topics of our next two sections.

OB has three levels of focus: individual, group, and organizational. In this chapter we examine individual behavior, and in chapter 9 we discuss group behavior. Organizational behavior is covered in chapter 5 (as organizational development). There are also several areas of OB. Power, politics, conflict, negotiation, collaboration, and managing stress are areas of OB that are discussed in this chapter.[9]

Personality

Look around you. You will see outgoing, shy, loud, quiet, warm, cold, aggressive, and passive people—we are diversified. These differences are what behaviorists call individual traits. **Personality** is the combination of traits that compose individuals. Our personality affects our behavior, our perceptions, and our attitudes. Take sport announcers. Quiet announcers—no matter how good their knowledge or skill—could hurt Monday Night Football on ESPN or NFL on Fox. Only extroverts need apply for announcer jobs. Think about Billy Packer, John Madden, Charles Barkley, and Deion Sanders—where would their viewership be if they didn't have lively on-air personalities? Personalities are pivotal in garnering viewership.[10]

Our personalities are shaped by our genes and by the environment. Our genes we are born with; the environment that forms us is composed of our families, our friends, and our life experiences. Researchers have developed numerous ways to classify personality. Two widely recognized ones are the single traits system and the Big Five personality traits, our first two topics of this section, followed by the perception process and bias in perception. Either way, personality is a good predictor of team performance.[11]

Single Traits System of Personality

Key traits in the single traits system are locus of control, optimism, risk propensity, self-esteem, and self-efficacy. (Self-esteem and self-efficacy are based on perception, so they are discussed with perception.) This system places each trait on a continuum.

Locus of Control

This trait, which deals with who we believe controls our destiny, lies on a continuum with externalizers at one end and internalizers at the other. Externalizers believe that they have no control over their fate and that their behavior has little to do with their performance. Internalizers believe just the opposite—that they control their fate and that their behavior directly affects their performance. Internalizers obviously tend to perform better. Do you believe you can succeed if you work hard? Do you take responsibility for your actions, or do you blame others when things go wrong?

Optimism

The continuum here is between optimists and pessimists. Optimists believe that things will go well, and they approach life with a can-do attitude. Pessimists believe that everything that can go wrong will go wrong, and this infuses their approach to life. Optimists take action to meet objectives because they believe they can make a difference, whereas pessimists give up easily and are defeated much earlier than optimists. You may have heard the old saying "Winners never quit and quitters never win." As Winston Churchill said, "Success is the ability to go from failure to failure without losing your enthusiasm." Are you persistent, or do you give up?

Optimistic people are happier. Do you like to be around unhappy people who complain all the time? As Lou Holtz said, "You choose to be happy or sad; happiness is nothing more than a poor memory for the bad things that happen to you." Are you an optimist or pessimist, and are you happy? To be more optimistic and happy, quit complaining, take responsibility for your actions, and focus on the good things in your life.[12]

Risk Propensity

This trait lies on a continuum between risk takers and risk avoiders. To be innovative, you must take risk.[13] Successful organizations seek managers who take reasonable risks; ESPN and the cable networks continue risk taking with various combinations of former players and media personalities in the broadcast booth. ESPN has tried various combinations of traditional play-by-play hosts (Mike Tirico), former coaches (Bill Parcells), players (Keyshawn Johnson), and many other football experts, looking for the right combination of personalities to attract viewers to its pre- and postgame shows. Part of the attraction of watching football is seeing and hearing from these personalities during shows such as *NFL Live* and *Sunday NFL Countdown*.[14] Are you a reasonable risk taker or a risk avoider?

Big Five Personality Traits

◀ LEARNING OUTCOME 1
Describe the Big Five personality traits.

Before reading about the Big Five, complete the Self-Assessment personality profile on page 238 to better understand your personality.

The Big Five trait system is the most widely accepted way to classify personalities. The five personality traits, presented here, are also defined as continuums.

- **Extroversion:** This trait lies on a continuum between extroverts and introverts. Are you outgoing or shy? Review your answers to the Self-Assessment extroversion column for items 1, 6, 11, 16, and 21.

> **TIME-OUT 1**
> Use the five traits given in the Self-Assessment to characterize the personality of your current boss or coach.

- **Agreeableness:** This trait lies on a continuum between cooperators and competitors. Do you cooperate with your coworkers or do you compete with them? Teams whose members cooperate with each other and compete with external teams show higher levels of performance than teams whose members compete with each other. Review your answers to the Self-Assessment agreeableness column for items 2, 7, 12, 17, and 22.

- **Emotionalism:** The continuum here is between emotionally stable and emotionally unstable. Stable people are calm, secure, and positive, whereas unstable people are nervous, insecure, and negative. Can you take trash talk during the game, or do you get emotional? Review your answers to the Self-Assessment emotionalism column for items 3, 8, 13, 18, and 23.

- **Conscientiousness:** This continuum has responsible-dependable at one end and irresponsible-undependable at the other. Conscientious people are more satisfied with life than nonconscientious people.[15] Can your family, team, and coworkers count on you to get the job done well? Review your answers to the Self-Assessment conscientiousness column for items 4, 9, 14, 19, and 24.

- **Openness to experience:** This aspect varies from being very willing to try new things to being very afraid to try new things. Do you like change, or do you prefer routines? Review your answers to the Self-Assessment openness to experience column for items 5, 10, 15, 20, and 25.

Big Five at Work

From an individual perspective, there are no simple right and wrong ways to be, but from the organization's perspective, there are. Organizations therefore go to great lengths to recruit and retain people with positive traits because understanding personality helps to predict performance.[16] For example, extroverts tend to do well in sales, whereas introverts don't. Firms want agreeable, cooperative team players who can self-regulate their behavior.[17] Conscientious people tend to follow the rules, are more ethical, and outperform irresponsible people.[18] In today's quickly changing global economy, organizations want employees who are open to new experiences; they are more creative.[19] Do you have the Big Five personality that organizations want?

The good news is that you very likely fall on the positive personality trait side. Why? Because people who score low in every trait don't get very far in life (e.g., extreme pessimists and externalizers don't have the determination to get into college, let alone succeed there). The bad news is that you're not perfect, so there are probably aspects of yourself that you need to work on. As you assess each trait in the Self-Assessment, realize that you can change if you work at it every day throughout the day. For example, if you catch yourself being negative, stop and replace your thoughts and words with positive ones. To be more extroverted, reach out to others every day until it feels natural. If you get emotional, calm down rather than go with it. Make a greater effort to be conscientious every time you have something to do, and remember that doing more than you are asked to do is a key to career

Your Big Five Personality Profile

There are no right or wrong answers, so be honest and you will really increase your self-awareness. Using the scale shown, rate each of the 25 statements according to how accurately it describes you. Place a number from 1 to 7 on the line before each statement.

Like me			Somewhat like me			Not like me
7	**6**	**5**	**4**	**3**	**2**	**1**

_____ 1. I enjoy meeting new people.

_____ 2. I am concerned about getting along well with others.

_____ 3. I have good self-control; I don't get emotional or angry and yell.

_____ 4. I'm dependable; when I say I will do something, it's done well and on time.

_____ 5. I try to do things differently to improve my performance.

_____ 6. I feel comfortable speaking to diverse people (different age, race, gender, religion, and intelligence).

_____ 7. I enjoy having lots of friends and going to parties.

_____ 8. I perform well under pressure.

_____ 9. I work hard to be successful.

_____ 10. I go to new places and enjoy traveling.

_____ 11. I am outgoing and initiate conversations, rather than being shy and waiting for others to approach me.

_____ 12. I try to see things from other people's point of view.

_____ 13. I am an optimistic person who sees the positive side of situations (the cup is half full).

_____ 14. I am a well-organized person.

_____ 15. When I go to a new restaurant, I order foods I haven't tried.

_____ 16. I am willing to go talk to people to resolve conflicts rather than say nothing.

_____ 17. I want other people to like me and consider me to be very friendly.

_____ 18. I give people lots of praise and encouragement; I don't put people down and criticize.

_____ 19. I conform by following the rules of an organization.

_____ 20. I volunteer to be the first to learn and do new tasks at work.

_____ 21. I try to influence other people to get what I want.

_____ 22. I enjoy working with others more than working alone.

_____ 23. I view myself as being relaxed and secure rather than nervous and insecure.

_____ 24. I am considered to be credible because I do a good job and come through for people.

_____ 25. When people suggest doing things differently, I support them and help bring it about. I don't make statements like these: "It won't work," "We've never done it before," "No one else has ever done it," "We can't do it."

Next determine your personality profile: (1) In the blanks, place a number from 1 to 7 that represents your score for each statement. (2) Add up each column—your total should be a number from 5 to 35. (3) On the number scale to the right of each column, circle the number that is closest to your total score. Each column in the chart represents the specific personality dimension listed.

success.[20] Be open to new experience; try new foods, play other sports or engage in other forms of recreation, go to new places, and volunteer for new assignments.

Your answers to the Self-Assessment are telling you something very important. This is the real you that you are looking at—do you really want to change? More importantly, are you willing to work at changing?

Perception Process

◀ LEARNING OUTCOME 2

Understand the perception process and the two factors on which it is based.

Referees make mistakes,[21] but why do some of us view a referee's videotaped decision as fair whereas others do not? We all see the same videotaped play, but we don't perceive it the same way. Because perceptions are the starting point of behavior, they affect our behavior.[22] For example, African Americans, relative to white Americans, perceive race and opportunity as limiting their ability to obtain a head coaching position, and thus fewer apply for coaching jobs.[23]

Perception is the process through which we select, organize, and interpret information from the surrounding environment. Our behavior follows our perceptions of people, events, learning, work, and organizations. Because this perception process colors everything, no two people experience anything exactly the same way.

How Perception Influences Behavior

We tend to treat people we perceive as likable differently than people we perceive as unlikable. We tend to work harder for someone we perceive as a good transformational manager than for someone we perceive as ineffective.[24] Perception is our individual interpretation of reality. Right or wrong, rational or irrational, it is the lens through which we view life. To improve the accuracy of your perception, try to see things through the eyes of your rivals.[25]

How we select, organize, and interpret information is based on numerous internal individual factors—our personality, self-esteem, attitudes, intelligence, needs, and values. These compose the internal component of perception. Self-esteem, or self-concept, is our perception of ourselves. Self-esteem derives from interpersonal comparisons of our traits, abilities, goals, and performance with those of others. When you compare yourself with others, be realistic. Don't compare yourself with former NBA star Michael Jordan; compare yourself with your peers. And never put yourself down. Everyone makes errors, but don't simply justify your mistakes; you need to learn from your mistakes and go on to improve.[26]

Why is it debated whether the USADA is doing a good job of managing doping issues in Olympic sport? Some see the USADA as doing a great job, and others think it is too powerful. What is your perception of how powerful the USADA is in Olympic sport?

As we noted earlier, self-esteem is also a personality trait; it varies between high-positive and low-negative. Do you like yourself? Do you consider yourself a valuable person or employee? Do you believe you are a capable person? Organizations endeavor to recruit people with positive self-esteem, because people with high self-esteem (and positive self-efficacy—belief in ability to succeed in a given situation) perform better on the job.[27]

 Do you believe that the USADA should investigate an athlete based on rumors?

The second component of this process is the information itself—this is the external component. The more accurate our information, the more closely our perception will resemble reality. Inaccurate information causes our perceptions to veer wildly from reality and can be a serious problem for organizations. The USADA must deal with all types of rumors (e.g., that lab technicians make errors, or that athletes are asked to inform on other athletes) and determine whether they are violations of USADA rules.

Others' perceptions of us, which build our reputation, are important to career progression. If your boss and higher-level managers perceive you as highly competent you will advance, but if you get a bad reputation you won't advance. Reputation explains why iconic athletes such as former NBA player Michael Jordan are highly paid to endorse products, whereas boxer Mike Tyson is not.[28] In 2010, golfer Tiger Woods went from fan favorite to unloved after a series of extramarital affairs went public. After 2 years, some people were happy to see Tiger regain his winning form, while other fans continued to dislike Tiger because of the poor choices he had made in the past.[29]

Customer and fan perception is also important to organizations, including teams. Perhaps nowhere are the topics of identity, image, and reputation more relevant than in the arena of sport. Teams with good reputations, often based on winning, tend to have good reputations and high levels of fan support and attendance; and reputations and fan loyalty can change from season to season, again often based on winning, because people generally love a winner.

Why We Attribute Reasons for Behavior

Attribution is the process of determining why we behave certain ways. Most of us continually try to find reasons behind behavior—our own behavior or that of those around us. The process (shown in figure 8.1) begins when we observe an act directly or learn of it indirectly (by reading or hearing about it). We want to know if the person's intent was situational (accidental or beyond the person's control) or intentional (within the person's control). We may not use these words, but this is what we are doing. We judge intent (or lack thereof) by three variables: distinctiveness (does Metta World Peace, formerly known as Ron Artest and unfortunately known for some on-court physical controversies and off-court outspoken behavior,[30] behave this way in other situations?), consensus (does his whole team behave this way?), and consistency (does Metta World Peace behave this way most—or all—of the time?). We also look for reasons for the behavior (did Metta decide that publicity, even negative publicity, was a good way to set himself apart—that is, a good career strategy?). Last, we decide on a response—we may abhor Metta's behavior or be amused by it or even admire it. Or we may simply not care. All of these responses drive our behavior—we may abstain from watching any game he is in, we may drive long distances to see him play, or we may affect his style of dress and buy T-shirts emblazoned with his name. See figure 8.1 for the attribution process.

Attribution is how we determine reasons for our behavior and that of others. However, most of us spend more time mulling over why other people behave the way they do. We spend less time examining our own behavior; but when we do look at our own behavior, we tend to credit our successes as being intentional. Conversely, when we fail, we tend to blame the situation. We also tend to reverse intention (Sally failed because she didn't practice enough) and situation (Jamal just got lucky) when we attribute reasons for other people's behavior. This is a classic example of perception differences.

TIME-OUT 2 Explain how you used the attribution process (a) in a recent incident in professional sport and (b) in a recent incident at work.

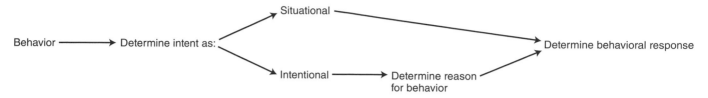

FIGURE 8.1 The attribution process.

We can't see people's motives for their behavior; we can only perceive the reason for the behavior through attribution. If a teammate makes a negative remark to us, is it because the player doesn't like us or is the person just kidding around? We sometimes misperceive motives and let them damage relationships; misunderstandings are common. So when in doubt about why someone did something to offend you, talk to the person about it. Others may not even realize that their behavior bothers you. Later in this chapter, you will learn how to resolve conflicts without hurting relationships.

Bias in Our Perception

Why does each of us perceive the same behavior differently? In two words, personal bias. Bias has several components—selectivity, frame of reference, stereotypes, and expectation—and we are all subject to these biases.

Selectivity

 Do you tend to select positive or negative information about the USADA?

Selectivity is the manner in which we screen information to favor the outcome we desire. We often go to great lengths to find information that supports our point of view yet ignore information that does not. In other words, we hear only what we want to hear. For example, we might hear 10 good points about the USADA and only one bad point. If we want the outcome of receiving this information (our response) to square with the fact that we like to disparage the USADA, we will focus on the one negative point and disregard the positive information. This enables us to conclude that the USADA doesn't do a good job of managing doping in Olympic sport. A related bias is the halo–horns effect, in which we judge others based on our perception of a single trait of theirs. (A person with a halo can do no wrong—a person with horns can do no right.)

Frame of Reference

Could athletes create a win–win situation by complying with USADA requirements?

Our frame of reference is our bias of seeing things from our own point of view. Do you and your parents always agree? Managers and employees tend to have different perceptions. Do you and your boss or coach agree on how well you perform?

Thus, as a manager or coach, don't be surprised if your team doesn't perceive things the way you do. Remember, it is not your perception but the employees' perceptions that will influence their behavior and performance. Try to see things from others' perspective,[31] and create a win–win situation so that all parties get what they want.

Stereotyping

Stereotyping happens when we project the characteristics or behavior of an individual onto a group. Women and minorities continue to be stereotyped in sport,[32] and stereotyping leads to discrimination.[33] Think about breakthrough athletes like MLB's Jackie Robinson or high school female wrestlers. All faced stereotypes that charged (falsely) that they shouldn't play with other groups or couldn't be good at what they did. Don't let stereotyping get in your way of seeing true strengths and true weaknesses. Researchers hope that people in the sport industry can debunk stereotypical myths of what an ideally fit body should look like. Managers can then provide opportunities for nonstereotypical, qualified applicants and show fitness customers what group fitness instructors and personal trainers can look like.[34] Keep an open mind when you are hiring sport employees and managers.

Expectations

Read the phrase in figure 8.2.

Did you read *the* word the twice? Or, like most people, did you read what you expected to read, only one *the*? Our expectations also bias our perceptions. Many of us, especially when we know each other well, don't really listen to each other. We hear what we expect to hear.

Another expectation bias is the "like us" assumption—that others perceive things as we do because they are like us. Don't expect others to behave as you do or perceive things the way you do, and don't judge others' behavior as wrong on the sole basis that it differs from yours. Remember to value diversity. As discussed in chapter 6, there are benefits of having cultural diversity in sport organizations.

FIGURE 8.2   Check your expectations.

TIME-OUT 3 Think about a misunderstanding that arose when you and another person perceived the same situation differently. Which perceptual biases do you think contributed to the misunderstanding?

LEARNING OUTCOME 3 ▶

Explain how personality, perception, and attitude are related and why they are important.

Attitudes

Attitudes are positive or negative evaluations of people, things, and situations. Attitude is a major factor in determining performance,[35] and your self-esteem and self-efficacy have a significant effect on your attitude.[36] Therefore, organizations look for people with high self-esteem and positive attitudes toward their careers and personal lives, because such people tend to be loyal and reliable workers. Our personalities, perceptions, and input from others (family, friends, teachers, coworkers, the mass media) form our attitudes. Collective attitudes influence sport organization performance. Sport fans' attitudes influence attendance at events and merchandise purchases.[37] In this section, we examine how the attitudes of management affect employee performance and the importance of job satisfaction.

TIME-OUT 4 Relate incidents in which your attitude affected your workplace behavior negatively and positively.

How the Attitudes of Management Affect Performance

Managers affect employee self-efficacy, job satisfaction, and performance.[38] The **Pygmalion effect** has to do with how management's attitude toward workers, expectations of workers, and treatment of workers affect their performance. It's pretty simple—how you view your staff is what you get! That is, your attitude toward your staff directly affects the quality of their work. There is much research to support this. When you as a manager view your staff as competent and highly skilled (even though they might not be initially), they will rise to the occasion (it may happen slowly, but it will happen). Likewise, when you don't believe your staff to be competent or trustworthy, guess what—they won't surprise you! Management's attitudes become a self-fulfilling prophecy. In summary, then, your attitude is an essential part of your effectiveness as a manager. John Wooden, the legendary former basketball coach at UCLA, expected excellence from every player. The result was 10 NCAA National Championships. Wooden constructed his "pyramid of success" (check it out at www.coachwooden.com) out of such concepts as "keep it simple" and "teamwork is not a preference, it's a necessity."[39]

All this said about the Pygmalion effect and self-fulfilling prophecies, you as an employee or a manager are still responsible for your own actions. Others' attitudes can affect your behavior and performance, but only if you let them. Ignore negative comments, stay away from people with negative attitudes, and continue to get better at what you do. Look at a negative boss as a gift—you need to learn how to work with difficult people; just don't let them defeat you. Show them you have what it takes to succeed.

TIME-OUT 5

Describe how expectations of you on the part of someone (a parent, friend, teacher, coach, or boss) strongly affected your success or failure.

Attitudes and Job Satisfaction

◄LEARNING OUTCOME 4
State what job satisfaction is and why it is important.

Job satisfaction is how content we are (or are not) with our jobs. The continuum ranges from high satisfaction (positive attitude) to low satisfaction (negative attitude). Job attitudes and job performance are perhaps the two most central and enduring sets of constructs in individual-level organizational research. Why? Because job satisfaction affects employee absenteeism, morale, performance, and turnover. Thus, organizations measure job satisfaction in organizational development surveys (chapter 6) and create cultures to maintain and increase job satisfaction. A person has to fit the task (P–T fit) and the organization (P–O fit) to achieve job satisfaction.[40]

Have you ever been unhappy on a team or at work because you just didn't fit in? P–O fit has a lot to do with finding a job that you like to perform and that you are also good at. Will you be happy performing a job you don't like or that you fail to do well? Were you happier as a star of the team or sitting on the bench? Were you happier playing on winning teams than on losing teams? Also, job satisfaction affects our satisfaction with life—having a job that satisfies us affects the way we view our lives outside work.

What determines job satisfaction? According to management guru Ken Blanchard, the number-one indicator of job satisfaction is the relationship you have with your boss.[41] But your boss is not the only determining factor. To find out the others, complete the Self-Assessment ahead.

Because job satisfaction is based on personality and perception, it can be changed. If you work at being more positive by focusing on the good parts of your job and spend less time thinking about and especially complaining to others about your job, your job satisfaction will improve. Thus, managers need to recruit and retain employees with positive attitudes. If you ask job candidates about their prior jobs and they make negative statements, cannot think of anything good to say, or hesitate, they may have a negative personality and job attitude. Improving your human relationship skills can help you get along better with coworkers and managers and increase your job satisfaction, as well as your chances for growth and opportunity for advancement and higher compensation.

Power

◄LEARNING OUTCOME 5
Define power and explain the difference between position and personal power.

It is important to understand power structures within sport organizations.[42] To be effective in an organization, you need to understand how people gain power and how they use power. Power used properly enhances your job effectiveness and organizational performance.[43] Therefore, in this section you will examine power—its importance, its bases, and its implications—so that you can use power wisely.

Organizational Power

Power is often viewed as one's ability to make people do something or as one's ability to do something to people or for them. These definitions are valid, but they also cast power as manipulative, or even destructive, as does Lord Acton's saying "Power corrupts and absolute

SELF-ASSESSMENT 8.2

Job Satisfaction

Select a present or past job or, if you prefer, a sport team. For each of the following determinants of job satisfaction, identify your level of satisfaction by placing a check on the continuum.

Personality
I have a positive self-esteem. _____ _____ _____ / _____ _____ _____ I have a negative self-esteem.

Work Itself
I enjoy doing the tasks I perform. _____ _____ _____ / _____ _____ _____ I do not enjoy doing the tasks I perform.

Compensation
I am fairly compensated. _____ _____ _____ / _____ _____ _____ I am not fairly compensated.

Growth and Upward Mobility
I have the opportunity to learn new things and get better jobs. _____ _____ _____ / _____ _____ _____ I have no opportunity to learn new things and get better jobs.

Coworkers
I like and enjoy working with my coworkers. _____ _____ _____ / _____ _____ _____ I do not like and enjoy working with my coworkers.

Management
I'm happy with the working relationship I have with my boss. _____ _____ _____ / _____ _____ _____ I do not enjoy my working relationship with my boss.
I believe that managers are doing a good job. _____ _____ _____ / _____ _____ _____ I do not believe managers are doing a good job.

Overall Job Satisfaction

When determining overall job satisfaction for yourself, you cannot simply add up a score based on these six determinants, because they are most likely of different importance to you. Thus, thinking about the six factors, rate your overall satisfaction level with your job. It is quite normal to have high job satisfaction and not like some aspects of your job.

I am satisfied with my job (high level of satisfaction)					I am dissatisfied with my job (low level of satisfaction)
6	5	4	3	2	1

 How might the USADA use its power constructively to solve some of the troubling doping issues facing Olympic sport?

power corrupts absolutely." Unfortunately, some people abuse power.[44] The imbalance of power has constrained women and minorities in sport organizations.[45] Power can intoxicate us and blind us to our flaws, and makes some people more comfortable committing unethical acts that they might otherwise be reluctant to commit, like lying.[46] But it is important to look at power as a constructive tool, as a way to organize action and get something done.

For our purposes, then, **power** is the ability to influence the actions of others. Mark Emmert, president of the NCAA, is thus a powerful person, as is every effective coach and athletic director. FIFA is a powerful organization because of the influence it wields around the world. Some charge that the USADA uses its power coercively; others say the USADA is just doing what needs to be done.

Without power, organizations and managers cannot achieve objectives. Leadership and power go hand in hand.[47] Employees are not influenced without a reason, and the reason is often the power a manager has over them. You don't always have to *use* your power to direct people. Often it is the perception of power, rather than the wielding of it, that influences others. An estimated 83.9 million Americans spend an average of 3.6 hours per week volunteering, with an estimated 20% of them volunteering in sport and recreation.[48]

Power can be derived from one's position and from one's personal attributes. Management has the power of position. You can also have personal power based on your personality, abilities, and skill. Position power is more effective when it is accompanied by personal power. The most effective leaders toggle between the two power sources. Just as it can be gained, every type of power can also be lost (ask Pete Rose, all-time base hit champion, who was banned from the Baseball Hall of Fame for betting on baseball games).

Bases of Power

The seven bases of power, along with their two sources, are shown in figure 8.3. People who get results and who have good people skills are often granted power (either formally by promotion or informally by general agreement of the group). Note that building a power base does not necessarily mean taking power away from others. People who are willing to step forward and do the work are given power.

Coercive Power

The source of coercive power is position power; coercive power uses threats or punishment to achieve compliance. It gets its effectiveness from our fear of humiliation (in the form of reprimands, probation, suspension, or dismissal). Coercive power also uses verbal abuse and ostracism (both dramatic but not very productive). Group members may use coercive power to enforce norms. Coercion does have appropriate uses—for example, when employees or players break the rules. The USADA uses coercive power routinely, as do innumerable governing bodies.

 Should the USADA have coercive power over Olympic athletes?

Connection Power

When people use their relationship with influential or important people to influence your behavior or attitudes, they are using connection power. Connection power is therefore a combination of position and personal power. Connections can help you find work and get the resources you need to succeed.[49] Networking is about developing relationships to increase connection power. We discuss networking in a later section.

Reward Power

As a manager, you will have the ability to praise, recognize achievement, raise wages, and promote people. This is reward power—the ability to influence others by giving them something they value. As we noted in chapter 7, as a manager you will get what you reward. You will learn how to give praise that motivates in chapter 11.

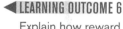 **◄ LEARNING OUTCOME 6**
Explain how reward power, legitimate power, and referent power differ.

Legitimate Power

Power given to people by organizations or by society is legitimate power. Managers have legitimate power. So do police officers. (And both have coercive power as well.) Legitimate power is position power. When our boss asks us to do something, we typically think we should do it because it's a legitimate request that is part of our job, so we do the task. If

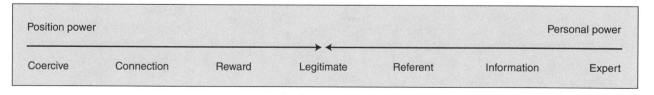

FIGURE 8.3 Sources and bases of power.

we don't think it is a legitimate request, for example if it seems unethical, we may try to get out of doing the task.

Referent Power

Referent power is about voluntarily giving someone power over you. Therefore, in your behavior you will refer to what you think the power holder would do or would want you to do. People using referent power don't give orders; they make relationship-related requests like "Please do this as a favor for me" and "Will you please do this for me?" Star athletes such as NBA star and Los Angeles Lakers shooting guard Kobe Bryant and WNBA star and Los Angeles Sparks forward Candace Parker have referent power over their fans. This is personal power, of course. It is about the referent's charisma, interpersonal openness, and experience as someone older and wiser or more successful and more skilled. Managers gain this power when they are respected by their work group.

Information Power

In this age of information, people who have knowledge or data that others need have information power. This is personal power, although sometimes it is also position power, because you happen to be in the right place (position) to acquire the knowledge or gather the data. As a manager, you will need to rely on information supplied by others. They will therefore have power over you because your work can be only as good as the information it is based on. You will also be a conveyer of information—to your staff and to your bosses—and as such will also have information power. You will improve your communication skills in chapter 10.

Expert Power

People who have expertise or specialized skills that others need have expert power. This too is personal power. NBA forward LeBron James and MLB outfielder Ichiro Suzuki have expert power that their teams need. The fewer the people who possess a particular expertise, the more power the expert has. The best managers and coaches are not always the ones with the most expertise. Expert power is essential to people who work with other departments and other organizations. They have no direct position power, but being seen as an expert gives them credibility and standing.

Gaining Power

Why do some people want and seek power whereas others refuse it even if it's pressed on them? D. McClelland and D.H. Burnham wrote that the answer is based on one's need for power.[50] (You can measure your need for power in the Self-Assessment in chapter 11.) Power needs to be used wisely and ethically; greed and the need for power have ruined careers and organizations. Successful companies have great managers, but poor management can sink a company.[51]

Do you want to increase your power? Power is gained only with time, experience, success, and the increasing respect of your colleagues. Power grabbers may succeed for a while, but they usually ultimately fail. People are easy to lead when they believe you have legitimate power and impossible to lead when they sense that you are a power grabber.

If you are highly competent, have good people skills, and develop good relationships, you will gain power easily. To gain more power, you can use coercion sparingly and only when necessary, network to gain

TIME-OUT 6 Think about several bosses or coaches whom you are in a position to observe. Describe the types of power they have and the ones that they use. Do you think they use their power well? Why or why not?

APPLYING THE CONCEPT 8.1

Using Power

Identify the appropriate power to use in each situation.

a. coercive
b. connection
c. reward or legitimate
d. referent
e. information or expert

_____ 1. Bridget, one of your top people, normally needs very little direction. However, recently her performance has faltered. You suspect that Bridget's personal problems are affecting her work.

_____ 2. You need a new computer to help you organize ticket sales more efficiently. Computers are allocated by a committee, which is very political in nature.

_____ 3. Jean, a promising assistant coach, wants a promotion. Jean has talked to you about getting ahead in sport management and has asked you to help prepare her for when the opportunity comes.

_____ 4. John, one of your worst players, has ignored one of your directives once again.

_____ 5. Whitney, who continually needs direction and encouragement, is not working to standard today. As she does occasionally, she claims that she doesn't feel well but can't afford to take time off. You have to get an important customer order for golf clubs shipped today.

connections, praise and reward others for a job well done, make only legitimate requests of others, gain information about your field and organization, and develop your expertise so that others come to you.

Politics in the Office and on the Field

Before you read about the nature of politics at work, political behavior, and how to develop political skills, complete the Self-Assessment that follows.

◀ LEARNING OUTCOME 7
Understand how power and politics are related.

Nature of Politics in the Workplace

Politics is the efforts of groups or individuals with competing interests to obtain power and positions of leadership. Like power, office politics has a negative connotation because it can be manipulative and destructive. So we have to be ethical in using power and political behavior. However, you can't really do a job well without political skills. In the economy, the medium of exchange is money; but you don't use money to get what you want at work: You use politics. Politics is about give and take. Research supports that successful managers spend more time using political behavior than average managers, that you need to be political to climb the corporate ladder (or at least keep from being thrown off), and that the higher up you get, the more important politics becomes.

Political Behavior

Networking, reciprocity, and coalitions are important political skills. The goal is to build a net that works (networking) and helps you to develop useful relationships. Developing relationships is easier if you learn to use reciprocity and build solid coalitions.

◀ LEARNING OUTCOME 8
Explain what networking, reciprocity, and coalitions have in common.

SELF-ASSESSMENT 8.3

Political Behavior

Select the response that best describes your behavior on your job or team.

Rarely	Seldom	Occasionally	Frequently	Usually
1	2	3	4	5

_____ 1. I get along with everyone, even difficult coworkers.

_____ 2. I avoid giving my personal opinion on controversial issues, especially when I know others don't agree with me.

_____ 3. I try to make people feel important by complimenting them.

_____ 4. I often compromise when I work with others, and I also avoid telling people they are wrong.

_____ 5. I try to get to know key managers and find out what is going on in every department.

_____ 6. I dress the way the people in power dress and pursue the same interests (watch or play sports, join the same clubs) as they do.

_____ 7. I network with higher-level managers so they will know who I am.

_____ 8. I seek recognition and visibility for my accomplishments.

_____ 9. I get others to help me get what I want.

_____ 10. I do favors for others and ask favors from them in return.

To determine your score, add your answers. The higher your score, the more political your behavior in the workplace. Place your score here _____ and on the continuum.

Nonpolitical	10	20	30	40	50	Political

Networking

Networking is about developing relationships to gain social or business advantage. Networking is important to career success. Companies are using social media for business,[52] and young people today are called the greatest networkers, as they use social media effectively.[53] More people get jobs through networking than through all other methods combined.[54] Some companies are using social media to hire people.[55] However, some young people are not good at networking face-to-face, which is also important on the job.[56] Many people develop networks through playing and talking about sports. For example, people have been offered a job on the playing field. Many business deals have been made on the golf course. People network by taking up sports that their boss and people at other higher levels play and watch, even when they have no interest in the sport. Talk sports to those who are interested, but talk about other topics of interest to people who are not into sports.

Reciprocating

Reciprocating is about returning in kind. **Reciprocity** thus involves using mutual dependence to accomplish objectives. Have you heard the expressions "I owe you one" and "You owe me one"? When someone does something for you, you incur an obligation that the person may expect to be repaid in kind. Likewise, when you do something for someone, you create a debt that you may be able to collect later when you need a favor. Reciprocity is commonly used to get the job done.

Coalition

A **coalition** is an alliance of people with similar objectives who have a better chance of achieving their objectives together than alone. It often takes a coalition to get changes that you want to make. Networking and reciprocity are work in continual progress. In contrast, coalitions often come together temporarily and then dissolve once their objectives are accomplished.

Most important decisions are made by coalitions outside of the formal meeting in which the decision is made. For example, let's say you are on a team and the captain is selected by a nomination and vote of the team members. If you want to be captain, you can "politic" by asking close teammates whom they will vote for and trying to get their votes, and if they are supportive you can ask them to ask others to vote for you. If the majority of the team say they will vote for you, you won the election before the coach even starts the meeting. If you don't get any support from your close teammates and others, you drop the effort to build a coalition, knowing that you will lose. This same coalition-building process is used to influence all types of decisions.

Developing Political Skills

If climbing the corporate ladder is your goal, political skills should be in your tool kit. Review the statements in the Self-Assessment and strive to become comfortable with networking, reciprocating, and working with coalitions. Learn what it takes in the organization where you work as you follow the guidelines in figure 8.4.

TIME-OUT 7 Give examples of how your firm or team uses networking, reciprocity, and coalitions to achieve objectives.

Learn the Organizational Culture of Success

By now, you know how important organizational culture is (chapter 6). Make sure you learn yours well—culture defines the ground rules for politicking at work, so watch how your managers use political behavior. It is very important to understand what it takes to get ahead in the organization. Unfortunately, both managers and staffers are often clueless about the ingredients for success. So in addition to asking, observe the people who are

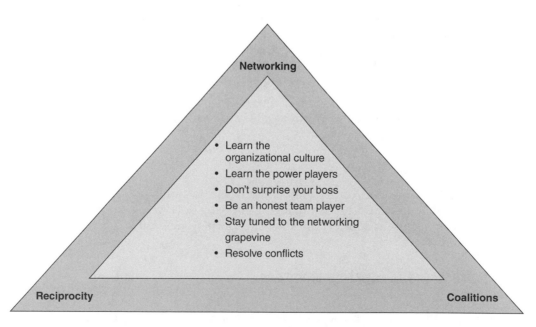

FIGURE 8.4 Developing political skills.

advancing and figure out why, and learn to read between the lines. Promote yourself in politically acceptable and ethical ways.

Learn the Power Players

Power players are people who have the ability to help you in your career. When you understand the power players in your group, department, and organization, you can tailor your presentations to meet their pet criteria. For example, some managers want details; others are impatient with the details and just want the big picture. Do things your boss's way, or convince the boss that your way is better and get support for your work so you stand out for advancement.

Develop a Good Working Relationship With Your Boss

When the performance appraisal system is subjective, it doesn't objectively indicate ranking of performance; having a good relationship with your boss—not results—gets you ahead.[57] And even with objective measures, if you want to get ahead, you need to have good working relationships with your managers. Here are some tips on how to succeed:
Know what the boss expects from you and do it, and give more than asked for.

- Get your boss's advice and inclusion in your coalition when you think that forming a coalition is the best strategy.
- Give your boss the good news—and the bad news. Let the boss know early on if you're having a problem. No boss wants to find out about your problem from somebody else.
- Don't talk negatively about your boss behind his back, because he will likely find out and it will hurt your chances of advancement. So follow the old rule—if you can't say something nice, don't say anything at all.
- Don't criticize your boss in public, even if asked to, because most bosses don't really want to hear anything negative about themselves.
- Don't show up a boss in public.
- Be very, very careful about going over your boss's head to complain, because if your boss has a good relationship with the person higher up, you will lose, and your boss may take revenge on you.
- If your boss doesn't give you excellent performance reviews, find out why and what it takes to get an excellent review—and do it if you want to get ahead.
- If you are not capable of meeting your boss's expectations or not willing to do so, consider looking for another job within the firm or at another organization. If you seek another job, don't complain about your boss; the manager you want to work for may think that you were the problem and not want to take a chance on you.
- If you make a political mistake that hurts your working relationship with your boss, the consequences may be isolation, extra work, bad tasks, and unfavorable evaluation of your performance.

Be an Honest Team Player

Secrecy breeds politics, so be open and honest.[58] High-functioning organizations are built on respect, confidence, and trust. If you are caught lying or cheating, your boss and team will not trust you. Self-discipline, teamwork, and fair play are great values on the playing field and in the office.

Stay Tuned to the Networking Grapevine

The grapevine can be a good thing—it can help you learn your organization's culture and its key players. It can also let you know what is going on in the organization and what is coming up, such as job openings. Your grapevine should include people both inside and outside your organization. Be active in trade or professional associations to keep up in your field and increase your skills and knowledge.[59]

TIME-OUT 8

Which suggestions for developing political skills feel least comfortable to you? Explain.

Resolve Conflicts

As you climb the corporate ladder, take care not to get thrown off. Choose your stands carefully. Avoid fights you can't win. If you find yourself suddenly out of the information loop, or if your boss or coworkers start treating you differently, find out why. Use your network or grapevine to find out whether someone is trying to undermine you and why. Understand where your enemies are coming from, how they operate, who's behind them, and what weapons they might use. Confront individuals or groups you suspect of instigating conflict. If you did something to offend a coworker, an apology from you may be in order. Admit mistakes; don't try to justify them.[60] In any case, approach your adversary and try to resolve the conflict using the ideas in the next section.

Managing Conflict

A **conflict** exists whenever argument becomes antagonistic. Conflict is inevitable in business, and well-meaning people differ all the time. When the issues are important and the opposing opinions strong, conflict can ensue. Managers spend hours weekly sorting out personality conflicts among staff members. Thus, effective conflict resolution and negotiation skills are imperative if you want to succeed as a manager. How well you handle conflict also affects your own job satisfaction and stress levels.

Conflict occurs everywhere. Part of the reason that Shaq left the LA Lakers was conflict with Kobe Bryant. In an effort to stay ahead of any conflicts in golf attributable to steroids, the Ladies Professional Golf Association (LPGA) started to conduct steroid testing back in 2008. In this section you will learn why people get into conflict, how conflict helps and hurts at work, and five styles of handling conflict.

Ground Rules

Implicit in all of our interactions with others is a psychological contract that we'll call the ground rules. These are our—and others'—expectations. At work, we all have a set of expectations about

APPLYING THE CONCEPT 8.2

Political Behavior

Identify each behavior as (a) effective or (b) ineffective.

_____ 6. Jill is taking golf lessons so she can join the Saturday golf group that includes some higher-level managers.

_____ 7. Paul tells his boss's boss about mistakes his boss makes.

_____ 8. Sally avoids socializing so that she can be more productive on the job.

_____ 9. John sent a very positive performance report about himself to three higher-level managers to whom he does not report. They did not request copies.

_____ 10. Carlos has to drop off daily reports by noon. He brings them around 10 on Tuesday and Thursday so that he can run into some higher-level managers who meet at that time near the office where the report goes. On other days, Carlos drops the report off around noon on his way to lunch.

what we will contribute to the organization (effort, time, skills) and what this will provide us (compensation, job satisfaction, status). These are our unspoken, implicit ground rules, and we don't want them violated. We may believe that there is mutual agreement on the ground rules, when in fact this may not be true. And therein lies the problem.

Thus, we get into conflict because our ground rules get broken. We fail to make explicit our own expectations, and we fail to inquire into the expectations of other parties. We further assume that other parties hold the same expectations as we do. As long as people meet our expectations, everything is fine; but when they don't, the result very often is conflict. Thus, sharing expectations, figuring out all the hidden agendas, and carefully negotiating explicit ground rules are key to avoiding conflicts.

Functional and Dysfunctional Conflict

Mention conflict, and people think of fighting and disruption. This is **dysfunctional conflict**—conflict that prevents groups from achieving their objectives. **Functional conflict** fosters disagreement and opposition that actually help achieve a group's objectives. We would all agree that too much conflict is dysfunctional. It so happens that so is too little conflict. Too little conflict means resistance to change and lack of diverse viewpoints. Too few viewpoints means that not enough alternatives are being explored and that opportunities in the environment are being overlooked. Functional conflict is one way to get to innovation and increased performance.[61] So the issue, then, is how to manage conflict so that it doesn't impair group functioning and so that it benefits team and organization performance.

The NCAA needs to resolve two very important but conflicting goals—the increasing commercialism of college sport and the development of young amateur athletes. If growing revenue through sponsorships and commercials becomes the NCAA's primary goal, it will be harder and harder to square this with keeping college athletes in amateur status. The NCAA has grappled with this dilemma for many years.[62]

LEARNING OUTCOME 9 ▶

Describe the five conflict management styles.

Styles of Conflict Management

Conflict management is based on two dimensions (concern for others' needs and concern for your own needs), which result in three types of behavior (passive, aggressive, and assertive). Taken together, these five components give us five different styles of conflict resolution, which are presented in figure 8.5 and discussed next.

Avoiding

Some employees try to manage conflict by avoiding it. They refuse to take a stance, withdraw mentally, or simply leave. This approach is neither assertive nor cooperative, and it resolves nothing. Both sides lose.

The advantage of avoidance is that it maintains relationships that would be hurt through resolving the conflict. The first disadvantage, of course, is that nothing gets resolved. The second disadvantage is that habitual avoiders become "rugs," and people who get walked on internalize a lot of conflict and stress. People walk all over avoiders, which can cause passive–aggressive behavior (in which the avoider loses control and really turns up the heat by getting into a yelling match).[63] Avoider managers allow employees to perform poorly without confronting them. This, of course, just makes the problem worse. The longer people wait to confront others, the more difficult the confrontation.

All this said, there are times when avoidance is appropriate: (1) when the conflict is trivial (trivial issues are not worth conflict), (2) when your stake in the issue is not high (you have everything to lose and nothing to win), (3) when confrontation could damage an important relationship (no sense burning big bridges), (4) when you don't have time to resolve the conflict (hurried resolutions are rarely good resolutions), and (5) when emotions are high (wait until heads are cooler).

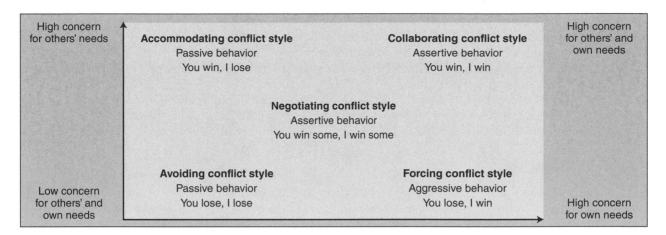

FIGURE 8.5 Styles of conflict management.

Accommodating

People who resolve conflict by passively giving in are managing conflict by accommodation. Accommodators satisfy the other party but neglect their own needs in the process. The opposing party wins; the accommodator loses.

Avoidance and accommodation differ in one significant way. Avoiders basically do nothing, but accommodators have to do something they don't really want to do. For example, if your professor asked the class for a volunteer to pick up and distribute course evaluation forms and you don't want to do it, you can simply avoid volunteering. However, if the professor asks you personally and you do it, you have used the accommodating style.

Habitual accommodation maintains relationships by doing things the other person's way. However, relationships built on one side's continual capitulation are not healthy ones and don't last. And giving in is counterproductive if the accommodator has the better solution. As with avoiders, people also take advantage of accommodators.

Accommodation, however, is appropriate in certain situations: (1) when you enjoy doing things for others (it's part of friendship), (2) when maintaining the relationship outweighs all other considerations, (3) when the changes agreed to are not important to you but are to the other party, (4) when time is limited, and (5) when you have an autocratic boss who resolves conflicts by force.

Forcing

People who use aggression to get their way resolve conflict by "going to combat." Forcers are uncooperative and aggressive—they do whatever it takes to satisfy their needs at the expense of others. Forcers threaten, intimidate, and call for majority rule when they know they will win. They also enjoy dealing with avoiders and accommodators because these are easy wins. Forcers win; everyone else loses.

When forcers have the better idea, the organization wins, but at a cost—in the form of low morale and wounds that may affect later situations. Plus, forcers make enemies right and left. Forceful managers use position power to force others to do things their way.

Force is appropriate in conflict resolution (1) when unpopular action must be taken on important issues, (2) when maintaining relationships is not critical, (3) when the conflict resolution is urgent, and (4) when you are dealing with an insubordinate employee.

Negotiating

People who resolve conflict through assertive give-and-take sessions are managing conflict by negotiation (also called compromise). Negotiators are both assertive and cooperative. Everyone wins some and loses some.

Negotiators typically resolve conflict quickly, and because everybody has given and gotten something, working relationships are maintained. The disadvantage is that the compromises negotiated may be suboptimal decisions. Negotiators often ask for more than they need in order to get what they want, particularly in collective bargaining, which can result in playing games.

Negotiation is appropriate to use (1) when the issues are complex and critical and there is no simple, clear-cut solution, (2) when parties have about equal power and are interested in different solutions, (3) when a solution will be only temporary, and (4) when time is short.

Collaborating

People who jointly and assertively try to get to the best solution, one that all parties can buy in to, resolve conflict by collaboration. Collaborators are problem solvers. They are both assertive and cooperative. Of the five styles, only collaborating focuses on finding the best solution. Avoiders and accommodators focus on avoiding conflict, and forcers focus on winning at all cost. Collaborators are willing to change positions if a better solution is presented. Negotiation is often based on secret information, whereas collaboration is based on open and honest communication.[64] This is the only conflict management style in which all parties win.

Collaboration often leads to strong solutions. The disadvantage is that greater skill, more effort, and more time are required to get there. Collaboration is difficult in the four situations in which negotiation is appropriate to use, and also when a forcer blocks the process. Collaboration offers the most benefits to individuals, groups, and organizations.

TIME-OUT 9
Which style of conflict management does your current boss or coach use most often? Explain using a typical example.

Collaboration is appropriate (1) when an important issue requires an optimal solution and compromise would result in a suboptimal solution, (2) when people place the group goal before self-interest, (3) when maintaining relationships is important, (4) when time is available, and (5) when the conflict is among peers.

There is no one best style for resolving conflict. The style we prefer personally may meet our needs but not the needs of the situation. If you wish to become a truly effective leader, you must become proficient at all five styles. And you must learn to judge a conflict and select the style that will best resolve it. Avoidance, accommodation, and force are the easiest to learn—indeed we've been using them for a long time. Most people find negotiation and collaboration the hardest to learn. Therefore, we explore negotiation and collaboration in more depth in the next two sections.

TIME-OUT 10
Which one style of conflict management do you use most often? Why? Give several examples.

Negotiation

Negotiating is about trying to get what you want, and you do it every day, even though you may not realize it. Good negotiators get better jobs with higher pay. Does this interest you? Negotiators attempt to hammer out agreements in which everyone gets something and everyone gives something. Negotiation is used to complete business deals, resolve disagreements, and reduce conflicts. Negotiation is appropriate and common in collective bargaining, buying and selling goods and services, and (sometimes) getting a job and raises. "Take it or leave it" situations, of course, leave no room for negotiation. Power and politics are important negotiating tools.

Negotiation often occurs in zero sum conflicts, in which one party's gain is the other party's loss. For example, each knockdown in price that athletic directors can negotiate for

APPLYING THE CONCEPT 8.3

Selecting Conflict Management Styles

Identify the most appropriate conflict management style for each situation.

    a. avoidance

    b. accommodation

    c. forcing

    d. negotiation

    e. collaboration

_____ 11. While serving on a committee that allocates athletic funds for building a new football stadium, you make a recommendation that another member opposes quite aggressively. Your interest in what the committee does is low, although you can see quite clearly that yours is the better idea.

_____ 12. The task force you've been assigned to has to select new fitness equipment. The four alternatives will all do the job. Members disagree on their brand, price, and service.

_____ 13. You manage golf cart sales for the Hole in One stores. Beth, who makes a lot of the sales, is in the midst of closing the season's biggest sale, and you and she disagree on which strategy to use.

_____ 14. You're late and on your way to an important meeting. As you leave your office, at the other end of the work area you see Chris, one of your employees, goofing off instead of working.

_____ 15. You're over budget for labor this month. Work is slow, so you ask Kent, a part-time employee, to leave work early. Kent tells you he doesn't want to because he needs the money.

a new scoreboard is their gain and the seller's loss. Thus, negotiators must sell the other party on their ideas, or they must exchange something for what they want. For a deal to work over a period of time, all parties in the negotiation need to believe they got a good deal. If a players' union believes that management won, player morale may dip, which could affect performance. Also, if fans (who are the nonrepresented third party in the wrangle between owners and the players' union) believe they got a bad deal, attendance might drop dramatically, as it has following past strikes.

Let's now describe the four stages of the negotiation process presented in figure 8.6. Skill-Builder 8.1 on page 272 gives you practice using the process.

Planning for the Negotiation

Solid preparations, or lack thereof, can mean the difference between success and failure. Be clear about what it is you are negotiating—is it price or salary, options, delivery time, sales quantities, or all of these? Planning entails four steps:

    1. Research the other party.

        Know the key players, know the issues, and know the context. Before you negotiate, try to find out what the other parties want and what they are and are not willing to give up. Use your networking grapevine to size up negotiators' personalities and negotiation style. The more you know about the other side, the better your chances of reaching an agreement. Think about what worked and did not work in previous negotiations with these parties. People often say that Donald Trump moves quickly in negotiating deals, but he says the reason he moves fast is that he prepares himself thoroughly.

    2. Set objectives.

        Based on your research, what can you expect? Limit your goals. Focus on just a few important points that you actually might be able to get.

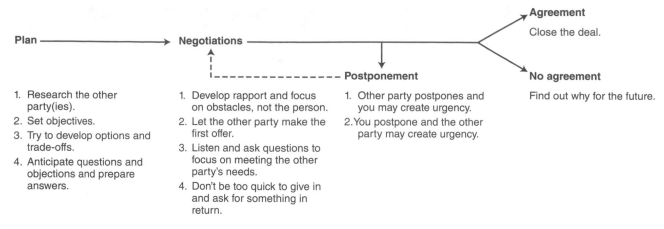

FIGURE 8.6 The negotiation process.

- Set a lower limit below which you are willing to agree. This lets you know when to walk away from a negotiation and not make a deal.

- Set a target objective that you believe is fair.

- Set an objective for the opening offer that is higher than you expect to get.

People in the other party may be doing the same thing, so don't view their opening offer as final. The key to successful negotiations is for all parties to get between their minimum and their target. This is the "I win some, you win some" situation that negotiations strive to achieve. It is helpful to have "must" and "want" criteria (chapter 3).

3. Try to develop options and trade-offs.

Suppose you are a free-agent NBA player. If you have multiple offers from other teams, you are in a strong power position to get your target salary. Remember context, however. If the job market is soft or you really want a particular job for whatever reason, dickering over salary may not be in your best interest. But don't shortchange yourself; explore your alternatives. If you have to give up something or cannot get exactly what you want, be prepared to ask for something else in return. If you cannot get the salary or raise you want, maybe you can get more days off or more in your retirement account.

4. Anticipate questions and objections and prepare answers.

The other party may want to know why you are negotiating. Be prepared to answer the unasked question—what's in it for you? Don't focus on what you want but on how your deal will benefit the other team. Talk in terms of *you* and *we*, not *I*, unless you are telling others what you're going to do for them.

There is a good chance that the other side will raise objections—reasons why the negotiations won't result in agreement. When agents ask for a raise, management typically says the team can't afford it. If, however, agents have done their homework, they strengthen their case by quoting profit numbers to prove their point. Unfortunately, parties don't always state their real objections. Thus, you need to listen and ask questions to find out what is preventing the agreement.

Make sure that you fully understand yourself, your position, and your deal and that you project confidence. If the other party doesn't trust you or believes the deal is not a good one, you won't reach an agreement. Thus, it's your job to convince the other party that she is getting a good deal. When you are being interviewed for a job, you have to convince the manager that you can do the job.

Negotiating

Now you are ready to negotiate the deal. Face-to-face negotiations are preferable because you can assess nonverbal behavior (discussed in chapter 10) and better understand objections. However, telephone and written negotiations work, too. Again, know the other party's preference.

1. Develop rapport and focus on obstacles, not the person.

Building rapport is important.[65] Smile and call the other party by name as you greet him. A smile tells people you like them, are interested in them, and enjoy them. Open with some small talk. How much time to wait until you get down to business depends on the other party's style. Some people like to get right down to business, but others want to get to know you before they discuss business. However, you want the other party to make the first offer, so don't wait too long or you may have to make the first move.

Never attack people on the other side or put them down with negative statements like "You're being unfair to ask for such a salary cut." The other party will become defensive, you will end up arguing, and prospects for agreement will dim if not disappear altogether. Instead, ask questions like "You think my salary request is too high?" Then state your competitive advantage in a positive way. If people perceive that you're pushing, threatening, or belittling, they won't trust you and negotiations will stall or reach an impasse. Avoid the "take it or leave it" approach, and if others use it, ask why they are refusing a deal that you believe is fair. Use open-ended questions to keep the other side talking.

2. Let the other party make the first offer.

There is always the possibility that the other party will offer you more than your target objective—you can then close the deal and be on your way. On the other hand, if offered less than your target, you can work from the assumption that this is a lowball offer and negotiate up by asking questions like "What is the salary range for this position?"

When others pressure you to make the first offer with questions like "Give us your salary requirement, and we'll tell you whether we'll take it," put the ball back in their court by asking, "What do you expect to pay?" If things go well during steps 1 and 2, you simply close the deal—you agree to agree. If you're not close to agreement, all is not yet lost.

3. Listen and ask questions to focus on meeting the other party's needs.

Again, focus on what's in the deal for the other party, not you. Create opportunities for revealing reservations and objections. When you're speaking, you may be revealing more than you want to; but when you're listening, the other person is doing the talking, which is what you want. That is, you are receiving information that will help you to overcome objections. If you go on and on about what you have to offer, you're not finding out what the other person is really interested in, and you may be killing the deal. Ask questions— "Is the salary out of the ballpark?" "Is it a reasonable amount?"—and then listen. Don't forget to listen. Perhaps the other person's objection involves a "want" criterion: Human resources wants to hire someone with 2 years of experience and you have only one. Play up the features you have that are wanted, and you may get an agreement. If the objection is a "must" criterion that you cannot meet, at least you know and you can stop chasing a deal that is not going to happen.

4. Don't be too quick to give in—ask for something in return.

Those who don't ask don't get. You want to satisfy the other party without giving up too much, and you want to get something in return. Don't go below your minimum objective—if it is realistic, you may have to walk away. If you do walk away, you may or may not be called back; and if not, you still may be able to come back for the same low salary, but not always. If the other side knows you are weakening and will accept a low agreement, they will be less likely to move from their stance. Think about "Must sell—need cash" signs. What type of price do you think they get? Don't let comments such as "Are you kidding me, that's too much" intimidate you. Also, when you are not getting what you want, having other options in your bag—fallback positions—can give you bargaining power.

Avoid giving in quickly. Recall your planned trade-offs. Don't give something for nothing. If the other party asks you to accept a lower salary, ask for a concession such as an extra year added to the contract.

Postponing

When you are not making progress, it is often wise to postpone the negotiations. Be prepared to postpone and to deal with the other party's postponing.

They Postpone—You Create Urgency

The other party says, "I'll get back to you." When you're not getting what you want, you can create urgency—for example, "This specific deal ends today." But don't be dishonest. The primary reason negotiations work is mutual trust and respect. Establishing a relationship of trust is key to closing a deal. Indeed, honesty and integrity are the most important assets a negotiator can possess. That doesn't mean you can't look at your options. Maybe you do have other job offers—in which case, it's perfectly acceptable to say, "I've got another job offer pending. When will you let me know what you've decided?"

But what if urgency doesn't work and the other person says, "I'll think about it"? Your response? "That's a good idea." But you also should quickly review the parts of your deal that the other person does like—leave her thinking about what she is walking away from. Putting her in the position of having second thoughts may keep the door open. If the other person doesn't appear to have second thoughts, then don't let the session end without pinning her down: "When can I expect to hear whether I get the job offer?" Ask for a specific time and note that if you don't hear from her by that date, you will call. Follow up with a letter, e-mail, or fax, thanking the other person for her time and highlighting the features she liked.

When the other party becomes resistant, the hard sell won't work. Take the pressure off by backing off. Ask where she wants to go from here, but don't press for an answer. This is the place to leave things open-ended. Waiting and giving the other person some breathing room may keep the door open. This is where you say, "Why don't we think about it and discuss it some more later?" Learn to read between the lines. Some people will not come right out and tell you "no deal."

You Postpone—They Create Urgency

Don't be hurried by others, and don't rush yourself. If you're not satisfied with the deal or you want to shop around, tell the other party that you want to think about it. You may also need to check with others for advice or approval (your boss) before you can finalize the deal. If the other party is creating urgency, be sure it is real. In many cases, you can get the same deal at a later date, so don't be pressured into making a deal you are not satisfied with or may regret later. If you do want to postpone, give a specific time that you will get back to the other person, and do so with more prepared negotiations, or simply say you cannot make an agreement.

Agreeing or Not Agreeing

Negotiations eventually end up with or without making a deal. Sometimes we agree and make a deal, but sometimes we don't agree to the terms of the other party, so we don't make a deal.

Agreeing

Once you've got an agreement, restate it. It is common to follow up an agreement with a letter of thanks that restates the agreement to ensure that the other parties have not changed their mind regarding the terms. After the deal is made, stop selling it. Change the subject to a nonbusiness one or leave, whichever is appropriate. The MLB and the Major League Baseball Players Association realized there was a drug problem in professional baseball. The two sides negotiated an agreement to try to stem the use of drugs in baseball. Some researchers believe that the two sides negotiated a more rigorous agreement than necessary.[66] However, the drug problem that had plagued MLB since 2002 required a rigorous set of rules to restore respect for players and for the game.

Failing to Agree

Not making an agreement is not necessarily a failure. Why should you settle for less than you deserve? It's not uncommon to lose one deal only to get a better one later. Refusal and failure happen to everyone—no one wins them all. The difference between also-rans and successful people lies in how they respond to failure. Successful people keep trying, learn from their mistakes, and continue to work hard. If you cannot come to an agreement, analyze the situation, determine why the negotiation failed, and get it right the next time.

Collaboration

◀ LEARNING OUTCOME 10

Use collaboration to resolve conflict.

To understand how collaboration works, we need to define two new terms. **Initiators** are people who approach other parties to resolve conflicts. Skillful initiators use BCF statements and then get involved parties to respond in BCF statements. **BCF statements** describe conflicts in terms of behavior, consequences, and feelings. That is to say, when you do B (behavior), C (consequences) happens, and I feel F (feelings). The sequence can be varied to fit the situation. An example of a BCF statement is "I fear [feeling] that the advertisement is not going to work [behavior] and that our hockey team will lose money [consequences]."

The idea is to resolve the conflict while maintaining the relationship.[67] So keep people from becoming defensive. When we become defensive, we go into behavior modes that are counterproductive. Two things are sure to make people defensive—when you don't let them talk and when you fix blame. Therefore, when you develop your opening BCF statement, be descriptive, not evaluative. Keep your opening statement short. The longer your statement, the more defensive you are likely to make the other party. And don't assess blame. Timing is also important. If people are busy, make arrangements to see them later to discuss the conflict. In addition, don't confront a person on several unrelated issues at once.

Now that you know what BCF statements are, you can use them to collaboratively resolve conflict. Figure 8.7 outlines the process of collaboration, and Skill-Builder 8.2 on page 273 gives you practice using the process. Next, we focus on initiating resolution and mediating conflict.

Initiating conflict resolution	Responding to conflict resolution	Mediating conflict resolution
Step 1. Plan a BCF statement that maintains ownership of the problem.	Step 1. Listen to and paraphrase the conflict using the BCF model.	Step 1. Have each party state the complaint using the BCF model.
Step 2. Present your BCF statement and agree on the conflict.	Step 2. Agree with some aspect of the complaint.	Step 2. Agree on the conflict problem(s).
Step 3. Ask for or give alternative conflict resolutions.	Step 3. Ask for or give alternative conflict resolutions.	Step 3. Develop alternative conflict resolutions.
Step 4. Make an agreement for change.	Step 4. Make an agreement for change.	Step 4. Make an agreement for change.
		Step 5. Follow up to make sure the conflict is resolved.

FIGURE 8.7 Resolving conflict by collaboration.

Initiating Conflict Resolution

As presented in figure 8.7, there are four steps to successfully initiating a conflict resolution.

1. Plan a BCF statement that maintains your ownership of the problem.

First let's look at what "ownership of the problem" means. Suppose you don't smoke and someone who is visiting you starts smoking. Who "owns" this problem? The smoke bothers you, not your visitor, so it's your problem. BCF statements that call on respondents to help you solve your problem don't assess blame or evaluate the behavior yet state the problem behavior clearly. State exactly what behavior bothers you.[68] This approach reduces defensiveness and establishes an atmosphere of problem solving that keeps doors open. Telling the other person he is stupid to smoke and will get cancer will only make him defensive and will likely start an argument rather than resolve the problem.

Put yourself in the other person's position. What presentation would keep you most open to solutions? Show concern for his issues as well as concern for your issues. Finally, if possible, practice your BCF statement before you approach the other party—you don't want to lose your cool. An example of a BCF statement is "When you smoke in the locker room [behavior], I have trouble breathing and become nauseous [consequence], and I feel uncomfortable and irritated [feeling]."

2. Present your BCF statement and agree on the conflict.

After you make your statement, let the other party respond. If she doesn't understand or refuses to acknowledge the problem, persist gently but firmly. You can't resolve a conflict if the other party won't acknowledge its existence. Explain the problem in different terms until you get an acknowledgment or realize that it's hopeless. But don't give up too easily.

3. Ask for and give alternative conflict resolutions.

Ask the other party what he thinks can be done to resolve the conflict. If you agree, great; if not, offer your solution. The idea is to get to collaboration. If the other party acknowledges the problem but is not responsive to resolving it, appeal to common goals. Make him realize the benefits—to him and to the organization.

4. Make an agreement for change.

Find specific actions you can both take. Clearly state, or for complex agreements write down, the specific changes that all parties must do to resolve the conflict. People don't always live up to their agreements, so follow up to make sure the conflict is resolved.

 TIME-OUT 11 Use figure 8.7 to outline how you could have resolved a conflict you recently faced.

Mediating Conflict

Frequently, parties in conflict cannot resolve their dispute alone. In these cases, mediators can be very helpful. A **mediator** is a neutral third party who helps resolve conflict. In non-unionized organizations, managers are commonly the mediators. But some organizations have trained staff who are designated mediators. In unionized organizations, mediators are usually professionals from outside the organization. However, resolution should be sought internally first. As a manager you may be called on to mediate a conflict. In this case, remember that you are a mediator, not a judge, and your job is to remain impartial. Get the employees to resolve the conflict themselves if possible.

If the conflict is not resolved through mediation, an arbitrator may be used as a follow-up. An **arbitrator** is a neutral third party whose decisions are binding. Arbitrators commonly use negotiation. Arbitration should be kept to a minimum because it is not a collaborative style. Arbitration is more commonly used in sport than is mediation. The reason is that collective bargaining agreements in sport focus on arbitration instead of mediation.

Dealing with different personality types, varying perceptions and attitudes, power, politics, and conflict can be very stressful. Therefore, in the next section we examine the causes and consequences of stress and how to manage it.

Stress

Our lives today abound with tension caused by deadlines, traffic jams, long hours at work and school, the need to excel in an uncertain competitive climate, lack of time to fulfill our responsibilities—the list is seemingly endless. **Stress** is our body's internal reaction to external stimuli coming from the environment. Our emotional reactions drive our bodies' physical reactions. How well do you handle stress? In this section, you will learn about functional and dysfunctional stress, causes of stress, signs of stress, and, most important, how to manage stress and play the stress tug-of-war.

Functional and Dysfunctional Stress

Stress is functional when it helps us perform better by challenging and motivating us to meet objectives. We all perform best under some pressure. When deadlines approach and the clock is ticking, our adrenaline flows and we often rise to the occasion with better than usual performance. The operative word here is *some:* some pressure but not too much. Think of stress as existing on a bell-shaped curve. On the left side, when you have too little stress, performance is lower; optimum stress is at the peak of the curve; but too much stress moves you to the right side of the curve, which lowers your performance.[69] Or, think of a race car "stress-o-meter." In low gear you go slow; when the gage is in the yellow zone, it's at its peak (time to shift), but going into the red can burn out the engine.[70]

Too much pressure is a serious, endemic problem in today's workplace. Excessive physical and mental stress can cause physical illness as well as mental and emotional problems.[71] Too much stress increases appetite and cravings and causes abdominal fat; so it makes you soft, flabby, and much older than you truly are.[72] As you may know, you can overtrain or compete and burn out, which results in lower athletic performance.[73]

Stressors are situations in which people feel overwhelmed by anxiety, tension, and pressure. Stress that is constant, chronic, and severe can cause burnout. *Burnout* is the constant lack of interest and motivation to perform one's job because of stress. From the organizational side, high stress results in job dissatisfaction, absenteeism, turnover, and lower levels of productivity.

Our abilities to handle pressure vary. In the same situation one person will be comfortable and stress free and another will be overwhelmed and stressed out. What stresses you out?

Causes of Stress

To overcome stress, it is important to understand what causes you stress.[74] There are five common job stressors. Before you read further, complete the Self-Assessment ahead to determine your stress personality type, which affects how you handle stress.

Type A, Type B Personality

Are you a type A or a type B personality? This is an important question for your health, because how much stress we personally set up in our lives is attributable, in part, to our personality type. Type A personalities are characterized as fast moving, hard driving, time conscious, competitive, impatient, and preoccupied with work. And as you have no doubt discerned, type A people set up fast-moving, hard-driving lives: They choose stressful lives. Type B personalities are just the opposite of type A personalities. As you can well imagine, type A people are more stressed than type Bs. Therefore, if you are a high type A personality, you may want to implement the stress management ideas presented here to offset the stress.

Even though personality types A and B are the most well-known classifications, other personality types exist. For instance, the type T personality has been described by various psychologists as a thrill-seeking or risk-taking personality. People with type T personality

SELF-ASSESSMENT 8.4

Stress Personality Type

Identify how frequently each item applies to you at work or when you are playing on a team.

Rarely	Seldom	Occasionally	Frequently	Usually
1	2	3	4	5

_____ 1. I enjoy competition and I work and play to win.

_____ 2. I skip meals or eat fast when there is a lot of work to do.

_____ 3. I'm in a hurry.

_____ 4. I do more than one thing at a time.

_____ 5. I'm aggravated and upset.

_____ 6. I get irritated or anxious when I have to wait.

_____ 7. I measure progress in terms of time and performance.

_____ 8. I push myself to work to the point of getting tired.

_____ 9. I work on days off.

_____ 10. I set short deadlines for myself.

_____ 11. I'm not satisfied with my accomplishments for very long.

_____ 12. I try to outperform others.

_____ 13. I get upset when my schedule has to be changed.

_____ 14. I consistently try to get more done in less time.

_____ 15. I take on more work when I already have plenty to do.

_____ 16. I enjoy work or school more than other activities.

_____ 17. I talk and walk fast.

_____ 18. I set high standards for myself and work hard to meet them.

_____ 19. I'm considered a hard worker.

_____ 20. I work at a fast pace.

_____ Total. Add up your scores (1-5) for all 20 items.

Your total score will fall between 20 and 100. Place an × on the continuum that represents your score.

Type A personality 100 90 80 70 60 50 40 30 20 **Type B personality**

find an outlet by participating in extreme sports.[75] Type T people can use their creativity to develop new sports like snowboarding and BMX or motocross racing.

Organizational Culture

Employee stress levels are directly affected by whether the culture is a cooperative one or an autocratic one and whether morale is high or low. The more positive an organization's culture, the less stress employees experience. Organizations that push their people to high levels of performance create stress, of course, but this can also give them high job satisfaction, which is de-stressing. So what type of culture is a good fit for you?

Management's Skill at Managing

The more effectively managers supervise their employees, the less stress experienced by all. Today's successful managers are making an effort to be nice to employees to help reduce stress, but at the same time they continue to work employees hard to get results, creating a better balance. How much stress does your boss cause you and the rest of the team?

Work Performed

Some work is more stressful than other work, and part of our stress comes from whether we enjoy our work. Those of us who enjoy the work itself handle stress better than those of us who don't. Thus, finding work that you enjoy is a wise move. University of Kentucky coach Rick Pitino became the Boston Celtics' coach. However, Pitino discovered that his coaching style, which had worked so well in college basketball, did not work with pro players. His response was to return to what he did well; he left the Celtics to coach college basketball at the University of Louisville, doing what he loves and what he does best—the secret of career success.

Human Relations

When people don't get along, stress increases. Our relationships with our coworkers are a very important factor in our job satisfaction. People who don't like their work but enjoy the people they work with can still be happy at work. However, when both components are missing—employees don't like the work *and* don't fit with coworkers—high absenteeism and turnover are often the result.

Signs of Stress

It is important to understand when stress is coming on so that you can deal with it.[76] Mild signs of stress include an increased breathing rate and an excessive amount of perspiration. When stress continues for a period of time, disillusionment, irritableness, headaches and other body tension, a feeling of exhaustion, and stomach problems can result. When you continually feel pressured and fear that you aren't going to meet deadlines, you are experiencing stress. When you start to think about failing (missing that shot or striking out), you are feeling stress.

People under stress do many things to find relief. They watch TV, movies, or video games (too much); drink (too much) and take illegal drugs; eat (too much); sleep (too much); and turn to pornography and abusive sex. Do you do these things to relieve stress? Using these escapes for a short time to get through a bad situation may not have negative long-term effects. However, be careful, because over a longer period of time people who watch too much TV often lose their interest in exercising and playing sports; people who drink or take drugs can become addicted; people who overeat become overweight; and most miss out on experiencing life. Obesity is a major problem, and employee alcohol and drug use costs American businesses billions annually in lost production, absenteeism, and health costs. No one starts out thinking *I'm going to become inactive, fat, or addicted to substances*; it happens over time.

Former University of North Carolina head basketball coach Dean Smith and former University of Nebraska head football coach Tom Osborne helped launch a nationwide campaign to rid televised college sports of alcohol advertising. Still, alcohol producers (especially beer companies) have a long tradition of advertising during college sporting events, and this trend will be hard to change. Unfortunately, well-known athletes have experienced alcohol problems; NFL wider receiver Hines Ward of the Pittsburgh Steelers and Diana Taurasi of the WNBA Phoenix Mercury were arrested for drinking and driving. Taurasi spent a full day behind bars, and this made her realize that "Once you make a mistake and put the control of your life in someone else's hands, it's scary."[77] Sadly, Josh

Hancock of the St. Louis Cardinals died while driving drunk. These are stories that point to the need for better methods to relieve stress.[78]

Managing Your Stress

As already discussed, first you have to identify the stressors in your life. Next, you look at what's causing them and the consequences of living with them (and without them—maybe you really don't want to quit college!). Finally, you find ways to eliminate or decrease the stressors. Helping employees stay fit increases productivity and is cost-effective. To combat the negative effect of stress, organizations are offering a variety of wellness programs. Harvard researchers found that medical costs dropped by about $3.27 for every dollar a company spent on wellness programs.[79] The stress management techniques we present here are widely effective, and you don't need to stress about using all of them.

Manage Your Time

Good time management skills can decrease job stress. Chapter 14 gives details on time management.

Relax

Start by getting enough rest and sleep to rejuvenate your body.[80] The average American doesn't get enough sleep; there is no magic number for everyone, but hardworking athletes generally need more sleep than the average person to perform at the top of their game. Here are some signs that you may not be getting enough sleep: trouble retaining information, irritability, minor illnesses, poor judgment, increased mistakes, and weight gain. Are you energetic, and do you recover sufficiently from your workouts?

Have some fun and laugh; try to slow down and enjoy yourself. Take some breaks during work and eat lunch; this reduces stress and mistakes. You will find that time down and time off make you more effective at school, on the field, and at work and may actually save you time! Pursue some enjoyable off-the-job interests. Socialize with friends and family, listen to music, pray, meditate—all of these options work for different people.[81] Find the ones that work for you.

Use Relaxation Exercises

Simple relaxation exercises can relieve stress. One of the most popular and simplest is deep breathing because it relaxes the entire body and can be done anywhere.[82] Consciously relaxing your entire body going from toe to head is another. Table 8.1 describes some relaxation exercises that you can do almost anywhere.

Deep breathing can be done during or between the other exercises. Simply take a slow deep breath, preferably through your nose, hold it for a few seconds (count to five); then let it out slowly, preferably through lightly closed lips. Make sure that you inhale by expanding the stomach, not the chest. Breathe in without lifting your shoulders or expanding your chest. Think of your stomach as a balloon. Slowly fill it, and then empty it. As you inhale, visualize breathing in healing energy that makes you feel better, more energetic, and less pained. As you exhale, visualize breathing out tension, pain, illness, and other stress. Use this visualizing technique during the other relaxation exercises.

Eat Right

Good health is essential to everyone's performance, and nutrition is a major factor in health. Obesity is a pervasive health problem. Stress often leads to overeating and compulsive dieting, and being overweight is itself stressful. Accurate and helpful information about nutrition and healthy eating habits is widely available. Here's the short version: Limit your

TABLE 8.1   Quick Tricks for Relaxation

Muscles relaxed	Exercise
All	Take a deep breath, hold it for about 5 seconds, and then let it out slowly. See page 264 for details. Deep breathing may be performed during or between other relaxation methods.
Forehead	Wrinkle your forehead by trying to make your eyebrows touch your hairline for 5 seconds. Relax.
Eyes, nose	Close your eyes tightly for 5 seconds. Relax.
Lips, cheeks, jaw	Draw the corners of your mouth back tightly (grimace) for 5 seconds. Relax.
Neck	Drop your chin to your chest, and then slowly rotate your head without tilting it backward. Relax.
Shoulders	Lift your shoulders up toward your ears and tighten for 5 seconds. Relax.
Upper arms	Bend your elbows and tighten your upper arm muscles for 5 seconds. Relax.
Forearms	Extend your arms out against an invisible wall and push forward with your hands for 5 seconds. Relax.
Hands	Extend your arms in front of you and clench your fists tightly for 5 seconds. Relax.
Back	Lie on your back on the floor or a bed and arch your back up off the floor while keeping your shoulders and buttocks on the floor. Tighten for 5 seconds. Relax.
Stomach	Suck in and tighten your stomach muscles for 5 seconds. Relax. Repeating this exercise several times throughout the day can help reduce the size of your waistline.
Hips, buttocks	Tighten buttocks for 5 seconds. Relax.
Thighs	Press your thighs together and tighten them for 5 seconds.
Feet, ankles	Flex your feet with toes pointing up as far as you can and tighten for 5 seconds, then point your feet down and tighten for 5 seconds. Relax.
Toes	Curl your toes under and tighten for 5 seconds, and then wiggle them. Relax.

For all exercises, tighten your muscles as much as you can without straining, and perform as many tightening–relaxing repetitions as needed to feel relaxed without straining.

intake of sugar and white flour (which most processed foods are full of); eat breakfast; don't eat junk food; consume less fat, caffeine, and salt; limit starchy carbohydrates (breads, grains, potatoes, rice, and so on); and eat more fruits and vegetables.[83] To assist with eating right, many firms are offering healthier meals at work.[84] If you have an eating disorder, acknowledge it (because it can kill you) and get professional help. Your college most likely offers free counseling or can get you to the right people.

Are soft drinks bad for you? Do diet drinks contribute to weight gain? A study indicated that diet soda does in fact lead to weight gain. People who consumed one or more soft drinks per day (regular or diet) were 44% more likely to have metabolic syndrome, 31% more likely to be obese, 25% more likely to have high blood sugar, and 18% more likely to have high blood pressure.[85] Sounds like a good reason to delete these drinks from your diet.

Exercise

It is well established that physical exercise has numerous beneficial effects on our health. Many firms pay all or part of gym memberships and have exercise facilities and offer classes. Google offers 230 exercise classes. More gyms leads to more sport management jobs. Exercising is an excellent way to break up your workday and release stress.[86] Always check with a doctor before starting an exercise program. Because your objective is to relax and reduce stress, not increase it, you should avoid the no pain–no gain mentality—leave that on the court or playing field. Aerobic exercises that increase the heart rate for 30 minutes three or more times a week are generally recommended. The key is to pick an exercise you enjoy doing; if you hate to jog, how long will you stick with it?

Think Positively

Optimists experience less stress than pessimists because they focus on the positive, not dwelling on the negative.[87] Get rid of your negative self-talk. Talk to yourself in the affirmative: "This is easy" or "I can do this." Repeat positive statements while doing deep breathing, but be realistic. Positive thinking doesn't guarantee that you will be free of stress headaches, but pessimism and negative self-talk push many people into headaches and various illnesses.

Don't Procrastinate: Don't Be a Perfectionist

Procrastinating is stressful. When you procrastinate, you don't accomplish tasks that you're supposed to do. The resulting feeling of failure causes stress, and the longer you wait to do the task, the more stressed you get. Even if you eventually complete the task, the results will be poorer than they might have been had you not procrastinated.

> **TIME-OUT 12**
> Choose a major stressor in your life right now and develop a plan to manage it, using the suggestions noted here or others that you think would work well for you.

Striving for perfectionism is stressful. Here we are talking about work tasks, not athletic performance. Reworking something excessively usually isn't worth the time and effort and may make you rush through another task that is more important. Sometimes reworking actually makes things worse. Define a job as done "perfectly enough" and stop.

Build a Support Network

Talking to others about your stressful situation helps reduce stress. Talk to your friends, family, teammates, and coworkers—that's what they are there for.[88] Don't be proud and clam up when things are getting you down. But don't continually complain and whine either; you'll wear out the welcome mat. Be there for others in return; that's what networking is all about.

> **TIME-OUT 13**
> Which of the stress management techniques noted here are you best at and worst at? Develop a plan to improve your weakest stress management skills.

LEARNING OUTCOME 11 ▶

Explain the stress tug-of-war analogy.

Stress Tug-of-War

Think of stress as a tug-of-war with you in the center, as shown in figure 8.8. On your left are ropes (causes of stress) pulling you to burnout. Stress that is too powerful will pull you off center. On your right are ropes (stress management techniques) that you can use to pull yourself back to the center. The stress tug-of-war is an ongoing game. On easy days you move to the right, and on overly tough days you move to the left. Your objective in this game? Find ways to stay centered. But when you can't, it is also important to recover after being stressed out.[89]

Managing stress well doesn't mean that you have to use all the techniques. Use what works best for you, but be aware that taken together, the techniques add up to a pretty good definition of a healthy life. What if you are using these techniques and your stress levels are still off the charts? Consider getting out of the situation. Ask yourself two questions: "Is my long-term health important?" and "Is this situation worth hurting my health?" If you answered yes and no, in that order, it may be time to drop the ropes and walk away.

We've covered a lot in this chapter; you have learned about OB and creating win–win situations, about the Big Five and your personality profile, about your attitudes and how

APPLYING THE CONCEPT 8.4

Stress Management Techniques

Identify the technique being used in each statement.

   a. time management
   b. relaxation
   c. nutrition
   d. exercise
   e. positive thinking
   f. support network

_____ 16. I talk to myself to be more optimistic about my foul shooting.

_____ 17. I've set up a schedule for myself to meet season ticket sales goals.

_____ 18. I get up earlier and eat breakfast to improve my performance.

_____ 19. I'm talking to my partner about my problems in acquiring funding for our athletic department.

_____ 20. I pray.

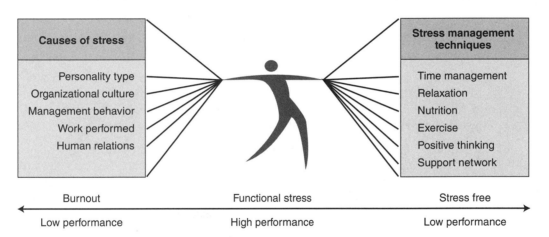

FIGURE 8.8   The stress tug-of-war.

they affect your performance and job satisfaction, how to use power and politics ethically to get what you want, how to manage conflicts, how to negotiate and collaborate, and how to manage your stress. Now it's time to apply this knowledge in your personal and professional life to develop the OB people skills that employers seek and to improve your quality of life and that of the people you interact with.

@ TAKE IT TO THE NET

Please visit www.HumanKinetics.com/AppliedSportManagementSkills and go to this book's companion web study guide, where you will find the following:

   A list of websites associated with the concepts in this chapter

   Exercises that you will need Internet access to complete

   Online versions of chapter exercises and end-of-chapter learning aids

   An exercise that helps you define the Key Terms

LEARNING AIDS

CHAPTER SUMMARY

1. Describe the Big Five personality traits.

   Five continuum traits exist: extrovert and introvert (the extroversion trait); cooperative and competitive (the agreeableness trait); stable and unstable (emotionalism); dependable and not dependable (conscientiousness); and willingness and unwillingness to try new things (openness to experience).

2. Understand the perception process and the two factors on which it is based.

   Perception is the process of selecting, organizing, and interpreting information from the external environment. How we do this is based on internal individual factors that include our personality and our attitudes. The second factor in the perception process is the information itself.

3. Explain how personality, perception, and attitude are related and why they are important.

   Our personalities affect our perceptions and our attitudes. Perception affects attitudes, and vice versa. Changing self-esteem and adjusting attitudes actually change single personality traits such as optimism. Personality, perception, and attitude are important because combined, they directly affect behavior and performance.

4. State what job satisfaction is and why it is important.

   Job satisfaction is a person's attitude toward her job. Job satisfaction is important because it has direct relationships with absenteeism, turnover, and performance.

5. Define power and explain the difference between position and personal power.

   Power is the ability to influence others' behavior. Position power is derived from top management and delegated down the chain of command, whereas personal power is derived from the followers based on the individual's behavior.

6. Explain how reward power, legitimate power, and referent power differ.

   The difference is based on how the person with power influences others. Reward power is the user's ability to influence others with something of value to them. Legitimate power is given by the organization and is a type of position power. Referent power has to do with the user's personal power relationship with others.

7. Understand how power and politics are related.

   Power is the ability to influence the behavior of others. Politics is the process of gaining and using power. Therefore, political skills are a part of power.

8. Explain what networking, reciprocity, and coalitions have in common.

   Networking, reciprocity, and coalitions are all political behaviors. Networking is used to develop relationships to gain social or business advantage. Reciprocity is used to create obligations and develop alliances and then use them to accomplish objectives. Coalitions are alliances of people with similar objectives who together have a better chance of achieving their objectives.

9. Describe the five conflict management styles.

   Avoiders passively ignore conflict rather than resolve it. Accommodators resolve conflict by passively giving in to the other party. Forcers use aggressive behavior to get their own way. Negotiators resolve conflict through assertive give-and-take concessions. Collaborators resolve the conflict by finding the best solution that is agreeable to all parties.

10. Use collaboration to resolve conflict.

    Collaboration involves (1) planning a BCF statement that maintains your ownership of the problem, (2) presenting your BCF statement, (3) agreeing on the conflict,

(4) asking for or giving alternative solutions, (5) agreeing on change, and (6) following up to see whether the conflict was truly resolved.

11. Explain the stress tug-of-war analogy.

The stress tug-of-war puts us between stressors that try to pull us off balance and stress management techniques that can keep us centered so that our stress is at functional levels and our performance high. If the causes of stress pull us off center, we burn out and our performance suffers.

REVIEW AND DISCUSSION QUESTIONS

1. Are the conflicts that the USADA faces functional or dysfunctional?

2. How could the USADA use negotiation to solve some of its conflicts?

3. Could the USADA use mediation to solve some of its conflicts?

4. Can college athletes use stress management to improve their performance?

5. What are the Big Five personality traits?

6. What are the four biases in perception?

7. What factors determine job satisfaction? Are they of equal importance to everyone?

8. What are the seven bases of power?

9. Can management order the end of power and politics in the organization? Should it? Why or why not?

10. Why should you learn your organization's culture and identify power players where you work?

11. How do you know when you are in conflict?

12. What is the difference between functional and dysfunctional conflict, and how does each affect performance?

13. What is the primary reason for your personal conflicts? Your work conflicts?

14. What is meant by "ownership of the problem"?

15. How are BCF statements used?

16. What is the difference between a mediator and an arbitrator?

17. What are the characteristics of type A personalities?

18. What type T sports do you like to either participate in or watch on screen?

19. What are some stress management techniques?

20. Draw a simple diagram of John Wooden's pyramid of success. You can find it at the official Wooden website www.coachwooden.com/index2.html.

CASE

What Is Involved in Scheduling College Football and Basketball Games?

So, you still think being an athletic director for a major university is an easy job? Think again. For instance, scheduling games in all sports and at all divisions has become increasingly more complex. The need to have open dates to play in busy arenas, transportation costs for each team, referee availability, weather concerns, gasoline costs, and housing costs all make the process very complex.

The first case is the scheduling of a University of Michigan versus University of Massachusetts (UMass) football game in 2012. This would be a rematch against Michigan and would be played at Michigan Stadium.

Why would Michigan, with a stadium that sits around 100,000 fans, want to play UMass, with a home stadium that fits only a few thousand fans? First of all, on April 20, 2011, UMass announced its move to the Football Bowl Subdivision (FBS) and the Mid-American Conference (MAC) and would play a full FBS and MAC schedule beginning with the 2012 football season. Thus it wanted to develop a strong nonconference schedule that would help build its growing football program.[90] Secondly, Michigan athletic director Dave Brandon was looking for a game with a lower-tier opponent since Michigan had a difficult schedule against many college football powerhouses, such as Alabama, Notre Dame, and Nebraska.[91] Lastly, UMass was happy to receive $650,000 to help build its football program.

A second case involving UMass was an unfortunate cancellation of the University of Kentucky versus UMass basketball game during the 2007-2008 basketball season. Travis Ford, the UMass coach, had a personal connection with Kentucky since he had been a star basketball player for Kentucky. Kentucky coach Tubby Smith helped arranged a game between Kentucky and Ford's UMass team, which was to be played in Boston. However, Tubby changed coaching jobs (he went to the University of Minnesota) soon after the 2006 season. The new Kentucky coach, Billy Gillispie, decided not to play UMass in Boston as prearranged. The result was not only a cancellation of a single game, but also a great deal of dysfunctional conflict between the athletic administrations at the two schools. Instead of having started a positive long-term relationship, it seemed more likely that the two colleges would be unwilling to trust each other. In essence, Kentucky used its long history as a basketball powerhouse to coerce UMass into making last-minute changes. There might have been a good basketball reason for Kentucky to cancel the game, but it felt more as though Kentucky was exhibiting its superior attitude as a team that had a much richer tradition of success in collegiate basketball.

What could be some of the reasons to cancel a scheduled game and create so much dysfunctional conflict between the two parties? First, it is possible that Gillispie wanted to minimize the number of road trips during the season. Second, he might have believed that the long road trip to Boston was not worth the effort. Third, he might have preferred to play (and hopefully win) against a higher-ranked opponent that would give Kentucky a higher ranking at the end of the season. Fourth, the personal connection that Ford had with Kentucky was not strong enough for either Ford or UMass AD John McCutcheon to use to save the game. Either way, Kentucky and Gillispie controlled the situation and forced the cancellation. Kentucky paid a prearranged cancellation fee of U.S.$50,000. UMass ultimately lost an expected U.S.$300,000 in revenue that the game would have generated. Maybe the real lesson was learned by UMass AD McCutcheon, who said, "This is a bad practice and maybe next time we should have a higher buyout."[92]

For more information on the game that was never played, visit the following ESPN website: http://sports.espn.go.com/ncb/news/story?id=2877223.

Case Questions

Support your answers to the following questions with specifics from the case and text or with information you get from the web and other sources.

1. Which type of power base did the University of Kentucky use when it cancelled its game with UMass?

   a. coercive

   b. connection

   c. reward

   d. legitimate

    e. referent

    f. information

2. Which type of power did Michigan's AD use when Michigan worked closely with UMass?

    a. coercive

    b. connection

    c. reward

    d. legitimate

    e. referent

    f. information

3. The scheduling of collegiate basketball games has nothing to do with organizational politics.

    a. true

    b. false

4. Are attitudes an issue in the Kentucky–UMass case?

    a. yes

    b. no

5. What style of conflict management was used by the Kentucky athletic department to resolve the problem with UMass?

    a. avoiding

    b. accommodating

    c. forcing

    d. negotiating

6. Did Michigan and UMass achieve a win–win situation?

    a. yes

    b. no

7. Did the University of Kentucky and UMass achieve a win–win situation?

    a. yes

    b. no

8. What type of conflict was involved in the Kentucky–UMass case?

    a. functional

    b. dysfunctional

    c. resolve

    d. psychological

9. What type of stress was placed on the UMass athletic director John McCutcheon?

    a. functional

    b. dysfunctional

    c. management

    d. organizational

10. Why do conflicts arise when scheduling collegiate basketball and football games?

SKILL-BUILDER EXERCISES

Skill-Builder 8.1: Contract Negotiation

Objective
To develop negotiation skills

Preparation
Reread the section on the negotiating process (pp. 254-259).

In-Class Application
Activity (10-20 minutes):

- Break into partners.
- One of you is Butch Steel, your team's star football player, and one of you is the general manager. Negotiations to re-sign Butch with the team are about to begin.
- Your instructor has just handed you your confidential sheets. Read them and jot down some plans for the lunch meeting you are about to have (your basic strategy, what you will say).
- As part of your preparation, read the following negotiating checklist and keep it by you during the negotiations for reference and note taking:

1. The appropriate plan for this situation:
   _____ general single-use project plan_____ detailed standing-policy plan

2. Your basic plan:
   _____
   _____
   _____

3. Your lower limit, target, and opening salary:
   _____

4. Can you imply that you have other options or trade-offs? If so, what are they?
   _____
   _____
   _____

5. Can you anticipate questions and objections? If so, what are they, and what are your answers?
   _____
   _____
   _____

6. Did you develop rapport and focus on obstacles, not the person? If not, why not?
   _____
   _____
   _____

7. Did you let the other party make the first offer? If not, why not?
   _____
   _____
   _____

8. Did you listen? Did you ask questions that focused on meeting the other party's needs? Did you ask for something in return for concessions? If so, what?

_____

9. Were you able to use postponement as a strategy? If so, how did the other side create urgency?

_____
_____
_____

10. Did you reach agreement? If so, state the final offer. If not, why not?

_____
_____
_____

- You do not have to finalize the contract. Begin negotiations.
- After you sign the contract, or agree not to sign, read your partner's confidential sheet and discuss the experience.

Choose one (10-20 minutes):

- Volunteers present their negotiations, and class critiques them.
- Hold informal, whole-class discussion of student experiences.

Wrap-Up

Take a few minutes to write your answers to the following questions:

What did I learn from this experience? How will I use this knowledge?

_____
_____
_____

Had the stakes been real, would this task have caused you some stress?

_____

As a class, discuss student responses.

Skill-Builder 8.2: Initiating a Collaboration

Objective

To develop your ability to resolve conflict

Preparation

During class you will role-play a conflict you are currently facing or have faced in the past. Students have told us that this exercise helped them successfully resolve real conflicts with roommates, coworkers, and teammates. Fill in the following information before class:

Other party or parties (use fictitious names):

_____

Pertinent information (relationship to you, knowledge of the situation, age, background):

_____

Describe the conflict:

_____
_____
_____

The other party's possible reaction to your initiating a discussion to resolve the conflict (how receptive will he or she be to collaborating? What might he or she say or do during the discussion to resist change?):

_____

_____

_____

How will you overcome this resistance to change?

_____

_____

_____

Write your opening BCF statement (keep it short, maintain ownership of the problem, and don't assess blame):

_____

_____

_____

In-Class Application

Complete the preceding skill-building preparation before class. Break into groups of three, and use the conflict papers you prepared before class to role-play a possible resolution. Take turns acting as initiator, responder, and observer. Observers will make notes on the feedback sheets provided in class (or use the form provided) and then lead a short discussion on the collaboration's effectiveness. Change groups and role-play the same conflicts with different people.

Choose one (10-15 minutes):

- Volunteers present examples of effective and ineffective resolutions. Select one student's example and as a group present it to the entire class.
- Conduct informal, whole-class discussion of student experiences.

Wrap-Up

Take a few minutes to write your answers to the following questions:

What did I learn from this experience? How will I use this knowledge?

_____

_____

_____

_____

As a class, discuss student responses.

Observer's Feedback Form

Note comments for improving each step in the collaboration. Cast them in positive terms, if you can. Be descriptive and specific, and for all improvements have an alternative positive behavior (APB) (if you had said or done _____, it would have improved the conflict resolution by _____).
Was the initiator's opening BCF statement well planned and effective? Give specifics on how to improve it.

_____

_____

_____

Did the initiator present the BCF statement effectively? Why or why not?

_____

_____

_____

Did the initiator and responder agree on the conflict? If not, why not?

_____

_____

_____

Who suggested alternative solutions? Was the suggestion made effectively? How could it have been improved?

_____

_____

_____

Was there an agreement for change? If so, was it a reasonable resolution? If not, why not?

_____

_____

_____

Other suggestions:

_____

_____

_____

_____

_____

SPORTS AND SOCIAL MEDIA EXERCISES

Use espn.com and search for articles related to conflict. Review three articles that discuss conflict in a sport situation.

1. _____

   _____

2. _____

   _____

3. _____

   _____

GAME PLAN FOR STARTING A SPORT BUSINESS

Power, politics, conflict, and stress are part of every organization. What is one thing you learned from the chapter that you will implement to help manage each of these behaviors that organizations exhibit?

Power _____

Politics _____

Conflict _____

Stress _____

Team Development

LEARNING OUTCOMES

After studying this chapter, you should be able to

1. explain how groups and teams differ;
2. explain the group performance model;
3. categorize groups by their structure;
4. define the three major roles group members play;
5. explain how rules and norms differ;
6. describe cohesiveness and why it is important to teams;
7. describe the five major stages of group development and the leadership style appropriate for each stage;
8. explain how group managers and team leaders differ; and
9. lead a meeting.

KEY TERMS

group	command groups	group roles
team	task groups	norms
group performance model	group composition	group cohesiveness
group structure dimensions	group process	status
group types	group process dimensions	stages of group development

DEVELOPING YOUR SKILLS

For groups to maximize their performance, they must have effective organizational context, group structures, group process, and group development. In this chapter, the skills focus is on developing group process skills, analyzing the group's development stage, and selecting the leadership style appropriate to the stage. You can also develop your skills at leading and participating in meetings, including dealing with problem team members in meetings.

REVIEWING THEIR GAME PLAN

Getting Kids to Team Play

Playing together, learning together, working together: These activities start early in life and continue throughout our lives. They shape us in crucial and fundamental ways into functioning adults, functioning communities, and functioning societies. Set them up wrong and you can take the word *functioning* out of the preceding sentence. Our society endeavors in numerous ways to keep *functioning* as a descriptor for our nation. Groups like the Boys & Girls Clubs of America, the YMCA, Jewish Community Centers (JCCs), town sport leagues, and Little League Baseball—to name only a very few—all work to shape kids into team players and high-functioning adults.

The mission of the Boys & Girls Clubs of America is simple—to be available for kids. As the organization notes in its mission statement, "In every community, boys and girls are left to find their own recreation and companionship in the streets. An increasing number of children are at home with no adult care or supervision. Young people need to know that someone cares about them." Boys & Girls Clubs offer that and more. Club programs and services instill a sense of competence, usefulness, belonging, and influence. "Boys & Girls Clubs are a safe place to learn and grow—all while having fun. They are truly The Positive Place for Kids."[1]

Whether leading basketball at the YMCA, coaching softball at the JCC, or leading a Boy Scouts or Girl Scouts troop, the men and women in these organizations devote their lives to helping kids and being positive role models. Their dream? That eventually the kids they coach will carry forward the torch of good sport conduct; integrity and hard work; and a love of sport as coaches, parents, teammates, teachers, and community leaders.

These organizations also need you. Join them—it's time for you to pass the torch forward. You can either volunteer or look for careers helping these organizations. You will find that this is a boomerang endeavor. What you give away will come back in deep satisfaction, in surprising joy, in strength you never knew you had, and in wisdom you won't gain anywhere else. For example, the 2012 NBA All-Star Game in Orlando helped the Boys & Girls Clubs in Central Florida. LeBron James, along with Sprite, installed a new outdoor play area, including an all-new baseball diamond, soccer pitch, and picnic area at the Walt Disney World Branch of the Boys & Girls Clubs of Central Florida. LeBron also donated new sport equipment to help with athletic programming. Tony Parker's victory in the Taco Bell Skills Challenge resulted in a $25,000 scholarship for a young club member. The members were also able to watch practices of the East and West teams.[1]

For current information on local recreation centers, see www.bgca.org for the Boys & Girls Clubs of America, www.ymca.net for the YMCA, and www.jcca.org for the Jewish Community Centers of North America.

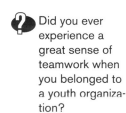 Did you ever experience a great sense of teamwork when you belonged to a youth organization?

Importance of Teamwork to Performance

Kids learn to work with each other when they join a youth organization like the Boys & Girls Clubs. They learn there are good times (winning games and laughing) and bad times (losing games and getting hurt), but either way they learn to stand with each other. Performance is important, and individuals working together make teams.[2] You might be familiar with the saying "There is no 'I' in 'team.'" On the other hand, managers have to be sure there is 'team' in 'teamwork'! Cal Ripken and Tony Gwynn retired with great individual accomplishments and accolades; but the Seattle Mariners won more American League games as a *team* than any team ever before.[3] Although there are great leaders, they know that success belongs to the team.[4]

You already understand the importance of teamwork to athletic performance. The same teamwork skills need to be applied to both athletics and sport management. Organizations are increasingly using groups as their fundamental unit of organizational structure to respond more flexibly and quickly to rapidly changing environments.[5] Thus, teamwork skills are becoming more important, and recruiters are looking to hire job candidates with the ability to work well within teams.

You have developed some teamwork skills that will help you get a job, so including team experience on your resume is a sure winner. But in hiring sport managers, firms are seeking candidates who possess team leadership–related knowledge and skills, especially for dealing with team challenges. By reading this chapter, you can improve your teamwork skills, but more important to sport management, you can understand the factors that contribute to team performance, learn how to improve team performance, and develop some team leadership skills. Team skills are part of people skills, so essentially all of the skills covered in other chapters will improve your teamwork. But before reading on, complete the Self-Assessment to determine whether you are more of an individual player or a team player.

SELF-ASSESSMENT 9.1

Are You a Team Player?

Answer the questions on a scale from 1 to 5. Place the number (1-5) on the line before the question.

Describes me				Does not describe me
5	4	3	2	1

_____ 1. I focus on what I accomplish during team projects.

_____ 2. I don't like to compromise.

_____ 3. I depend on me to get things done.

_____ 4. I prefer to work alone, rather than in a group, when I have a choice.

_____ 5. I like to do things my way.

_____ 6. I do things myself to make sure the job gets done right.

_____ 7. I know that teams do better when each member has a separate job.

_____ 8. I'm more productive when I work alone.

_____ 9. I try to get things done my way when I work with others.

_____ 10. It bothers me if I can't get the group to do things my way.

Add up your scores, place the number here, and put it on the continuum below.

Individual								Team player
50	45	40	35	30	25	20	15	10

There is no right or wrong here, but the manager's job is to get the work done through others. If you have a very high score, indicating individuality, you may want to work at being more of a team player. You may also consider seeking a professional job (sales) within the field of sport management rather than a supervisory position.

Lessons of the Geese

Ever wondered why geese fly south for the winter in "V" formations? What scientists have found has implications that teams would do well to learn and apply.

- Each bird flapping its wings creates an uplift (thrust) for the bird following. Flying in a "V" adds 71% greater flying range compared to flying in disorganized clusters or flying alone.

    Lesson: Travel on the thrust of each other (synergy). A common direction and a sense of community can get your team to the finish line faster and easier.

- Falling out of formation causes individual birds to feel the sudden drag and the higher (and more difficult) resistance of going it alone. This helps them continually adjust their flying to keep the formation.

    Lesson: There is strength, power, and safety in members who travel in the same direction.

- When lead birds get tired, they rotate to the back of the formation, and another goose flies point.

    Lesson: Take turns doing the hard jobs.

- Geese at the back of the "V" honk to encourage front flyers to keep speed.

    Lesson: We all need to be reminded with active support and praise.

- When a goose gets sick or is wounded and falls out of the "V," two geese follow it down to help and protect it. They stay with the downed goose until the crisis is resolved, and then they launch out on their own in a "V" formation to catch up with their group.

    Lesson: Stand by each other in times of need.

LEARNING OUTCOME 1 ▶

Explain how groups and teams differ.

There Are Groups and There Are Teams

Although we often use the words *group* and *team* interchangeably, they are different. All teams are groups, but not all groups are teams. **Groups** have a clear leader and two or more members who perform independent jobs with individual accountability, evaluation, and rewards. **Teams** are groups whose members share leadership and whose members perform interdependent jobs, with individual and group accountability, evaluation, and rewards. Table 9.1 and figure 9.1 further distinguish between groups and teams.

TIME-OUT 1

Describe a current work group or team you play for in terms of figure 9.1 and the six characteristics given in table 9.1. Use this group or team for the remaining Time-Outs in this chapter.

As table 9.1 and figure 9.1 show, it's not always easy to clearly distinguish when a group is also a team. The reason is that there are shades of team and group structures—they exist on a continuum—and most groups lie somewhere in between "extreme groups" (with little latitude in autonomy) and "extreme teams" (with great latitude in autonomy). The terms *management directed, semiautonomous,* and *self-managed* (or *self-directed*) are commonly used to differentiate groups along this continuum. Management-directed groups are clearly groups, self-directed groups are clearly teams, and semiautonomous groups are somewhere in between.

LEARNING OUTCOME 2 ▶

Explain the group performance model.

Group Performance Model

Several factors contribute to team effectiveness. The performance of groups is based on four factors (as shown in figure 9.2). In the **group performance model,** performance is a function of organizational context, group structure, group process, and group development stage.

TABLE 9.1   Differences Between Groups and Teams

Characteristics	Groups	Teams
Size	Two or more; can be large.	Typically 5 to 12 members.
Leadership	One clear leader makes decisions.	Leadership is shared among members.
Jobs	Jobs are distinct and clear-cut; individual members do one independent part of the work.	Jobs are fluid and overlap in responsibility and tasks performed. Members perform numerous interdependent tasks with complementary skills; the team completes an entire task or project.
Accountability and evaluation	Leader evaluates each member's performance.	Members evaluate each other's individual performance and the group's performance.
Rewards	Rewards are based on individual performance.	Rewards are based on both individual and group performance.
Objectives	Set by the organization and group leader.	Objectives are set by the organization and the team.

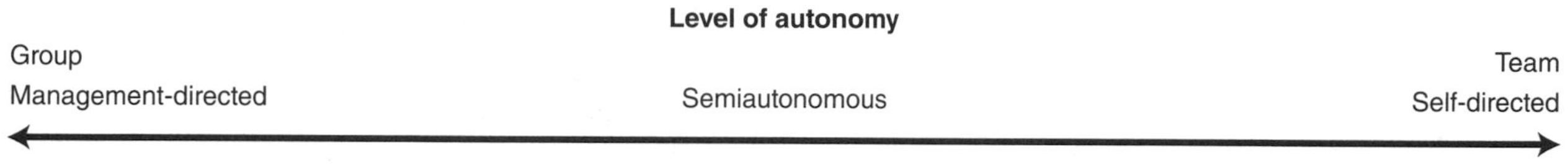

Level of autonomy

Group
Management-directed   Semiautonomous

Team
Self-directed

FIGURE 9.1   Level of autonomy.

APPLYING THE CONCEPT 9.1

Is It a Group or Is It a Team?

Identify each statement as characteristic of (a) groups or (b) teams.

_____ 1. My boss conducts my performance appraisals, and I get good ratings.

_____ 2. We don't have departmental goals; we just do the best we can to accomplish our mission.

_____ 3. My compensation is based primarily on my club's performance.

_____ 4. I get the assembled tennis racket from Jean; then I paint it and send it to Tony for packaging.

_____ 5. There are about 30 people in my department.

Each factor is like a link on a chain; if any factor is weak, the team can fall apart. Before we get into the details of the four factors, read about pro team success next.

High Performance and Evaluating Team Worth

Bill Belichick's phenomenal success in leading the New England Patriots to three Super Bowl victories in five appearances is the stuff legends are made of. Belichick no doubt has other pro teams scratching their heads. Patriot star players are willing to be paid less than market value to be part of a team with a strong chance of winning the Super Bowl again. How does he do it? Everyone on the team knows that star players, such as Tom Brady and Wes Welker, set examples of team behavior that any new players joining the team are expected to follow.

What is the key to making teams in pro sport and in business work? Valuing everyone's contributions. This means that team members must understand and accept the idea that

Group performance	(f)	Organizational context	Group structure	Group process	Group development stage
High to low		Environment Mission Strategy Culture Structure Systems and processes	Type Size Composition Leadership Objectives	Roles Norms Cohesiveness Status Decision making Conflict resolution	Orientation Dissatisfaction Resolution Production Termination

(f) = a function of

FIGURE 9.2 Group performance model.

some players or workers are the stars and are key to the team's success. Of course, the flip (and equally important) side is that star players and star workers need to understand that they can't win alone—the team must work together seamlessly. This is especially true for the Patriots.[6]

Determining the value of pro teams is a sport unto itself these days. *Forbes* valued NFL Dallas Cowboys (U.S.$1.850 billion), the Washington Redskins (U.S.$1.555 billion), and the Patriots (U.S.$1.4 billion) as the three most valuable teams.[7] *Why* is this of such interest? Because pro sport teams are first and foremost businesses, and increasing the value of a franchise is good business (buy, make money, and sell higher). Building a strong team brand is a surefire way to increase the value of a franchise, because each league can produce only one champion a year. Losing teams need to make money, too.[8] Building fan trust in the team is more important than focusing too much on player identification, and it's more important in the long run compared to a short-term strategy of attracting star players.[9]

Organizational Context

A number of factors in the organization and the environment—called context—affect how groups function and their level of performance. We discussed these factors in previous chapters.

LEARNING OUTCOME 3 ▶

Categorize groups by their structure.

Group Structure

Group structure dimensions include group leadership, type, size, composition, and objectives (see figure 9.3).

Group Leadership

To a large extent, leaders both provide and determine group structure. Teams succeed or fail based on leadership.[10] The leader's relationships with team members are different, and the relationships affect team performance. Generally, better relationships lead to higher performance. Thus, your success and the fate of your teams will be determined by how effectively you lead them. Table 9.1 highlights the fact that the leadership requirements for groups and teams are different. Leadership is often a response to environment, context, group size, composition, and objectives.

Types of Groups

Group types can be formal or informal, functional or cross-functional, and command or task. We spend a great deal of our life working in groups. Thus, you need to understand the different types of groups that you will be part of during your career.

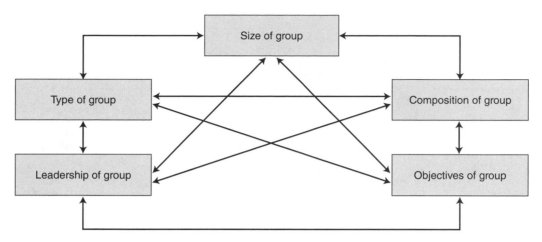

FIGURE 9.3 How groups are structured. The arrows indicate the effect that each dimension has on the others (or systems interrelationship).

Formal or Informal

Formal groups, such as departments, are created by organizations as their official structures. Informal groups are not part of the organization's official structure: They are spontaneous creations that occur when members come together voluntarily because of similar interests. You get a job in formal groups, and you develop informal relationships and form informal groups. Kids join a formal team when they join a Little League Baseball team. They join an informal team when they play a pickup game of baseball at a Boys & Girls Club.

 Do you recall having a better experience on formal or informal teams when you were younger?

Functional or Cross-Functional

Groups organized by function (vertically) perform work of one type. Accounting, human resources, and sales departments are functional groups. Groups whose members come from different functional areas are cross-functional (horizontal) groups. Groups organized around projects are typically cross-functional groups. Managers coordinate activities between functional and cross-functional groups and thus serve as their links (see figure 9.4). Rensis Likert called this the linking-pin role. Higher-level managers need to make important decisions across functional areas.[11] The use of cross-functional groups is on the rise because of the need to coordinate functional areas.[12]

Command or Task

Command groups consist of managers and their staffs, and they get the job done—whatever the job is. People are hired to be a part of a command group. Command groups can be either functional or cross-functional. The

 TIME-OUT 2 Identify the task groups in the organization you work for or play for. Specify whether they are task forces or standing committees.

president and vice presidents in an organization form a cross-functional command group; each vice president and his managers are a functional command group.

Task groups are composed of staff who work on a specific objective, in other words, committees. There are two primary forms of task groups: task forces and standing committees.

Task forces are temporary groups formed for a specific purpose. Project teams and ad hoc committees (chapter 5) are task groups in which members have a functional leader and work with cross-functional departments as needed. One person from each functional area involved in the work serves on the task force. Volunteers in sport organizations are often placed on task forces (temporary committees) to help with specific tasks. For instance, at the Olympics, volunteers coach, perform marketing activities, assist in medical situations,

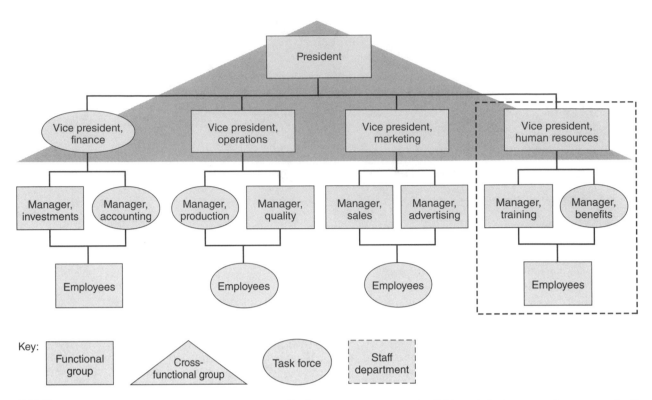

FIGURE 9.4   Functional and cross-functional groups. Each manager serves as the linking pin between each group vertically and horizontally.

and distribute food and water at events. At the Athens Olympics, volunteers were motivated to help because of nostalgia, camaraderie and friendship, Olympic connection, and sharing and recognition of expertise.[13]

Standing committees are permanent groups that work on ongoing organizational issues. Membership in standing committees is often rotated every year so that new ideas and fresh perspectives are brought in. For example, membership may be for 3 years, with one-third of the committee replaced every year. Some firms have budget committees and sport event committees.

Command groups and task groups differ in several ways. One difference is the membership. Command groups are usually (although not always) functional, whereas task groups are typically cross-functional. Another difference is in who belongs to which type of group. Everyone in an organization belongs to a command group, but employees often work for organizations for many years without ever serving on a task force or standing committee. Generally, the higher the level of management, the more time is spent serving in task groups.

 Did you like smaller or larger groups in your youth?

Group Size

There is no ideal group size. The sizes of groups vary depending on their purpose. Groups that are too small limit ideas and creativity and tend to be too cautious. Issues of overwork and burnout can also arise because the workload is not distributed over enough members. On the other hand, groups that are too large tend to be slow; individuals don't always get to contribute as much as they can in smaller groups, and some members just sit back and let the others do all the work—*social loafers* or *free riders*.

Group size affects group process, so leadership style must be tailored to the size of the group. The larger the group, the more formal or autocratic the leadership should be. Smaller groups need less formal and more participative management styles. Larger groups inhibit equal participation. Generally, participation is most equal in groups of around five. This is why teams are small in size. The larger the group, the more the members need support in the form of formal structured plans, policies, procedures, and rules.

Managers typically have no say in the size of the groups they manage. However, managers of large departments can choose to organize their department into teams. Committee chairs are often able to select the group's size and in doing so should keep the group size appropriate for the task.

Teams are often small (10-15 players) when kids join a formal Little League Baseball team. The small number of players on the team allows the players to get to know each other very well over the course of a season. Kids would not be able to feel as close to all of their classmates in a physical education class at school with 100 students.

Composing the Group

Group composition is the mix of members' skills and abilities. Research in sport has supported the importance of team composition.[14] Deciding whom to put on a project or a team is one of the biggest challenges facing a manager or team leader, and determining how to mix and match newcomers with old-timers to form new configurations is an important decision in designing teams. Coaches in the NFL, the NCAA, and high school face this decision every season.

New England Patriots coach Bill Belichick is known for bringing in a few key players every year and bringing in a few complementary players at the same time. Belichick blends the acquisition of key star players and a few complementary players and stockpiles draft picks, techniques that have been used as a blueprint for many teams in the NFL.[15]

Attracting, selecting, and retaining the best people for the job are among the most important functions of a manager, and this really hits home in building teams. Diversity is an important issue for sport managers today, so try to assemble a diverse group.[16] Your management skills may be stretched, but it will be worth it; as we have noted previously, diverse groups often outperform homogeneous groups. When assembling teams, select people with complementary knowledge and skills to maximize performance.[17]

 Did you prefer to belong to competitive teams when you played sports as a youth?

 Were the teams you played on as a youth cohesive? Were they diversified?

Objectives

In chapter 4 we explored the benefits of setting objectives. These benefits apply to both individuals and groups. In groups, objectives are commonly very broad—usually about fulfilling the organization's mission. Teams

TIME-OUT 3 State the type of group or team you belong to and describe its size, composition, leadership, and objectives.

frequently develop their own objectives. One reason teams often outperform groups is that having developed their objectives, they own them in a way that groups do not. A sport team, for example, might set goals to best last year's win–loss record, to make the playoffs, or to win the championship. Recreational sport teams might emphasize teamwork and exercise. Work teams might set objectives to increase customer satisfaction, team rapport, sales, or profits.

Setting and then achieving objectives lead to increased confidence, motivation, and job satisfaction. This is why effective managers pay close attention to objective setting. They guide their team in setting objectives that can be met, that are clear, and that can solve the problem. If your group or team doesn't have any objectives, consider taking the lead to help the team set some goals.

Group Process

Group process is the patterns of interactions that emerge as group members work together. *Group dynamics* is another word for group process. Dynamics are about how people work together as they get the work done, not the work itself. Group process often changes over time, and it is not something people figure out on their own. Women tend to be more sensitive to group dynamics,[18] but careful and thoughtful training in group process is crucial for teams to be effective.

The six components of **group process dimensions** are roles, norms, cohesiveness, status, decision making, and conflict resolution.

Group Roles

LEARNING OUTCOME 4 ▶

Define the three major roles group members play.

Group roles are different from job roles, because group roles focus on how people interact as they do the job, and they help or hinder getting the job done.[19] **Group roles** are task, maintenance, and self-interest.

Group members play task roles when they do and say things that help to accomplish the group's objectives. Task roles are often described as structuring, job centered, production, task oriented, and directive.

Group members play maintenance roles when they do and say things that shape and sustain the group process. Maintenance roles are described as consideration, employee centered, relationship oriented, and supportive.

Members play self-interest roles when they do and say things that help the individual but hurt the group. When members put their own needs before those of the group, the group's performance can suffer.

How Group Roles Affect Performance

To be effective, groups need their members to focus on both their task roles and their maintenance roles while minimizing self-interest roles. When members focus only on tasks, performance can suffer because maintenance roles not only help members deal with conflict effectively but also develop relationships. Group process without maintenance roles may even become dysfunctional. Obviously, groups whose members focus solely on having a great time don't get the job done. And groups whose members place self-interest ahead of group interest don't produce to their fullest potential.

Of course, many situations benefit both the individual and the group. As you strive to achieve objectives, you need to distinguish between self-interests that benefit both the individual and the organization (win–win situations) and those that benefit the individual but hurt the organization (win–lose situations). Group performance typically increases dramatically when members aren't concerned about who gets credit for specific accomplishments (teamwork of passing rather than trying to score all the points yourself).

TIME-OUT 4 State the primary group roles played in your current work group or team.

Leadership Implications

Savvy group leaders and members watch the roles being played in their group and facilitate helping behaviors among members. They step in to guide the group back to balance when members shift too far to a task focus or a maintenance focus, and leaders reign in star members who put their self-interest ahead of the group's interest. For example, hockey players who strive to score the most goals themselves are acting in their own self-interest, not necessarily the interest of the team. Such athletes might cost the team goals because they don't pass to teammates who are in better positions to score. Thus, the coach has to take leadership action, such as talking to the player and benching.

Group Norms

LEARNING OUTCOME 5 ▶

Explain how rules and norms differ.

Whether or not policies, procedures, and rules are in place to guide behavior, every group eventually develops group norms—unwritten and unspoken rules about how things are

APPLYING THE CONCEPT 9.2

Roles

Identify the role fulfilled in each statement.

a. task
b. maintenance
c. self-interest

_____ 6. Wait. We can't decide yet—we haven't heard Rodney's idea.

_____ 7. I don't understand. Could you explain why we're practicing our power play again?

_____ 8. We've tried that play before; it doesn't work. My play is much better.

_____ 9. What does who's going to the dance have to do with the game tonight? We're getting sidetracked.

_____ 10. Ted's solution is much better than mine. Let's go with his idea.

done. Our behavior and attitudes (chapter 8) are shaped by what people around us consider appropriate, correct, or desirable.[20] **Norms** are the group's shared expectations of members' behavior. Norms determine what should, ought, or must be done for the group to maintain consistent and desirable behavior. Developing the norm of trusting the other team members is important to performance.[21] Team norms can develop in four situations: during practices, during competition, in social situations, and during the off-season. Norms affect our behavior, but they also affect our attitudes.[22]

How Norms Develop

Norms develop spontaneously as members interact. Each group member brings to the group cultural values and past experiences (beliefs, attitudes, and knowledge) that shape norms. If working hard becomes a group norm, the entire group will perform to that expectation; if it doesn't, the group will not.

Groups develop their own rules for what is acceptable (and not acceptable) in humor, socializing, ways of talking (smearing), ways of letting new members know what is acceptable and not acceptable—the list is endless and encompasses obvious behavior and subtle, nuanced behavior.

How Norms Are Enforced

Group pressure is a powerful influence over health behaviors, including alcohol and drug use, smoking, and exercise.[23] Have you ever seen peers pressure others to comply with norms? Think about how you and others have experienced peer pressure, and you know how norms are enforced. Have any of your peers ever pressured you to push harder (or back off) or change your game at practice or during play?

Group norms can help or hinder a group. Norms can promote healthy group process—for example, when helping each other, working hard, being the best performers, and not being a prima donna are group norms. Or they can sabotage performance—for example, when bending the rules, heavy social drinking, using drugs, and underperforming are the group norms. Negative norms have hindered teams, including women and minorities.[24] Rarely does any one individual

 TIME-OUT 5 Identify at least two norms in your current work group or team. How do you know these are norms? How does the group enforce these norms?

set an entirely new norm, but group leaders help perpetuate or shift norms.[25] So as a group leader or member, be aware of your group's norms. Work to develop positive norms and try to eliminate negative ones.

Group Cohesiveness

The extent to which a group abides by and enforce its norms depends on its cohesiveness. **Group cohesiveness** is the extent to which members stick together. The more cohesive the group, the more it sticks together as a team. Members identify themselves with the team and want to be with the team.[26] The more desirable membership in the group is, the more willing members will be to comply with the group's norms. In highly cohesive groups, all members follow the norm even if the norm is to produce less than required or, conversely, if it is to work a lot harder than the company expects. This doesn't happen in groups that have moderate or low cohesion; the members produce at varying levels, and the norms are not strongly enforced. This has important consequences; for example, if a highly cohesive group's norm is social or performance-enhancing drug use, some group members will use drugs that they wouldn't use on their own simply to be accepted by the group. The authors of one study interviewed athletes and coaches from eight teams in the Atlanta Olympics about their performance. The four teams that failed to meet performance expectations had problems with team cohesion.[27]

Factors Influencing Cohesiveness

Six factors influence cohesiveness:

1. Objectives: The stronger the agreement and commitment made to achieving the group's objectives, the higher the group's cohesiveness. Lack of commitment leads to lower cohesiveness and performance.[28]

2. Size: The smaller the group, the higher the cohesiveness. Three to nine members appears to be a good group size for cohesiveness.

3. Homogeneity: Generally, the more similar group members, the higher the group's cohesiveness. People tend to be attracted to people who are similar to themselves. The dilemma here is that diverse groups often outperform homogeneous ones.

4. Participation: The more equal the member participation, the higher the group's cohesiveness. A study that examined cohesion and performance in team sports concluded that a "positive cohesion-performance relationship was linked to a stronger perception that athletes would train in the off-season."[29]

5. Competition: The focus of the competition affects cohesiveness. If the group focuses on internal competition, members try to outdo each other, and low cohesiveness results. If the group focuses on external competition, members tend to pull together as a team to beat rivals.

6. Success: The more successful a group is at achieving its objectives, the more cohesive it becomes. Success breeds cohesiveness, which breeds more success. People want to be on a winning team.

Many studies have compared cohesive and noncohesive groups. Think about teams you played for. Did you push harder and play better with teammates you really liked and got along well with, versus when you didn't? Did the truly cohesive teams do better and enjoy playing on the team more? One study found that NBA teams with a high shared experience and a low turnover tended to improve their win–loss records significantly.

Managing a lower turnover of players led to improved win–loss records for both winning teams and losing teams. This is important because it would appear that losing teams have little reason for keeping their roster intact. Teams with more losses than wins in 1 year won an average of 5.7 more games in the following year if their level of shared experience also rose. However, teams won only 1.2 more games on average if they had shuffled their rosters. In other words, teams that stayed together tended to play a lot better together.[30]

Cohesiveness is associated with performance in the following ways:

TIME-OUT 6 — Identify your work group or team's cohesiveness as high, medium, or low. Support your assessment with examples.

- Groups with the highest productivity were highly cohesive and accepted management's directives on productivity levels.

- Groups with the lowest productivity were also highly cohesive but rejected management's directives on productivity levels; they set and enforced their own levels, which were below those of management. This can happen in organizations with unions that have an "us against them" attitude.

- Groups with intermediate productivity were low-cohesive groups, irrespective of their acceptance of management's directives. The widest variance in individuals' performance was among the groups with the lower cohesiveness. They tended to be more tolerant of nonconformity with group norms.

Leadership Implications

Your goal as a leader is to develop cohesive groups that hold high productivity as a group norm. Participative management style helps groups develop cohesiveness and builds agreement on, and commitment toward, objectives. All members need to be included and feel as though they are part of the team; no one should be left out. Coaching also encourages cohesiveness. Some intragroup competition may be helpful, but leaders should focus primarily on intergroup competition. Winning teams become cohesive very naturally, which in turn motivates the group to higher levels of success. The trick is to develop a cohesive but diversified group.

Status Within the Group

As group members interact, they develop respect for one another in numerous ways. The more respect, prestige, influence, and power a group member has, the higher her status within the group. **Status** is the perceived ranking of one member relative

TIME-OUT 7 — List each member in your current work group or team, including you, and identify each person's status in the group. Support your assessment with reasons.

to other members in the group. Status is based on several factors—one's performance, job title, salary, seniority, expertise, people skills, appearance, and education, among others. Depending on the group's norms, the sports and the levels at which members play affect their status, with professional status at the top.[31]

Members who conform to the group's norms typically have higher status than members who don't. Conversely, a group is more willing to listen to and overlook a high-status member who breaks the norms, but group leaders tend to conform to the group norms. High-status members also have more influence on the development of norms and on decisions made by the group. Because members with less status often find their ideas ignored, they tend to copy high-status members' behavior.[32] They also find acceptance by agreeing with the high-status members' suggestions. When people need help and advice, they go to a person with high status.

How Status Affects Group Performance

High-status members have a major impact on the group's performance. If high-status members support positive norms and high productivity, chances are the group will too.

Another important factor influencing group performance is *status congruence*, which is the acceptance and satisfaction that members receive from their status in the group. Members dissatisfied with their status may not participate as actively as they would if they were satisfied with their status. Dissatisfied members may therefore physically or mentally escape from the group and not perform to their full potential. Or they may cause conflict as they strive to gain status.

Leadership Implications

To be effective, leaders need high status. Therefore, it behooves leaders to maintain good relations with the group, particularly with high-status informal leaders, and to be sure they endorse positive norms and objectives. However, the leader also needs to have good relationships with lower-status members to help them feel comfortable with their status. In addition, leaders should be aware of conflicts that may be the result of status incongruence. White males tend to have higher status than women and minorities, and it's the manager's job to value diversity so that everyone's status is based on performance only. The most productive groups consist of members with equal or close to equal status, in which all members feel they are contributing.

Decision Making and Conflict Resolution

Organizations depend on teams to make important decisions, and how decisions are made by groups directly affects performance. In youth programs, coaching performance would be better if parent volunteers were required to receive training and education to be a coach.[33] Volunteer organizations need to focus on empowering their volunteers through the fit of the volunteer to the task, organization, and appropriate managerial treatment.[34]

Conflict is common in groups and teams, and unresolved conflicts can have a negative effect on performance.[35] In chapter 8 you developed your skills at resolving conflict. Understanding and applying group process will make you a more effective group and team member and leader. Figure 9.5 summarizes the six group processes.

LEARNING OUTCOME 7 ▶
Describe the five major stages of group development and the leadership style appropriate for each stage.

Stages of Group Development and Leadership Styles

As we have noted, groups have organizational contexts, structures, and processes. They also go through developmental stages as they grow from a collection of individuals to a

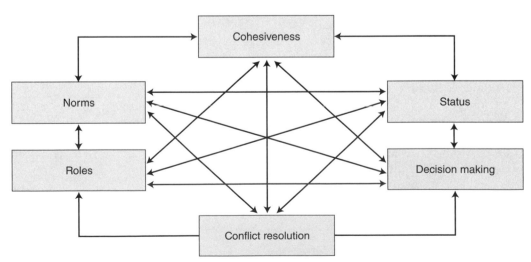

FIGURE 9.5 Six group processes. The arrows indicate the effect that each dimension has on the others (or systems interrelationship).

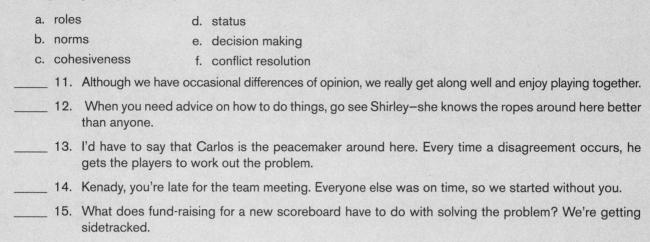

Group Process

Identify the group process operative in each statement.

a. roles   d. status
b. norms   e. decision making
c. cohesiveness   f. conflict resolution

_____ 11. Although we have occasional differences of opinion, we really get along well and enjoy playing together.

_____ 12. When you need advice on how to do things, go see Shirley—she knows the ropes around here better than anyone.

_____ 13. I'd have to say that Carlos is the peacemaker around here. Every time a disagreement occurs, he gets the players to work out the problem.

_____ 14. Kenady, you're late for the team meeting. Everyone else was on time, so we started without you.

_____ 15. What does fund-raising for a new scoreboard have to do with solving the problem? We're getting sidetracked.

smoothly operating and effective group or team. As organizations rely more on teams, the role of leaders in developing teams is crucial. The **stages of group development** are orientation, dissatisfaction, resolution, production, and termination. Savvy managers change their leadership style as the group develops. See figure 9.6 for an illustration of the stages as you read about each stage in this section.

Stage 1: Orientation

Command groups are rarely started with all new members. Therefore, the orientation stage is more characteristic of task groups that are clearly beginning anew. Orientation, also known as the *forming stage,* is characterized by low development (D1, high commitment and low competence). When people first form a group, they often come with a moderate to high commitment to it. However, because they haven't worked together, they lack competence as a team, even though they may be highly competent individuals.

During orientation, members must work out structure issues about leadership and group objectives. The size of the group and its composition are checked out. Members may be anxious over how they will fit in (status), what will be required of them (roles and norms), what the group will be like (cohesiveness), how decisions will be made, and how members will get along (conflict). These issues must be resolved if the group is to progress to the next developmental stage.

In teams in athletics, it is common to start the season having newcomers replace players who have left the team (age, graduation, retirement), joining those who stay. Thus, mixing and matching newcomers with old-timers is a big challenge facing managers. Training camps held before a season begins are an important mechanism not only for deciding which players will make the team but also for developing group norms and resolving orientation issues. Thus, a swimming league not only trains before school starts but also has social functions so that swimmers (and sometimes parents) can get to know each other.

The appropriate leadership style during orientation is autocratic (high task and low maintenance). When groups first come together, leaders need to help the group clarify its objectives and provide clear expectations for members. Leaders can also set a friendly tone that helps members start to get to know one another.

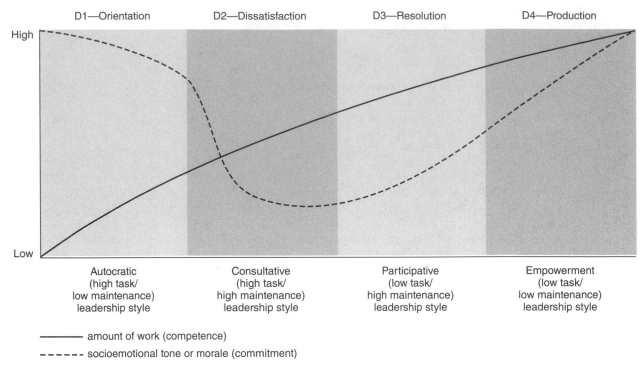

| | D1—Orientation | D2—Dissatisfaction | D3—Resolution | D4—Production |

Autocratic (high task/ low maintenance) leadership style

Consultative (high task/ high maintenance) leadership style

Participative (low task/ high maintenance) leadership style

Empowerment (low task/ low maintenance) leadership style

———— amount of work (competence)

- - - - - socioemotional tone or morale (commitment)

FIGURE 9.6   Group development stages and leadership style.

Stage 2: Dissatisfaction

This stage, also known as the *storming stage,* is characterized by moderate development level (D2, lower commitment and some competence). After working together for a time, members typically become dissatisfied in some way with the group. Uncomfortable questions arise: Why am I a member? Are we ever going to win or accomplish anything? Why don't other members do what's expected of them? Often the task is more complex and difficult than anticipated; members mask their own feelings of incompetence with frustration. The group has developed some competence to perform the task, but not as much as members would like, so there is impatience as well.

During dissatisfaction, the group needs to resolve its structure and process issues before it can progress to the next developmental stage. This is a dangerous stage because groups can get stuck in dissatisfaction and never progress to becoming a fully functioning team. Coaches in the swimming league may be frustrated with certain participants because they are trying to balance swim practice with band camp, and beginning swimmers may question whether they will ever get in good enough shape.

The appropriate leadership style during the dissatisfaction stage is consultative (high task and high maintenance). When satisfaction drops, leaders need to focus on the maintenance role to encourage members to continue to work toward the objectives. At the same time, leaders must continue to focus on the task—swimming skills and endurance.

Stage 3: Resolution

Resolution, also called the *norming stage,* is characterized by a high development level (D3, variable commitment and high competence). With time, members often resolve the incongruence between their initial expectations and the realities that the objectives, tasks, and skills represent. As members develop competence, they typically grow more satisfied with the group. Relationships develop that satisfy group members' affiliation needs. Members learn to work together as they develop a structure and process with acceptable leadership, norms, status, cohesiveness, and decision-making styles. During periods of conflict or change, the group will return to resolve these issues yet again.

Commitment varies from time to time as the group interacts. If the group does not deal effectively with its process issues, it may regress to stage 2 (dissatisfaction), or it may plateau and stagnate in both commitment and competence. If the group succeeds at developing positive structures and processes, it will develop to the next stage. The swimming league developed a series of organized practices that fit all of the swimmers' schedules. This resolution was not an easy task, but accomplishing it made the team close-knit as they worked together to find ways to carpool.

The appropriate leadership style during resolution is participative (low task and high maintenance). Once group members know what to do and how to do it, there is little need to direct their task behavior. Groups in resolution need their leaders to focus on maintenance. When commitment varies, this is usually attributable to some problem in group process, such as a conflict. Leaders should then focus on maintenance behavior to get groups through the issues they face. If leaders continue to overmanage task behavior, groups can become dissatisfied and regress or plateau at this level.

Stage 4: Production

The production stage, also called the *performing stage*, is characterized by a high level of development (D4, high commitment and high competence). At this stage, commitment and competence don't fluctuate much. Groups function smoothly as teams with high levels of satisfaction. They maintain positive structures and processes. The fact that members are very productive further fuels positive feelings. Group structure and process may change with time, but issues are resolved quickly and easily; members are open with each other. The swimming team in our example moved into the production stage and routinely takes swimmers to national competitions.

The appropriate style during the production stage is empowerment (low task and low maintenance). Groups that achieve this stage play appropriate task and maintenance roles; by this stage, leaders don't need to play either role, unless there is a problem, because the group is effectively sharing leadership.

Stage 5: Termination

Termination, also called the adjourning stage, is not reached in command groups unless there is some drastic reorganization. However, task groups do terminate. During this stage, members experience feelings of loss as they face leaving the group. Closure is important. The swimming league's annual awards dinner, which carefully honors every team member, helps swimmers who are going on to college—and their parents—say good-bye to members who have become friends.

 **TIME-OUT 8** Identify your work group's or team's developmental stage and the leader's management style. Is his or her style appropriate for your group's stage? What could be done to improve your group's structure and process?

Two key variables identified through each stage of group development are work on the task (competence) and the socioemotional tone or morale (commitment). These two variables do not progress in the same manner. As figure 9.6 shows, competence continues to increase steadily through stages 1 to 4, whereas commitment fluctuates—it starts out high in stage 1, drops in stage 2, and then rises through stages 3 and 4. The success and failure of a team are often based on the manager.[36] Thus, selecting the appropriate leadership style is important. You will develop the skill of analyzing a team and selecting the appropriate leadership style to use in Skill-Builder 9.2 on page 305.

LEARNING OUTCOME 8 ▶

Explain how group managers and team leaders differ.

Developing Groups Into Teams

As table 9.1 on page 281 shows, groups and teams are different. The trend is to empower groups to become teams because teams are more productive than groups. As you work to make groups into teams, consider the size of the department or group. If your group has 20 or more members, break it into two or three teams. In this section, we examine training and the functions of management—planning, organizing and staffing, leading, and controlling teams—and how group managers and team leaders differ.

If teams are to succeed, members need training in group process skills so they can make decisions and handle conflict. A team-building program, as discussed in chapter 6, is also very helpful in turning groups into teams. The management functions are handled differently in groups and teams. Here we discuss how the manager's job changes with teams.

- **Planning:** Setting objectives and decision making are important parts of planning. In teams, team members set objectives, develop plans, and make the decisions. The manager's role is to involve and coach members and make sure they understand the objectives, accept them, and are committed to achieving them.

- **Organizing and staffing:** Team members participate in selecting, evaluating, and rewarding members. Jobs are more interchangeable and are assigned by members as they perform interdependent parts of the task.

- **Leading:** Although teams share leadership, most teams identify someone as leader; the difference is that these chosen leaders lead with the permission of the team and are leading a group of leaders, so to speak. Thus, the official team leader doesn't tell people what to do. Effective team leaders are highly skilled in group process and team building. Leaders spend a great deal of time developing group structure and process. Effective leaders work to bring the team to the production stage, and they change leadership styles with the team's developmental stage.

TIME-OUT 9 State whether your current boss or coach is a group manager or a team leader. Give reasons for your choice.

- **Controlling:** Team members monitor their own progress, take corrective action, and perform quality control. Successful team leaders tend to have strong people skills and develop relationships that motivate members to high levels of performance. These leaders don't spend much of their time checking on employees; rather, they spend time developing leadership skills of all team members.

In summary, the roles of group manager and team leader differ in significant ways. Group managers perform the four functions of management. Team leaders empower members to perform the management functions and focus on shaping group structure and group process, and these leaders get the team to the mature developmental stage, that of production.

LEARNING OUTCOME 9 ▶

Lead a meeting.

Getting to Better Meetings

With the increasing use of teams, meetings take up an increasing amount of time in organizations. Therefore, leading effective meetings is an important skill. Successful meetings depend on the leader's skill at managing group process. People commonly complain that there are too many meetings, they are too long, and they are unproductive—a waste of time.[37] Committees have been known to keep minutes and waste hours. Therefore, in this section, we give you pointers on how to plan and conduct meetings and how to handle problem group members.

Planning Meetings

Your preparations and those of your team are crucial for conducting effective meetings. Unprepared leaders conduct unproductive meetings. Planning is needed in at least five areas: (1) setting objectives, (2) selecting participants, (3) making assignments, (4) setting the agenda and the time and place for the meeting, and (5) leading the meeting. A written copy of the plan should be sent to members before the meeting (see "Meeting Plans").

Objectives

Have an objective—or don't call a meeting. Amazing numbers of meetings are called without a clear purpose. Before you call a meeting, clearly define its purpose and set out the objectives that you wish to accomplish.[38] Clarifying the purpose of the meeting will ensure that all participants start the meeting with the same purpose and objective.

Participants and Assignments

Before you call a meeting, decide who needs to attend.[39] When too many people attend, your ability to complete the work slows down considerably. Look at your objectives and decide who is affected by them and who should have input. Do you need an outside specialist to provide expertise? Participants should know in advance what is expected of them.

Meeting Plans

Content

- Time: List date, place, and time (both beginning and ending).
- Objectives: State the objectives and purpose of the meeting. The objectives can be listed with agenda items, as shown in the following example, rather than as a separate section. Make sure that objectives are specific (chapter 4).
- Participation and assignments: If all members have the same assignments, list them. If different members have different assignments, list their names and assignments. Assignments may be listed as agenda items, as shown for Ted and Karen in the example.
- Agenda: List each item to be covered in priority order with its approximate time limit. Accepting the minutes of the last meeting may be an agenda item.

Example

Boys Club Baseball Team Meeting

December 15, 2013, Boys Club Central Office, 1 to 2 p.m.

Participation and Assignments

All members will attend and should have read the list of players available for each of the six teams before the meeting. Be ready to discuss your preferences for selecting players.

Agenda

Ted will lead a discussion of the process to be used in selecting players—15 minutes.
Karen will lead the process of selecting players—40 minutes.
Ted and Karen will present dates for teams to hold practice without discussion—5 minutes. Discussion will take place at the next meeting after you have given the possible practice dates some thought.

Give adequate notice if any preparation is required on their part (reading material, doing research, or writing a report). Make sure members are accountable for their assignments.

Agenda

Before you call a meeting, identify the activities that will take place and list them in order by importance—this is your agenda. Agendas tell people what is expected and how the meeting will progress.[40] Setting time limits for each item keeps everyone on task and avoids the needless (and endless) discussion and getting off topic that are so common at meetings. When digression occurs, take the group back to topic. But be flexible and allow more time when it is really needed. Members may also submit agenda items they want included. The reason for listing items in order of priority is that if the group doesn't get to every item, the least important items will carry forward.

Date, Place, and Time

To determine which days and times of the week are best for meetings, get members' input. People tend to be more alert early in the day. When members work in close proximity, it is better to have more frequent, shorter meetings that focus on one or just a few items. However, when members have to travel, meetings must be fewer and longer. Select an adequate place for the group and plan for their physical comfort.

A current trend is to hold important meetings at sport stadiums. Conference rooms in newer stadiums are often larger than those available at hotels. Holding a meeting at a sport stadium such as Yankee Stadium or at Madison Square Garden in New York City lends a lot of prestige to the event.

Leadership

Think about what leadership style best fits your objectives for the meeting. Each agenda item may need to be handled differently. For example, some items simply call for disseminating information; others may require a discussion, vote, or consensus; still other items require a simple, quick report from a member. Develop your team members' leadership skills by rotating meeting leaders.

Technology

E-mail, teleconferences, and videoconferences have reduced the need for some meetings. These technologies save travel costs and time, and they may result in better and quicker decisions. Minutes (notes on what took place during a meeting) can be taken on laptops or tablets (and by some on smart phones), and hard copies or e-mails can be distributed at the end of the meeting.

Conducting Meetings

At a group's first meeting, the group is in the orientation developmental stage. Therefore, develop objectives, but give members time to get to know one another. Introductions set the stage for subsequent interactions. A simple technique is to start with introductions and then move on to the group's purpose, objectives, and members' jobs or assignments. Sometime during or following this procedure, take a break to enable members to interact informally. If members see that their social needs will not be met, dissatisfaction may occur more quickly.

Effective meetings have three parts:

1. Begin the meeting on time and identify objectives. Waiting for late-arriving participants penalizes those who are on time and develops a norm for coming late. Begin by

reviewing progress to date, the group's objectives, and the meeting's purpose or objective. If minutes are recorded, they are usually approved at the beginning of the next meeting. For most meetings, a secretary should be appointed to take minutes.

2. Cover agenda items in priority order. Try to keep to the approximate times, but be flexible. However, if the discussion begins to digress or becomes a destructive argument, move on.

3. Summarize and review assignments, and end the meeting on time. Whoever is leading the meeting should summarize what took place and whether the meeting's objectives were achieved. Review the assignments given. The secretary or leader should record all assignments. This sets up accountability and follow-up on assignments to ensure results.

Meeting leaders need to focus on group structure, process, and development. As already noted, leadership needs change with the group's developmental level. Assess the stage your group is in as you decide how to lead meetings. Provide appropriate task or maintenance behavior only as it is needed, and avoid self-interest roles and problem members.

Problem Members

As groups and teams develop, certain personalities emerge that can cause the group to be less efficient. We call these personalities Silent Ones, Talkers, Wanderers, Arguers, the Bored, and the Social Loafer. Personality, position, and status affect meeting behavior.[41]

Silent Ones

In effective groups, every member participates. Silent Ones do not give the group the benefits of their input. Encourage Silent Ones to participate, without being obvious or overdoing it. One technique that works well is rotation, in which all members take turns giving input. Rotation is generally less threatening than being called on directly. However, rotation is not appropriate all the time. To build up the confidence of Silent Ones, call on them with questions they can easily answer.

If you are a Silent One, push yourself to participate. Remind yourself that you have good ideas too and that others in the meeting feel as you do. Preparing what you will say before the meeting will give you confidence to speak up.[42]

Talkers

Talkers have something to say about everything. They dominate discussions and drown out other voices. Talkers can cause intragroup problems such as low cohesiveness and conflicts. Your job is to slow Talkers down, not to shut them up. But above all, don't let them dominate. Rotation works well here too because it limits Talkers' amount of "floor." When rotation isn't appropriate, gently interrupt Talkers and present your own ideas or call on other members to present theirs.

If you are a Talker, restrain yourself. Remember, powerful people listen. As a Talker, you are likely a leader, and thus it is your job to help others develop, so give them a chance to speak.

Wanderers

Wanderers are distracters. They digress, they joke too much, they change the subject, and they provide roadblocks to getting anything done. Your job is to keep the group on track. If Wanderers want to socialize, cut it off. Be kind. Thank them for their contribution, and then throw out a question to the group to get it back on topic.

If you are a Wanderer, you are likely high maintenance and low task oriented. Change your habits and try to develop a balance between these two roles. Check your urge to stray from the topic, and pull your thoughts and comments back on track. Think about why you wander—are you subconsciously trying to sabotage the group?

Arguers

Like Talkers, Arguers like to be the center of attention. For Arguers, arguing is an end in itself. Whether it is constructive or destructive doesn't concern them. They view everything as a win–lose situation, and they cannot stand losing. Your job is to resolve conflict, but not in an argumentative way. Don't get into an argument with Arguers; that is exactly what they want. Should they start an argument, bring others into the discussion. If the argument gets personal, cut it off. Make it clear that you will not tolerate personal attacks. Keep the discussion moving, and keep it on target.

If you are an Arguer, practice backing off. Lose on purpose—it is not the end of the world. Think about why you have to be the center of attention. What makes you need to fight and win? Strive to change your win–lose view of life. (Win–win is much more pleasant.) Learn to convey your views assertively, not aggressively—by the way, this is good for your blood pressure! All of us get to be wrong. Learn to admit mistakes gracefully.

The Bored

The Bored are not interested in the meeting, the group, or its objectives. Maybe they are preoccupied. Maybe they feel superior. Whatever their reason, they don't pay attention and they don't participate. Assign the Bored tasks. Have them record ideas on the easel or record minutes. Call on the Bored; bring them into the group. Don't allow the Bored to sit back—boredom is contagious, and you don't want it to spread.

If you are one of the Bored, think about why. Should you change jobs? If not, then participate—you owe this to your team and to yourself. Remember, motivation comes from within. Take more of a leadership role.

The Social Loafer

This *Social Loafer* (or *free rider*) problem member doesn't want to take individual responsibility and do a fair share of the work. Following all the previously mentioned meeting guidelines helps, especially giving clear individual assignments. Don't let the group develop norms that allow social loafing, and use peer pressure to get people to do their work. Confront Social Loafers assertively using the conflict resolution model in chapter 8. When necessary, threaten to go to the boss. If these methods do not work, go to the supervisor (professor or boss) and explain the situation; specify the behavior that is lacking and explain that you and the group have tried to resolve the problem but that the Social Loafer refuses to perform to standards.

If you are a Social Loafer, step up to the plate and do your fair share of the work.

Working With Problem Members

Here are the rules you do not want to break: Do not embarrass, do not intimidate, and do not argue with any members, no matter how much they provoke you. If you do, they will be martyrs and you will be a bully. If you have serious problem members who don't respond to the preceding techniques, talk with them individually outside the group. Review the BCF statements (behavior, consequences, feelings) in chapter 8, and maintain ownership of the problem. Be honest, be firm, and lay your cards on the table.

As we bring this chapter to a close, recall the importance of teamwork, the lessons of

TIME-OUT 10 Recall a recent meeting you attended. Write a critique of the meeting, laying out what went well and why and what went wrong and why. Were there problem members? How did the leader handle them?

the geese, and the differences between groups and teams. Know the group performance model—group performance is a function of organizational context, group structure, group process, and group development. Develop effective group structure for the type of group; select the appropriate size, composition, and leadership style; and set objectives. Manage group process through group roles, set positive norms, develop cohesiveness, maintain status congruence, make good decisions, and resolve conflict. Analyze the group's development stage and use the appropriate leadership style, and bring groups to the production stage of development. Develop groups into teams by training and empowering your members to participate in management functions. Run effective meetings so you don't waste the group's time.

APPLYING THE CONCEPT 9.4

People Who Sabotage Meetings

Identify the person in each statement as

   a. Silent one
   b. Talker
   c. Wanderer
   d. Bored
   e. Arguer
   f. Social loafer

_____ 16. Charlie is always first or second to give his ideas. He elaborates and expounds and then elaborates again.

_____ 17. One of the usually active team members is sitting back quietly today for the first time. The other members are doing all the discussing and volunteering for assignments.

_____ 18. As the team discusses game strategy for next Saturday, Billy asks if they heard about the team owner and the mailroom clerk.

_____ 19. Eunice usually shrinks from giving her ideas. When asked to explain her position, she often changes her answers to agree with others in the group.

_____ 20. Dwayne loves to challenge members' ideas. He likes getting his own way. When someone doesn't agree with Dwayne, he makes wisecracks about the person's prior mistakes.

@ TAKE IT TO THE NET

Please visit www.HumanKinetics.com/AppliedSportManagementSkills and go to this book's companion web study guide, where you will find the following:

   A list of websites associated with the concepts in this chapter
   Exercises that you will need Internet access to complete
   Online versions of chapter exercises and end-of-chapter learning aids
   An exercise that helps you define the Key Terms

CHAPTER SUMMARY

1. Explain how groups and teams differ.

   Groups and teams differ by size, leadership, jobs, accountability and evaluation, rewards, and objectives. Groups have a clear leader and two or more (possibly many more) members who perform independent jobs with individual accountability, evaluation, and rewards. Teams typically have fewer members who share leadership and who perform interdependent jobs with both individual and group accountability, evaluation, and rewards.

2. Explain the group performance model.

   Group performance is a function of organizational context and the group's structure, process, and developmental stage.

3. Categorize groups by their structure.

   Groups can be structured as formal or informal, functional or cross-functional, and command or task. Formal groups are part of the organizational structure; informal groups are not. Functional group members come from one area; cross-functional members come from different areas. Command groups are composed of managers and their staff working to get the job done; task groups work on specific objectives. Task forces are temporary; standing committees are ongoing.

4. Define the three major roles group members play.

   Group task roles are played when members do and say things that directly aid in the accomplishment of the group's objectives. Group maintenance roles are played when members do and say things that develop and sustain the group process. Self-interest roles are played when members do and say things that help the individual but hurt the group.

5. Explain how rules and norms differ.

   Rules are formally established by management or by the group itself. Norms are the group's shared but unspoken expectations of its members' behavior. Norms develop spontaneously as members interact.

6. Describe cohesiveness and why it is important to teams.

   Group cohesiveness is the extent to which members stick together. Group cohesiveness is important because highly cohesive groups that accept management's directives for productivity levels perform better than groups with low levels of cohesiveness.

7. Describe the five major stages of group development and the leadership style appropriate for each stage.

   (1) Orientation is characterized by low development level (D1—high commitment and low competence), and the appropriate leadership style is autocratic. (2) Dissatisfaction is characterized by moderate development level (D2—lower commitment and some competence), and the appropriate leadership style is consultative. (3) Resolution is characterized by high development level (D3—variable commitment and high competence), and the appropriate leadership style is participative. (4) Production is characterized by outstanding development level (D4—high commitment and high competence), and the appropriate leadership style is empowerment. (5) Termination is not reached in command groups unless there is some drastic reorganization. However, task groups do terminate.

8. Explain how group managers and team leaders differ.

   The group manager takes responsibility for performing the four functions of management. The team leader empowers the members to take responsibility for performing the management functions and focuses on developing effective group structure, group process, and group development.

9. Lead a meeting.

Make sure the meeting has a purpose. Begin meetings by covering the objectives for the meeting. Cover agenda items in priority order. Keep people on track. Conclude with a summary of what took place and assignments to be completed for discussion at future meetings.

REVIEW AND DISCUSSION QUESTIONS

1. Which are usually larger, groups or teams?

2. Give one reason the New England Patriots is a successful team.

3. One study found that NBA teams with a high shared experience and a low turnover tended to have significantly better win–loss records. Why?

4. Why is diversity important to group composition?

5. Why are objectives important to groups?

6. How do groups enforce norms?

7. Recall the study cited in the text that examined the performance of eight U.S. teams in the 1996 Olympics at Atlanta. What was the reason given that four of the teams failed to meet expectations?

8. Does members' commitment to the group continue to increase through the first four stages of group development?

9. Are the four functions of management equally important to both groups and teams?

10. Why is it important to keep records of meeting assignments?

11. Describe the five types of problem members in meetings. How do they cause problems?

12. What are four reasons that volunteers gave for volunteering to work at the 2004 Athens Olympics?

13. Describe the team structure for a volunteering effort you have been involved with at your college.

14. Which lesson of the geese is most lacking and needed in teams today? Why?

15. Is it really worth making a distinction between groups and teams? Why or why not?

16. Which part of the group performance model is the most important to high levels of performance? Why?

17. Select any type of group (work, school, sport) that you belong to or have belonged to in the past. Explain how each of the group's five structure components affected its performance.

18. Select any type of group you belong to or have belonged to in the past. Explain how each of the group's six group process components affected its performance.

19. Based on your experience in meetings, and what you have read and heard from others, which part of planning a meeting is most lacking?

20. Which type of group problem member is most annoying to you? Why? How can you better work with this type in the future?

CASE

Building a Fantasy Sport Team

Fantasy Sports used to be called Rotisserie Baseball. Back In the 1980s, it was called roto for short. What is really involved in building a fantasy team? The fantasy business has been growing rapidly, and fantasy sports have become popular with sport fans. One study found that fans play for entertainment and escape, competition, social interaction, or some combination of these.[43]

A league first needs to be formed. Many leagues use yahoo.com or espn.com as a platform for managing their teams. Owners need to be found to select players. In the early stages of selecting teams, owners do not usually know everybody who is selecting a team. Still, a date is selected and agreed upon by all owners.

Next, a commissioner, or leader, is selected to start the league on one of the sites. The owner of each team then drafts his team in a rotating sequence. Owners often have a sum of fantasy dollars to spend on their time. It takes great skill to build a team that performs to a high standard, is not injury prone, hits for home run power yet also for a high batting average, and so on.

But, how does an owner form a team? Does he pick players who work well together? Does he pick players on his favorite professional teams? Do you pick a few high-salaried players and fill in with a few extra players on the bench? Do you make trades with other owners in the league who you feel are similar to you? What looks like an unorganized group of players is actually a well-orchestrated selection of players who work together like a team.

At this stage, owners are beginning to know all the other owners in the league. They establish some normal behavior. For instance, all changes in a lineup have to be completed before game time. Injured players can be replaced by the pool of players who are not currently selected. One of the reasons fantasy baseball is addictive is that owners can add, delete, and trade players for most of the season. Owners like to have rules, since this helps to keep the league on track.

At the end of the regular season, the fantasy season also finishes. A playoff takes place, and one team is crowned champion. In reality, the team of owners is disbanded until the new season takes place next year.

Case Questions

1. Why do people play fantasy baseball?
   a. entertainment
   b. competition
   c. social interaction
   d. escape
   e. all of the above

2. When owners meet for the initial drafting of players, what developmental stage are the owners experiencing?
   a. orientation
   b. dissatisfaction
   c. resolution
   d. production
   e. termination

3. When owners trade players during the season, what developmental stage are the owners experiencing?
   a. orientation
   b. dissatisfaction

    c. resolution

    d. production

    e. termination

4. You would expect group cohesiveness to be stronger during the initial drafting of players as compared to the productive stage of making trades with other owners during the season.

    a. true

    b. false

5. Being an owner in a fantasy league requires little teamwork.

    a. true

    b. false

6. Describe any experiences you have had with fantasy sports. Are these experiences that you would like to build a career on?

SKILL-BUILDER EXERCISES

Skill-Builder 9.1: Group Performance

Objective

To use group structure, process, development, and meetings to improve group performance. Note: This exercise is designed for class groups that have worked together for some time. (Five or more hours of prior class work is recommended.)

Preparation

Answer the following questions as they apply to your class group or team.

1. Using figure 9.1 and table 9.1, would you classify your members as a group or a team? Why?

    _____

    _____

    _____

Group Structure

1. Our group or team is structured (circle one in each category)

    formally/informally

    functionally/cross-functionally (by majors)

    by command/by task

2. There are _____ students in our group or team, which is (circle one)

    too large   too small   just right

3. Describe the composition of your group or team.

    _____

    _____

    _____

4. Is there a clear group or team leader? Name the leaders.

    _____

5. List your group's or team's objectives.

_____

_____

_____

6. List some ways in which your group's or team's structure could be improved to achieve its objectives.

_____

_____

_____

Group Process

1. List each member of your group or team (including you) and the major roles you each play.

   1. _____   4. _____

   2. _____   5. _____

   3. _____   6. _____

2. Identify at least three group or team norms. Are they positive or negative? How does the group or team enforce them?

_____

_____

_____

3. Is your group or team a high-, moderate-, or low-cohesive group?

_____

4. List each group or team member, including you, in order of status. If this does not apply, tell why.

   1. _____   4. _____

   2. _____   5. _____

   3. _____   6. _____

5. How does your group or team make decisions?

_____

_____

_____

6. How does your group or team resolve conflict?

_____

_____

_____

7. List some ways in which your group's or team's group process could be improved to achieve its objectives.

_____

_____

_____

Developmental Stage

1. At what stage of group development is your group or team? Explain.

   _____
   _____
   _____

2. List some ways in which your group or team can move to a higher developmental stage to increase group performance.

   _____
   _____
   _____

Meetings

1. List some ways in which your group or team meetings could be improved to increase group performance.

   _____
   _____
   _____

2. Does your group or team have any problem members? What can be done to make them more effective?

   _____
   _____
   _____

In-Class Application

Complete the preceding skill-building preparation before class.
   Choose one (10-30 minutes):

- Meet with your assigned group or team and present your findings on the preceding questions. Brainstorm ways to improve your group's or team's structure, process, developmental stage, and meetings.
- Conduct informal, whole-class discussion of student findings.

Wrap-Up

Take a few minutes to write your answers to the following questions:

What did I learn from this experience? How will I use this knowledge?

_____
_____
_____
_____
_____

Skill-Builder 9.2: Group Development and Leadership Style

Objective

To develop your skill at determining the group's level of development and selecting the appropriate leadership style

Preparation

Read about and understand the stages of group development and leadership styles. To help you with this exercise, use figure 9.7. For this exercise, read and complete the 12 situations following these steps.

1. Select the level of development. Place D1, D2, D3, or D4 on the D _____ line following the situation.

2. Read the four alternative leadership actions. Each action represents one of the four leadership styles. Determine the leadership style (LS) and place each letter (A, C, P, E) on the LS _____ lines.

3. Circle the letter of the one style that matches the development level.

Using the Group Development and Leadership Style Model

1. The first step is to use the top of the model to determine the level of group development (D1-4).

2. The second step in using the model is to select the leadership style (LS1A, 2C, 3P, 4E) to match the level of development. Just follow the development arrow down to the leadership style.

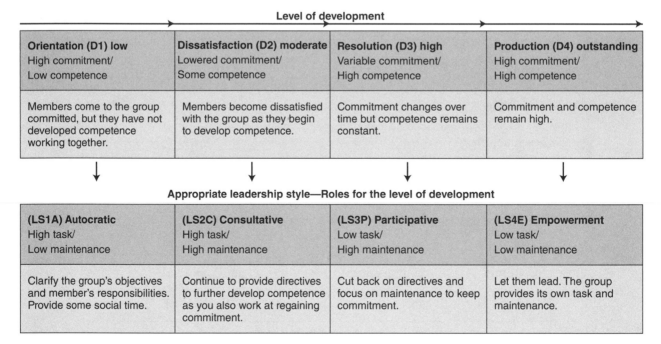

FIGURE 9.7 The group development and leadership style model.

Situations

1. Your group works well together; members are cohesive and have positive norms. They maintain a fairly consistent level of production that is above the organizational average, as long as you continue to play a maintenance role. You have a new assignment for them. To accomplish it, you would D _____.

   a. Explain what needs to be done and tell them how to do it. Oversee them while they perform the task. LS _____

    b. Tell the group members how pleased you are with their past performance. Explain the new assignment, but let them decide how to accomplish it. Be available if they need help. LS _____

    c. Tell the group what needs to be done. Encourage them to give input on how to do the job. Oversee task performance. LS _____

    d. Explain to the group what needs to be done. LS _____

2. You have been promoted to a new supervisory position. The group you supervise appears to have little talent to do the job, but they do seem to care about the quality of the work they do. The last supervisor was fired because of the group's low productivity level. To increase productivity, you would D _____

    a. Let the group members know you are aware of their low production level, but let them decide how to improve it. LS _____

    b. Spend most of your time overseeing group members as they perform their jobs. Train them as needed. LS _____

    c. Explain to the group that you would like to work together to improve productivity. Work together as a team. LS _____

    d. Tell the group how productivity can be improved. With the members' ideas, develop methods and make sure they are implemented. LS _____

3. Your department continues to be one of the top performers in the organization. The members work well as a team. In the past, you generally let them take care of the work on their own. You decide to D _____ .

    a. Encourage group members on a regular basis. LS _____

    b. Define members' roles and spend more time overseeing performance. LS _____

    c. Continue things the way they are; leave the members alone. LS _____

    d. Hold a meeting. Recommend ways to improve, and get members' ideas as well. After agreeing on changes, oversee the group to make sure it implements the new ideas and does improve. LS _____

4. You have spent much of the past year training your employees. However, they do not need you to oversee production as much as you used to. Several group members no longer get along as well as they did in the past. You've played referee lately. You D _____ .

    a. Have a group meeting to discuss ways to increase performance. Let the group decide what changes to make. Be supportive. LS _____

    b. Continue things the way they are now. Supervise them closely and be the referee when needed. LS _____

    c. Leave the group alone to work things out for themselves. LS _____

    d. Continue to supervise closely as needed but spend more time playing a maintenance role; develop a team spirit. LS _____

5. Your department has been doing such a great job that it has increased in size. You are surprised at how fast the new members are integrated. The team continues to come up with ways to improve performance, without prompting from you. Because it has grown so large, the department will be moving to a larger location. You decide to D _____.

    a. Design the new layout and present it to the group to see if the members can improve on it. LS _____

    b. Allow the group to design the new layout. LS _____

    c. Design the new layout and put a copy on the bulletin board so employees know where to report for work after the move. LS _____

d. Hold a meeting to get employees' ideas on the layout of the new location. After the meeting, think about their ideas and finalize the layout. LS _____

6. You are appointed to head a task group. Because of the death of a relative, you had to miss the first meeting. At the second meeting, you notice that the group seems to have developed objectives and some ground rules. Members have volunteered for assignments that have to be accomplished. You D _____.

   a. Take over as a strong leader and change some ground rules and assignments. LS _____

   b. Review what has been done so far, and keep things as they are. However, you take charge and provide clear direction from now on. LS _____

   c. Take over the leadership but allow the group to make the decisions. Be supportive and encourage them. LS _____

   d. Given that the group is doing so well, leave and do not attend any more meetings. LS _____

7. Your group was working at, or just below, standard. There has been a conflict within the group, and as a result, production is behind schedule. You D _____.

   a. Tell the group how to resolve the conflict. Then closely supervise to make sure people do what you say and production increases. LS _____

   b. Let the group work it out. LS _____

   c. Hold a meeting to work as a team to come up with a solution. Encourage the group members to work together. LS _____

   d. Hold a meeting to present a way to resolve the conflict. Sell the members on its merits, ask for their input, and follow up. LS _____

8. Your organization allows flextime. Two of your employees have asked if they can change work hours. You are concerned because the busy work hours need adequate coverage. The department is very cohesive and has positive norms. You decide to D _____.

   a. Tell them things are going well; we'll keep things as they are now. LS _____

   b. Hold a department meeting to get everyone's input, and then reschedule their hours. LS _____

   c. Hold a department meeting to get everyone's input; then reschedule their hours on a trial basis. Tell the group that if there is any drop in productivity, you will go back to the old schedule. LS _____

   d. Tell them to hold a department meeting. If the department agrees to have at least three people on the job during the busy hours, they can make changes, giving you a copy of the new schedule. LS _____

9. You have arrived 10 minutes late for a department meeting. Your employees are discussing the latest assignment. This surprises you because in the past, you had to provide clear direction and employees rarely would say anything. You D _____.

   a. Take control immediately and provide your usual direction. LS _____

   b. Say nothing and just sit back. LS _____

   c. Encourage the group to continue, but also provide direction. LS _____

   d. Thank the group for starting without you and encourage them to continue. Support their efforts. LS _____

10. Your department is consistently very productive. However, occasionally the members fool around and someone has an accident. There has never been a serious injury. You hear a noise and go to see what it was. From a distance you can see Sue sitting

on the floor, laughing, with a ball made from company material in her hand. You D _____.

   a. Say and do nothing. After all, she's OK, and the department is very productive; you don't want to make waves. LS _____

   b. Call the group together and ask for suggestions on how to keep accidents from recurring. Tell them you will be checking up on them to make sure the behavior does not continue. LS _____

   c. Call the group together and discuss the situation. Encourage them to be more careful in the future. LS _____

   d. Tell the group that's it; from now on you will be checking up on them regularly. Bring Sue to your office and discipline her. LS _____

11. You are at the first meeting of an ad hoc committee you are leading. Most of the members are second- and third-level managers from the marketing and financial areas; you are a supervisor from production. You decide to start by D _____.

   a. Work on developing relationships. Get everyone to feel as though they know each other before you talk about business. LS _____

   b. Go over the group's purpose and its authority. Provide clear directives. LS _____

   c. Ask the group to define its purpose. Because most of the members are higher-level managers, let them provide the leadership. LS _____

   d. Provide both direction and encouragement. Give directives and thank people for their cooperation. LS _____

12. Your department has done a great job in the past. It is getting a new computer system. You have been trained to operate the computer, and you are expected to train your employees to operate it. To train them, you D _____.

   a. Give the group instructions and work with people individually, providing direction and encouragement. LS _____

   b. Get the group together to decide how they want to be instructed. Be very supportive of their efforts to learn. LS _____

   c. Tell them it's a simple system. Give them a copy of the manual and have them study it on their own. LS _____

   d. Give the group instructions. Then supervise their work closely, giving additional instructions as needed. LS _____

In-Class Application

Complete the preceding skill-building preparation before class (10-50 minutes):
The professor goes over the first few situations using the model explaining the answers. The class can meet in groups of two or three to go over the remaining situations. Or the professor may simply give the answers.

Wrap-Up

Take a few minutes to write your answers to the following questions:
What did I learn from this experience? How will I use this knowledge?

_____

_____

_____

_____

_____

SPORTS AND SOCIAL MEDIA EXERCISES

Sport Business Radio is a new age site that uses all facets of social media. For now, go to the site at www.sportsbusinessradio.com/audio/interviews and listen to the Erik Spoelstra interview. What comments does he have about coaching his Miami Heat team?

_____

_____

_____

_____

_____

GAME PLAN FOR STARTING A SPORT BUSINESS

Not many people run a business all alone. It normally takes a team of people to help start and grow a business. List four people you know that you would want on your team.

Team member 1 _____

Team member 2 _____

Team member 3 _____

Team member 4 _____

Communicating for Results

LEARNING OUTCOMES

After studying this chapter, you should be able to

1. understand how communication flows through organizations;
2. list the four steps in the communication process;
3. use transmissions channels well;
4. communicate effectively in person;
5. select appropriate channels for your messages;
6. solicit feedback properly;
7. explain how we receive messages;
8. choose appropriate response styles; and
9. calm an emotional person.

KEY TERMS

communication	encode	feedback
vertical communication	receiver	paraphrasing
horizontal communication	transmit	message-receiving process
grapevine	decode	listening
communication process	nonverbal communication	reflecting
sender	message-sending process	empathy

311

DEVELOPING YOUR SKILLS

Humans are all about talk, and, frankly, the best managers talk better than the rest of us. They stay on target and get their messages across time and again to all manner of recipients, from staff to stockholders to the news media. Fortunately, this is a skill you can develop. Through this chapter you will understand the communication process and develop your skills at sending, receiving, and responding to messages through the use of models. You can also develop skills at dealing with emotional people and improve your ability to give and receive criticism.

REVIEWING THEIR GAME PLAN

Courting the Changing Media

Think about your favorite "viewer sports" (the ones you like to watch) for a moment. Short of envisioning yourself playing them, you are just as likely to conjure up a TV image or favorite radio announcer's voice as you are to think of a game or tournament you watched live. Like eyeglasses and contact lenses for those of us who don't have perfect vision, TV, Internet, radio, and print media are the lenses through which most of us view most of the sports we follow. This makes the media especially important to sport organizations. Sport organizations that don't have great relationships with their market's media aren't doing their job.

Often the first way in which fans and customers access an organization's products, whether the product is a star shortstop or a hotly desired catcher's mitt, is through the media. The conduits of sport information that first come to mind are, of course, television, radio, and print media. However, media sources are proliferating. Online magazines, blogs, chat networks, e-mail marketing, and websites buzz 24 hours a day, 7 days a week—all over the globe. For example, SiriusXM satellite radio broadcasts over our radios but also through our computers and cell phones via the Internet. Sirius has stations for NFL, MLB, NASCAR, and the Professional Golfers' Association (PGA), to name a few. Comcast makes available Red Zone, which is part of Comcast's Sports Entertainment Package for less than $8 per month and is produced by NFL Network. The channel airs every Sunday from 11:30 a.m., providing fans with live look-ins, game highlights, fantasy stats, and more.[1] ESPN increased its online presence with live feeds on its interactive website, ESPN360. com. ESPN shows over 3,500 events per year. Some of the events, such as lacrosse and cricket, are smaller niche sports.

Savvy organizations monitor a great variety of media to see how their team or company is being portrayed. "Dish" is ever more important. If a false rumor spread on the Internet can send a company's stock plummeting, think about what a crank fan's website or a cranky sport columnist can do. Media conglomerates such as Time Warner, which owns *Sports Illustrated,* FOX, CNN, and Warner Brothers music and movies, wield great power. In an entertainment-driven world, not talking about your team—the silent treatment—can be just as devastating as false buzz.

Company websites allow customers and fans to e-mail comments and suggestions. Customers get to vent and applaud, and fans get to feel as though they are part of the action. Not surprisingly, more and more fans and customers are hitting the "Send" button. The response has been so great that companies have had to hire new personnel to support their websites. Website marketing communication does activate attitude change within consumers.[2] There is the potential to use website communication for sport event organizers to enhance consumer attitudes toward the event and increase attendance.[3]

The importance of building strong relationships with the media, then, cannot be stated too strongly. Your organization, be it the Seattle Mariners, a local high school, or a private youth sport league, needs to garner the interest of local newspapers to continually generate public interest. Watching children play in local leagues is a wonderful experience, but without media attention, few people beyond the players' families know about these games. That may be OK. Then again, it may not if you need to grow your team. This may mean courting local reporters to help them cover your team extensively and responsibly. It may mean courting local sport talk shows to rev up excitement about the team.

A positive example of using sport talk shows to keep fans at a fever pitch was the long-running afternoon radio talk show *Mike & the Mad Dog* on New York's WFAN radio station. This show had been at or near number one in the market ratings since its conception in 1989. Mike (Francesa) and the Mad Dog (Chris Russo) were voted two of the most powerful sport figures in New York year in and year out. The simple (and brilliant) idea behind their show was basically two guys in a bar talking sports. "The words tumble out of [Mad Dog's] mouth in a strange stew, the L's and R's smoosh into W's particularly when he's talking fast. This is most of the time."[1]

But WFAN morning talk show host Don Imus learned a difficult lesson when he was fired from his position after making racial remarks against the Rutgers women's basketball team.[4] Thus, all talk show hosts (including Mike and the Mad Dog) need to be careful when they are communicating with their audience members. As a sign of the changing nature of sport communication, Mad Dog left WFAN for his own show on SiriusXM. As a satellite radio station, Sirius provides Mad Dog a chance to reach sport fans outside of the New York area. Even without Mad Dog, Mike's show on WFAN, *Mike'D Up*, is carried live on the YES television network.[5]

ESPN has its own New York radio stations—ESPN 1050 AM and ESPN 98.7 FM. *Mike & Mike in the Morning* competes directly with Mike Francesa. Mike Greenberg and Mike Golic *(Mike & Mike),* in particular, have a lively show every morning with the full support of all the ESPN resources.

Of course, the Olympics, NCAA, NFL, NBA, and MLB are covered widely by ESPN, ABC, CBS, NBC, and FOX. Think about some American traditions. Where would football be without Monday Night Football and friendly crowds at local sport bars watching their alma maters ravage a long-time rival on fall Saturdays? Will the WNBA, women's professional basketball in the United States, become an American tradition? If it does, this will be in large part because its games are shown on ABC, ESPN2, and NBATV. The jury on the WNBA's fate is still out—only a few viewers are opting to watch WNBA games. However, ESPN signed a 9-year agreement to broadcast WNBA games until 2016 on ABC-ESPN. ESPN's executive vice president for content, John Skipper, said, "We've had very good success with the women's college basketball tournament, with women's college softball, and women's soccer. This is an important part of that commitment."[6]

Large organizations have public relations (PR) departments to court the media, talk to them, keep their interest up, and occasionally put a spin on things. In small organizations, however, the PR hat is worn by many and, sometimes, by everyone. In one sense, every person in an organization represents the company—people need to realize this and be trained in communications.

For current information on Mike Francesa, see www.wfan.com.

Understanding the Importance of Good Communication

◀ LEARNING OUTCOME 1

Understand how communication flows through organizations.

Communication is the process of transmitting information and meaning. The world of work revolves around communications—effective communications may mean a problem solved in its infancy or sidestepped altogether. Ineffective communications may mean problems created. Unfortunately, miscommunication is common in organizations.

How much time do you spend reading, listening to, and watching sport media? The communication industry media is big business for sport. Comcast spent $4.4 billion to broadcast the London Olympic Games.[7] The field of sport management relies on communication to better understand the role of stakeholders in sport.[8] Communication within an athletic department affects its success.[9] Owners, managers, athletes, and all the employees of a sport organization need to realize that their personal communications with the media, clients, fans, suppliers, and customers are part of an environment where the spoken word can be transmitted instantly and globally via the Internet.

Effective leadership and coaching are based on communication skills.[10] So it's no wonder that communication and interpersonal skills were ranked first among what recruiters look for when hiring college grads.[11] Personal and professional relationships are based on communications, as is networking. So your communication skills will have a direct impact on your career success as well as on your personal relationships.

Although there are lots of jobs in sport media and we do discuss sport media briefly, we focus on communicating within sport organizations, which include ESPN and other media companies, throughout this chapter. For our purposes, there are two types of communication: organizational and interpersonal. Organizational communication takes place between organizations and among an organization's divisions, departments, projects, and teams. Interpersonal communication takes place between individuals.

Using Organizational Communication

If an organization is to thrive, its mission, strategy, goals, and culture all must be communicated effectively within and outside the firm. "For today's athlete and coach, winning is no longer enough. The stakes have risen considerably, and so has the scrutiny on every aspect of their lives. Those who excel as communicators distinguish themselves from the rest."[12] Athletic directors (ADs) have to spend more time on image and exposure to make sure their universities are able to maintain good reputations. ADs need to know what traditional media (television, radio) and new media (blogs, fan-generated sites) are saying about their teams. To this end, sport managers are developing communication strategies.[13]

ESPN is known as a cable television station that communicates well with sport fans. It uses creative, humorous advertisements to gain attention for its shows and to reinforce the idea that true sport fans must watch ESPN's *SportsCenter* to know what is happening in sport. A review of the history of ESPN, *Those Guys Have All the Fun: Inside the World of ESPN*, explains how the station grew from a small cable network in 1979 to a dominant sport brand. The authors also detail how the show hosts on ESPN are jealous of each other, as compared to the locker room type of joking around on set.[14]

Think about how communications flow through an organization. The first thing that comes to mind is the formal channels. These can be vertical—down from the top (from the CEO and corporate executives on down the chain of command) and up from the bottom (from staff at the front line on up the chain). Communications can also be horizontal—same-level communications between salespeople and between vice presidents, for example. Then there are the informal channels (the grapevine) that every organization has; these channels resemble the ricochet of bullets.

Formal Vertical and Horizontal Communication

Vertical communication is the downward and upward flow of information through the organization. It is formal communication because it is officially sanctioned transmission of information. To be successful, sport policies, procedures, and rules must be communicated effectively.[15] Top management's strategies are communicated down the chain of command to instruct employees. The delegation process is downward communication.

Upward communication, on the other hand, involves staff sending information up through the different management levels. Managers often learn about what is going on in the organization and with customers through staff on the front lines. To facilitate upward communication (because it is often people on the front line who first sense changes in the business climate), most organizations encourage open-door management styles and communications, with the idea of making people feel at ease in talking to managers. Coaches often meet with their

 Can you provide an example of horizontal communication for a sport talk radio show you listen to?

| TIME-OUT 1 | Give examples of vertical communication and horizontal communication, and list a piece of information you got from your organization's grapevine. |

APPLYING THE CONCEPT 10.1

Communication Flow

Identify each communication as

a. downward

b. upward

c. horizontal

d. grapevine

_____ 1. Hey, Carl, did you hear that our two linebackers, Tom and Frankie, were drinking at the prom last week?

_____ 2. Juanita, you know when you hand the baton off to me, you need to quickly move out of my way.

_____ 3. Dwayne, here's the team roster you needed. Check it, and I'll make changes.

_____ 4. Robin, I've got two new customers who want to set up charge accounts. Please rush the credit check so we can increase ticket sales.

_____ 5. Ted, please run this letter over to the athletic funding committee before noon.

teams when they are performing below par to get feedback from players on how the team can start winning. Depending on the issue, the coach's style, and the team's culture, the information flow is downward (the coach tells players what they need to do), upward (players tell the coach what needs to happen), or (ideally) both.

Horizontal communication is information shared between peers. Horizontal communication is the coordination that goes on within a department, among team members, and among different departments. Managers meet with people from different departments (in person and electronically) to coordinate their efforts and resolve conflicts between them.[16] More experienced players encourage each other and rev up their teammates for a big game. Mike's' "chewing the fat" is also horizontal communication with the listener (the audience), which is why his fans love the show so much.

Informal Grapevine Communication

The **grapevine** is the flow of information through informal channels. It is informal communication because it isn't official or sanctioned. This rumor mill begins anywhere in the organization and flows in any direction. Grapevines spread false good news (the Los Angeles Kings will be trading for Pittsburgh Penguin MVP Evgeni Malkin) and true bad news (the media whispers appear to indicate that star Philadelphia Phillies first baseman Ryan Howard will be out for the rest of the season) with equal aplomb and almost always ahead of when the formal information is put out.

Grapevines are a powerful means of communication. They can be useful, and they can be destructive. Gossip has wrecked homes, friendships, and organizations. Organizations sometimes use grapevines to their advantage, but reining them in during times of uncertainty can be a daunting undertaking. Effective managers provide formal information truthfully and quickly to prevent gossip and to correct errors spreading through the grapevine.[17] You should spread good news through the grapevine. When you hear false rumors, try to nip them in the bud. Unlike many talk show hosts, Mike Francesa carefully verifies the information he receives, and this has paid off handsomely. One reason he is so highly regarded is that fans know he isn't dishing out unsubstantiated rumors. Some people prefer not to know the dirt on their coworkers. How active are you in the grapevine at work? Do you spread accurate information? Are you being ethical?

2. Message transmitted through a channel.

1. Encodes the message and selects the transmission channel.

Sender

3. Decodes the message and decides if feedback is needed.

Receiver

4. Feedback, response, or new message may be transmitted through a channel.

The sender and receiver may continually change roles as they communicate.

FIGURE 10.1 The communication process.

Using Interpersonal Communication

The **communication process** is the transmission of information, meaning, and intent. In this section, we discuss the interpersonal communication process (see figure 10.1).

LEARNING OUTCOME 2 ▶

List the four steps in the communication process.

1. A **sender** (the person doing the communicating) **encodes** the message (puts it into a form that the **receiver** of the message will understand).

2. The sender **transmits** the message by using a form of communication to send the message (by talking, phoning, e-mailing) to the receiver.

3. The receiver **decodes** the message by translating the message into a meaningful form (interprets it).

4. The receiver may (or may not) give feedback.

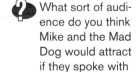 What sort of audience do you think Mike and the Mad Dog would attract if they spoke with a British accent? A Texas drawl?

Encoding Your Message

When you send a message, you initiate the communication. Your message is the information, meaning, or intent that you want to get across to the receiver. Make sure you have a clear intent for your messages—if you don't have a clear idea of what you want to get across, neither will the receiver. To clarify your intent, consider your receivers and determine what they need to hear to understand your message. Avoid barriers that block communication (see figure 10.2). Mike encodes the content (message) of his show in typical New York working-class speech, accent, and slang. This not only creates the ambience (shooting the breeze in a bar) that the producers want listeners to imagine; it also cinches a broad listenership. New Yorkers, from Wall Street power brokers to taxi cab drivers, have great affection for this accent; it is part of the mystique, and they are very comfortable with it. When encoding, be careful about the words you select because they can get people to tune in to your message or tune out.[18] Selecting the right words can help you overcome the barriers leaders face,[19] which we discuss next.

First Barrier—The Words We Choose

Semantics and jargon can be formidable barriers for your receivers, because words mean different things to different people (semantics), and jargon excludes people outside its originating group. Thus, "triple double" is an expression that will be totally misinterpreted by receivers who are unfamiliar with it and will cause them to puzzle futilely over your

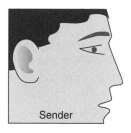
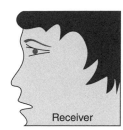

The words we choose
Information overload
Logic and order
The channel "shoe" doesn't fit
Trust and credibility
Failure to listen
Our emotions
Distortion

Sender

Receiver

FIGURE 10.2 Barriers to communication.

message. Triple double means that a player in basketball accumulates more than double digits (i.e., 10 or more) in three of the following five categories in a single game: points, steals, rebounds, assists, and blocked shots. It is a fairly rare accomplishment. However, Jason Kidd, formerly of the Dallas Mavericks, became quite prolific at completing the triple double.

To overcome problems of misinterpretation, consider what your receivers need in the way of language to understand your message, and then tailor the language you choose to fit their needs. Effective communicators don't use jargon with people who are not familiar with the terminology and especially with people from different cultures. Think for a moment about the many ways we use sport terms. For example, take the expressions "sure shot" (pool), "slam dunk" (basketball), and "tap in" (golf)—used outside sport, they are all metaphors for success. Sport metaphors are so embedded in everyday language that we don't give them a second thought. People trying to learn American English, however, don't have a clue as to what these phrases mean. So watch the use of jargon and if you need to, explain it.

Second Barrier—Information Overload

All of us have limits on the amount of information we can take in and process at any given time. New employees commonly experience information overload during their first few days at work because they are given so much new information. With so much information available so instantly via the Internet, we are often dazzled and overwhelmed and don't know what to do with it all. You would think that all of this information would help companies make decisions, but increasingly, the opposite is true. Overload is now the norm. We have reached the too-much-information age.

To minimize information overload, limit the information in your message to an amount the receiver can reasonably take in. Don't give monologues, and check periodically to be sure that the receiver is keeping up with you. Give the receiver a chance to process the message and feed it back to you so that you can check for misunderstandings or lapses in attention. If you talk too long, the receiver will become bored or lose the thread of the message.

> **TIME-OUT 2**
> List three important messages you recently sent at work, on your team, or in your personal life and tell how you encoded them, how you transmitted them, and how they were received. State which barriers were operative and why. If there were no barriers, tell why. Now do this for a message your boss or coach sent you or someone else.

Third Barrier—Logic and Order

Make sure that your message makes sense. One of the simplest ways to do this is to check the order of your points. Outlines really help here. You want the receiver to be able to follow your message easily and not become confused.

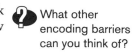 What other encoding barriers can you think of?

Transmitting Your Message

After you encode your message, you must select the channel (oral or written, phone or text or e-mail, video conference or face-to-face meeting) through which you will transmit the message.

Different channels work for different messages. Use of an inappropriate channel can kill a communication. E-mails or cold calls just won't work in some situations. Using a phone call to clinch a deal with a star player isn't the same as meeting with him in person. Before you send an important message, give careful thought to which channel will help you get your message across. In the next section, we examine various channels in detail, so let's continue with barriers.

Decoding the Message

Decoding occurs when receivers translate or interpret your message. They mix the content in your message with other ideas or information they have and with emotions they are feeling at the time, and they also look at your message through their own perceptual filters. All of these can be barriers (see figure 10.2) to receiving a message accurately.

First Barrier—Trust and Credibility

Trust is important to collaboration. Trust opens us to working and communicating effectively with others.[20] All of us as receivers consider whether we trust the sender and whether the sender has credibility. Sport managers need to deliver the sport product effectively to gain credibility.[21] When we don't trust senders—for whatever reason (they don't know what they're talking about, they don't have all the facts, they don't have good judgment, they've betrayed others before)—we are reluctant to accept their messages at face value. Once doubt enters the equation, it is extremely difficult to rebuild trust.

So be honest and authentic in all your communications.[22] If you can't be honest about something (and this happens), don't send the message! Know what you're talking about. Get the facts straight before you send your message. Trust and credibility are precious; don't squander them.

Second Barrier—Failure to Listen

We are all guilty of this. Our attention wanders; we're more interested in how we're going to respond than in hearing what the sender is saying (we've thought of something clever to say, and we stop listening and start framing it). We want to get to the "end of the story"—we don't want to hear the details, or they bore us.

So help your receivers receive your message—help them listen. Question them in such a way that they must paraphrase your message and play it back to you. Stop during a long message and give receivers a chance to ask questions and to think about what you've just said. Ask for their thoughts on what you've said so far. Make your message interesting. If you are a problem talker (chapter 9), people will not listen to you. Later in this chapter we discuss how to be a better listener when receiving messages.

> **TIME-OUT 3**
> Take three important messages you recently received at work, on your team, or in your personal life and tell how they were encoded and transmitted, and how they were received. State which barriers were operative and why. If there were no barriers, tell why. Now do this for a message recently received by your boss or coach.

Third Barrier—Our Emotions

Emotions are an important part of our relationships. But getting emotional can cloud our judgment, so being calm helps communication. Our emotions color how we decode mes-

APPLYING THE CONCEPT 10.2

Barriers to Communication

Identify the barriers in the following messages or responses as

a. perceptual filter

b. information overload

c. wrong transmission channel

d. emotions

e. trust and credibility

f. distortion

g. failure to listen

_____ 6. Relax. You shouldn't be so upset that our young team didn't win the championship.

_____ 7. I don't have any questions. (Really thinking, "I was lost back on step one and don't know what to ask.")

_____ 8. We are right on schedule in building our new athletic facility. (Really thinking, "We are actually behind, but we'll catch up.")

_____ 9. I said I'd do it in a little while. It's only been 15 minutes. Why do you expect it done by now?

_____ 10. You don't know what you're talking about when you give your opinions on how to play defense. I think we will do it my way.

sages. When we are angry, sad, or irrationally attached to an idea, concept, or person, we find it difficult to be objective and to hear the real message. Take the fans who call Mike Francesa. These folks by definition are not exactly objective about their favorite teams and favorite players or about teams and players they love to hate and hate to love—they will hear an honest but negative appraisal as an attack or as anything but the truth.

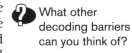 What other decoding barriers can you think of?

Take the receiver's emotions into consideration when you have to send a difficult message. Try not to get the person emotional. Also consider how your own emotions are coloring the message you are sending. Later in this chapter we give you ways to calm emotional people.

Fourth Barrier—Distortion

Distortion occurs when we alter information that we send and receive; it's a nice word for lying. We don't want to use the word "lying" because we may offend someone. We may do this for innumerable reasons. We don't like the truth, so we twist a message to fit our version of the incident and the "facts"—we believe what we want to believe. Tell the truth. Many people have said that things are going well only to get burned at the last minute when they can't deliver. This results in lost trust and credibility; it's better to let people know of problems early, because they may be able to help you. Likewise, when receiving messages, we hear what we want to hear. In these situations, you may have to repeat your message. You may have to reframe it. Asking for feedback helps you discern what the receivers are hearing. Listen carefully. Avoid having "yes" employees who filter out bad news—problems get solved only when they are faced honestly. Some executives are building truth-telling cultures.[23]

Using the Channels

Sometimes the difference between failed communications and those that hit their mark is your choice of channel. The channels through which we transmit our messages are nonverbal, oral, written, and visual (see table 10.1).

◀ LEARNING OUTCOME 3

Use transmission channels well.

TABLE 10.1   Channels for Transmitting Messages

Nonverbal	Oral	Written	Visual
Facial expressions (smile, frown; eye contact)	Face-to-face	Memos	Television
Vocal quality (emotional, emotionless, loud, quiet)	Meetings	Letters	Posters
Gestures (hand and body movements)	Presentations	Reports	Websites
Posture (sitting up, slouching)	Telephone	Bulletin boards	
Setting	Voice mail	Newsletters	
		Electronic means (e-mails, faxes, instant messages, text messages)	

Nonverbal Channels

Every time we talk to someone, we use words, but we also communicate nonverbally. **Nonverbal communication** consists of the messages we send without words. Nonverbal communication is thus our body language. Try talking without body language of any kind—it's difficult. Your image and reputation, and those of your team, are affected by your nonverbal communications.[24]

You can send some pretty complex messages nonverbally. Our frowns, chuckles, hand gestures, posture, and tone of voice all signal excitement, purpose, despair, confidence or lack thereof, disapproval, affection, enthusiasm, and the whole host of human responses. Being able to read people's facial expressions and other nonverbal messages is an important skill.

Chicago Bears coach Lovie Smith doesn't yell at his players. When he gets mad, he stares straight ahead in silence. His players call it "the Lovie Look" and say it's more frightening—and more effective—than a torrent of angry words. Lovie Smith believes he can get his team to compete more fiercely and win more games by giving directives calmly and treating players with respect.[25] Screaming managers are often resented and their messages ignored.

The adage "Actions speak louder than words" is true. So be aware of your nonverbal signals. Make them consistent with your message or, rather, make your message consistent with your body language. When your body language is inconsistent with your message, your receiver will know. Likewise, notice other people's body language to understand their real messages. All of us have the ability to read body language, but some people are better at paying attention to it. Do you consciously read nonverbal messages? Work on it.

How you arrange your office signals numerous things (nonverbally) about your management style. If you want open communication, make your office conducive to open communication. Don't sit behind your desk and have the other person sit in front of the desk, unless you want to signal that you are in charge. Sitting side by side signals that you are willing to be open, that you are willing to meet the person halfway, and that you respect what she has to contribute.

LEARNING OUTCOME 4 ▶

Communicate effectively in person.

Oral Channels

We transmit messages orally by talking with each other directly (face-to-face), in meetings, in presentations, by telephone, and by voice mail. Using oral channels is easy and fast and allows immediate feedback. The disadvantages are that such channels are often less accurate than other channels and may provide no record. Regardless of your career path, you will need to excel at presenting your ideas, be it face-to-face, in meetings, or in presentations.[26]

Face-to-Face Communications

Face-to-face communications are appropriate for delegating tasks, coaching, disciplining, sharing information, answering questions, checking progress toward objectives, and developing and maintaining rapport. Don't be boring.[27] As you learned in chapter 8, common advice when in conflict is to sit down face-to-face and initiate a resolution. In the next section, you will learn a step-by-step process to follow when sending messages face-to-face.

Meetings

Meetings are appropriate for coordinating team activities, delegating tasks to groups, and resolving conflicts.[28] The most common meeting is the brief, informal get-together with two or more employees. As you learned in chapter 9, with the increased use of teams, much more time is spent in meetings, and the ability to lead effective meetings is an important skill to acquire.

 **TIME-OUT 4** Think about a task your boss or coach recently assigned you. Note which of the preceding steps he or she took, which ones he or she didn't, and how he or she could have sent the message more effectively.

Presentations

Whether you are accepting an award, promoting a charity, or fulfilling sponsorship requirements, your ability to use words gracefully, lucidly, and accurately and to deliver them well is a sure way to garner positive attention from your colleagues and your bosses. Speaking skills are needed in virtually every job.[29] Presentation skills are not only for formal speeches. The grace and confidence you gain in giving presentations are essential ingredients for working with others individually and in groups. Here are a few pointers.

Begin speeches with an attention-grabbing opener—a quote, a joke, or an interesting story that ignites interest in your topic. Following the opener, your presentations should have three parts: (1) a beginning—a purpose statement and an overview of the main points to be covered; (2) a middle—a discussion of the main points in enough detail to get the message across (but not so much detail that you lose your audience); and (3) an end—a summary of the purpose, main points, and any action required of the audience. Stories are good at getting your message across, but they can't be boring.[30] If you are uncomfortable giving presentations, practice. Then practice some more. Join your local Toastmasters club—these clubs have shaped many an effective speaker from the clay of pure terror. There are numerous books on giving effective presentations.

PowerPoint is a great presentation enhancer, and you should learn how to use it. To use PowerPoint effectively, follow these two tips. First and foremost, don't just read your slides, unless you want to bore people senseless—death by PowerPoint is common. To help avoid reading, go easy on the text. Just use an outline to aid you in talking to your audience. If you can't talk to people, just show them your slides and let them read the slides for themselves to save everyone's time. Second, the purpose of PowerPoint is to help you get your point across, so don't go crazy with special effects. They may be impressive, but they often distract from the point you are trying to make. Avoid laser pointers; they are distracting.

Telephone and Cell Phone Calls

The amount of time you spend on the phone will depend on your job. Phones are inappropriate for personnel matters (such as disciplining) but are good for quick exchanges of information. They are especially useful for saving travel time. Although e-mail and texting have gained in popularity, they are terrible for conversations, so use the phone and save time.

Here are a few pointers to keep in mind when you talk on a phone at work. Before making calls, set an objective and list what you plan to discuss. Use your list for jotting notes during the call. When receiving calls, determine the caller's purpose and decide whether you or another person should handle it. When calls come in at inconvenient times, arrange to call the person back. Use your cell phone responsibly and politely. Other people (in restaurants, airports, and other public places) don't want to hear your business conversations; but they will if you're not considerate, because cell phone users always talk louder than normal even though they are not aware of it. So step aside in private. And avoid using your cell phone (especially texting) when you're driving—your life isn't the only one on the line.

Mobile phones have evolved as a personal assistant for many professionals. Phones can be used to schedule and organize your personal calendar, deliver and receive e-mails, browse the web, and help you get to a meeting on time by providing guided directions. They give you an alarm clock for your hotel wake-up call; a calculator; and bar code scanning capabilities, replacing the need to carry credit cards. However, a mobile phone also means that your employer (if he has your phone number) can reach you at all times of the day.[31]

Voice Mail

Productivity took a giant leap forward when we stopped having to call back innumerable times because someone was away from her desk or on the phone.

Written Channels

Today, every time we text, e-mail, post, tweet, or use social media, we are writing.[32] Social media are increasing in popularity of use for business.[33] So every organization demands that its people have good writing skills; nothing reveals your weaknesses more clearly (and more permanently!) than poorly written communications. Poor writing skills hinder your college performance, job search, and career development and advancement. It is fine to text your friends in abbreviated jargon, but not for most formal business communications.[34] So learn to write effectively. Written communications allow for accuracy and precision and provide the all-important record. But it often takes longer to text and e-mail back and forth than it does to just pick up the phone and talk. And don't let social media communications take over your face-to-face and phone communications to maintain good working (and social) relationships.

Here are the written channels you will continually use in your work.

1. Memos—commonly used to send intraorganizational messages
2. Letters
   1. "Snail mail" for getting your formal messages to people outside the organization, on company letterhead
   2. Faxes for when the instant communication needs to be hard copy
3. Reports for formally conveying information, evaluations, analyses, and recommendations
4. Newsletters for conveying general information to the entire organization
5. Bulletin board notices for supplementing other channels and for wide dissemination of public information
6. Signs for permanent reminders of important information, such as mission statements and safety instructions

Use written channels for all manner of communications—to send general information, to send specific and detailed information, to thank people, to send messages that require future action, or to send messages that affect several people in a related way, to name but a few.

E-Mail, Texting, and Instant Messaging (IM)

Together, let's call them e-comm. E-comm is commonly used for all the channels, to send memos, letters, reports, and newsletters, and it can serve as a bulletin board and sign.

E-comm is great for instant 24/7 communications (both formal and informal). E-comm has been called the greatest productivity tool of our time. Conversely, some employees and friends complain that e-comm causes information overload, wastes work time, and is annoying.[35]

Personal e-comm takes up employees' work time, at great expense to employers. As a manager, don't let e-comm and talking on cell phones interfere with productivity on the job.

Writing Tips

Here is a (very) short course for improving your writing. Before you write, organize your thoughts. Decide on the content that will help your audience understand your point—outlines are good for this. Check the message that you've laid out in your outline for focus. Weed out ideas and information that receivers don't need. Consider what you want your receivers to hear, to think, and to do. Now write from your outline.

As with effective presentations, effective written communications have a beginning (the purpose of the communication), a middle (support for the purpose—facts, figures, reasoning), and an end (a summary of the major points and a clear statement of conclusions or of action, if any, to be taken by you and the receivers). If you want your message to sizzle, reread it and rewrite it. Do it again. Great writers use multiple drafts, and for important business issues, so can you.

Write as though you are talking to the person.[36] Write to communicate clearly, not to impress. Keep your message short and simple. Follow the 1–5–15 rule. Limit each paragraph to one topic, with an average of five sentences that average 15 words. Vary paragraph and sentence length, but never let paragraphs get too long, because this discourages the person from reading your message. Write in the active voice ("I recommend . . . ") rather than the passive voice ("It is recommended . . . ").

Check your work for spelling and grammar errors. Have others edit your work. If you are writing a paper or report, search out articles in the *Journal of Sport Management*, a leading journal in the field, and other sport journals.

Press Releases

You could end up working in a collegiate sport information department (SID). Among many other responsibilities, SIDs are responsible for organizing and writing press releases. Press releases are crisply written letters that SIDs disseminate to local media about the sport teams, coaching staff, student-athletes, and the entire athletic department.

Many websites provide tips on writing a press release, such as the following. Make sure the information is newsworthy and substantial; tell the audience that the information is intended for them and why they should continue to read it; make sure the first 10 words of your press release are effective; avoid excessive use of adjectives and fancy language; deal with facts; provide as much contact information as possible; and make it as easy as possible for media representatives to do their jobs. See the example that follows.

Visual Channels

Sporting event telecasts (on TV and increasingly on the Internet) are big business.[37] Two notions dominate discussions of links between sport media and sport attendance. One side says that media use in sport both escalates with and provokes event attendance. The other side holds that media use can act as a recreational substitute for attendance.[38] What do you think? If you aspire to work for Division IA or pro teams, you should realize that telecasting of games is big money for teams. You may also want to consider a career in sport media. There are lots of jobs behind the scenes, or should we say screens, of visual channel sports.

Visuals are also critical to coaching in improving performance. Many teams watch game videos to identify strengths and areas to improve on for the next game. But watching video right after a performance is also important in coaching, for example after a dive. Engineers

---

Example of a Press Release

Springfield SLAMM Ready for 2014 Summer Pro-Am League

May 15, 2014
For Immediate Release
Media Relations Contact: Info@DrSteveSobel.com or 565-5000.
Head Coach Dr. Steve Sobel of Longmeadow, announced that The Springfield SLAMM, one of the pro-am summer basketball teams in New England, will be playing in the 2014 Greater Hartford Pro-Am League this season as well as selected appearances in the Greater Springfield area.

The team is NCAA sanctioned and approved for inclusion of Division I basketball players. Former players include first round NBA draft pick Jeremy Lamb, Deandre Daniels, and Ryan Boatright, all of the University of Connecticut. Additional former players include Missouri star Alex Oriakhi, Boston College graduate Joe Trapani, and the University of Vermont American East Player of the Year candidate Michael Trimboli.

Gary Forbes of the NBA's Denver Nuggets played in 2010 as well as UMass product Stephan Lasme.

The SLAMM reached the semi-finals last year and Sobel said he "is looking to make another significant run to the championship in August."

The coaching staff for the 2014 campaign includes Assistant Coaches Ethan Sobel, Aaron Patterson, Ike Miller and Community Relations Director Charles Kittredge. Robert Zeller has been appointed director of player personnel.

The SLAMM players will also continue to visit hospitals to do clinics as they did last year at The Connecticut Children's Medical Center for Children and their Families. There will also be basketball shooting clinics for junior high and high school players of all ages on June 25 and 26.

The SLAMM's first game will take place on June 29 at the Mass Mutual Center.

Used with permission of Steve Sobel.

---

from BMW (yes, the car people) developed a machine that not only videos long jumps; it spits out three crucial numbers: horizontal velocity, vertical velocity leaving the board, and angle of flight. Bryan Clay, two-time decathlon Olympic medalist, used it in preparation for tryouts and the London Olympics.[39] At the Olympic tryouts, he set the world record.[40]

Combining Channels

 Do you think broadcasting the *Mike Francesa* show on television reduces or enhances the normal communication process of radio?

Repetition helps ensure that important messages are received and that their meaning is understood and remembered. This is where combining channels can be very useful; for example, to convey an important message, you might send a memo (sometimes several) and then follow up with personal visits or phone calls to see whether receivers have questions. There are times when you will want to formally document a face-to-face meeting, particularly in disciplinary situations (we discuss this more in chapter 13). Mike Francesa uses multiple channels to distribute his show. The daily radio broadcast is on WFAN; the video simulcast is on the YES television network. The show is simultaneously broadcast using both mediums to enrich the experience for viewers.

 **TIME-OUT 5** Identify the channel used for an oral message and a written one that you recently received at work or on your team. State whether the sender's choice of channel was effective and, if it was not, which channel would have been better and why.

LEARNING OUTCOME 5 ▶
Select appropriate channels for your messages.

Choosing Channels

To choose the best channel for a given message, look at the media's richness. Media richness is the amount of information and

APPLYING THE CONCEPT 10.3

Choosing Channels

Select the most appropriate channel for transmitting the following messages (which haven't been encoded yet). When combined media will be most effective, indicate which ones.

a. face-to-face
b. meeting
c. presentation
d. phone call

e. memo
f. letter
g. report

h. bulletin board
i. poster
j. newsletter

_____ 11. You want to know whether an important shipment of uniforms has arrived.

_____ 12. You want staff and players to turn the lights off in the locker room when no one is in it.

_____ 13. You need to explain the new community relations program to your team.

_____ 14. John has come in late for work again; you want him to shape up.

_____ 15. You've exceeded your ticket sales goals and want your boss to know about it, because it should have a positive influence on your upcoming performance appraisal.

meaning that the channel can convey. The more information and meaning, the "richer" is the channel. Face-to-face talk is therefore the richest channel because the full range of oral and nonverbal communication is used. Phone calls are less rich than face-to-face meetings because many nonverbal cues are lost. Written messages can be rich, but they must be very well written to qualify. Video is rich because body language is evident. Key your channel choice to how difficult, complex, or important your message is.

Sending Messages

The sender of a message should plan the message, send it effectively, and check understanding (get feedback). Sending a message might seem like an easy part of proper communication. But think about how a manager you like seems to communicate ideas so much more easily than a manager you dislike. It is rather likely that the successful manager took the time to send the message as described in this section.

Planning the Message

Before you send a message, use this short checklist to make sure your message is on target: Ask yourself what, who, how, which, where, and when.

- What is my goal in this message?[41] (What do you want the end result of the communication to be? Set an objective.)
- Who should receive my message?
- How should I encode my message?
- Which channel is appropriate for my message, my receivers, and the situation?
- Where should I deliver my message? (In your office, the locker room, or the receiver's workplace? Choose a place that keeps distractions to a minimum.)
- When should I transmit my message? (Timing is important. Think about your receiver and be considerate—for example, don't approach someone 5 minutes before quitting time to transmit a 15-minute message. Make appointments when appropriate.)

Sending Oral Messages

As noted earlier, oral channels are richer than other channels, and face-to-face, oral communication is best when the message you must transmit is a difficult or complex one. When sending a face-to-face message, follow these steps in the **message-sending process**: (1) develop rapport, (2) state your communication objective, (3) transmit your message, (4) check the receiver's understanding, (5) get a commitment and follow up.

Step 1: Develop rapport. Put the receiver at ease. It is usually appropriate to begin communication with small talk related to the message.

Step 2: State your communication objective. It is helpful for the receiver to know the objective (end result) of the communication before you explain the details.

Step 3: Transmit your message. Tell the receiver whatever you want him to know.

Step 4: Check the receiver's understanding. When giving information, ask direct questions or paraphrase. Simply asking "Do you have any questions?" does not check understanding. (Later we describe how to check understanding.)

Step 5: Get a commitment and follow up. If the message involves assigning a task, make sure that the message recipient can do the task and have it done by a certain time or date. When employees are reluctant to commit to the necessary action, managers can use persuasive power within their authority. Follow up to ensure that the necessary action has been taken.

LEARNING OUTCOME 6 ▶

Solicit feedback properly.

Getting Receivers to Get It—Feedback

We all need feedback to know how we are doing.[42] For communication to take place, at some point you and your receiver must reach a mutual understanding about your message's meaning. Therefore, after you transmit your message, you will need to know whether the receiver "gets it." This is where you check understanding by soliciting feedback. Feedback is needed to ensure performance.[43]

Senders use feedback to verify that their meaning has been communicated (understood). **Feedback** is the process of verifying messages. It literally feeds back to the sender the original information, meaning, or intent transmitted in the message. Questioning, paraphrasing, and soliciting comments and suggestions are all ways senders can check understanding through feedback. Requiring feedback from receivers motivates them to achieve high levels of performance and improves their attention and their retention. Indeed, the most common reason that messages fail to communicate information, meaning, or intent is a lack of feedback. Actionable feedback produces both learning and good performance.[44] Before we look at effective ways to solicit feedback, let's look at what can go wrong.

How Not to Solicit Feedback

One sure way to block feedback is to send your entire message and then ask, "Do you have any questions?" Most of the time, you have very effectively killed any chances for discussion, because very few people will ask questions. Here is why they don't.

1. They feel ignorant. No one wants to look like the dim bulb in the group.
2. They are ignorant. Sometimes people don't know enough about the topic to ask questions. That is, they don't know whether the information given is complete, correct, or subject to interpretation.
3. They don't want to point out your ignorance. This commonly occurs when the sender is a manager and the receivers are staff. Asking a question in this situation may suggest that you have done a poor job of preparing and sending the message or that you are wrong. Neither is a comfortable situation for your receivers.

After senders ask whether there are questions (and thereby end the discussion), they often make yet another leap in the wrong direction. They assume that if receivers had no questions, the receivers understood the message. If only this were true! When receivers don't understand the message, they will act upon the message incorrectly (e.g., perform a task incorrectly). When this happens, the message has to be sent again; the task has to be done again; and time, materials, and effort are wasted in the meantime. Taking a few minutes to get feedback often saves hours of needless work.

How to Solicit Feedback

Proper questioning and proper paraphrasing help ensure that when you send your message, your receivers get the message. In **paraphrasing,** receivers restate the message in their own words. Be sure to use your own words, to say it differently, because some people don't want you to parrot back what they said. Keep the following in mind when getting feedback.

1. There are no dumb questions. Never sneer at a question (no matter how stupid you think it is). Always answer patiently and explain clearly. If people sense impatience in you, you've just stopped any question dead in its tracks. To encourage good questions, praise good questions.

2. Tune into your own nonverbals. Match your walk to your talk. If your nonverbal messages are discouraging feedback, no amount of verbal pleading on your part will bring forth the harvest of questions you desire.

3. Tune into your receivers' nonverbals. Seeing a lot of puzzled or blank looks out there? It's time to stop, backtrack, and clarify.

4. Ask your receivers questions. Ask anything (except, of course, "Do you have any questions?"). Ask for specific information you have given. If responses are off track or muddled, repeat the message, give more examples, or elaborate further. Ask indirect questions: "How do you feel about such and such?" Ask "If you were me" questions (e.g., "If you were me, how would you solve our lack of focus during games?"). Ask third-party questions, such as "How will players respond when they have to bring their grades up to stay on the team?" If you get receivers to talk, the feedback gates will open.

5. Have receivers paraphrase your message. Paraphrasing is a valuable way to check understanding. Soliciting it gracefully is also an art. Clumsy soliciting of paraphrasing makes people feel stupid. Saying "Joan, tell me what I just said so that I can be sure you won't make your typical mistakes" is not going to work—in fact, it's going to backfire big time! You probably will need to practice soliciting of paraphrasing. In the beginning, before it becomes second nature, have some paraphrasing questions worked out beforehand; with practice they will eventually roll off your tongue. "Now tell me what you are going to do so that we will be sure we are in agreement." "Would you tell me what you are going to do so that I can be sure that I explained myself clearly?" This is known as "making feedback people-friendly."

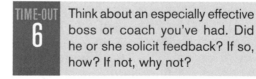

TIME-OUT 6

Think about an especially effective boss or coach you've had. Did he or she solicit feedback? If so, how? If not, why not?

Receiving Messages

So far, we've discussed the communication process from the viewpoint of the sender. Now it's time to become a good receiver. If someone asked you if you are a good listener, most likely you would say yes. However, unfortunately, a recent survey found that the number-one thing lacking in new college grads is listening skills.[45] Can you pay attention and listen

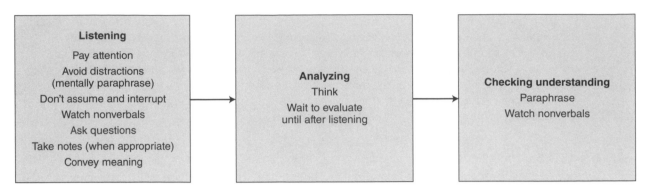

FIGURE 10.3 The message-receiving process.

effectively at school, in sport, and at work? Complete the Self-Assessment to determine the level and quality of your listening skills; be honest.

Careful listening clues you in to others' needs and desires and to important information that can make you more effective and more skillful. This is why sport managers, salespeople, negotiators, and conflict resolution experts have to be good listeners.[46] Before we sharpen your listening skills, consider how people receive messages, summarized in figure 10.3. The **message-receiving process** involves listening, analyzing, and checking understanding. To receive the real message the sender is transmitting, you have to do all three. Receiving doesn't end with good listening. By using the message-receiving process, you can become a better listener.

Becoming a Listener

Failure to listen is the killer of many an otherwise effective communication. Here is how to improve your listening skills. Spend 1 week focusing on listening. This is going to be a very quiet week for you. Talk as little as possible, and listen, listen, listen. When your attention wanders, bring it back. Get quiet. Take special pains to concentrate on what other people say and on the nonverbal signals they send. Note when verbal and nonverbal messages are particularly consistent and when they are blatantly out of sync. Note when nonverbal messages reinforce the speaker's words and when they detract from them. Talk only when necessary. (You can do this—it's just for a week! Try it.)

Listening is the process of giving the speaker your undivided attention (and we emphasize the word *undivided*). Poor listening is caused in part by the fact that we speak on average about 120 words a minute, but we can comprehend 600 or so words a minute. Our ability to comprehend words five times more quickly than speakers can talk results in—you guessed it—wandering minds. Our minds don't like to be empty, so they pack in irrelevant thoughts. The result, of course, is that with all the background chatter, the sender's message loses out. Here are some reminders on how to provide undivided attention:

- **Pay attention.** It's that simple and that hard—because paying attention *is* hard, or we would all be great listeners. So, relax (quickly) and clear your mind, and then focus on the sender. This gets you on track right now. If you miss the first few words, you may miss the whole gist of the message. Practice this: The next time someone interrupts your work in order to talk, stop whatever you are doing (now, or ask for a minute to finish), and give the person your full and complete attention. Don't multitask when people want to talk to you; your nonverbals will be saying "Go away, I'm too busy to talk to you."

- **Avoid distractions.** Keep your eyes on the speaker. Do not fiddle with pens, papers, your belt loop, or your new haircut. Put your phone on "take a message" mode. If the area is noisy or full of distractions, move to a quiet spot.

- **Stay tuned in.** If your mind wanders to other topics (and it will), gently bring it back. Continue to bring it back every time you notice yourself straying. Don't tune out because you don't like something about the speaker or because you disagree with what is being said. Don't tune out because the topic is difficult—ask questions instead. Don't think about what you're going to say in reply. Stay tuned in by silently paraphrasing the message. The next time your mind wanders, repeat what the person is saying to yourself; repeating really forces you to stay tuned in. Try it! It works.

SELF-ASSESSMENT 10.1

Listening

Select the response that best describes the frequency of your behavior. This Self-Assessment is easiest to complete online.

Almost always	Usually	Frequently	Occasionally	Seldom
A	U	F	O	S

_____ 1. To encourage others to talk, I show interest, ask them questions about themselves, and smile and nod.

_____ 2. I pay closer attention to people who are similar to me than to those who are different from me.

_____ 3. I evaluate people's words and nonverbal signals as they talk.

_____ 4. I avoid distractions; if it's noisy, I suggest moving to a quiet spot.

_____ 5. If people interrupt me when I'm doing something, I put what I was doing out of my mind and give them my complete attention.

_____ 6. When people are talking, I allow them time to finish. I don't interrupt them, anticipate what they're going to say, or jump to conclusions.

_____ 7. I tune out people who don't agree with me.

_____ 8. My mind wanders to personal topics when someone else is talking or professors are lecturing.

_____ 9. I pay close attention to nonverbal signals to help me fully understand what the other person is really saying.

_____ 10. When the topic is difficult, I tune out and just pretend I understand.

_____ 11. When the other person is talking, I think about what I'm going to say in reply.

_____ 12. When I think something is missing or contradictory in a discussion, I ask questions to get the person to explain her ideas more fully.

_____ 13. I let the other person know when I don't understand something.

_____ 14. When listening to other people, I try to put myself in their place and see things from their perspective.

_____ 15. When someone gives me information or instructions, I repeat them in my own words and ask the sender whether I'm correct.

Have some of your friends fill out this assessment, giving their impressions of your listening habits.

Scoring. For statements 1, 4, 5, 6, 9, 12, 13, 14, and 15, give 5 points for an A answer; 4 for U; 3 for F; 2 for O; and 1 for S. For items 2, 3, 7, 8, 10, and 11, the score reverses: 5 points for S; 4 for O; 3 for F; 2 for U; and 1 for A. Place these scores on the lines next to your responses and add them to get your total. Your score should be between 15 and 75. Place your score on the following continuum.

Poor listener												Good listener
15	20	25	30	35	40	45	50	55	60	65	70	75

- **Don't assume and don't interrupt.** Most mistakes in receiving messages are made when we hear the first few words of a sentence, think we know what is about to be said, finish it in our own minds, and then miss the real message. Listen to the entire message, without interrupting, because you really do not know what the speaker is going to say.

- **Watch nonverbals.** People sometimes say one thing and mean something else. Watch as you listen to be sure that the speaker's eyes, body, and face are in sync with the verbal message. If something seems out of sync, ask questions to clarify.

- **Ask questions.** Check your understanding. When you feel something's missing or contradictory, or you just don't understand, don't be afraid to ask for clarification. The speaker will be grateful, as will other listeners. If you don't understand a message, chances are they don't understand it either.

- **Take notes.** Write down important things. This helps you concentrate on what is being said and helps you remember later. Always have something to write on and something to write with. Taking notes also tells the sender nonverbally that you want to get the message right.

- **Convey that you are listening.** Use verbal clues ("You feel . . . ," "Yes," "I see," "I understand") and nonverbal cues (eye contact, nodding your head, leaning slightly forward) to indicate that you are interested and listening.

Once you've put in your week of listening, take some time and think about what it felt like to listen more than you talked. Was it hard? Now take the Self-Assessment on page 329 again. Did your answers change? Do you still talk more than you listen? Regardless of how much and how well you listen, if you follow these guidelines, you will improve your conversational ability and become someone people want to talk to and listen to. To become an active listener, take responsibility for ensuring mutual understanding. Work to change your behavior to become a better listener. Review the 15 statements in the Self-Assessment on page 329. Make a habit of doing items 1, 4, 5, 6, 9, 12, 13, 14, and 15. And avoid doing items 2, 3, 7, 8, 10, and 11.

Analyzing the Message

When we analyze a message, we think about it, decode it, and evaluate it. Therefore, as speakers send their messages, you should be doing two things:

- Thinking: Use your excess capacity for comprehending to listen actively. Silently paraphrase, organize, summarize, review, and interpret. When this is not working, repeat every word to yourself. This marshals all your forces for decoding the message.

- Waiting to evaluate: When people try to listen and evaluate what is said at the same time, they miss part or all of the message. So listen to the entire message and then make your conclusions. When you evaluate the message, base your conclusions on the facts presented rather than on stereotypes and politics.

 **TIME-OUT 7** Now that you've listened for a week and have done the Self-Assessment twice, what do you think is your weakest listening skill? What are you going to do about it?

LEARNING OUTCOME 8 ▶
Choose appropriate response styles.

Responding to Messages

Not every message requires a response, of course, but many do. With each response, the communication process both begins again (you encode and transmit, and the receiver decodes) and continues (because this is a response, not the initiating message). The roles of receiver and sender continue to flip throughout every conversation. So feedback goes both ways.[47]

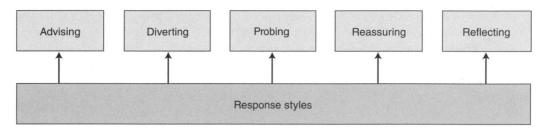

FIGURE 10.4   Response styles.

The way you respond to a message directly affects the communication process. You, of course, want to respond appropriately, and you have five response styles from which to choose (see figure 10.4): advising, diverting, probing, reassuring, and reflecting. To demonstrate the different response styles, let's look at five responses to a rather confrontational message from a person on your team: "You supervise me so closely that I can't do my job—I have no breathing room."

Advisor's Responses

"You need my directions to do a good job; you lack experience." "I disagree. You need my instructions and you need for me to check your work." (Note that advice was not asked for, but it was given anyway.) Advisors evaluate, give their personal opinion, direct, or instruct. Advisors tend to close, limit, or redirect the flow of communication.

Giving advice is appropriate when you are asked for it. Remember, however, that giving advice too quickly builds dependence. Developing your staff's ability to think things through and to make decisions is an important part of your job. When asked for advice by employees who you believe don't really need it, ask, "What do you think is the best way to handle this situation?" "What do you think we should do?"

Diverter's Responses

"You've reminded me of a manager I once had who. . . . Did you see the game last night?"

Diverters switch the focus to a new message—what we commonly call changing the subject. Diverters tend to redirect, close, or limit the flow of communication. Diversions used early on in the conversation may cause senders to think that their message is not worth discussing or that the other party's message is more important.

Diversion is appropriate when either party is uncomfortable with the topic. Diversion may be helpful when someone is sharing personal experiences or feelings but the other person wants to edge the conversation away from something too personal, too embarrassing, or too "close." Religious and political discussions rarely change people's minds but often end in arguments, so divert to another subject to avoid conflict.

Prober's Responses

"What do I do to cause you to say this?" (Not "Why do you feel this way?") "How long have you felt this way?"

Probers ask the sender to give more information about some aspect of the message so the prober can better understand the situation. When probing, use "what" questions in preference to "why" questions.

Probe during the early stages of the message to ensure that you fully understand the situation. After probing, you often may need to use some of the other response styles.

Reassurer's Responses

"Don't worry, I won't do it for much longer." "Your work is improving, so I may be able to provide less direction soon."

331

Reassurers endeavor to reduce the intensity of the emotions associated with the message. They're saying, "Don't worry; everything will be OK." They are pacifying the sender.

This technique works well when the other person lacks confidence, because it can include giving praise to help people develop confidence. How often do you say something like "Don't worry, you will pass the test" or ". . . get a hit" or ". . . win the game" or ". . . get 'em next time"?

Reflector's Responses

"My checking up on you annoys you?" "You don't think I need to check up on you; is this what you mean?" (Note that these responses allow the person to express feelings and direct the path of the exchange.)

Reflecting paraphrases the message and communicates understanding and acceptance. When reflecting, do not to use the sender's exact words; it is mimicking (and thus patronizing). When reflecting is used gracefully, senders feel listened to, understood, and free to explore the topic in more depth. Use reflective responses early in the conversation to find out what the real meaning of the message is.

Sometimes we just want someone to listen to us—so we can get our frustration out. At these times, we don't want advice or lots of annoying questions, and we don't want someone to change the subject or say that everything is OK. We just want a good listener with reflective responses. When you lose a close game after giving 100%, what do you want to hear from a friend? "You need to work harder." "Why didn't you pass the ball more?" "Don't worry; you will do better next time." "It was a tough game." Which response tells you that your friend is willing to listen to your frustration?

 **TIME-OUT 8** State two oral messages you received recently and your responses to them. Identify your response style for each message. Give two different responses using other styles and state why each is appropriate or inappropriate.

Dealing With Emotional People

Someone with whom you work—player, coach, parent of player, boss, work group member, customer—is going to start an emotional exchange with you. Emotions can shut down accurate communications and divert from the real message. If you want to succeed, understand emotions and learn to deal with them. Realize that feelings are

- subjective—they reveal people's attitudes and needs,
- often disguised as factual statements, and
- neither right nor wrong.

We cannot choose feelings or control the feelings themselves. However, we can control how we express our feelings. We choose our behavioral responses (what we say and do). For example, if Rachel in the heat of a win exults in Louise's humiliating loss in their tennis match, Louise can choose to lower herself to Rachel's level with a confrontational and emotional response, and she can even become violent. Or she can rise to the occasion and show grace, dignity, and the courage to face her loss. Louise's response can cause the exchange to rapidly deteriorate, or it can remind Rachel that some things are more important than winning.

Don Imus certainly didn't control his emotions very well while discussing the Rutgers women's basketball team. The lesson here? Each of us chooses our responses in emotional exchanges, and we always have a chance to shape these exchanges into something positive. How do you respond when players talk trash to you during the game—can you ignore them, or do you let your emotions hurt your game?

APPLYING THE CONCEPT 10.4

Identifying Response Styles

Identify each response to the given situation as

    a. advising

    b. diverting

    c. probing

    d. reassuring

    e. reflecting

Irate parent: Coach, do you have a minute to talk?

Coach: Sure, what's up?

Irate parent: Can you do something about all the swearing that players do on the team? It's disgusting. I'm surprised you haven't done anything.

Coach:

_____16. I didn't know anyone was swearing. I'll look into it.

_____17. You don't have to listen to it. Just ignore the swearing.

_____18. Are you feeling well today?

_____19. So you find this swearing offensive?

_____20. What words are they saying that offend you?

Calming an Emotional Person

◀ LEARNING OUTCOME 9

Calm an emotional person.

If someone explodes at you in anger, what can you do? Fortunately, there are a lot of positive ways to handle the situation. But first, here is what you shouldn't do:

- Don't put the person down.
- Don't deny the anger.
- Don't accuse back.
- Don't patronize the person.
- Don't show who's boss.

This means that the following statements should never be said (even if you are thinking them):

- "You shouldn't be angry." (How do you know? Don't judge feelings as wrong.)
- "Don't be upset." (Too late—the person is already upset.)
- "You're acting like a baby." (Like this is going to get you somewhere?)
- "Just sit down and be quiet." (This may shut the person up, but it will fuel emotions. Think about it. If someone tells you to be quiet, will you calmly listen and agree to the lecture?)
- "I know how you feel." (No, you don't. No one, even someone who has experienced the same thing, knows how others feel.)

 Can you list other statements that you should not make when you're trying to calm someone?

These statements only raise the temperature of the exchange. Belittlers cause emotional distress and undermine confidence. Contributing to a person's anger, fear, and panic hampers performance. So avoid emotional responses, which you often will regret later anyway. Try to get away from an emotional exchange and get to communication.

First, you have to deal with the emotion and then you can deal with the issue, because you can't successfully deal with the issue when emotions are high.

Fortunately, there are many productive ways you can respond. For one thing, make sure you know chapter 8 inside and out. For another, learn to empathize. **Empathy** is the ability to understand and relate to someone else's situation and feelings. Empathic responders deal with feelings, content, and the underlying meaning expressed in the message.

Empathic people are good listeners—in fact, with good listening comes empathy; they are natural by-products of each other. So, remember to use good listening skills. Pay attention to what people are saying; don't assume and don't interrupt; let them know you are listening (honor their feelings, in other words); and withhold evaluative responses.

Carefully reflect feelings back like this. "Were you hurt when you didn't get first-string position?" "You resent Charlie for not pulling his weight on the team—is that what you mean?" "Are you doubtful that the job's going to get done on time?" Very often, simply understanding the sender's feelings is the solution—only venting is wanted, not advice. Other times, solutions must be found. As emotions cool (and they will if you give them enough time), you can proceed to the crux of the problem and begin solving it. If emotions continue to run high, you may have to wait until a later time before you can consider solutions.

Giving and Receiving Criticism

You're going to give some criticism and you're going to get some. It's easier to give it than to get it, isn't it? As with other important endeavors, you may as well do both well.

TIME-OUT 9

Recall an emotional exchange that you witnessed at work or on your team. Did the responder calm the person effectively? Write a paragraph about the exchange showing where the responder went right or went wrong.

Giving Criticism

Most managers dislike giving critical feedback to underperformers.[48] This is part of the reason so many people don't do a good job. Avoid personal criticism, and don't criticize things people can't change. It doesn't help to tell a player she dropped the ball; she knows it and most likely already feels bad about it. Don't waste time placing blame. The team wins or loses; saying it's someone's fault doesn't change anything in a positive way, but it will hurt cohesiveness. Never criticize someone publically, especially your bosses. Criticism of work, reports, progress on schedules, and the like, of course, is part of the manager's job. Giving (and taking) criticism is just another tool in your tool kit—one that you can learn, hone, and turn to your competitive advantage. Good coaching is all about giving criticism to improve performance, and the way you give the criticism determines its effectiveness, both on and off the field.

Here are some guidelines for giving motivational criticism to improve performance. You will learn how to deal with problem employees and to discipline in chapter 13. Practice empathy when you're giving criticism. Don't focus on the negative and don't belittle someone, because it isn't constructive; in fact, it often leads to lower performance.[49] Avoid making judgments. Don't tell people they are wrong, unless it is necessary, for example when you are disciplining employees. When you tell people they are wrong, they tend to get defensive and become less open to

TIME-OUT 10

Think about what sorts of criticism you accept without getting emotional and defensive. Use this insight when you give criticism.

change. Instead, make feedback actionable; don't criticize without giving a recommendation on how the person can improve. For example, don't tell an employee that he's picking up boxes wrong. Say, "Instead of lifting the boxes using your back, try bending at the knees and use your legs to lift so you don't hurt yourself." You may also demonstrate the better way.

The employees whom you manage are more likely to accept your criticism than are your family and friends and coworkers. When you are not the boss, follow the guidelines just presented, but change your approach. Rather than just telling people they are doing something wrong and telling them how to do it better, ask whether they want criticism. For example, don't say, "You're doing that wrong; do it this way." Instead, say, "Would you like me to show you how you can save time doing that?"

Getting Criticism

None of us enjoy being criticized, even when it is constructive, and many people detest receiving it. A big part of the problem is that people are so poor at giving criticism. Now that you know how to give criticism, you will be effective at it. But you're going to get some criticism, maybe lots of it, so you might as well take it well. In fact, if you are wise, you will want constructive criticism. How else are you going to realize your full potential? View constructive criticism through the perceptual lens of wanting it. This will put you in a position to use it constructively and to see it not as a personal attack on you but as what it is—help, encouragement, and teaching. And taking criticism gracefully gives you power.

If you are overly sensitive and become defensive, people will avoid giving you the criticism you need if you are to grow. Think about how you will gain when you take the pain. If your coach simply says "Good game," which we love to hear, can you improve in the next game? Only if the coach or others criticize you with actionable feedback can you improve. Think of criticism as what it is—feedback to improve your performance.

Remember that even jerks can help you improve. So no matter how poorly the person gives criticism, don't get defensive; stay open to ways to improve. Take responsibility. Admit your mistakes, learn from them, and, most important, don't repeat them.[50] Don't dwell on your mistakes, or you will make even more mistakes. If you drop the ball or miss a shot, get back out there with confidence and focus on getting it right.

Even extraordinary talents get their share of criticism. If you watch sports, you see lots of coaches yelling. In 2004, New York Giants quarterback Eli Manning was criticized for not wanting to play for the San Diego Chargers. He was again criticized for forcing a trade to the New York Giants. By 2006, Manning was being criticized for not trusting his wide receivers. Manning was still looking for success on the football field. Manning took the criticism very professionally, and that was hard to do because he plays in the media frenzy of New York City.[51] Manning's patience was rewarded when he calmly led the Giants to a Super Bowl XLII victory over the heavily favored, and previously unbeaten, New England Patriots.

@ TAKE IT TO THE NET

Please visit www.HumanKinetics.com/AppliedSportManagementSkills and go to this book's companion web study guide, where you will find the following:

A list of websites associated with the concepts in this chapter

Exercises that you will need Internet access to complete

Online versions of chapter exercises and end-of-chapter learning aids

An exercise that helps you define the Key Terms

LEARNING AIDS

CHAPTER SUMMARY

1. Understand how communication flows through organizations.

   Formal communications flow vertically (down and up through the chain of command) and horizontally (between coworkers). Informal communication flows through the grapevine in many directions.

2. List the four steps in the communication process.

   The sender (1) encodes a message and then (2) transmits it. (3) The receiver decodes the message. (4) The receiver decides whether feedback is needed and, if it is, encodes a message (a response) and transmits it—and the process begins again.

3. Use transmission channels well.

   Although oral communication is easy and fast and encourages feedback, it is also less accurate than other methods and provides no record. Written communication is more accurate and provides a record, but it also takes longer, and feedback is not immediate.

4. Communicate effectively in person.

   (1) Develop rapport. (2) State your message using a beginning, middle, and end. (3) Check the receiver's understanding. (4) Get a commitment, and follow up.

5. Select appropriate channels for your messages.

   As a general guide, use rich oral channels for sending difficult and unusual messages, written channels for transmitting simple and routine messages to several people, and combined channels for important messages.

6. Solicit feedback properly.

   Do not simply ask whether anyone has questions. Ask receivers to paraphrase your message. Ask them for specific information you have given. Ask indirect questions, "if you were me" questions, and third-party questions. Just get them talking.

7. Explain how we receive messages.

   To receive a message well, we listen (give the speaker our undivided attention), analyze (think about, decode, and evaluate the message), and check our understanding (often by giving feedback).

8. Choose appropriate response styles.

   Heated exchanges are best handled by advising, diverting, probing, reassuring, and reflecting, but not in this order. Depending on the exchange, reflecting, reassuring, or diverting is typically a good first response. Probing is appropriate later in the process, and advising is typically the last step if it is used at all.

9. Calm an emotional person.

   Avoid statements that put the person down, patronize her, or show her who is boss. Instead, pay attention, don't assume, and don't interrupt; let her know you are listening (honor her feelings), and withhold your evaluation. Let her vent. Later, carefully reflect her feelings back to her.

REVIEW AND DISCUSSION QUESTIONS

1. What are the differences among vertical, horizontal, and grapevine communications?

2. What is the difference between encoding and decoding?

3. What is distortion?

4. Give an example of nonverbal communication in baseball, in poker, and in soccer.

5. What forms of communications do you personally use to gather information about sports?

6. What is the 1–5–15 rule?

7. What is media richness?

8. What should you include when you send an oral message? A written one? What makes each effective and why?

9. Which response style do you use most often?

10. When we calm emotional people, why don't we simply show them who is boss?

11. Visit your college library and find an article in the *Journal of Sport Management* that mentions communication. In what context is the term used?

12. What athletes can you name who received criticism in a professional manner? What athletes or coaches responded in an aggressive, reactionary manner?

13. Practice writing a press release for a local sporting team. You might also write a press release for a fantasy sport team (if you are part of a fantasy league) you manage.

14. Is the grapevine helpful or harmful to most organizations? Should managers try to stop grapevine communications? Why or why not?

15. Wireless phones and handheld devices are blurring work and home life. Is this positive or negative? Should people stay connected and work while on vacation?

16. Which communication barrier do you think is the most common, and which barrier do you believe has the most negative effects on communication?

17. Which message transmission channel do you use most often in your personal and professional lives? What is your strongest and weakest channel? How can you improve on your weakness?

18. When sending messages, how effective are you at checking the receiver's understanding? How can you improve?

19. When receiving messages, how effective are you at listening? How can you improve?

CASE

BDA Sports Management Speaks Baron Davis' Language

Do you think you would be good at babysitting egos? Think you can handle the fickle media, long hours, and first-class seats on airplanes and at sporting events? Then become a sport agent—it's good work if you can get it. And life will never be dull again. Some very large sport agencies—IMG and ProServ are two that come to mind—represent professional athletes in all sports. But many pro players use independent agents, and a growing number of these are lawyers.

Agents handle all or part of a professional athlete's business affairs, including contract negotiations, product endorsements, licensing arrangements, personal appearances, public relations, and financial counseling. Although agents don't like to reveal the commissions they get on the contracts they negotiate for their players, it appears that the average commission on players' contracts is between 3% and 5%—a good income when you consider how much some players earn.

Agents are regulated fairly carefully because the opportunities for defrauding players or misrepresenting them are legion. Regulators include state and federal governments, the agents themselves, the NCAA, and players' associations. All of these groups have, with varying success, adopted certification programs in attempts to monitor player agents.[52] The best attempt so far has been spearheaded by the NCAA. The NCAA's endeavor to establish a uniform system for regulating athlete agents—the Uniform Athlete Agents Act (UAAA)—has been passed in the United States in 41 states, the District of Columbia, and the U.S. Virgin Islands. The act requires agents to register with a state authority to be able to act as an athlete agent in that state.[53]

Agents who represent MLB players must jump through a few hoops. To be certified by the players' association, for example, an agent must represent at least one member on a 40-man roster of an MLB club.[54] The association has more than 300 agents on record.

Why all the emphasis on regulating agents? It's because there are a lot of rules and regulations to meet, and also because large amounts of money can tempt people to bend the rules. So unfortunately, there is too much monkey business in the business of sport agency. Agents are not supposed to communicate with college players, but some agents do this anyway. And when they get caught, everyone pays—the athletes, the colleges, the sport programs, and the fans. Athletes such as basketball players Marcus Camby (University of Massachusetts) and Ricky Moore (University of Connecticut) received gifts while in college. Gifts can range from money to airline tickets.[55]

College athletes often select an agent when they turn professional. One reputable agency is BDA Sports Management in Walnut Creek, CA. One of the most famous athletes represented by BDA Sports Management is Baron Davis who has played with Charlotte, New Orleans, Golden State, the LA Clippers, the Cleveland Cavaliers, and most recently the New York Knicks of the NBA. Davis has founded the Baron Davis Foundation, which is designed to serve the common welfare of youth.

Like Baron himself, Todd Ramasar, Baron's agent at BDA Sports Management, attended UCLA. Prior to joining BDA, Todd originally built Life Sports Management where he represented Baron. He has a mission to help athletes on and off the court. He looks for players with ability on the court, a willingness to learn the business side of basketball, and a desire to succeed when their playing career is over. BDA is a smaller agency than IMG or ProServ, and it is promoted as a full-service athlete management agency and marketing firm to professional basketball players. Davis has said, "Todd is one of the most brilliant individuals I have ever met. He runs his company with the utmost respect and care for his clients. Having been with two previous agents, I have now found a home in BDA Sports Management. I trust him with my life! Period!"[56]

Baron Davis did trust Todd Ramasar one more time, and they negotiated a $1.4 million one-year contract with the New York Knicks for the 2012 NBA season.[57] Even better, Davis is still owed a guarantee of $27 million of a $30 million deal he signed with Cleveland Cavaliers. It is fair to say that Ramasar has shown Davis the money![58]

Information about BDA Sports Management can be found at www.bdasports.com.

Case Questions

Answer the following questions about communication between an agent and a player.

1. College athletes are not allowed to communicate with which of the following professionals?
   a. baker
   b. postman
   c. agent
   d. media personnel

2. Todd Ramasar and Baron Davis made a great team because they both went to UCLA.

   a. true

   b. false

3. Baron Davis has had the same agent his entire professional career.

   a. true

   b. false

4. IMG is an independent agency that represents

   a. football players

   b. baseball players

   c. tennis players

   d. players from all sports

5. No rules govern the conduct of sport agents.

   a. true

   b. false

6. Marcus Camby was found to have communicated with agents while he was an amateur player in college.

   a. true

   b. false

7. What step of the communication process is being used if a player's agent and the team are working on the wording of the first draft of the player's contract?

   a. encoding

   b. transmitting

   c. decoding

   d. feedback

8. What step of the communication process is being used if BDA Sports Management faxes a copy of a revised player contract back to the team?

   a. encoding

   b. transmitting

   c. decoding

   d. feedback

9. Name three agents who represent athletes from the NFL and MLB.

10. Name two athletes who have had problems with their agents. What sort of communication barriers do you think were operative in each case?

SKILL-BUILDER EXERCISES

Skill-Builders 10.1, 10.2, 10.3: Strong Messages, Strong Receivers

Objective

To hone your ability to send and receive messages

Preparation

Read and understand this chapter. Your instructor will inform you as to which one or more of the three exercise messages you will be transmitting. Exercise 10.1 will be given in class. Exercises 10.2 and 10.3 will require some research and brainstorming.

In-Class Application

Choose one or more of the three exercises:

- For exercise 10.1, break into pairs. You will each be sender and receiver in turn.

- For exercises 10.2 and 10.3, break into groups of five to eight members and transmit your messages to the group. Select one of the group's messages for presentation to the class. If this is an exercise 10.3 message, your group will present their "decoding" to the class as well.

Exercise 10.1: Giving Instructions. Your instructor will pass out drawings of objects. Your job as encoder is to direct your receiver to draw the objects. Your receiver may not look at the drawing. You are not to tell him or her what the object is or how it is used. You may not use hand signals or drawings of your own—only words are permitted. You have 15 minutes to get the drawing done.

Exercise 10.2: Delivering a Message. Find a sport-related message by a coach, athlete, player's agent, MLB manager, or head of the NFL that was difficult to deliver or hard to receive. This could be a coach who lost his or her cool, a coach who rallied a team that was on its knees, a player who was retiring, a leader involved in a strike, or a parent involved in a youth league scandal—there are many possibilities. Use the Internet, old copies of *Sports Illustrated*, or biographies of sport figures to find the exact quotation, the context in which it was delivered, and the receivers of the message. If the sport figure delivered the message poorly, reenact the original delivery to your group (to the best of your imagination), and then deliver the message in a more effective way. If the sport figure did a great job of encoding a difficult message, enact a poor encoding first and then the original, great rendition.

Exercise 10.3: Explaining a Sport or Game. Research an obscure sport (such as curling or boomeranging) or game (such as a little-known card game); one you are pretty sure your classmates don't know how to play. Develop some interesting ways to explain the rules (in 10 minutes or less) of this sport or game to your receiving group. You may not tell the name of the sport or the names of objects used in the sport. Your receivers will demonstrate that they received your message by giving a very quick demonstration of the game. Ask the class to guess the sport.

Wrap-Up

Take a few minutes to write your answers to the following questions:

What did I learn from this experience? How will I use this knowledge?

_____

_____

_____

As a class, discuss student responses.

SPORTS AND SOCIAL MEDIA EXERCISES

Mark Cuban, president and owner of the NBA Dallas Mavericks, wrote "the last few years have brought about a lot of change in how people publish and receive information. It might just be time to change how teams communicate as well. What do you think ?" Review Cuban's blog and find three communications-related quotes. Go to http://blogmaverick.com/2011/04/04/whats-the-role-of-media-for-sports-teams.

1. _____

2. _____

3. _____

GAME PLAN FOR STARTING A SPORT BUSINESS

Your own sport business needs to develop a comprehensive strategic social media plan.

1. Write a complete plan on what social media you plan to use for your sport business.

   _____

2. Determine approximately how much each form of media will cost you to implement.

   _____

3. What skills do you have to develop your social media plan? How much of the plan will require you to hire someone else to accomplish your social media goals?

   _____

Motivating to Win

Controlling Planning Organizing Leading Controlling Planning Organizing Leading Controlling Planning
zing Leading Controlling Planning Organizing Leading Controlling Planning Organizing Leading C
g Planning Organizing Leading Controlling Planning Organizing Leading Controlling Planning O
Leading Controlling Planning Organizing Leading Controlling Planning Organizing Leading Controlling
g Organizing Leading Controlling Planning Organizing Leading Controlling Planning Organizing Leading
ling Plan

LEARNING OUTCOMES

After studying this chapter, you should be able to

1. explain how motivation works;
2. use the performance equation;
3. discuss the four content-based motivation theories;
4. discuss the three process-based motivation theories;
5. discuss reinforcement theory; and
6. compare content, process, and reinforcement theories.

KEY TERMS

motivation

motivation process

performance equation

content-based motivation theories

hierarchy of needs theory

ERG theory

two-factor theory

acquired needs theory

process-based motivation
  theories

equity theory

goal-setting theory

expectancy theory

reinforcement theory

Organizing Leading Controlling Planning Organizing Leading Controlling Planning Organizing Lea
Controlling Planning Organizing Leading Controlling Planning Organizing Leading Controlling Planning Org
Leading Controlling Planning Organizing Leading Controlling Planning Organizing Leading Contr
Planning Organizing Leading Controlling Planning Organizing Leading Controlling Planning Organ
ading Controlling Planning Organizing Leading Controlling Planning Organizing Leading Controlling

DEVELOPING YOUR SKILLS

You can't win in business or sport without motivated players. In this chapter, you will learn about the motivation process and one reinforcement-based motivation theory, and four content-based and three process-based theories, as well as getting tips on motivating with each theory. Giving praise is motivational and is not used nearly enough. You can develop this skill using a four-step model for giving praise.

REVIEWING THEIR GAME PLAN

Famous Motivational and Leadership Quotes

Sport coaches and athletes are known for their many memorable quotes about motivation and leadership. Vince Lombardi is well known for his amazing words of wisdom. We use a few of his quotes here to focus your attention on how exciting motivation can be.

Vince Lombardi

"Leaders aren't born, they are made. And they are made just like anything else, through hard work. And that's the price we'll have to pay to achieve that goal, or any goal."

"It is essential to understand that battles are primarily won in the hearts of men."

"In great attempts, it is glorious even to fail."

"Leaders are made, they are not born. They are made by hard effort, which is the price which all of us must pay to achieve any goal that is worthwhile."

"The harder you work, the harder it is to surrender."

"It's not whether you get knocked down, it's whether you get up."

"The quality of a person's life is in direct proportion to their commitment to excellence, regardless of their chosen field of endeavor."

"There's only one way to succeed in anything, and that is to give it everything. I do, and I demand that my players do."

"If you aren't fired with enthusiasm, you'll be fired with enthusiasm."

"Once you learn to quit, it becomes a habit."

"Winning isn't everything—but wanting to win is."

Special Olympics Motto

"Let me win, but if I cannot win, let me be brave in the attempt."

Coach Darrell Royal

"Luck is what happens when preparation meets opportunity."

Babe Didrikson Zaharias

"Luck? Sure. But only after long practice and only with the ability to think under pressure."[1]

LEARNING OUTCOME 1 ▶

Explain how motivation works.

Motivation and Performance

Researchers and sport managers want answers to the following types of questions: What motivates athletes and employees to work hard? What motivates people to volunteer to coach for the Olympics? What motivates volunteers at sport organizations?[2] And most important, how can we motivate our employees, athletes, and consumers? Motivated, engaged employees give companies and teams a competitive advantage through increased performance.[3] Let's face it, motivation leading to effort has long been recognized as an

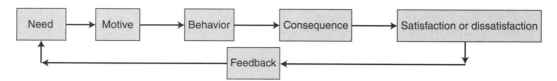

FIGURE 11.1 The motivation process loop.

important determinant of achievement.[4] In this chapter, you will read about what motivates you and others, and you will learn how to motivate others. Let's begin this section with an explanation of the motivation process, the role of expectations, the performance equation, and an overview of the motivation theories presented throughout this chapter.

Motivation Process

Motivation is based on our feelings and needs. It is what drives us to satisfy our needs. **Motivation** is the willingness to achieve organizational objectives.

Motivation is also a process. Through the **motivation process,** people go from need to motive to behavior to consequence and finally to either satisfaction or dissatisfaction. Let's say you work up a powerful thirst (need) while working out and want some water (motive). You get a drink (behavior) that quenches (consequence) and thus satisfies your thirst. In many endeavors, our satisfaction is short-lived. For this reason, the motivation process loops back and begins anew as we continually strive to meet our needs (see figure 11.1).

Our needs and wants thus motivate every aspect of our behavior. Because our needs and wants are typically more complex than our thirst after a workout, we don't always know what they are and therefore don't always know why we do what we do. That is why organizational behaviorists study needs—understanding needs often explains behavior. We can't observe motives directly, but we can observe behavior and thereby infer motive. But humans are vastly trickier than this simple model, because different motives frequently drive the same behavior. Add to this mix the fact that we also strive to satisfy several needs at once. Thus, motivation is complex.

Role of Expectations

Motivation is the key to success or failure as it affects performance.[5] So, what causes poor performance? Many things, but a key factor is managers themselves. Don't look first at the inadequacies of your staff (poor skills, lack of experience, bad attitude—you know the list). Look first at your own expectations. Remember the Pygmalion effect (chapter 8)—your expectations and your treatment of people affect their motivation and hence their performance. Sam Walton (founder of Walmart) said, "High expectations are the key to everything." If you have high expectations for your staff and treat your workers as high achievers, you will get their best. Vince Lombardi treated his players as champions, and his players made history season after season.

You need to realize that what works to motivate you may not motivate others. Thus, rule number one is to know your people. Get to know them as individuals and learn what meets their unique and diverse needs. It is crucial to instill a self-perception of competence in individuals.

People's expectations of themselves also affect their performance. This is the self-fulfilling prophecy. We will live up—or down—to our own expectations, so each of us must seek ways to be positive, confident, and optimistic. A negative outlook can be changed, but it takes effort (chapter 8). Vince Lombardi said, "We would accomplish many more things if we did not think of them as impossible."[6]

Henry Ford said that if you believe you can, or you believe you can't, you are right. If you think you will be successful, you will be. If you think you will fail, you will, because you will fulfill your own expectations. For example, if you go to the hoop and shoot believing

 Have you ever had a job that was fun? How did this affect your motivation?

you will miss, what most often happens? Think about other sports you play and things you do. But we have to believe realistically based on hard work. You can't walk into a test or game unprepared and expect to do well. Hard work and practice give us the realistic confidence to believe we can succeed and to excel. And it takes motivation to work hard.

Performance Equation

Motivated people try harder, but this is not the complete explanation for one's performance. Performance takes more than motivation:

LEARNING OUTCOME 2 ▶

Use the performance equation.

$$\text{Performance} = \text{Ability} \times \text{Motivation} \times \text{Resources}$$

This is the **performance equation.** To get maximum performance, you need high levels of ability and motivation and resources—it's that simple. It is also that complicated, because this is not easy to pull off, as every organization knows all too well. What this equation does is focus your thinking. Is your group's performance suffering? Then examine what is missing from the equation and why. For example, if your tennis player isn't winning any matches, is the reason lack of ability (we can't all be stars no matter how much we practice), motivation (missing practice, not working hard, not following your coaching instruction), or resources (will a new racket help?)?

World champion swimmer Missy Franklin clearly has ability, but her coach Todd Schmitz helps keep her motivated with fun activities and with less hard training than Michael Phelps' coach assigns, and the team doesn't have their own pool so they go to multiple places to practice.[7] Pat Riley, former coach of the two-time NBA champion Los Angeles Lakers and current president of the Miami Heat, is convinced that when a (high ability) player gets to see himself making a mistake, the player can correct it, and when he sees himself making a great play, he can replicate it over and over again. Riley firmly believes that analyzing game video (resources) in great detail improves motivation in sport and gives his team the mental edge.[8]

One of the frustrating parts of teaching, coaching, and managing is having motivated, hardworking people who just don't have the ability to make the cut. This takes us back to our model of success. You need to find things that you are good at (ability) and enjoy (motivation) to do well and be satisfied. If you realize you can't be a pro athlete but you love sport and recreation and think you can be happy as a sport manager, you are on the right track. Your next step is to narrow down your career path.

It is also frustrating not to have the resources. How many coaches and sport managers think, If we only had a bigger budget (more specifically, if we only had the court or field for more practice time, more assistant coaches, more money to attract better pros or more college scholarships, a new field), we could do a better job?

The third frustration is working with people who have ability but lack the motivation to reach their full potential. That is the focus of this chapter. (We teach you about budgeting in chapter 13, and if you develop your management skills you will increase your ability to get more and better resources.)

Only when you know what is missing can you develop strategies that will solve the problem. Coaches constantly look for ways to improve their team's performance equation. For instance, if a team's ability is not up to snuff, a coach needs to laser in on specifics, adjust training accordingly, and recruit to fix holes in the team. Great football coaches, such as Bill Belichick of the New England Patriots, make adjustments to their offense and defense during the game and at halftime.

Motivating People

How do we motivate our workers, our players, and ourselves to be our best?[9] There is no single best way. However, keep in mind that the basic motivation is self-interest and that

TABLE 11.1 Major Motivation Theories

Classification of theories	Specific theories and types of reinforcement
1. **Content-based theories**—focus is on identifying and understanding people's needs.	**Hierarchy of needs**—people are motivated by five levels of needs: physiological, safety, social, esteem, and self-actualization (Maslow).
	ERG—people are motivated by three needs: existence, relatedness, and growth (Alderfer).
	Two-factor theory—motivator factors (higher-level needs) are more important than maintenance factors (lower-level needs) (Herzberg).
	Acquired needs—people are motivated by their need for achievement, power, and affiliation (McClelland).
2. **Process-based theories**—focus is on how people choose behaviors to fulfill their needs.	**Equity**—people are motivated when their perceived inputs equal outputs (Adams).
	Goal setting—difficult but achievable goals motivate people (Locke).
	Expectancy—people are motivated when they believe they can accomplish the task and the rewards for doing so are worth the effort (Vroom).
3. **Reinforcement theory**—focus is on consequences for behavior (Skinner).	**Positive reinforcement**—attractive consequences (rewards) for desirable performance encourage continued behavior.
	Avoidance—negative consequences for poor performance encourage continued desirable behavior.
	Extinction—withholding reinforcement for an undesirable behavior reduces or eliminates that behavior.
	Punishment—undesirable consequences (punishment) for undesirable behavior prevent the behavior.

the pursuit of happiness is fundamental to human motivation. So if you want to motivate people, answer their often unasked question: *"What's in it for me?"* If you give people what they want, they will in turn give you what you want—creating win–win situations.[10] This process is easier said than done, so it is the focus of this chapter. Self-awareness and introspection about what motivates you can help you to motivate yourself. To this end, we present two Self-Assessments to help you better understand what motivates you. It's time for some theories. To get an overview, peruse table 11.1, and read about these motivation theories in the following sections.

Content-Based Motivation Theories

◀ LEARNING OUTCOME 3
Discuss the four content-based motivation theories.

According to content-based theorists, to create a satisfied workforce, organizations must meet their employees' needs. **Content-based motivation theories** thus focus on identifying and understanding people's needs. The key to success is to meet the needs of the workforce and the objectives of the organization. As you strive to create this win–win situation, you need to sell the benefits that meet the employees' needs.

Hierarchy of Needs Theory

Abraham Maslow developed the hierarchy of needs theory in the 1940s,[11] but it is still being researched today.[12] The **hierarchy of needs theory** proposes that people are motivated by five levels of needs: physiological, safety, social, esteem, and self-actualization. Maslow operated under four major assumptions. (1) Only unmet needs motivate. (2) People's needs are arranged in order of importance (a hierarchy) from basic to complex. (3) People will not be motivated to satisfy a high-level need unless their lower-level needs have been

APPLYING THE CONCEPT 11.1

Performance Equation

Identify which part of the performance equation is operative in each situation.

a. ability

b. motivation

c. resources

_____ 1. Calling on one of her golf club retailers, Latoya realizes belatedly that she has forgotten her product display book. No visuals–no interest. She loses the sale.

_____ 2. Frank is definitely the team's slacker–as coach says; Frank's got the goods, he just doesn't use them.

_____ 3. I train longer and harder, but Heather and Linda continually beat my times.

_____ 4. Yeah, my grades could be better, but, hey, I made the team, so it's time to relax and have some fun.

_____ 5. FIFA would be more efficient if it cut down on waste.

_____ 6. Amateur athletes have to pinch pennies to pay for training.

_____ 7. Our athletic director says we need money for the lacrosse program.

_____ 8. When team cuts loom, players train harder.

_____ 9. Before Title IX, women did not enjoy equal opportunities to play collegiate sports.

_____ 10. Women collegiate basketball teams have plenty of applicants now that WNBA pro basketball is an option after players finish school.

at least minimally satisfied. (4) People have five types of needs (presented here in order of importance from lowest to highest).

1. Physiological needs: Our primary or basic needs are air, water, food, shelter, sex, and relief from or avoidance of pain.

2. Safety needs: Our safety and security are our next level of need.

3. Social needs: After we establish a safe and secure life, we look for love, friendship, acceptance, and affection. MLB pitcher C.J. Wilson decided to play for the Los Angeles Angels since he is from the West Coast. He wanted to be closer to his family and friends back home.[13]

4. Esteem needs: These include ego, status, self-respect, recognition for our accomplishments, and a feeling of self-confidence and prestige. Pro athletes are paid very well, but that doesn't preclude their wanting to achieve excellence on the playing field for the sake of excellence itself.

5. Self-actualization needs: This is our highest level of needs—our need to develop our full potential. And some people go to incredible lengths to do this. (Think about the people who pursue extreme sports.)

Interestingly, decades before self-directed teams became popular in the 1990s, Maslow called for them, because this is a straightforward way to meet self-actualization needs. Figure 11.2 lists ways in which managers attempt to meet these five needs.

 TIME-OUT 1

Where in the hierarchy of needs are you for a specific professional aspect of your life? For a specific aspect of a sport? Explain why you are at this level.

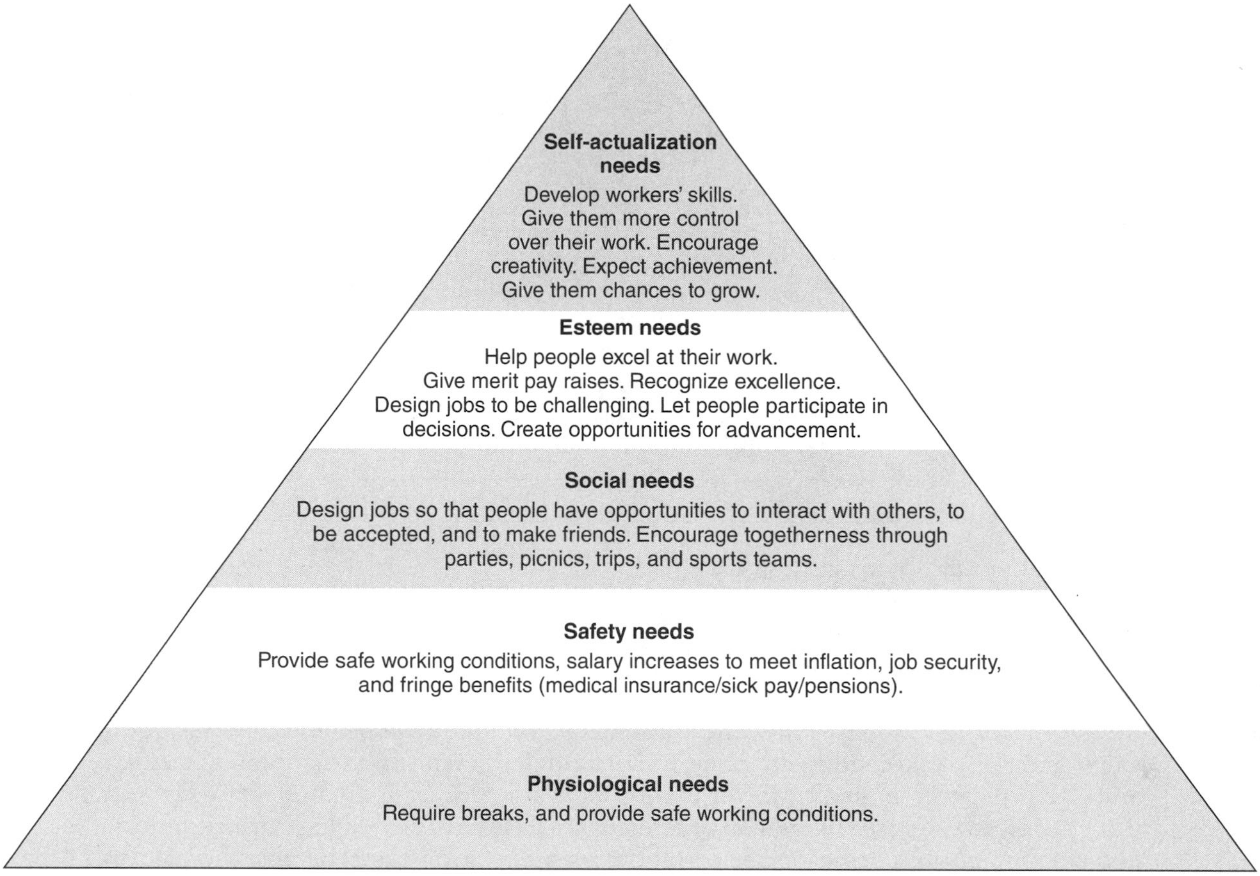

FIGURE 11.2 How organizations satisfy the hierarchy of needs.

ERG Theory

ERG is a well-known simplification of the hierarchy of needs. Psychologist Clayton Alderfer developed the **ERG theory** by reorganizing Maslow's needs hierarchy into three needs: existence (physiological and safety needs), relatedness (social), and growth (esteem and self-actualization). Alderfer agreed with Maslow that unsatisfied needs motivate individuals but disagreed that only one need level is active at a time.[14]

To use this theory, first determine which needs have been met and which ones have not. Then work on meeting the unsatisfied needs and progress to growth needs.

Kevin Durant is an interesting example of the ERG theory. It is fair to say that Durant (like most well-paid professional athletes) does not have to worry about his existence needs. Durant is a three-time NBA scoring champion. He led the Oklahoma City Thunder basketball team to the 2012 NBA Finals; they lost to the Miami Heat. Surprisingly, some question what drives Durant's motivation. Before each game, he hugs his mother at the court sideline (relatedness needs). However, it is fair to say that as a fairly inexperienced and youthful player (he entered the NBA at 19 years old), he is still growing (growth) in his role as the leader of OKC.[15]

Two-Factor Theory

Let's focus on you for a moment. What motivates you? Take the following Self-Assessment and find out before you learn about two-factor theory.

In the 1950s, Frederick Herzberg classified two sets of needs. Herzberg and his associates disagreed with the traditional view that satisfaction and dissatisfaction are at opposite ends

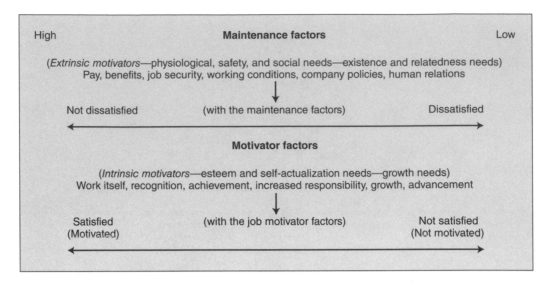

High   **Maintenance factors**   Low

(*Extrinsic motivators*—physiological, safety, and social needs—existence and relatedness needs)
Pay, benefits, job security, working conditions, company policies, human relations

Not dissatisfied   (with the maintenance factors)   Dissatisfied

Motivator factors

(*Intrinsic motivators*—esteem and self-actualization needs—growth needs)
Work itself, recognition, achievement, increased responsibility, growth, advancement

Satisfied   (with the job motivator factors)   Not satisfied
(Motivated)   (Not motivated)

FIGURE 11.3   Herzberg's two-factor theory.

of one continuum.[16] They proposed two continuums: One continuum is our satisfaction or dissatisfaction with the work environment; the other continuum is our satisfaction or dissatisfaction with the job itself. Herzberg called the first continuum the maintenance or hygiene factor (pay, job security, title, working conditions, fringe benefits, and relationships) and the second continuum the motivator factor (achievement, recognition, challenge, and advancement). In the **two-factor theory,** motivator factors, not maintenance factors, drive people to excel (see figure 11.3). Maintenance factors are also called extrinsic factors because they are outside the job itself.[17] Motivators are intrinsic factors because they derive from the work itself.[18]

Herzberg contended that maintenance factors minimize or even prevent employee dissatisfaction, but they do not satisfy or motivate workers. Thus, dissatisfied employees who get a pay raise will, for a time, not fault their pay—they will be "not dissatisfied" for a while. Before long, however, they will grow accustomed to the pay, and dissatisfaction will creep back in. They will soon need another "fix" of money, which becomes a repeating cycle.

Herzberg's stance is that organizations must ensure that maintenance factors are adequate, but they do not have to go to excessive lengths. Once employees are no longer dissatisfied with their environment, the intrinsic factors in their jobs will kick in and motivate them. The current view of money as a motivator is that, yes, money matters, but money does not in and of itself motivate people to work harder. Recall (chapter 8) that people can experience overall job satisfaction without being satisfied with every determinant of job satisfaction, including pay.

Pro athletes are paid very well today; many people would argue that these athletes' compensation is excessive. Does Alex Rodriguez, earning U.S.\$32 million for the 2012 season,[19] need more money to motivate him? Do you think giving him a raise will get him to play any harder or better? Or would he be better motivated by such intrinsic factors as his reputation, setting records, and the chance to win the MLB World Series? You can see how intrinsic factors are important in the motivational equation.[20]

Two-factor theory implies that the best way to motivate employees is to ensure that they are not dissatisfied with maintenance factors and then to focus on motivator factors. This means building challenge and opportunity for achievement into the job itself. To motivate employees, you can make their jobs more interesting and challenging,

TIME-OUT 2   List the maintenance and motivator factors in your current job or team and rate your level of dissatisfaction or satisfaction in each continuum. Give reasons for your rating.

SELF-ASSESSMENT 11.1

What Motivates You?

For the following 12 factors, rate how important each one is to you on a scale of 1 to 5.

Not important				Very important
1	2	3	4	5

_____ 1. An interesting job I enjoy doing

_____ 2. A boss who treats everyone the same regardless of the circumstances

_____ 3. Getting praise, recognition, and appreciation for the work that I do

_____ 4. A job that is routine without much change from day to day

_____ 5. The opportunity for advancement

_____ 6. A prestigious job title regardless of the pay and work

_____ 7. A job that gives me freedom to do things my way

_____ 8. Working conditions (safe environment, cafeteria)

_____ 9. The opportunity to learn new things

_____ 10. An emphasis on following company rules, regulations, procedures, and policies

_____ 11. A job I can do well and can succeed at

_____ 12. Job security (staying with the same organization for my entire career)

Record your answer scores and total each column. Are motivator factors or maintenance factors more important to you?

Motivating factors	Maintenance factors
1. _____	2. _____
3. _____	4. _____
5. _____	6. _____
7. _____	8. _____
9. _____	10. _____
11. _____	12. _____
_____ Total points	_____

give them more responsibility, provide them with opportunities for growth, and offer them recognition for a job well done. Job enrichment and delegation (chapter 5) are two methods of doing this.

Acquired Needs Theory

The **acquired needs theory** proposes that employees are motivated by their need for achievement, power, and affiliation. Henry Murray developed the original general needs theory[21]; it was later adapted by John Atkinson and David McClelland, who developed a specific acquired needs theory.[22]

McClelland did not classify lower-level needs. His affiliation needs are the same as social and relatedness needs, and his power and achievement needs resemble esteem, self-

SELF-ASSESSMENT 11.2

Which Acquired Need Drives You?

For the following 15 statements, rate how similar each one is to you on the following scale.

Not like me				Very much like me
1	2	3	4	5

_____ 1. I enjoy working hard.

_____ 2. I like to compete, and I like to win.

_____ 3. I take good care of my friends.

_____ 4. I don't shrink from difficult challenges.

_____ 5. I usually end up deciding which movie or restaurant we'll go to.

_____ 6. I want other people to really like me.

_____ 7. I check on how I'm progressing as I complete tasks.

_____ 8. I confront people who do things I disagree with.

_____ 9. I love parties.

_____ 10. I go to great lengths to set and achieve realistic goals.

_____ 11. I try to influence other people to get my way.

_____ 12. I belong to lots of groups and organizations.

_____ 13. The satisfaction of completing a difficult task is as good as life gets.

_____ 14. I take charge when a group I'm in is floundering.

_____ 15. I prefer to work with others rather than alone.

Enter your scores here and total each column. The column with the highest score is your dominant or primary need.

Achievement	Power	Affiliation
1. _____	2. _____	3. _____
4. _____	5. _____	6. _____
7. _____	8. _____	9. _____
10. _____	11. _____	12. _____
13. _____	14. _____	15. _____
_____	_____	_____ Total points

actualization, and growth needs. Unlike Maslow, McClelland believed that our personality determines our needs, which are further developed as we interact with our environment. Personality does affect motivation.

All of us need some amount of achievement, power, and affiliation, just in varying degrees. One of the three needs tends to dominate in each of us and thus drives our behavior. Before we discuss the three needs in detail, complete Self-Assessment 11.2 to see which need drives you.

Need for achievement   People with high need for achievement (nAch) typically take personal responsibility for solving problems. They are goal oriented and set moderate, realistic, and attainable goals. They seek challenge and excellence and choose the road less traveled (i.e., they are often highly individualistic). They take calculated, moderate risk and desire concrete feedback on their performance. They are willing to work hard. High nAchs think about how they can do a better job, how they can accomplish something unusual or important, and how they can fast-forward their careers. They perform well in nonroutine, challenging, and competitive situations (in which low nAchs do not perform well).

McClelland's research showed that only about 10% of the U.S. population has a high dominant need for achievement. Evidence of a correlation exists between high achievement need and high performance.[23] High nAchs tend to enjoy sales jobs and are often entrepreneurs. Olympic and other highly successful athletes have high nAch.

Motivating high nAchs requires not getting in their way—high nAchs motivate themselves! Assign them the nonroutine, challenging tasks that they crave. Give them frequent feedback on their performance. Increase their responsibility as they gain competence.

Need for power   People with high need for power (nPow) typically like to control situations. They want influence or control over others; they enjoy competitions in which they can win (they do not like to lose); and they are willing to confront others. High nPows think about controlling situations and others, and they seek positions of authority and status. They tend to have a lower need for affiliation.

Motivating high nPows requires letting them plan and control their jobs as much as possible. Try to include them in decision making, especially when the decision affects them. They tend to perform best alone rather than as team members. Try to assign them to a whole task rather than just part of a task.

Need for affiliation   People with high need for affiliation (nAff) seek close relationships with others. They very much want to be liked. They enjoy social activities and endeavor to fit in. They join groups and organizations. High nAffs think in terms of friends and relationships. They enjoy developing, helping, and teaching others. They derive satisfaction from working with the group rather than from the task itself. They typically have low nPow.

Effective teams typically have a good number of high nAffs. Very often the "heart" of great teams is nonstar players who are important because they are easy to get along with, develop relationships that make the team cohesive (chapter 9), and do whatever it takes to help the team.

Motivating high nAffs is important because you want these people on board—they will make your group effective. Make sure they are assigned to teams. Praise them and value them. Assign them the tasks of orienting and training new employees. They make great mentors. However, teams need a balance of all three types.

 TIME-OUT 3   Explain how your need for achievement, power, or affiliation affects your behavior at your job or on your team.

Managerial Needs Profile

McClelland found that the common motivational needs profile of managers is high nPow, high nAch, and low nAff. Here are the reasons. People with a high nAff typically want to be one of the group, not the leader. They want everyone to like them, so they don't want to evaluate performance and discipline and fire employees. People with low nAch don't tend to strive to be managers, but people with high nPow and high nAch do. Do you have the managerial needs profile? If you do, it doesn't guarantee success, but it helps. If you don't, you still can be a successful manager, especially if you work at it. Or you may want to consider other career paths. There are lots of great professional nonmanagement sport and recreation positions. Also, many people start out wanting to coach, but later in their career move to managerial athletic director (AD) positions.

Table 11.2 compares the four content-based theories of motivation.

TABLE 11.2   A Comparison of Content-Based Motivation Theories

Hierarchy of needs (Maslow)	ERG theory (Alderfer)	Two-factor theory (Herzberg)	Acquired needs theory (McClelland)
Self-actualization	Growth	Motivators	Achievement and power
Esteem	Relatedness	Maintenance	
Social	Existence		Affiliation
Safety			Not classified
Physiological			
Notes			
Needs must be met in a hierarchical order.	Needs at any level can be unmet simultaneously.	Maintenance factors do not motivate employees.	Motivating needs are developed through experience.

LEARNING OUTCOME 4 ▶

Discuss the three process-based motivation theories.

Process-Based Theories

Process-based motivation theories focus on understanding how employees choose behavior to fulfill their needs. Process-based theories are more complex than content-based theories. Content-based theories simply identify and then endeavor to understand our needs. Process-based theories go a step further and try to understand several things:

- Why we have different needs
- How and why we choose to satisfy needs in different ways[24]
- The mental process we go through as we understand situations
- How we evaluate how well we are satisfying our needs[25]

Equity Theory

Equity theory, primarily J. Stacy Adams' motivation theory, proposes that we seek social equity in the rewards we receive (output) for our performance (input).[26] **Equity theory** proposes that employees are motivated when their perceived inputs equal outputs.

According to equity theory, all of us compare our inputs (effort, experience, seniority, status, intelligence) and outputs (praise, recognition, pay, benefits, promotions, increased status, supervisor's approval) with those of relevant others. A relevant other may be a coworker or a group of employees from the same or a different organization or even in a hypothetical situation. Notice that the definition says *perceived*, and not *actual*, in the comparison of inputs to outputs. Equity may actually exist. However, if we believe that inequity exists, we will change our behavior to create perceived equity.[27] That is, we need to perceive that we are being treated fairly, relative to others.

Diversity is a major issue facing sport managers, and you need to treat everyone fairly and justly.[28] If you don't, you may face a lawsuit or a legislation issue. Title IX was passed because females were not given equality in sport. Still today, some girls are bringing lawsuits against schools that will not let them play on boys' teams. NCAA coaches and ADs struggle with fairness. Should resources be distributed equally based on program needs, or should they be distributed based on program contributions?[29] Which do you perceive as fair?

Unfortunately, part of the problem with equity theory is that we are motivated by self-interest. What we perceive as fair to us is often not seen as fair to others. Many of us also tend to inflate our own efforts and performance when we compare ourselves with others. Have you ever seen players on teams who believe that they are much better than they really are? It's often the case that no one, not even their teammates, can convince them otherwise.

We also tend to overestimate what others earn. We may be very satisfied and motivated until we find out that a relevant other earns more for the same job or earns the same for less work. When we perceive inequity, we may try to reduce it by reducing input or by increasing output.

A comparison with relevant others leads to three conclusions: We are underrewarded, overrewarded, or equitably rewarded. When underrewarded, people try to create equity by doing things like less work, changing the situation (like getting a raise), or getting another job. Most people don't change behavior if they believe they are overrewarded, and with equity there is no problem.

Some pro athletes negotiate extremely lucrative contracts that suddenly become hard to fulfill because of injury, age, or declining skills. The athlete may still be motivated to excel, but physical ability no longer warrants his compensation. Management has to accept the responsibility of the large contract and find alternative methods to make the team competitive. In MLB, payment for a contract is fully guaranteed. NFL contracts are fulfilled only until the time a player is a cut from the team—the contracts are not fully guaranteed. At times, an NFL contract is announced and it seems as if a player is being overrewarded—but only if he plays out the entire contract. In contrast, when an MLB contract is announced and it seems as if a player is being overrewarded, he just might be, because the contract is guaranteed.[30]

People tend to be dissatisfied and unmotivated if they don't believe they are being treated fairly, rather than actually being motivated by equity. So don't expect people to work hard just because you are treating them fairly, but be ready to deal with perceptions of unfair treatment by you or by the organization.

Using equity theory in practice can be difficult, because you as a manager don't necessarily know the employee's reference group, nor do you know her view of inputs and outcomes. However, equity theory does offer some useful general recommendations:

TIME-OUT 4
Give an example of how your perception of equity or inequity affected your motivation and performance in a job or team. Were you underrewarded, overrewarded, or equitably rewarded?

1. Be aware that equity is based on perception, and perception may not be correct. Managers sometimes create equity and inequity by favoring certain workers.

2. Go to great lengths to make rewards equitable. When employees perceive that they are not treated fairly, morale and performance suffer. Employees who produce at the same level should be given equal rewards.

3. Reward excellence. Make sure employees understand the inputs needed to attain certain outputs. When using incentive pay, clearly specify what the employee must do to achieve the incentive. You should be able to objectively justify to others why one person got a high merit raise.

Goal-Setting Theory

Goal-setting theory is one of the most valid theories.[31] It complements Herzberg's and McClelland's theories because goals lead to higher levels of motivation and performance. Goals can challenge us to worker harder; they energize us.[32] **Goal-setting theory** proposes that achievable but difficult goals motivate employees. (Chapter 4 discusses objectives in detail.) The idea behind goal setting is that behavior has purpose—to fulfill needs. Setting goals helps us identify ways we can meet our needs, and attaining objectives reinforces effective behavior. Thus, setting goals can increase performance.[33]

There are three types of goals: easy, "do your best," and difficult but achievable. Easy goals are not recommended because we tend to stop when we achieve the objective, performing below our ability. The goal of just doing the best you can doesn't work for most people either; we tend to say we did the best we can when we really didn't. That

TIME-OUT 5
Give an example of how a goal affected your motivation and performance or that of someone with whom you work or play.

leaves difficult but achievable goals as the best because they push us (they are also called stretch goals). To have high levels of performance, you need to set high standards—goals.[34] When we set difficult but achievable goals, with reasonable deadlines, we work efficiently and effectively to complete the task in the allotted time.

Expectancy Theory

Expectancy theory is based on Victor Vroom's equation[35]:

$$\text{Motivation} = \text{Expectancy} \times \text{Valence}$$

Expectancy theory proposes that employees are motivated when they believe that they can accomplish the task and that the rewards for doing so are worth the effort. Two important variables, expectancy and valence, must be met in order for people to be motivated.

Expectancy is our perception of our ability to accomplish an objective (i.e., the probability that we will succeed). Generally, the higher our expectancy, the better are our chances of being motivated. When we don't believe we can accomplish objectives, we stop trying. Also important is our perception of the relationship between performance and the outcome or reward (called instrumentality). Generally, the higher our expectancy of attaining the outcome or reward, the higher our motivation.[36]

Valence is the value we place on the outcome or reward—that is, its importance. Generally, the more highly we value the outcome or reward, the higher our motivation. If we don't value the reward, we are less likely to work hard for it.

Expectancy theory does work. People are motivated when the following happen:

1. Objectives are clearly defined and are doable (goal-setting theory).

2. Performance is tied to rewards, and high performance is rewarded.[37]

3. Rewards have value to the employee. (It thus behooves you to know what makes workers or players on your team tick—yelling at one player may be motivational, while a look of disappointment may work better with another.)

4. Employees believe that you will give them the reward. (As we have noted numerous times, trust is a key to success.[38])

> **TIME-OUT 6** Give an example of how your expectancy has affected your motivation at your job or team. Specify your expectancy and valence.

LEARNING OUTCOME 5 ▶

Discuss reinforcement theory.

Reinforcement Theory

B.F. Skinner, the famed psychologist and influential theorist of behaviorism, contended that to motivate people we don't need to identify and understand their needs (content theories) or understand how they choose behaviors to fulfill their needs (process theories). Instead, we must understand the relationship between behavior and consequence and then arrange contingencies that reinforce desirable behaviors and discourage undesirable ones.[39] **Reinforcement theory** proposes that consequences for behavior cause people to behave in predetermined ways. The idea behind reinforcement is that we learn what is, and is not, desired behavior as a result of consequences for our behavior, which we get through feedback.[40] Because behavior is learned through experiences of positive and negative consequences, Skinner proposed three components, as shown in figure 11.4.

LEARNING OUTCOME 6 ▶

Compare content, process, and reinforcement theories.

So reinforcement is about getting people to do what we want them to do by answering their often unasked question, "What's in it for me?" In essence you are saying, "If you do this behavior [stimulus calling for response behavior], I will give you this reward—or this punishment if you don't [consequence, i.e., types of reinforcement]—and this is how often I will give you the reward or punishment [schedules of reinforcement]."[41] In this section, we discuss different types of reinforcement done on schedules (operant conditioning), how to motivate with reinforcement, and giving praise to motivate employees.

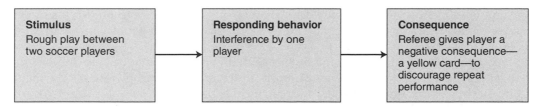

FIGURE 11.4 Skinner's three components of reinforcement theory.

Employee behavior	Type of reinforcement	Manager action (consequence)	Employee behavior modification (future)
Improved performance	Positive	Praise improvements	Repeat quality work
Improved performance	Avoidance	Do not give any reprimand	Repeat quality work
Performance not improved	Extinction	Withhold praise/raise	Do not repeat poor work
Performance not improved	Punishment	Discipline action, i.e., written warning	Do not repeat poor work

FIGURE 11.5 Types of reinforcement. Assuming that the employee improved performance, positive reinforcement is the best motivator.

Types of Reinforcement

There are four types of reinforcement you can use to get your staff to do what you ask (positive, avoidance, extinction, and punishment). Deciding on the right time to use each type of reinforcement is an important step in producing the desired consequences. The ultimate goal is to use positive reinforcement as frequently as possible. However, certain situations might require the use of avoidance, extinction, and (unfortunately) punishment. Figure 11.5 illustrates the four types of reinforcement.

Positive reinforcement   This is a powerful way to attain desired behaviors. You encourage desired behaviors and offer attractive consequences (rewards) for desirable performance. Here's a simple example: An employee arrives on time for a meeting and is rewarded with thanks. The praise reinforces punctuality. Other reinforcements include pay raises, promotions, time off, increased status—the list is endless. Positive reinforcement is an excellent way to increase productivity, and positive incentives are therefore routinely used to motivate individuals and teams. Giving players a day off from practice after a well-played game is an effective, no-cost positive reinforcement. Offering rewards is thus positive reinforcement.[42] It is also a proven way of increasing motivation.[43] Many pro athletes get extra compensation when they win their division, make the playoffs, or win the championship.

Negative reinforcement   This is the flip side of positive reinforcement. There are three types of negative reinforcement:

Avoidance works because we all prefer to avoid negative consequences. With avoidance there is no actual punishment; rather the threat of negative consequences controls our behavior. Standing plans, especially rules, are designed to make us avoid certain behavior. We don't break the rules because we don't want to get punished. Employees see that breaking a rule, like being late, will cause them to miss rewards or to be punished, so they think twice about being late.

Extinction attempts to reduce or eliminate an undesirable behavior by withholding reinforcement when the behavior occurs: in other words, ignore the behavior and it will go away. This approach works sometimes, such as with an employee who wants attention. But ignoring bad behavior usually leads to more bad behavior, so in most cases, you need to take action. One way to do so is to withhold a reward of value, such as a pay raise, until the employee performs to set standards. The other, our next topic, is to punish the undesirable behavior. Managers can also inadvertently extinguish good performance if they do not reward it in some way.

Punishment is an undesirable consequence and can thus be used to change undesirable behavior. For example, if employees are reprimanded for being late, this may cause them to be on time. Punishments in the workplace include probation, fines, demotion, loss of privileges, and termination, to name but a few. Employees violating the company code of conduct, such as expectations regarding sexual harassment, need to be punished to send the message that the behavior is not acceptable and that it will be punished. Firms and sport teams are also punishing bad behavior off the job and field.

Punishment is the least effective way to motivate people. These are several reasons. We get accustomed to punishment (weird, but true!). Punishment can also cause other undesirable behaviors, such as lowered productivity (because of resentment or poor morale) and theft or sabotage.

The commissioner of the NFL, Roger Goddell, suspended New Orleans Saints coach Sean Payton for 1 year because his defensive players organized a bounty system. Defensive players were rewarded with cash when they injured opponents.[44] Payton accepted his punishment. However, Jonathan Vilma appealed his own year suspension as a player who was part of the bounty system.[45]

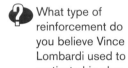

What type of reinforcement do you believe Vince Lombardi used to motivate his players?

You Get What You Reinforce

Employees will do what they are rewarded for doing. If managers say that quality is important but employees who do quality work are not rewarded and nothing happens

TIME-OUT
7
Illustrate the four types of reinforcements with examples from your current job or team.

to employees (e.g., extinction or punishment) who do not do quality work, no one will be motivated to continue to do quality work. If a professor tells students to read this book but does not test them on the book (reward or punishment based on test performance), what percentage of students do you think will read and study this book?

Schedules of Reinforcement

The second consideration in modifying behavior is when to reinforce it. Behaviorists have developed two schedules: continuous reinforcement and intermittent reinforcement.

- *Continuous reinforcement:* With continuous schedules, every instance of the desired behavior is reinforced. Thus, machines with automatic counters that display exactly how many units have been produced provide continuous reinforcement, as do managers who comment on every customer report or provide a commission for every sale.

- *Intermittent reinforcement:* Intermittent schedules are of two types: time-based schedules called interval schedules, and output-based schedules called ratio schedules. Ratio schedules are generally better motivators than interval schedules. Either type can use a fixed interval or ratio or a variable interval or ratio. For example, you are paid a salary every 2 weeks regardless of the number of hours worked (fixed interval). A coach gives praise only for outstanding performance (variable ratio).

Motivating With Reinforcement

Positive reinforcement is by every measure the best all-around motivator. Here are some guidelines:

1. Make sure people know exactly what is expected of them. Set clear objectives.
2. Select appropriate rewards. A reward to one person may be a punishment to another. Know your employees' needs.

3. Use an appropriate reinforcement schedule. (For example, continual praise doesn't sound genuine.)

4. Do not reward mediocre or poor performance.

5. Look for the positive and praise it; don't focus on the negative and on criticizing. Use the Pygmalion effect—make people feel good about themselves.

6. Make sure your praise is genuine and generously given—don't be miserly with your praise.

7. Do things *for* your employees, not *to* them.

Positive reinforcement should be a manager's first choice. Positive reinforcement creates win–win situations by meeting both employees' and the organization's needs. Avoidance and punishment create lose–win situations. Employees lose, because they are punished. The organization or manager may win initially by forcing people to do (or not do) something, but the organization ultimately loses if highly skilled and trained people quit.

TIME-OUT 8

Give examples of behavior at your current job or team that was modified by reinforcement. State the type of reinforcement and the schedule used.

Recognition Praise

In the 1940s, research revealed that what people want most from their job is full appreciation for their work. Similar studies performed over the years confirm this—people want to be recognized for what they contribute. A study of Best Buy found that a 0.1% increase in employee engagement drove U.S.$100,000 in operating income to the bottom line of each store per year. The most important factor in increased performance was simple recognition.[46] Praise develops positive self-esteem and leads to better performance—the Pygmalion effect and self-fulfilling prophecy rolled into one tidy package. Praise motivates because it meets employees' needs for esteem, self-actualization, growth, and achievement. Giving praise creates win–win situations. It is probably the most powerful, most simple, least costly, and yet most underused motivational technique.[47]

Older managers need to realize that the new employees coming in today are the most praised generation. They are used to being praised just for showing up in school, and their experience is that everyone on the team gets a trophy regardless of individual or team performance. So you should give them praise. However, unearned praise is condescending and destructive; incentives become entitlements, and we've ruined our kids by celebrating mediocrity. So set a high standard with clear goals, and give praise when the goals are achieved.

Ken Blanchard and Spencer Johnson popularized praise through their best-selling book *The One-Minute Manager*, in which they showed how to give 1 minute of feedback in the form of praise. Figure 11.6 adapts their method.[48]

1. Tell the employee exactly what was done correctly. Be sincere; look the person in the eye. (Eye contact shows sincerity and concern.) Be specific and descriptive.[49] General statements such as "You're a good worker" are not effective. On the other hand, don't talk for too long, or the praise loses impact—keep the entire praise to less than 1 minute.

Jose: "Al, I just watched you deal with that in-your-face reporter. Great job! You kept your cool; you were polite. That reporter came to the game angry and left happy."

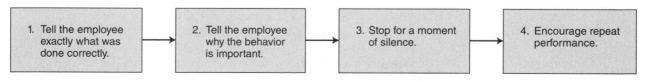

| 1. Tell the employee exactly what was done correctly. | 2. Tell the employee why the behavior is important. | 3. Stop for a moment of silence. | 4. Encourage repeat performance. |

FIGURE 11.6   Giving praise.

2.   Tell the employee why the behavior is important. State (briefly) how everyone benefits from the action. Also, tell the employee how you feel about the behavior. Be specific and descriptive.

Jose: "Without reporters, we don't reach our fans. But one dissatisfied reporter can cost us thousands of dollars in lost sales. It really made me proud to see you handle that tough situation the way you did."

3.   Stop for a moment of silence. Being silent is tough for many of us. The rationale for the silence is to give the employee the chance to feel the impact of the praise. Think of this as "the pause that refreshes." When you are thirsty and take the first gulp of a refreshing drink, it's not until you stop and say "Ah" that you feel your thirst being quenched.

(Jose silently counts to 5.)

4.   Encourage repeat performance. This reinforcement motivates the person to continue the desired behavior.

Jose: "Thanks, Al, keep up the good work."

Giving praise is easy, and it doesn't cost a penny. Managers who give praise genuinely and generously say it works wonders. It is also a much better motivator than raises or other monetary rewards. One manager told about an employee who was taking his time stacking tennis ball cans on a display. The manager praised the employee for stacking the cans so straight. The employee was so pleased with the praise that the display went up about 100% faster. Note that the manager looked for the positive and used positive reinforcement rather than punishment. The manager could have reprimanded the worker by saying, "Quit goofing off and get the job done." That statement would not have motivated the employee to increase productivity. However, it would have hurt human relations and could have ended in an argument. Had the manager's praise not worked as hoped, the manager could have then used another reinforcement method.

In today's global business world, you may never see people you work with face-to-face, but you can video conference or Skype them. Even with e-mail, you can praise people following steps 1, 2, and 4. Plus, even now, the old-fashioned handwritten note of praise is considered a very powerful motivator.[50]

Putting Theory to Work Within the Motivational Process and Motivating Yourself

In this section, we illustrate how the motivation theories complement each other. We then provide ideas on how you can motivate yourself to higher levels of performance.

Putting the Theories Together

Researchers are seeking an integration of motivation theories, which is the topic of this section. The motivation theories we've been discussing are important because they help us understand why people behave the way they do. At this point, you're probably wondering, "Do these theories fit together? Is one best? Or should I try to pick and choose for particular situations?" (The answers are yes, no, and yes.)

The theories fit together in that they complement each other. That is, each category of theories focuses on a different stage in the motivation process. So they all answer different questions. Content-based theories address what needs people have that should be met on the job. Process-based theories address how people choose behavior to fulfill their needs. Reinforcement theory addresses how managers can help employees to meet organizational objectives.

Earlier in this chapter, we discussed how the motivation process progresses from need to motive to behavior to consequence and then to satisfaction or dissatisfaction. The motivation theories fit within the motivation process as shown in figure 11.7. Note the loop between step 4 and step 3; this occurs because behavior is learned through consequences

APPLYING THE CONCEPT 11.2

Motivation Theories

Identify the theory behind each statement.

a. hierarchy of needs   d. acquired needs   g. expectancy

b. ERG theory   e. equity   h. reinforcement

c. two-factor   f. goal setting

_____ 11. I make sure every job in our racket stores is interesting and challenging.

_____ 12. I treat everyone in our sporting goods store fairly.

_____ 13. I know Kate likes people, so I give her jobs in which she works with other employees.

_____ 14. Carl yelled at umpires because he knew it bothered me. So I decided to ignore his yelling, and he stopped.

_____ 15. I know my employees, what they like to do, and what about work excites them. And I know what sorts of rewards light a fire under their performance.

_____ 16. Our sporting goods company now offers good working conditions, salaries, and benefits, so we are working at developing employee camaraderie by having TGIF parties at 4 p.m. on Fridays.

_____ 17. Whenever my staff at the fitness center does a good job, I thank them.

_____ 18. I used to try to improve working conditions to motivate my staff. But I now focus on giving people more responsibility so they can grow and develop new skills.

_____ 19. I realize I tend to be autocratic because this fills my needs. I'm working at giving the team that makes baseball gloves more autonomy.

_____ 20. I focus on three needs and realize that needs can be unmet at more than one level at a time.

(behavior modification). The loop between step 5 and step 1 is always a given, because meeting our needs is a never-ending process. Finally, note that step 5 is two separate continuums (satisfied–not satisfied or dissatisfied–not dissatisfied), based on the need factor being met (motivator or maintenance).

As we near the end of this chapter, recall that we are motivated to meet our needs and that self-interest drives motivation as we pursue happiness. Your expectations affect others' motivation. When performance is below expectation, use the performance equation (Performance = Ability × Motivation × Resources) to determine how to improve performance. Refer to table 11.1 on page 347 to review the motivation theories and figure 11.7 to put them together within the motivational process.

Motivating Yourself

Next we present a four-step model you can use to motivate yourself, followed by some other advice if you are not motivated and feel bored or trapped on the job. In either case, you have to take responsibility for motivating yourself and being happy.

Set Objectives

First, you've got to know what you want—objective—and be willing to work hard to get whatever it is you want. What do you want? To be motivated, develop objectives using the writing objectives model in chapter 4, table 4.2.

Drive and persistence are the key to success. Intelligence is overrated; the drive to win[51] and persistence are better predictors of success.[52] Are you willing to work hard and keep at it until you accomplish your objective?

Develop Plans— Willpower Alone Fails

Why do so many people make New Year's resolutions and fail to keep them? The reason is that willpower or self-discipline alone, without a plan, doesn't work.[53] What exactly are you going to do step by step to accomplish your objective? Do you need to improve your skills and qualifications, for example by getting a college degree and passing a certification exam, to meet your objective?

Measure Results

Get feedback to know how you are progressing toward your objective. Compare your actual performance to your objective.[54] For longer-term objectives, check regularly, not only at the end. How are you progressing—are we there yet?

Reinforce Results

Be sure to use reinforcement theory on yourself. If you are missing the objective, consider punishing yourself; for example if your weight is up, eat less next time. If you are on track to meet the objective, reward yourself in some way—have a special dessert.

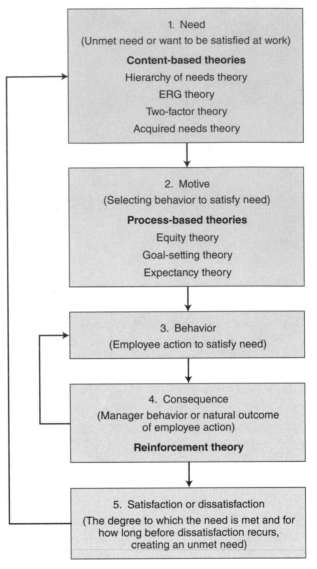

FIGURE 11.7 Motivation theories within the motivation process.

Remember, what you think about is how you feel, and what you feel is how you behave. So develop a self-motivation objective; then plan, measure, and reinforce—and think about it and visualize yourself accomplishing the objective. The self-motivation model in figure 11.8 reviews the steps of self-motivation.

Bored or Feeling Trapped on the Job?

If you are in these situations, you can keep things the same, or you can take responsibility and change the situation; you have two major alternatives. One, you can look for another

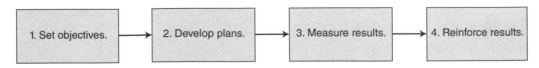

FIGURE 11.8 Self-motivation model.

job (within or leaving the firm) following the four steps of self-motivation model, which may require developing new skills, getting more education, or getting some type of certification. Two, you can think about how your job can be enriched or change the design. With ideas in mind, talk to your boss about implementing ways to improve your job to make it more interesting and challenging, such as taking on new responsibilities.

@ TAKE IT TO THE NET

Please visit www.HumanKinetics.com/AppliedSportManagementSkills and go to this book's companion web study guide, where you will find the following:

A list of websites associated with the concepts in this chapter

Exercises that you will need Internet access to complete

Online versions of chapter exercises and end-of-chapter learning aids

An exercise that helps you define the Key Terms

LEARNING AIDS

CHAPTER SUMMARY

1. Explain how motivation works.

   People go through a five-step process to meet their needs. This is a circular process because needs recur.

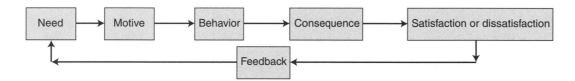

2. Use the performance equation.

   The performance equation states that

   $$Performance = Ability \times Motivation \times Resources.$$

   If any one of these components is weak, performance is negatively affected. When performance stumbles, managers need to determine which component of the equation is causing performance to suffer and take action to correct the problem.

3. Discuss the four content-based motivation theories.

   All four content theories identify and then seek to understand people's needs. The theories identify similar needs but differ in the classification of needs. Hierarchy of needs theory classifies needs as physiological, safety, social, esteem, and self-actualization. ERG theory classifies needs as existence, relatedness, and growth. Two-factor theory lists motivator factors and maintenance factors. Acquired needs theory uses achievement, power, and affiliation needs. (See table 11.1 on p. 347 and table 11.2 on p. 354 for a comparison of the four content-based theories.)

4. Discuss the three process-based motivation theories.

   All three process theories seek to understand how people choose behaviors to fulfill their needs. The process theories differ in their explanations of what motivates people. Equity theory proposes that the perception of inputs equaling outputs motivates people. Goal-setting theory proposes that achievable but difficult goals are the driving factor in motivation. Expectancy theory proposes that motivation occurs when people believe they can accomplish the task and when the rewards for doing so are worth the effort.

5. Discuss reinforcement theory.

   Positive reinforcement rewards the person for performing the desired behavior. Avoidance reinforcement encourages the person to perform the desired behavior to avoid a negative consequence. Extinction reinforcement withholds a positive consequence to get the person to stop an undesirable behavior. Punishment reinforcement gives the person a direct negative consequence to get him to stop an undesirable behavior.

6. Compare content, process, and reinforcement theories.

   Content-based theories focus on identifying and understanding employees' needs. Process-based theories seek to understand how people choose behavior to fulfill their needs. Reinforcement theory is not concerned with need; it focuses on getting people to perform desirable behavior through consequences and reinforcement.

REVIEW AND DISCUSSION QUESTIONS

1. What is motivation and why is it important to know how to motivate employees?

2. Do managers' attitudes and expectations affect employee motivation and performance? Explain your answer.

3. Do you agree with the performance equation? Will you use it on the job?

4. Do people really have diverse needs?

5. Apply Maslow's hierarchy of needs to a sport organization you are familiar with.

6. Which of the three process-based motivation theories do you prefer? Why?

7. What reinforcements have been used to get you to go to work and to be on time?

8. True or false: Reinforcement theory is unethical because it is used to manipulate employees. Explain your reasoning.

9. What athletes in the past 6 months have been punished as a way to discourage a certain behavior? What was their punishment?

10. Which motivation theory do you plan to use on your job or as a coach? If you plan to use a hybrid, explain which parts of which theories you will emphasize.

11. Do you think that incentive-laden contracts motivate athletes to perform at their highest level?

12. What are the three major classes of motivation theories?

13. What are the four content motivation theories?

14. What are the two factors in two-factor theory?

15. What is the role of perception in equity theory?

16. What are the two parts of expectancy theory?

17. What are the two schedules of reinforcement?

18. What are the four steps of giving praise?

CASE

Living His Tennis Passion: Al Dunbar

Al Dunbar can normally be found at the Springfield, Massachusetts, Jewish Community Center (JCC) teaching the fine art of playing tennis. As a coach he has a profound impact on youth. He is the father of two daughters and one son. When his girls were young, he would set up a tent on the grounds of the JCC for the girls so that he could teach and be a hands-on parent during the summer.[55] As his own children grew up, Al went on to coach and train many other children in the skills of playing recreational, high school, and collegiate-level tennis. For his commitment, Al was voted a Key Players Ambassador. Key players are noted for making a difference in children's lives.

However, Al is more than just a tennis instructor. He is truly passionate about the game of tennis. He has been a member of the U.S. Tennis Association national board. He attends the U.S. Open, where the largest stadium is named after his late friend Arthur Ashe. He still plays tennis and often wins his age bracket.

Al is one of the tennis directors for the Shelly Rosenthal tournament held at Forest Park in Springfield. The tournament is often the first chance young players have to play in a competitive tennis event.[56]

Al has also been a schoolteacher all of his life. He started with a distinguished career teaching and coaching at high school. After a short and restless retirement from teaching, Al returned as a media teacher in a different high school. As would be expected, he is also the tennis coach.

Al is very compassionate and loving with his junior players. His primary goal is for the players to love the game of tennis. He nurtures the students and helps them learn more about the game and the famous players they watch on television. He often organizes trips to professional tennis matches so they can watch live events.

As his players get older, he instills a greater sense of competitiveness. As they enter a high school with a competitive tennis team, he tells his players to be ready to practice hitting with the older students. At some point it will be their turn to play on their high school team, and they should be ready for either singles or doubles play.

On a good day (which can also be a cold snowy day), you can find Al out coaching tennis to players of all ages. He motivates them with his passion for tennis.[57]

Case Questions

1. Al focuses on motivation and performance.
   a. true
   b. false

2. Al focuses on which factor in the performance equation?
   a. ability
   b. motivation
   c. resources

3. Al's junior tennis players appear to be on which level in the hierarchy of needs?
   a. physiological
   b. safety
   c. social
   d. esteem
   e. self-actualization

4. Al focuses on which level of ERG needs with his junior tennis players?

    a. existence

    b. relatedness

    c. growth

5. Al's approach has less emphasis on meeting which need?

    a. achievement

    b. power

    c. affiliation

6. Herzberg would say that Al is using

    a. maintenance

    b. motivators

7. Vroom would agree that Al uses expectancy motivation theory.

    a. true

    b. false

8. Adams would say that Al offers

    a. equitable rewards

    b. underrewards

    c. overrewards

9. Al uses goal-setting theory.

    a. true

    b. false

10. Al uses which types of reinforcement?

    a. positive

    b. extinction

    c. avoidance

    d. punishment

11. What type of motivation do you think Al uses with his players? Do you know any sport organizations that use Al's motivating techniques?

12. In a position of authority, would you use Al's motivational style? Explain your answer.

13. Could Al's technique work in all organizations? Explain your answer.

SKILL-BUILDER EXERCISES

Skill-Builder 11.1: Giving Praise

Objective

To hone your ability to praise

Preparation

Think of a situation in which you did something well in a sport, something deserving of praise and recognition—you made a great save in a game, or you turned an unhappy teammate into a happy one. Put yourself in your coach's position and write the praise you would give yourself.

Briefly describe the situation.

_____

_____

_____

_____

1. Tell yourself exactly what you did correctly.

    _____

    _____

    _____

    _____

2. Tell why your behavior was important.

    _____

    _____

    _____

    _____

3. Stop for a moment of silence. (Count to 5 silently.)
4. Encourage your repeat performance.

    _____

    _____

    _____

    _____

In-Class Application

Complete the preceding skill-building preparation before class. Break into groups of three to five members, and take turns giving your praise to a member of the group.

1. Explain the situation to the group.
2. Give the person praise as you would in real life. (Do not read it off your paper.)
3. Ask the group for feedback:

    Was the praise specific and descriptive? Did the giver look the receiver of the praise in the eye?

    Was the importance of the behavior clearly stated?

    Did the giver stop for a moment of silence?

    Did the giver encourage repeat performance?

    Did the giver of praise touch the receiver (optional)?

    Did the praise take less than 1 minute? Did the praise seem sincere?

Wrap-Up

Take a few minutes to write your answers to the following questions:

What did I learn from this experience? How will I use this knowledge?

_____

_____

_____

_____

As a class, discuss student responses.

Skill-Builder 11.2: Self-Motivation

Objective

To better understand what motivates you

Preparation

Review the two Self-Assessment exercises on pages 351 and 352 in this chapter and figure 11.8 and the self-motivation model, and think about how the other theories apply to you as well.

What did you learn about yourself? What motivates you in your personal relationships, in school, in sport, and on the job?

_____

_____

_____

_____

How can you improve your self-motivation to do better in your personal relationships, in school, in sport, and on the job? Select one area and follow the four steps in figure 11.8, the self-motivation model.

_____

_____

_____

_____

_____

_____

_____

_____

_____

_____

_____

_____

_____

_____

_____

_____

_____

_____

_____

_____

_____

_____

_____

_____

In-Class Application

Complete the preceding skill-building preparation before class. Break into groups of four to six members and take turns sharing your answers. Give each other ideas on how to improve motivation.

Wrap-Up

Take a few minutes to write down answers to the following questions:

What did I learn from this experience? How will I use this knowledge?

_____
_____
_____
_____

As a class, discuss student responses.

SPORTS AND SOCIAL MEDIA EXERCISES

The academic fields of management and coaching have many leaders that give motivational speeches. Use YouTube to find three coaches who you feel gave an inspiring speech to their teams.

1. _____
   _____
2. _____
   _____
3. _____
   _____

GAME PLAN FOR STARTING A SPORT BUSINESS

You will need to motivate yourself and your employees to run your own sport business. What specific motivational theory from this chapter will you use to motivate yourself and your employees?

_____
_____

Leading to Victory

LEARNING OUTCOMES

After studying this chapter, you should be able to

1. explain why managers are not always leaders;
2. compare the trait, behavioral, and contingency theories of leadership;
3. explain leadership trait theory;
4. contrast two-dimensional leaders and grid leaders;
5. identify the management levels where charismatic, transformational, transactional, and symbolic leaders work best;
6. contrast the various contingency models of leadership;
7. critique the continuum and the path–goal models; and
8. describe normative leaders.

KEY TERMS

leaders	charismatic leaders	continuum leaders
trait theorists	transformational leaders	path–goal leaders
behavioral theorists	transactional leaders	normative leaders
leadership style	symbolic leaders	contingency managers
two-dimensional leaders	contingency leaders	substitutes for leadership
Leadership Grid	situational favorableness	

Organizing Leading Controlling Planning Organizing Leading Controlling Planning Organizing Lea
ntrolling Planning Organizing Leading Controlling Planning Organizing Leading Controlling Planning Org
Leading Controlling Planning Organizing Leading Controlling Planning Organizing Leading Contro
anning Organizing Leading Controlling Planning Organizing Leading Controlling Planning Organ
ading Controlling Planning Organizing Leading Controlling Planning Organizing Leading Controlling Pla
ganizing Leading Controlling Planning Organizing Leading Controlling Planning Organizing Leading Lea

DEVELOPING YOUR SKILLS

Leaders substantively affect the performance of organizations.[1] Thus, organizations are increasingly looking for ways to train and develop leaders; one current focus is team leadership as more and more organizations turn to teams. The good news is that everyone has leadership potential. This means that you, too, can become an effective leader. In this chapter, you will learn about leadership traits, behavior, and contemporary and situational leadership theories. Through the use of the contingency management model, you can develop your ability to analyze employees' capability level and select the appropriate leadership style to maximize performance in a given situation.

REVIEWING THEIR GAME PLAN

Paul Fenton: Leading by Example

Paul Fenton was determined to be a hockey player in the NHL. Although he did play in the NHL from 1984 to 1992, his true success has come off the ice and in the boardroom. Fenton played for the Hartford Whalers, New York Rangers, Los Angeles Kings, Winnipeg Jets, Toronto Maple Leafs, and San Jose Sharks. He is considered the first American player to have scored 50 goals in a season, which he accomplished while playing for the Binghamton Whalers in the AHL.

But every professional athlete has to retire at some point—often before the age of 40. Paul was able to rely on a network of friends he had made during his lengthy journey through the NHL. His college coach at Boston College, Jack Parker, was his mentor as he entered the NHL. Former assistant general manager of the Whalers, Jack Ferreira, had coached Fenton when he was just 16 years old. Ultimately, Ferreira, as the general manager (GM) of the newly founded Anaheim Ducks, asked Fenton to take charge of the organization's professional scouting.

After 5 years in Anaheim with the Ducks, Fenton moved to the Nashville Predators, where he served as director of player personnel for 8 years. Paul is now in his 15th season with the Predators and his seventh as the club's assistant general manager. Paul was in charge of all player acquisitions when he drafted Ryan Suter and Shea Weber in 2003. In 2012, Suter signed as a free agent with the Minnesota Wild for 13 years and $98 million. Weber decided to stay with the Predators after the Philadelphia Flyers offered a 14 year, $110 million offer sheet. Apparently, Paul is a good evaluator of talent.[2]

Paul Fenton has a pleasant demeanor. He is quick with a smile and even quicker with an upbeat assessment of new young players he has scouted. These likable traits were evident even when Paul Fenton played Pee Wee and high school hockey. He always led by example. He wasn't the most graceful skater, but he worked hard, passed the puck to his teammates, and had a knack for scoring goals in bunches.

Early in Paul's career a scout told him, "You're not Bobby Orr. You've got your degree, you should use it." Paul, though, showed determination and did have a successful playing career. Better yet, he parlayed that experience into a professional management career. His position as assistant GM requires him to travel around the world scouting for talent. He is also involved in many day-to-day decisions to help the team run properly—he is not afraid to get his hands dirty and do some work around the Bridgestone Arena. Once again, his honesty and hard work have paid off, and he has been promoted through the Predator organization. Paul Fenton continues to lead by example. The lessons here are many: Have a dream—yes; follow your dream—sure; but most of all, have the wherewithal to make it happen. You have to *work hard* to stay in the sport that you love.

For more information on the Nashville Predators and Paul Fenton, visit predators.nhl.com/club/page.htm?id=36986.

Leadership

Leadership is one of the most talked about, written about, and researched management topics.[3] If you search "leadership" on the website www.scholar.google.com, you will find some 2,250,000 academic articles on the subject. You can refine the search to include just business-related articles for the past 2 years, and you will have about 136,000 journal articles on leadership![4] Strong leadership is needed,[5] as great things often come down to the work of a single leader.[6] Great companies and teams have great leaders, and a bad leader can tank them.[7] But with today's focus on teamwork, leadership ability is important to everyone in the organization, not just managers.[8]

Leadership in sport is important. Although leadership has been an immensely popular area of study, there are still many areas of the topic to explore. For example, a recent study concluded that a change in coaching leadership at a university initially lead to poorer performance. However, as the coaches' tenure increased, team performance improved.[9] Can you provide examples of this happening at your favorite university?

Can Leadership Be Taught?

There are two common questions about leadership: "Are leaders made or born?" and "Can leadership skills be developed?" The answer to the first question is both; we are all born with leadership potential, but some of us have more natural ability than others. As Vince Lombardi said, "Leaders are made, they are not born. They are made by hard effort, which is the price which all of us must pay to achieve any goal that is worthwhile."[10] Another view is that experts are definitely made, not born. A study highlighted the experiences of nine women as mothers and sport leaders. Potential constraints for these mothers to be a sport leader included guilt, exhaustion and stress, social disapproval, and organizational resistance to children in sport settings. These women overcome the constraints with a passion for sport and leadership, strong support networks, and development of integrated strategies to blend work and family issues together.[11] Do you have a passion for sport, and will you work at leadership in sport like these mothers?

The answer to the second question is yes. Leadership can be taught.[12] However, even though leadership skills can be taught, recruiters say they often see a lack of interpersonal and leadership skills in job applicants.[13] Firms are offering leadership training.[14] If we can't develop leadership skills, why are organizations spending millions on leadership training? So yes, through studying and applying this chapter, you can develop your leadership skills.

Leaders Versus Managers

Leaders influence people to work to achieve the organization's objectives.[15]

We frequently use the words *manager* and *leader* interchangeably. We shouldn't, because they are not necessarily the same.[16] Leading is a management function (remember, there are four—planning, organizing, leading, and controlling). Unfortunately, not all managers are leaders. And, of course, there are leaders who are not managers.[17] Many of us have been in situations in which one of our peers had more influence in the department or team than did the manager or coach. Also, as we strive as a team to meet objectives, we influence each other, or leadership is shared.[18] So anyone can be a leader within any group[19]; and regardless of your position, you are expected to share leadership, because leadership is a shared activity.[20]

◀ LEARNING OUTCOME 1
Explain why managers are not always leaders.

Traits of Effective Leaders

Researchers first studied leadership in the early 1900s. They wanted to identify a set of characteristics or traits that distinguished leaders from followers and effective leaders from ineffective ones. Their investigations led to the trait, behavioral, and contingency theories

◀ LEARNING OUTCOME 2
Compare the trait, behavioral, and contingency theories of leadership.

of leadership, which have done much to help us understand what makes leaders tick and what makes them effective.

Early studies assumed that leaders are born, not made, but exactly what makes a person a leader has proved to be elusive. Using one of the original approaches, **trait theorists** look for characteristics that make leaders effective. Over the years in more than 300 studies, these theorists analyzed numerous physical and psychological qualities, such as appearance, aggressiveness, self-reliance, persuasiveness, and dominance, in an effort to identify a set of traits that successful leaders possess. Your personality characteristics and traits also affect your leadership style[21] and your creativity.[22] The idea was that this list of traits would guide the promotion of promising candidates to leadership positions.

The problem was that no one has been able to compile a list of traits that successful leaders universally possess. There are always exceptions. The lesson here, of course, is that leaders are an extremely diverse lot. In addition, some people could lead in one position but not in another.

Even though it is generally agreed that no universal set of leadership traits exists, we continue to study and write about leadership traits.[23] Why? Even though leaders don't universally possess the same qualities, a lot of leaders do possess certain qualities. And the good news is that these qualities can be learned.

Ghiselli's Study

As we noted chapter 1, Edwin Ghiselli conducted a widely publicized study of leadership traits. He studied more than 300 managers from 90 different U.S. businesses and

TIME-OUT
1
Which of the Ghiselli traits does your current boss or coach exhibit, and which ones does he or she lack?

published his results in 1971.[24] He concluded that certain traits are important to effective leadership, but not all of them are necessary for success. Ghiselli identified the following six traits, in order of importance, as significant. Effective leaders generally have (1) supervisory ability (using the four functions of management—planning, organizing, leading, and controlling—that you learn in this course), (2) a need for occupational achievement, (3) intelligence, (4) decisiveness, (5) self-assurance, and (6) initiative. Paul Fenton took the initiative to turn his experience as a professional hockey player into a lifetime career as an executive with the Nashville Predators. He continues to travel around the globe looking for new players to sign for the Predators.

Ethics and Spirituality in the Workplace

People want leaders with integrity. Recall the importance of business ethics (chapter 2). Once again, we want to emphasize the importance of diversity and being ethical with everyone.

Related to ethics and values is spirituality. Evangelist Billy Graham identified four main character traits as personal qualities of leadership: integrity, personal security, sense of priority, and vision. Zig Ziglar, a world-famous motivational speaker and best-selling author who trains people to be successful, and Peter Lowe, who conducts success seminars all over the world, both say that proper emphasis on the spiritual aspects of life is extremely important to success. Research has shown that people who attend church regularly make more money, have better health, are happier with their jobs and family life, and have a much lower divorce rate than others. As Zig puts it, "In short, they get more of the things that money can buy and all of the things that money can't buy."[25] Of course, not all successful leaders are spiritual, but most are ethical.

Behavior of Effective Leaders

By the late 1940s, most research into leadership had shifted from analyzing traits to analyzing what leaders do. In the continuing quest to identify which leadership styles work and which ones fail, researchers compared the behavior of effective and ineffective leaders in search of the one best leadership style. **Behavioral theorists** look at the leadership style of effective leaders. This focus has also provided insights into the leader–follower dynamic. The leadership style used by superiors in the organization heavily influences the styles of lower-level managers. For example, if your boss is autocratic, very likely you will be too. But before we examine these theories, complete the following Self-Assessment to determine your theory X, theory Y leadership style.

SELF-ASSESSMENT 12.1

Theory X, Theory Y Leadership Style

Note the frequency with which you do (or would do, if you have not yet held a position of leadership) each action. Be honest. There are no right or wrong answers. This Self-Assessment is easiest to complete online.

Usually	Frequently	Occasionally	Seldom
U	F	O	S

_____ 1. I set objectives for my department alone; I don't include staff input.

_____ 2. I allow staff members to develop their own plans, rather than develop them myself.

_____ 3. I delegate to staff several of the tasks that I enjoy doing, rather than do them myself.

_____ 4. I allow staff members to solve problems they encounter, rather than solve them myself.

_____ 5. I recruit and select new employees alone; I don't solicit input from staff.

_____ 6. I orient and train new employees myself, rather than have members of my team do it.

_____ 7. I tell staff members only what they need to know, rather than give them access to anything they want to know.

_____ 8. I praise and recognize staff efforts; I don't just criticize.

_____ 9. I set controls for the team to ensure that objectives are met, rather than allow the team to set its own controls.

_____ 10. I frequently observe my group to ensure that it is working and meeting deadlines.

For items 1, 5, 6, 7, 9, and 10, give each U answer 1 point; F, 2 points; O, 3 points; and S, 4 points. For items 2, 3, 4, and 8, give each S answer 1 point; O, 2 points; F, 3 points; and U, 4 points. Total your score, which should be between 10 and 40. Place your score here _____.

You have just measured your theory X, theory Y behavior. This theory was developed by Douglas McGregor (1906-1964), who contrasted the two theories based on the assumptions managers make about workers. Theory X managers assume that people dislike work and need managers to plan, organize, and closely direct and control their work in order for them to perform at high levels. Theory Y managers assume people like to work and do not need close supervision. Place a check on the continuum that represents your score.

Theory X behavior			Theory Y behavior
10	20	30	40
Autocratic			Participative

The lower your score (10), the more you tend toward theory X behavior; the higher your score (40), the more you tend toward theory Y behavior. A score of 20 to 30 shows a balance between the two extremes of the continuum. Note: Your score may or may not accurately reflect how you would behave in an actual job; however, it can help you understand your underlying attitudes.

Basic Styles of Leadership

Leadership style is the combination of traits, skills, and behaviors that managers use to interact with employees. In the 1930s, before behavior theory became popular, researchers at the University of Iowa studied leadership styles of managers and identified three basic styles.[26] (1) *Autocratic:* The manager makes the decisions, tells employees what to do, and closely supervises them—basically Theory X behavior. (2) *Democratic:* The manager encourages employee participation in decisions, works with employees to determine what to do, and doesn't supervise them closely—Theory Y behavior. (3). *Laissez-faire:* The manager lets employees go about their business without much input—that is, employees decide what to do and take action, and the manager does not follow up.

LEARNING OUTCOME 4 ▶

Contrast two-dimensional leaders and grid leaders.

Two-Dimensional Leaders

Two-dimensional leaders focus on job structure and employee considerations, a focus that results in four possible leadership styles. In 1945, Ralph Stogdill[27] at Ohio State University and Rensis Likert[28] at the University of Michigan began independent studies of leadership styles. Although the research teams used different terminology, they identified the same two dimensions. UM's team called the two dimensions job centered and employee centered; OSU's team called them initiating structure and consideration. The OSU and UM leadership models also differed in structure: UM placed the two dimensions at opposite ends of the same continuum. OSU considered the two dimensions independent of one another. Both dimensions measure the manager's behavior when interacting with employees:

- Initiating structure, job centered: the extent to which managers take charge to plan, organize, lead, and control as employees perform tasks. This dimension focuses on getting the job done.

- Consideration, employee centered: the extent to which managers develop trust, friendship, support, and respect. This dimension focuses on developing rapport with employees.

TIME-OUT 2 Which of the two-dimensional leadership styles does your coach or boss use? Describe his or her behavior using this model.

In the two-dimensional model, managers get the job done by directing people and developing supportive relationships. Combinations of the two dimensions result in four leadership styles, as shown in the OSU 2 × 2 matrix in figure 12.1. Although the OSU and UM studies are now dated, they are still written about today, and they influence the current theories.

Leadership Grid

In the 1960s, Robert Blake and Jane Mouton developed the Managerial Grid, which later became the **Leadership Grid**, developed by Blake and Anne Adams McCanse.[29] The Leadership Grid uses the same dimensions as the two-dimensional model; in the grid, these dimensions are called concern for production and concern for people. The Leadership Grid identifies the ideal leadership style as having a high concern for both production and people. Because the grid measures the two dimensions on a scale from 1 to 9, 81 possible permutations are possible, from which Blake and McCanse categorized five major leadership styles:

- (1,1) Impoverished leaders show low concern for both production and people. They do the minimum required to remain employed.

TIME-OUT 3 Describe your boss's leadership style. Which of the Leadership Grid styles does your boss use?

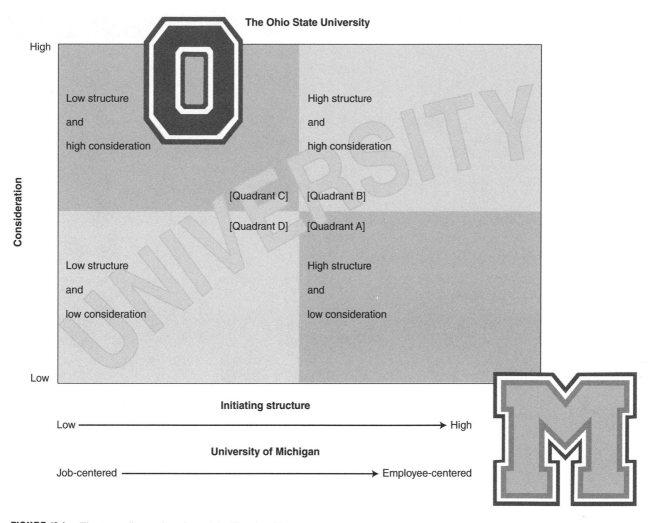

FIGURE 12.1 The two-dimensional model of leadership.

- (9,1) Authority–compliance leaders show a high concern for production and a low concern for people. They focus on getting the job done by treating people like machines.
- (1,9) Country club leaders show a low concern for production and a high concern for people. They strive to maintain a friendly atmosphere without much regard for production.
- (5,5) Middle-of-the-road leaders balance their concerns for production and people. They strive for performance and morale levels that are minimally satisfactory.
- (9,9) Team leaders show a high concern for both production and people. They strive for maximum performance and maximum employee satisfaction.

The trend toward teams has resulted in demands for leaders who have a balanced directive and supportive style but not necessarily high concern for both at the same time. For example, a coach may focus on a skills drill, showing high concern for performance. At another time, the coach may give a motivational speech, focusing on players. Tony Dungy, when he coached the Indianapolis Colts, came close to creating an overall 9,9 situation. The players were happy to play for the Colts, and the team was very productive on and off the field. Figure 12.2 is an adaptation of the Leadership Grid.

According to Blake, Mouton, and McCanse, the team leadership style (9,9) is the most appropriate style to use in "all" situations. However, most researchers have called

APPLYING THE CONCEPT 12.1

Grid Leaders

Identify the five statements by leadership style.

a. 1,1 (impoverished)

b. 1,9 (country club)

c. 9,1 (authority-compliance)

d. 5,5 (middle-of-the-road)

e. 9,9 (team)

_____ 1. The marketing group's morale is high, and its members enjoy their work, but the department's productivity is one of the lowest in the company. The marketing manager is a people person but doesn't always get around to business.

_____ 2. The HR group's morale is adequate; its productivity is average. The HR manager is somewhat concerned about people and production.

_____ 3. The fitness center group's morale is at one of the lowest levels in the company, but this group is also one of the top performers. Its manager focuses on production but not on the needs of her staff.

_____ 4. The maintenance department is one of the lowest performers and has low morale. Its manager is not concerned with people or production.

_____ 5. The ticket sales group is a top performer in the company, and its morale is high. Its manager focuses on both people and production.

this belief a myth, stating that there is no one best style in all situations, or that leadership is situational.

LEARNING OUTCOME 5 ▶

Identify the management levels where charismatic, transformational, transactional, and symbolic leaders work best.

Contemporary Behavioral Perspectives

The contemporary focus is on behavior but not on seeking the one best style in all situations. Current researchers focus on which behaviors make top-notch managers outstanding, even though the managers' individual leadership styles may vary dramatically.[30] These researchers have identified charismatic, transformational, transactional, and symbolic leaders.

Charismatic leaders inspire loyalty, enthusiasm, and high levels of performance. Charisma is determined by the leader's personality or behavior. Charismatic leaders have a vision and a strong personal commitment to their goals; they communicate their goals to others, display self-confidence, and are viewed as able to make the radical changes needed to reach the goals. Charismatic leaders have a strong influence on employee commitment to the organization. Followers buy into the belief systems of charismatic leaders, feel affection for them, obey them, and develop emotional ownership of their goals, all of which lead to higher levels of performance. Thus, charismatic leaders can be more effective than their less charismatic counterparts.[31]

Charismatic CEOs and star athletes bring recognition to companies and sport teams. Many contemporary leaders are charismatic, including Michael Jordan and LeBron James (NBA), Derek Jeter (MLB), David Beckham (soccer), and Tom Brady and Tim Tebow (NFL). Charisma comes from the followers, who also can take away charisma. For example, NFL player Michael Vick lost charisma because of his involvement in dogfighting.

Transformational leaders emphasize change, innovation, and entrepreneurship as they continually take their organizations through three acts. They (1) recognize the need for revitalization; (2) they create a new vision; and they (3) institutionalize change. Transformational leadership is one of the most widely accepted leadership paradigms.[32] These leaders articulate a vision of the future, foster group-oriented work, set high expectations, challenge followers' thinking, support individual needs, and act as role models.[33] Although every manager can be a transformational leader, these leaders are typically top-level managers.[34] Note that a leader can be charismatic, transformational, both, or neither.

Theo Epstein while he was with the Boston Red Sox was a transformational leader. When he arrived, the Red Sox had not won a World Series since 1918. Epstein was brought in to inspire the team and lead it to win. He succeeded by finding players who were positive role models and who worked well together. In a similar situation, Pat Gillick, then GM of the Toronto Blue Jays, brought an attitude that winning should be fun—as he said, "Be positive. Be upbeat. Be supportive."[35]

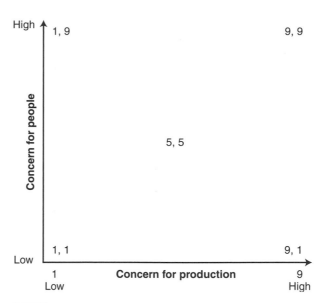

FIGURE 12.2 The Leadership Grid.

TIME-OUT 4 Think about the top manager in your firm or team. Is he or she a charismatic leader or a transformational leader? Why or why not?

Transactional leaders emphasize exchange. Transactional leadership is often contrasted with transformational leadership.[36] Exchange is about rewarding or punishing based on follower performance. The exchange process can be both constructive (promising rewards for performance) and corrective (correcting mistakes before or after they happen). Transactional leaders are typically middle and first-line managers.

Symbolic leaders establish and maintain a strong organizational culture. An organization's workforce learns the organization's culture (shared values, beliefs, and assumptions about how workers should behave in the organization—chapter 6) through its leadership. Symbolic leadership starts with top management and flows down to middle and first-line managers. Symbolic leaders go beyond looking out for their own self-interests and focus on meeting the needs of others. As detailed in chapter 6, the Indianapolis Colts' Tony Dungy and the Chicago Bears' Lovie Smith used a servant leadership style. Do you believe that Paul Fenton is a charismatic, transformational, transactional, or symbolic leader or some combination of these?

Situational Leadership Models

LEARNING OUTCOME 6
Contrast the various contingency models of leadership.

Both the trait and behavioral theories attempted to identify the best leadership style for all situations—a one-size-fits-all approach. In the late 1960s, it became apparent that this approach doesn't work very well. Contingency leaders, commonly called situational leaders, analyze the situation and use the appropriate leadership style for the situation, and contingency leadership is still being studied today.[37]

Contingency Leaders

In 1951, Fred E. Fiedler began to develop the first situational leadership theory—the contingency theory of leader effectiveness.[38] Fiedler believed that our leadership style reflects our personality and remains basically constant. That is, leaders do not change their styles. **Contingency leaders** are task or relationship oriented, and their style should fit the situation. The first step is to determine whether your leadership style is task or relationship oriented. You can do this by using the Least Preferred Coworker Scale, an instrument developed at the University of Washington that is still being used today. After determining your leadership style, you look at situational favorableness.

Situational favorableness is the degree to which a situation enables leaders to exert influence over followers. The three variables, in order of importance, are as follows:

1. Leader–member relations: Is this relationship good or poor? Do followers trust, respect, accept, and have confidence in their leader? Is it a friendly, tension-free situation? Leaders with good relations have more influence. The better the relations, the more favorable the situation. Paul Fenton has a good relationship with the people who work for him.

2. Task structure: Is the task structured or unstructured? Do employees perform repetitive, routine, unambiguous, and standard tasks that are easily understood? Leaders in structured situations have more influence. The more repetitive the jobs, the more favorable the situation.

3. Position power: Is the manager's position power strong or weak? Does he have the power to assign work, reward and punish, hire and fire, and give raises and promotions? Leaders with position power have more influence. The more power, the more favorable the situation.

To determine whether a task or relationship orientation is appropriate, use the Fiedler contingency model and answer three questions (pertaining to situational favorableness) set up as a decision tree—figure 12.3 shows an adapted model. Users answer question 1 and follow the decision tree to *good* or *poor* depending on their answer. After answering question 3, users end up in one of eight possible situations.

A major criticism of Fiedler's model concerns his view that leaders cannot change their style (a task vs. a relationship style) and that if the leader's style does not fit the situation, the leader should change the situation to fit his style. The other contingency writers suggest changing your leadership styles, not the situation. Do you believe you can or cannot change your leadership style?

TIME-OUT 5

Is your current boss or coach task oriented or relationship oriented? Using figure 12.3, identify your boss's situation by number and then identify the appropriate style to use for this situation. Does your boss use the appropriate style?

LEARNING OUTCOME 7 ▶

Critique the continuum and the path–goal models.

Continuum Leaders

In Robert Tannenbaum and Warren Schmidt's model (developed in 1964), leadership occurs on a continuum from boss-centered (autocratic) to employee-centered (participative) leadership. Their model focuses on who makes the decisions. Tannenbaum and Schmidt identified seven major styles from which leaders can choose. Figure 12.4, an adaptation of their model, lists the seven styles.[39] **Continuum leaders** choose their style based on boss-centered or employee-centered leadership.

Before selecting one of the seven styles, managers consider the following three variables: (1) the manager's preferred leadership style, (2) the subordinates' preferred style for their leader, and (3) the situation.

Even though the continuum model was very popular in the 1960s, one major criticism of it charges that the model is too subjective. In other words, determining which leadership style to use in which situation is complex.

TIME-OUT 6

Which leadership style (1-7) in figure 12.4 does your boss or coach use? Is it the most appropriate style? Why or why not?

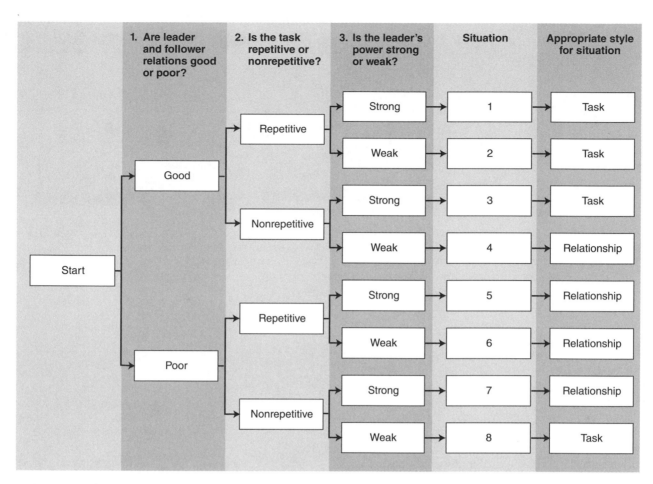

FIGURE 12.3 The contingency model of leadership. If the manager's preferred leadership style matches the situation, the manager does nothing. If the preferred leadership style does not match the situation, the manager changes the situation to match her preferred leadership style.

APPLYING THE CONCEPT 12.2

Contingency Leaders

Use figure 12.3 to first identify which of the eight situations best fits the following descriptions and indicate whether the appropriate leadership style is (a) task oriented or (b) relationship oriented.

_____ 6. Saul oversees the assembly of mass-produced golf tees. He has the power to reward and punish. He is considered a hard-nosed boss.

_____ 7. Karen manages corporate event planning. She helps other departments plan events. Karen is viewed as a dreamer, someone who doesn't understand the various departments. Employees are often rude to Karen.

_____ 8. Juan manages the processing of checks. He is well liked by his staff. Juan's boss enjoys hiring employees and evaluating their performance.

_____ 9. Sonia, the event manager, assigns dates and times for each event. The event-planning atmosphere is tense.

_____ 10. Louis owns a professional soccer team. He is highly regarded by volunteer members on the board of directors. The board members recommend ways to increase season-ticket sales.

APPLYING THE CONCEPT 12.3

Continuum Leaders

Use figure 12.4 to identify the continuum leadership style (1-7) implied in each statement.

_____ 11. Chuck, I recommended that you be transferred to the new public relations department, but you don't have to go if you don't want to.

_____ 12. Sam, go clean the tables in the stadium restaurant right away.

_____ 13. From now on, this is the way security at all games will be done. Does anyone have any questions about the procedure?

_____ 14. These are the 2 weeks in which we can schedule the high school basketball tournament. You select one.

_____ 15. I'd like your ideas on how to stop the bottleneck on the production line making hockey pucks. But I have the final say on the solution we implement.

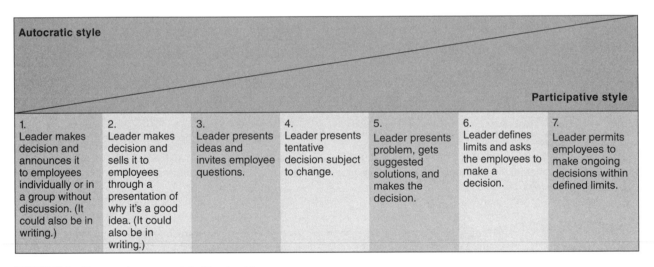

FIGURE 12.4 The continuum model of leadership.

Path–Goal Leaders

Robert House developed the path–goal leadership model in the 1970s. **Path–goal leaders** determine employee objectives and achieve them using one of four styles. The focus is on how leaders influence employees' perceptions of their goals and the paths they follow to attain goals.[40] As shown in figure 12.5 (an adaptation of the model), House's model uses situational factors to determine which leadership style best achieves goals by influencing employee performance and satisfaction.

Subordinate situational characteristics include (1) authoritarianism, the degree to which employees defer and want to be told what to do and how to do the job; (2) locus of control, the extent to which employees believe they control goal achievement (internal) or whether goal achievement is controlled by others (external); and (3) ability, the extent of employee ability to perform tasks to achieve goals. Environmental situational factors include (1) task structure, the extent of repetitiveness of the job; (2) formal authority, the extent of the leader's power; and (3) work group, the extent to which coworkers contribute to job satisfaction.

FIGURE 12.5   The path–goal model of leadership.

After considering situational factors, managers select the most appropriate leadership style by following these guidelines:

1. Directive: Leaders provide high structure. Directive leadership is appropriate when subordinates want authority, have external locus of control, and have low ability. This style is also appropriate when the task is complex or ambiguous, formal authority is strong, and the work group provides job satisfaction.

2. Supportive: Leaders provide high consideration. Supportive leadership is appropriate when subordinates do not want autocratic leadership, have internal locus of control, and are of high ability. This style is also appropriate when tasks are simple, formal authority is weak, and the work group does not provide job satisfaction.[41]

3. Participative: Leaders solicit employee input. Participative leadership is appropriate when subordinates want to be involved, have internal locus of control, and are of high ability. This style is also appropriate when the task is complex, authority is either strong or weak, and job satisfaction from coworkers is either high or low.

4. Achievement-oriented: Leaders set difficult but achievable goals, expect subordinates to perform at their highest level, and reward them for doing so. That is, leaders provide both high structure and high consideration. Achievement-oriented leadership is appropriate when subordinates are open to autocratic leadership, have external locus of control, and are of high ability. Achievement-oriented leadership is also appropriate when the task is simple, authority is strong, and job satisfaction from coworkers is either high or low.

 TIME-OUT 7 Which path–goal leadership style does your boss or coach use? Is this the most appropriate style for the situation? Explain.

Academics tend to like path–goal leadership because it is based on research. However, one major criticism by managers is that like continuum leadership, the path–goal model is too subjective. Another criticism is that it is difficult to determine which style to use when.

Normative Leaders

◀ **LEARNING OUTCOME 8**
Describe normative leaders.

In 1973, Victor Vroom and Philip Yetton published a decision-making model,[42] which Vroom and Arthur Jago refined and expanded to four models in 1988.[43] The models incorporate two factors: individual versus group decisions and time-driven versus development-driven decisions. In 2000, Vroom published a revised version of his model.[44]

Vroom's model is called a normative model because it provides a sequential set of questions that are rules (norms) to follow to determine the best decision style for the given situation.

To determine the appropriate style for a specific situation, users of the normative model answer seven questions (not discussed here), some of which may be skipped depending on prior answers. The questions are sequential and are presented in a decision-tree format similar to that of Fiedler's contingency model.

Normative leaders use one of five decision-making styles appropriate for the situation. Vroom identified the five leadership styles based on the level of participation of group members in the decision.

- Decide: The leader makes the decision alone and announces it, or sells it, to the group. The leader may get information from others outside the group and within the group without specifying the problem.

- Consult individuals: The leader describes the problem to individual group members, gets information and suggestions, and then makes the decision.

- Consult group: The leader holds a group meeting and describes the problem to the group, gets information and suggestions, and then makes the decision.

- Facilitate: The leader holds a group meeting and acts as a facilitator as the group works to define the problem and the limits within which a decision must be made. The leader seeks participation, debate, and concurrence on the decision without pushing her ideas. However, the leader has the final say on the decision.

- Delegate: The leader lets the group diagnose the problem and make the decision within stated limits. The role of the leader is to answer questions and provide encouragement and resources.

Vroom's model is popular with academics because it is based on research. However, the model is not popular with managers, who find it cumbersome to select one of two models, then answer seven questions, and finally determine the appropriate leadership style. Because of this complexity, we don't show the two models with seven questions and five leadership styles.

 TIME-OUT 8 Which normative leadership style does your boss or coach use? Is this the most appropriate style for the situation? Explain.

Legendary NFL coach Vince Lombardi often used the "decide"-style leadership. Does the decide style work today? It depends. The leadership style used by Pat Summitt (former University of Tennessee women's basketball coach) is quite similar to Lombardi's. So is that of Bill Parcells, who took the New York Giants to Super Bowl victories in 1986 and 1990. Other coaches prefer group-style leadership. Phil Jackson, coach of the NBA champion Chicago Bulls and Los Angeles Lakers, uses Zen-like philosophy to motivate and train his players. He has been blessed with superstar players, but he has also used a group attitude to produce results.

Contingency Management

The contingency models we have described so far are complex, making it difficult to determine which leadership style to use in what situations. In this section, we present the contingency management model developed by Robert N. Lussier.[45] **Contingency managers** analyze employee capability level and select the autocratic, consultative, participative, or empowerment style for the situation. Lussier's model makes it relatively easy to select the appropriate style for the given situation. Before you learn how to be a contingency manager, complete the Self-Assessment to determine your preferred contingency management style.

Analyzing the Employee Capability Level in a Given Situation

There are two distinct aspects of employee capability. Notice that to determine capability level, we are combining the first two dimensions of the performance formula discussed in chapter 11 (Performance = Ability × Motivation × Resources).

Assess Your Preferred Management Style

Following are 12 situations. Select the one alternative that most closely describes what you would do in each situation. Don't be concerned with trying to pick the right answer; select the alternative you would really use. Circle *a, b, c,* or *d*. (Ignore the *C* preceding each situation and the *S* following each answer choice; these will be explained later in Skill-Builder 12.2 on p. 397.)

1. *C* _____ Your rookie crew seems to be developing well. Their need for direction and close supervision is diminishing. What do you do?

    a. Stop directing and overseeing performance unless there is a problem. *S* _____

    b. Spend time getting to know the members personally, but make sure they maintain performance levels. *S* _____

    c. Make sure things keep going well; continue to direct and oversee closely. *S* _____

    d. Begin to discuss new tasks of interest to them. *S* _____

2. *C* _____ You assigned Jill a task, specifying exactly how you wanted it done. Jill deliberately ignored your directions and did it her way. The job will not meet the customer's standards. This is not the first problem you've had with Jill. What do you decide to do?

    a. Listen to Jill's side but be sure the job gets done right. *S* _____

    b. Tell Jill to do it again the right way, and closely supervise the job. *S* _____

    c. Tell her the customer will not accept the job and let Jill handle it her way. *S* _____

    d. Discuss the problem and solutions to it. *S* _____

3. *C* _____ Your employees work well together and are a real team; the department is the top performer in the organization. Because of traffic problems, the president has approved staggered hours for departments. As a result, you can change your department's hours. Several of your workers are in favor of changing. What action do you take?

    a. Allow the group to decide the hours. *S* _____

    b. Decide on new hours, explain why you chose them, and invite questions. *S* _____

    c. Conduct a meeting to get the group members' ideas. Have them select new hours together, with your approval. *S* _____

    d. Send out a memo stating the hours you want. *S* _____

4. *C* _____ Bill, a new employee you hired, is not performing at the level expected after a month's training. Bill is trying, but he seems to be a slow learner. What do you decide to do?

    a. Clearly explain what needs to be done and oversee his work. Discuss why the procedures are important; support and encourage him. *S* _____

    b. Tell Bill that his training is over and it's time to pull his own weight. *S* _____

    c. Review task procedures and supervise his work closely. *S* _____

    d. Inform Bill that his training is over and that he should feel free to come to you if he has any problems. *S* _____

5. *C* _____ Helen has had an excellent performance record for the past 5 years. Recently you have noticed a drop in the quality and quantity of her work. She has a family problem. What do you do?

    a. Tell her to get back on track and closely supervise her. *S* _____

    b. Discuss the problem with Helen. Help her realize that her personal problem is affecting her work. Discuss ways to improve the situation. Be supportive and encourage her. *S* _____

    c. Tell Helen you're aware of her productivity slip and that you're sure she'll work it out soon. *S* _____

    d. Discuss the problem and solution with Helen and supervise her closely. *S* _____

6. C _____ Your organization does not allow smoking in certain areas. You just walked by a restricted area and saw Joan smoking. She has been with the organization for 10 years and is a very productive worker. Joan has never been caught smoking before. What action do you take?

   a. Ask her to put the cigarette out; then leave. S _____

   b. Discuss why she is smoking and what she intends to do about it. S _____

   c. Give her a lecture about not smoking and check up on her in the future. S _____

   d. Tell her to put the cigarette out, watch her do it, and tell her you will check on her in the future. S _____

7. C _____ Your employees usually work well together with little direction. But recently, a conflict between Sue and Tom has caused problems. What action do you take?

   a. Call Sue and Tom together and make them realize how this conflict is affecting the department. Discuss how to resolve it and how you will check to make sure the problem is solved. S _____

   b. Let the group resolve the conflict. S _____

   c. Have Sue and Tom sit down and discuss their conflict and how to resolve it. Support their efforts to implement a solution. S _____

   d. Tell Sue and Tom how to resolve their conflict, and closely supervise them. S _____

8. C _____ Jim usually does his share of the work with some encouragement and direction. However, he has migraine headaches occasionally and doesn't pull his weight when this happens. The others resent doing Jim's work. What do you decide to do?

   a. Discuss his problem and help him come up with ideas for maintaining his work; be supportive. S _____

   b. Tell Jim to do his share of the work and closely watch his output. S _____

   c. Inform Jim that he is creating a hardship for the others and should resolve the problem by himself. S _____

   d. Be supportive but set minimum performance levels and ensure compliance. S _____

9. C _____ Barbara, your most experienced and productive worker, has come to you with a detailed idea that could increase your department's productivity at a very low cost. She can do her present job and this new assignment. You think it's an excellent idea. What do you do?

   a. Set some goals together. Encourage and support her efforts. S _____

   b. Set up goals for Barbara. Be sure she agrees with them and sees you as being supportive of her efforts. S _____

   c. Tell Barbara to keep you informed and to come to you if she needs any help. S _____

   d. Have Barbara check in with you frequently so that you can direct and supervise her activities. S _____

10. C _____ Your boss asked you for a special report. Frank, a very capable worker who usually needs no direction or support, has all the necessary skills to do the job. However, Frank is reluctant because he has never done a report. What do you do?

   a. Tell Frank he has to do it. Give him direction and supervise him closely. S _____

   b. Describe the project to Frank and let him do it his own way. S _____

   c. Describe the benefits to Frank. Get his ideas on how to do it and check his progress. S _____

   d. Discuss possible ways of doing the job. Be supportive; encourage Frank. S _____

11. *C* _____ Jean is the top producer in your department. However, her monthly reports are constantly late, and they contain errors. You are puzzled because she does everything else with no direction or support. What do you decide to do?

    a. Go over past reports, explaining exactly what is expected of her. Schedule a meeting so that you can review the next report with her. *S* _____

    b. Discuss the problem with Jean and ask her what can be done about it; be supportive. *S* _____

    c. Explain the importance of the report. Ask her what the problem is. Tell her that you expect the next report to be on time and error free. *S* _____

    d. Remind Jean to get the next report in on time without errors. *S* _____

12. *C* _____ Your workers are very effective and like to participate in decision making. A consultant was hired to develop a new method for your department using the latest technology in the field. What do you do?

    a. Explain the consultant's method and let the group decide how to implement it. *S* _____

    b. Teach the workers the new method and supervise them closely as they use it. *S* _____

    c. Explain to the workers the new method and the reasons it is important. Teach them the method and make sure the procedure is followed. Answer questions. *S* _____

    d. Explain the new method and get the group's input on ways to improve and implement it. *S* _____

To determine your preferred management style, circle the letter you selected for each situation.

	Autocratic	Consultative	Participative	Empowerment
1	C	B	D	A
2	B	A	D	C
3	D	B	C	A
4	C	A	D	B
5	A	D	B	C
6	D	C	B	A
7	D	A	C	B
8	B	D	A	C
9	D	B	A	C
10	A	C	D	B
11	A	C	B	D
12	B	C	D	A
Total				

Add up the number of circled items per column. The column with the most items circled suggests your preferred management style. Is this the style you tend to use most often? We will explain each style in this section.

Your management style flexibility is reflected in the distribution of your answers. The more evenly distributed the numbers, the more flexible your style. A total of 1 or 0 for any column may indicate a reluctance to use that style.

Note that there is no right or wrong preferred style. What we want to do is use the most appropriate management style for the situation. You will learn how to do that in this section.

Now that you have determined your preferred management style, you will learn how to determine employee capability level and how to select the appropriate management style based on capability, followed by putting it all together in figure 12.6. We end by illustrating how to use the model in a given situation on page 390.

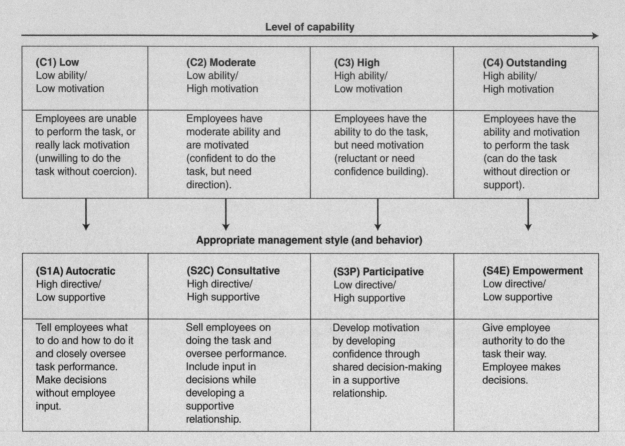

Level of capability

(C1) Low	(C2) Moderate	(C3) High	(C4) Outstanding
Low ability/ Low motivation	Low ability/ High motivation	High ability/ Low motivation	High ability/ High motivation
Employees are unable to perform the task, or really lack motivation (unwilling to do the task without coercion).	Employees have moderate ability and are motivated (confident to do the task, but need direction).	Employees have the ability to do the task, but need motivation (reluctant or need confidence building).	Employees have the ability and motivation to perform the task (can do the task without direction or support).

Appropriate management style (and behavior)

(S1A) Autocratic	(S2C) Consultative	(S3P) Participative	(S4E) Empowerment
High directive/ Low supportive	High directive/ High supportive	Low directive/ High supportive	Low directive/ Low supportive
Tell employees what to do and how to do it and closely oversee task performance. Make decisions without employee input.	Sell employees on doing the task and oversee performance. Include input in decisions while developing a supportive relationship.	Develop motivation by developing confidence through shared decision-making in a supportive relationship.	Give employee authority to do the task their way. Employee makes decisions.

FIGURE 12.6   The contingency management model.

- Ability: Do employees have the knowledge, experience, education, skills, and training to do a particular task without direction?
- Motivation: Do employees have the confidence to do the task? Do they want to do the task? Are they committed to performing the task? Will they perform the task without encouragement and support?

Employee capability may be measured on a continuum from low to outstanding. As a manager, you assess each employee's capability level.

- Low: The employees can't do the task without detailed directions and close supervision. Employees in this category are either unable or unwilling to do the task.
- Moderate: The employees have moderate ability and need specific direction and support to get the task done properly. The employees may be highly motivated but still need direction.
- High: The employees have high ability but may lack the confidence to do the job. What they need most is support and encouragement to motivate them to get the task done.

- Outstanding: The employees are capable of doing the task without direction or support.

Most people perform a variety of tasks on the job, and employee capability may vary depending on the specific task. For example, a bank teller may handle routine transactions with great ease but falter when opening new or special accounts. Employees tend to start working with low capability, needing close direction. As their ability to do the job increases, managers can begin to be supportive and cease close supervision. As a manager, you gradually develop your employees from low to outstanding levels over time.

Selecting the Appropriate Leadership Style in a Given Situation

As discussed earlier with reference to OSU's two-dimensional leadership model, when you interact with the employees you manage, your behavior can focus on directing or supporting employees.

- Directive behavior: The manager focuses on getting the task done by directing and controlling behavior to ensure that tasks get done and closely oversees performance.
- Supportive behavior: The manager focuses on developing relationships by encouraging and motivating behavior without telling the employee what to do. The manager explains things and listens to employee views, helping employees make their own decisions by building confidence and self-esteem.

Based on the two dimensions of behavior (directive and supportive), four management styles have been described. The four situational management styles are autocratic, consultative, participative, and empowerment. Which style to use is based on the employee capability level, as discussed next.

An *autocratic style* is highly directive and little concerned with building relationships. The autocratic style is appropriate when you are interacting with low-capability employees. When interacting with such employees, give very detailed instructions describing exactly what the task is and when, where, and how to perform it. Closely oversee performance and give some support. You will spend the majority of your time with the employees, giving directions. Make decisions without input from the employees.

A *consultative style* involves highly directive and highly supportive behavior and is appropriate when you are interacting with moderately capable employees. Give specific instructions and oversee performance at all major stages of a task. At the same time, support the employees by explaining why the task should be performed as requested and answering their questions. Work on relationships as you explain the benefits of completing the task your way. Give fairly equal amounts of time to directing and supporting employees. When making decisions, you may consult employees, but retain the final say. Once you make the decision, which can incorporate employees' ideas, direct and oversee employees' performance.

A *participative style* is characterized by less directive but still highly supportive behavior and is appropriate when you are interacting with employees with high capability. When interacting with such employees, spend a small amount of time giving general directions and a great deal of time giving encouragement. Spend limited time overseeing performance, letting employees do the task their way while focusing on the end result. Support the employees by encouraging them and building their self-confidence. If a task needs to be done, don't tell them how to do it; ask them how they will accomplish it. Make decisions together or allow employees to make decisions subject to your limitations and approval.

An *empowerment style* requires providing very little direction or support for employees and is appropriate when you are interacting with outstanding employees. You should let them know what needs to be done and answer their questions, but it is not necessary to oversee their performance. Such employees are highly motivated and need little, if any, support. Allow them to make their own decisions, subject to your approval. Other terms for empowerment are *laissez-faire* and *hands off.* A manager who uses this style leaves employees alone to do their own thing.

Contingency Management Model

The contingency management model puts the preceding information into an easy-to-use form. Note that figure 12.6 is somewhat similar to the group development and leadership style model seen in figure 9.7 on page 306; figure 12.6 presents the same four management styles using the terms directive and supportive, rather than task and maintenance.

Using the Contingency Management Model

Let's take the first situation from the Self-Assessment on page 385 and select the appropriate management style using figure 12.6. Follow the steps listed after you read the situation.

1. *C* _____ Your rookie crew seems to be developing well. Their need for direction and close supervision is diminishing. What do you do?

   a. Stop directing and overseeing performance, unless there is a problem. *S* _____

   b. Spend time getting to know them personally, but make sure they maintain performance levels. *S* _____

   c. Make sure things keep going well; continue to direct and oversee closely. *S* _____

   d. Begin to discuss new tasks of interest to them. *S* _____

Follow these steps:

1. Using figure 12.6, select the capability level. Put the number 1, 2, 3, or 4 after the *C* _____ preceding question 1.

2. Each alternative option *(a, b, c,* and *d)* is one of the four management styles. Place the management style letters (1A, 2C, 3P, 4E) illustrated for each alternative on the *S* _____ that follows each option.

3. Match the style to the capability by putting an *X* next to the most appropriate management behavior.

Here are the answers.

1. As a rookie crew, the employees' capability started at a low level, but they have now developed to the moderate level. Did you place a 2 after the *C*?

2. Alternative *a* is 4E, the empowerment style, involving low direction and support. Alternative *b* is 2C, the consultative style, involving both high direction and high support. Alternative *c* is 1A, the autocratic style, involving high direction but low support. Alternative *d* is 3P, the participative style, involving low direction and high support (in discussing employee interests). Did you get them all correct?

3. Based on C2 capability, the appropriate management style is S2C, consultative, which is option *b.* If you selected *b* as the management style that best matches the situation, you were correct.

However, in the business world, there is seldom only one way to handle a situation successfully. Therefore, you are given points based on how successful your behavior would be in each situation. In situation 1, *b* is the most successful alternative because it involves developing the employees gradually; answer *b* is worth 3 points. Alternative *c* is the next best alternative, followed by *d.* It is better to keep things the way they are now than to try to rush employee development, which would probably cause problems. So *c* is a 2-point answer, and *d* gets 1 point. Alternative *a* is the least effective because you are going from one extreme of supervision to the other. This is a 0-point answer because the odds are great that this approach will cause problems that will diminish your management success. The better you match your management style to employees' capabilities, the greater are your chances of being a successful manager. You will develop this ability in Skill-Builder 12.2 on page 397.

When Leaders Are Not Necessary

The leadership theories we've presented thus far assume that some type of leader should be directing every situation. What happens when leaders are not what the situation requires? That is, given the circumstances or environment, they either cannot be effective or simply are not needed. **Substitutes for leadership** eliminate the need for a leader. In certain circumstances, three characteristics can counteract or neutralize the efforts of leaders or render them unnecessary.

The following variables can substitute for or neutralize leadership because they provide the needed direction or support. (1) Characteristics of subordinates—because of their ability, knowledge, and experience they don't need much supervision. (2) Characteristics of the task—because the job is routine, they don't need much supervision. (3) Characteristics of the organization—because of the structure, they don't need much supervision (for example, when teams share leadership).

 **TIME-OUT 9** Do the characteristics of your peers, the work you do, or your organization's culture eliminate the need for a designated leader? In other words, is your boss necessary? Explain.

Getting to Your Personal Style of Leadership

You may be wondering, "Where do I start? Which style will work for me? How will I know which route to take in a given situation?" These are reasonable questions. And we have no nifty sound-bite response for you. Leadership is a much studied and not always well understood concept. Suffice it to say that you are not today the manager or leader you will be in the future. You will have many opportunities in your future jobs and teams to see which leadership shoe fits your foot, which shoe works really well for you in some situations but not in others, and which shoe should work for you but doesn't.

True leadership is like a masterpiece painting. You can paint by the numbers (lead by the rules, theories, and models), but your painting won't look like Rembrandt's or Picasso's. This doesn't mean that Rembrandt and Picasso—like other masters (be they legendary coaches or legendary entrepreneurs)—didn't know the rules. They knew them very well indeed—they were just able to take them to another level. That is what masterful leaders do—they take the rules, models, and theories to another level, and, when they do, they sometimes make history. (And then researchers study them—just think of Vince Lombardi of the Green Bay Packers). There's another thing: Masterful painters, coaches, or leaders don't start out as masters—they all start out as apprentices, practicing, learning, and living the rules. So, let's start you out on Earth—only time will tell how high you can fly.

 TIME-OUT 10 State the leadership style you prefer and why.

As we bring this chapter to a close, to help you through this maze we've gathered the various models and theories in figure 12.7. Study it carefully. It will help you understand the similarities and differences in the approaches to leadership we've examined in this chapter.

	Two-dimensional leadership styles			
	HD/LS	HD/HS	LD/HS	LD/LS
I. Trait leadership	X	X	X	X
II. Behavioral leadership				
Basic leadership styles	Autocratic	Democratic		Laissez-faire
Two-dimensional	Quadrant A	Quadrant B	Quadrant C	Quadrant D
Leadership grid	9,1 Authority	9,9 Team; Moderate D&S 5,5 Middle-of-the-road	1,9 Country club	1,1 Impoverished
Charismatic leadership	X	X	X	X
Transformational leadership	X	X	X	X
Transactional leadership	X	X	X	X
Symbolic leadership	X	X	X	X
III. Contingency leadership				
Contingency leadership	Task		Relationship	
Leadership continuum	1	2 & 3	4 & 5	6 & 7
Path-goal	Directive	Achievement	Supportive	
			Participative	
Normative leadership	Decide	Consult	Facilitate	Delegate
Leadership substitutes	X	X	X	X

FIGURE 12.7 A comparison of leadership models. H = high; L = low; D = directive; S = supportive. X = no two-dimensional leadership style used with this theory.

@ TAKE IT TO THE NET

Please visit www.HumanKinetics.com/AppliedSportManagementSkills and go to this book's companion web study guide, where you will find the following:

A list of websites associated with the concepts in this chapter

Exercises that you will need Internet access to complete

Online versions of chapter exercises and end-of-chapter learning aids

An exercise that helps you define the Key Terms

LEARNING AIDS

CHAPTER SUMMARY

1. Explain why managers are not always leaders.

Just the fact that someone is a manager doesn't mean he understands how to lead people.

2. Compare the trait, behavioral, and contingency theories of leadership.

Trait theorists look for distinctive characteristics of effective leaders. Behavioral theorists look at the behavior of effective leaders and try to find one leadership style that works for all situations. Contingency theorists try to fit leadership style to the situation.

3. Explain leadership trait theory.

    Trait theory assumes that distinctive characteristics account for leadership effectiveness. According to Ghiselli, supervisory ability is the most important leadership trait. Supervisory ability is the aptitude to perform the four management functions (planning, organizing, leading, and controlling).

4. Contrast two-dimensional leaders and grid leaders.

    These two types of leaders use the same two dimensions of leadership, but the two models describe and structure the dimensions somewhat differently. The two-dimensional model defines four leadership styles (high structure–low consideration, high structure–high consideration, low structure–high consideration, low structure–low consideration), whereas the Leadership Grid uses five leadership styles (1,1—impoverished; 9,1—authority-compliance; 1,9—country club; 5,5—middle-of-the-road; and 9,9—team).

5. Identify the management levels where charismatic, transformational, transactional, and symbolic leaders work best.

    Charismatic and transformational leaders are typically top-level managers. Transactional leaders are usually middle and first-line managers. Symbolic leaders work in top management, and, if successful, their vision flows down to middle and first-line management.

6. Contrast the various contingency models of leadership.

    Fiedler's contingency model recommends changing the situation, not the leadership style. The other contingency models recommend changing the leadership style, not the situation.

7. Critique the continuum and the path–goal models.

    Both models are subjective, making them difficult and cumbersome to use.

8. Describe normative leaders.

    Normative leaders use one of five decision-making styles, depending on the situation.

REVIEW AND DISCUSSION QUESTIONS

1. What is leadership and why is it important?

2. What traits do you think are important to leaders?

3. Based on your responses to the Self-Assessment on page 375, are you a theory X or a theory Y leader?

4. Name several pro athletes who are charismatic leaders and explain why.

5. What are the two dimensions of leadership and the four possible leadership styles?

6. Why do you think most sport management studies have focused on the leadership skills of coaches instead of those of athletic administrators?

7. Describe Phil Jackson's (Los Angeles Lakers) leadership style in terms of the Leadership Grid. Defend your answer.

8. Describe and compare the two leadership styles of the contingency model of leadership.

9. Describe and compare the two dimensions of the continuum model of leadership.

10. Describe and compare the four leadership styles of the path–goal model of leadership.

11. Give examples of MLB general managers who are transformational leaders.

12. What are three substitutes for leadership?

13. Do you believe that men and women lead differently?

14. Do you believe results differ when men coach women's college teams? What about women coaching men's college teams? Defend your answers.

15. Review the coaching examples provided in the discussion of Vroom and Yetton's normative model of leadership. Do you agree with our analysis of the leadership styles of these coaches? Why or why not?

16. Using "leadership" and "sport" as your key words, use www.scholar.google.com to search for the top five listed academic journal articles.

17. Find three additional leadership quotes attributed to Vince Lombardi at www.vincelombardi.com.

18. Which situational leadership model do you prefer? Why? Will you use it? Why or why not?

CASE

Who Would Lead Topps?

The battle for leadership was set. Topps Trading Cards had been producing baseball cards for more than 50 years. New York–based Topps was ready to accept an offer from Michael Eisner's Tornante Co. and its partner Madison Dearborn Partners to buy Topps. Eisner's group was willing to pay U.S.$9.75 per share—which is roughly U.S.$440 million. Topps would be the beneficiary of Eisner's 20 years of experience as CEO at the Walt Disney Company. His contact with media moguls would help sell more cards to more consumers. Eisner is a charismatic leader with an inviting smile, but he is also known as a demanding leader.[46] Eisner often treated the Disney CEO job as if he were the king of the kingdom. He tended to micromanage and in doing so lost many top-level executives to other media companies. However, Disney parks, movies, and stores were all built into large businesses under his leadership.

Topps, meanwhile, had been languishing in a sports card market that hadn't seen a booming sales year since Shaquille O'Neal was a rookie back in the 1992-1993 season. A strong leader such as Eisner could really energize Topps, even though he had never worked in the sports card industry.

Topps's main competitor, Carlsbad, California–based Upper Deck, jumped into the negotiations and attempted its own buyout of Topps at a slightly higher per share stock price of U.S.$10.75. If approved, the deal would give Upper Deck more than 80% of the two largest trading card manufacturers. Then, the U.S. government would have to rule whether Upper Deck would have a monopoly in the sports card market. The potential that a monopoly situation existed might be fairly easy to prove because Topps and Upper Deck easily dominated the sports card industry. Upper Deck produces memorabilia for a stable of players such as Michael Jordan, Ken Griffey, Jr., Tiger Woods, and Kobe Bryant.

In the end, Eisner's Tornante Co. and buyout firm Madison Dearborn Partners agreed to take Topps private for $9.75 a share after a majority of the company's board voted for the deal. Approval of the deal was quite close since three of the newer board members felt that Eisner had not paid enough for Topps.[47]

More important, what type of leadership would be needed to manage Topps? Eisner would bring to the table the superstar CEO leadership style from his Disney years. However, Ryan O'Hara was installed as CEO and kept Topps looking for new opportunities. He acquired GMG Entertainment, which creates digital currency cards sold at retail stores for online game, entertainment, and social media sites. Digital currency cards are used by social media companies; for example, people use them to play games on Facebook.[48]

To read more about each trading company, see www.topps.com and www.upperdeck. com. You can watch a video of former CEO Ryan O'Hara at www.sportscollectorsdaily.com/ topps-renews-nyc-lease-ceo-talks. To learn more about the card industry, try www.beckett. com or www.tuffstuff.com.

Case Questions

1. Michael Eisner's basic management style appears to be _____.
   a. democratic
   b. autocratic
   c. laissez-faire

2. Michael Eisner _____ be considered a charismatic leader.
   a. should
   b. should not

3. After watching the video, would you consider Ryan O'Hara a charismatic leader?
   a. yes
   b. no

4. It appears that Michael Eisner _____ focus on symbolic leadership in his attempt to buy Topps.
   a. did
   b. did not

5. Did all the board members at Topps agree that it was a good idea to accept Eisner's offer to buy their company?
   a. yes
   b. no

6. Michael Eisner _____ created an atmosphere of substitutes for leadership at Topps.
   a. would have
   b. would not have

7. Ryan O'Hara _____ create an atmosphere of substitutes for leadership at Topps.
   a. will
   b. will not

8. Use the Leadership Grid in figure 12.2 on page 379 to decide what type of leadership style Eisner might be inclined to use if he were the CEO of Topps.
   a. 1,1
   b. 1,9
   c. 9,1
   d. 5,5
   e. 9,9

9. Use the Leadership Grid in figure 12.2 on page 379 to decide what type of leadership style Ryan O'Hara will be inclined to use as CEO of Topps.
   a. 1,1
   b. 1,9
   c. 9,1
   d. 5,5
   e. 9,9

10. Would the leadership methods used by Michael Eisner work at your organization? Why or why not?

SKILL-BUILDER EXERCISES

Skill-Builder 12.1: Leadership Styles

Objective

To better understand what makes a leadership style effective or ineffective

Preparation

Recall the best coach or boss and the worst coach or boss you ever had and complete the assignment.

Theory	Best coach or boss	Worst coach or boss
1. List leadership traits (i.e., Ghiselli's list) that the person had or lacked and how they affected performance.		
2. List some of the behaviors of the person and how they affected performance. Was the person charismatic, transformational, transactional, or symbolic?		
3. Identify which of the seven continuum leadership styles the person used most often. Did the person change leadership styles to match the situation effectively?		
4. Identify which of the four contingency management leadership styles the person used most often. Did the person change leadership styles to match the situation effectively?		

In-Class Application

Complete the preceding skill-building preparation before class.

Procedure 1 (10-15 minutes)

Break into groups of five or six members and come to an agreement, based on your answers in the Skill-Builder, on what makes a leader effective or ineffective. Focus on the most important traits, behaviors, and leadership styles that make the difference. Write the group summary here:

Effective leaders:

_____

_____

_____

Ineffective leaders:

_____

_____

_____

Procedure 2 (10-15 minutes)

Each group selects a spokesperson to present the group's answer to procedure 1.

Wrap-Up

Take a few minutes to write your answers to the following questions:

What did I learn from this experience? How will I use this knowledge?

_____

_____

_____

As a class, discuss student responses.

Skill-Builder 12.2: Contingency Management Styles

Objective

To improve your skill at selecting the most appropriate leadership style in a given situation

Preparation

For this exercise, you should understand the contingency management styles material.

In-Class Application

During class, you will use the 12 situations from the Self-Assessment on pages 385-388 that determined your preferred management style. However, as was illustrated in "Using the Contingency Management Model" on page 390, you will select the most appropriate style using figure 12.6 on page 388.

Procedure 1 (15-30 minutes)

A. Your instructor will illustrate how to use figure 12.6, the contingency management model, in analyzing situation 2. Recall that situation 1 was analyzed on page 390. Follow these steps.

1. Using figure 12.6, your instructor will explain the capability level for situation 2 on page 385. You will put the number 1, 2, 3, or 4 on the C _____ of situation 2.

2. Your instructor will go over each alternative option, stating each management style. You will place one of the management style designators (1A, 2C, 3P, 4E) on the S _____ of situation 2.

3. Your instructor will match the style to the capability, and you will put an X next to the most appropriate management behavior alternative.

B. Your instructor will analyze situation 3 following the same steps.

C. Analyze situation 4 on your own, following the same steps. Afterward, your instructor will go over the answers. When doing situations 4 through 12, don't be too concerned whether you get the best or second-best style because in real-life situations, you will better understand the situation, and the best two styles do get good results.

Procedure 2 (15-30 minutes)

Break into groups of three. As a group, complete situations 5 through 12 or as many as you can during the allotted time. Your instructor will give you the recommend answers during or after you complete the situations. As you work, your instructor will be available to come to your group to answer questions.

Wrap-Up

Take a few minutes to write your answers to the following questions:

What did I learn from this experience? How will I use this knowledge?

_____

_____

_____

As a class, discuss student responses.

SPORTS AND SOCIAL MEDIA EXERCISES

Sometimes it is hard to impress upon students how much has been written about leadership. It is certainly one of the most written about topics in sport and business. Describe three of the books listed at Leadership Now: Building A Community of Leaders, www.leadershipnow.com.

1. _____

2. _____

3. _____

GAME PLAN FOR STARTING A SPORT BUSINESS

Your own sport business needs leadership if you expect it to be successful. Will you use a Theory X or Theory Y style of leadership to run your business, and which leadership theory or theories will you use to run your business? Describe the type of leader you want to be.

_____

_____

PART V

Controlling

Controlling is the fourth and final function that an effective manager needs to perform. Controlling (chapter 13) requires setting objectives and standards, measuring progress, and taking corrective action. Established financial controls monitor the operating budget, capital budget, and projected income statement and balance sheet. Human controls are organized around a coaching model designed to provide motivational feedback to maintain and improve performance. Information about managing sport facilities and sporting events is presented in chapter 14, including sales forecasting techniques, scheduling tools, and time management techniques. A special section at the end of the book includes thoughts about the future of sport management, and the appendix gives you career management ideas.

Controlling for Quality and Productivity

LEARNING OUTCOMES

After studying this chapter, you should be able to

1. explain how controls function within the systems process;
2. understand why feedback is a control;
3. describe the control process;
4. list which control methods are used with which frequency;
5. differentiate between static and flexible budgets and between incremental and zero-based budgets;
6. explain how capital budgets and operating budgets differ;
7. state what the three basic financial statements entail;
8. use motivational feedback;
9. understand the role of EAP staff; and
10. state three ways to increase productivity.

KEY TERMS

preliminary controls

concurrent controls

rework controls

damage controls

standards

critical success factors (CSFs)

control frequencies

management audits

budgets

operating budgets

capital budgets

financial statements

coaching

management by walking around (MBWA)

management counseling

employment assistance programs (EAPs)

discipline

productivity

Organizing Leading Controlling Planning Organizing Leading Controlling Planning Organizing Lead
ntrolling Planning Organizing Leading Controlling Planning Organizing Leading Controlling Planning Orga
Leading Controlling Planning Organizing Leading Controlling Planning Organizing Leading Contro
anning Organizing Leading Controlling Planning Organizing Leading Controlling Planning Organi
ading Controlling Planning Organizing Leading Controlling Planning Organizing Leading Controlling Pla
anizing Leading

DEVELOPING YOUR SKILLS

Every effective manager needs to be a pro at controlling. It is the only way you will know whether you and your department are on the right track. In this chapter, we present models for control systems and the control process to help develop your controlling skills. You will also learn about financial controls—budgeting and financial statements—and how to calculate productivity. Understanding accounting is vital because you won't be in business for long if you can't generate profits, and controlling is your key to making a profit. Take a least one course on accounting, often called the language of business. You will also develop your skills at getting the job done through others by using coaching and disciplining models to improve performance.

REVIEWING THEIR GAME PLAN

It Takes Three to Golf

In the story of the Ranch Golf Club in Southwick, Massachusetts, the three protagonists are a dairy family, a Jiffy Lube owner couple, and a few investors. The dairy family owned the dream, the Jiffy Lube couple owned the willingness, and the investors had more capital. How did this unlikely trio turn a dream into reality and a fledgling golf club into a four-star course in less than a year of operation? The answer is expertise—in this instance, in the form of Rowland Bates, a Realtor. The Hall family approached Bates with the idea that the family dairy farm was good turf for golf. The Halls would provide the land, and Bates would find the investors.

Enter Pete and Korby Clark, young part-owners of some 50 Jiffy Lubes in the northeastern United States, who had jingles in their pockets from a recent sale of most of their franchises and a desire to try something new. The Clarks had been looking at various ventures since 1991, but nothing much interested them until Rowland Bates approached them with his plan. What was different about Bates' proposal? Rowland offered the Clarks a hands-on deal—they would be in on the creation and management; he didn't want just their money.

The Clarks soon found that building a golf course requires money, and lots of it. And although banks were willing to loan them plenty of money if they built Jiffy Lubes, they could not borrow much for their golf course. Again, Bates' expertise, connections, and tireless beating of the investor bushes soon netted them enough investors to cut the deal. The final deal hammered out by Bates involved one-third ownership by the Halls, one-third by the Clarks, and one-third by other investors.[1]

The idea from the beginning was to create a state-of-the-art, premier golf course. The trio had plenty of natural advantages to work with in the Halls' dairy land, which was rich in beauty, vistas, woods, and the all-important differing elevations. The owners hired California architect Damian Pascuzzo to design a grand golf course. And design one he did. The course boasts 7,100 yards (6,492 meters) in length and a 140 slope rating (a very good rating). Each golf car is equipped with a ParView GPS system that diagrams each hole and provides current yardage from the pin and other helpful facts and figures.[2] Peak-season green fees are around U.S.$100; service is unsurpassed, similar to that in Arizona, where the Clarks played golf to learn about excellent service. On the course at all times, player assistants provide all types of help, including golf tips, retrieval of left-behind clubs, and cool towels on hot days. The two massive 19th-century barns have been completely remodeled and painted their original and distinctive yellow color; and they now serve as clubhouse, restaurant and lounge, golf shop, and function facility.[3]

The Clarks wanted to create a new business—they didn't necessarily want to be involved in its day-to-day operation, so they turned to Willowbend, a professional golf management team, for four reasons. (1) They needed expertise. (2) They had other things to do with their life—a family to raise, community service they were keenly committed to, and coaching, among others. (Pete was the head baseball coach and assistant football coach for Agawam High School and has also coached for Trinity College.) (3) The mix was right—Pete and Korby oversaw the important strategic decisions and had input when they wanted, but Willowbend handled the day-to-day decisions. (4) The employees worked for Willowbend, which offered a good benefits package. The key to successful comanaging for the Clarks and Willowbend was clear, open communication of expectations.

However, in 2005 Willowbend stopped managing golf courses and sold the business. By now the Clarks had gained enough experience running the Ranch and no longer needed professional management. Peter Clark increased his management role to become the managing partner, overseeing day-to-day operations, and Korby works full-time too. During the summer, 80 people work at the Ranch, and the professional staff gets benefits through the human resources function. The club has a sophisticated information system for its three departments—golf (greens and practice, tournaments and outings, golf shop), maintenance (the course and other facilities), and food and beverage (the Ranch Grille, bar, and functions)—that includes many performance measures. The partners also have a separate real estate business selling land and houses near the golf course.

Pete says there are more similarities than differences between running Jiffy Lubes, golf courses, and baseball and football teams. The focus is the same—high-quality service. You have to treat the customer or player right. He uses the same "three I's" philosophy with Jiffy Lubes, the Ranch, and his coaching: intensity (to be prepared to do the job right), integrity (to do the right thing when no one is watching), and intimacy (to be a team player).

The three I's are turning into money. The Ranch is striving to be the best golf club in New England. In less than a year, the Ranch earned a four-star course rating, one of only four in New England. In the January 2003 issue of *Golf Digest,* the Ranch was rated number three in the country in the "new upscale public golf course" category, and it was ranked as the best public course in Massachusetts in 2007. The Ranch was voted in the top 50 of all public golf courses in *Golf World's* 2010 Readers' Choice Awards; it was one of only two courses in all of New England that made the list.

For current information on the Ranch Golf Club, visit www.theranchgolfclub.com, which features a virtual visit of the golf course.

Quality and Control Systems

As defined in chapter 1, controlling establishes mechanisms to ensure that objectives are achieved. The key to long-term success is satisfied customers. Organizations need to monitor progress toward their objectives,[4] and they need control systems.[5] Therefore, controlling is an important managerial competency.[6] In this section, we discuss quality, controlling from outside the firm, organizational systems control, and controlling functional areas.

Quality

Recall (chapter 2) that quality involves comparing actual use to requirements in order to determine value, and that total quality management (TQM) is the process in which everyone in an organization focuses on the customer to continually improve value. Without continuous improvement, the firm will lose business to competitors. Clearly, effective control mechanisms are needed to ensure quality goods and services. Controlling to ensure high quality and productivity is what this chapter is all about.

The International Organization for Standardization (ISO) is the world's largest developer of voluntary International Standards. International Standards give state-of-the-art specifications for products, services, and good practice, helping to make industry more efficient and effective. ISO certifies firms that meet set quality standards. As part of ISO 9000 certification, the firm must document policies that address quality management, continuous improvement, and customer satisfaction.[7] Most multinational organizations have ISO certification, and they require suppliers they do business with to be certified to ensure quality. To learn more about ISO, visit its website (www.iso.org).

The American Society for Quality (ASQ) is the world's leading membership organization devoted to quality. ASQ provides the Quarterly Quality Report, which measures customer perceptions of the quality and reliability of products and services.[8] A prior report contained an evaluation of consumer perception of the difference in quality between Reebok-Adidas and Nike. Reebok had recently merged with Adidas, so the ASQ report concerned how well the Reebok and Adidas cultures would work together. The results showed Reebok footwear firmly ahead of Nike's quality rating.[9] To learn more about ASQ, visit its website (www.asq.org).

Controlling From the Outside

Government laws and regulations serve as controls to all organizations. Many sport organizations are also monitored and controlled by external bodies of governance. We have discussed many of these bodies: FIFA and its executive committee monitor all soccer activities; the IOC monitors all Olympic activities; the PGA is the regulating body for golf; each Jewish Community Center is monitored by the JCCA (Jewish Community Centers of America); and each individual YMCA is governed by the rules of the World Alliance of YMCAs. College athletics are governed by the rules and policies set forth by the NCAA. These organizations establish rules and regulations that every member must follow; but sport authorities, such as the IOC, look out for the interests of all stakeholders.[10]

These governing bodies are dedicated to their particular sport. For example, the IOC approves the sports and events in the Olympics. The IOC picks locales for the Summer and Winter Games 7 years in advance. Cities bid for the right to hold the Games and must prove they have the necessary facilities to host the Games, house the athletes and spectators, and provide officiating.[11] For more information on the IOC, visit its website (www.olympic.org).

Organization Systems Control

LEARNING OUTCOME 1 ▶

Explain how controls function within the systems process.

To determine whether performance is up to expectations, it must be measured and controlled.[12] Because of the diversity in types of organizations and types of stakeholders, no performance measure or control system is universally applicable—the measure or system must be tailored to each situation.[13] In this chapter, we focus on how various controls are used to measure and evaluate each stage of the system. In chapter 2, we examined the systems process; now we examine how controls are used at each stage to ensure that objectives are met—because control mechanisms are used to accomplish organizational goals.[14] Figure 13.1 shows how this works. Four different types of controls are needed in different parts of the systems process, which we discuss here.

Preliminary Controls

Preliminary controls anticipate and prevent possible problems. One major difference between successful and unsuccessful managers is their ability to anticipate and prevent problems, rather than solve problems after they occur. If preliminary controls work, a manager doesn't need to use concurrent, rework, or damage control to fix a problem.

Planning and organizing are key functions in preliminary control, which is also called feedforward control. The organization's mission and objectives guide the use of all of its resources. Standing plans control

TIME-OUT
1
Use figure 13.1 to identify the primary inputs, transformation, outputs, and customers of your firm or team. Also, identify the level of customer satisfaction. (Remember, customers can be fans, users of the golf course, buyers of your merchandise, players on your youth league soccer team, employees at your organization if your department is human resources, stockholders if you are the CEO, or suppliers of input to your company if you are the finance department that pays them. Employees, stockholders, and suppliers are also called stakeholders—stakeholders can thus be considered customers from certain viewpoints.)

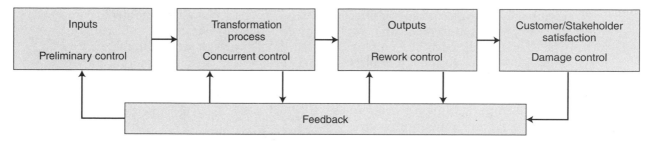

Inputs	Transformation process	Outputs	Customer/Stakeholder satisfaction
Preliminary control	Concurrent control	Rework control	Damage control

Feedback

FIGURE 13.1   Controlling the systems process.

employee behavior in recurring situations to prevent problems, and contingency plans tell employees what to do if problems occur.

A typical preliminary control is preventive maintenance. Many production departments and transportation companies or departments routinely tune up their machines and engines to prevent breakdowns. Another preliminary control is to purchase only quality inputs in order to prevent production problems. The practice area, the golf course itself, golf cars, and tee times are the major inputs that require preliminary control at the Ranch.

Concurrent Controls

Concurrent controls are actions taken during transformation to ensure that standards are met. The key to success here is quality control.[15] It is more efficient to reject faulty input than to rework output that does not function properly. Checking quality is also crucial during the transformation process and, of course, at the output stage. At the Ranch, the transformation is the actual playing of golf. A major concurrent control is player assistance out on the course. If players are not satisfied, player assistants know it early on and fix the problem before the game is over.

Rework Controls

Rework controls are actions taken to fix output. Rework is necessary when preliminary and concurrent controls fail. Most organizations inspect output before it is sold or sent as input to other departments in the organization. Sometimes rework is neither cost-effective nor possible, and outputs have to be accepted as is, discarded, or sold for salvage, all of which can be costly. For example, if Wilson Sporting Goods makes defective golf balls (outputs), it is too late; the company cannot change the past.

Damage Controls

Damage controls are actions taken to minimize negative impacts on customers attributable to faulty output. When a faulty product or service gets to the customer, damage control is needed. The longer problems go unrecognized or unresolved, the more damage occurs to the firm and the more difficult it is to solve the problems. Warranties (a form of damage control) refund the purchase price, fix the product, reperform the service (a form of rework), or replace the product with a new one. Handling customer complaints is a controlling technique. When sport teams lose a lot of games, attendance tends to fall, and damage control is needed to try to get fans back to the venue.

Feedback

Feedback helps organizations continually increase customer satisfaction, so feedback is an important control and must be used at every stage of the system. The only way

 TIME-OUT 2 Give examples of preliminary, concurrent, rework, and damage controls in your current organization or team.

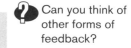 Can you think of other forms of feedback?

to continually increase customer satisfaction is to use feedback from the customer to continually improve products.[16] Customer evaluation cards are only one example of feedback.

The Clarks spend much of their time at the Ranch talking to players about the service, looking for ways to improve the players' experience. Within an organization, output groups give feedback to transformation and input groups. Transformation groups give feedback to input groups for continuous improvement through the entire system.

TIME-OUT 3 Describe the controls you personally use in your department.

Control Focus

Good coaches and sport managers know that the controls that lead to success are preliminary and concurrent, so that is where they spend more time and effort—which prevents the need for rework and damage control. Think about it. If you are not properly prepared for the game (preliminary) and are losing, you will not win (concurrent). After losing (although viewing game films and so on is helpful) you don't get a do-over (rework), and after you lose fans, it is hard to bring them back (damage).

Controlling Functional Areas

Recall from chapter 5 that firms are commonly organized into four functional areas: operations, marketing, human resources, and finance. Information is a fifth functional area, which can be a stand-alone department or part of finance. Organizations have other departments as well; however, these five key functional areas serve our purposes here, as shown in figure 13.2.

TIME-OUT 4 Use figure 13.2 to diagram the systems process for the department you work in.

Although in most organizations the operations area is the only functional area that transforms inputs into the external outputs of goods and services (products), all functional areas have inputs and outputs. Although external customer damage control is primarily the function of marketing, damage control is also necessary when internal outputs are faulty and thus is required in every functional area.

APPLYING THE CONCEPT 13.1

Using Appropriate Controls

Choose the appropriate control for each situation.

   a. preliminary

   b. concurrent

   c. rework

   d. damage

_____ 1. The new golf shirt I bought today has a button missing.

_____ 2. I just got my monthly budget report telling me how much of its budget the marketing department spent.

_____ 3. Coach is reviewing the plays she will use in Sunday's big game.

_____ 4. As I was jogging in my new nylon shorts, they split down the side.

_____ 5. The manager uses the time management system on Fridays.

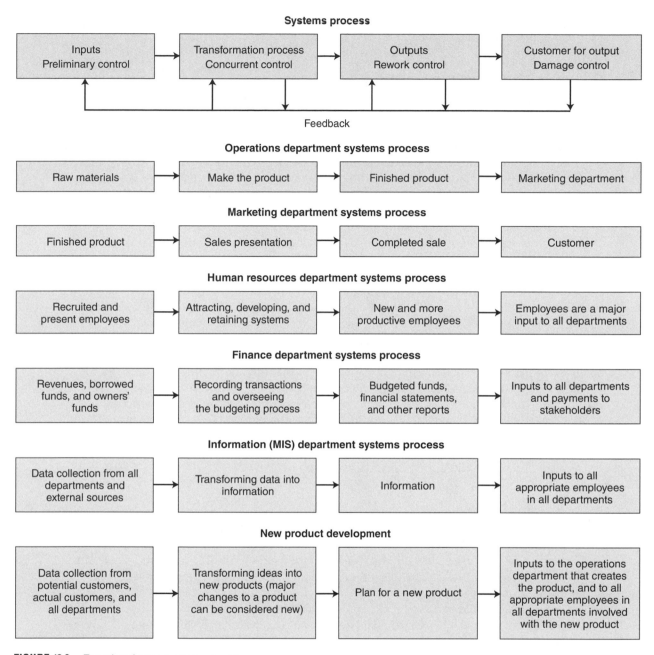

FIGURE 13.2 Functional-area systems processes.

Operations

The operations (also called production and manufacturing) functional area makes the goods or performs the service. For example, the Ranch uses a sophisticated scheduling system to maintain the golf course turf. Seeding, fertilizing, watering, and mowing are well planned and computerized. In the next chapter, you will learn about operations.

Marketing

Marketing, which includes sales, is the functional area responsible for selling the organization's products. The four key areas (called the four Ps) of marketing are pricing, promoting (personal selling and advertising), placing (sales locations), and product attributes (features, packaging, brands, installation, and instructions). Marketing also identifies target markets.

Marketing deals primarily with external customers and undertakes damage control outside the organization, whereas other departments perform damage control inside the organization. Marketing measures customer satisfaction in order to attract and retain customers. Marketing also distributes customer and competitor feedback to other departments.

The Ranch markets in a variety of ways. First, its best marketing is through word of mouth. Golfers are always on the lookout for great courses, and players are pleased to recommend the Ranch. The Ranch also runs TV ads and print ads in newspapers and golf magazines. And, as mentioned earlier, at its cutting-edge website (www.theranchgolfclub.com), professionals and amateur players can take a virtual tour of the course.

Sport marketers have to evaluate how effectively the marketing media they used (television, magazines, catalog, Internet, radio, and so on) reached the customers or fans who were expected to view the ads. Companies such as Rawlings, Nike, and Adidas pay for sponsorship of sporting events expecting a certain number of fans to see their company message. Banner ads placed on an Internet site are expected to lead new customers to the company's website. Or, how well did a radio ad placed in a specific geographic market succeed in driving more fans to a sporting event?[17]

A key topic in sport marketing is *ambush marketing*. In ambush marketing, a sport manufacturer, normally at a large sporting event, advertises its product without paying a sponsorship fee. For example, suppose that Adidas is an official sponsor of the Olympics. Nike could buy billboard space along the roads heading into the stadium. Or, Nike could create an online contest using Olympic sports to divert consumer or fan interest away from the paid-for advertising. Ambush marketing has frustrated major sport event organizers and sponsors for years. It has been legal as long as the firm ambushing the competitor has stopped short of trademark infringement or false advertising.[18] However, ambush marketing is often considered a gray area in terms of when it occurs. When does a competitor cross the line and infringe on the paid sponsor? Did a group of women in bright orange dresses ambush a soccer match? FIFA officials accused them of marketing an unlicensed beer brand by wearing orange mini-dresses, the color of the beer sold by the smaller unlicensed beer brand.[19] Do you think ambush marketing should be illegal?

Human Resources

Inputs for human resources (HR) are the potential employees whom HR attracts (recruits and selects). In HR's transformation process, it develops (orientation, training and development, and performance appraisal) and retains (compensation, health and safety, and labor relations) employees. Its outputs are new and more productive employees, who are also major inputs to every functional area.[20]

For details on HR processes, see chapter 7. Large organizations such as Wilson Sporting Goods fund a separate HR department. The Ranch has approximately 80 summer employees with equal staffing numbers in its three major departments. The Ranch performs most of the HR functions itself.

Finance

Finance (which includes accounting) is the functional area responsible for recording all financial transactions (primarily paying for inputs and costs involved in the sale of outputs), obtaining funds needed to pay for inputs (loans plus sale of bonds and stocks), and investing any surplus funds (various forms of savings accounts and the purchasing of assets, such as another company's stock holdings). Finance also prepares the budgets and financial statements.

Inputs for finance include collected revenues, borrowed funds, and owners' funds. The transformation process includes recording transactions and overseeing the budgeting process. Outputs are budgets, financial statements, and other reports (such as tax returns, employee tax withholding, and annual reports). The finance department's primary customers are other departments (through their budgets) and stakeholders (employees via their paychecks and suppliers and lenders via payments to them). You will learn more about finance in the next chapter.

Information

Control mechanisms have inherent information-processing properties. Management information systems (MISs) control information in a central location and for networks. MIS departments are typically responsible for the organization's computers. MIS departments collect data from all departments and external sources as their inputs. (Data in this context refers to unorganized facts and figures.) This department then transforms data into information. Information is data organized in a meaningful way that helps workers make decisions.

Cross-Functional Product Development

Not all organizations fund product development teams. Therefore, we don't list this as a major functional area. However, it is an important function in many firms and usually falls within the purview of either marketing or operations. Ideas for major improvements and new products often come from external sources, especially potential customers, as well as from other areas of the firm. For example, Nike's marketing department collects data so that product development can design a line of footwear that will appeal to new and existing customers. The operations department looks into the practical aspects of producing the new footwear. Finance works up numbers on the cost and pricing effects. The final plan for producing the new footwear then goes to operations. The marketing department plans how to promote and sell the new footwear. Finance works up the costs and budget for the footwear and keeps records (information) on performance. The HR department may need to make personnel changes or attract creative engineers or marketers to the company. Meanwhile, top managers control the entire process, making sure the new product development is completed successfully.

Feedback Process

◀ LEARNING OUTCOME 2
Understand why feedback is a control.

Every employee in an organization transforms inputs into outputs in some way. For example, a production worker makes a part of a sneaker, which becomes input for the next person down the line and so on until the footwear is completed. Every employee should therefore also use preliminary, concurrent, rework, and damage controls.

Feedback is essential if the system is to improve (see figure 13.3). Throughout the system, feedback circulating through all the functional areas improves inputs, transformations, and outputs while continually increasing customer satisfaction. Note that operations, marketing, finance, and HR provide feedback to each other and to MIS as well.

Control Process

◀ LEARNING OUTCOME 3
Describe the control process.

The control process involves the four steps shown in figure 13.4. The steps are the same whether the control is an organization-wide control or a functional-area control, even though the controls themselves may be very different. Effective control mechanisms provide knowledge for continuous improvement through the four phases of the control process.

1. Set objectives and standards. The first step in the control process is to set objectives and standards. Objectives and standards are part of the input process and are preliminary controls. Objectives, in a sense, are standards, but they are big-picture standards. Thus, detailed and specific standards are also needed to determine whether the objectives are being met.[21]

Objectives are often qualitative or, at least, broadly quantitative. Controls are quantitative in much greater detail. To be comprehensive and complete, standards must address five criteria. **Standards** minimize negative impacts on customers attributable to faulty output

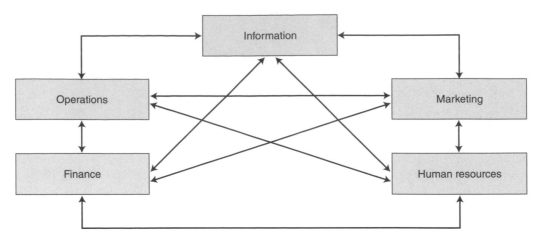

FIGURE 13.3　The feedback process. The arrows represent the flow of feedback throughout the systems process.

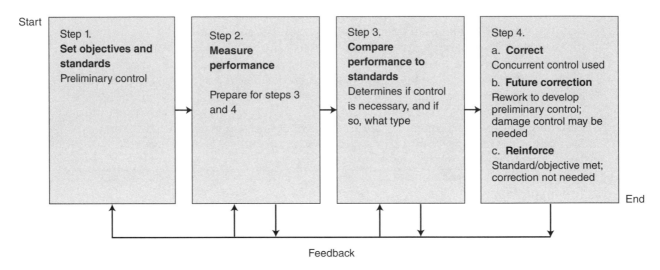

FIGURE 13.4　The control process.

by controlling quantity, quality, time, cost, and behavior. You need to measure success,[22] but be careful how you measure with standards.[23] Albert Einstein said, "Not everything that can be counted counts, and not everything that counts can be counted."[24] Teams need to adhere to standards,[25] and incomplete standards often lead to negative results. Workers respond to what is measured, so developing balanced standards is a key management function that drives business success.

　　• Quantity: How many units should employees produce to earn their pay? Examples of quantitative standards include number of sales made, home runs hit, quarterback sacks made, or classes taught. Measuring performance quantitatively tends to be relatively clear-cut.

　　• Quality: How well must a job be done? How many errors are acceptable? Qualitative standards are essential if the control is to be effective. Quality can often be measured quantitatively. Quantitative examples include the number of interceptions thrown, coaching mistakes made in games, and poor teaching evaluations received from students. But other aspects of qual-

TIME-OUT 5　Give an example of a standard your organization or team uses that satisfies the five criteria for complete standards.

ity are often difficult to establish and measure. How does an administrator determine how good the teachers are in a sport management program? It isn't easy, but quality must be measured and evaluated.

• Time: When should the task be completed? How fast should it be completed? When you assign tasks, it is important to specify time frames. Deadlines are a time-honored, time-based standard. Performance is also measured against specific periods—goals scored per season, annual graduation rate, home runs in a season, or profits per quarter.

• Cost: How much should the job cost to do? This is part of the budgeting function. Some production departments use cost-accounting methods to ensure accuracy. Most departments have set budgets. Examples include expense account limits for entertaining customers, fixed overhead costs to keep expenses down (long-term rent agreements or outsourced secretarial help), and so on. Cost standards for the professor may include a salary limit set by the state or private college board of trustees and a limit for overhead costs such as travel. In pro sport, the cost of athletes keeps going up; the cost is a major concern for team owners, and it is often passed on to the fans in the form of ticket prices and other costs of attending the sport event.

• Behavior: Which behaviors are appropriate and which ones are not appropriate? Standing plans, especially rules, guide and control behaviors of workers. Players are expected to be on time for practice. Players are also expected to behave morally on and off the field. Penn State assistant football coach Jerry Sandusky was convicted of child sexual abuse on campus in 2012, and the administration had helped to cover up the abuse.[26] NASCAR fined Kurt Busch $50,000 for his poor behavior during the 2011 Sprint Cup finale at Homestead-Miami Speedway. NASCAR cited both an obscene gesture Busch made inside his car and verbal abuse toward a reporter.[27] Other methods to control behavior are also effective, and we discuss a few of them later in this chapter.

2. Measure performance. If you can't measure objectives and standards, you can't control them. The second step in the control process is to measure performance, which helps organizations determine whether they are meeting their objectives and also helps them find ways to beat their current performance and beat or match that of their competitors.[28] Professional sport teams are measuring brand association to increase long-term franchise value.[29] An important consideration in the control process is what to measure and how frequently to measure it.[30]

It is important to identify critical success factors. **Critical success factors (CSFs)** are pivotal areas in which satisfactory results will ensure successful achievement of the objective or standard. In other words, we cannot control everything; but as organizations, departments, teams, and individuals, we can identify the few most important objectives, goals, and standards without which we fail and with which we succeed. One important measure is customer satisfaction, because without customers you don't have a business. These are the CSFs, and you must control them very carefully. For example, possible CSFs for the WNBA include improving team competitiveness, maintaining national television exposure, and improving marketing.

3. Compare performance with standards. The third step in the control process is to compare performance with standards. This step is relatively easy if the first two steps have been done correctly.

A performance or variance report, such as the one shown in table 13.1, is commonly used to measure performance. Performance reports typically show standards, actual performance, and deviations from the standards. In table 13.1, the golf club

TIME-OUT 6 Give several CSFs for your current job. Place them in order of importance and explain why they are critical.

TABLE 13.1　Operations Performance Report

Outputs and inputs	Standard or budgeted amount	Actual	Variance
Units produced (golf clubs– the outputs)	100,000	99,920	−80
Production cost (inputs)			
Labor, including overtime	U.S.$700,000	U.S.$698,950	+U.S.$1,050
Materials	U.S.$955,000	U.S.$957,630	−U.S.$2,630
Supplies	U.S.$47,500	U.S.$47,000	+U.S.$500
Totals	U.S.$1,702,500	U.S.$1,703,580	−U.S.$1,080

production results, although under the production goal and over cost, are good because they both deviate less than 1% from the standard. (To determine deviation, the variation is divided by the standard.) Managers need to be accountable for meeting the objectives and standards.[31] When variances are significant, they should be examined carefully and fixed. We discuss this in more detail later in this section.

4. Correct or reinforce. The last step of the control process is to correct or reinforce. During the transformation process, concurrent controls are used to correct performance to meet standards. But when the job is done (the product is made or the service is delivered), if it is faulty and it is too late to correct the problem, then it is time to (1) figure out why the standard was not met, (2) use the information to develop new preliminary controls, and (3) implement the new controls so that the standard is met next time. When performance affects others, damage control may also be required. So learn from errors and mistakes by understanding their causes, and implement changes that will prevent future errors or reduce negative consequences when errors reoccur.[32]

TIME-OUT
7
Think about a situation in which you or your boss had to take corrective action to meet a standard. Describe the action taken.

Of course, when the standard has been met, there is no need for corrective action. Keep things running smoothly. This does not mean that the control process ends here. It's time for a little gratitude—don't forget to praise your team for a job well done and to give other rewards, such as bonuses. Also, continue to find ways to increase performance.

LEARNING OUTCOME 4 ▶

List which control methods are used with which frequency.

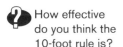 How effective do you think the 10-foot rule is?

Frequency of Controls

An important consideration in the control process is how frequently to measure performance.[33] You need controls, but don't be a control freak.[34] Ten methods, which can be categorized by frequency of occurrence, are used to measure and control performance. **Control frequencies** are constant, periodic, and occasional.

Constant Controls

Constant controls are in continuous use and include self-control, clan control, and standing plans. The three I's that Pete Clark uses at the Ranch are constant controls. One constant-control standing plan at the Ranch is the 10-foot rule: If you come within 10 feet (3.04 meters) of customers, you always greet them cheerfully and ask whether they need any assistance.

Self-Control

A big question facing every manager is, Will my staff do their job if they are not monitored closely? The answer is that you must know your staff. Some groups need much less control than others. The issue here is one of balance—self-control (internal in employees) versus imposed control (external from managers). Too much external control causes problems, and so does too little control. So use contingency management (chapter 12).

Clan Control

This control is about organizational culture and norms, which are powerful ways to shape desired behavior. Organizations that use teams often rely on clan control—peer pressure. See chapter 9 for details on group control (another term for clan control), norms, and enforcing norms. Self-control and clan control are used throughout the control process and in conjunction with the four control types.

Standing Plans

Policies, procedures, and rules exist to influence behavior in recurring predictable situations. Standards can be thought of as a type of standing plan. When standing plans and standards are developed, they are preliminary controls. When standing plans and standards are implemented to solve problems, they become concurrent, rework, or damage controls. Standing plans are developed in sport by governing bodies to see to it that uniform policies, procedures, and rules are implemented locally (an example in the United States is Springfield Recreation Department), nationally (NCAA, another U.S. example), and globally (IOC).

Periodic Controls

Periodic controls are used on a regular, fixed basis, such as hourly, daily, weekly, monthly, quarterly, or annually. Periodic controls include regularly scheduled reports, budgets, and audits. The Ranch management provides the owners with monthly reports. Together they develop annual and monthly budgets, and they have an annual audit performed.

Scheduled Reports

Oral reports in the form of daily, weekly, and monthly meetings to discuss progress and problems are common in all organizations. Written reports required on a schedule are also common, and they are typically being sent via e-mail. At Wilson Sporting Goods, the sales manager gets weekly sales reports. Vice presidents get monthly income statements. Regularly scheduled reports are designed as a preliminary control. But the report itself is used (when there is a problem) as a concurrent, rework, or damage control, depending on the situation.

Budgets

Budgets are a widely used control tool. They are also essential. Budgets need to be constructed carefully, always with an eye on where costs can be cut even more, and actual costs need to be measured against budgeted costs relentlessly. Think of budgets as your reality check. New budgets are preliminary controls. As the year progresses, they become concurrent controls. At year end, they are reworked for the next year. A budget may also require damage control if significant changes such as overspending take place. The damage control might involve disciplining or firing the employee who overspent. You will learn more about budgeting in the "Financial Controls" section.

Audits

Organizations use two types of audits: internal and external. Part of the accounting function is to maintain careful and extremely detailed records of the organization's transactions and assets. (Accounting transparency is a cornerstone of the U.S. economy, as we explain later—careful records are one way to ensure transparency.) Large organizations maintain internal auditing departments whose responsibility it is to make sure assets are reported accurately. Internal auditors also serve as watchdogs to keep theft (embezzlement and fraud) to a minimum. Most large organizations hire outside auditors to verify their financial statements.

Management audits look at ways to improve the organization's planning, organizing, leading, and controlling functions. This analysis examines the past and present so that future performance can be improved. Management audits are conducted both internally and externally.

The International Standards Organization has an environmental management standards certification (called ISO 14000) to help ensure that managers are implementing global management practices to minimize harmful effects on the environment caused by a company's activities and are continually improving the company's environmental performance.[35] ISO 14000 requires a management audit as part of the environmental certification process. For more information, visit the ISO website (www.iso.org).

After a series of financial scandals revealed a weakness in the American auditing system, new controls (laws and regulations) were implemented to help prevent future problems. The Sarbanes-Oxley Act (SOA) of 2002 represents a huge change to federal securities law. SOA requires all financial reports to include an Internal Controls Report. This shows that a company's financial data are accurate and that adequate controls are in place to safeguard financial data.[36] The paperwork to comply with SOA can be a tremendous problem for small companies. Legislation is being reviewed to give smaller business (less than $1 billion in revenue) extra time to comply with all the regulations.[37]

Occasional Controls

Occasional controls are used on an as-needed basis. They include observation, the exception principle, special reports, and project controls. Unlike periodic controls, they are not conducted at set intervals. The management team comes in unannounced to observe operations at the Ranch to ensure that everything is up to standard. The Clarks provide special reports to managers to help them continually improve. Project controls are also in place for special golf events that involve corporate clients and other organizations.

Observation

This is exactly what it sounds like—designated people, video cameras, and electronic devices observing work in progress, whether the work involves a professor giving a lecture, a pro athlete in training, or a machine making a golf ball. Observation is used with all four types of control. Management by walking around (MBWA) is an especially effective method of observation that we will examine in more detail later in this chapter.

Exception Principle

This is about placing control in the hands of staff unless problems occur, in which case people go to their supervisors for help. Corrective action is then taken to get performance back to standard. However, people—be they production line workers or CEOs—often shrink from asking for help or reporting on poor performing until it is too late to take corrective action. Therefore, it is important for managers and staff to agree in detail on what constitutes an exception.

Special Reports

When problems or opportunities are identified, management often requests special reports, which may be compiled by a single employee, a committee, or outside consultants. The intent of such reports is to identify causes of problems and possible solutions. Reports can be as simple as a manager asking an employee what the problem is or asking for recommendations on improving the situation.

Project Controls

With nonrecurring projects, project managers still need to install controls to ensure that such projects are completed on time and on budget. Because planning and controlling are so closely linked, planning tools, such as Gantt charts and PERT networks (Performance Evaluation and Review Technique, chapter 14), are also project control methods. Project controls are designed as a preliminary control but can be used with any of the other three types of controls when schedules are not being met.

Organizations understand that controls are crucial to their success. Therefore, it behooves you to get comfortable with the control process and learn to use controls well. Table 13.2 summarizes controls. The types, frequency, and methods of control are listed separately because all four types of control may be used with any method. Recall how a budget changes its type of control over time and that more than one control method can be used at once. You need to be aware of which stage of the system you are working in and of the controls that will be most effective for what you are doing in that stage (see figure 13.1 on p. 405). Also, don't forget the four steps of the control process used within the types, frequency, and methods of controls.

TIME-OUT 8 Give an example of a constant, a periodic, and an occasional control used by your organization or team. Explain why each control is classified as such.

Financial Controls

Budgets and financial statements are important tools. The information they contain is key in making decisions of all kinds, including allocating money among teams and hiring coaches.[38] Therefore, you need to get very comfortable with budgets and financial statements. You may find that not only must you bring your costs in line with budgets, but that you will also be expected to develop budgets and to use spreadsheet software to present them. Accounting is the language of business and, as such, is a key way to understand your

TABLE 13.2 The Control System

Types of controls	The control process	Frequency and methods of control		
Inputs (preliminary)	1. Set objectives and standards	*Constant controls*	*Periodic controls*	*Occasional controls*
Transformation (concurrent)	2. Measure performance	Self Clan Standing plans	Scheduled reports	Observation Exception
Outputs (rework)	3. Compare performance to standard		Budgets Audits	principle Special reports
Customer satisfaction (damage)	4. Correct or reinforce			Project

Control Methods

Identify the appropriate control method for each situation.

Constant	Periodic	Occasional
a. self	d. regularly scheduled reports	g. observation
b. clan	e. budgets	h. exception principle
c. standing plans	f. audits	i. special reports
		j. project

_____ 6. The boss asks the floor supervisor to meet to explain why imprinting the current golf ball run with the corporate logo is behind schedule.

_____ 7. Posted signs state that helmets are to be worn throughout the factory—no exceptions.

_____ 8. The manager's desk faces the work floor.

_____ 9. Accounting staff members are working on supply contracts alone today because the boss is out of the office.

_____ 10. The manager assembles the monthly operations performance report.

organization. Financial statements can tell you a great deal if you speak their lingo. Also, many current and former pro athletes are investing in or launching their own businesses. So, there are some sport managers who need to understand financials. For example, NBA's Steve Nash has nine business ventures, including Vancouver Nutrition, OneBode, and a string of gyms with his name.[39] Michael Jordan became the majority owner of the Charlotte Bobcats after 4 years as part of the team's ownership group and its managing member of basketball operations; he is now chairman and the first former player to become the majority owner of an NBA franchise.[40] Former NBA star player Magic (Earvin) Johnson invested $50 million for about a 3% to 4% ownership of the MLB Los Angeles Dodgers team.[41] Are you thinking about starting your own business, or climbing the corporate ladder? You can't do it without being financially savvy.

Some students fear budgeting because they believe they are not a good match for accounting. Don't fear, because the spreadsheet will do the math for you, and budgeting is not about a bunch of debits and credits. It is about figuring out how much it will cost you to run your team or department, usually for a season or year, and in most cases you have a prior budget to use as a template anyway. And until you make it to the top, someone will be helping you with and approving your budget.

Master Budget

Preparing and following budgets are every manager's business. **Budgets** are plans for allocating resources to specific activities. Notice that our definition does not use terms pertaining to money. That is because organizations budget all types of resources—HR, machines, time, space, and, yes, funds. However, in the following discussion our focus is on financial budgets, the part of the picture that involves money.

To construct master budgets, organizations develop operating budgets and capital budgets; organizations then measure costs and revenue flow through the income statement, the balance sheet, and the statement of cash flow (see figure 13.5). Notice that information from two of the end products of the process, the income statement and the balance sheet, is used to construct future master budgets, because these two statements tell managers how much money they have to work with and therefore how much they may need to borrow to cover operating expenses and capital expenditures.

Budgets usually cover 1 year, broken down by month. The controller, the chief finance officer (CFO), oversees the budgeting process that results in the master budget. In other words, the master budget is the end result of the budgeting process. Although organizations commonly follow the three steps we noted previously, how each step is performed varies widely from organization to organization.

Each department submits a proposed budget to the controller or committee for approval. During the budgeting process, which by its very nature deals with finite resources, power politics often come into play as managers defend their turf and their budgets. Budgeting is therefore also about negotiating (see chapter 8) and hard bargaining.

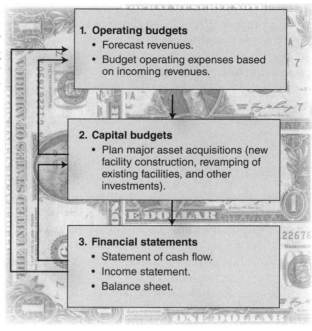

FIGURE 13.5 The master budget.

Operating Budgets

As it had for the last five Summer Olympics, Nike geared up for London 2012 by signing athletes to wear its brands (expenses) and forecasting increased sales (revenues) after the Games as medal winners promoted the Nike Swoosh label[42] (revenues – expenses = profits). Nike was the U.S. Olympic team sponsor, but it lost out to Adidas as the official sportswear of the 2012 Games.[43] **Operating budgets** use revenue forecasts to allocate funds to cover projected expenses. Only after organizations determine how much money they have, and expect to have, can they plan how it should be spent to make more money. Therefore, the first step in the master budgeting process is to forecast revenue.

Forecasting Revenue

This is the forecast of total income for the year. Before the season even begins, the team has to predict attendance revenues for the entire year and for the long term as well. The New York Yankees baseball team generated $325 million in revenue from regular-season tickets and luxury suites in 2010.[44] Although sales are the most common form of revenue, many organizations also have other forms of revenue. Some pro teams now make more on media deals than they do in ticket revenue.[45] Pro football, America's most popular and profitable sport, has rising media revenues but has been trying to tackle a decrease in game attendance. Ticket sales have been down every year since 2007.[46]

Here are some other forms of sport revenues. MLB and other pro sport teams have sales (tickets, luxury boxes, concessions and logo product sales, and sponsor ads); they also have revenue sharing and TV and cable revenue. College athletic programs and high school programs commonly have sales, school funding, donations, and fund-raising. Research supports that good athletic programs lead to increased athletic donations and increased academic support.[47] Some teams, primarily large NCAA Division IA teams, get to enjoy large sums of money from TV, cable, and merchandise. The University of Notre Dame receives U.S.$9 million a year in television revenues from NBC to broadcast its football games. The University of Texas is regularly counted as the most valuable college franchise, worth $139 million. Texas' worth was a combination of ticket sales, club seats, luxury seats, and sponsorship from Coca-Cola, Pepsi, and Nike.[48] You may think there is big money to be made in college sports, but the reality is that only 22 of 337 Division I colleges (6.5%) made a profit in 2011.[49] Even if one or two teams are making money, they have to support all the teams that lose lots of money. So thousands of college athletic department budgets are very heavily subsidized with funds outside the athletic department.

Revenue forecasts project and then total all sources of income. Marketing commonly provides revenue figures for the entire firm. Revenue forecasts are therefore primarily built on sales forecasts (chapter 14). In one sense, the sales forecast is the building block on which all budgets are based. Major sources of revenue at the Ranch, by department, include membership, golf green and practice fees, restaurant, pub, functions, and golf shop.

Budgeting Expenses

Operating budgets use expense projections to allocate total operating spending for the year. It is true, of course, that controlling expenses is important. Each functional area has an operating budget. Because of the systems effect, every functional-area budget affects the others. The operations department needs sales forecasts to determine how many products or services to produce (and to estimate the related expenses of doing so). The HR department needs staffing requirements before it can determine how many people it needs to hire (and to estimate the related expenses of doing so). And so it goes through every functional area and every department. Therefore, it is imperative that managers share information.

Things can happen that increase expenses dramatically. For example, free agency in the NHL, NFL, and MLB increased the cost of players, a cost that was passed on to fans through increased ticket and concession prices. The average NHL team values hit a record U.S.$240 million, but operating income (revenues minus expenses) fell 21% thanks to soaring player salaries.[50] A large unexpected jump in energy cost can ruin a budget. Ticket scalping has cost teams and fans who buy tickets. Major expenses at the Ranch include golf course maintenance, building maintenance, purchasing for all departments (fertilizer and chemicals, food and beverages, clothes and golf equipment), management and administrative expenses, employee compensation, and energy.

LEARNING OUTCOME 5

Differentiate between static and flexible budgets and between incremental and zero-based budgets.

Types of Operating Budgets

Two costs are important in operating budgets. *Fixed costs* are costs that don't change as business activity fluctuates. The rent remains the same regardless of whether the facility is used once a year or every day. *Variable costs*, however, do change as business activity fluctuates. The total cost of sales catalogs and mailing increases or decreases as the number printed and mailed changes.

Static Versus Flexible Budgets

Static budgets have only one set of expenses, whereas flexible budgets have a series of expenses for a range of activities. Static budgets are appropriate in stable environments in which demand for the product is unchanging. Flexible budgets are appropriate in turbulent environments in which demand for the product varies dramatically. With spreadsheet software, it is easy to make flexible budgets because as you change the "what if scenarios," all the calculations change for you. The Ranch has a static budget for each month, which it tries hard to meet.

Incremental Versus Zero-Based Budgets

These two types of budgets differ in how allocations are justified. With incremental budgeting, justification of funds from past budget periods and approval of previously allocated expenses are not required; only new expenses are justified and approved. With zero-based budgeting (ZBB), all expenses are justified and approved with each new budget. That is, ZBB assumes that the previous year's budget should not be the base on which next year's budget is constructed. Zero-based budgets focus on the organization's mission and objectives and what it will cost to achieve them. ZBB is especially appropriate in turbulent environments in which some departmental activities or products are increasing dramatically and others are decreasing.

Activity-Based Cost Accounting

Activity-based cost accounting (ABC) allocates costs by tasks performed and resources used. ABC is not as widely used as the preceding approaches. However, it is particularly useful to organizations that produce numerous goods and services whose production requires a wide diversity of tasks and resources. For example, recreation facilities offer a variety of services. Some are simple activities that use few resources and take little time (such as a weekly exercise class for 10 adults—about 3 hours a week). Others use many resources and take a lot of time (such as a sport camp for 300 campers—an all-summer endeavor). How does the facility calculate the cost of these two services? Eight times the cost of the weekly exercise class does not accurately reflect the expenses that will be incurred in the more complex summer camp.

TIME-OUT 9 Identify the major sources of revenue and expenses at your firm or team.

Capital Budgets

◀ LEARNING OUTCOME 6
Explain how capital budgets and operating budgets differ.

An important part of the master budget process is to estimate funds for capital expenditures. **Capital budgets** allocate funds for improvements. It takes money to make money; that is what capital budgeting is all about.

Capital expenditures are used to purchase or improve long-term assets. These are the assets from which the organization expects to receive benefits for several years, that are paid for over several years, and that are depreciated over several years. They include land, new buildings, new stadiums and arenas, and—today—existing companies that the organization acquires. They also include replacements for expensive machinery and equipment or for outmoded arenas that must be updated if the organization is to remain competitive. In every case, the objective is to earn a satisfactory return on invested funds. Raising money to buy capital assets is an important function of finance.

Building new sport stadiums is a capital budget decision. Many professional teams want the city to pay for all or part of the cost of stadiums and arenas. Unfortunately, public financing of sport stadiums can be a cost that exceeds the benefits.[51] The Yankees built a new stadium and expected the increase in revenue to pay off; many figured it would be a gold mine that would dramatically improve the team's value should it be sold. The Yankees paid the entire U.S.$800 million cost of construction; New York State and New York City kicked in the remaining U.S.$400 million in the form of land acquisition, infrastructure improvements, and tax breaks.[52] At times, the economic recession and high ticket prices at the new Yankee Stadium resulted in management's having to lower prices on premium seats.[53] So the Yankees are hard at work with capital budgeting.

The British government spent an estimated U.S.$43 billion to host the Summer Olympics in 2012, calculating that it would pay off; China claims it made a profit on the Beijing Olympics in 2008.[54] NBC spent U.S.$4.38 billion to secure Olympic broadcasting rights from 2012 to 2020, expecting advertising and other revenues to exceed the cost and to return a profit on the deal. However, there are no sure capital investments, as some doubt that China made a profit, and NBC lost $223 million on the Vancouver Games in 2010.[55] To help ensure profitability, NBC aired the Olympics (TV channels and streaming) for 5,535 hours, an increase of 35% over the 2008 Olympics (3,600 hours).[56]

Financial Statements

TIME-OUT 10 Identify several of your firm's or team's capital expenditures.

◀ LEARNING OUTCOME 7
State what the three basic financial statements entail.

The last step in the master budgeting process is preparation of the projected (or pro forma) financial statements. After the other budgets are complete, the accountants put it all together to predict the financial status of the organization after a year of projected operations. In developing pro forma financial statements, accountants and managers may change other budgets, for example by cutting expenses or capital investments, to ensure financial stability in the long run. However, it is often a good decision to forgo short-term profits (even to take a loss) in preparation for long-term growth and profits, for example by increasing capital investments to take on debt that will eventually pay off. The pro forma statements are not shown to the public; only the actual statements are made public.

The financial statements lay out, for the world to see, the organization's financial health or lack of health. As such, they are used internally (as the organization monitors its own health) and externally (as investors decide whether they will invest in the firm, creditors decide whether they will lend it money, and suppliers decide whether the firm will stand good on its credit line). As you can see, financial statements are important pieces of paper. Well done, they are transparent and allow stakeholders (investors, credit markets, and suppliers) to evaluate a company's performance, its growth rate, and its reserve funds.

The three **financial statements** are the income statement, the balance sheet, and the statement of cash flow. We present them in the usual order in which they appear in companies' annual reports.

Income Statement

The income statement shows the company's revenues and expenses and its profit or loss for the stated period. In annual reports, income statements show year-to-year figures. Why? Because a U.S.$10 million profit is meaningless unless you know that the company made U.S.$5 million last year and U.S.$20 million the year before that. (Stakeholders need a context, and year-to-year numbers give them this context so that they can identify trends.) Organizations also use monthly and quarterly income statements to measure interim performance and to catch performance problems early on. Table 13.3 shows an abbreviated income statement and balance sheet for an example golf company.

What are the two primary ways organizations increase net income? They increase revenues and decrease expenses. Unfortunately, this is more easily said than done. Capital expenditures are one way in which companies endeavor to increase revenues; they use operating budgets to see where they can decrease costs.

Profit is not the same as cash. In fact, a company can be earning substantial profits and still need to borrow cash to operate. Cash therefore does not appear on the income statement; it appears on the balance sheet and the statement of cash flow. When you make a sale, you increase assets (cash—balance sheet) and increase sales (revenues—income statement).

Balance Sheet

The balance sheet lists assets, liabilities, and owners' equity. Assets are what the organization owns. Liabilities are what it owes to others. Subtract the organization's liabilities from its assets and you have the owners' or stockholders' equity (that share of the assets owned free and clear). This statement is called a balance sheet because assets always equal liabilities plus owners' equity at a particular point in time (see table 13.3).

Operating costs affect current (less than a year) assets and liabilities. Capital expenditures affect long-term assets and liabilities in the form of property or plant and equipment. Long-term liabilities are the payments (such as mortgage payments and bond debt) that the organization has contracted for in order to purchase major assets (capital budget).

Statement of Cash Flow

This statement shows cash receipts and payments for the stated period. You can't pay your bills without cash flowing into the firm,[57] and you can't get credit and bank loans without showing steady cash flow.[58] So you need to keep tabs on cash flow.[59] This statement

TABLE 13.3 Income Statement and Balance Sheet for The Golf Company

The Golf Company Income Statement

	Dec 11	Dec 10	Dec 09
Revenue	886.5	967.7	950.8
Cost of Goods Sold	575.2	602.2	607.0
Gross Profit	311.3	365.5	343.8
Gross Profit Margin	35.1%	37.8%	36.2%
SG&A Expense	358.1	348.2	342.1
Depreciation & Amortization	38.6	40.9	40.7
Operating Income	(81.1)	(26.6)	(30.5)
Operating Margin	−9.1%	−2.7%	−3.2%
Nonoperating Income	(8.1)	(11.0)	0.0
Nonoperating Expenses	(1.1)	2.0	0.9
Income Before Taxes	(90.3)	(35.6)	(29.6)
Income Taxes	81.6	(16.8)	(14.3)
Net Income After Taxes	(171.8)	(18.8)	(15.3)
Continuing Operations	(171.8)	(18.8)	(15.3)
Discontinued Operations	–	–	–
Total Operations	(171.8)	(18.8)	(15.3)
Total Net Income	(171.8)	(18.8)	(15.3)
Net Profit Margin	−19.4%	−1.9%	−1.6%
Diluted EPS from Total Net Income	(2.82)	(0.46)	(0.33)
Dividends per Share	0.04	0.04	0.10

The Golf Company Balance Sheet

Assets	Dec 11	Dec 10	Dec 09
Current Assets			
Cash	43.0	55.0	78.3
Net Receivables	119.3	154.9	159.5
Inventories	233.1	268.6	219.2
Other Current Assets	23.9	66.1	56.0
Total Current Assets	419.3	544.6	513.0
Net Fixed Assets	117.1	129.6	143.4
Other Noncurrent Assets	190.6	210.8	219.5
Total Assets	727.1	885.0	875.9

Liabilities	Dec 11	Dec 10	Dec 09
Current Liabilities			
Accounts Payable	39.0	–	31.8
Short-Term Debt	–	–	0.0
Other Current Liabilities	128.8	175.2	119.7
Total Current Liabilities	167.8	175.2	151.5
Long-Term Debt	–	–	–
Other Noncurrent Liabilities	49.4	16.6	17.2
Total Liabilities	217.2	191.7	168.7
Shareholder's Equity			
Preferred Stock Equity	0.0	0.0	0.0
Common Stock Equity	509.9	693.2	707.2
Total Equity	510.0	693.2	707.3
Shares Outstanding (thou.)	64,886.9	64,406.4	64,472.6

All amounts (except percentages) are in millions of U.S. dollars.

commonly has two sections: operating and financial activities. Checks are considered cash. Statements of cash flow typically cover 1 year. However, monthly and quarterly statements of cash flow are also computed to measure interim performance and to stop cash flow problems. Operating costs and capital expenditures affect the statement of cash flow as revenue is received and cash expenditures are paid for. It is not unusual for firms to have uneven cash flow. For example, NHL teams take in most of their money during their season, but they have to pay the bills in the off-season with cash. Some companies need to borrow money during their off-season, which they pay back during the season.

Unfortunately, some companies spend more than they take in. Frank McCourt bought the MLB Los Angeles Dodgers with debt, added more debt, spent lavishly, and went through an ugly public divorce. He ended up putting the Dodgers in bankruptcy.[60] Prince pioneered oversized and long tennis rackets only to fall prey to better-equipped rivals Head and Wilson Sporting Goods, which both offer a wider product range. Price tried to get acquired in 2010 but received no acceptable bids, filed for bankruptcy, and was acquired by Authentic Brands in 2012.[61]

Bonds Versus Stocks

A company with a growth strategy needs money to expand. Two commonly used options for large corporations are to sell bonds and to sell stock. The sale of bonds and stocks doesn't affect the income statement, but it affects the balance sheet and cash flow statements. So what's the difference between bonds and stock? Let's say the company wants to raise $1 million.

Bonds If the company sells bonds, it must pay back the bond holders plus the rate of interest specified. The firm increases its assets of cash and its liabilities by $1 million. No ownership in the company has been given away. Bonds have been sold to raise money for sport stadiums.

Stock If the company sells stock, it never has to pay back the stockholders because they become owners of the company. The firm increases its assets of cash and its owners' equity by $1 million. So if you buy stock, you hope that the value of the stock goes up and that the company will pay dividends, but you can lose money if you sell the stock for less than you paid for it.

Investor owners in pro sport teams want to make a yearly profit, but they want to see the valuation of the team increase for capital gains. Manchester United soccer team is the most valuable team in all of sport at U.S.$2.235 billion.[62] Magic Johnson and the Guggenheim Baseball Management group bought the MLB Los Angeles Dodgers in 2012 for the highest price ever paid for ownership of a pro team, U.S.$2 billion. This was a premium price at 8.7 times 2011 revenue, when the last three teams had sold at about three times revenue. Whether the investment deal is a hit or strikeout depends on the TV rights in 2014.[63]

Note that the only time the company gets any money is when it first sells the stock—an initial public offering (IPO). When a stockholder sells the shares to another person, the company gets nothing and has to record the new owner of the stock. Stockbrokers make their money (commission) by buying and selling stock for their client investors.

The financial statements are prepared last because they use information from the operating and capital budgets. The cash flow statement is prepared first because it is used to prepare the other two statements. The income statement is prepared next because this information is used on the balance sheet. If the financial statements do not meet expectations, next year's capital budget

TIME-OUT
11
Does your organization make its financial statements available to the public? If so, get a copy and review them. Also, does it develop operating and capital budgets? Try to get copies of those as well. If you are not sure, ask your boss.

and operating budgets will need to be revised—hence the feedback loop in the master budget process in figure 13.5 on page 417. Revisions are common when a net loss is projected.

Human Controls

Control systems also need to be established to help employees complete their jobs properly. As a manager, to get the job done, you will have to deal with people problems.[64] This section covers the roles of properly coaching employees, providing positive feedback, and using the proper corrective actions when monitoring employees.

Coaching

Many people who hear the word *coaching* immediately think of athletes, but coaching is also an important sport management skill that is used to get the best results from each employee.[65] A great boss, like a sport coach, can inspire employees to new heights.[66] Before reading about coaching, complete the Self-Assessment on coaching to determine how well you do or can coach people to improve performance.

Coaching involves giving motivational feedback to maintain and improve performance. If you have ever had a good coach, think about what he or she did to maintain and improve your performance and that of other team members. The next time you watch a sporting event, keep an eye on the coaches and watch their technique.

The Ranch's approach to motivation is a coaching approach. Each employee goes through an extensive orientation and training program. Managers continue to motivate staff by working on the basics to continually improve performance through (coach) Pete Clark's three I's.

Importance of Motivational Feedback

◀ LEARNING OUTCOME 8
Use motivational feedback.

As implied in our definition, feedback is the mainstay of coaching and should be motivational and developmental.[67] The idea is to give more positive feedback than negative feedback. A culture of positive feedback creates an abundance of enthusiasm and energy in an organization.[68] So, cheer your people on with an immediate response to their excellent work. When athletes make good plays, the coach and team cheer them on—the same technique motivates people in the workplace.

Ineffective and frustrated managers spend more time criticizing than praising. Managers who only criticize staff undermine their motivation. Unmotivated workers play it safe, do the minimum, focus on not making errors, and cover up errors to avoid criticism—not exactly the way you want your team to work. If you find yourself criticizing more often than praising, it's time to consider what you are doing.

Now think about your best and worst bosses and coaches. Who gave you more positive feedback? For whom did you do your best work? (We think we already know the answer.) So, remember the Pygmalion effect and give praise (chapter 11). Use this coaching technique daily.

Coaching Corrective Action

Coaching is needed when performance falls below aspiration levels.[69]

Remember the performance equation (chapter 11)? Use it to think about the situation: Performance = Ability × Motivation × Resources. When ability is holding back performance, consider training. When motivation is lacking, find out why. Talk to the person—he may have some insight—and develop a plan together.

If motivation does not work, you may have to use discipline, which we discuss later. When resources are lacking, work to obtain them. Management by walking around (discussed soon in this section) increases your knowledge and thus will give you ideas for possible solutions, whether they are resource problems or ability or motivation problems.

Coaching

For each of the following 15 statements, select the response that best describes your actual behavior or what you would do when coaching others to improve performance. Place the number 5, 4, 3, 2, or 1 on the line before each statement.

Describes my behavior				Does not describe my behavior
5	**4**	**3**	**2**	**1**

_____ 1. I know when to coach, counsel, and discipline people.

_____ 2. I don't try to be a psychological counselor or offer advice to solve personal problems, but I do refer people who need help to professionals.

_____ 3. I deal with mistakes as a learning opportunity, rather than a reason to place blame and punish.

_____ 4. I make sure people are clear about my expectations, rather than let them guess.

_____ 5. I take action to make sure people do at least the minimum, rather than let them perform below standard.

_____ 6. I maintain a relationship with people when I coach them, rather than let coaching hurt our relationship.

_____ 7. I coach soon after the incident, rather than wait for a later time to talk about it.

_____ 8. I focus on showing concern for people and helping them improve performance for their own benefit, rather than to get what I want done.

_____ 9. I show people how they can benefit by taking the action I suggest, rather than just tell them what to do.

_____ 10. I offer very specific suggestions for improving, rather than say general things like "You're not doing a good job" or "You need to do better."

_____ 11. I don't use words like "always" and "never" when talking about what the person does that needs to be improved. For example, I would say, "You were late twice this week," not "You're always late" or "You're never on time."

_____ 12. I focus on the behavior that needs to be improved, rather than on the person. For example, I would say, "Why not set an earlier time to get to work—say, 7:45 instead of 8:00?" not "Why can't you be on time?"

_____ 13. I walk around and talk to people to help them improve, rather than wait for them to come to me.

_____ 14. I feel comfortable giving people feedback, rather than feeling uncomfortable or awkward.

_____ 15. I coach differently depending on the problem, rather than always in the same way.

_____ Total score

To determine your coaching score, add up the numbers for your 15 answers (between 15 and 75) and place the score on the total score line and on the following continuum.

Effective coaching							Not effective coaching
75	**70**	**60**	**50**	**40**	**30**	**20**	**15**

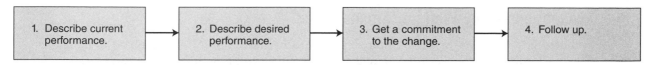

FIGURE 13.6 The coaching model.

The Coaching Model

What do managers often shrink from doing? In three words, advising problematic employees. Managers all too often hesitate to work with an employee who needs help. They hope that the person will somehow turn around on her own, but they find that the situation often worsens. When you see that an employee is having problems, you need to take corrective action quickly. Part of the problem is that managers don't know how to coach. Coaching is easier if you view it as a way to provide ongoing feedback to help people improve their performance[70]—and if you follow the steps in the coaching model in figure 13.6.

1. Describe current performance. Using specific examples, describe the current performance that needs to be changed. Tell the person, in a positive way, exactly what he is doing that needs to be improved.

- Don't say: "You're picking boxes up wrong."

- Do say: "Billie, there's a more effective and safer way to pick boxes up than bending at the waist."

2. Describe desired performance. Tell the person in detail exactly what the desired performance is. Explain how he will benefit from following your advice. If the problem is ability related—that is, lack of knowledge or experience—demonstrate the proper way.[71] If the problem is motivational, simply describe the desired behavior and ask the person to state why the behavior is important.

- Ability: "If you squat down and pick up the box using your legs instead of your back, it is easier and there is less chance of injuring yourself. Let me demonstrate for you."

- Motivation: "Why should you squat and use your legs rather than your back to pick up boxes?"

3. Get a commitment to the change. When the issue is ability, it usually isn't necessary to get a verbal commitment to the change if the person seems willing to make it. However, if the person defends his way and you're sure it's not effective, explain why your proposed way is better. If you cannot get the person to understand and agree, get a verbal commitment. This step is also important if the issue is motivation, because if employees are not willing to commit to a change, they will most likely not make the change.

- Ability and motivation: "Will you squat rather than use your back from now on?"

4. Follow up. Remember, most employees will do what managers inspect (imposed control), not what they expect. Therefore, you're doing both yourself and the employee a favor by following up to ensure that change is occurring as desired. In ability situations (and if the person was receptive in step 3), say nothing—just watch to be sure the task is done correctly in the future. Coach again, if necessary. In motivation situations, clearly state that you will follow up and that there are consequences if performance doesn't improve.

- Ability: Say nothing, but observe.

- Motivation: "Billie, picking up boxes using your back is dangerous; if I see you doing it again, I will take disciplinary action."

Management by Walking Around

Coaching focuses on helping employees succeed by monitoring performance through giving feedback to praise progress and to redirect inappropriate behavior, and you can extend coaching with management by walking around.[72] **Management by walking around (MBWA)** is about listening, teaching, and facilitating.

1. If you want to find out what's going on, listen more than you talk, and be open to feedback. Learn to talk last, not first. Open with a simple question like "How are things going?" Then use the communication skills you honed in chapter 10 as you pry useful information out of everyone.[73]

2. Teaching is not about telling people what to do—it's about training (chapter 7), so use job instructional training when needed. Teaching is also about development by empowering employees to solve their own problems. Therefore, coaches say, "What do you think should be done?" and "How can we improve?"

3. Facilitating is about taking action that helps people to do their jobs and to satisfy customers. The focus is on improving the system. Your team members know their jobs and they know (often all too well) the stumbling blocks, because they deal with them every day. Your job is to run interference and to remove stumbling blocks so that the team can get on with its business.

Now it's your turn to give feedback. Tell the team what is going to be done about the problem—if anything—and when. If you listen but don't facilitate, your staff will stop talking and you will lose your most important source for improving the system. The Clarks and their managers are classic MBWA-ers. They are constantly around and following the three steps of MBWA with both employees and golfers. The result? A four-star golf course almost from the get-go and a highly motivated staff.

Problem Employees

When you coach, you are fine-tuning the performance of someone who wants to improve. When you counsel and discipline, you are dealing with a very different situation—a problem employee who is not performing to standard or who is violating standing plans.

Who are the problem employees? They fall into four categories:

1. Employees who do not have the *ability* to meet the job performance standards. This is an unfortunate situation, but after training reveals that such employees cannot do a good job, they should be dismissed. Many employees are hired on a trial basis; this is the time to say, "Sorry, but you have to go."

TIME-OUT 13 Think about a problem employee or teammate whom you are aware of. Describe how the person affected your department's or team's performance.

2. Employees who do not have the *motivation* to meet job performance standards. These employees often need discipline.

3. Employees who intentionally *violate standing plans*. As a manager, it is your job to enforce the rules through disciplinary action.[74]

4. Employees with *problems*. These employees may have the ability but have a problem that affects job performance. The problem may not be related to the job. It is common for personal problems, such as child care and relationship or marital problems, to affect job performance. Employees with problems should be counseled before they are disciplined.

Review the list of problem employees you may encounter. It is not always easy to distinguish between the types of problem employees. Therefore, it is often advisable to start with coaching, then move to counseling, and finally change to discipline if the problem persists.

Management Counseling

◀ LEARNING OUTCOME 9
Understand the role of EAP staff.

Organizations realize that part of their job is to help employees deal with their problems. When most people hear the term *counseling,* they think of professional therapy. People who are not professional counselors—and that includes managers—should not attempt this level of help. Management counseling is something very different; it consists solely of recognition and referral. The manager's job is to refer employees to professional counselors.

Management counseling helps employees recognize that they have a problem and then refers them to the employee assistance program. **Employee assistance programs (EAPs)** help employees get professional assistance in solving their problems.

More and more companies are offering EAPs, because they improve employee retention and productivity. The San Francisco Giants have one of the best-organized EAP programs in professional sport. Michael Paolercio is the director. The program provides work-life and wellness services for ballplayers and full-time, year-round employees including managers, coaches, scouts, retirees, game-day workers, and family members. Paolercio has earned the trust of the Giants community with regard to helping them with their mental health screenings, wellness programs such as yoga and massage, legal and financial referrals, mental health and substance-abuse crisis interventions, and informal consultations.[75]

Former Cleveland Indians pitcher Sam McDowell became a certified and licensed therapist in sport psychology and addiction after his retirement. For more than 14 years, he was the director of EAPs and sport psychology programs for the Texas Rangers and Toronto Blue Jays. The recent suicide of former NFL player Junior Seau led McDowell to write a passionate letter about how B.A.T. (Baseball Assistance Team) has helped former baseball players by providing medical, financial, and psychological assistance.[76]

Managers need to confront employees quickly but give them a chance to improve, and getting the problem employee to agree to counseling is sometimes necessary. Ozzie Guillen, former coach of the Chicago White Sox, was ordered to receive sensitivity training from the MLB EAP staff. The commissioner of baseball, Bud Selig, believed this was necessary after Guillen often made slurs during media sessions.[77]

Management counseling is not about delving into someone's personal life. There is a line here that must not be crossed—for the employee's sake and also for yours. You don't need to know the details; in fact, it is better that you not know them. Knowing too much can hurt your effectiveness as a manager, and it is not your job. Issues of privacy play a big role in these situations; that's why your organization has a separate department—the assistance program. Your role is simply to help the person realize she has a problem that is affecting her work.

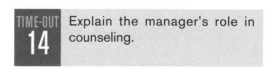

TIME-OUT 14 Explain the manager's role in counseling.

So, don't give advice. If you do, you are putting both yourself and your organization at risk for litigation. To make the referral, you can say, "Are you aware of our employee assistance program? Would you like me to set up an appointment with Jean in HR to see if she can help?" If job performance continues to suffer, then discipline becomes an appropriate choice.

Remember, your first obligation is to your organization—it is not to individual employees. Not taking action because you feel uncomfortable approaching people, because you feel sorry for them, or because you like them helps neither you nor the employees. Don't forget that problem employees cause more work for you and for the rest of the team. This is not good for morale. Taking action is the right thing to do; just make sure it is the right action.

Problem Employees

The late employee	The insubordinate employee
The absent employee	The employee who steals
The dishonest employee	The sexual or racial harasser
The violent or destructive employee	The safety violator
The alcoholic or drug user	The sick employee
The nonconformist	The employee who's often socializing or doing personal work
The employee with a family problem	

Discipline

You've taken the coaching route. You've taught and facilitated and fed back positive reinforcements. And you've been down the EAP road. Nothing has worked. Now what do you do? You take disciplinary action. **Discipline** is corrective action to get employees to meet standards and to follow the rules. Discipline can be effective if it makes the person realize the seriousness of the situation. The first objective of discipline is to change behavior.[78] There are some important secondary objectives. One is to let employees know that action will be taken when rules are broken or performance is not met. The second objective is to maintain your authority when challenged.

When you find yourself having to take disciplinary action, it's time to involve your boss and the HR department to make sure you discipline appropriately without violating any company policies or laws. HR procedures outline grounds for specific sanctions and dismissal based on the violation. Common offenses include breaking rules, theft, sexual or racial harassment, substance abuse, and safety violations. The following list provides some guidelines.

Progressive Discipline

Many organizations use a series of escalating actions. Progressive discipline typically occurs in this order: (1) oral warning, (2) written warning, (3) suspension, and finally (4) dismissal. For most violations, all four steps are followed. However, for certain violations, such as theft or sexual or racial harassment, offenders may be dismissed immediately. Documenting each step is extremely important. At the Ranch, employees are well trained and clearly informed

Guidelines for Legal and Effective Discipline

- Clearly communicate the standards and standing plans to all employees.
- Be sure that the punishment fits the violation.
- Follow the standing plans yourself.
- Take consistent, impartial action when the rules are broken.
- Discipline immediately, but stay calm and get all the necessary facts before you discipline.
- Discipline in private.
- Document discipline.
- When the discipline is over, resume normal relations with the employee.

APPLYING THE CONCEPT 13.3

Guidelines for Effective and Legal Discipline

Use the guidelines for legal and effective discipline to identify which guideline is or is not being followed in each situation.

_____ 11. To yell that loudly, the coach must have been very upset about our not trying hard enough.

_____ 12. It's not fair. The star players come back from winter break late all the time; why can't I?

_____ 13. When I miss my defensive assignment, coach reprimands me. When Chris does it, nothing is ever said.

_____ 14. Coach gave me a verbal warning for smoking inside the locker room, which is a restricted area, and placed a note in my file.

_____ 15. I want you to come into my office so that we can discuss this matter.

of expectations. Employees who do not meet the standards are warned and terminated if they don't perform to standard. The managers, with the Clarks, are involved in performance appraisals, discipline, and termination.

When You Have to Discipline Someone

The steps shown in figure 13.7 set up an effective model for you to use to discipline an employee. These steps would also serve a team well if it is faced with low performance by a team member.

1. Refer to past feedback. Begin by refreshing the employee's memory. Refer to the coaching or counseling the person has received or to the fact that the person has been warned about breaking the rule in question.

- Prior coaching: "Billie, remember my showing you the proper way to lift boxes with your legs?"

- Rule violation: "Billie, you know the safety rule about lifting boxes with your legs. We discussed it two days ago—do you remember?"

2. Ask why the undesired behavior was used. Giving the employee a chance to explain the behavior is part of getting all the necessary facts before you discipline. The employee may or may not have justification for the behavior.

Example: "Two days ago you agreed to lift boxes by the rules. Is there a good reason you're still using your back?"

3. Give the discipline. Review the guidelines set up by your HR department and follow them carefully. If there is no good reason for the undesirable behavior, give the discipline. The discipline will vary with the stage in the disciplinary progression.

Example (first discipline): "I'm giving you a verbal warning."

4. Get a commitment to change and develop a plan. If the employee refuses to commit to change, make note of this in the critical incidents file and follow your organization's

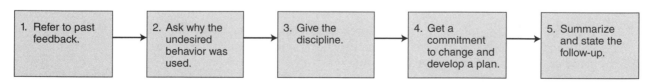

FIGURE 13.7 The disciplining model.

next procedure. If a plan was developed in the past, review it with the employee, discuss what changes might make the plan more useful, and ask the person to commit to it again. Offer recommendations for change and develop a new plan, if necessary.[79] Statements like "Your previous attempt didn't work; there must be a better way" are often helpful. With a personal problem, offer professional help again.

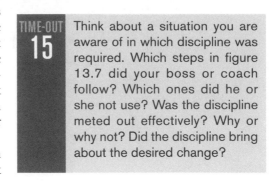

TIME-OUT 15

Think about a situation you are aware of in which discipline was required. Which steps in figure 13.7 did your boss or coach follow? Which ones did he or she not use? Was the discipline meted out effectively? Why or why not? Did the discipline bring about the desired change?

Example: "Is there something you can think of that will help you remember to lift boxes the correct way?" "Will you lift with your legs from now on?"

5. Summarize and state the follow-up. Part of your follow-up is to document the discipline. If a warning or suspension has been triggered, get the employee's signature to document that the employee was warned and knows the consequences if the behavior doesn't change.

Example: "To recap our discipline session, you agree to use your legs instead of your back when you lift. I've given you a verbal warning. If I catch you again, you will be given a written warning, which is followed by a suspension, and you will be fired if necessary. I want you to sign this document summarizing our discipline session that will be placed in your personnel file."

Productivity

All of us would like to get paid more. However, if we earn more without producing more, the only way for the company to maintain profits is to raise prices to offset the increased wage cost. Not only does this cause inflation, but increased prices damage an organization's competitiveness. For example, as pro athlete salaries increase, so does the cost of tickets and other expenses of attending the game and buying apparel. Some fans come to fewer games or stop coming. Therefore, increasing productivity is the area that organizations continually do battle in as they wage their war against loss of market share and inflation. Effective managers understand how to measure productivity, and they constantly look for ways to increase productivity.[80] Unfortunately, ways to reduce cost include layoffs, downsizing, early retirement buyouts, and restructuring, which tend to occur during recessions.[81] And many people who are unemployed can't afford to attend pro sports.

TaylorMade-adidas Golf has been successful in a perpetual race to increase the distance (productivity) people can hit a golf ball with its golf clubs.[82] Gatorade has a Sports Science Institute in Florida to improve Gatorade drinks so that they better enhance athletes' performance. It developed the G, with before-, during-, and after-workout drinks in the G Series, G Series Fit, and G Series Pro lines.[83] The Ranch maintains productivity by keeping players to average game-completion times. Slow players or parties hold up players in the pipeline and can hurt customer satisfaction. The golf cars' GPS systems tell the players if they are on schedule, and player assistants help players stay on schedule.

Measuring Productivity

You can improve only what you measure.[84] Measuring productivity can be complex, but it doesn't have to be. In this section, we outline a simple yet realistic approach that you can use on the job to measure productivity.

Productivity measures performance by dividing outputs by inputs. Let's say Exxon-Mobil wants to know the productivity of its new Formula One racing fuel. In this test, the Formula

One car traveled 1,000 miles (1,609 kilometers) and used 100 gallons (378.5 liters) of the new fuel. Its productivity was 10 miles to the gallon (16 kilometers/3.78 liters):

Productivity = Output = 1,000 miles traveled = 10 miles per gallon

Input 100 gallons of fuel

Now let's say a Wilson Sporting Goods manufacturer wants to know the weekly productivity of its accounts payable department. We are going to simplify things here a bit, but this example will give you an idea of how to get a realistic idea of your group's productivity rate.

1. Select a time period, such as an hour, a day, a week, a month, a quarter, or a year. In this example, the accounts payable manager decides to look at a week.

2. Determine how many bills (outputs) were sent out during that period. The manager checks the records and finds out that the three-person department sent out 800 bills last week.

3. Determine the "quick cost" of sending out the bills (inputs). Determining costs can be complicated if you determine total cost, which includes overhead, depreciation, and many other variables. In this instance, our manager uses only direct labor charges for the three employees, who are each paid U.S.$10 an hour. They all worked 40 hours during the week in question for a total of 120 hours. The total quick cost then is U.S.$10 an hour × 120 hours, or U.S.$1,200.

4. Dividing the number of outputs (bills sent out) by the inputs (direct labor charges) gives the productivity ratio, 0.67 (800/U.S.$1,200 = 0.666), which of course can be expressed as a percentage (67%). It can also be stated as labor cost per unit. To determine labor cost per unit, simply reverse the process and divide inputs by outputs (U.S.$1,200/800). It thus cost U.S.$1.50 to send out each bill.

Calculating Productivity Rate Changes

Our manager now sets the 0.67 productivity rate as the base rate. In the next week, the accounting department again sends out 800 bills, but because of computer problems, the three employees have to work overtime at an additional cost of U.S.$100. The productivity rate thus decreases to 0.62 (800/U.S.$1,300). The labor cost per unit goes up to U.S.$1.63 (U.S.$1,300/800). To determine the percentage change, use the following formula:

Current productivity rate (62%) – Base productivity rate (67%) = Change (5%)

Change/Base productivity rate (5/67) = 0.0746, or a 7.46% decrease in productivity

Production Versus Productivity

It is important to think in terms of your productivity rate and not just in terms of increasing output, because productivity can decrease even though output increases. Suppose Wilson's accounts payable department sends out 850 bills, but doing so requires 10 hours of overtime (time-and-a-half at U.S.$15.00 an hour × 10 hours = $150)—productivity has decreased to 63%, which is below the 67% standard (850/1,350). In other words, if you measure only output and it increases, you can be fooled into thinking you are doing a better job, when in reality you are doing a worse job.

Increasing Productivity

◀ LEARNING OUTCOME 10
State three ways to increase productivity.

There are three ways to increase productivity:

- Increase output value and maintain input value ($\uparrow$ O $\leftrightarrow$ I).
- Maintain output value and decrease input value ($\leftrightarrow$ O $\downarrow$ I).
- Increase output value and decrease input value ($\uparrow$ O $\downarrow$ I).

APPLYING THE CONCEPT 13.4

Measuring Productivity

The standard monthly productivity rate in the golf club department is as follows:

Productivity = Outputs / Inputs = 6,000 units / U.S.$9,000 cost = 0.67, or 67%

Calculate the current productivity rate for each month and show it as both a ratio and a percentage. Then calculate the percentage productivity change compared to the standard, stating whether it was an increase or a decrease.

16. January: outputs = 5,900; inputs = U.S.$9,000

ratio: _____ percent: _____; change: _____ %

_____

17. February: outputs = 6,200; inputs = U.S.$9,000

ratio: _____ percent: _____; change: _____ %

_____

18. March: outputs = 6,000; inputs = U.S.$9,300

ratio: _____ percent: _____; change: _____ %

_____

19. April: outputs = 6,300; inputs = U.S.$9,000

ratio: _____ percent: _____; change: _____ %

_____

20. May: outputs = 6,300; inputs = U.S.$8,800

ratio: _____ percent: _____; change: _____ %

_____

Always compare your productivity to the standard and during one period to previous periods, because productivity during any given period by itself is meaningless. What is important is whether productivity is changing for the better or worse or whether it is stagnating. Unfortunately, as your level of productivity increases, it often becomes increasingly difficult to continuously improve it.[85]

Measuring Functional-Area Productivity

Productivity measures are important for another reason—they indicate how well an organization is being managed. It therefore behooves organizations to look at functional-area productivity as they strive to drive down costs.[86] Table 13.4 lists the various ratios that are used to measure functional areas. The numbers used to calculate the financial ratios are taken from the income statement and balance sheet (examples of which are shown in table 13.3 on p. 421). As indicated in table 13.4, these ratios are easy to calculate and understand, and they are used commonly as controls. To make meaningful year-to-year comparisons, analysts commonly use 3 years of data.

TABLE 13.4 Financial Ratios

Functional area	Ratio	Calculation	Information
Profitability	Gross profit margin	$\dfrac{\text{Sales-COGS}}{\text{Sales}}$	Measures efficiency of operations and product pricing.
	Net profit margin	$\dfrac{\text{Net profit and income}}{\text{Sales}}$	Measures product profitability.
	Return on investment	$\dfrac{\text{Net profit and income}}{\text{Total assets}}$	Measures return on total capital expenditures or ability of assets to generate a profit.
Liquidity	Current ratio	$\dfrac{\text{Current assets}}{\text{Current liabilities}}$	Measures ability to pay short-term debt.
	Quick ratio	$\dfrac{\text{Current assets-inventory}}{\text{Current liabilities}}$	This is a stronger measure of bill-paying ability, because inventory may be slow to sell for cash.
Leverage	Debt to equity	$\dfrac{\text{Total liabilities}}{\text{Owners' equity}}$	Shows proportion of the assets owned by the organization.
Operations	Inventory turnover	$\dfrac{\text{COGS}}{\text{Average inventory}}$	Shows how efficient the organization is in controlling its investment in inventory. The larger the number, the better, because this means that products are being sold faster.
Marketing	Market share	$\dfrac{\text{Company sales}}{\text{Total industry sales}}$	Measures the organization's competitive position. The larger, the better, because this means the organization is outselling its competitors.
	Sales to presentations	$\dfrac{\text{Sales completed}}{\text{Sales presentations made}}$	Shows how many presentations it takes to make a sale.
Human resources	Absenteeism	$\dfrac{\text{Number of absent employees}}{\text{Total number of employees}}$	Shows the ratio of employees not at work for a given time period.
	Turnover	$\dfrac{\text{Number of employees leaving}}{\text{Total number of employees}}$	Shows the ratio of employees who must be replaced for a given period (usually 1 year).
	Workforce composition	$\dfrac{\text{Number of a specific group}}{\text{Total number of employees}}$	Shows the ratio of women, Hispanics, African Americans, and so on in the organization's workforce.

COGS = cost of goods sold.

Measuring the Organization's Overall Performance

Financial ratios indicate the organization's overall performance; they do not measure the performance of the finance area itself. Thus, the profitability ratios are based heavily on sales, which is a marketing function. However, the performance of the other functional areas is affected by how well finance does its job. Finance controls the budget, which helps (or hinders) the other functional areas. Marketing sells the products on credit, and finance (through its accounting function) collects the payments and pays for purchases made throughout the organization. Management uses a variety of financial ratios and percentages to measure performance at the Ranch.

Measuring Productivity in Marketing and Operations

Marketing and operations in an organization can be likened to the heart and lungs in the body. The key to business success is for these two areas, with the aid of the other functional areas, to continually increase customer value. If marketing and operations do not work well and do not work well together, the organization may fail to thrive. Gross profit margin and net profit margin are also considered marketing ratios because they are based on sales.

Inventory turnover is primarily the responsibility of operations. However, the operations department depends on marketing's sales forecasts, which it uses to decide how much product to produce. If sales forecasts are too optimistic, operations will produce too much product, which will sit in inventory, which decreases the turnover rate.

As we bring this chapter to a close, you need to understand types of controls, the control process, and frequencies and methods of controls; see table 13.2 for a review. Budgeting is also important. The master budget includes operating budgets, capital budgets, and financial statements; see figure 13.5 for a review. You should develop your coaching skills and improve your ability to handle problem employees with management counseling and discipline, when needed; learn figures 13.6 and 13.7. Lastly, you should be able to measure productivity and know how to increase it.

@ TAKE IT TO THE NET

Please visit www.HumanKinetics.com/AppliedSportManagementSkills and go to this book's companion web study guide, where you will find the following:

A list of websites associated with the concepts in this chapter

Exercises that you will need Internet access to complete

Online versions of chapter exercises and end-of-chapter learning aids

An exercise that helps you define the Key Terms

LEARNING AIDS

CHAPTER SUMMARY

1. Explain how controls function within the systems process.

 The first stage of the systems process is inputs. Preliminary controls are designed to anticipate and prevent possible problems. The second stage is the transformation process. Concurrent controls are actions taken during the transformation to ensure that standards are met. The third stage is outputs. Rework controls are actions taken to fix an output. The fourth stage is customer or stakeholder satisfaction. Damage controls are actions taken to minimize negative impacts on customers attributable to faulty outputs. Feedback is used at each stage to improve the process to continually increase customer satisfaction.

2. Understand why feedback is a control.

Feedback is circulated through all the functional areas to improve organizational performance in the input, transformation, and output processes and to continually increase customer satisfaction.

3. Describe the control process.

The four steps in the control process are (1) set objectives and standards; (2) measure performance; (3) compare performance to standards; and (4) correct or reinforce, with a feedback loop for continuous improvement.

4. List which control methods are used with which frequency.

Self-control, clan control, and standing plans are used constantly (continuously). Routine reports, budgets, and audits are used periodically. Observation, the exception principle, special reports, and project controls are used occasionally.

5. Differentiate between static and flexible budgets and between incremental and zero-based budgets.

A static budget has only one set of expenses, whereas a flexible budget has a series of expenses for a range of activities. With incremental budgeting, past funds are allocated with only new expenses being justified and approved. With zero-based budgeting, all funds must be justified each year.

6. Explain how capital budgets and operating budgets differ.

The capital expenditures budget includes all planned major asset investments. It consists of funds allocated for investments in major assets that will last, and be paid for, over several years. The expense budget contains funds allocated to pay for operating costs during the budgeting year. With expense budgets, the focus is on cost control. With capital expenditures, the focus is on the more important role of developing ways to bring in additional revenues through new and improved products and projects that will create customer value.

7. State what the three basic financial statements entail.

The income statement details revenue and expenses and the profit or loss for the stated time period. The balance sheet presents assets, liabilities, and owners' equity. The statement of cash flow presents the cash receipts and payments for the stated time period.

8. Use motivational feedback.

The objective of coaching is to improve performance. Positive feedback, such as giving praise, motivates employees to maintain and improve their performance.

9. Understand the role of EAP staff.

The manager's role in counseling is to recognize that an employee has a problem and refer the person to the employee assistance program. EAP staff members then help employees get professional help to solve their problems.

10. State three ways to increase productivity.

To measure productivity, outputs are divided by inputs. Productivity is increased by (1) increasing output value while maintaining input value; (2) maintaining output value while decreasing input value; and (3) increasing output value while decreasing input value.

REVIEW AND DISCUSSION QUESTIONS

1. Why is damage control important?

2. Name five sport governing bodies.

3. Discuss the role of governing bodies in managing and controlling their sport.

4. Who are the primary customers or stakeholders for the outputs of operations, marketing, human resources, finance, and MIS departments?

5. Why do organizations measure performance?

6. What is shown in a performance report?

7. What is the role of reinforcement in the control process?

8. List the three constant-control methods, the three periodic-control methods, and the four occasional-control methods.

9. What are the three steps in the master budgeting process?

10. Why is the capital budget the most important budget?

11. State what the three financial statements show.

12. What is the objective of coaching?

13. How do managers commonly undermine employees' motivation?

14. What is the performance equation and how is it used with coaching?

15. What are the three activities of management by walking around, and what is the role of facilitating?

16. How do coaching, counseling, and disciplining differ?

17. Which of the eight discipline guidelines is most relevant to you personally? Explain.

18. Name the major ratio measures in finance, marketing, and human resources and explain what they measure.

19. Do you agree with the ASQ study that determined Reebok had a better quality score than Nike?

CASE

Lean and Mean Manufacturing at Rawlings

Since 1887, Rawlings Sporting Goods has been a leading manufacturer and marketer of sporting goods in the United States. Rawlings' mission has always centered on enabling participation by developing and producing innovative, high-performance equipment and protective apparel for the professional, amateur, and entry-level player. Rawlings advisors include former baseball stars and current players such as Derek Jeter.[87]

Lean manufacturing is one of the latest trends in making sure quality is built into products. Just like automobiles, sporting goods need to be built with the highest of expectations. One of the newer concepts is called lean manufacturing.

Executives at Rawlings Sporting Goods knew they were in an increasingly competitive marketplace—from the likes of Nike and Reebok. The management team decided (in a management audit) that they needed to focus on improving cost, quality, delivery, and innovation.

Rawlings was introduced to lean manufacturing in the early 1990s. The major goal of lean manufacturing might be summarized as the elimination of waste throughout the entire supply chain of an organization. Waste was eliminated not only in the production process but also in the way the managers forecast customer demand, scheduled the facilities, and programmed the operations to run different lines at once.

The entire process was measured, and improvement was noticeable. The manufacturing shop employees received extensive training. Setup time for machines was cut in half. Managers walked around the manufacturing facility and mapped the flow of materials through the process. Job functions were timed. Bottlenecks were removed. It took at least 18 months for employees to become familiar with the new methods.

One of the keys to the process was balancing supply and demand. Rawlings relied on an older Japanese method of just-in-time inventory to keep their own inventories down and yet have sporting goods available just when customers needed them. Sales, marketing, operations, and product development had to learn to communicate with each other better to improve their own knowledge of the supply and demand cycle.

K2, a leader in sporting goods manufacturing with at least 35 different brand names, ended up buying Rawlings. However, Rawlings' mission remains the same, which is to continually improve the quality of the product by using lean manufacturing techniques.[88]

In 2012, Rawlings Sporting Goods partnered with ESI for a line of electronics accessories. The new line of Rawlings-branded accessories will include headphones, ear buds, pedometers, and protective cases. Although Rawlings is moving away from sport, its goal is to be a part of its customers' on-the-go lifestyles.[89]

To learn more about Rawlings and the products it offers, visit www.rawlings.com. To watch a video of the manufacturing of a Rawlings bat, log into www.youtube.com/Rawlings1887. Look for the video "The Making of a Rawlings Wood Bat."

Case Questions

1. What type of financial control was used at Rawlings?
   a. Costs were analyzed.
   b. Discipline was instituted.
   c. Damage control was conducted.
   d. Control frequencies were instituted.

2. The employee's receiving immediate training on lean manufacturing is an example of
   a. coaching
   b. discipline
   c. damage control
   d. controlling

3. Which of the following is most likely an example of a concurrent control at Rawlings?
   a. Financial reporting was improved.
   b. Setup time was cut in half.
   c. CSFs were established.
   d. Creativity was improved.

4. Which of the following is most likely an example of a rework control at Rawlings?
   a. Bottlenecks were removed.
   b. Balance sheets were prepared.
   c. A CSF was developed.
   d. Creativity was improved.

5. Which of the following issues was not identified in the management audit at Rawlings?

   a. improving costs

   b. improving quality

   c. improving accounting

   d. improving creativity

6. Which of the following is most likely a critical success factor (CSF) at Rawlings?

   a. improving creativity

   b. preparing financial statements

   c. instituting a management audit

   d. improving quality

7. Which of the following is most likely an example of damage control at Rawlings?

   a. improving creativity

   b. implementing JIT inventory

   c. falsifying financial statements

   d. performing management audits

8. Which of the following is an example of management by walking around at Rawlings?

   a. Managers set preliminary controls.

   b. Management offers counseling.

   c. Managers visit the shop floor.

   d. Managers write financial statements.

9. Which of the following is the main goal of lean manufacturing?

   a. improving accounting procedures

   b. eliminating waste

   c. conducting managerial audits

   d. improving standards

10. How did Japanese management theory affect the Rawlings process?

    a. controlling expenses

    b. improving inventory control

    c. conducting managerial audits

    d. analyzing financial statements

SKILL-BUILDER EXERCISES

Skill-Builder 13.1: Coaching

Objective

To develop your skill at improving performance through coaching

Preparation

Review the section on coaching.

In-Class Application

Complete the preceding skill-building preparation before class.

1. Role-play (10-30 minutes): Break into groups of three and role-play the three situations, taking turns being the manager or coach and the employee. Remember that as the employee you are unwilling to follow the standing plan. The odd person out in each role-play is to observe and "coach the coach."

2. Compare student-written motivational feedback forms.

3. Conduct informal, whole-class discussion of student experiences.

The Situations

1. Employee 1 is a clerical worker in the ticket office. The person uses files, as do the other 10 employees in the department. The employees all know that they are supposed to return the files when they are finished so that others can find the files when they need them. Employees should have only one file out at a time. The supervisor notices that employee 1 has five files on the desk, and another employee is looking for one of them. The supervisor thinks that employee 1 will complain about the heavy workload as an excuse for having more than one file out at a time.

2. Employee 2 is a server in the concession area of the stadium. The employee knows that the tables should be cleaned up quickly after customers leave so that new customers don't have to sit at dirty tables. It's a busy night. The supervisor finds dirty dishes on two of this employee's occupied tables. Employee 2 is socializing with some friends at one of the tables. Employees are supposed to be friendly; employee 2 will probably use this as an excuse for the dirty tables.

3. Employee 3 is an assistant fitness instructor in a fitness center. All employees at the fitness center where this person works know that they are supposed to clean a fitness machine if a member does not. When the fitness manager arrived at the fitness center, he noticed that employee 3 did not clean machines after members used them. Employee 3 normally does excellent work and will probably make reference to this fact when coached.

Make some notes on how you will coach employees 1, 2, and 3.

1. Describe current performance.

   _____

   _____

2. Describe desired behavior.

   _____

   _____

3. Get a commitment to the change.

   _____

   _____

4. Follow up.

   _____

   _____

Observer, use the following form or use your coaching skills to develop a motivational feedback form. Feel free to research quotations of the great coaches and paraphrase them in your own coaching style.

1. How well did the manager describe current behavior?

   _____

2. How well did the manager describe desired behavior? Did the employee state why the behavior is important?

_____

3. How successful was the manager at getting a commitment to the change? Do you think the employee will change?

_____

4. How well did the manager describe how he or she was going to follow up to ensure that the employee performed the desired behavior?

_____

Wrap-Up

Take a few minutes to write down answers to the following questions:

What did I learn from this experience? How will I use this knowledge?

_____

_____

_____

_____

As a class, discuss student responses.

Skill-Builder 13.2: Disciplining

Objective

To develop your ability to discipline an employee

Preparation

Review the section on disciplining.

In-Class Application

You will discipline, be disciplined, and observe a discipline session using figure 13.7. This is a follow-up exercise to the preceding Skill-Builder.

Procedure 1 (2-4 minutes)

Break into groups of three. Form some partner pairs, if necessary. Each member selects one of the three situations from the preceding Skill-Builder. Decide who will discipline employee 1, the clerical worker; employee 2, the concession server; and employee 3, the fitness instructor. Also select a different group member to play the employee being disciplined.

Procedure 2 (3-7 minutes)

Prepare for the discipline session. Write an outline of what you will say to employee 1, 2, or 3; follow the steps in the discipline model.

1. Refer to past feedback. (Assume that you have discussed the situation before, using the coaching model.)

_____

_____

2. Ask why the undesired behavior was used. (The employee should make up an excuse for not changing.)

_____

_____

3. Give the discipline. (Assume that an oral warning is appropriate.)

_____

_____

4. Get a commitment to change and develop a plan.

_____

_____

5. Summarize and state the follow-up.

_____

_____

Procedure 3 (5-8 minutes)

a. Role-play. The manager of employee 1, the clerical worker for a ticket office, disciplines him or her as planned. (Use the actual name of the person playing the employee.) Talk—do not read your written plan. Employee 1, put yourself in the worker's position. You work hard; there is a lot of pressure to work fast. It's easier when you have more than one file. Both the manager and employee will need to ad lib.

The person not playing a role is the observer. He or she makes notes on the following observer form. For each of the steps, try to make a statement about the positive aspects of the discipline and a statement about how the manager could have improved. Give alternative things the manager could have said to improve the discipline session. Remember, the objective is to change behavior.

Observer Form

1. How well did the manager refer to past feedback?

_____

_____

2. How well did the manager ask why the undesired behavior was used?

_____

_____

3. How well did the manager give the discipline?

_____

_____

4. Did the manager get a commitment to change? Do you think the employee will change his or her behavior?

_____

_____

5. How well did the manager summarize and state the follow-up? How effective will the follow-up be?

_____

_____

b. Feedback. The observer leads a discussion of how well the manager disciplined the employee. The employee should also give feedback on how he or she felt and what might have been more effective in getting him or her to change. Do not go on to the next interview until you are told to do so. If you finish early, wait until the others finish or the time is up.

Procedure 4 (5-8 minutes)

Same as procedure 3, but change roles so that employee 2, the food server in a sport arena, is disciplined. Employee 2, put yourself in the worker's position. You enjoy talking to your friends, and you're supposed to be friendly to the customers.

Procedure 5 (5-8 minutes)

Same as procedure 3, but change roles so that employee 3, the assistant fitness instructor, is disciplined. Employee 3, put yourself in the worker's position. You are an excellent fitness instructor. Sometimes you forget to clean the fitness machines after members use them.

Wrap-Up

Take a few minutes to write your answers to the following questions:

What did I learn from this experience? How will I use this knowledge?

_____

_____

_____

_____

SPORTS AND SOCIAL MEDIA EXERCISES

1. The world of finance is a bit easier to understand because of the many blogs devoted to finance. The following link helps athletes better organize their personal finances: www.mint.com/blog/family/mintfamily-with-beth-kobliner-sports-heroes-as-financial-role-models-062012/.

2. What three suggestions does Beth Kobliner provide for athletes to follow to improve their financial situation?

_____

_____

GAME PLAN FOR STARTING A SPORT BUSINESS

Create a 1-year budget for your sport business. Be realistic in forecasting your revenues. What types of expenses will you incur with the type of business you have selected?

Facilities and Events

Controlling Planning Organizing Leading Controlling Planning Organizing Leading Controlling Planning
zing Leading Controlling Planning Organizing Leading Controlling Planning Organizing Leading C
ng Planning Organizing Leading Controlling Planning Organizing Leading Controlling Planning O
g Leading Controlling Planning Organizing Leading Controlling Planning Organizing Leading Controlling
ng Organizing Leading Controlling Planning Organizing Leading Controlling Planning Organizing Leading
lling Planning Controlling Planning Organizing Leading Controlling Planning
g Leading Controlling Planning Organizing Leading Controlling Planning Organizing Leading Controlling
ng Organizing Leading Controlling Planning Organizing Leading Controlling Planning Organizing Leading
lling Planning Organizing Leading Controlling Planning Organizing Leading Controlling Planning
g Leading Controlling Planning Organizing Leading Controlling Planning Organizing Leading Controlling
ng Organizing Leading Controlling Planning Organizing Leading Controlling Planning Organizing Leading
lling Planning Organizing Leading Controlling Planning Organizing Leading Controlling Planning
g Leading Controlling Planning Organizing Leading Controlling Planning Organizing Leading Controlling
ng Organizing Leading Controlling Planning Organizing Leading Controlling Planning Organizing Leading
lling Planning Organizing Leading Controlling Planning Organizing Leading Controlling Planning
g Leading Controlling Planning Organizing Leading Controlling Planning Organizing Leading Controlling

LEARNING OUTCOMES

After studying this chapter, you should be able to

1. describe what managing a sport facility entails;

2. describe what is involved in event planning;

3. explain how standing plans and single-use plans differ;

4. explain when, and why, contingency plans are necessary;

5. discuss how sales forecasts shape strategy;

6. explain how qualitative and quantitative forecasting techniques differ;

7. explain how the jury of executive opinion and the three sales composites differ;

8. explain how past sales and time series forecasting techniques differ;

9. know when to use planning sheets, Gantt charts, and PERT diagrams;

10. use a time log; and

11. manage your time better.

KEY TERMS

standing plans

policies

procedures

rules

single-use plans

contingency plans

sales forecast

market share

qualitative forecasting techniques

quantitative forecasting techniques

time series

scheduling

planning sheets

Gantt charts

(PERT) Performance Evaluation and Review Technique diagrams

critical path

time management

time management systems

DEVELOPING YOUR SKILLS

If you want to manage a sport facility or work as an athletic director, you're going to plan and control events at one time or another. In this chapter, you will learn about dimensions of plans and how to use scheduling tools: the planning sheet, Gantt charts, and PERT. You will also learn the methods for forecasting sales for events and ongoing business such as ticket, concession, and apparel sales. In addition, you can use the time management system and 50 tips to improve your time management skills that can help develop you into a skillful planner and controller of facilities and events.

REVIEWING THEIR GAME PLAN

Making the JCC Maccabi Games a Hit

Sport events don't just happen. Events that come off without a hitch mean that a whole team of event planners have been at work behind the scenes, scrambling, smoothing, and problem solving for months, if not years. Events like the Senior Olympics, the Goodwill Games, and the Maccabi Games, which have dramatically expanded opportunities for people of all ages and all walks of life to participate in sport, exemplify event planning at its best. An offspring of the Israeli Maccabiah Games—the "Jewish Olympics" held in Israel—the U.S. JCC Maccabi Games attract thousands of young athletes aged 13 to 16 to compete at different sites in the United States. The games have helped to develop top Jewish athletes, many of whom (Mark Spitz, 1968 and 1972 Olympics; Mitch Gaylord, 1984 Olympics; and Lenny Krayzelburg, 2000 Olympics, to name a few) went on to achieve fame in the Olympics.[1]

Stuart Greene was the games director for the 2002 and the 2011 U.S. JCC Maccabi Games in Springfield, Massachusetts. He has also helped organize games in many communities across the United States. He works hard to make sure that each event, which takes more than a year to plan, is a success. First on his agenda is securing a host community center. Greene negotiates with the management of potential host centers, alerts local governments so they can prepare for the influx of people, organizes volunteers, finds homes for the participants to stay in during the games, and secures sites at local colleges where games such as soccer and volleyball can be played. He has his committees in place by August of the previous year, a kickoff campaign ready 2 months later in October, and host families selected at least 6 months before the games begin.[2] Additionally, Greene has helped raise nearly U.S.$500,000 in donations and products to support the games.

The umbrella organization, the Maccabi World Union, is of great assistance to Greene in these endeavors. The organization circulates a yearly planning calendar to assist in the design of the games. Although Greene faces different issues with each site, he says the union's calendar gives him a strong base on which he can build a great event.

For current information on the JCC Maccabi Games in your area, visit www.jccmaccabi.org.

LEARNING OUTCOME 1 ▶

Describe what managing a sport facility entails.

Sport Facilities Management

Recall that the value of sport in each case depends on the ways in which sport is managed and that without facilities, there is no sport.[3] There are many sport management jobs related to facilities management, including facility financing, construction, facility operations, user agreements, and insurance; and the job of sport facility security has increased in importance since September 11, 2001. Sport management professionals often find careers in managing various types of facilities. Such work includes managing private health clubs, hotel fitness centers, YMCA or JCC athletic facilities; monitoring the manufacture of sporting apparel such as footwear and baseball caps; and managing anything from indoor sporting centers to entire stadiums. Sport management students can build a career working in facilities used to play the sport about which they are passionate.[4] In this chapter, we don't expect to make you an expert in facilities management. Your college or university may offer one or more courses related to facilities and events.

In chapter 4, we examined strategic planning, which focuses on the long term. In this chapter we examine operational planning (also called short-term action planning) and controlling issues. We discuss planning and controlling together because they are inseparable. When you plan, you also need to build in controls, because without controls, the plans will not meet the objective. This chapter focuses on events and facilities because most high-level sport managers at one time or another manage (plan and control) a facility and put on events. For example, your college or university might ask you to plan a three-on-three basketball tournament for charity, host a sport-related event for Special Olympics, or manage the daily operation of the fitness center on your campus.

Renovating and New Facilities

If an existing facility is not adequate and another one is not available, facility management may decide to renovate the existing facility to fit their criteria. For example, the Boston Red Sox games always sell out for the season; the team would like to have a new stadium, but it wants to stay in Boston, where little land is available. To help sell more tickets, the team's management renovated the stadium to add more seats and boxes, but it hasn't solved the problem of constantly sold-out games and disappointed fans. As of early 2012, the Red Sox ticket sellout streak was over 300 straight games, which was a MLB record.[5]

When facilities are not adequate, the firm may decide that moving to another existing facility is more cost efficient. Twenty years ago, the Naismith Memorial Basketball Hall of Fame in Springfield, Massachusetts, moved from a small building on the Springfield College (SC) campus (the actual birthplace of basketball—SC alumnus and professor James Naismith, invented basketball in his physical education class held at the YMCA in 1891 in a building owned by SC in downtown Springfield). The collection eventually outgrew the downtown facility, and in 2002 a brand-new Basketball Hall of Fame almost twice the size of the original facility opened its doors.[6] In the new Hall of Fame, fans enjoy multimedia tributes to the game's great players, coaches, and other figures of interest. The Volleyball Hall of Fame in Holyoke, Massachusetts (the birthplace of volleyball—invented in 1895 by SC alumnus William G. Morgan at the Holyoke YMCA) opened in 1987 and has had renovations over the years.[7]

At the professional level, facilities help to attract attendance, and stadium capacity is important. Economic development has provided large sections of the public with access to sport facilities. Teams constantly look for public financing of facilities, and a lot of political maneuvering is involved in getting large public expenditures for stadiums and arenas. We discussed earlier that the New York Yankees built a new stadium, ready for the 2009 season, paying the U.S.$800 million cost of construction, with U.S.$400 million kicked in by New York State and New York City in the forms of land acquisition, infrastructure improvements, and tax breaks. The cross-town New York Mets also built a new stadium. Since the early 1980s, more than a dozen NFL, MLB, NBA, and NHL franchises relocated to new cities, and an important part of the reason for moving is facilities.[8]

Hosting major sport events, including the Olympics, requires expensive investments in sport facilities, which are commonly used for local sport after the games.[9] Recall that the British government spent an estimated U.S.$43 billion to host the Summer Olympics in London in 2012.[10] Many colleges and universities have renovated and built new athletic facilities to attract top athletes, to appeal to students who want to work out, and to get more media coverage. At the high school level, facilities and event management is also critical to an athletic program's success. Teams with the best facilities may not always win, but having excellent facilities helps.

Many steps are needed in facility planning. Feasibility assessments must be conducted to determine the need and the demand of the marketplace for such a building. Funding needs to be addressed. An architect must be selected to draw a detailed conceptual design. An operational plan will be needed to implement the stages of construction. Facility audits will have to be prepared to ensure that all areas of construction are abiding by safety regulations. The Sports Management Group is a facility planner that has worked with more than 200 communities and 100 universities to help transform their vision of a sport facility into a reality.[11] These are only some of the steps required to plan a facility, and the process is a huge undertaking. However, being part of a committee overseeing the development of a modern athletic building can be very exciting and rewarding.

Managing Facilities

Once an athletic or recreational facility is open for business, the continual process of managing and training the people who will run the facility on a day-to-day basis begins. Planning daily operations also includes soliciting and scheduling various events to keep the facility's calendar full and revenues coming in. With multiple events taking place, project management skills are needed as you manage the facilities.[12]

A good example is Mike Crum, chief operating officer for the Charlotte Regional Visitors Authority and the former director of Charlotte's Auditorium-Coliseum-Convention Center Authority. The son of former University of North Carolina at Chapel Hill head football coach Dick Crum, Mike presides over a U.S.$25 million budget; 200 full-time and 1,800 part-time employees; and all maintenance and operations for the Charlotte Convention Center, Charlotte Coliseum, Ovens Auditorium, Cricket Arena, and the NASCAR Hall of Fame, which opened May 11, 2010.[13] Although Mike seriously considered coaching, he eventually decided on sport management. He desired to be in the sport business but didn't like the insecurity of coaching.

Crum spent 8 years under former director Steve Camp learning the ropes. Crum's responsibilities included expanding the convention center, building a new arena, and trying to keep the NBA's Charlotte Hornets in town (unfortunately, the Hornets did move the franchise to New Orleans). Crum characterizes his job as constantly putting out fires. The challenge is balancing political skirmishes with constantly changing demands. The job also requires that he attend a never-ending series of meetings and conferences and a large portion of the 450 concerts, ball games, and other events hosted by the arenas and auditoriums he manages. "You're never really off," Camp notes. "That takes a while to get used to. It's a big job."[14]

Hiring Professional Facility Management Firms

In 1976, the Louisiana Superdome became the first major sporting facility to use outside professionals to manage its operations. This means that the owners pay a firm to manage facility operations. Recall that the Ranch Golf Club hired the professional golf management team Willowbend.[15] Today, the Louisiana Superdome is managed by Spectator Management Group (SMG). Philadelphia-based SMG is the world leader in facility management, marketing, and development. It manages public facilities including stadiums, arenas, theaters, and exhibition and convention centers. SMG manages using long-term contracts and is responsible for both the financial and operating success of the facilities.[16]

Facility managers are challenged daily as the facility management industry continues to grow. Managers are involved in scheduling events, arranging for transportation, managing event security, and making sure food concessions are ready for game time. In the aftermath of Hurricane Katrina, SMG had to literally rebuild the Louisiana Superdome. The Dome was shut down for nearly a year, and approximately U.S.$168 million was spent to repair the entire building. The rebuilding process did allow SMG to update the Dome with the latest in high-end telecommunications and broadband connectivity.[17]

Sport Event Management

◀ LEARNING OUTCOME 2

Describe what is involved in event planning.

Sport event management is management and thus requires the four functions of management—planning, organizing, leading, and controlling. Hosting a sport event requires a great deal of planning and controlling,[18] and a mega-event, such as the Olympics, takes years of planning.[19] Sport events are often organized by committees. Sport mega-event organizing committees grow rapidly; they are temporary, and they are responsible for the symbolic significance of the event.[20] However, without effective leadership, events will fail to achieve objectives. Sport managers plan many types of events. They coordinate games, provide food for teams, arrange team transportation, hire officials, manage ticket sales, plan and monitor concession sales, schedule the various leagues, and organize tournaments. Table 14.1 gives a partial list of the activities involved in planning the Maccabi Games.

To prepare for a Maccabi Games for 1,000 athletes, the event planner must accomplish the following:

- Set an event budget in line with the overall budget allowances for events. For instance, how much money will be spent buying Ping-Pong tables or preparing the gymnasium floor for volleyball games?

- Find out whether the caterers being considered are licensed and insured. The caterer must be able to serve 1,000 athletes and provide foods that will appeal to teens. Also, the caterer needs to serve food quickly because the athletes have a very busy schedule.

- Ask the caterer for a list of past clients and check with those clients to make sure the caterer is reliable.

- Find out whether the caterer can accommodate various dietary restrictions. For instance, the Maccabi Games need to have kosher foods available for athletes who follow Jewish dietary laws.

- Plan evening social activities. Visiting local amusement parks, museums, and dance clubs costs money and requires security and transportation.

TABLE 14.1   Typical Activities in Planning the Maccabi Games

People activities	Athletic activities	Financial activities
Forming an administrative games management team (games director, assistant games director)	Training coaches and players on the rules of compassion for other coaches, athletes, and spectators	Securing sponsorship from businesses and individuals; sponsorship at the game sponsor level (top sponsors) and the gold, silver, bronze, or patron sponsor levels
Forming operations committees to organize food, water, opening and closing ceremonies, transportation, and security	Conducting tryouts for teams	Developing budgets for all the administrative functions and athletic events
Recruiting coaches for each sport	Recruiting athletes for sports that do not have enough players	Managing cash activities that range from collecting entrance fees from the athletes to paying suppliers (such as the bus company and security forces)
Developing public relations material (optional—only if you want the games to have media exposure)	Organizing a caring-and-sharing event to allow athletes to take time out from competition to volunteer within their community	Determining final revenue and cost comparison after the games have ended and the athletes have returned home

 **What activities do you think are involved in planning for parking at a Maccabi event?**

- Arrange for security. Police escorts to all events are required. Security at sporting events is monitored by having all athletes, coaches, and friends wear credentials around their necks at all times.
- Develop transportation networks to move all the athletes and coaches from venue to venue. All buses should be coordinated at a hub. Jewish Community Center buses need to run on tight schedules to ensure that athletes arrive at their events on time.

As we discussed in chapter 2, events such as the September 11 terrorist attacks have made the world of planning events much more difficult than it was in previous decades. High-profile mega-events, such as the Super Bowl, the World Series, and the Olympics, are likely targets for terrorists trying to make their point. The National Center for Spectator Sports Safety and Security (NCS4) at the University of Southern Mississippi has emerged as a leader in researching sport security awareness; improving sport security policies and procedures; and enhancing emergency response through evacuation, recovery operations, and crowd management training.

NCS4 focuses on awareness and preparedness of sport managers with regard to security at sporting events. Sport managers need to be aware of the possibility of catastrophic events and elevated terrorist activity. Because sporting and entertainment venues are places where many people come together in an exciting environment, the potential exists for damage to property, personal injury, and loss of life.

Being prepared means that key personnel responsible for security operations at sporting events be familiar with risk assessment methods. These methods include adequate training in identifying vulnerabilities and threats, improving physical protection systems, enhancing emergency response and recovery operations, and building multi-agency and evacuation capabilities.[21]

The recent NCS4 Conference covered the following sport security and safety topics:

1. Rising rates of spectator injuries and fatalities
2. Active shooter scenarios
3. Risk management
4. Americans with Disabilities Act issues
5. Weather issues
6. Game-day management issues
7. Nonattendee event spectators and their impact on security
8. Crowd control
9. Emergency management, fire, EMS, first responder unified planning[22]

Two weeks before the 2012 Summer Olympics in London began, G4S, the firm charged with providing guards to Olympic venues, told the British government that it would fall 3,000 guards short. G4S was contracted to provide 10,000 guards and could provide only 7,000. G4S was paid hundreds of millions of dollars and still failed to hire the correct number of guards. The British government had to use military and local police to overcome the shortfall.[23]

Planning and Controlling Sports

In this section, we discuss planning dimensions, standing plans and single-use plans, contingency plans, why managers don't plan and control, and flags that indicate poor planning and controlling.

Planning Dimensions

Plans are characterized by five dimensions: (1) the management level that develops the plan; (2) the type of plan—strategic or operational; (3) the scope covered in the plan—broad (for

TABLE 14.2 The Five Dimensions of Plans

Management level	Type of plan	Scope	Time	Repetitiveness
Upper and middle	Strategic	Broad	Long range	Single-use plan
Middle and lower	Operational	Narrow	Short range	Standing plan

the entire organization or a business unit) or narrow (for a functional department or part of a department); (4) the time frame—long range or short range; and (5) repetitiveness—a single-use plan or a standing plan. Chapter 4 covered the first four dimensions; here we cover the operational repetitiveness dimension. To get an overview of planning, examine table 14.2; note that upper-level managers use single-use planning more frequently than do first-level and middle managers, who typically use standing plans. Planning skills are important,[24] and strategic plans must be implemented through operational plans. It is important to plan how you will use the resources you manage.[25]

Standing Plans and Single-Use Plans

◄ LEARNING OUTCOME 3
Explain how standing plans and single-use plans differ.

Plans are either standing plans, which are designed to be used repeatedly, or single-use plans, which are designed to be used just once. Figure 14.1 gives the different uses for standing and single-use plans.

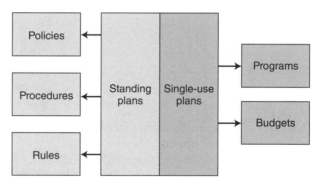

Standing Plans

Standing plans are the policies, procedures, and rules for handling situations that arise repeatedly. These plans save everyone involved

FIGURE 14.1 Uses for standing and single-use plans.

valuable time because the plans are used over and over, and they guide future decision making. Standing plans, properly used, help organizations meet objectives. Thus, achieving employee adherence to the policies, procedures, and rules contained in standing plans is critical for successful coordination and functioning within organizations.

Policies are general guidelines for decision making. They provide guidelines in implementing strategies.[26] Policies exist at all levels of organizations. Boards of directors develop broad policies, with the input of top management, for the entire organization. Managers then implement these policies. In doing so, they often establish more detailed policies for their own work groups. External groups such as governments, labor unions, and accrediting associations also dictate certain policies. Examples of typical policy statements are "We promote qualified employees from within" and "Employees will receive due process in grievances." Notice that policy statements are intentionally general—managers have much discretion in how they implement policy. As a manager, your daily decisions will be guided by policies. It will be your job to interpret, apply, and explain company policies to your team.

Procedures (also called standard operating procedures and methods) are sequences of actions to be followed to achieve an objective. Procedures are more specific than policies; they entail a series of decisions and may involve more than one functional area.[27] For example, to meet a client's needs, the personnel from sales, accounting, production, and shipping may follow a set procedure. Procedures ensure that recurring, routine situations are handled in a consistent, predetermined manner. Large organizations typically develop procedures for ticket sales, purchasing, inventory, grievances, and so forth.

Rules state exactly what should or should not be done. In addition to the company, the government and sport organizations such as the NCAA develop rules. As you can see from the following examples, rules do not allow for discretion or leeway: "No shoes on the ice." "No smoking or eating in the locker room." "Helmets are required on the field." Rule violations tend to be unethical

TIME-OUT 1 — Give an example of a policy, procedure, and rule from an organization you work for or play for.

and illegal activities.[28] Violations of rules involve penalties that vary in severity according to the seriousness of the violation and the number of offenses. As a manager, you will be responsible for establishing and enforcing rules in a uniform manner.

Policies, procedures, and rules are all standing plans. They differ in terms of their scope—policies provide general guides, procedures set a sequence of activities, and rules govern specific actions—but they all guide behavior in recurring situations as controls. It is important that you distinguish between them so that you know when you can do something your way and when you cannot.

Single-Use Plans

Single-use plans include programs and budgets that address nonrepetitive situations. Single-use plans, unlike standing plans, are developed for a specific purpose and most likely will not be used again in the same form. However, an effective single-use plan may become a model for future programs, budgets, or contracts. The plan for building the new Yankee Stadium was a single-use plan, which also required controls. Nike had to plan for the 2012 Olympics by increasing inventory of selected items related to this one-time event.[29] But the plan was based on prior Olympic game plans.

TIME-OUT 2 — Give an example of a program your firm or team has in place and assess whether it was set up following the guidelines described previously.

A program describes a set of activities designed to accomplish an objective over a specified period, which can be short (days, weeks, months) or long (years, decades). Programs are set up for objectives as varied as developing products, expanding facilities, and taking advantage of new opportunities in the environment.

When you're developing a program, you will follow these steps: (1) Set broad program objectives; (2) break the project down into specific objectives and goals; (3) assign responsibility for each objective and goal; (4) establish starting and ending times for each objective and goal; and (5) determine the resources needed for each objective and goal. This process is illustrated later when we discuss planning sheets.

We examined budgets in detail in chapter 13. The following definition will suffice for our purposes here: Budgets are the funds allocated to operate a department or program for a fixed period. Budgets are crucial tools in both planning (they help you develop realistic plans) and control (they help you assess how implementation is going), and you need to operate within your budget.[30] One of Stu Greene's most important responsibilities is to ensure that the Maccabi Games are within their budget.

What sorts of planning activities might Stu Greene engage in to accomplish this objective?

LEARNING OUTCOME 4 ▶

Explain when, and why, contingency plans are necessary.

Contingency Plans

No matter how effective your plan, there will be times when things go wrong.[31] Maybe the computer on which all the ticket information is stored goes down or your star player is sidelined for the season because of injuries. Just the fact that something is uncontrollable doesn't mean it is not foreseeable. Effective managers have contingency plans for just such situations. **Contingency plans** are alternative plans that can be implemented if uncontrollable events occur. So you need to have contingency plans,[32] which are also called *scenario plans*.[33] Wise coaches and managers take great pains to develop backup players and employees who will be ready to step in should a first-string player or employee be sidelined for any reason. For example, MLB managers keep close tabs on promising minor league players, who are their contingency plans for sidelined players.

APPLYING THE CONCEPT **14.1**

Categorizing Plans

Categorize each of the following items or statements as follows:

   a. an objective

   b. a policy

   c. a procedure

   d. a rule

   e. a program

   f. a budget

_____ 1. Programs that build healthy spirit, mind, and body for all (YMCA)

_____ 2. An athletic director's plan to improve the performance of the college's women's swim team

_____ 3. To increase our attendance by 10% next year

_____ 4. Employees will be given a 2-month maternity leave after the birth of their child.

_____ 5. Next month's cost to operate your department

_____ 6. Safety glasses are required for touring the new sport arena's construction site.

_____ 7. Leaves of absence must be approved by the manager and the forms submitted to the personnel office 1 month in advance of their effective dates.

_____ 8. Maintain the reject rate on sneakers under 1%.

_____ 9. U.S.$1,000 has been allotted for conducting a facilities management seminar.

To develop a contingency plan for your department or team, answer these three questions:

   1. What might go wrong?

   2. How can I prevent it from happening?

   3. If it does occur, what can I do to minimize its effect?

 TIME-OUT 3 Describe a situation in which a contingency plan is appropriate, and then briefly describe a possible plan for it.

Pose questions 1 and 2 to everyone involved. Your answer to question 3 is your contingency plan. It is also a good idea to talk to others both inside and outside your organization who have implemented similar plans. They may have encountered problems you haven't thought of, and their contingency plans can serve as models for yours.

Why Managers Don't Plan and Control

 How would you address a lack of time if you were in his shoes?

Stu Greene notes that by far the most common reason managers don't plan is lack of time—this is one reason he makes sure to allot time for this all-important activity.

This is also one reason we cover time management in this chapter. Many crises can be avoided, or controlled, if you carve out time for planning. Managers who always find time to do a job over but don't find the time to do it right in the first place (plan and control, in other words) are not doing the right job. Managers who plan have fewer crises; they are in better control of their departments. Managers who don't plan find themselves scrambling from one fire to the next. Planning is a continuous activity, and plans don't have to be complicated or take lots of your time. Make planning an integral part of your work routine.

If you are tempted to skip the planning stage, remember the adage "When you fail to plan, you plan to fail."

Flags That Indicate Poor Planning and Controlling

Signs of poor planning include the following:

- Unmet objectives: Deadlines, delivery dates, and schedules are not met.

- Continual crises: Every job is a rush job, and overtime is overused to complete jobs.

TIME-OUT 4 How would you rate the planning ability of a current or past boss or coach? Give examples of inadequate planning.

- Idle resources: Physical resources are idle, financial resources are accumulating interest and not being put to immediate use, or staff are kept waiting for the manager to assign tasks.

- Lack of resources: Resources are not available when needed.

- Duplication: The same task is done more than once.

Sales Forecasting Techniques

LEARNING OUTCOME 5 ▶

Discuss how sales forecasts shape strategy.

Forecasting is the process of predicting what will happen in the future. Managers pay particular attention to sales forecasts to predict consumer expenditure on sport,[34] as did Nike in predicting extra sales for the 2012 Olympics.[35] In this section, we discuss qualitative and quantitative sales forecasting techniques.

A **sales forecast** predicts the dollar amount of product that will be sold during a specified period. Accurate sales forecasts are crucial in planning because many activities hinge on them—staffing and laying off workers, ordering in adequate supplies to meet production needs, and avoiding under- and overstocking. Marketing departments typically forecast short-term sales out for 1 year. The forecasts are reviewed by the sales manager, who submits them for approval and possible adjustment by upper management. Marketing then uses the forecasts to set sales quotas. The operations department uses the forecasts to decide how much product or service to produce. Marketing also monitors inventory levels (production and customer) to adjust the forecasts as needed. Finance uses forecasts to determine how much money the organization will take in so that the finance team can budget expenditures, and also how much money the organization will need to borrow to cover short-term and long-term expenses. The human resources department uses the forecasts to increase staffing or plan for layoffs. For example, since the Yankees sold 3,765,807 tickets in 2010 and 3,653,680 in tickets 2011, the New York Yankees could forecast selling at least 3,500,000 tickets for the 2013 season.[36] The team will use this number to forecast its net revenues (which will also include advertising and media sales forecasts and team merchandise sales forecasts). Revenue forecasts help the team determine how much budget it can allocate to acquiring new talent.

Companies use total industry sales to calculate their market share. **Market share** is the organization's percentage of total industry sales. For example, Nike's market share of the global athletic shoe market grew to 18.7% in 2011.[37] Professional and trade publications forecast industry sales numbers to help organizations analyze the environment and forecast their own sales. Organizations also take local conditions, especially local competition, into account when they forecast sales.

Accurate forecasts often determine whether an organization survives tough times and whether it thrives in good times. The recession in the United States between 2007 and 2009, caused by a financial meltdown of the home mortgage industry, lingered long afterward with an unemployment rate of around 8%. The European financial crisis started with high debt levels within the Greek government. Both financial situations helped to lower financial projections in nearly all industries,[38] so some sports saw decreases in spending on tickets sales and apparel.

◄ LEARNING OUTCOME 6
Explain how qualitative and quantitative forecasting techniques differ.

Sales forecasting techniques are either qualitative or quantitative. **Qualitative forecasting techniques** primarily use subjective judgment, intuition, experience, and opinion to predict sales. (Some math is also used.) **Quantitative forecasting techniques** use objective, mathematical techniques and past sales data to predict sales. Organizations typically combine quantitative and qualitative techniques to increase accuracy.

Qualitative Sales Forecasting

As table 14.3 shows, qualitative techniques include individual opinion, a jury of executive opinion, sales force composites, customer composites, operating unit composites, and surveys. Only qualitative techniques can be used for new products or by new companies because no past sales data exist on which to base a quantitative forecast (although new companies can be influenced by all sorts of quantitative data if they are going into an established industry).

Individual Opinion

We all use our personal experience, intuition, and past events to predict what we think will happen in the future. A person starting a new business alone has no option but to form an educated (based on industry analysis) individual opinion.

Jury of Executive Opinion

In this technique, a group of managers or experts pool their opinions to forecast sales. The typical format is a group meeting in which ideas are shared and an attempt is made to reach consensus on the sales forecast. A jury of executive opinion is often used among partners, which is the form of ownership of some pro franchisers.

Sales Force Composite

◄ LEARNING OUTCOME 7
Explain how the jury of executive opinion and the three sales composites differ.

This technique combines forecasts made by each sales rep. Each rep predicts his sales for a future period; these are then totaled to give the composite forecast. Sales reps tend to know their customers and can be a good source. However, many company managers believe that their salespeople are too optimistic or that they put in for lower numbers so they can exceed quotas, so these managers balance the composite with other forecast techniques. Sales force composites work well when sales reps sell relatively expensive products (or total orders) with a clear-cut customer base or territory.

Customer Composite

In this technique, the purchase forecasts of major customers are combined. Customer composites work well when an organization has relatively few customers with large-volume

TABLE 14.3 Summary of Common Sales Forecasting

Qualitative (subjective)	Quantitative (objective)
Individual opinion	Past sales
Jury of executive opinion	Time series
Sales force composite	Regression
Customer composite	
Operating unit composite	
Survey	

sales. Nike, with large retail accounts like Modell's and Foot Locker, no doubt uses customer composites, among other techniques, to build forecasts.

Operating Unit Composite

In what situations do you think the Maccabi Games staff would use qualitative forecasting techniques?

This is the total sales forecast for multiple units. Businesses with multiple operating units, such as chain stores like Dick's and Modell's, commonly predict the sales for each operating unit and then add them to forecast total company sales.

In department composites, a business with multiple departments (such as a sporting goods store with golf, fitness, footwear, and clothing departments) can treat each department as an operating unit. In product composites, a business with multiple products forecasts sales for each product or service and combines them to create a total forecast. Adidas might choose to do this with its footwear, golf, and cycling divisions.

Survey

This forecasting technique uses mail or e-mail questionnaires or telephone or personal interviews to predict future purchases. A sample of a population (e.g., people whose hobby is kayaking) is surveyed, and a forecast for the entire population is made based on the responses. Stu Greene and the administrative committee of the Maccabi Games interviewed the leaders of a local community to gauge their interest in hosting the games. The interview results indicated that the community leaders weren't sure if their community was large enough to host an event of this magnitude. From this information, Stu determined that his strategy would be to convince the community that by working together they would be able to properly host the games.

TIME-OUT 5 Describe a situation in which your firm or team might forecast sales or team growth using qualitative techniques.

LEARNING OUTCOME 8 ▶

Explain how past sales and time series forecasting techniques differ.

Quantitative Sales Forecasting

Quantitative techniques include past sales, time series, and regression. Qualitative techniques can be combined with quantitative ones as long as the products and companies have existed long enough to accrue an adequate database for sales. Time series and regression techniques require at least a year of data, and a longer period will give better results. This technique amounts to business forecasting by data, and although numbers can't tell the future, data do help.

Past Sales

This technique assumes that past sales will be repeated or can be subjectively adjusted for environmental factors. For example, the Red Sox have sold around 2 million tickets annually for the past 20 years no matter how well the team has been performing on the field. Slight structural changes to venerable Fenway Park allowed the Red Sox to reach 3,046,443 fans in 2010 and 3,054,001 fans in 2011. The Sox's past sales therefore indicated a strong likelihood that this pattern would continue.[39]

Time Series

Time series predicts future sales by extending the trend line of past sales into the future. Sales data are collected weekly, monthly, quarterly, or yearly and then plotted to show the trend. The trend line can be extended by hand (an upward-trending line implies increasing sales, a horizontal line implies flat sales, and a downward-trending line implies decreasing sales) and the sales estimated manually, but computer time series programs are much more accurate. Time series is also used to plot seasonal trends. With time series, adjustments for environmental factors are still made but are more objective.

APPLYING THE CONCEPT 14.2

Sales Forecasting Techniques

Choose the most appropriate forecast techniques for the following organizations:

a. individual opinion

b. jury of executive opinion

c. sales force composite

d. customer composite

e. operating unit composite

f. survey

g. past sales

h. time series analysis

i. regression analysis

_____ 10. The Sports Authority footwear chain

_____ 11. AND1 sports apparel with a sales force that calls on specific stores in the sales area

_____ 12. A sole proprietor who sells her own new, very different sport cream for pain

_____ 13. Jim and Betty's mom-and-pop sport store

_____ 14. Nike sneakers

_____ 15. Ticket sales to a game between your championship team and last year's second-place finisher

Regression

Regression (using line of best fit), which is beyond the scope of this book, is a mathematical modeling technique that helps you minimize error as you find a line that best fits your sales data. Regression analysis therefore makes forecasts more accurate. As a manager, you will find regression analysis very useful (simple regression analysis is not especially difficult); make sure you master it in your statistics classes. Stu Greene uses his experience at previous Maccabi Games to forecast what will be needed at upcoming games. For instance, you can use past data on the number of athletes at previous games and the amounts of food, housing, and security and the number of venues that were used. You can adjust these figures based on the number of athletes who will be competing in upcoming games.

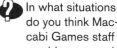 In what situations do you think Maccabi Games staff would use quantitative forecasting techniques?

Sport managers and researchers are combining forecasting techniques. For example, researchers developed a forecasting model to predict Minor League Baseball (MiLB) teams' ability to capture attendance and the long-term viability of the franchise. Regression was used to help predict the decline in attendance.[40] It is generally easier to more accurately predict sales at regularly scheduled team games than for special events.

TIME-OUT 6 Describe a situation in which your team might forecast sales or team growth using quantitative techniques.

◄ LEARNING OUTCOME 9

Scheduling Tools

Know when to use planning sheets, Gantt charts, and PERT diagrams.

After marketing completes its sales forecast and receives customer orders for the product, the operations department begins to produce the product. To ensure ready availability of products without excessive carrying costs (inventory costs), many organizations include customer input in their scheduling activities. This is particularly important with just-in-time (JIT) operations, which is a widely used method of reducing carrying costs. Scheduling is about planning and controlling to ensure that sales are completed. Scheduling is one of the most important tasks a business does.[41]

Scheduling is the process of listing essential activities in sequence with the time needed to complete each activity. The details of the schedule answer the "what," "when," "where," "how," and "who" questions. For example, Stu needs to schedule a number of things for the Maccabi Games. When will the games take place (exact dates and times)? Where are the venues located? What size buses will be needed? Who will greet the athletes and make sure they are picked up and dropped off properly? Effective schedulers define the objective to be accomplished; break it into finite, doable tasks; and make sure resources are available when needed. All managers schedule resources, including their own time, which we discuss in the next section.

Organizations routinely use computers to schedule resources. A wide variety of scheduling software is available. However, just as with math skills, you strengthen your scheduling skills if you understand the underlying concepts before you turn to computers. To get you started, we will explore simple planning sheets, Gantt charts, and PERT diagrams using the old-fashioned paper and pencil in this section.

But first let's discuss two simple, fundamental tools we use daily—our calendars and to-do lists. Don't underestimate their value in maximizing your efficiency. Planning calendars can be bought in every office supply store; a to-do list is as close as a scrap of paper; and as you know, you can use your smart phone, and there are plenty of apps to help you. Use them.

Planning Sheets

Planning sheets state an objective and list the sequence of activities, when each activity will begin and end, and who will complete each activity to meet the objective. The Maccabi operational plan shows a planning sheet for a monthly marketing letter, developed by Stu for staff and volunteers involved in the Maccabi Games. Before continuing, review the operational plan and identify the five planning dimensions involved in this plan (table 14.2). (The answers are at the bottom of the plan.) Planning sheets work best with single activities that are fairly simple and accomplished in independent sequential steps. Use the Maccabi operational plan as a template for the planning sheets you use.

Set Objectives

Obviously, the first step in planning is to clearly state the end result you desire, using the guidelines for writing objectives that we presented in chapter 4. Next, fill in who will be responsible for achieving the objective, the starting and ending dates, the priority (high, medium, low), and the control checkpoints for monitoring progress. The American Society for Quality (ASQ) compliments both Reebok-Adidas and Nike for improving their codes of conduct, objectives, and their techniques for monitoring contract manufacturers in other countries

Plan and Schedule

List the sequence of steps stating what, where, how, resources needed, and so on in the first column of the planning sheet. In the second and third columns, place the start and end time for each step. The fourth column indicates the person responsible for each step.

The planning sheet can be used for charitable events (such as walks to raise funds for cancer research) that have become quite popular and are an increasingly popular form of exercise. Participants are more attached to the goals of the event than to the sponsor images. Rays of Hope is a walk to raise money for breast cancer research. Although people continue to participate increasingly in recreation and sport, there is also an increase in participants

Maccabi Operational Plan

Objective: To mail a personalized letter to everybody involved in the Maccabi Games by the 15th of each month

Person responsible: Joel

Due date: 15th of each month

Control checkpoints: 7th and 12th of each month

Starting date: 1st of each month

Priority: High

Activities	Start	End	Who
1. Write letter	1st	2nd	Stu
2. E-mail letter for mass production	3rd or 4th		Stu
3. Print letters on Maccabi stationery using computer's mail merge feature to print names and addresses on letters and envelopes	5th	9th	Joel
4. Put Stu's stamped signature on each letter for a personal look	10th	11th	Joel
5. Stuff envelopes	10th	11th	Joel
6. Bundle to meet bulk-mailing specifications	12th	13th	Joel
7. Deliver to U.S. Postal Bulk Mail Center	13th		Joel
8. Mail letters	14th or 15th		U.S. Postal Service

Five planning dimensions are used as follows: (1) This plan was developed by Stuart. Stuart is the top-level manager who works closely with Maccabi headquarters in New York. (2) Plan type—operational. (3) Plan scope—narrow. (4) Time frame—short range. (5) Repetitiveness—standing plan.

in these types of charitable sport events. Rays of Hope had over 20,000 walkers, who raised over $1 million to help fund breast cancer research. Many nonathletes who walk 5 miles become more recreational walkers after the event is completed.[42]

 TIME-OUT 7 Describe a situation in which your team might forecast sales or team growth using quantitative techniques.

Gantt Charts

Popularized by Henry Gantt in the early 1900s, **Gantt charts** use bar graphs to illustrate progress on a project. Activities are shown vertically, and time is shown horizontally. The resources to be allocated, such as people or machines, are shown on the vertical axis. Alternatively, a variety of department projects can be shown on the same chart. Gantt charts, like planning sheets, are appropriate for plans with independent sequential steps. Two advantages of Gantt charts over planning sheets are that the chart's control is built in (progress can be seen at a glance) and you can view multiple projects on one chart. This is very helpful when you are prioritizing and scheduling activities that use the same resources.

 TIME-OUT 8 Give an example of one of your team's plans that could be tracked effectively using a Gantt chart.

Figure 14.2 is a hypothetical Gantt chart for multiple orders at a manufacturing company in its operations department. Each bar represents the start to end time, and the filled-in part represents order completion to date. The chart shows at a glance how orders are progressing. Knowing instantly when a project is behind schedule is crucial for taking corrective action.

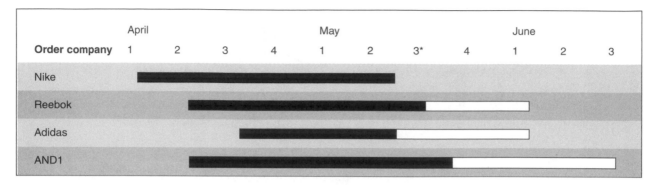

FIGURE 14.2 Multiple-project Gantt chart (order by week). *Today. The Nike project is done; Reebok is on schedule to be completed this week; Adidas is behind schedule and needs to become a high priority; AND1 is ahead of schedule.

Assume that "today" is day 1 of week 3 in May (the end of the dark color of the bar should be directly under the 3 to be on schedule). What is the status of each of the four projects on the chart in figure 14.2? The answer is in the figure caption.

Performance Evaluation and Review Technique (PERT)

Multiple activities are independent when they can be performed simultaneously; they are dependent when one activity must be completed before the next activity can begin. The planning sheet and Gantt chart are useful tools when the activities follow each other in a dependent series. However, when activities are both dependent on and independent of each other, PERT diagrams are more appropriate. **PERT (Performance Evaluation and Review Technique) diagrams** highlight the interdependence of activities by diagramming their "network." Figure 14.3 shows a PERT diagram.

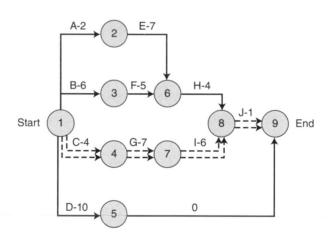

FIGURE 14.3 PERT diagram.

The key components in a PERT diagram are activities, events, time, the critical path, and possibly cost. With complex programs, it is common for one "event" to represent multiple activities. For example, in producing a racing car, building the engine (which comprises multiple tasks) might be represented as one event. Time can be measured in a variety of units from seconds to decades, depending on the tasks being tracked. The strength of PERT diagrams is that they show which tasks form the project's critical path. The **critical path** tracks the most time-consuming series of activities and therefore determines the length of time it will take to complete a project. The double arrows in figure 14.3 show this particular project's critical path. Any delay in completing the critical path delays the entire project. Many organizations are focusing on shortening the time it takes to complete each activity (time-based competition). Cost for each activity can also be tracked in a PERT diagram.

The following steps explain how the PERT diagram in figure 14.3 was completed:

1. List every activity (event) that must be completed to reach the objective. Assign each event a letter. Figure 14.3 shows 10 activities labeled A to J.

2. Determine the time it will take to complete each event. In figure 14.3, time is measured in days—A-2 (event A is slated to take 2 days), B-6 (event B, 6 days), C-4 (event C, 4 days), and so on.

3. Arrange the events in the sequence in which they must be completed. In figure 14.3, event A must be completed before event E can begin, event E before event H can begin, and so forth. If these were golf balls, before a store can stock its shelves (J), the golf balls must be ordered (A), received (E), and priced (H). Notice that activity D is independent. Arrows point in the direction of the event that follows. Numbered circles signify the completion of an event. All activities originate and terminate at a circle. In figure 14.3, 1 represents the start of the project, and 9 its completion.

4. Determine the critical path. To do this, total the time it takes for each path from start (1) to end (9). Path 1–2–6–8–9 takes 2 + 7 + 4 + 1 days, or a total of 14 days to complete. Path 1–3–6–8–9 takes 6 + 5 + 4 + 1 = 16 days; path 1–4–7–8–9 takes 4 + 7 + 6 + 1 = 18 days; and path 1–5–9 takes 10 + 0 = 10 days. The critical path (indicated by the double arrows) is therefore path 1–4–7–8–9. So this project should take 18 days to complete. If your customer has requested delivery of the product 2 weeks hence, you know instantly that you cannot make the delivery date. This enables to you to consider other strategies early on, including renegotiating the delivery date.

In summary, planning sheets and Gantt charts are typically used to develop procedures for routine standing plans, whereas PERT diagrams are used with single-use plans for complex projects with dependent activities. However, all three can be used for standing and single-use plans. There are computerized versions of Gantt charts and Pert diagrams. The first Skill-Builder at the end of the chapter gives you practice in constructing a Gantt chart and a PERT diagram by hand.

 TIME-OUT 9 Give an example of one of your team's plans that could be tracked effectively using a PERT diagram.

Time Management

How much of your time can you devote to playing and watching sports?

Time management enables people to get more done in less time with better results. The average person could improve time use by 20%.[43] Developing time management skills is

APPLYING THE CONCEPT 14.3

Scheduling Tools

Select the most appropriate scheduling tool for each situation:

a. planning sheet
b. Gantt chart
c. PERT diagram

_____ 16. A high school with six teams and three practice fields

_____ 17. Planning the construction of a new sport arena

_____ 18. Developing procedures for a new way to track ticket sales

_____ 19. A plan to restructure the athletic department at a university

_____ 20. Scheduling the use of the YMCA's weight training rooms and courses

an effective way to reduce stress (chapter 8). Time management skills can therefore have a direct effect on your productivity and on your career.[44] You need to make a conscious choice about how to spend your time and resources.[45] The idea is to work smarter, not harder, or to work less and do more.[46] The good news is that time management skills can be developed. This section is all about time, and it shows you how to analyze your use of time, learn a time management system, and select from 50 time management techniques to improve your time management skills.

LEARNING OUTCOME 10 ▶

Use a time log.

Analyzing Your Use of Time

The first step to successful time management requires that you figure out how you spend (and waste) time. We often don't realize how much time we waste until we analyze how we use our time.[47] How much time do you spend looking for a lost folder, being interrupted for trivial reasons, deleting spam e-mails, or being on hold on a phone call? If you don't think you need to analyze your use of time, think again. Everyone can benefit from this endeavor. If you are an effective user of time, you will become more effective. If you are ineffective, it's time to improve.

Keep a Time Log

The biggest mistakes people make are not knowing how much time they actually do waste and how they waste time.[48] The time log tracks your daily activities and helps you figure out "where all the time goes." You can use figure 14.4 as a template for creating your own time logs. Track your time every day for 1 or 2 weeks. (Make sure these are typical weeks. Tracking atypical weeks won't be of much use.) Take the time log with you throughout the day, and fill in each 15-minute time slot, if possible.

Starting time	Description	Evaluation of time use
8:00		
8:15		
8:30		
8:45		
9:00		
9:15		
9:30		
9:45		
10:00 (etc., to ending time)		

Daily time log for: Day _____ Date _____

FIGURE 14.4 Daily time log.

From R. Lussier and D. Kimball, 2014, *Applied Sport Management Skills, Second Edition* (Champaign, IL: Human Kinetics).

If you use a computer much of the day, services you can purchase for a low monthly fee (www.slifelabs.com, www.rescuetime.com) and websites with free downloads (manictime. com, getklok.com) will help you keep track of your time on the computer and improve your time management. Just knowing that the lengths of their sessions on Facebook or other websites are going to be recorded makes people think twice about the visit.[49]

Analyze It

After logging your time for 5 or 10 typical working days, you need to analyze your data. Using the following evaluation list and the abbreviations noted in parentheses, review your logs and answer the questions. We give you ideas for solutions in the following discussion, but first take a moment and annotate your time logs.

- How did you spend most of your time? Note how much time you spent on your high priorities (HP) and on your low priorities (LP).
- Where did you spend too much time (TT)?
- Where could you have spent more time? That is, where did you not spend enough time (NT)?
- What major interruptions (I) kept you from doing what you wanted to get done? Do you interrupt yourself by constantly checking your phone and e-mail and get sidetracked doing unimportant things, rather than staying with important things until they are done? How could you eliminate these in the future?
- What tasks could you delegate to someone else (D)? To whom can you delegate these tasks? (You learned about developing delegation skills in chapter 5.)
- How much time does your boss control (B)? How much time do your employees control (E)? How much time do others outside your department control (O)? How much time do you actually control (M)?
- How can you gain more control of your own time?
- Look for crisis situations (C). Were they caused by something you did or did not do? Do you have recurring crises? What changes can you make to help eliminate recurring crises? Do you have effective contingency plans?
- Look for habits, patterns, and tendencies. Do they help you get the job done or prevent you from getting the job done? How can you change them to your advantage?
- List three to five of your biggest time wasters (W). What can you do to eliminate them?
- Ask yourself, "How can I manage my time more efficiently?"

A Time Management System

◀ LEARNING OUTCOME 11
Manage your time better.

Are you accomplishing all the things you want to get done? If not, maybe you need a time management system.[50] The time management system we present here has a proven track record with thousands of managers. Try it for 3 weeks. After that, you can tailor it to your own needs.

TIME-OUT 10 Use your time log data to identify your three biggest time wasters. Read the following discussion and develop some strategies for minimizing them.

The problem we all face is not a shortage of time but rather ineffective use of our time. Could you use an extra 2 hours every day? Experts say most people waste at least this much time every day.

The four key components of an effective time management system are these:

- Prioritize: Seldom—if ever—do we have enough time to do everything we want to do. However, there is usually enough time to do what is really important. Prioritizing tasks helps you decide where you should spend your time and prevents you from squandering it on trivial matters.[51]

- Set objectives: We've been here before (chapter 4), but it's important. People who get things done set objectives. Write down your objectives—the important things you need to accomplish.

- Plan: Plan how you are going to get your objectives done. Don't skip this step.

- Make a schedule: Schedule each week and workday.

Time management systems all boil down to two things—develop a game plan and stick to it. **Time management systems** involve planning each week, scheduling each week, and scheduling each day.

1. Plan each week. Ideally, you will plan the coming week on the last day of the current week, so that on Monday, you will be ready to go. However, some jobs require that you plan the week on the first day of the week. Using figure 14.5 as a template, think about your objectives and list the ones you think you can accomplish in the week. Focus on nonroutine tasks, not routine ones you do weekly or daily.

After setting a few major objectives, list the activities you need to accomplish for each objective in column 1. If an objective calls for multiple activities, use one of the three scheduling tools given earlier. Prioritize each activity.[52] High priorities must be done first; medium and low priorities can be pushed into the future (see chapter 5 on setting priorities).

In the last two columns, fill in the time you think you will need and the most promising day to do each task. Total the time you have allotted for your objectives for the week. Is this time realistic given that you still need to do routine tasks and deal with unexpected events? With experience, you will become more accurate about what you can and cannot accomplish in a given week. Planning to do more than you can actually get done is not only frustrating—it guarantees failure. Not planning enough activities, of course, wastes time.

2. Schedule each week. Scheduling your work is critical because it gets you organized and focused,[53] and you should plan time to schedule for each task.[54] Make your schedule as you plan your week or do it afterward, whichever you prefer. These two tasks should take 30 minutes or less. Using figure 14.6, fill in time slots that are already spoken for, such as standing weekly meetings. Next, schedule events over which you have control, like performance appraisals. Most managers leave about 50% of their week unscheduled to

Plan for the week of: _____			
Objectives:			
Activities	**Priority**	**Time needed**	**Day to schedule**
Total time for the week			

FIGURE 14.5 Weekly planner.

From R. Lussier and D. Kimball, 2014, *Applied Sport Management Skills, Second Edition* (Champaign, IL: Human Kinetics).

Schedule for the week of: _____					
Time	Mon.	Tues.	Wed.	Thurs.	Fri.
8:00 8:15 8:30 8:45					
9:00 (etc., to ending time)					

FIGURE 14.6   Weekly schedule.

From R. Lussier and D. Kimball, 2014, *Applied Sport Management Skills, Second Edition* (Champaign, IL: Human Kinetics).

Schedule for the day of: _____
Time
8:00 8:15 8:30 8:45
9:00 (etc., to ending time)

FIGURE 14.7   Daily schedule.

From R. Lussier and D. Kimball, 2014, *Applied Sport Management Skills, Second Edition* (Champaign, IL: Human Kinetics).

accommodate unexpected events. Your job may require more or less unscheduled time. With practice, you will find the balance that works for you.

The key to time management is not to prioritize your schedule but to schedule your priorities. In other words, control your schedule: Don't let it control you. Allocate time to get your important objectives accomplished, and don't get diverted with nonproductive activities.[55]

3. Schedule each day. At the end of each day, schedule the following day. Or you can schedule your day first thing in the morning. This should take 15 minutes or less. Base the day's schedule on your plan and schedule for the week, using figure 14.7 as a template. Daily schedules help you adjust for unplanned events. Pencil in already scheduled activities like meetings. Strive to keep your daily schedule flexible. As we noted earlier, most managers leave 50% of their time unscheduled to handle unexpected events. Here are some other scheduling tips:

- Don't be too optimistic; schedule enough time to do each task. Many managers find that doubling their initial estimate works well. Don't despair; you will improve with practice.

- Focus on only one thinking task at a time. Some people seem to get an incredible number of things done—if you watch them closely, you will see they have the discipline to laser in on one task at a time. First, as shown by research, the human mind is not capable of doing more than one thinking task at a time (multitasking).[56] Think of it like a single-screen TV; you can't watch more than one show at a time. However, you can watch two shows during the same half hour by flipping back and forth between channels. You will get the gist of both shows, but you will lose some of the details that could be important. This is what happens every time you multitask. To truly learn something, and remember it, you have to pay full attention.[57] So tackle one task at a time.[58]

- Schedule high-priority items during your "prime time," the time when you are at your best. For most people this is early in the morning. Others start slow and build momentum through the day. Figure out your MO and use your prime time to work on tasks that require your full attention. Do routine tasks, such as checking your mail, at other times.

- Try to schedule a time for unexpected events. Tell employees to see you with routine matters during a set time, such as 3 p.m. Have people call you, and plan to call them, during this set time. Depending on your job, don't be checking your phone and e-mail constantly; do so at set times to avoid interruptions in getting your high-priority items done.[59]

- Don't perform an unscheduled task without determining its priority. If you are working on a high-priority item and a medium-priority matter arises, let it wait.[60] Even so-called urgent matters can often wait.

Time management works well for managers whose jobs entail a variety of nonrecurring tasks. For managers and employees who deal primarily with routine tasks, the time management system we've outlined here may not be necessary. If you are in a routine situation, a good to-do list that prioritizes items (shown in chapter 5) may be all you need. Skill-Builder 14.2 on page 473 helps you analyze your time use. Forms similar to those in figures 14.4 through 14.7 can be purchased in pad, book, and even computer versions. You can also copy these examples.

Time Management Techniques

The following Self-Assessment contains 50 time management techniques arranged by management function. Planning and controlling are placed together because they are so closely related. Organizing and leading are separated.

As we bring this chapter to a close, you should understand the important role of facilities and event management. Facilities and event management includes developing the sales forecast to predict attendance and profitability and scheduling to plan and control activities. You should have ideas on how to improve your time management skills.

 TIME-OUT 11 Using your answers from the Self-Assessment, choose the three most important techniques you should use. Explain how you will implement each technique.

Time Management Techniques

Here are 50 ideas that you can use to improve your time management skills. Check the appropriate box for each idea.

Time management techniques	Should do	Could do	Do not do	Does not apply to me
Planning and controlling management functions				
1. I use the time management system presented in the text.	☐	☐	☐	☐
2. I use a to-do list and prioritize items on it. I do the important things rather than the "urgent" ones.	☐	☐	☐	☐
3. I get an early and productive start on my top-priority items.	☐	☐	☐	☐
4. I do only high-priority items and unpleasant or difficult tasks during my prime time.	☐	☐	☐	☐
5. I don't spend time on unproductive activities to avoid or escape job-related anxiety. I get the job done.	☐	☐	☐	☐
6. Throughout the day I ask myself, "Should I be doing this now?"	☐	☐	☐	☐
7. I plan before I act.	☐	☐	☐	☐
8. I do contingency planning—that is, I have plans in place for recurring crises.	☐	☐	☐	☐
9. I am decisive. It is better to make a wrong decision than none at all.	☐	☐	☐	☐
10. I schedule enough time to do the job right the first time. I try to be realistic about the amount of time it takes to do a job.	☐	☐	☐	☐
11. I schedule a quiet hour during which my staff interrupts me only for true emergencies. I have someone take messages, or I ask people to call me back.	☐	☐	☐	☐
12. I've established a quiet time for my team. I've found that the first hour of the day works best.	☐	☐	☐	☐
13. I schedule large blocks of uninterrupted (emergencies only) time for projects and so forth.	☐	☐	☐	☐
14. If this doesn't work, I hide somewhere.	☐	☐	☐	☐
15. I break big tasks into smaller, more doable tasks.	☐	☐	☐	☐
16. Before I stop work on a scheduled item to do something unscheduled, I ask, "Is doing this unscheduled task more important than the scheduled event?"	☐	☐	☐	☐
17. I schedule a time for doing similar activities (making and returning calls, writing letters and memos).	☐	☐	☐	☐
Organizing management function				
18. I schedule time for unexpected events (my "office hours") and let people know when I'm open for calls and questions. I ask people to see me or call me during those hours, unless it's an emergency. I answer mail and do other routine tasks during this time. If people ask to see me—"Got a minute?"—I ask them whether it can wait until my office hours.	☐	☐	☐	☐
19. I schedule a time, set up an agenda, set a time limit for all visitors, and keep on topic.	☐	☐	☐	☐

Time management techniques	Should do	Could do	Do not do	Does not apply to me
Organizing management function *(continued)*				
20. I keep a clean, well-organized work area and desk.	☐	☐	☐	☐
21. I remove all non-work-related or distracting objects from my work area and desk.	☐	☐	☐	☐
22. I do one task at a time.	☐	☐	☐	☐
23. With paperwork, I make a decision at once. I don't reread it later and decide later.	☐	☐	☐	☐
24. My files are systematically arranged and labeled as active or inactive. When I file an item, I note a throwaway date on it.	☐	☐	☐	☐
25. When appropriate, I call rather than write or visit.	☐	☐	☐	☐
26. I delegate appropriate tasks when I can.	☐	☐	☐	☐
27. I use form letters and a word processor.	☐	☐	☐	☐
28. I answer letters (memos) on the letter itself.	☐	☐	☐	☐
29. I have someone read and summarize appropriate things for me.	☐	☐	☐	☐
30. I divide reading requirements with others and share summaries.	☐	☐	☐	☐
31. I have calls screened to make sure the right person handles them.	☐	☐	☐	☐
32. I plan before I call. I have an agenda and all pertinent information handy, and I take notes on the agenda.	☐	☐	☐	☐
33. I ask people to call me back during my office hours. I also ask about the best time to call them.	☐	☐	☐	☐
34. I have a specific objective or purpose for every meeting I conduct. If I can't state the meeting's purpose, I don't have the meeting.	☐	☐	☐	☐
35. When I do hold meetings, I invite only the necessary participants and I keep them only as long as needed.	☐	☐	☐	☐
36. I always have an agenda for a meeting and I stick to it. I start and end as scheduled.	☐	☐	☐	☐
37. I set objectives for travel. I list everyone I will meet with, and I e-mail them agendas. I have a file folder for each person with all the necessary data for our meeting.	☐	☐	☐	☐
38. I combine and modify activities to save time.	☐	☐	☐	☐
Leading management function				
39. I set clear objectives for my staff with built-in accountability; I give them feedback often.	☐	☐	☐	☐
40. I don't waste others' time. I don't make my team wait idly for decisions, instructions, or materials in meetings. I wait for a convenient time—I don't interrupt team members or others and waste their time.	☐	☐	☐	☐
41. I train my staff carefully. I don't do their work for them.	☐	☐	☐	☐
42. I delegate activities in which I don't need to be personally involved.	☐	☐	☐	☐
43. I set deadlines earlier than the actual deadline.	☐	☐	☐	☐
44. I use the input of my staff. I don't try to reinvent the wheel.	☐	☐	☐	☐
45. I teach time management skills to my team.	☐	☐	☐	☐
46. I don't procrastinate; I do it.	☐	☐	☐	☐

Time management techniques	Should do	Could do	Do not do	Does not apply to me
Leading management function (*continued*)				
47. I'm not a perfectionist—I define what is acceptable and stop there.	☐	☐	☐	☐
48. I try to stay calm. Getting emotional only causes more problems.	☐	☐	☐	☐
49. I've found ways to reduce socializing without rocking the team spirit.	☐	☐	☐	☐
50. I communicate well. I don't confuse my staff with vague, poorly planned directives.	☐	☐	☐	☐

After you have completed the Self-Assessment, implement your "Should do" items. Next, work on your "Could do" items. Try to keep a mind-set of continually improving your time management skills. Once in a while, reread the "Does not apply to me" column to see if any of these items apply now.

@ TAKE IT TO THE NET

Please visit www.HumanKinetics.com/AppliedSportManagementSkills and go to this book's companion web study guide, where you will find the following:

A list of websites associated with the concepts in this chapter

Exercises that you will need Internet access to complete

Online versions of chapter exercises and end-of-chapter learning aids

An exercise that helps you define the Key Terms

LEARNING AIDS

CHAPTER SUMMARY

1. Describe what managing a sport facility entails.

    Sport management personnel frequently help plan, design, and manage new facilities. A crucial part of their job is to generate interest in the organization or the local community for the new facility. Forming a committee of interested people early in the process ensures doing the right job. Once the facility is open for business, the job shifts to managing and training staff to run the facility on a day-to-day basis.

2. Describe what is involved in event planning.

    Sport managers plan many types of events. They coordinate games, provide food for teams, arrange team transportation, hire officials, manage ticket sales, plan and monitor concession sales, juggle league schedules, and organize tournaments.

3. Explain how standing plans and single-use plans differ.

    They differ in repetitiveness. Standing plans are policies, procedures, and rules for handling repetitive situations. Single-use plans are programs and budgets for handling nonrepetitive situations.

4. Explain when, and why, contingency plans are necessary.

Contingency plans are plans that may need to be implemented if uncontrollable events occur. There are many events managers cannot control that can prevent achievement of objectives. By identifying what can go wrong and planning how to handle it, managers increase their chances of achieving objectives.

5. Discuss how sales forecasts shape strategy.

Sales forecasts sometimes determine strategy. If forecasts indicate a slowdown in the economy (environment), companies can elect to defend market share. If forecasts indicate stable demand for a product or service, companies may choose to use a cash cow to fund new products. If sales forecasts indicate that the economy is turning up, companies may choose to market aggressively to open up new markets.

6. Explain how qualitative and quantitative forecasting techniques differ.

Qualitative forecast techniques use subjective judgment, intuition, experience, and opinion, with some math. Quantitative techniques use past sales data and mathematical (objective) analysis to predict sales. However, the two methods are often used in combination to improve forecasting.

7. Explain how the jury of executive opinion and the three sales composites differ.

The jury of executive opinion seeks a consensus from managers or experts. Composite sales methods combine the independent forecasts of salespeople, customers, or operating units to predict total company sales without reaching consensus. The composite techniques are more objective than the jury of executive opinion.

8. Explain how past sales and time series forecasting techniques differ.

With past sales, future sales are predicted to be the same or are subjectively adjusted for environmental factors. With time series, future sales are predicted by extending the trend line over time.

9. Know when to use planning sheets, Gantt charts, and PERT diagrams.

Planning sheets and Gantt charts work best for plans with independent, sequential activities. Gantt charts have two advantages over planning sheets: They show progress directly on the chart and can show multiple projects on one chart. PERT diagrams are more appropriate when activities are dependent on each other.

10. Use a time log.

A time log is a daily diary that shows how we use our time. It identifies areas to work on to improve time use.

11. Manage your time better.

The basic steps in the time management system are (1) plan each week, (2) schedule each week, and (3) schedule each day.

REVIEW AND DISCUSSION QUESTIONS

1. What are the five planning dimensions?

2. What is the difference between a policy, a procedure, and a rule?

3. Why do some sport managers fail to plan?

4. Why is sales forecasting important?

5. What are some of the activities involved in planning a youth Olympics-style games?

6. What types of events do sport managers plan?

7. What is the mission of the University of Southern Mississippi National Center for Spectator Sports Safety and Security?

8. When would you use a PERT diagram rather than a Gantt chart?

9. Why are time management skills important to a team manager?

10. What does a time log show?

11. What are the four key components of the time management system?

12. What are the most likely major opportunities and threats to be concerned about in sport management in the next few years?

13. What do you believe is the most important issue facing sport management today?

14. What is your vision of the future of sport management?

CASE

Controlling Fans at Professional Sporting Events

Every sporting event needs to be concerned about the potential for hooligan-type behavior. The term *hooligan* is often associated with European football games. Some rowdy fans get out of control and can create chaos for the majority of well-behaved fans. All too often the rowdy hooligan behavior leads to the death of a few fans.

Unfortunately, examples of rowdy fan behavior are all too common. For instance, fans were warned to behave properly at the EURO 2012 football tournament. However, 183 fans of Poland and Russia were arrested when they clashed. Water cannons, tear gas, and rubber bullets were used to disperse a mob, while fireworks, bottles, and other makeshift missiles were thrown by fans on both sides.[61]

At a 2007 soccer game in Sicily, a police officer died after being hit by a blunt object as fans fought with police inside and outside Catania's Angelo Massimino Stadium during an Italian league game against local rival Palermo. About 100 people were injured, and Italian soccer authorities postponed an entire round of games and closed down stadiums that didn't satisfy safety regulations.[62]

German soccer federation president Theo Zwanziger acknowledged in 2007 that fan violence in Germany had reached a new level. "It's scary," Zwanziger said, "That is a dangerous environment. . . . You just have to put a match to the fuse and everything will explode.[63]

Examples of hooligan-type behavior can be found in other sports. A prime example occurred when athletes and fans interacted during a 2004 game between the NBA Indiana Pacers and Detroit Pistons. The incident was not a single, short-term tussle. The Pacers and Pistons' fight with fans lasted for a few minutes (a chair, beer, and popcorn were thrown at Pacers players), and the entire affair ended up in a court of law. As a result, the NBA limited the size of alcoholic drinks to 24 ounces (710 milliliters), placed a limit of two alcoholic drinks per customer, and banned alcohol sales after the third quarter.[64]

In 2011, four San Francisco Giants baseball fans took a road trip to Los Angeles to watch the Opening Day game between their Giants and the Dodgers. The four Giants fans wore their Giants clothing while they attended the game in L.A. After the game, they were attacked unprovoked in the parking lot. Giants fan Bryan Stow was seriously injured and ended up permanently disabled and would be unable to return to his work as a paramedic.[65]

Event planners determine security objectives before the event, implement the security plan, monitor and control the actual event, and then have a postevent security meeting. You can be proactive and plan for potential problems before they happen. Security considerations include perimeter security around the outside of the civic center, field, or stadium, and training for security personnel. A postevent analysis helps you to better plan future events. The 2013 Super Bowl experienced a power outage for nearly 35 minutes in the second half of the game. A complete postevent analysis between SMG which manages the Superdome, the local utility company Entergy Services, and the NFL was conducted to determine the exact reason why the power outage occurred during the biggest sport event of the year.[66]

Measures to reduce hooliganism at soccer games include providing family enclosures; trying to reduce racist chanting and remarks; promoting cooperation between clubs, police, and media in finding and prosecuting hooligans; and making sure that banned hooligans are not allowed at games. Standing plans can be used to improve efficiency through development of some regular steps and procedures to implement in all events.

Fans want a safe environment to watch a game. When Barry Bonds hit his historic home run to pass Hank Aaron, the resulting scrum to claim the ball looked quite dangerous. However, police personnel were strategically placed around the ballpark to control the situation. Two police officers did help a lucky fan catch the ball, and the only real harm was that his New York Mets shirt was torn. Proactive planning eliminated a potential chaotic situation and instead created a positive moment for all fans.[67]

For more information on hooliganism, visit http://news.bbc.co.uk/hi/english/static/in_depth/programmes/2002/hooligans/. This website allows you to watch a three-part BBC series devoted to hooligan-type behavior.

Case Questions

Select the best alternative for the following questions. Be able to explain your answers.

1. Event planners gain efficiency primarily from their
   a. standing plans
   b. single-use plans

2. Protecting the perimeter of an event is a(n)
   a. objective
   b. policy
   c. procedure
   d. rule
   e. program
   f. budget

3. Protecting fans at an event is a(n)
   a. objective
   b. policy
   c. procedure
   d. rule
   e. program
   f. budget

4. When looking for events that can attract an attendance appropriate to maintaining fan safety and that can generate profits for all involved parties, event planners must be careful to stay within their
   a. objective
   b. policy
   c. procedure
   d. rule
   e. program
   f. budget

5. The planning tools that would be most effective in helping event planners to schedule events and security are
   a. planning sheets
   b. Gantt charts
   c. PERT diagrams

6. Event planners are most likely to use which quantitative sales forecasting technique to determine expected attendance?
   a. past sales
   b. time series

7. Event planners are most likely to use which qualitative sales forecasting technique?
   a. sales force composite
   b. customer composite
   c. operating unit composite
   d. survey

8. Time is a competitive advantage for an event planner.
   a. true
   b. false

9. Time management skills are an important part of an event manager's skill kit.
   a. true
   b. false

10. Event planners who have a pre-event security strategy will have a good long-term plan.
    a. true
    b. false

11. What other sporting events do you think would be appropriate for a pre-event security plan? Describe the success (or struggles) a local sporting event had with security.

SKILL-BUILDER EXERCISES

Skill-Builder 14.1: Planning to Make a Dream Come True

Objective

To develop your planning skills using a Gantt chart (see p. 457) and a PERT diagram (see pp. 458-459)

Preparation

You're about to take the plunge and realize your dream—your own sporting goods store: _____ (name it here). You've set April 1 for your grand opening. It is now late December. You need to move in 1 month before you open in order to set everything up. By March you need to have hired and trained an assistant. Your Aunt Matilda, who is financing this undertaking, has asked that you go over your plan with her on January 2. You intend to put the plan in motion on January 3.

You're still new at this, so to be sure you've got everything covered, you're going to use both a Gantt chart and a PERT diagram. Construct them both, in your order of preference, using the guidelines given in the chapter. Make sure that you include the activities (plus others that you identify) and completion times listed next, which are not necessarily in sequence.

a. Lease store fixtures for displaying sneakers, clothing, and sport equipment (2 weeks needed to receive and arrange them).

b. Order and receive sneakers, clothing, and sport equipment (1 week).

c. Recruit and select an assistant (3 weeks or less).

d. Install the fixtures, paint, and decorate (2 weeks).

e. Form a corporation (4 weeks).

f. Arrange to buy your merchandise on credit (2 weeks).

g. Find a store location (6 weeks or less).

h. Unpack and display merchandise (1 week).

i. Train assistant (1 week).

j. Select sneakers, clothing, and sport equipment (1 week).

k. Determine start-up cost and cash outflow per month through April 30 (1 week).

Gantt Chart

When developing your Gantt chart, use the following week-based format. You may want to change the letter sequence to match starting dates.

	Gantt Chart												
Activity (letter)	**January**				**February**				**March**				**April**
	1	**2**	**3**	**4**	**1**	**2**	**3**	**4**	**1**	**2**	**3**	**4**	**1**
_____													
_____													
_____													
_____													
_____													
_____													
_____													
_____													
_____													
_____													
_____													
_____													

PERT Diagram

To construct your PERT diagram, first draw arrows from your start date, January 2, to circles for activities (events) that do not depend on other events—these are your independent events. Then work on dependent events. Place event letters inside each circle. On each arrow, place the number of weeks it will take to complete the event. Then draw an arrow to the end date, April 1. Once every event and the time to complete it are shown on the diagram, determine your critical path and add the second arrows to highlight this. Hint: Using only the events listed previously (not including the events you have added), you should have five arrows coming from your start date to events. A promising place to start may be finding your store location.

PERT
(with critical path)

Start   End

In-Class Application

Complete the preceding skill-building preparation before class.
Choose one (10-30 minutes):

- Break into groups of three to five members and critique each other's Gantt charts and PERT diagrams. Brainstorm ways to improve them.
- Conduct informal, whole-class discussion of student charts and diagrams.

Wrap-Up

Take a few minutes to write your answers to the following questions:

Which is more appropriate for this situation—Gantt charts or PERT diagrams?

_____

What did I learn from this experience? How will I use this knowledge?

_____
_____
_____
_____

Skill-Builder 14.2: Time Management

Objective

To learn to get more done in less time with better results

Preparation

For this Skill-Builder you will use figures 14.5 through 14.7 as templates. Before using the time management system, it is helpful to keep a time log (figure 14.4) for 1 or 2 (typical) weeks to identify areas where you would like to improve your use of time. (However, this is optional.)

Step 1: Plan Your Week

Using figure 14.5, develop a plan for the rest of this week. Begin with today, and include the time you spend at work, at home, at school, and on recreational and sporting activities.

Step 2: Schedule Your Week

Using figure 14.6, schedule the rest of this week. Be sure to schedule a 30-minute period to plan and schedule next week, preferably on the last day of this week.

Step 3: Schedule Your Day

Using figure 14.7, schedule each day. Do this for every day at least until the class period when this Skill-Builder is due.

In-Class Application

Complete the preceding skill-building preparation before class.
Choose one (10-30 minutes):

- Break into groups of three to five members and discuss your schedules and planning calendars. Pass them around so that you can compare time management styles. Brainstorm ways to improve each other's use of time.
- Conduct informal, whole-class discussion of student findings.

Wrap-Up

Take a few minutes to write your answers to the following questions:

What did I learn from this experience?

_____

_____

_____

How will I use this knowledge?

_____

_____

_____

As a class, discuss student responses.

SPORTS AND SOCIAL MEDIA EXERCISES

Find five different examples of sport facilities at the following blog for SMG Worldwide: http://smg-world.blogspot.com.

1. _____
2. _____
3. _____
4. _____
5. _____

GAME PLAN FOR STARTING A SPORT BUSINESS

Create a timeline for a sport event you would like to hold for your sport business.

AFTERWORD

The Future of Balance in Sport

One of the newest techniques used to monitor the success of an organization is the balanced scorecard (BSC). The BSC is one of the most highly touted management tools today. The scorecard balances financial concerns with other issues that are important to the firm. The theory was developed by Harvard Business School professor Robert Kaplan and management consultant David Norton.[1] There are four areas that should be measured and reinforced.

- Financial performance (How profitable are we? How do our shareholders view our performance?)

- Customer service performance (Do we exceed our fans' expectations? How do our customers view our performance?)

- Internal business practices (How effective are our operations and processes? How can we continually improve and increase productivity?)

- Learning and growth performance (Are we continually developing our employees? Is our organizational culture working? How do our players and employees view the firm and their jobs?)

All four dimensions of the BSC are equally important, and results relate to one another through the systems effect. A BSC doesn't simply measure the past; rather, it sets targets and measures that focus on the future, because the BSC is both a planning and a controlling method. If your team is without a scorecard, it isn't playing the game; it's only practicing.

Nike measures its overall performance with a BSC that includes human rights compliance measures in addition to cost, delivery, and quality measures. Sport managers, especially in sports such as baseball that are heavily into statistics, find that they can blend the financial issues of the team (revenue, ticket prices) with other issues (fan satisfaction, ballpark condition, attendance trends, player development, player and team performance). A model can be built to help control both financial and nonfinancial issues.

Sport management students are fond of keeping the scorebook at various games. So it is going to be quite natural to keep track of the success of a sport-related business by using a balanced scorecard approach.

Balancing the Major Issues in Sport Management

As we near the close of this book, we would like to present our own version of a balanced report on some of the problems and opportunities facing professional sport management. Not coincidentally, this discussion integrates many of the important issues we have discussed throughout the text. We use four current issues that will likely affect sport for the next decade. Personal ethics and steroid use are the two major threats. Globalization and the financial health of sport are two major opportunities as sport gets deeper into a new decade.

Personal Ethics and Honesty

Sports are one of the true forms of mass entertainment. Like rock singers and movie stars, athletes are constantly followed by the media. When star athletes do something wrong, their actions are major news. Incidents such as the bounty system employed by the New Orleans Saints, which rewarded players with cash for injuring opponents, are illegal and unethical. These cases are heavily followed by the media and tarnish the sport.[2]

Athletes are not alone in the need to improve ethical behavior. Coaches such as Sean Payton have to be punished if they allow bounty systems. NBA referee Tim Donaghy pled guilty to betting on games while officiating some of those same games. He later resigned his position as an official. David Stern, commissioner of the NBA, was visibly upset over the entire affair. But the problem occurred under his management tenure, and thus he had to be held accountable.[3] Penn State assistant football coach Jerry Sandusky was found guilty of sexual child abuse, and head coach Joe Paterno and administrators were guilty of covering up the scandal. The NCAA fined Penn State U.S.$60 million and took away all Coach Paterno's victories from 1998 to 2011, and his statue was taken down.[4]

Steroid Use and Drug Testing

The use of illegal drugs in sport will need to be continually monitored. The U.S. government failed to convict three high-profile athletes of steroid usage—Barry Bonds, Lance Armstrong, and Roger Clemens. Only Bonds was convicted of obstruction of justice.[5] However, new allegations against Lance Armstrong were filed by the U.S. Anti-Doping Agency.[6] Monitoring steroid use will help athletes live longer and have more productive lives after their playing days are over.

Financial Health of Sport

The U.S. economy is growing slowly, but has failed to return to the full employment levels seen prior to the 2008 recession. Although the economy is fairly stable, it still lacks high growth with respect to adding new jobs. So, jobs in all industries, including sport, are harder to find. The appendix offers insights into starting and developing your own career.

Games are being broadcast using satellite television, wireless communications, and the Internet. Fans often find that it is cheaper, easier, and just as enjoyable to watch sporting events from home, from a local sport-themed restaurant, or on their laptop or cell phone. However, nothing replaces the excitement of watching live events at a packed stadium. Will teams be able to raise ticket prices to cover higher costs? Many teams have made sure to announce when they lowered ticket prices to help fans feel more comfortable buying "live" tickets.

Globalization of Sport

The world of sport is still growing. Sporting events are held throughout the world, and sport managers are needed to plan, organize, manage, and control sporting events of all sorts.

At the same time, new leagues, fitness programs, athletic clubs, domed soccer and lacrosse training facilities, and local sport magazines are popping up in all areas of the world. The NBA and MLB are scheduling games in Japan. David Beckham moved from the United Kingdom to the United States to play MLS to bring soccer to a new level of interest in America. Future NHL hockey players are regularly scouted throughout Europe and Russia. Kobe Bryant and LeBron James were global stars—not just U.S. stars—who headed to the 2012 Olympic Games.

Future of Sport Management

As a student of sport management and as a future manager, you must ask questions that people in the industry should be asking themselves: What are the bad management decisions being made? What do these issues portend for the future of pro sports? What ripple effects might a severe recession in the pro sport team industry have on industries that depend on the financial health of pro sport teams? The sport industry is an odd-duck industry—by its very nature, it will always have winning teams and losing teams. How can they all win at the biggest game of all—the bottom-line game?

The good news is that America's love affair with sport has lost none of its bloom. Look around you: There are fencing teams, dance studios, soccer teams, and figure skating clubs. The list is long and diverse, and people from all walks of life build their free time around sports—doing them, watching them, teaching them, and traveling great distances to participate in them. The future of sport management is bigger, brighter, and more diverse than it has ever been. Whereas pro sport teams have some serious white water directly ahead that they badly need to find ways to negotiate, sports are thriving in America and around the world. Managers trained in sport management are in great demand. Opportunities abound in managing sporting goods stores; organizing athletic departments at educational institutions; shaping the future of sports in governing bodies such as FIFA, the NCAA, and the IOC; planning events; working in local community recreation centers and youth leagues; officiating; coaching; broadcasting; and numerous professional leagues. Maybe you took this course because you want to work for a professional team. However, we hope this book has helped you see just how many different sport organizations need great managers. (See the appendix for a discussion of careers in sport management over the next few years.)

Organizational success is not just about focusing on profits; using a balanced scorecard actually leads to better results. Be aware of issues and the future of sport management, and keep up with the latest issues in your field.

Careers in Sport Management

A wide array of career opportunities is available to you in the field of sport management. In this appendix, we offer tips for the job search and suggest ways to gain valuable work experience. We also describe various resources that may be helpful as you begin to investigate your career options.

Career Search

A career search in the field of sport management is no different than any other career search. A wise man who taught with us once said, "Nobody who completes a job search ends up without a job." The central idea is that any career management process requires a good understanding of yourself, your personal goals, your interests, your salary and benefits requirements, and your willingness to travel extensively for business. Any job in the field that interests you can, and should, lead to more responsible, higher-paying work later in your career. However, you typically have to start at the bottom and work your way up the organization.

Many career books are available to help you learn about conducting a job search. Our favorite career management book has been on the market for 40 years: *What Color Is Your Parachute?* by Richard Nelson Bolles is an annual best-seller. Bolles asks two basic career questions: What do you want to do? Where do you want to do it?[1] We add, What are you good at doing? The book helps you answer these questions.

Specific Fields in Sport Management

Chapter 1 provides an overview of the field of sport management. Review the various careers you can enter, which are outlined in that chapter. These careers include such areas as sport broadcasting, athletic administration, coaching, officiating, fitness center management, retail sport management, sporting goods manufacturing, and recreation and youth centers. In addition, the cases provided in this book cover different areas within sport in which a student might like to find a job and build a career.

Internships

Internships are a valuable method to gain on-the-job experience that can either lead to a full-time position with the same organization or help you get a job in another organization. Pick your internship wisely by selecting an organization you can see yourself with for a long time. If you like facility management or event planning, contact the arenas and stadiums in your area. If you like recreation management, contact the YMCA or JCC in your area. Retail sporting goods stores are also good places to contact, because you will find this type of store in most every area. A recent "sport man" student just completed an internship with Dream Bat Company in the small town of Somers, Connecticut. The intern is now a product representative for the company and will receive a commission on all the Dream Bats that he sells. You can find Dream Bat Company on Facebook and become one of its fans.

Some students are fortunate enough to land paid internship positions. However, most internships are unpaid and call for 120 to 150 hours to fulfill academic requirements. Most internships require the student to write a paper or complete a journal of the experience. We have found that students who develop an interesting PowerPoint presentation on their sport internship can show future employers what they actually did during their internship.

Networking

Most students underestimate the power of networking. We take the word "networking" for granted, but think about it. It is really two words—"net" and "working." Is your net working? Do you know people in the sport field? Did you ever try to contact a sport administrator at your local sport arena? Fitness center? Recreation center? Television station? Newspaper? In the electronic age, it is possible to e-mail these people and begin a relationship. Often, you can find their e-mail addresses at the end of an article in the newspaper or on their organization's website. Be polite and make sure to tell the professional that you are a student looking for assistance in your quest to understand the field of sport management. These people are often very supportive of students' efforts to learn about their business.

Keep a log of the people you meet in your networking endeavors. Add their e-mail addresses to your Internet address book. Send them quick notes on events you attended at their organization and tell them how you enjoyed the experience. Building a good network is not about finding a job right away but rather about developing a long-lasting relationship that is beneficial to both parties. Networking is not exactly about who you know. It is more about whether the sport professional knows you. So, you need to make sure these professionals learn about you. Send important sport leaders in industries where you want to work an e-mail, a Facebook message, a LinkedIn invitation, or a Twitter tweet. Live the journey!

Websites for Sport Careers

The best way for us to help you find specific jobs in sport is to tell you about websites that are geared toward this goal. These sites are excellent sources of information about jobs in sport, although some sites provide more information than others. Some sites are more interested in having people sign up for their monthly service; others provide job titles, short descriptions, and addresses to which you can send a resume and cover letter. It is a good idea to visit multiple websites, as some list jobs that others don't.

Here are some general websites that offer advice to all new college grads:

- www.collegerecruiter.com: Career test to identify possible jobs; internships and entry-level jobs
- student.fins.com: Jobs and tips for new college grads
- www.careerbuilder.com: Jobs and advice
- www.jobs.com: Advice for job seekers
- www.monster.com: Primarily business jobs

Here are some sport websites. Some require membership fees, but you can usually view job descriptions without paying to help you identify the type of job that interest you.

- www.sportscareerfinder.com: Helps with selecting and finding a sport job.
- www.womensportsjobs.com: Lists hot jobs for the week. Don't let the name of the site fool you; it's good for men as well as women and also good for finding intern-

ships. For example, the page as of this writing listed Director of Sports Marketing for ESPN and Regional Development Director for the American Heart Association.

- www.teamworkonline.com: Provides ongoing listings of sport positions. For example, at the time of this writing the site listed Inside Sales Account Executive with the Minnesota Wild.
- www.jobsinsports.com: Has internships
- www.workinsports.com
- www.sportsmanagementworldwide.com
- www.ihiresportsandrecreation.com
- www.sportscareers.com

GLOSSARY

acquired needs theory—Proposes that employees are motivated by their need for achievement, power, and affiliation.

acquisition—Occurs when one business buys all or part of another business.

adaptive strategies—Prospecting, defending, and analyzing.

arbitrator—Neutral third party whose decisions are binding.

assessment centers—Places where job applicants undergo a series of tests, interviews, and simulated experiences to determine their managerial potential.

attitudes—Positive or negative evaluations of people, things, and situations.

attribution—The process of determining why people behave in certain ways.

authority—The right to make decisions, issue orders, and use resources.

BCF statements—Statements that describe conflicts in terms of behavior, consequences, and feelings.

behavioral theorists—Theorists who look at the leadership style of effective leaders.

bona fide occupational qualification (BFOQ)—Allows discrimination where it is reasonably necessary to normal operation of a particular organization.

brainstorming—The process of suggesting many possible alternatives without evaluation.

budgets—Plans for allocating resources to specific activities.

business portfolio analysis—The corporate process of determining which lines of business the corporation will be in and how it will allocate resources among them.

capital budgets—Budgets that allocate funds for improvements.

centralized authority—Important decisions are made by top managers.

charismatic leaders—Inspire loyalty, enthusiasm, and high levels of performance.

coaching—Giving motivational feedback to maintain and improve performance.

coalition—An alliance of people with similar objectives who have a better chance of achieving their objectives when they work together versus separately.

collective bargaining—The negotiation process resulting in a contract that covers employment conditions at the organization.

command groups—Consist of managers and their staffs.

communication—The process of transmitting information and meaning.

communication process—The transmission of information, meaning, and intent.

communication skills—The ability to get your ideas across clearly and effectively.

comparable worth—Jobs that are distinctly different but that require similar levels of ability, responsibility, skills, and working conditions are valued equally and paid equally.

compensation—The total cost of pay and benefits to employees.

competitive advantage—Specifies how the organization offers unique customer value.

components of culture—Behavior, values and beliefs, and assumptions.

conceptual skills—The ability to understand abstract ideas.

concurrent controls—Actions taken during transformation to ensure that standards are met.

conflict—Exists whenever disagreement becomes antagonistic.

consensus mapping—The process of developing group agreement on a solution to a problem.

consistent decision style—Taking time but not wasting time; knowing when more information is needed and when enough analysis has been done.

content-based motivation theories—Focus on identifying and understanding people's needs.

contingency leaders—Are task or relationship oriented, and their style should fit the situation.

contingency managers—Contingency managers analyze employee capability level and select the autocratic, consultative, participative, or empowerment style for the situation.

contingency plans—Alternative plans that can be implemented if unpredictable events occur.

continuum leaders—Choose their style based on boss-centered or employee-centered leadership.

control frequencies—Constant, periodic, and occasional.

controlling—The process of establishing and implementing mechanisms to ensure that objectives are achieved.

core values of TQM—A companywide focus on (1) delivering customer value and (2) continuously improving the system and its processes.

corporate growth strategies—Concentration, backward and forward integration, and related and unrelated diversification.

creative process—The three stages are (1) preparation, (2) incubation and illumination, and (3) evaluation.

creativity—A way of thinking that generates new ideas.

criteria—The standards that must be met to accomplish an objective.

critical path—The most time-consuming series of activities in a PERT network.

critical success factors (CSFs)—Pivotal areas in which satisfactory results will ensure successful achievement of the objective or standard.

customer value—The purchasing benefits used by customers to determine whether to buy a product.

damage controls—Actions taken to minimize negative impacts on customers caused by faulty output.

decentralized authority—Important decisions are made by middle and first-level managers.

decision making—The process of selecting an alternative course of action that will solve a problem.

decision-making conditions—Certainty, risk, and uncertainty.

decision-making skills—The ability to select alternatives to solve problems.

decode—The receiver's process of translating a message into a meaningful form.

delegation—The process of assigning responsibility and authority for accomplishing objectives.

delegation model—Steps are to (1) explain the need for delegating and the reasons for selecting the employee; (2) set objectives that define responsibility, the level of authority, and the deadline; (3) develop a plan; and (4) establish control checkpoints and hold employees accountable.

departmentalization—The grouping of related activities into work units.

development—Ongoing education that improves skills for present and future jobs.

devil's advocate—Group members defend the idea while others try to come up with reasons why the idea won't work.

direct investment—Occurs when a company builds or purchases operating facilities (subsidiaries) in a foreign country.

discipline—Corrective action to get employees to meet standards and to follow the rules.

dysfunctional conflict—Conflict that prevents groups from achieving their objectives.

empathy—The ability to understand and relate to someone else's situation and feelings.

employee assistance programs (EAPs)—Programs that help employees get professional assistance in solving their problems.

encode—The sender's process of putting a message into a form that the receiver will understand.

equity theory—Proposes that employees are motivated when their perceived inputs equal outputs.

ERG theory—Proposes that people are motivated by three needs: existence, relatedness, and growth.

ethics—Standards of right and wrong that influence behavior.

expectancy theory—Proposes that employees are motivated when they believe they can accomplish the task and the rewards for doing so are worth the effort.

external environment—The factors that affect an organization's performance from outside its boundaries.

feedback—The process of verifying messages.

financial statements—The income statement, the balance sheet, and the statement of cash flow.

force-field analysis—Assesses current performance and then identifies the forces hindering change and those driving it.

free agent—A player who is free to negotiate a contract with any team.

functional conflict—Disagreement and opposition that help achieve a group's objectives.

Gantt charts—Charts that use bars to graphically illustrate progress on a project.

global sourcing—The use of worldwide resources for inputs and transformation.

goals—General targets to be accomplished.

goal-setting theory—Proposes that achievable but difficult goals motivate employees.

grand strategies—The corporate strategies for growth, stability, turnaround, and retrenchment, or a combination thereof.

grapevine—The flow of information through informal channels.

group—Two or more members with a clear leader who perform independent jobs with individual accountability, evaluation, and rewards.

group cohesiveness—The extent to which members stick together.

group composition—The mix of group members' skills and abilities.

group performance model—Group performance is a function of organizational context, group structure, group process, and group development stage.

group process—The patterns of interactions that emerge as group members work together.

group process dimensions—Include roles, norms, cohesiveness, status, decision making, and conflict resolution.

group roles—Expectations shared by the group of how members will fulfill the requirements of their various positions.

group structure dimensions—Include group type, size, composition, leadership, and objectives.

group types—Formal or informal, functional or cross-functional, and command or task.

hierarchy of needs theory—Proposes that people are motivated by the five levels of needs: physiological, safety, social, esteem, and self-actualization.

horizontal communication—Information shared between peers.

human resources management—Planning, attracting, developing, and retaining employees.

initiators—People who approach other parties to resolve conflicts.

innovation—The implementation of a new idea.

internal environment—Factors that affect an organization's performance from within its boundaries.

international business—A business primarily based in one country that transacts business in other countries.

job characteristics model—Comprises core job dimensions, critical psychological states, and employee growth-need strength to improve quality of working life for employees and productivity for the organization.

job description—Identifies the tasks and responsibilities of a position.

job design—The process of combining tasks that each employee is responsible for completing.

job enrichment—The process of building motivators into a job by making it more interesting and challenging.

job evaluation—The process of determining the worth of each job relative to other jobs in the organization.

job specifications—Qualifications needed to staff a position.

joint venture—Created when firms share ownership (partnership) of a new enterprise.

labor relations—Interactions between management and unionized employees.

leaders—Influence employees to work to achieve the organization's objectives.

Leadership Grid—Identifies the ideal leadership style as having a high concern for both production and people.

leadership style—The combination of traits, skills, and behaviors that managers use to interact with employees.

leading—The process of influencing employees to work toward achieving objectives.

learning organization—An organization that learns, adapts, and changes as its environment changes to continuously increase customer value.

levels of authority—Inform, recommend, report, and full.

levels of management—Top, middle, and first-line.

line authority—The responsibility to make decisions and issue orders down the chain of command.

listening—The process of giving the speaker your undivided attention.

lockout—When management refuses to let employees work.

management audits—Look at ways to improve the organization's planning, organizing, leading, and controlling functions.

management by objectives (MBO)—The process by which managers and their teams jointly set objectives, periodically evaluate performance, and reward according to the results.

management by walking around (MBWA)—Is about listening, teaching, and facilitating.

management counseling—Helps employees recognize that they have a problem and then refers them to the employee assistance program.

management functions—The activities all managers perform, such as planning, organizing, leading, and controlling.

management information systems (MISs)—Formal systems for collecting, processing, and disseminating information that aids managers in decision making.

management roles—The roles managers undertake to accomplish the management function, including interpersonal, informational, and decisional.

management skills—Include (1) technical skills, (2) people skills, (3) communication skills, (4) conceptual skills, and (5) decision-making skills.

manager's resources—Include human, financial, physical, and informational resources.

market share—An organization's percentage of total industry sales.

mediator—Neutral third party who helps resolve conflict.

merger—Occurs when two companies form one corporation.

message-receiving process—Includes listening, analyzing, and checking understanding.

message-sending process—(1) develop rapport, (2) state your communication objective, (3) transmit your message, (4) check the receiver's understanding, (5) get a commitment and follow up.

mission—An organization's purpose or reason for being.

motivation—The willingness to achieve organizational objectives.

motivation process—Process through which people go from need to motive to behavior to consequence and finally to either satisfaction or dissatisfaction.

multinational corporation (MNC)—A business with significant operations in more than one country.

networking—Developing relationships to gain social or business advantage.

nominal grouping—The process of generating and evaluating alternatives using a structured voting method.

nonprogrammed decisions—With significant and nonrecurring and nonroutine situations, the decision maker should use the decision-making model.

nonverbal communications—Messages sent without words.

normative leaders—Use one of five decision-making styles appropriate for the situation.

norms—The group's shared expectations of members' behavior.

objectives—State what is to be accomplished in specific and measurable terms by a certain target date.

OD interventions—Specific actions taken to implement specific changes.

operating budgets—Use revenue forecasts to allocate funds to cover projected expenses.

operational planning—The process of setting short-term objectives and determining in advance how they will be accomplished.

operational strategies—Strategies used by every functional-level department to achieve corporate- and business-level objectives.

organizational behavior (OB)—The study of actions that affect performance in the workplace.

organizational culture—The shared values, beliefs, and standards for acceptable behavior.

organizational development (OD)—The ongoing planned change process that organizations use to improve performance.

organization chart—A graphic illustration of the organization's management hierarchy and departments and their working relationships.

organizing—The process of delegating and coordinating tasks and resources to achieve objectives.

orientation—Introduces new employees to the organization, its culture, and their jobs.

paraphrasing—The process of having receivers restate the message in their own words.

path–goal leaders—Determine employee objectives and achieve them using one of four styles.

people skills—The ability to work well with people.

perception—The process through which we select, organize, and interpret information from the surrounding environment.

performance—A measure of how well managers achieve organizational objectives.

performance appraisal—The ongoing process of evaluating employee performance.

performance equation—Performance = Ability × Motivation × Resources.

personality—The combination of traits that characterizes individuals.

PERT (Performance Evaluation and Review Technique) diagrams—These diagrams highlight the interdependence of activities by diagramming their network.

planning—The process of setting objectives and determining in advance exactly how the objectives will be met.

planning sheets—State an objective and list the sequence of activities, when each activity will begin and end, and who will complete each activity to meet the objective.

policies—General guidelines for decision making.

politics—The efforts of groups or individuals with competing interests to obtain power and positions of leadership.

power—The ability to influence the actions of others.

preliminary controls—Anticipate and prevent possible problems.

problem—Exists whenever objectives are not being met.

problem solving—The process of taking corrective action to meet objectives.

procedures—Sequences of actions to be followed in order to achieve an objective.

process-based motivation theories—Focus on understanding how employees choose behavior to fulfill their needs.

process consultation—An OD intervention designed to improve team dynamics.

productivity—Measures performance by dividing outputs by inputs.

programmed decisions—With recurring or routine situations, the decision maker should use decision rules or organizational policies and procedures to make the decision.

Pygmalion effect—Manager's attitudes and expectations of employees and how the manager treats employees affect their performance.

qualitative forecasting techniques—Use subjective judgment, intuition, experience, and opinion to predict sales.

quality—Actual use is compared to requirements to determine value.

quantitative forecasting techniques—Use objective, mathematical techniques and past sales data to predict sales.

receiver—The person to whom the message is sent.

reciprocity—Using mutual dependence to accomplish objectives.

recruiting—The process of attracting qualified candidates to apply for job openings.

reflecting—Paraphrasing the message and communicating understanding and acceptance to the sender.

reflective decision style—Taking plenty of time to decide, gathering considerable information, and analyzing numerous alternatives.

reflexive decision style—Making snap decisions without taking time to get all the information needed and without considering alternatives.

reinforcement theory—Proposes that consequences for behavior cause people to behave in predetermined ways.

reserve clause—Allowed teams to automatically resign their players at the end of the season.

responsibility—The obligation to achieve objectives by performing required activities.

rework controls—Actions taken to fix output.

rules—State exactly what should or should not be done.

salary caps—The maximum amount of money a team can spend on players.

sales forecast—Predicts the dollar amount of a product that will be sold during a specified period.

scheduling—The process of listing essential activities in sequence with the time needed to complete each activity.

selection—The process of choosing the most qualified applicant recruited for a job.

sender—Initiates communication by encoding and transmitting a message.

single-use plans—Programs and budgets developed for handling nonrepetitive situations.

situational favorableness—The degree to which a situation enables leaders to exert influence over followers.

situation analysis—Draws out those features in a company's environment that most directly frame its strategic window of options and opportunities.

social responsibility—The conscious effort to operate in a manner that creates a win–win situation for all stakeholders.

span of management—The number of employees reporting to a manager.

sport management—A multidisciplinary field that integrates the sport industry and management.

sport manager—The person responsible for achieving the sport organization's objectives through efficient and effective utilization of resources.

staff authority—The responsibility to advise and assist other personnel.

stages in the change process—Denial, resistance, exploration, and commitment.

stages of group development—Orientation, dissatisfaction, resolution, production, and termination.

stakeholders—People whose interests are affected by organizational behavior.

stakeholders' approach to ethics—Creating a win–win situation for all stakeholders so that everyone benefits from the decision.

standards—Minimize negative impacts on customers attributable to faulty output by controlling quantity, quality, time, cost, and behavior.

standing plans—Policies, procedures, and rules for handling situations that arise repeatedly.

status—The perceived ranking of one member relative to other members in the group.

strategic human resources planning—The process of staffing an organization to meet its objectives.

strategic planning—The process of developing a mission and long-term objectives and determining how they will be accomplished.

strategic process—In this process, managers develop the mission, analyze the environment, set objectives, develop strategies, and implement and control the strategies.

strategy—A plan for pursuing the mission and achieving objectives.

stress—Our body's internal reaction to external stimuli coming from the environment.

stressors—Situations in which people feel overwhelmed by anxiety, tension, and pressure.

strike—When employees collectively refuse to go to work.

structure—The way in which an organization groups its resources to accomplish its mission.

substitutes for leadership—Eliminate the need for a leader.

survey feedback—An OD technique that uses a questionnaire to gather data to use as the basis for change.

SWOT analysis—Used to assess strengths and weaknesses in the internal environment and opportunities and threats in the external environment.

symbolic leaders—Establish and maintain a strong organizational culture.

synectics—The process of generating novel alternatives through role-playing and fantasizing.

systems process—The method used to transform inputs into outputs.

task groups—Consist of employees who work on a specific objective.

team—A group with shared leadership whose members perform interdependent jobs with both individual and group accountability, evaluation, and rewards.

team building—Helps work groups increase structural and team dynamics performance.

technical skills—The ability to use methods and techniques to perform a task.

three levels of strategies—Corporate, business, and functional.

time management—Techniques that enable people to get more done in less time with better results.

time management systems—Planning each week, scheduling each week, and scheduling each day.

time series—Predicts future sales by extending the trend line of past sales into the future.

total quality management (TQM)—The process by which everyone in the organization focuses on the customer to continually improve product value.

training—Acquiring the skills necessary to perform a job.

trait theorists—Look for characteristics that make leaders effective.

transactional leaders—Emphasize exchange.

transformational leaders—Emphasize change, innovation, and entrepreneurship as they continually take their organization through three acts.

transmit—Use a form of communication to send a message.

two-dimensional leaders—Focus on job structure and employee considerations, which results in four possible leadership styles.

two-factor theory—Proposes that motivator factors, not maintenance factors, are what drive people to excel.

types of managers—General, functional, and project.

variables of change—Strategy, structure, technology, and people.

vertical communication—The downward and upward flow of information through an organization.

vestibule training—Develops skills in a simulated setting.

win–win situation—A situation in which both parties get what they want.

REFERENCES

TO THE STUDENT

1. www.vincelombardi.com/quotes.html (accessed July 20, 2012).

CHAPTER 1

1. K. Danylchuk, "Internationalizing Ourselves: Realities, Opportunities, and Challenges," *Journal of Sport Management* 25 (2011): 1-10.

2. National Association for Sport and Physical Education, www.aahperd.org/naspe/careers/sportmgmt.cfm.

3. B. Dwyer and Y. Kim, "For Love or Money: Developing and Validating a Motivational Scale for Fantasy Football Participation," *Journal of Sport Management* 25 (2011): 70-83.

4. D.F. Mahony, M. Mondello, M.A. Hums, and M. Judd, "Recruiting and Retaining Sport Management Faculty: Factors Affecting Job Choice," *Journal of Sport Management* 20 (2006): 414-430.

5. R.S. Weinberg and D. Gould, *Foundations of Sport and Exercise Psychology*, Champaign, IL: Human Kinetics, 2011.

6. S.D. Parks, *Leadership Can Be Taught: A Bold Approach for a Complex World*, Boston: Harvard Business School Press, 2005.

7. L. Chalip, "Toward a Distinctive Sport Discipline," *Journal of Sport Management* 20 (2006): 1-21.

8. North American Society for Sport Management, www.nassm.org (accessed September 21, 2011).

9. J. Malacko, "Preventive Management in Sport – A Challenge of New Ideas," *Sport Science* 4(1) (2011): 55-59.

10. J. Reynoso, "Value Creation and Sport Management," *Journal of Service Management* 22(3) (2011): 431-434.

11. M.K. Srivastava and D.R. Gnyawali, "When Do Relational Resources Matter? Leveraging Portfolio Technological Resources for Breakthrough Innovation," *Academy of Management Journal* 54(4) (2011): 797-810.

12. *Ibid.*

13. D. Shull, "Norman on the Economy: 'It is the worst I've ever seen America with the confidence level.'" *Street & Smith's Sport Business Journal* (August 15-21, 2011): 6.

14. J. De Avila, "A Wider World of Sports, Online," *Wall Street Journal* (March 10, 2009): D1.

15. *Wall Street Journal* (November 14, 1980): 33.

16. C. Gamble, "CFOs Cite Integrity As Most Important Trait," *T+D* 64(12) (December 2010): 18.

17. P. Martel, S. Maltbie, and J. Bond, "What Will Help Next Generation Leaders Advance?" *Public Management* 93(4) (May 2011): 18-20.

18. A.C. Cosper, "How to Be Great," *Entrepreneur* (March 2010): 12.

19. K.M. Bloomfield and R.A. Price, "So You Want to be a Billionaire," *Forbes* (August 30, 2010): 64-67.

20. C. Verzat, J. Byrne, and A. Fayolle, "Tangling With Spaghetti: Pedagogical Lessons From Games," *Academy of Management Learning and Education* 8(3) (2009): 356-369.

21. R.W. Stackman and K. Devine, "Leadership and Emotional-Rational Coherence: A Start?" *Academy of Management Perspectives* 25(1) (2011): 42-44.

22. M.F. Malinowski, "Essential Project Management Skills," *Project Management Journal* 42(2) (March 2011): 94.

23. M. McDonald and J.D. Westphal, "My Brother's Keeper? CEO Identification with the Corporate Elite, Social Support among CEOs, and Leader Effectiveness," *Academy of Management Journal* 54(4) (2011): 661-693.

24. P. Martel, S. Maltbie, and J. Bond, "What Will Help Next Generation Leaders Advance?" *Public Management* 93(4) (May 2011): 18-20.

25. G.A. Van Kleef, A.C. Homan, B. Beersma, D. Van Knippenberg, and F. Damen, "Searing Sentiment or Cold Calculation? The Effects of Leader Emotional Displays on Team Performance Depend on Follower Epistemic Motivation," *Academy of Management Journal* 52(3) (2009): 562-580.

26. M.J. Mills, "High-Involvement Work Practices: Are They Really Worth It?" *Academy of Management Perspectives* 23(3) (2009): 93-95.

27. R.S. Rubin and E.C. Dierdorff, "How Relevant is the MBA? Assessing the Alignment of Required Curricula and Required Managerial Competencies," *Academy of Management Learning and Education* 8(5) (2009): 208-224.

28. North American Society for Sport Management, www.nassm.org (accessed September 21, 2011).

29. E. Ghiselli, *Explorations in Management Talent*, Santa Monica, CA: Goodyear, 1971.

30. S.M. Farmer, X. Yao, and K.K. Mcintyre, "The Behavioral Impact of Entrepreneur Identity Aspiration and Prior Entrepreneurial Experience," *Entrepreneurship Theory and Practice* 35(2) (March 2011): 245-273.

31. *Ibid.*

32. R.W. Stackman and K. Devine, "Leadership and Emotional-Rational Coherence: A Start?" *Academy of Management Perspectives* 25(1) (2011): 42-44.

33. H. Mintzberg, *The Nature of Managerial Work,* New York: Harper & Row, 1973.

34. E. Morrison, "From the Editors," *Academy of Management Journal* 53(5) (2010): 932-936.

35. A. Murray, "The End of Management," *Wall Street Journal* (August 21-22, 2010): W3.

36. J.L. Stinson and D.R. Howard, "Athletic Success and Private Giving to Athletic and Academic Programs at NCAA Institutions," *Journal of Sport Management* 21 (2007): 235-264.

37. S.D. Parks, *Leadership Can Be Taught: A Bold Approach for a Complex World,* Boston: Harvard Business School Press, 2005.

38. L. Dragoni, P.E. Tesluk, J.E.A. Russell, and I. Oh, "Understanding Managerial Development: Integrating Developmental Assignments, Learning Orientation, and Access to Developmental Opportunities in Predicting Managerial Competencies," *Academy of Management Journal* 52(4) (2009): 731-742.

39. S. Overly, "Partnership with Under Armour Gets Attention for U-Md.'s Football Team," *Washington Post* (September 1, 2011).

CHAPTER 2

1. M. Steininger, "What Germans think of Dallas Mavericks star Dirk Nowitzki," *Christian Science Monitor* (June 13, 2011).

2. *Ibid.*

3. *Ibid.*

4. F.M. Santos and K.M. Eisengardt, "Constructing Markets and Shaping Boundaries: Entrepreneurial Power in Nascent Fields," *Academy of Management Journal* 52(4) (2009): 643-671.

5. B.R. Agle, N.J. Nagarajan, J.A. Sonnenfeld, and D. Srinivasan, "Does CEO Charisma Matter? An Empirical Analysis of the Relationship Among Organizational Performance, Environmental Uncertainty, and Top Management Team Perceptions of CEO Charisma," *Academy of Management Journal* 49 (2006): 161-174.

6. D. Ravasi and M. Schultz, "Responding to Organizational Identity Threats: Exploring the Role of Organizational Culture," *Academy of Management Journal* 49 (2006): 433-458.

7. R.S. Livengood and R.K. Reger, "That's Our Turf! Identify Domains and Competitive Dynamics," *Academy of Management Review* 35(1) (2010): 48-66.

8. *Ibid.*

9. N.A. Gardberg and C.J. Fombrun, "Corporate Citizenship: Creating Intangible Assists Across Institutional Environments," *Academy of Management Review* 31 (2006): 329-346.

10. J. He and H.C. Wang, "Innovation Knowledge Assets and Economic Performance: The Asymmetric Roles of Incentives and Monitoring," *Academy of Management Journal* 52(5) (2009): 919-938.

11. J. Woiceshyn and L. Falkenberg, "Value Creation in Knowledge-Based Firms: Aligning Problems and Resources," *Academy of Management Perspectives* 22(2) (2008): 85-99.

12. K.E.M. De Stobbeleir, S.J. Ashford, and D. Buyens, "Self-regulation of Creativity at Work: The Role of Feedback-Seeking Behavior in Creative Performance," *Academy of Management Journal* 54(4) (2011): 811-831.

13. W.D. Sine, H. Mitsuhashi, and D.A. Kirsch, "Revisiting Burns and Stalker: Formal Structure and New Venture Performance in Emerging Economic Sectors," *Academy of Management Journal* 49 (2006): 121-132.

14. M.K. Srivastava and D.R. Gnyawali, "When Do Relational Resources Matter? Leveraging Portfolio Technological Resources for Breakthrough Innovation," *Academy of Management Journal* 54(4) (2011): 797-810.

15. R.L. Priem, "A Consumer Perspective on Value Creation," *Academy of Management Review* 32 (2007): 219-235.

16. D. Sirmon, M.A. Hitt, and R.D. Ireland, "Managing Firm Resources in Dynamic Environments to Create Value: Looking Inside the Black Box," *Academy of Management Review* 32 (2007): 273-292.

17. K.E.M. De Stobbeleir, S.J. Ashford, and D. Buyens, "Self-regulation of Creativity at Work: The Role of Feedback-Seeking Behavior in Creative Performance," *Academy of Management Journal* 54(4) (2011): 811-831.

18. Press release, "Campbell's Chunky Soup Teams Up With NFL Legends Tony Dungy and Jerome Bettis to get Dads Off the Couch and on the Field," campbellsoup.com (September 21, 2010).

19. W. Tsai, K.H. Su, and M.J. Chen, "Seeing Through the Eyes of a Rival: Competitor Acumen Based on Rival-Centric Perceptions," *Academy of Management Journal* 54(4) (2011): 761-778.

20. S. Kesenne, "Competitive Balance in Team Sports and the Impact of Revenue Sharing," *Journal of Sport Management* 20 (2006): 39-51.

21. J. Maxcy and M. Mondello, "The Impact of Free Agency on Competitive Balance in North American Professional Team Sports Leagues," *Journal of Sport Management* 20 (2006): 39-51.

22. M. Maske, "Nike to Become NFL's Official Uniform Manufacturer," *Washington Post* (October 12, 2010).

23. C. Bode, S.M. Wagner, and L.M. Ellram, "Understanding Responses to Supply Chain Disruptions: Insights from Information Processing and Resource Dependence Perspectives," *Academy of Management Journal* 54(4) (2011): 833-856.

24. J. Maxcy and M. Mondello, "The Impact of Free Agency on Competitive Balance in North American Professional Team Sports Leagues," *Journal of Sport Management* 20 (2006): 39-51.

25. T. Raphael, "What a $252,000,000 Contract Means to You," *Workforce* 80(2) (2001): 112.

26. A. Shipley, "Lengthy NBA Lockout Looms, with Owners and Players Deeply Divided," *Washington Post* (June 29, 2011).

27. N. Davis and M.C. Duncan, "Fantasy Sports and Masculinity," *Journal of Sport and Social Issues* 30 (2006): 244-264.

28. E. Malcolm, "Paying the Price, Athletes Who Have Gotten in Trouble Over Twitter," www.associated-content.com/article/8046569/paying_the_price_athletes_who_have.html?cat=15 (May 22, 2011).

29. L. Chalip, "Toward a Distinctive Sport Discipline," *Journal of Sport Management* 20 (2006): 1-21.

30. F. Lera-Lopez and M. Rapun-Grarate, "The Demand for Sport: Sport Consumption and Participation Models," *Journal of Sport Management* 21 (2007): 103-122.

31. J. Maxcy and M. Mondello, "The Impact of Free Agency on Competitive Balance in North American Professional Team Sports Leagues," *Journal of Sport Management* 20 (2006): 39-51.

32. M.P. Sam and S.J. Jackson, "Developing National Sport Policy Through Consultation: The Rules of Engagement," *Journal of Sport Management* 20 (2006): 366-386.

33. S. Inglis, "Creative Tensions and Conversations in the Academy," *Journal of Sport Management* 21 (2007): 1-14.

34. R. Ackoff, *Creating the Corporate Future*, New York: Wiley, 1981.

35. H.J. Sapienza, E. Autio, G. George, and S.A. Zahra, "A Capabilities Perspective on the Effects of Early Internationalization of Firm Survival and Growth," *Academy of Management Review* 31 (2006): 914-933.

36. K. Danylchuk, "Internationalizing Ourselves: Realities, Opportunities, and Challenges," *Journal of Sport Management* 25 (2011): 1-10.

37. P. Navarro, "The Hidden Potential of 'Managerial Macroeconomics' for CEO Decision Making in MBA Programs," *Academy of Management Learning and Education* 5 (2006): 213-224.

38. S. McKelvey and A.M. Moorman, "Bush-Whacked: A Legal Analysis of the Unauthorized Use of Sport Organizations' Intellectual Property Campaign Advertising," *Journal of Sport Management* 21 (2007): 79-102.

39. D.S. Mason, L. Thibault, and L. Misener, "An Agency Theory Perspective on Corruption in Sport: The Case of the International Olympic Committee," *Journal of Sport Management* 20 (2006): 52-73.

40. S. Kesenne, "Competitive Balance in Team Sports and the Impact of Revenue Sharing," *Journal of Sport Management* 20 (2006): 39-51.

41. North American Society for Sport Management, www.nassm.org (accessed September 23, 2011).

42. S.D. Sidle, "Building a Committed Global Workforce: Does What Employees Want Depend on Culture?" *Academy of Management Perspectives* 23(1) (2009): 79-80.

43. R.N. Lussier, R. Baeder, and J. Corman, "Measuring Global Practices: Global Strategic Planning Through Company Situational Analysis," *Business Horizons* 37(5) (1994): 56-63.

44. J. Branch, "N.F.L. Experiment Aims to Spread Game's Appeal," www.nytimes.com (October 23, 2007).

45. Margin note, *BusinessWeek* (January 25, 2010): 9.

46. S. Hall, "Dentsu, Infront Sports & Media Launch Joint Venture to Distribute World Cup Broadcast Rights in Asia," *Japan Corporate News Network*, http://japancorp.net/ (October 17, 2006).

47. S.E. Feinberg and A.K. Gupta, "MNC Subsidiaries and Country Risk: Internalization as a Safeguard Against Weak External Institutions," *Academy of Management Journal* 52(2) (2009): 381-399.

48. K.L. Wakefield and D.L. Wann, "An Examination of Dysfunctional Sport Fans: Method of Classification and Relationships With Problem Behaviors," *Journal of Leisure Research* 38 (2006): 168-186.

49. S. Hall, "Introducing a Risk Assessment Model for Sporting Venues," *Sport Journal* 10(20) (2007): 294-312.

50. L. Thibault, "Globalization of Sport: An Inconvenient Truth," *Journal of Sport Management* 23 (2009): 1-20.

51. R. Audi, "Objectivity Without Egoism: Toward Balance in Business Ethics," *Academy of Management Learning and Education* 8(2) (2009): 263-274.

52. AACSB, *AACSB Standards 2011 Update Report:* 72.

53. P. Godfrey, "Corporate Social Responsibility in Sport: An Overview and Key Issues," *Journal of Sport Management* 23 (2009): 698-716.

54. J.B. Evans, L.K. Trevion, and G.R. Weaver, "Who's in the Ethics Driver's Seat? Factors Influencing Ethics in the MBA Curriculum," *Academy of Management Learning and Education* 5 (2006): 278-293.

55. E.M. Hartman, "Can We Teach Character? An Aristotelian Answer," *Academy of Management Learning and Education* 5 (2006): 68-81.

56. J.D. McMillen, "Sport Law: A Managerial Approach," *Journal of Sport Management* 21 (2007): 137-138.

57. B.E. Litzky, K.A. Eddlestan, and D.L. Kidder, "The Good, the Bad, and the Misguided: How Managers Inadvertently Encourage Deviant Behavior," *Academy of Management Perspectives* 20 (2006): 91-103.

58. Y. Mishina, B.J. Dykes, E.S. Block, and T.G. Pollock, "Why Good Firms Do Bad Things: The Effects of High Aspirations, High Expectations, and Prominence on the Incidence of Corporate Illegality," *Academy of Management Journal* 53(4) (2010): 701-722.

59. D.B. Montgomery and C.A. Ramus, "Calibrating MBA Job Preferences for the 21st Century," *Academy of Management Learning and Education* 10(1) (2011): 9-26.

60. E.A. Locke, "Business Ethics: A Way Out of the Morass," *Academy of Management Learning and Education* 5 (2006): 324-332.

61. *Ibid.*

62. *Ibid.*

63. B.E. Litzky, K.A. Eddlestan, and D.L. Kidder, "The Good, the Bad, and the Misguided: How Managers Inadvertently Encourage Deviant Behavior," *Academy of Management Perspectives* 20 (2006): 91-103.

64. R.A. Giacalone and K.R. Thompson, "Business Ethics and Social Responsibility Education: Shifting the Worldview," *Academy of Management Learning and Education* 5 (2006): 266-277.

65. D.O. Neubaum, M. Pagell, J.A. Drexler, F.M.M. Ryan, and E. Larson, "Business Education and Its Relationship to Student Personal Moral Philosophies and Attitudes Toward Profits: An Empirical Response to Critics," *Academy of Management Learning and Education* 8(1) (2009): 9-24.

66. S. Shaw and W. Frisby, "Can Gender Equity Be More Equitable? Promoting an Alternative Frame for Sport Management Research, Education, and Practice," *Journal of Sport Management* 20 (2006): 483-509.

67. G.B. Cunningham and J.S. Fink, "Diversity Issues in Sport and Leisure," *Journal of Sport Management* 20 (2006): 483-509.

68. C.A. Henle, "Bad Apples or Bad Barrels? A Former CEO Discusses the Interplay of Person and Situation With Implications for Business Education," *Academy of Management Learning and Education* 5 (2006): 346-355.

69. D.L. McCabe, K.D. Butterfield, and L.K. Trevino, "Academic Dishonesty in Graduate Business Programs: Prevalence, Causes, and Proposed Action," *Academy of Management Learning and Education* 5 (2006): 294-305.

70. R.A. Giacalone and K.R. Thompson, "Business Ethics and Social Responsibility Education: Shifting the Worldview," *Academy of Management Learning and Education* 5 (2006): 317-323.

71. D.L. McCabe, K.D. Butterfield, and L.K. Trevino, "Academic Dishonesty in Graduate Business Programs: Prevalence, Causes, and Proposed Action," *Academy of Management Learning and Education* 5 (2006): 294-305.

72. V. Tonoyan, R. Strohmeyer, M. Habib, and M. Perlitz, "Corruption and Entrepreneurship: How Formal and Informal Institutions Shape Small Firm Behavior in Transition and Mature Market Economies," *Entrepreneurship Theory and Practice* 34(5) (2010): 803-831.

73. E.A. Locke, "Business Ethics: A Way Out of the Morass," *Academy of Management Learning and Education* 5 (2006): 324-332.

74. "Infractions Appeals Committee Upholds Findings, Penalties of Former Head Women's Basketball Coach at Howard University," www.ncaa.org.

75. C.A. Henle, "Bad Apples or Bad Barrels? A Former CEO Discusses the Interplay of Person and Situation With Implications for Business Education," *Academy of Management Learning and Education* 5 (2006): 346-355.

76. D.S. Mason, L. Thibault, and L. Misener, "An Agency Theory Perspective on Corruption in Sport: The Case of the International Olympic Committee," *Journal of Sport Management* 20 (2006): 52-73.

77. S. Foy, "Can Physical Educators Do More to Teach Ethical Behavior in Sports?" *Journal of Physical Education, Recreation and Dance* 72(5) (2000): 12.

78. C. Bradish and J.J Cronin, "Corporate Social Responsibility in Sport," *Journal of Sport Management* 23 (2009): 691-697.

79. P.C. Godfrey, "Corporate Social Responsibility in Sport: An Overview of Key Issues," *Journal of Sport Management* 23 (2009): 698-716.

80. P. Navarro, "The MBA Core Curricula of Top-Ranked U.S. Business Schools: A Study of Failure?" *Academy of Management Learning and Education* 7(1) (2008): 108-123.

81. N.A. Gardberg and C.J. Fombrun, "Corporate Citizenship: Creating Intangible Assists Across Institutional Environments," *Academy of Management Review* 31 (2006): 329-346.

82. M. Henricks, "Three Are Better Than One," *Entrepreneur* (December 2006): 30.

83. R. Perrini, "Corporate Social Responsibility: Doing the Most Good for Your Company and Your Cause," *Academy of Management Perspectives* 20 (2006): 90-93.

84. T. Gardner, "Bruce Pearl Fired as Head Basketball Coach at Tennessee," *USA Today* (March 21, 2011).

85. http://liveunited.org/partners/national-football-league (accessed September 24, 2011).

86. Definition developed by the Brundtland Commission. Cited from Colvin interview of Linda Fisher, *Fortune* (November 23, 2009): 45-50.

87. A.A. Marcus and A.R. Fremeth, "Green Management Matters Regardless," *Academy of Management Perspectives* 23(3) (2009): 17-26.

88. Call for Papers, "Sustainability in Management Education," *Academy of Management Learning and Education* 8(3) (2009): 312.

89. K. Belson, "Gentlemen Start Conserving," www.nytimes.com (September 12, 2011).

90. *Ibid.*

91. P. French, "Beijing 2008—China's Olympic reputation risk," www.ethicalcorp.com.

92. D. Owen, "New Olympic Committee Chief Plans Reform Panel," www.ft.com (July 17, 2001).

93. A. Hughes, "Rogge worries about ethics and backs China to shine in 2012," www.morethanthegames.

co.uk/london-2012/1413242-rogge-worries-about-ethics-and-backs-china-shine-2012 (November 14, 2010).

94. J. Macur and E. Pfanner, "London Rioting Prompts Fear Over Soccer and Olympics," www.nytimes.com (August 9, 2011).

CHAPTER 3

1. Earnings call transcript, "Nine Months 2011 Results," www.adidas-group.com (accessed February 1, 2013).

2. "Reebok's shine dims post Adidas deal," *Boston Business Journal* (April 16, 2009).

3. T. Lefton, "What's Next for Reebok? 'Fun and Fit,'" *Sports Business Journal Daily* (April 13, 2009).

4. Earnings call transcript, "Nine Months 2011 Results," www.adidas-group.com (accessed February 1, 2013).

5. P. Martel, S. Maltbie, and J. Bond, "What Will Help Next Generation Leaders Advance?" *Public Management* 93(4) (May 2011): 8-20.

6. J. Samuelson, "The New Rigor: Beyond the Right Answer," *Academy of Management Learning and Education* 5 (2006): 356-365.

7. M. McDonald and J.D. Westphal, "My Brother's Keeper? CEO Identification with the Corporate Elite, Social Support among CEOs, and Leader Effectiveness," *Academy of Management Journal* 54(4) (2011): 661-693.

8. C. Tien, H. Lo, and H. Lin, "The Economic Benefits of Mega Events: A Myth or a Reality? A Longitudinal Study on the Olympic Games," *Journal of Sport Management* 25 (2011): 11-23.

9. K. Roach and M.A. Dixon, "Hiring Internal Employees: A View From the Field," *Journal of Sport Management* 20 (2006): 137-158.

10. M. Reiss, "Little Return on Secondary Investments," espn.com (accessed October 28, 2011).

11. H.D. Ireland and C.C. Miller, "Decision-Making and Firm Success," *Academy of Management Executive* 18 (2004): 8-12.

12. T. Archer, "Pressure will be on Jerry Jones as GM," espn.com (accessed July 19, 2011).

13. M. Parent, "Decision Making in Major Sport Events Over Time: Parameters, Drivers, and Strategies," *Journal of Sport Management* 24 (2010): 291-318.

14. M. Mazzeo, "Offseason Investment Paying off for Eli," espn.com (accessed October 21, 2011).

15. J. Taylor, "Tony Romo's blunders here to stay," espn.com (accessed October 4, 2011).

16. M.J. O'Fallon and K.D. Butterfield, "Moral Differentiation: Exploring Boundaries of the 'Monkey See, Monkey Do' Perspective," *Journal of Business Ethics* 102(3) (2011): 379-399.

17. M.E. Brown and M.S. Mitchell, "Ethical and Unethical Leadership: Exploring New Avenues for Future Research," *Business Ethics Quarterly* 20(4) (2010): 583-616.

18. M.K. Srivastava and D.R. Gnyawali, "When Do Relational Resources Matter? Leveraging Portfolio Technological Resources for Breakthrough Innovation," *Academy of Management Journal* 54(4) (2011): 797-810.

19. M. Parent, "Decision Making in Major Sport Events Over Time: Parameters, Drivers, and Strategies," *Journal of Sport Management* 24 (2010): 291-318.

20. *Ibid.*

21. D.S. Mason, L. Thibault, and L. Misener, "An Agency Theory Perspective on Corruption in Sport: The Case of the International Olympic Committee," *Journal of Sport Management* 20 (2006): 52-73.

22. K.E.M. De Stobbeleir, S.J. Ashford, and D. Buyens, "Self-regulation of Creativity at Work: The Role of Feedback-Seeking Behavior in Creative Performance," *Academy of Management Journal* 54(4) (2011): 811-831.

23. A. Joshi, "The Influence of Organizational Demography on the External Networking Behavior of Teams," *Academy of Management Review* 31 (2006): 583-595.

24. E.A. Locke and G.P. Latham, "Has Goal Setting Gone Wild, or Have Its Attackers Abandoned Good Scholarship?" *Academy of Management Perspective* 23(1) (2009): 17-23.

25. R.C. Litchfield, "Brainstorming Reconsidered: A Goal-Based View," *Academy of Management Review* 33(3) (2008): 649-668.

26. *Ibid.*

27. D.J. Haines and A. Farrell, "The Perceived Barriers to Research in College Recreational Sports," *Recreational Sports Journal* 30 (2006): 116-125.

28. K.E.M. De Stobbeleir, S.J. Ashford, and D. Buyens, "Self-regulation of Creativity at Work: The Role of Feedback-Seeking Behavior in Creative Performance," *Academy of Management Journal* 54(4) (2011): 811-831.

29. E.M. Spektor, M. Erez, and E. Naveh, "The Effect of Conformist and Attentive-to-Detail Members on Team Innovation: Reconciling the Innovation Paradox," *Academy of Management Journal* 54(4) (2011): 740-760.

30. S. Shellenbarger, "Better Ideas Through Failure," *Wall Street Journal* (September 27, 2011): D1, D4.

31. *Ibid.*

32. M.K. Srivastava and D.R. Gnyawali, "When Do Relational Resources Matter? Leveraging Portfolio Technological Resources for Breakthrough Innovation," *Academy of Management Journal* 54(4) (2011): 797-810.

33. K.E.M. De Stobbeleir, S.J. Ashford, and D. Buyens, "Self-regulation of Creativity at Work: The Role of Feedback-Seeking Behavior in Creative Performance," *Academy of Management Journal* 54(4) (2011): 811-831.

34. K. Roach and M.A. Dixon, "Hiring Internal Employees: A View From the Field," *Journal of Sport Management* 20 (2006): 137-158.

35. D.J. Haines and A. Farrell, "The Perceived Barriers to Research in College Recreational Sports," *Recreational Sports Journal* 30 (2006): 116-125.

36. www.moneyball-movie.com (accessed November 18, 2011).

37. D.J. Haines and A. Farrell, "The Perceived Barriers to Research in College Recreational Sports," *Recreational Sports Journal* 30 (2006): 116-125.

38. D.S. Mason, L. Thibault, and L. Misener, "An Agency Theory Perspective on Corruption in Sport: The Case of the International Olympic Committee," *Journal of Sport Management* 20 (2006): 52-73.

39. K. Roach and M.A. Dixon, "Hiring Internal Employees: A View From the Field," *Journal of Sport Management* 20 (2006): 137-158.

CHAPTER 4

1. M. Futterman and J. Revill, "Scandal–Hit FIFA Reelects President," *Wall Street Journal* (June 2, 2011): 7.

2. "Repeat Offender: FIFA's Chief Blatter's Remarks," http://news.sky.com/home/world-news/article/16112139 (November 17, 2011).

3. North American Society for Sport Management (www.nassm.org); S. Inglis, "Creative Tensions and Conversations in the Academy," *Journal of Sport Management* 21 (2007): 1-14.

4. M.L. McDonald and J.D. Westphal, "My Brother's Keeper? CEO Identification with the Corporate Elite, Social Support Among CEOs, and Leadership Effectiveness," *Academy of Management Journal* 54(4) (2011): 661-693.

5. L. Ferkins, D. Shilbury, and G. McDonald, "Board Involvement in Strategy: Advancing the Governance of Sport Organizations," *Journal of Sport Management* 23 (2009): 245-277.

6. C. Brennan, "US Players Weather Storm, But Their Rain Gear Doesn't," *USA Today* (October 1, 2010).

7. T. Weir, "Company Apologizes for Rain Suit Failure at Ryder Cup," *USA Today* (March 10, 2010).

8. H.A. Solberg and H. Preuss, "Major Sport Events and Long-Term Tourism Impacts," *Journal of Sport Management* 21 (2007): 213-234.

9. D.S. Mason, L. Thibault, and L. Misener, "An Agency Theory Perspective on Corruption in Sport: The Case of the International Olympic Committee," *Journal of Sport Management* 20 (2006): 52-73.

10. "Adidas Group to acquire outdoor specialist Five Ten," www.adidas-group.com/en/pressroom/archive/2011/03Nov2011_2.aspx (November 3, 2011).

11. "TaylorMade-adidas Golf Strategy," www.adidas-group.com/en/investorrelations/strategy/taylormade/default.aspx (accessed November 27, 2011).

12. *Ibid.*

13. FIFA Mission and Statutes, www.fifa.com/aboutfifa/organisation/mission.html (accessed November 27, 2011).

14. www.nassm.com/ (accessed November 27, 2011).

15. F. Lera-Lopez and M. Rapun-Grarate, "The Demand for Sport: Sport Consumption and Participation Models," *Journal of Sport Management* 21 (2007): 103-122.

16. W. Tsai, K.H. Su, and M.J. Chen, "Seeing Through the Eyes of a Rival: Competitor Acumen Based on Rival-Centric Perceptions," *Academy of Management Journal* 54(4) (2011): 761-778.

17. M. Porter, "How Competitive Forces Shape Strategy," *Harvard Business Review* 57(2) (1979): 137-145.

18. D. Rovell, "Nike Fights Back Against Toning Shoes: Will It Win?" cnbc.com (August 2, 2010; accessed October 11, 2011).

19. R. Channick, "Chicago Firm Will Help Introduce U.S. to Chinese Sports Apparel Giant," *Chicago Tribune* (January 12, 2011).

20. C. Bode, S.M. Wagner, and L.M. Ellram, "Understanding Responses to Supply Chain Disruptions: Insights from Information Processing and Resource Dependence Perspectives," *Academy of Management Journal* 54(4) (2011): 833-856.

21. G. Dutton, "How Nike Is Changing the World: One Factory at a Time," http://ethisphere.com/how-nike-is-changing-the-world-one-factory-at-a-time/ (March 26, 2008).

22. W. Tsai, K.H. Su, and M.J. Chen, "Seeing Through the Eyes of a Rival: Competitor Acumen Based on Rival-Centric Perceptions," *Academy of Management Journal* 54(4) (2011): 761-778.

23. G. Toczydlowski, Presentation at Springfield College (April 24, 2007).

24. W. Tsai, K.H. Su, and M.J. Chen, "Seeing Through the Eyes of a Rival: Competitor Acumen Based on Rival-Centric Perceptions," *Academy of Management Journal* 54(4) (2011): 761-778.

25. "Career Resolutions," *Wall Street Journal* (December 30, 1997): 1.

26. C. Ricketts, "Hit List/Lou Holtz," *Wall Street Journal* (December 23-24, 2006): 2; L. Holtz, "Setting a Higher Standard," in *Success Yearbook*, Tampa, FL: Peter Lowe International, 1998: 74.

27. P.C. Fiss, "Building Better Causal Theories: A Fuzzy Set Approach to Typologies in Organizational Research," *Academy of Management Journal* 54(2) (2011): 393-420.

28. M. Lewis, "Nike's $27B Growth Plans & Stats on $1.5B Action-Sports Group," *Transworld Business* (May 6, 2010).

29. Z. Miller, "Nike Sets Its Sights Higher for 2015 Sales Target," *Euromonitor International* (September 1, 2011).

30. A. Scarborough, "Nike Losing Ground in NCAA Arms Race," tuscaloosanews.com (May 18, 2011).

31. M.C. Sonfield and R.N. Lussier, "The Entrepreneurial Strategy Matrix Model for New and Ongoing Ventures," *Business Horizons* 40 (1997): 73-77.

32. P.C. Fiss, "Building Better Causal Theories: A Fuzzy Set Approach to Typologies in Organizational Research," *Academy of Management Journal* 54(2) (2011): 393-420.

33. *Ibid.*

34. *Ibid.*

35. M. Porter, *Competitive Strategy: Techniques for Analyzing Industries and Competitors,* New York: Free Press, 1980.

36. P.C. Fiss, "Building Better Causal Theories: A Fuzzy Set Approach to Typologies in Organizational Research," *Academy of Management Journal* 54(2) (2011): 393-420.

37. *Ibid.*

38. *Ibid.*

39. R. Batt and A.J.S. Colvin, "An Employment Systems Approach to Turnover: Human Resources Practices, Quits, Dismissals, and Performance," *Academy of Management Journal* 54(4) (2011): 695-717.

CHAPTER 5

1. This case is based on discussions with Michael Fioretti.

2. S. Cunningham, T. Cornwell, and L. Coote, "Expressing Identity and Shaping Image: The Relationship Between Corporate Mission and Corporate Sponsorship," *Journal of Sport Management* 23 (2009): 65-86.

3. J. Stevens, "The Canadian Hockey Association Merger and the Emergence of the Amateur Sport Enterprise," *Journal of Sport Management* 20 (2006): 74-100.

4. M. Farber, "Unlike in Other Leagues, a Captain in the NHL Not Only Wears His Rank on His Jersey but Also Can Wield as Much Influence Over his Teammates as the Coach," *Sports Illustrated* (October 16, 2000): 76-79.

5. C. Hann, "Control Issues," *Entrepreneur* (April 2012): 24.

6. A. Bernstein, "U.S. Olympic Committee on Notice with New CEO," *Washington Business Journal* (March 31, 2000): 22.

7. "Blake Resigns as CEO of USOC," http://robots.cnnsi.com/more/news/2000/10/25/usoc_blake_ap/.

8. "Forty Under Forty: Patrick Sandusky: United States Olympic Committee," *Sport Business Journal* (March 21, 2011): 15A.

9. P. Lawrence and J. Lorsch, *Organizations and Environment,* Burr Ridge, IL: Irwin, 1967.

10. S.H. Appelbaum, E. Adeland, and J. Harris, "Management of Sports Facilities: Stress and Terrorism Since 9/11," *Management Research News* 28(7) (2005): 69-83.

11. S. Walter, "Big Events Call for Even Bigger Security: Security in a Changing World: What Cities Are Doing to Prepare," *Nation's Cities Weekly* (January 21, 2002): 6.

12. C. Clarey, "SPECIAL REPORT: 2010 VANCOUVER OLYMPICS; Little Chill, but Vancouver Promises Plenty of Olympic Thrills," www.nytimes.com (February 12, 2010).

13. C. Hann, "Control Issues," *Entrepreneur* (April 2012): 24.

14. D.S. Mason, L. Thibault, and L. Misener, "An Agency Theory Perspective on Corruption in Sport: The Case of the International Olympic Committee," *Journal of Sport Management* 20 (2006): 52-73.

15. C. Hann, "Control Issues," *Entrepreneur* (April 2012): 24.

16. J. Reingold and J.L. Yang, "There's the Organization Chart—and Then There's the Way Things Really Work. Instead of Ignoring These Hidden Power Structures, Some Smart Companies Are Bringing Them Out of the Shadows," *Fortune* (July 23, 2007): 98-106.

17. M.K. Srivastava and D.R. Gnyawali, "When Do Relational Resources Matter? Leveraging Portfolio Technological Resources for Breakthrough Innovation," *Academy of Management Journal* 54(4) (2011): 797-810.

18. J. Reingold and J.L. Yang, "There's the Organization Chart—and Then There's the Way Things Really Work. Instead of Ignoring These Hidden Power Structures, Some Smart Companies Are Bringing Them Out of the Shadows," *Fortune* (July 23, 2007): 98-106.

19. *Ibid.*

20. A.A. King, M.J. Lenox, and A. Terlaak, "The Strategic Use of Decentralized Institutions: Exploring Certification With the ISO 14001 Management Standard," *Academy of Management Journal* 48 (2005): 1091-1106.

21. J. Reingold and J.L. Yang, "There's the Organization Chart—and Then There's the Way Things Really Work. Instead of Ignoring These Hidden Power Structures, Some Smart Companies Are Bringing Them Out of the Shadows," *Fortune* (July 23, 2007): 98-106.

22. L. Ferkins, D. Shilbury, and G. McDonald, "Board Involvement in Strategy: Advancing the Governance of Sport Organizations," *Journal of Sport Management* 23 (2006): 245-277.

23. http://investors.nikeinc.com/Theme/Nike/files/doc_financials/AnnualReports/2011/index.html.

24. K. Helliker, "Realignment Can't Make You Smarter," *Wall Street Journal* (September 22, 2011): D8.

25. R. Hackman and G. Oldham, *Work Redesign,* Reading, MA: Addison-Wesley, 1980.

26. W. Tsai, K.H. Su, and M.J. Chen, "Seeing Through the Eyes of a Rival: Competitor Acumen Based on Rival-Centric Perceptions," *Academy of Management Journal* 54(4) (2011): 761-778.

27. C. Hann, "Control Issues," *Entrepreneur* (April 2012): 24.

28. D.S. Mason, L. Thibault, and L. Misener, "An Agency Theory Perspective on Corruption in Sport: The Case of the International Olympic Committee," *Journal of Sport Management* 20 (2006): 52-73.

29. C. Hann, "Control Issues," *Entrepreneur* (April 2012): 24.

30. *Ibid.*

31. K. Langlois, "A Wild Ride," www.nba.com/pistons/features/davidson_partone.html.

CHAPTER 6

1. K. Armstrong, "Lifting the Veils and Illuminating the Shadows: Furthering the Explorations of Race and Ethnicity in Sport Management," *Journal of Sport Management* 25 (2011): 95-106.

2. G. Clavio and A. Eagleman, "Gender and Sexually Suggestive Images in Sports Blogs," *Journal of Sport Management* 25 (2011): 295-304.

3. E. Smith and A. Hattery, "Race Relations Theories: Implications for Sport Management," *Journal of Sport Management* 25 (2011): 107-111.

4. G. Cunningham, "Understanding the Diversity-Related Change Process: A Field Study," *Journal of Sport Management* 23 (2009): 407-428.

5. L. Burton, H. Grappendorf, and A. Henderson, "Perceptions of Gender in Athletic Administration: Utilizing Role Congruity to Examine (Potential) Prejudice Against Women," *Journal of Sport Management* 20 (2006): 483-509.

6. Yogi Berra, www.yogi-berra.com.

7. D. Hoch, "The Athletic Director and Change," *Coach & Athletic Director* 71(9) (April 2, 2002): 4-5.

8. J. Harris, "Sociology of Sport: Expanding Horizons in the Subdiscipline," *Quest* 58 (2006): 71-91.

9. District of Columbia State Data Center, *quarterly report*, "Super Bowl 1 (1967) vs. Super Bowl XLI" (January 2007).

10. W.J. Henisz, "Leveraging the Financial Crisis to Fulfill the Promise of Progressive Management," *Academy of Management Education and Learning* 10(2) (2011): 298-321.

11. M. Maske, "NFL Network Will Allow Simulcast of Patriots-Giants," *Washington Post* (December 27, 2007): EO6.

12. Associated Press, "Super Bowl to be streamed online" (December 20, 2011).

13. S. Mohammed and S. Nadkarni, "Temporal Diversity and Team Performance: The Moderating Role of Team Temporal Leadership," *Academy of Management Journal* 54(3) (2011): 489-506.

14. D. Hoch, "The Athletic Director and Change," *Coach & Athletic Director* 71(9) (April 2, 2002): 4-5.

15. www.cybexintl.com.

16. An excellent site on the history of fencing can be found at www.ahfi.org.

17. www.cybexintl.com/products/strength/BravoExt/default.aspx (accessed December 24, 2011).

18. "AIA: Conveyors Drive Productivity in Golf Ball Packaging," *assemblymag.com* (September 6, 2005).

19. C. Conway, "Physical Education and the Use of ICT," *British Journal of Teaching Physical Education* 31(3) (2000): 12-13.

20. R. Adams, "Extra Innings: The Secret to Winning After 40," *Wall Street Journal* (July 21-22, 2007): P1, P3.

21. S. Kuper, "Inside Baseball, Michael Lewis and Billy Beane talk *Moneyball,*" *Financial Times* (November 13, 2011).

22. D. Farrar, "Has ESPN created the perfect quarterback rating? Not just yet . . .", yahoo.com (August 1, 2011).

23. A. Gupta, "Leadership in a Fast-Paced World: An Interview With Ken Blanchard," *Mid-American Journal of Business* 20 (2005): 7-11.

24. A.H. Van de Ven and K. Sun, "Breakdowns in Implementing Models of Organizational Change," *Academy of Management Perspectives* 25(3) (2011): 58-74.

25. G.B. Cunningham and J.S. Fink, "Diversity Issues in Sport and Leisure," *Journal of Sport Management* 20 (2006): 483-509.

26. W.J. Henisz, "Leveraging the Financial Crisis to Fulfill the Promise of Progressive Management," *Academy of Management Education and Learning* 10(2) (2011): 298-321.

27. J. Lok, "Institutional Logics as Identity Projects," *Academy of Management Journal* 53(6) (2010): 1305-1335.

28. A. Gupta, "Leadership in a Fast-Paced World: An Interview With Ken Blanchard," *Mid-American Journal of Business* 20 (2005): 7-11.

29. P. Shrivastava, "Pedagogy of Passion for Sustainability," *Academy of Management Learning and Education* 9(3) (2010): 443-455.

30. A.H. Van de Ven and K. Sun, "Breakdowns in Implementing Models of Organizational Change," *Academy of Management Perspectives* 25(3) (2011): 58-74.

31. C. Fritz, C.F. Lam, and G.M. Spreitzer, "It's the Little Things That Matter: An Examination of Knowledge Workers' Energy Management," *Academy of Management Perspectives* 25(3) (2011): 28-39.

32. K. Hultman, *Resistance Matrix: The Path of Least Resistance,* Austin, TX: Learning Concepts, 1979.

33. A.H. Van de Ven and K. Sun, "Breakdowns in Implementing Models of Organizational Change," *Academy of Management Perspectives* 25(3) (2011): 58-74.

34. J. Lok, "Institutional Logics as Identity Projects," *Academy of Management Journal* 53(6) (2010): 1305-1335.

35. *Ibid.*

36. K. Roach and M.A. Dixon, "Hiring Internal Employees: A View From the Field," *Journal of Sport Management* 20 (2006): 137-158.

37. Y. Liu and J. Wang, "Discussion on Sports Team Culture," *Journal of Capital College of Physical Education* 13(1) (2001): 28-33.

38. E. Schein, *Organizational Culture and Leadership*, San Francisco: Jossey-Bass, 1985.

39. C. Hymowitz, "Executives Who Build Truth-Telling Cultures Learn Fast What Works," *Wall Street Journal* (June 12, 2006): B1.

40. J. Macmullan, "A Turn at Gates Is Just His Style," *bostonglobe.com* (April 4, 2002).

41. M. Feinsand, "Joe Torre Says MLB May Ban Alcohol From All Big-League Clubhouses After Red Sox Drinking Debacle," nydailynews.com (October 11, 2011).

42. Wilson Sporting Goods, www.wilson.com.

43. H. Williams, "The Backstretch Blog: NASCAR Needs to Go Soft," *Chicago Tribune* (August 16, 2011).

44. M. Kreidler, "Steve Jobs' Reach Into Sports," espn.com (October 7, 2011).

45. M. Reiss, "Belichick Breaks Silence on Spygate," *bostonglobe.com* (February 17, 2008).

46. G.B. Cunningham and J.S. Fink, "Diversity Issues in Sport and Leisure," *Journal of Sport Management* 20 (2006): 483-509.

47. *Ibid.*

48. G.B. Cunningham, "Opening the Black Box: The Influence of Perceived Diversity and a Common In-Group Identity in Diverse Groups," *Journal of Sport Management* 21 (2007): 58-78.

49. Census, *Wall Street Journal* (December 22, 2011): A1.

50. National Public Radio, news broadcast on WFCR (March 30, 2011).

51. C. Dougherty, "U.S. Nears Racial Milestone," *Wall Street Journal* (June 11, 2010): A3.

52. M. Jordan, "Births Fuel Hispanic Gains," *Wall Street Journal* (July 15, 2011): A3.

53. C. Dougherty, "New Faces of Childhood," *Wall Street Journal* (April 6, 2011): A3.

54. M. Jordan, "Illegals Estimated to Account for 1 in 12 U.S. Births," *Wall Street Journal* (August 12, 2010): A1-A2.

55. S. Reddy, "Latinos Fuel Growth in Decade," *Wall Street Journal* (March 25, 2011): A2.

56. G. Daddario and B.J. Wigley, "Prejudice, Patriarch, and the PGA: Defensive Discourse Surrounding the Shoal Creek and Augusta National Controversies," *Journal of Sport Management* 20 (2006): 466-482.

57. M.L. Sartore, "Categorization, Performance Appraisals, and Self-Limiting Behavior: The Impact on Current and Future Performance," *Journal of Sport Management* 20 (2006): 535-553.

58. G.B. Cunningham and J.S. Fink, "Diversity Issues in Sport and Leisure," *Journal of Sport Management* 20 (2006): 483-509.

59. S. Shaw, "Scratching the Back of 'Mr. X': Analyzing Gendered Social Processes in Sport Organizations," *Journal of Sport Management* 20 (2006): 510-534.

60. D.L. Gill, R.G. Morrow, K.E. Collins, A.B. Lucey, and A.M. Schultz, "Attitudes and Sexual Prejudice in Sport and Physical Activity," *Journal of Sport Management* 20 (2006): 554-564.

61. M.L. Sartore, "Categorization, Performance Appraisals, and Self-Limiting Behavior: The Impact on Current and Future Performance," *Journal of Sport Management* 20 (2006): 535-553.

62. G.B. Cunningham, J.E. Bruening, and J. Straub, "The Underrepresentation of African Americans in NCAA Division I-A Head Coaching Positions," *Journal of Sport Management* 20 (2006): 387-413.

63. C. Hymowitz, "Two Football Coaches Have a Lot to Teach Screaming Managers," *Wall Street Journal* (January 29, 2007): B1.

64. M. Klis, "Black power: Still in playoffs, Lovie Smith and Tony Dungy also part of strong core of African Americans in top NFL jobs," *denverpost.com* (January 21, 2007).

65. K. Russell, "The First Black Coach in Sports on The Super Bowl," huffingtonpost.com (February 4, 2007).

66. E. Smith and A. Hattery, "Race Relations Theories: Implications for Sport Management," *Journal of Sport Management* 25 (2011) 107-111.

67. *Ibid.*

68. National Women's Law Center, www.pay-equity.org/PDFs/PFA-FactSheet-2010.pdf (April 10, 2010).

69. S. Shaw and W. Frisby, "Can Gender Equity Be More Equitable? Promoting an Alternative Frame for Sport Management Research, Education, and Practice," *Journal of Sport Management* 20 (2006): 483-509.

70. L.P. McGinnis and J.W. Gentry, "Getting Past the Red Tees: Constraints Women Face in Golf and Strategies to Help Them," *Journal of Sport Management* 20 (2006): 216-247.

71. S. Shaw, "Scratching the Back of 'Mr. X': Analyzing Gendered Social Processes in Sport Organizations," *Journal of Sport Management* 20 (2006): 510-534.

72. A. Finley, "Billie Jean King Commemorates Title IX's 35th Anniversary," *Stanford Review Online* (May 11, 2007).

73. J. Steeg, "Hard time' for Vivas during tenure at Fresno State," *USA Today* (May 13, 2008).

74. A.H. Van de Ven and K. Sun, "Breakdowns in Implementing Models of Organizational Change," *Academy of Management Perspectives* 25(3) (2011): 58-74.

75. E.M. Spektor, M. Erez, and E. Naveh, "The Effect of Conformist and Attentive-to-Detail Members on Team Innovation: Reconciling the Innovation Paradox," *Academy of Management Journal* 54(4) (2011): 740-760.

76. *Ibid.*

77. A.H. Van de Ven and K. Sun, "Breakdowns in Implementing Models of Organizational Change," *Academy of Management Perspectives* 25(3) (2011): 58-74.

78. J. Glasser, "King of the Hill: In Big-Time College Sports, Athletic Directors Like Ohio State's Andy Geiger Rule," *U.S. News & World Report* (March 18, 2002): 52-60.

79. www.ohiostatebuckeyes.com/genrel/smith_gene00.html (accessed January 27, 2012).

80. L.J. Werteim, "The Program," *Sports Illustrated* (March 5, 2007): 54-62.

81. P. Thamel, "Ohio St. Receives One Year Bowl Ban," www.nytimes.com (December 20, 2011).

CHAPTER 7

1. I. Nooyi, "Role Models," *Entrepreneur* (March 2012): 63.

2. R. Batt and A.J.S. Colving, "An Employment Systems Approach to Turnover: Human Resources Practices, Quits, Dismissals, and Performance," *Academy of Management Journal* 54(4) (2011): 695-717.

3. S. Shaw, "Scratching the Back of 'Mr. X': Analyzing Gendered Social Processes in Sport Organizations," *Journal of Sport Management* 20 (2006): 510-534.

4. www.eeoc.gov/laws/statutes/titlevii.cfm (accessed December 30, 2011).

5. L.J. Burton, H. Grappendorf, and A. Henderson, "Perceptions of Gender in Athletic Administration: Utilizing Role Congruity to Examine (Potential) Prejudice Against Women," *Journal of Sport Management* 25 (2011): 36-45.

6. U.S. Equal Employment Opportunity Commission, www.eeoc.gov (accessed June 29, 2012).

7. M.L. Sartore and G.B. Cunningham, "Weight Discrimination, Hiring Recommendations, Person-Job Fit, and Attributions: Fitness-Industry Implications," *Journal of Sport Management* 21 (2007): 172-193.

8. R. Batt and A.J.S. Colving, "An Employment Systems Approach to Turnover: Human Resources Practices, Quits, Dismissals, and Performance," *Academy of Management Journal* 54(4) (2011): 695-717.

9. T. Taylor and C. Ho, "Global Human Resource Management Influences on Local Sport Organizations," *International Journal of Sport Management and Marketing* 1 (2005): 110-126.

10. This job description was used with permission from Elms College.

11. A.R. Connell, "Eye of the Beholder: Does What Is Important About a Job Depend on Who Is Asked?" *Academy of Management Perspectives* 24(2) (2010): 83-85.

12. Aon website, www.aon.com (accessed January 15, 2012).

13. T. Engelberg, D.H. Zakus, J.L. Skinner, and A. Campbell, "Defining and Measuring Dimensionality and Targets of the Commitment of Sport Volunteers," *Journal of Sport Management* 26 (2012): 192-205.

14. Higheredjobs.com (accessed January 13, 2012).

15. D. Snyder, "The Root: Stop Picking on Lebron," npr.org (July 9, 2010).

16. T. Miller, "Best Recruiting Programs Since 2007," http://espn.go.com/blog/pac10/post/_/id/34159/best-recruiting-programs-since-2007 (February 3, 2012).

17. K. Roach and M.A. Dixon, "Hiring Internal Employees: A View From the Field," *Journal of Sport Management* 20 (2006): 137-158.

18. *Ibid.*

19. NBA website, www.nba.com/dleague/fan_faq.html#fanfaq1 (accessed February 3, 2012).

20. R. Bachman, "Schools That Train the Enemy," *Wall Street Journal* (June 6, 2012): D6.

21. E. Clark, "The Best Baseball Coach in the NFL," *Wall Street Journal* (June 15, 2012): D9.

22. R. Batt and A.J.S. Colving, "An Employment Systems Approach to Turnover: Human Resources Practices, Quits, Dismissals, and Performance," *Academy of Management Journal* 54(4) (2011): 695-717.

23. *Ibid.*

24. R.E. Silverman, "Work Reviews Losing Steam," *Wall Street Journal* (December 19, 2011): D1.

25. E. Smith and A. Hattery, "Race Relations Theories: Implications for Sport Management," *Journal of Sport Management* 25 (2011): 107-117.

26. R. Batt and A.J.S. Colving, "An Employment Systems Approach to Turnover: Human Resources Practices, Quits, Dismissals, and Performance," *Academy of Management Journal* 54(4) (2011): 695-717.

27. S. Warner, B. Newland, and B.C. Green, "More Than Motivation: Reconsidering Volunteer Management Tools," *Journal of Sport Management* 25 (2011): 391-407.

28. R.E. Silverman, "Work Reviews Losing Steam," *Wall Street Journal* (December 19, 2011): D1.

29. K. Badenhausen, "The Heaviest Hitters," *Forbes* (April 2012): 78-81.

30. Staff, "Spend It Like Beckham," *Forbes* (May 7, 2012): 22.

31. D. Engbar, "Does OSHA Keep Tabs on the NFL?" www.slate.com (July 25, 2007).

32. Associated Press, "Vikes Take Precautions With Heavy Williams," www.sportingnews.com (July 31, 2006).

33. R.N. Lussier, "Maintaining Civility in the Laboratory," *Clinical Leadership and Management Review* 19(6) (2005): E4.

34. W. Williamson, "Broncos Make Front-Office Change," www.espn.com (accessed February 4, 2012).

35. A. Schwarz, "Word for Word/Blast From the Past—Baseball in Crisis? Nah. It's Déjà vu All Over Again," *New York Times* (July 14, 2002): 7.

36. L. Koppett, *Koppett's Concise History of Major League Baseball*, Philadelphia: Temple University Press, 1998.

37. *Ibid.*

38. N. David, "NFL, Players Announce New 10-year Labor Agreement," usatoday.com (July 25, 2011).

39. *Ibid.*

40. H. Beck, "N.B.A. Reaches a Tentative Deal to Save the Season," www.nytimes.com (November 26, 2011).

41. "2012 NBA Finals Tie Last Year's TV Rating," www.nba.com/2012/news/06/22/finals-ratings.ap/index.html (June 22, 2012).

42. R. Batt and A.J.S. Colving, "An Employment Systems Approach to Turnover: Human Resources Practices, Quits, Dismissals, and Performance," *Academy of Management Journal* 54(4) (2011): 695-717.

43. B. Fikes, "TaylorMade-adidas Cuts 41," www.nytimes.com (June 14, 2007).

44. NCAA Web site (www.ncaa.org). accessed February 4, 2012.

45. S. Silverthrone, "On Managing with Bobby Knight and 'Coach K,'" Harvard Business School, http://hbswk.hbs.edu/item/5464.html (August 14, 2006).

46. T. Gardner, "Pat Knight Fired as Head Coach at Texas Tech," *USA Today* (March 7, 2011), http://content.usatoday.com/communities/campusrivalry/post/2011/03/report-pat-knight-fired-as-coach-at-texas-tech/1.

CHAPTER 8

1. G. Lippi, M. Franchini, and G. Guidi, "Tour de Chaos," *British Journal of Sport Medicine* 41(10) (October 2007): 625-632.

2. J. Macur, "Landis's Positive Doping Test Upheld," www.*nytimes.com* (September 21, 2007).

3. M. Zalewski, "Landis Loses Final Appeal," cyclingnews.com (June 30, 2008).

4. A. Shipley, "Alberto Contador stripped of 2010 Tour de France title, given two-year ban for positive test," washingtonpost.com (February 6, 2012).

5. G. Risling, "Lance Armstrong Doping Probe Dropped," time.com (February 3, 2012).

6. B. Nightengale, "Ryan Braun Tests Positive for PED, Says 'It's BS,'" usatoday.com (December 11, 2011).

7. M. Fainaru-Wada and T.J. Quinn, "Ryan Braun Wins Appeal of Suspension," espn.com (February 24, 2012).

8. M. Schmidt, "Selig Says Steroid Era Is Basically Over," www.nytimes.com (January 11, 2010).

9. R. Sibson, "'I Was Banging My Head Against the Wall': Exclusionary Power and the Gendering of Sport Organizations," *Journal of Sport Management* 24 (2010): 379-399.

10. D. Goetzl, "New Sport: Personality Contests; Shows Turn to Comedy to Lure Bigger Audience," *Advertising Age* 72 (November 12, 2001): 18.

11. K.E.M. De Stobbeleir, S.J. Ashford, and D. Buyens, "Self-regulation of Creativity at Work: The Role of Feedback-Seeking Behavior in Creative Performance," *Academy of Management Journal* 54(4) (2011): 811-831.

12. E. Bernstein, "Therapy That Keeps on the Sunny Side of Life," *Wall Street Journal* (September 26, 2006): D1.

13. M.K. Srivastava and D.R. Gnyawali, "When Do Relational Resources Matter? Leveraging Portfolio Technological Resources for Breakthrough Innovation," *Academy of Management Journal* 54(4) (2011): 797-810.

14. B. Hofheimer, "ESPN Launches New NFL Shows, Expands Others," www.espnmediazone3.com/us/2011/09/08/espn-launches-new-nfl-shows-expands-others/ (September 8, 2011).

15. A. Haupt, "11 Health Habits That Will Help You Live to 100," MSN, http://health.msn.com/healthy-living/11-Health-Habits-That-Will-Help-You-Live-to-100#scptmd (January 30, 2012).

16. K.E.M. De Stobbeleir, S.J. Ashford, and D. Buyens, "Self-regulation of Creativity at Work: The Role of Feedback-Seeking Behavior in Creative Performance," *Academy of Management Journal* 54(4) (2011): 811-831.

17. *Ibid.*

18. A. Haupt, "11 Health Habits That Will Help You Live to 100," MSN, http://health.msn.com/healthy-living/11-Health-Habits-That-Will-Help-You-Live-to-100#scptmd (January 30, 2012).

19. K.E.M. De Stobbeleir, S.J. Ashford, and D. Buyens, "Self-regulation of Creativity at Work: The Role of Feedback-Seeking Behavior in Creative Performance," *Academy of Management Journal* 54(4) (2011): 811-831.

20. G. Toczydlowski, Presentation at Springfield College (April 24, 2007).

21. E. Hochuli, "Admit a Mistake," *BusinessWeek* (April 12, 2012): 78.

22. G.B. Cunningham, "Opening the Black Box: The Influence of Perceived Diversity and a Common In-Group Identity in Diverse Groups," *Journal of Sport Management* 21 (2007): 58-78.

23. G.B. Cunningham, J.E. Bruening, and J. Straub, "The Underrepresentation of African Americans in NCAA Division I-A Head Coaching Positions," *Journal of Sport Management* 20 (2006): 387-413.

24. B.J. Hoffman, B.H. Bynum, R.F. Piccolo, and A.W. Sutton, "Person-Organization Value Congruence: How Transformational Leaders Influence Work Group Effectiveness," *Academy of Management Journal* 54(4) (2011): 779-796.

25. W. Tsai, K.H. Su, and M.J. Chen, "Seeing Through the Eyes of a Rival: Competitor Acumen Based on Rival-Centric Perceptions," *Academy of Management Journal* 54(4) (2011): 761-778.

26. E. Hochuli, "Admit a Mistake," *BusinessWeek* (April 12, 2012): 78.

27. B.J. Hoffman, B.H. Bynum, R.F. Piccolo, and A.W. Sutton, "Person-Organization Value Congruence: How Transformational Leaders Influence Work Group Effectiveness," *Academy of Management Journal* 54(4) (2011): 779-796.

28. M.M. Parent and P.O. Foreman, "Organizational Image and Identity Management in Large-Scale Sporting Events," *Journal of Sport Management* 21 (2007): 15-40.

29. F. Evans, "Tiger triumphs again at AT&T," espn.com (July 1, 2012).

30. J. Hill, "Metta World Peace has history: Suspension for hitting James Harden should be at least 10 games," espn.com (April 23, 2012).

31. W. Tsai, K.H. Su, and M.J. Chen, "Seeing Through the Eyes of a Rival: Competitor Acumen Based on Rival-Centric Perceptions," *Academy of Management Journal* 54(4) (2011): 761-778.

32. Y. Lee, "A New Voice: Korean American Women in Sports," *International Review for the Sociology of Sport* 40 (2005): 481-495.

33. M.L. Sartore and G.B. Cunningham, "Weight Discrimination, Hiring Recommendations, Person-Job Fit, and Attributions: Fitness-Industry Implications," *Journal of Sport Management* 21 (2007): 172-193.

34. *Ibid.*

35. M.K. Srivastava and D.R. Gnyawali, "When Do Relational Resources Matter? Leveraging Portfolio Technological Resources for Breakthrough Innovation," *Academy of Management Journal* 54(4) (2011): 797-810.

36. B.J. Hoffman, B.H. Bynum, R.F. Piccolo, and A.W. Sutton, "Person-Organization Value Congruence: How Transformational Leaders Influence Work Group Effectiveness," *Academy of Management Journal* 54(4) (2011): 779-796.

37. K.L. Wakefield and D.L. Wann, "An Examination of Dysfunctional Sport Fans: Method of Classification and Relationships With Problem Behaviors," *Journal of Leisure Research* 38 (2006): 168-186.

38. B.J. Hoffman, B.H. Bynum, R.F. Piccolo, and A.W. Sutton, "Person-Organization Value Congruence: How Transformational Leaders Influence Work Group Effectiveness," *Academy of Management Journal* 54(4) (2011): 779-796.

39. A. Hill with J. Wooden, *Be Quick—But Don't Hurry: Learning Success From the Teachings of a Lifetime,* New York: Simon & Schuster, 2001. Visit www.coachwooden.com for an interactive tour of Wooden's pyramid of success.

40. Y.S. Choi, M. Seo, D. Scott, and J. Martin, "Validation of the Organizational Culture Assessment Instrument: An Application of the Korean Version," *Journal of Sport Management* 24 (2010): 169-189.

41. K. Blanchard, D. Hutson, and E. Wills, *The One Minute Entrepreneur,* New York: Currency/Doubleday, 2008.

42. S. Shaw and W. Frisby, "Can Gender Equity Be More Equitable? Promoting an Alternative Frame for Sport Management Research, Education, and Practice," *Journal of Sport Management* 20 (2006): 483-509.

43. A.C. Cosper, "The Zen Zone," *Entrepreneur* (March 2012): 12.

44. R. Sibson, "'I Was Banging My Head Against the Wall': Exclusionary Power and the Gendering of Sport Organizations," *Journal of Sport Management* 24 (2010): 379-399.

45. S. Shaw, "Scratching the Back of 'Mr. X': Analyzing Gendered Social Processes in Sport Organizations," *Journal of Sport Management* 20 (2006): 510-534.

46. J. Zweig, "What Conflict of Interest? How Power Blinds Us to Our Flaws," *Wall Street Journal* (October 16-17, 2010): C1.

47. A.C. Cosper, "The Zen Zone," *Entrepreneur* (March 2012): 12.

48. M. Kim, P. Chelladurai, and G.T. Trail, "A Model of Volunteer Retention in Youth Sport," *Journal of Sport Management* 21 (2007): 151-171.

49. M.K. Srivastava and D.R. Gnyawali, "When Do Relational Resources Matter? Leveraging Portfolio Technological Resources for Breakthrough Innovation," *Academy of Management Journal* 54(4) (2011): 797-810.

50. D. McClelland and D.H. Burnham, "Power Is the Great Motivator," *Harvard Business Review* (March/April 1978): 103.

51. S. Shaw, "Scratching the Back of 'Mr. X': Analyzing Gendered Social Processes in Sport Organizations," *Journal of Sport Management* 20 (2006): 510-534.

52. G.A. Fowler, "Are You Talking to Me?" *Wall Street Journal* (April 25, 2011): R5.

53. J. Zaslow, "The Greatest Generation (of Networkers)," *Wall Street Journal* (November 4, 2009): D1, D3.

54. A. Gumbus and R.N. Lussier, "Career Development: Enhancing Your Networking Skill," *Clinical Leadership and Management Review* 17 (2003): 16-20.

55. S. Raice, "Friend—and Possible Employee," *Wall Street Journal* (October 24, 2011): R4.

56. J. Zaslow, "The Greatest Generation (of Networkers)," *Wall Street Journal* (November 4, 2009): D1, D3.

57. A. Gupta, "Leadership in a Fast-Paced World: An Interview With Ken Blanchard," *Mid-American Journal of Business* 20 (2005): 7-11.

58. C. Hann, "The Masters," *Entrepreneur* (March 2012): 54-58.

59. R. Abrams, "Put Spring in Your Business," *Costco Connection* (April 2012): 13.

60. E. Hochuli, "Admit a Mistake," *BusinessWeek* (April 12, 2012): 78.

61. E.M. Spektor, M. Erez, and E. Naveh, "The Effect of Conformist and Attentive-to-Detail Members on

Team Innovation: Reconciling the Innovation Paradox," *Academy of Management Journal* 54(4) (2011): 740-760.

62. A. Kaburakis, "International Prospective Student-Athletes and NCAA Division I Amateurism," *International Journal of Sport Management and Marketing* 2 (2007): 100-118.

63. E. Bernstein, "Friendly Fight: A Smarter Way to Say I'm Angry," *Wall Street Journal* (April 19, 2011): D1, D4.

64. *Ibid.*

65. C. Hyatt, "Qualitative Methods in Sport Studies," *Journal of Sport Management* 21 (2007): 281-282.

66. B. Denham, "Government and the Pursuit of Rigorous Drug Testing in Major League Baseball: A Study in Political Negotiation and Reciprocity," *International Journal of Sport Management and Marketing* 2 (2007): 379-395.

67. E. Bernstein, "Friendly Fight: A Smarter Way to Say I'm Angry," *Wall Street Journal* (April 19, 2011): D1, D4.

68. *Ibid.*

69. American Psychological Association (APA) website, www.apa.org (accessed July 3, 2012).

70. S. Shellenbarger, "When Stress Is Good for You," *Wall Street Journal* (January 24, 2012): D1, D5.

71. American Psychological Association (APA) website, www.apa.org (accessed July 3, 2012).

72. N. Turner, "Beat Belly Fat," *Costco Connection* (January 2012): 85.

73. M. Futterman, "How Not to Ruin a Prodigy," *Wall Street Journal* (May 30, 2012): D6.

74. S. Shellenbarger, "When Stress Is Good for You," *Wall Street Journal* (January 24, 2012): D1, D5.

75. D. Self, E. Henry, C. Findley, and E. Reilly, "Thrill Seeking: The Type T Personality and Extreme Sports," *International Journal of Sport Management and Marketing* 2 (2007): 175-190.

76. S. Shellenbarger, "When Stress Is Good for You," *Wall Street Journal* (January 24, 2012): D1, D5.

77. K. Anderson, "The Trials of Diana Taurasi," http://sportsillustrated.cnn.com (September 12, 2011).

78. J. Adande, "This Wake-Up Call Too Late," www.latimes.com (May 6, 2007).

79. V. Harnish, "Looking to Make Employees Healthier and More Productive?" *Fortune* (March 19, 2012): 56.

80. A. Haupt, "11 Health Habits That Will Help You Live to 100," MSN, http://health.msn.com/healthy-living/11-Health-Habits-That-Will-Help-You-Live-to-100#scptmd (January 30, 2012).

81. American Psychological Association (APA) website, www.apa.org (accessed July 3, 2012).

82. S. Shellenbarger, "When Stress Is Good for You," *Wall Street Journal* (January 24, 2012): D1, D5.

83. N. Turner, "Beat Belly Fat," *Costco Connection* (January 2012): 85.

84. V. Harnish, "Looking to Make Employees Healthier and More Productive?" *Fortune* (March 19, 2012): 56.

85. T.P. Pope, "Exploring a Surprising Link Between Obesity and Diet Soda," *Wall Street Journal* (May 31, 2007): D1.

86. C. Suddath, "Sweating in Secret," *BusinessWeek* (April 2-8, 2012): 82-83.

87. S. Shellenbarger, "When Stress Is Good for You," *Wall Street Journal* (January 24, 2012): D1, D5.

88. American Psychological Association (APA) website, www.apa.org (accessed July 3, 2012).

89. S. Shellenbarger, "When Stress Is Good for You," *Wall Street Journal* (January 24, 2012): D1, D5.

90. www.umassathletics.com/sports/m-footbl/spec-rel/092711aab.html (accessed January 1, 2012).

91. K. Meinke, "Michigan Football Team Completes 2012 Schedule by Adding Rematch With Pesky UMass," www.annarbor.com (September 27, 2011).

92. R. Chimelis, "Kentucky Bounces UMASS Game," *The Republican* (May 22, 2007): C1.

CHAPTER 9

1. www.bgca.org/newsevents/TheScoop/Pages/NBA_All-Star_2012.aspx (accessed February 29, 2012).

2. E.M. Spektor, M. Erez, and E. Naveh, "The Effect of Conformist and Attentive-to-Detail Members on Team Innovation: Reconciling the Innovation Paradox," *Academy of Management Journal* 54(4) (2011): 740-760.

3. F. Reh, "There Is No 'I' in Team," www.about.com (August 1, 2007).

4. A.C. Cosper, "The Zen Zone," *Entrepreneur* (March 2012): 12.

5. G.B. Cunningham and J.S. Fink, "Diversity Issues in Sport and Leisure," *Journal of Sport Management* 20 (2006): 483-509.

6. S. Buckley, "Warts and All, Bill Belichick Stands at the Top for Both QB and Coach," bostonherald.com (February 2, 2012).

7. *K. Badenhausen, M.K. Ozanian, and C. Settimi,* "NFL Team Values: The Business of Football," forbes.com (September 7, 2011).

8. J. Gladden, R. Irwin, and W. Sutton, "Managing North American Major Professional Teams in the New Millennium: A Focus on Building Brand Equity," *Journal of Sport Management* 15 (2001): 298.

9. S. Wu, C. Tsai, and C. Hung, "Toward Team or Player? How Trust, Vicarious Achievement Motive, and Identification Affect Fan Loyalty," *Journal of Sport Management* 26 (2012): 179-191.

10. A.C. Cosper, "The Zen Zone," *Entrepreneur* (March 2012): 12.

11. R. Likert, *The Human Organization: Its Management and Value*, New York: McGraw-Hill, 1967.

12. M.E. Pfahl, "Strategic issues associated with the development of internal sustainability teams in sport and recreation organizations: A framework for action and sustainable environmental performance," *International Journal of Sport Management Recreation and Tourism* 6 (2010): 37-61

13. S. Fairley, P. Kellett, and B. Green, "Volunteering Abroad: Motives for Travel to Volunteer at the Athens Olympic Games," *Journal of Sport Management* 21 (2007): 41-57.

14. G.B. Cunningham, "Opening the Black Box: The Influence of Perceived Diversity and a Common In-Group Identity in Diverse Groups," *Journal of Sport Management* 21 (2007): 58-78.

15. P. Kirwin, "Always a Little Different Up in New England," www.nfl.com (July 20, 2007).

16. G.B. Cunningham and J.S. Fink, "Diversity Issues in Sport and Leisure," *Journal of Sport Management* 20 (2006): 483-509.

17. E.M. Spektor, M. Erez, and E. Naveh, "The Effect of Conformist and Attentive-to-Detail Members on Team Innovation: Reconciling the Innovation Paradox," *Academy of Management Journal* 54(4) (2011): 740-760.

18. E. Bernstein, "Speaking Up Is Hard to Do: Researchers Explain Why," *Wall Street Journal* (February 7, 2012): D1, D4.

19. E.M. Spektor, M. Erez, and E. Naveh, "The Effect of Conformist and Attentive-to-Detail Members on Team Innovation: Reconciling the Innovation Paradox," *Academy of Management Journal* 54(4) (2011): 740-760.

20. S.S. Wang, "Under the Influence: How the Group Changes What We Think," *Wall Street Journal* (May 3, 2011): D1.

21. S. Wu, C. Tsai, and C. Hung, "Toward Team or Player? How Trust, Vicarious Achievement Motive, and Identification Affect Fan Loyalty," *Journal of Sport Management* 26 (2012): 179-191.

22. S.S. Wang, "Under the Influence: How the Group Changes What We Think," *Wall Street Journal* (May 3, 2011): D1, D3.

23. *Ibid.*

24. M.H. Martin, "Embodying Contradictions: The Case of Professional Women's Basketball," *Journal of Sport and Social Issues* 30 (2006): 265-288.

25. S.S. Wang, "Under the Influence: How the Group Changes What We Think," *Wall Street Journal* (May 3, 2011): D1, D3.

26. G.B. Cunningham, "Opening the Black Box: The Influence of Perceived Diversity and a Common In-Group Identity in Diverse Groups," *Journal of Sport Management* 21 (2007): 58-78.

27. D. Gould, D. Guinan, C. Greenleaf, R. Medbery, and K. Peterson, "Factors Affecting Olympic Performance: Perceptions of Athletes and Coaches from More and Less Successful Teams," *Sport Psychologist* 13(4) (2000): 347-352.

28. S. Warner, M. Bowers, and M. Dixon, "Team Dynamics: A Social Network Perspective," *Journal of Sport Management* 26 (2012): 53-66.

29. *Ibid.*

30. S. Berman, J. Down, and C. Hill, "Tacit Knowledge as a Source of Competitive Advantage in the National Basketball Association," *Academy of Management Journal* 1 (2002): 13-31.

31. F. Lera-Lopez and M. Rapun-Grarate, "The Demand for Sport: Sport Consumption and Participation Models," *Journal of Sport Management* 21 (2007): 103-122.

32. S.S. Wang, "Under the Influence: How the Group Changes What We Think," *Wall Street Journal* (May 3, 2011): D1, D3.

33. L. Wiersma and C. Sherman, "Volunteer Youth Sport Coaches' Perspectives of Coaching Education/Certification and Parental Codes of Conduct," *Research Quarterly for Exercise and Sport* 76 (2005): 324-338.

34. M. Kim, P. Chelladurai, and G. Trail, "A Model of Volunteer Retention in Youth Sport," *Journal of Sport Management* 21 (2007): 151-171.

35. S. Kerwin and A. Doherty, "An Investigation of the Conflict Triggering Process in Intercollegiate Athletic Departments," *Journal of Sport Management* 26 (2012): 224-236.

36. C. Hann, "The Masters," *Entrepreneur* (March 2012): 54-58.

37. H.S. Luedtke, "Making the Most of Meetings," *Costco Connection* (April 2012): 13.

38. *Ibid.*

39. *Ibid.*

40. *Ibid.*

41. E. Bernstein, "Speaking Up Is Hard to Do: Researchers Explain Why," *Wall Street Journal* (February 7, 2012): D1, D4.

42. *Ibid.*

43. B. Dwyer and Y. Kim, "For Love or Money: Developing and Validating a Motivational Scale for Fantasy Football Participation," *Journal of Sport Management* 25 (2011): 70-83.

CHAPTER 10

1. M. Lederer, "NFL RedZone: Join In the Action!" comcast.com (September 8, 2011).

2. K. Filo, D. Funk, and G. Hornby, "The Role of Web Site Content on Motive and Attitude Change for Sport Events," *Journal of Sport Management* 23 (2009): 21-40.

3. *Ibid.*

4. E. Gill Jr., "The Rutgers Women's Basketball and Don Imus Controversy (RUIMUS): White Privilege,

New Racism, and the Implications for College Sport Management," *Journal of Sport Management* 25 (2011): 118-130.

5. "YES Network and WFAN's Multi-Year Agreement Includes Live Simulcasts of Mike Francesa's The NFL Show and Mike'd Up: Francesa on the FAN," www.cbscorporation.com/news-article.php?id=451 (March 2, 2009).

6. "WNBA Unveils TV Deal with ESPN/ABC through 2016," http://sports.espn.go.com/wnba/news/story?id=2937330 (July 15, 2007).\

7. D.A. Warshaw, "Comcast Bets Big on Sports," *Fortune* (March 19, 2012): 157-162.

8. P. Pedersen, P. Laucella, K. Miloch, and L. Fielding, "The Juxtaposition of Sport and Communication: Defining the Field of Sport Communication," *International Journal of Sport Management and Marketing* 2 (2007): 193-207.

9. G.B. Cunningham, "Opening the Black Box: The Influence of Perceived Diversity and a Common In-Group Identity in Diverse Groups," *Journal of Sport Management* 21 (2007): 58-78.

10. C. Hann, "Control Issues," *Entrepreneur* (April 2012): 24.

11. R. Alsop, "Something Old Something New," *Wall Street Journal* (September 20, 2006): R1-R3.

12. www.sportsmediachallenge.com/about/ (accessed July 11, 2012).

13. Y. Hur, Y.J. Ko, and J. Valacich, "A Structural Model of the Relationships Between Sport Website Quality, E-Satisfaction, and E-Loyalty," *Journal of Sport Management* 25 (2011): 458-473.

14. J. Miller and T. Shales, *Those Guys Have All the Fun: Inside the World of ESPN*, New York: Back Bay Books, 2011.

15. M.P. Sam and S.J. Jackson, "Developing National Sport Policy Through Consultation: The Rules of Engagement," *Journal of Sport Management* 20 (2006): 366-386.

16. S. Kerwin and A. Doherty, "An Investigation of the Conflict Triggering Process in Intercollegiate Athletic Departments," *Journal of Sport Management* 26 (2012): 224-236.

17. C. Hann, "The Masters," *Entrepreneur* (March 2012): 54-58.

18. R. McCammon, "Cool Rules," *Entrepreneur* (May 2012): 22-23.

19. B.J. Hoffman, B.H. Bynum, R.F. Piccolo, and A.W. Sutton, "Person-Organization Value Congruence: How Transformational Leaders Influence Work Group Effectiveness," *Academy of Management Journal* 54(4) (2011): 779-796.

20. S. Wu, C. Tsai, and C. Hung, "Toward Team or Player? How Trust, Vicarious Achievement Motive, and Identification Affect Fan Loyalty," *Journal of Sport Management* 26 (2012): 179-191.

21. D.C. Funk and J.D. James, "Consumer Loyalty: The Meaning of Attachment in the Development of Sport Team Allegiance," *Journal of Sport Management* 20 (2006): 189-217.

22. C. Hann, "The Masters," *Entrepreneur* (March 2012): 54-58.

23. C. Hymowitz, "Executives Who Build Truth-Telling Cultures Learn Fast What Works," *Wall Street Journal* (June 12, 2006): B1.

24. M.M. Parent and P.O. Foreman, "Organizational Image and Identity Management in Large-Sale Sporting Events," *Journal of Sport Management* 21 (2007): 15-40.

25. C. Hymowitz, "Two Football Coaches Have a Lot to Teach Screaming Managers," *Wall Street Journal* (January 29, 2007): B1.

26. R. McCammon, "Cool Rules," *Entrepreneur* (May 2012): 22-23.

27. *Ibid.*

28. S. Kerwin and A. Doherty, "An Investigation of the Conflict Triggering Process in Intercollegiate Athletic Departments," *Journal of Sport Management* 26 (2012): 224-236.

29. R. McCammon, "Talking Points," *Entrepreneur* (April 2012): 18-19.

30. *Ibid.*

31. D. Benton, "4 Communication Strategies for Managing Your Team Remotely," fastcompany.com (April 27, 2012).

32. R. McCammon, "Voice Lessons," *Entrepreneur* (March 2012): 28-21.

33. R. Abrams, "Put Spring in Your Business," *Costco Connection* (April 2012): 13.

34. R. McCammon, "Voice Lessons," *Entrepreneur* (March 2012): 28-21.

35. E. Bernstein, "The Miscommunicators," *Wall Street Journal* (July 3, 2012): D1, D3.

36. R. McCammon, "Voice Lessons," *Entrepreneur* (March 2012): 28-21.

37. Y. Hur, Y.J. Ko, and J. Valacich, "A Structural Model of the Relationships Between Sport Website Quality, E-Satisfaction, and E-Loyalty," *Journal of Sport Management* 25 (2011): 458-473.

38. M.P. Pritchard and D.C. Funk, "Symbiosis and Substitution in Spectator Sport," *Journal of Sport Management* 20 (2006): 299-321.

39. S. Cacciola, "Cracking the Long-Jump Code," *Wall Street Journal* (February 14, 2012): D8.

40. Bryan Clay website, www.bryanclay.com (accessed July 5, 2012).

41. K.E.M. De Stobbeleir, S.J. Ashford, and D. Buyens, "Self-regulation of Creativity at Work: The Role of

Feedback-Seeking Behavior in Creative Performance," *Academy of Management Journal* 54(4) (2011): 811-831.

42. R.E. Silverman, "Work Reviews Losing Steam," *Wall Street Journal* (December 19, 2011): D1.

43. M.L. Sartore and G.B. Cunningham, "Weight Discrimination, Hiring Recommendations, Person-Job Fit, and Attributions: Fitness-Industry Implications," *Journal of Sport Management* 21 (2007): 172-193.

44. K.E.M. De Stobbeleir, S.J. Ashford, and D. Buyens, "Self-regulation of Creativity at Work: The Role of Feedback-Seeking Behavior in Creative Performance," *Academy of Management Journal* 54(4) (2011): 811-831.

45. Public Radio, news broadcast, WFCR 88.5, aired May 28, 2010.

46. S. Kerwin and A. Doherty, "An Investigation of the Conflict Triggering Process in Intercollegiate Athletic Departments," *Journal of Sport Management* 26 (2012): 224-236.

47. R.E. Silverman, "Work Reviews Losing Steam," *Wall Street Journal* (December 19, 2011): D1.

48. *Ibid.*

49. M.L. Sartore and G.B. Cunningham, "Weight Discrimination, Hiring Recommendations, Person-Job Fit, and Attributions: Fitness-Industry Implications," *Journal of Sport Management* 21 (2007): 172-193.

50. E. Hochuli, "Admit a Mistake," *BusinessWeek* (April 12, 2012): 78.

51. B. Esiason, "Eli, Giants Receivers Must Believe in Each Other," www.nfl.com (November 22, 2006).

52. D.S. Mason and T. Slack, "Evaluating Monitoring Mechanisms as a Solution to Opportunism by Professional Hockey Agents," *Journal of Sport Management* 15(2) (April 2001): 107-134.

53. NCAA.org, "Frequently Asked Questions, "http://www.ncaa.org/wps/wcm/connect/public/NCAA/Resources/Latest+News/2010+news+stories/July+latest+news/FAQ+on+Uniform+Athlete+Agents+Act, July 29. 2010.

54. http://mlbplayers.mlb.com/pa/info/faq.jsp#agent.

55. E. Willenbacher, "Regulating Agents: Why Current Federal and State Efforts Do Not Deter the Unscrupulous Athlete-Agent and How a National Licensing System May Cure the Problem," *St. John's Law Review* 78 (Fall 2004): 1225-1255.

56. www.bdasports.com

57. M. Kurylo, "It's Official: Knicks Sign Free Agent Baron Davis," espn.com (December 19, 2011).

58. M. Stein, "Cavaliers Amnesty Baron Davis," espn.com (December 15, 2011).

CHAPTER 11

1. J. Alder and S. Khurana, "Sport: Motivation Quotes: A Select Collection of Motivational Sports Quotes,"

http://quotations.about.com/cs/inspirationquotes/a/Sports36.htm (accessed January 2, 2012).

2. S. Warner, B. Newland, and B.C. Green, "More Than Motivation: Reconsidering Volunteer Management Tools," *Journal of Sport Management* 25 (2011): 391-407.

3. B.L. Rich, J.A. Lepine, and E.R. Crawford, "Job Engagement: Antecedents and Effects on Job Performance," *Academy of Management Journal* 53(3) (2010): 617-635.

4. E.G. Love, D.W. Love, and G.B. Northcraft, "Is the End in Sight? Student Regulation of In-Class and Extra-Credit Effort in Response to Performance Feedback," *Academy of Management Learning and Education* 9(1) (2010): 81-97.

5. S. Lindenberg and N.J. Foss, "Managing Joint Production Motivation: The Role of Goal Framing and Governance Mechanisms," *Academy of Management Review* 36(3) (2011): 500-525.

6. P. Riley, *The Winner Within*, New York: Berkley, 1994.

7. M. Futterman, "How Not to Ruin a Prodigy," *Wall Street Journal* (May 30, 2012): D6.

8. P. Provost, www.motivational-story.com/motivation-in-sports.html.

9. S. Warner, B. Newland, and B.C. Green, "More Than Motivation: Reconsidering Volunteer Management Tools," *Journal of Sport Management* 25 (2011): 391-407.

10. K. Blanchard, D. Hutson, and E. Wills, *The One Minute Entrepreneur*, New York: Currency/Doubleday, 2008.

11. A. Maslow, "A Theory of Human Motivation," *Psychological Review* 50 (1943): 370-396; A. Maslow, *Motivation and Personality*, New York: Harper & Row, 1954.

12. N. Bozionelos, "Happiness Around the World: Is There More to It Than Money?" *Academy of Management Perspectives* 24(4) (2010): 96-97.

13. A. Gonzalez, "Angels land both Pujols and Wilson: Iconic slugger departs St. Louis; lefty goes home to West Coast," mlb.com (accessed December 8,2011).

14. C. Alderfer, "An Empirical Test of a New Theory of Human Needs," *Organizational Behavior and Human Performance* (April 1969): 142-175; C. Alderfer, *Existence, Relatedness, and Growth*, New York: Free Press, 1972.

15. J.A. Adande, "What's Kevin Durant's Motivation?" espn.com (June 18, 2012).

16. F. Herzberg, "One More Time: How Do You Motivate Employees?" *Harvard Business Review* (January/February 1968): 53-62.

17. J.D. Davis, M.R. Allen, and H.D. Hayes, "Is Blood Thicker Than Water? A Study of Stewardship Perceptions in Family Business," *Entrepreneurship Theory and Practice* 34(6) (2010): 1093-1116.

18. K.E.M. De Stobbeleir, S.J. Ashford, and D. Buyens, "Self-regulation of Creativity at Work: The Role of

Feedback-Seeking Behavior in Creative Performance," *Academy of Management Journal* 54(4) (2011): 811-831.

19. K. Badenhausen, "The Heaviest Hitters," *Forbes* (April 2012): 78-81.

20. B.L. Rich, J.A. Lepine, and E.R. Crawford, "Job Engagement: Antecedents and Effects on Job Performance," *Academy of Management Journal* 53(3) (2010): 617-635.

21. H. Murray, *Explorations in Personality*, New York: Oxford Press, 1938.

22. J. Atkinson, *An Introduction to Motivation*, New York: Van Nostrand Reinhold, 1964; D. McClelland, *The Achieving Society*, New York: Van Nostrand Reinhold, 1961; D. McClelland and D.H. Burnham, "Power Is the Great Motivator," *Harvard Business Review* (March/April 1978): 103.

23. M. Brettel, A. Engelen, and L. Voll, "Letting Go to Grow—Empirical Findings on a Hearsay," *Journal of Small Business Management* 48(4) (2010): 552-579.

24. S. Lindenberg and N.J. Foss, "Managing Joint Production Motivation: The Role of Goal Framing and Governance Mechanisms," *Academy of Management Review* 36(3) (2011): 500-525.

25. Y. Zhu, "Does the Relationship between Job Satisfaction and Job Performance Depend on Culture?" *Academy of Management Perspectives* 24(1) (2010): 86-87.

26. S. Adams, "Toward an Understanding of Inequity," *Journal of Abnormal and Social Psychology* 67 (1963): 422-436.

27. D. Loo, "Big Pharma Launches a Talent Raid in China," *BusinessWeek* (July 18-24, 2011): 21-22.

28. L.J. Burton, H. Grappendorf, and A. Henderson, "Perceptions of Gender in Athletic Administration: Utilizing Role Congruity to Examine (Potential) Prejudice Against Women," *Journal of Sport Management* 20 (2011): 36-45.

29. D.F. Mahony, H.A. Riemer, J.L. Breeding, and M.A. Hums, "Organizational Justice in Sport Organizations: Perceptions of College Athletes and Other College Students," *Journal of Sport Management* 20 (2006): 159-188.

30. S. Dubner, "N.F.L. vs. M.L.B. as a Labour Market: A Freakonomics Quorum," *http://freakonomics.blogs.nytimes.com/2007/11/28/nfl-vs-mlb-as-a-labor-market-a-freakonomics-quorum/* (November 28, 2007).

31. G. Hirst, D. Van Knippenberg, C.H. Chen, and C.A. Sacramento, "How Does Bureaucracy Impact Individual Creativity? A Cross-Level Investigation of Team Orientation-Creativity Relationships," *Academy of Management Journal* 54(3) (2011): 624-641.

32. L.V. Gerstner, "Fix This Education," *BusinessWeek* (October 17-23, 2011): 98.

33. K.E.M. De Stobbeleir, S.J. Ashford, and D. Buyens, "Self-regulation of Creativity at Work: The Role of Feedback-Seeking Behavior in Creative Performance," *Academy of Management Journal* 54(4) (2011): 811-831.

34. L.V. Gerstner, "Fix This Education," *BusinessWeek* (October 17-23, 2011): 98.

35. V. Vroom, *Work and Motivation*, New York: Wiley, 1964.

36. L.F. Edelman, C.G. Brush, T.S. Manolova, and P.G. Greene, "Start-up Motivations and Growth Intentions of Minority Nascent Entrepreneurs," *Journal of Small Business Management* 48(2) (2010): 174-196.

37. K.E.M. De Stobbeleir, S.J. Ashford, and D. Buyens, "Self-regulation of Creativity at Work: The Role of Feedback-Seeking Behavior in Creative Performance," *Academy of Management Journal* 54(4) (2011): 811-831.

38. C. Leahey, "Building Trust Inside Your Company," *Fortune* (March 19, 2012): 35.

39. B.F. Skinner, *Beyond Freedom and Dignity*, New York: Knopf, 1971.

40. E.G. Love, D.W. Love, and G.B. Northcraft, "Is the End in Sight? Student Regulation of In-Class and Extra-Credit Effort in Response to Performance Feedback," *Academy of Management Learning and Education* 9(1) (2010): 81-97.

41. Author statement to clearly inform the reader that this is his interpretation of Skinner's reinforcement theory.

42. K.E.M. De Stobbeleir, S.J. Ashford, and D. Buyens, "Self-regulation of Creativity at Work: The Role of Feedback-Seeking Behavior in Creative Performance," *Academy of Management Journal* 54(4) (2011): 811-831.

43. V. Harnish, "Tired of Reading the Same Old Advice?" *Fortune* (November 7, 2011): 52.

44. R. Lane, "Paging Drew Brees: Why Sean Payton's Suspension Was Way Too Lenient," forbes.com (March 21, 2012).

45. A. Breer, "Jonathan Vilma has hearing for restraining order set for July 26," nfl.com (July 17, 2012).

46. R. McCammon, "Approval Ratings," *Entrepreneur* (February 2012): 16-17.

47. K. Blanchard, D. Hutson, and E. Wills, *The One-Minute Entrepreneur* (New York: Currency/Doubleday, 2008.

48. K. Blanchard and S. Johnson, *The One-Minute Manager*, New York: Morrow, 1982.

49. R. McCammon, "Approval Ratings," *Entrepreneur* (February 2012): 16-17.

50. *Ibid.*

51. G.J. Kilduff, H.A. Eefenbein, and B.M. Staw, "The Psychology of Rivalry: A Relationally Dependent Analysis of Competition," *Academy of Management Journal* 53(5) (2010): 943-969.

52. J.C. Dencker, "Outliners: The Story of Success," *Academy of Management Perspectives* 24(3) (2010): 97-99.

53. M. Kimes, "New Guru on the Block," *Fortune* (December 26, 2011): 149-152.

54. E.G. Love, D.W. Love, and G.B. Northcraft, "Is the End in Sight? Student Regulation of In-Class and Extra-Credit Effort in Response to Performance Feedback,"

Academy of Management Learning and Education 9(1) (2010): 81-97.

55. www.umass.edu/keyplayers/ambassadors2003.html (accessed January 2, 2012).

56. J. Deburro, "The Republican's Sheldon Rosenthal Memorial Junior Tennis Tournament set for Forest Park," www.masslive.com/sports/index.ssf/2010/07/the_republicans_sheldon_rosent_2.html (July 6, 2010).

57. This case is based on an author interview with Al Dunbar.

CHAPTER 12

1. B. Soebbing and M. Washington, "Leadership Succession and Organizational Performance: Football Coaches and Organizational Issues," *Journal of Sport Management* 25 (2011): 550-561.

2. S. Gentile, "Top Shelf: Parise, Suter give Wild instant credibility," foxnews.com (July 4, 2012).

3. "Call for Papers—Teaching Leadership," *Academy of Management Journal* 53(4) (2010): 922.

4. These were the results of the author's own search using www.scholar.google.com on July 5, 2012.

5. M. Korn, "Analyze, Decide, Lead, Says Columbia's Business Dean," *Wall Street Journal* (July 7, 2011): B6.

6. A. Hann, "The Masters," *Entrepreneur* (March 2012): 54-58.

7. A.C. Cosper, "The Zen Zone," *Entrepreneur* (March 2012): 12.

8. B.J. Hoffman, B.H. Bynum, R.F. Piccolo, and A.W. Sutton, "Person-Organization Value Congruence: How Transformational Leaders Influence Work Group Effectiveness," *Academy of Management Journal* 54(4) (2011): 779-796.

9. B. Soebbing and M. Washington, "Leadership Succession and Organizational Performance: Football Coaches and Organizational Issues," *Journal of Sport Management* 25 (2011): 550-561.

10. www.vincelombardi.com/quotes.html (accessed July 17, 2012).

11. S. Leberman and F. Palmer, "Motherhood, Sport Leadership, and Domain Theory: Experiences from New Zealand," *Journal of Sport Management* 23 (2009): 305-334.

12. F. Walter, M.S. Cole, and R.H. Humphrey, "Emotional Intelligence: Sine Qua Non of Leadership or Folderol?" *Academy of Management Perspectives* 25(1) (2011): 45-59.

13. R.B. Kaiser and R.B. Kaplan, "The Deeper Work of Executive Development: Outgrowing Sensitivities," *Academy of Management Learning and Education* 5(4) (2006): 463-483.

14. I. Nooyi, "Role Models," *Entrepreneur* (March 2012): 63.

15. B. Soebbing and M. Washington, "Leadership Succession and Organizational Performance: Football Coaches and Organizational Issues," *Journal of Sport Management* 25 (2011): 550-561.

16. M. Brettel, A. Engelen, and L. Voll, "Letting Go to Grow—Empirical Findings on a Hearsay," *Journal of Small Business Management* 48(4) (2010): 552-579.

17. R.W. Stackman and K. Devine, "Leadership and Emotional-Rational Coherence: A Start?" *Academy of Management Perspectives* 25(1) (2011): 42-44.

18. N. Gillespie and G. Dietz, "Trust Repair After an Organization-Level Failure," *Academy of Management Review* 34(1) (2009): 127-145.

19. B.A. De Jong and T. Elfring, "How Does Trust Affect the Performance of Ongoing Teams? The Mediating Role of Reflexivity, Monitoring, and Effort," *Academy of Management Journal* 53(3) (2010): 535-549.

20. H.C. Lin and S.T. Hou, "Managerial Lessons from the East: An Interview with Acer's Stan Shih," *Academy of Management Perspectives* 24(4) (2010): 6-16.

21. M. Bolduc, "The Leadership Secrets of George Washington," *Wall Street Journal* (February 11-12, 2012): A11.

22. K.E.M. De Stobbeleir, S.J. Ashford, and D. Buyens, "Self-regulation of Creativity at Work: The Role of Feedback-Seeking Behavior in Creative Performance," *Academy of Management Journal* 54(4) (2011): 811-831.

23. *Ibid.*

24. E. Ghiselli, *Explorations in Management Talent*, Santa Monica, CA: Goodyear, 1971.

25. Z. Ziglar, "Formula for Complete Success," in *Success Yearbook*, Tampa, FL: Peter Lowe International, 1998: 30, 105.

26. K. Lewin, R. Lippet, and R.K. White, "Patterns of Aggressive Behavior in Experimentally Created Social Climates," *Journal of Social Psychology* 10 (1939): 271-301.

27. R.M. Stogdill and A.E. Coons (eds.), *Leader Behavior: The Description and Measurement*, Columbus: The Ohio State University Bureau of Business Research, 1957.

28. R. Likert, *New Patterns of Management*, New York: McGraw-Hill, 1961.

29. R. Blake and J. Mouton, *The Leadership Grid III: Key to Leadership Excellence*, Houston: Gulf, 1985; R. Blake and A.A. McCanse, *Leadership Dilemmas—Grid Solutions*, Houston: Gulf, 1991.

30. J.B. Wu, A.S. Tsui, and A.J. Kinicki, "Consequences of Differentiated Leadership in Groups," *Academy of Management Journal* 53(4) (2010): 90-106.

31. B.M Galvin, P. Balkundi, and D.A. Waldman, "Spreading the Word: The Role of Surrogates in Charismatic Leadership Processes," *Academy of Management Review* 35(3) (2010): 477-494.

32. J.B. Wu, A.S. Tsui, and A.J. Kinicki, "Consequences of Differentiated Leadership in Groups," *Academy of Management Journal* 53(4) (2010): 90-106.

33. L. Burton and J.W. Peachey, "Transactional or Transformational? Leadership Preferences of Division III Athletic Administrators," *Journal of Intercollegiate Sports* 2 (2009): 245-259.

34. B.J. Hoffman, B.H. Bynum, R.F. Piccolo, and A.W. Sutton, "Person-Organization Value Congruence: How Transformational Leaders Influence Work Group Effectiveness," *Academy of Management Journal* 54(4) (2011): 779-796.

35. L. Tischler, "The Road to Recovery," *Fast Company* (July 2002): 82-83.

36. M. Brettel, A. Engelen, and L. Voll, "Letting Go to Grow—Empirical Findings on a Hearsay," *Journal of Small Business Management* 48(4) (2010): 552-579.

37. M. Farjoun, "Beyond Dualism: Stability and Change as a Duty," *Academy of Management Review* 35(2) (2010): 202-225.

38. F. Fiedler, *A Theory of Leadership Effectiveness*, New York: McGraw-Hill, 1967.

39. R. Tannenbaum and W. Schmidt, "How to Choose a Leadership Pattern," *Harvard Business Review* (May/June 1973): 166.

40. R. House, "A Path Goal Theory of Leadership Effectiveness," *Administrative Science Quarterly* 16(2) (1971): 321-329.

41. D. Vincer and T. Loughead, "The Relationship Among Athlete Leadership Behaviors and Cohesion in Team Sports," *Sport Psychologist* 24 (2010): 448-467.

42. V.H. Vroom and P.W. Yetton, *Leadership and Decision Making*, Pittsburgh: University of Pittsburgh Press, 1973.

43. V.H. Vroom and A.G. Jago, *The New Leadership: Managing Participation in Organizations*, Englewood Cliffs, NJ: Prentice-Hall, 1988.

44. V.H. Vroom, "Leadership and the Decision-Making Process," *Organizational Dynamics* 28 (Spring 2000): 82-94.

45. The model was developed by R.N. Lussier and is used with his permission.

46. R. Karlgaard, "Two Paths to Leadership Greatness," www.forbes.com (June 6, 2005).

47. Z. Kouwe, "Eisner Buys Topps Cards for $385M," newyorkpost.com (March 7, 2007).

48. C. Olds, "Topps Acquires Digital Currency Card Company," beckett.com (July 11, 2011).

CHAPTER 13

1. Personal interviews with Pete and Korby Clark (July 2012).

2. www.theranchgolfclub.com.

3. P. White, "Back at the Ranch," *Commonwealth Golf* III (2002): 44-48.

4. G. Colvin, "Why talent is overrated," *Fortune* (October 27, 2008): 138-147.

5. P. Jarzabkowski, "Shaping Strategy as a Structuration Process," *Academy of Management Journal* 51(4) (2008): 621-650.

6. R.S. Rubin and E.C. Dierdorff, "How Relevant is the MBA? Assessing the Alignment of Required Curricula and Required Managerial Competencies," *Academy of Management Learning and Education* 8(5) (2009): 208-224.

7. International Standards Organization website, www.iso.org (accessed July 16, 2012).

8. ASQ website, www.asq.org (accessed July 16, 2012).

9. ASQ website, http://asq.org/quality-report/reports/quarterly-quality-report-20061114.pdf (accessed July 16, 2012).

10. D.S. Mason, L. Thibault, and L. Misener, "An Agency Theory Perspective on Corruption in Sport: The Case of the International Olympic Committee," *Journal of Sport Management* 20 (2006): 52-73.

11. IOC website, www.olympic.org (accessed July 16, 2012).

12. G. Colvin, "How Are Most Admired Companies Different? They Invest in People and Keep Them Employed—Even in a Downturn," *Fortune* (March 22, 2010): 82.

13. S. Kelman, "Public Service Performance: Perspectives on Measurement and Management," *Academy of Management Review* 33(2) (2008): 561-564.

14. S.E. Green, U. Li, and N. Nohria, "Suspended in Self-spun Webs of Significance: A Rhetorical Model of Institutionalization and Institutionally Embedded Agency," *Academy of Management Journal* 52(1) (2009): 11-36.

15. *Ibid.*

16. K. Blanchard, D. Hutson, and E. Wills, *The One Minute Entrepreneur*, New York: Currency, 2008.

17. D.Y. Pyun and J.D. James, "Enhancing Advertising Communications: Developing a Model of Beliefs About Advertising Through Sport," *International Journal of Sport Communication* 2(1) (2009): 1-21.

18. T. Scassa, "Ambush Marketing and the Right of Association: Clamping Down on References to That Big Event With All the Athletes in a Couple of Years," *Journal of Sport Management* 25 (2011): 354-370.

19. "World Cup 2010: Fifa detains 36 female Holland fans for 'ambush marketing,'" www.guardian.co.uk/football/2010/jun/15/holland-ambush-marketing-fifa-dresses (June 15, 2010).

20. S. Husin, P. Chelladurai, and G. Musa, "HRM Practices, Organizational Citizenship Behaviors, and Perceived Service Quality in Golf Courses," *Journal of Sport Management* 26 (2012): 143-158.

21. K. Blanchard, D. Hutson, and E. Wills, *The One Minute Entrepreneur*, New York: Currency, 2008.

22. J. Jantsch, "4 Metrics for Measuring Success," *Entrepreneur* (February 2009): 118.

23. R. Youngjohns, "How Can I Keep My Sales Team Productive in a Recession?" *Fortune* (March 2, 2009): 22.

24. Taken from N.J. Adler and A.W. Harzing, "When Knowledge Wins: Transcending the Sense and Nonsense of Academic Rankings," *Academy of Management Learning and Education* 8(1) (2009): 72-95.

25. E.M. Spektor, M. Erez, and E. Naveh, "The Effect of Conformist and Attentive-to-Detail Members on Team Innovation: Reconciling the Innovation Paradox," *Academy of Management Journal* 54(4) (2011): 740-760.

26. Staff, "Penn State," *Wall Street Journal* (July 14-15, 2012): A1.

27. Associated Press, "NASCAR fines Kurt Busch $50,000," espn.com (November 25, 2011).

28. J. He and H.C. Wang, "Innovation Knowledge Assets and Economic Performance: The Asymmetric Roles of Incentives and Monitoring," *Academy of Management Journal* 52(5) (2009): 919-938.

29. S.D. Ross, J.D. James, and P. Vargas, "Development of a Scale to Measure Team Brand Associations in Professional Sport," *Journal of Sport Management* 20 (2006): 260-279.

30. S. Kelman, "Public Service Performance: Perspectives on Measurement and Management," *Academy of Management Review* 33(2) (2008): 561-564.

31. G. Colvin, "How Are Most Admired Companies Different? They Invest in People and Keep Them Employed—Even in a Downturn," *Fortune* (March 22, 2010): 82.

32. G. Colvin, "Why talent is overrated," *Fortune* (October 27, 2008): 138-147.

33. P. Jarzabkowski, "Shaping Strategy as a Structuration Process," *Academy of Management Journal* 51(4) (2008): 621-650.

34. C. Hann, "Control Issues," *Entrepreneur* (April 2012): 26.

35. International Standards Organization, www.iso.org (accessed July 16, 2012).

36. "Welcome to Sarbanes Oxley 101," www.sarbanes-oxley-101.com/ (July 10, 2012).

37. T. Geron, "Will Sarbanes-Oxley Changes Help the IPO Market"? forbes.com (February 24, 2012).

38. S.W. Dittmore, D.F. Mahony, D.P.S. Andrew, and M.A. Hums, "Examining Fairness Perceptions of Financial Resource Allocations in U.S. Olympic Sport," *Journal of Sport Management* 23 (2009): 429-456.

39. K. Badenhausen, "The New Fame Game," *Forbes*, (June 4, 2012).

40. Bobcats website, www.bobcats.com (accessed July 16, 2012).

41. G. Klein, "Magic Johnson Will Be Point Guard in Dodgers' Ownership Group," www.latimes.com (May 3, 2012).

42. J. Kell, "Nike Races Ahead of Inventory Pileup," *Wall Street Journal* (June 24, 2012): B2.

43. Staff, "Losers—Phil Knight," *Forbes* (July 16, 2012): 22.

44. The Business of Baseball: New York Yankees, www.forbes.com/lists/2011/33/baseball-valuations-11_New-York-Yankees_334613.html (accessed January 8, 2012).

45. T. Van Riper, "The New Moneyball," *Forbes* (April 9, 2012): 70-82.

46. K. Clark, "Game Changer: NFL Scrambles to Fill Seats," *Wall Street Journal* (June 30-July 1, 2012): A1, A2.

47. J.L. Stinson and D.R. Howard, "Athletic Success and Private Giving to Athletic and Academic Programs at NCAA Institutions," *Journal of Sport Management* 21 (2007): 235-264.

48. C. Smith, "The Most Valuable College Football Teams," *forbes.com* (December 21, 2011).

49. Associated Press news posted on Charter home page (August 10, 2011).

50. K. Badenhausen, M.K. Ozanian, and C. Settimi, "Hockey Scores," *Forbes* (December 19, 2011): 26-27.

51. B.K. Johnson, M.J. Mondello, and J.C. Whitehead, "The Value of Public Goods Generated by an NFL Team," *Journal of Sport Management* 21 (2007): 123-136.

52. J. Birger and T. Arango, "The Yankees Face Life After George," *Fortune* (August 20, 2007): 56-64.

53. R. Sandomir, "Yankees Slash the Price of Top Tickets," www.nytimes.com (April 28, 2009).

54. Staff, "The (Big) Bucks Behind the Olympics," *Fortune* (June 11, 2012): 101.

55. D. Roberts, "Will NBC's Investment Pay Off?" *Fortune* (June 11, 2012): 105-106.

56. C.S. Stewart, "In Age of Twitter, NBC Rewrites Olympic Playbook," *Wall Street Journal* (July 14-15, 2012): A1.

57. M. Henricks, "Creative Ways to Get Cash Flowing," *Entrepreneur* (May 2009): 32.

58. D. Worrell, "Raising Money," *Entrepreneur* (September 2008): 58.

59. D. Worrell, "Keeping Tabs on Cash Flow," *Entrepreneur* (January 2009): 32.

60. B. Solomon, "Baseball Bandit: Frank McCourt Escapes Dodgers with $860 Million Profit," *Forbes.com.* (March 28, 2012).

61. D. Benoit and S. Gleason, "Prince Sports Files for Bankruptcy," *Wall Street Journal* (May 2, 2012): 810.

62. Staff, "Forbes Soccer Team Valuations 2012," *Forbes* (May 7, 2012): 42.

63. Staff, "Swing and a Miss?" *Forbes* (April 23, 2012): 24.

64. N. Tocher and M.W. Rutherford, "Perceived Acute Human Resource Management Problems in Small

and Medium Firms: An Empirical Examination," *Entrepreneurship Theory and Practice* 33(2) (2009): 455-479.

65. R. Hooijbert and N. Lane, "Using Multisource Feedback Coaching Effectively in Executive Education," *Academy of Management Learning and Education* 8(4) (2009): 483-493.

66. J. Welch and S. Welch, "An Employee Bill of Rights," *BusinessWeek* (March 16, 2009): 72.

67. T. Gutner, "Ways to Make the Most of a Negative Job Review," *Wall Street Journal* (January 13, 2009): D4.

68. M. Goldsmith, "What Got You Here Won't Get You There: How Successful People Became Even More Successful," *Academy of Management Perspective* 23(3) (2009): 103-105.

69. D.W. Lehman and R. Ramanujam, "Selectivity in Organizational Rule Violations," *Academy of Management Review* 34(4) (2009): 643-657.

70. J. Sinegal, "Show Don't Tell," *Fortune* (July 6, 2009): 44.

71. *Ibid.*

72. K. Blanchard, D. Hutson, and E. Wills, *The One Minute Entrepreneur*, New York: Currency, (2008).

73. S. Berfield, "Obituary: C.K. Prahalad," *BusinessWeek* (April 26-May 2, 2010): 20.

74. D.W. Lehman and R. Ramanujam, "Selectivity in Organizational Rule Violations," *Academy of Management Review* 34(4) (2009): 643-657.

75. R. Vesely, "EAP Proves a Giant Step for Ballplayers," workforce.com (February 20, 2012).

76. S. McDowell, "Baseball Assistance Team," http://bat.mlblogs.com/tag/baseball-assistance-team/ (May 5, 2012).

77. S. Merkin, "Guillen to Attend Sensitivity Training," www.mlb.com (June 6, 2006).

78. M. Goldsmith, "What Got You Here Won't Get You There: How Successful People Became Even More Successful," *Academy of Management Perspective* 23(3) (2009): 103-105.

79. T. Gutner, "Ways to Make the Most of a Negative Job Review," *Wall Street Journal* (January 13, 2009): D4.

80. N.J. Adler and A.W. Harzing, "When Knowledge Wins: Transcending the Sense and Nonsense of Academic Rankings," *Academy of Management Learning and Education* 8(1) (2009): 72-95.

81. R. Batt and A.J.S. Colving, "An Employment Systems Approach to Turnover: Human Resources Practices, Quits, Dismissals, and Performance," *Academy of Management Journal* 54(4) (2011): 695-717.

82. J.M. O'Brien, "Making the 3-Wood," *BusinessWeek* (April 9-25, 2012): 84-87.

83. D. Stanford, "Gatorade Goes Back to the Lab," *BusinessWeek* (November 28-December 2, 2011): 85-88.

84. J. Jantsch, "4 Metrics for Measuring Success," *Entrepreneur* (February 2009): 118.

85. B. Williamson, "Managing at a Distance," *BusinessWeek* (July 27, 2009): 64.

86. S. Baker, "A New Math for Cutting Costs," *BusinessWeek* (May 11, 2009): 57.

87. www.rawlings.com/aboutus.aspx (accessed July 24, 2012).

88. G. Toushek, "Rawlings Sporting Goods, Star Players," *Manufacturing in Action* (April 2005).

89. "Brand Central Scores Rawlings Deal," http://www.licensemag.com/licensemag/Sports/Brand-Central-Scores-Rawlings-Deal/ArticleStandard/Article/detail/782418 (July 24, 2012).

CHAPTER 14

1. Maccabi USA, Sports for Israel, www.maccabiusa.com.

2. David Kimball coaches Maccabi with Stu Greene.

3. S. Uhrich and M. Benkenstein, "Sport Stadium Atmosphere: Formative and Reflective Indicators for Operationalizing the Construct," *Journal of Sport Management* 24 (2010): 211-237.

4. D. Getz and A. McConnell, "Serious Sport Tourism and Event Travel Careers," *Journal of Sport Management* 25 (2011): 326-338.

5. B. Hohler and S. Lakso, "Red Sox Sellout Streak a Real Numbers Game," www.boston.com (May 4, 2012).

6. Basketball Hall of Fame, www.hoophall.com (accessed July 16, 2012).

7. Volleyball Hall of Fame, www.volleyhall.org/about.html (accessed July 16, 2012).

8. W.M. Foster and C. Hyatt, "I Despise Them! I Detest Them! Franchise Relocation and the Expanded Model of Organizational Identification," *Journal of Sport Management* 21 (2007): 194-212.

9. C. Tien, H. Lo, and H. Lin, "The Economic Benefits of Mega Events: A Myth or a Reality? A Longitudinal Study on the Olympic Games," *Journal of Sport Management* 25 (2011): 11-23.

10. Staff, "The (Big) Bucks Behind the Olympics," *Fortune* (June 11, 2012): 101.

11. The Sports Management Group, www.sportsmgmt.com (accessed July 18, 2012).

12. M.F. Malinowski, "Essential Project Management Skills," *Project Management Journal* 42(2) (2011): 94.

13. www.crva.com (accessed July 20, 2012).

14. E. Spanberg, "Diplomacy Counts (Mike Crum Runs the Charlotte Auditorium-Coliseum-Convention Center Authority)," *Business Journal Serving Charlotte and the Metropolitan Area* 6(10) (2001): 3.

15. Personal interviews with Pete and Korby Clark (July 2012).

16. Spectator Management Group, www.smgworld.com (accessed July 18, 2012).

17. F. Mitchell, "Superdome Makes Full Recovery," www.nytimes-institute.com (May 24, 2007).

18. M. Parent, "Decision Making in Major Sport Events Over Time: Parameters, Drivers, and Strategies," *Journal of Sport Management* 24 (2010): 291-318.

19. C. Tien, H. Lo, and H. Lin, "The Economic Benefits of Mega Events: A Myth or a Reality? A Longitudinal Study on the Olympic Games," *Journal of Sport Management* 25 (2011): 11-23.

20. M.M. Parent and P.O. Foreman, "Marching in the Glory: Experiences and Meanings When Working for a Sport Mega-Event," *Journal of Sport Management* 23 (2009): 210-237.

21. www.ncs4.com/ (accessed July 21, 2012).

22. "Annual Sports Safety and Security Conference, Exhibition set for July 31-Aug. 2," hattiesburgamerican.com (July 6, 2012).

23. V. Cavaliere, "London Olympics 2012: First Athletes Arrive to Security 'Shambles,' Traffic Jams," www.nytimes.com (July 17, 2012).

24. M.F. Malinowski, "Essential Project Management Skills," *Project Management Journal* 42(2) (2011): 94.

25. C. Bode, S.M. Wagner, and L.M. Ellram, "Understanding Responses to Supply Chain Disruptions: Insights from Information Processing and Resource Dependence Perspectives," *Academy of Management Journal* 54(4) (2011): 833-856.

26. D.F. Kuratko and D.B. Audretsch, "Strategic Entrepreneurship: Exploring Different Perspectives of an Emerging Concept," *Entrepreneurship Theory and Practice* 33(1) (2009): 1-17.

27. P.J. Derfus, P.G. Maggitti, C.M. Crimm, and K.G. Smith, "The Red Queen Effect: Competitive Actions and Firm Performance," *Academy of Management Journal* 51(1) (2008): 61-80.

28. D.W. Lehman and R. Ramanujam, "Selectivity in Organizational Rule Violations," *Academy of Management Review* 34(4) (2009): 643-657.

29. J. Kell, "Nike Races Ahead of Inventory Pileup," *Wall Street Journal* (June 24, 2012): B2.

30. K. Blanchard, D. Hutson, and E. Wills, *The One Minute Entrepreneur*, New York: Currency, (2008).

31. P.P. Heugens and M.W. Lander, "Structure! (and Other Quarrels): A Meta-Analysis of Institutional Theories of Organizations," *Academy of Management Journal* 52(1) (2009): 61-85.

32. S.A. Alvarez and S.C. Parker, "Emerging Firms and the Allocation of Control Rights: A Bayesian Approach," *Academy of Management Review* 34(2) (2009): 209-227.

33. J. McGregor, "There is no more normal," *BusinessWeek* (March 23 and 30, 2009): 30-34.

34. M. Milano and P. Chelladurai, "Gross Domestic Sport Product: The Size of the Sport Industry in the United States," *Journal of Sport Management* 25 (2011): 24-35.

35. J. Kell, "Nike Races Ahead of Inventory Pileup," *Wall Street Journal* (June 24, 2012): B2.

36. MLB Attendance Report 2011, http://espn.go.com/mlb/attendance/_/year/2011/sort/homeTotal.

37. www.trefis.com/company?hm=NKE.trefis&# (accessed July 17, 2012).

38. National Bureau of Economic Research, "Business Cycle Dating Committee, National Bureau of Economic Research," www.nber.org/cycles/sept2010.html (September 20, 2010).

39. http://espn.go.com/mlb/attendance/_/year/2011/sort/homeTotal.

40. J.T. Yokum, J.J. Gonzaiez, and T. Badgett, "Forecasting the Long-Term Viability of an Enterprise: The Case of a Minor League Baseball Franchise," *Journal of Sport Management* 20 (2006): 248-259.

41. J. Ankeny, "Appointments with Success," *Entrepreneur* (March 2012): 49.

42. K. Filo, D. Funk, and D. O'Brien, "The Antecedents and Outcomes of Attachment and Sponsor Image Within Charity Sport Events," *Journal of Sport Management* 24 (2010): 623-648.

43. A. Dizik, "Services to Help Us Stop Dawdling Online," *Wall Street Journal* (January 28, 2010): D2.

44. S. Shellenbarger, "No Time to Read This? Read This," *Wall Street Journal* (November 18, 2009): D1, D5.

45. E.J. Pollock, "How I Got a Grip on My Workweek," *BusinessWeek* (April 6, 2009): 84-86.

46. M. Lev-Ram, "Work Less, Do More," *Fortune* (November 2010): 56.

47. A. Dizik, "Services to Help Us Stop Dawdling Online," *Wall Street Journal* (January 28, 2012): D2.

48. C. Penttila, "Best Practices—Rush Hour," *Entrepreneur* (August 2008): 74.

49. A. Dizik, "Services to Help Us Stop Dawdling Online," *Wall Street Journal* (January 28, 2010): D2.

50. S. Shellenbarger, "No Time to Read This? Read This," *Wall Street Journal* (November 18, 2009): D1, D5.

51. S. Shellenbarger, "Conquering the To-Do List," *Wall Street Journal* (December 28, 2011): D1, D2.

52. *Ibid.*

53. J. Ankeny, "Appointments with Success," *Entrepreneur* (March 2012): 49.

54. S. Shellenbarger, "Conquering the To-Do List," *Wall Street Journal* (December 28, 2011): D1, D2.

55. S. Covy, "Time Management," *Fortune* (September 19, 2009): 28-29.

56. J. Robinson, "E-mail is Making You Stupid?" *Entrepreneur* (March 2010): 61-63.

57. *Ibid.*

58. M. Lev-Ram, "Work Less, Do More," *Fortune* (November 2010): 56.

59. *Ibid.*

60. S. Shellenbarger, "No Time to Read This? Read This," *Wall Street Journal* (November 18, 2009): D1, D5.

61. L. Edwards, "Euro 2012: 183 Arrested after Polish and Russian Clash as March Descends into Violence on Russia Day," www.telegraph.co.uk (June 13, 2012).

62. "Belgrade Violence, Dresden Threats Suggest Soccer Violence Increasing," www.sportsline.com (February 26, 2007).

63. *Ibid.*

64. M. Dodd, "Pacers, Pistons Have Taken a Fall Since Brawl," *usatoday.com* (December 25, 2004).

65. R. Polidoro, "Bryan Stow's friends describe brutal attack outside Dodger Stadium," http://rockcenter.msnbc.msn.com (December 19, 2011).

66. K. Belson, "Before Game Decided, Superdome Goes Dark," *New York Times.com*, (February 3, 2013).

67. "Queens Man in San Francisco for One Day Catches Famous Ball," http://espn.go.com (August 9, 2007).

AFTERWORD

1. R. Kaplan and D.P. Norton, "Using the Balanced Scorecard as a Strategic Management System," *Harvard Business Review* (January-February 1996): 75-85.

2. R. Lane, "Paging Drew Brees: Why Sean Payton's Suspension Was Way Too Lenient," forbes.com (March 21, 2012).

3. K. Berger, "Scandal Hasn't Brought NBA to a Halt," www.newsday.com (August 3, 2007).

4. T. Coyne and R.D. Russo, "Penn St fined $60M, wins vacated from '98-11," Associated Press (July 23, 2012).

5. Associated Press, "Barry Bonds found guilty of obstruction," espn.com (April 14, 2011).

6. Associated Press, "U.S. Anti-Doping Agency charges Lance Armstrong with drug use," www.cbc.ca (June 13, 2012).

APPENDIX

1. R.N. Bolles, What Color Is Your Parachute? A Practical Manual for Job-Hunters and Career-Changers, Berkeley, CA: Ten Speed Press, (2012).

INDEX

Page numbers followed by an *f* or a *t* indicate a figure or table, respectively.

ABOUT THE AUTHORS

Robert N. Lussier, PhD, is a professor of management at the birthplace of basketball, Springfield College in Springfield, Massachusetts, where more than one-third of the students compete in 27 intercollegiate athletic teams. He has taught undergraduate and graduate sport management students for more than 15 years. He has also supervised sport internships and serves as an advisor for sport management research projects.

Lussier has authored more than 385 publications, including texts in management, leadership, and human relations. He was an intercollegiate athlete and has coached at the college, high school, and youth levels. He works out daily and enjoys spending time with his wife and six children.

David C. Kimball, PhD, is a professor of management and director of the sport management program at Elms College in Chicopee, Massachusetts. He teaches sport management and sport marketing courses and coaches and supervises Maccabi athletes each summer. He has an expansive network of friends and acquaintances in the sport management field; many of the case studies in this book arose from these relationships.

He loves being personally involved in sports and runs 30 miles a week while participating in Les Mills training. He also enjoys watching sports on television almost as much as at the arena, ballpark, or stadium.